Oracle Press™

Applied Oracle Security: Developing Secure Database and Middleware Environments

Oracle Press™

Applied Oracle Security: Developing Secure Database and Middleware Environments

David C. Knox
Scott G. Gaetjen
Hamza Jahangir
Tyler Muth
Patrick Sack
Richard Wark
Bryan Wise

New York Chicago San Francisco
Lisbon London Madrid Mexico City Milan
New Delhi San Juan Seoul Singapore Sydney Toronto

The McGraw-Hill Companies

Cataloging-in-Publication Data is on file with the Library of Congress

McGraw-Hill books are available at special quantity discounts to use as premiums and sales promotions, or for use in corporate training programs. To contact a representative, please e-mail us at bulksales@mcgraw-hill.com.

Applied Oracle Security: Developing Secure Database and Middleware Environments

1234567890 DOC DOC 019

ISBN 978-0-07-161370-5
MHID 0-07-161370-6

Sponsoring Editor
Lisa McClain

Editorial Supervisor
Patty Mon

Project Editor
LeeAnn Pickrell

Acquisitions Coordinator
Meghan Riley

Technical Editors
Ben Ault, Tammy Bednar, Derrick Cameron, Sergio Leunissen, Robert Lindsley, Bill Maroulis, Raj Mattamal, Scott Spadafore, Peter Wahl

Copy Editor
Lisa Theobald

Proofreader
Martin Benes

Indexer
James Minkin

Production Supervisor
George Anderson

Composition
Apollo Publishing Service

Illustration
Lyssa Wald, Apollo Publishing Service

Art Director, Cover
Jeff Weeks

Cover Designer
Pattie Lee

I dedicate this book to all those who not only aspire for greater achievements, but also follow through on obtaining them. Dream big and do big!

—David Knox

I dedicate this book to my wife, Mary, and my two sons, Anthony and Jeffrey, for being patient and understanding while I worked on the book. I love you guys and we now have the summer free so we can play.

–Scott Gaetjen

To my parents, Panahul Alam Jahangir and Nargis Jahangir, my two greatest sources of warmth, support, and affection.

–Hamza Jahangir

I would like to dedicate this book to my loving wife, Sally, for her tireless support. She invested as many hours as I did in this project, caring for our new son, Colin, on weekends and evenings so that I could pursue this endeavor, and for that I am truly grateful.

–Tyler Muth

I dedicate this book to my wife, Wendi, and my sons, Collin, Ashtin, Giovanni, and Vinson. Thank you for your support and understanding during the production of this book. We have been through a lot this past year and have learned that family and friends is what really matters. Love to all of you, especially to my wife, Wendi. XOXO.

—Pat Sack

I dedicate this book to my dad, Robert Wark, for his wisdom and love.

—Richard Wark

I dedicate this book to my father, Ronald, whose love of brain-teasers, HP calculators, and spreadsheet macros started me down this wonderful road I find myself traveling.

—Bryan Wise

About the Authors

David C. Knox, Senior Director, Solution Engineering, Oracle Corporation, currently works as a Senior Director for Oracle's National Security Group. Prior to this role, he ran the Solution Engineering division for Oracle North American Sales and Consulting, where he would oversee Solutions Development and R&D innovation for all Oracle technologies. He has also held positions as Senior Director of the Oracle Protected Enterprise & Security Business and as Chief Engineer for Oracle's Information Assurance Center.

Since joining Oracle in 1995, Mr. Knox has worked with customer organizations including the Department of Defense, intelligence agencies, financial services, and a variety of other industries, giving him a broad understanding of key business drivers and processes. His expertise in computer security derives from both working knowledge and experience with Oracle's security products and database security, but also from his academic studies in the areas of multilevel security, cryptography, Lightweight Directory Access Protocol (LDAP), and Public Key Infrastructure (PKI).

Mr. Knox is the author of *Effective Oracle Database 10*g *Security By Design* (McGraw-Hill Professional 2004). His other published work includes security contributions to *Expert One on One Oracle* by Thomas Kyte (Worx Press 2001) and *Mastering Oracle PL/SQL: Practical Solutions* (Apress 2003). He has also authored several Oracle whitepapers. Mr. Knox earned a bachelor's degree in computer science from the University of Maryland and a master's degree in computer science from Johns Hopkins University.

Scott G. Gaetjen, Technical Director, Oracle National Security Group, conducts research and design on new security solutions, leveraging his 15 years of experience with Oracle technologies to provide advanced security capabilities to Oracle's customers. He has served as a technical lead and mentor for several customers in the U.S. Department of Defense, U.S. intelligence agencies, U.S. civilian government, and the financial industries. In the process of helping these customers meet their mission objectives, Mr. Gaetjen has developed a keen technical understanding of operating system security, Oracle database security, J2EE application security, and identity management.

Mr. Gaetjen has been involved in the research and development of the Oracle Data Vault technology since its inception as a solution in 2004 under Oracle's Consulting organization and participated in the efforts to make the solution into a true Oracle product.

He earned a bachelor's degree in mathematics from James Madison University and a master's degree in computer systems management from the University of Maryland University College.

Hamza Jahangir is currently a Principal Architect in the Enterprise Architecture group at Oracle. He has been with Oracle since 2004 and has been working with Oracle Database and middleware products for more than ten years. As an architect, he spends much of his time in a technical advisory capacity to help his clients better understand and apply security products and technologies to solve security challenges, mainly those that span database and middleware environments (such as Identity Management, Access Management, Directories, and J2EE security).

Mr. Jahangir also teaches security classes and spends time evangelizing best practices around bridging database and middleware security to Oracle user groups and professional communities around identity management, service-oriented architectures, and IT security. He spends the remainder of his working time on experimenting with new architectures and prototyping solutions around new application and enterprise security models.

When he is not working, he enjoys spending time with his family, friends, and a nylon-string classical guitar. He has a bachelor's degree in computer science from Northeastern and is currently working toward an MBA at Georgetown.

Tyler Muth is a Principal Technologist with the Oracle Public Sector division, specializing in database and application security. He leads Application Express workshops throughout the United States, advises customers on architecture decisions, and collaborates with customers to develop tactical applications. He is a passionate contributor to the security community through presentations at Oracle Technology Days and Oracle User Groups; his blog, www.tylermuth .wordpress.com; and participation on the Oracle Technology Network forums.

Prior to his current role, Mr. Muth was one of the early developers on the Application Express development team, where he worked for more than five years. He was a technical reviewer for several of Tom Kyte's books, a contributing author for asktom.oracle.com, and a manager for a production system in zero-gravity.

Patrick Sack, Technical Vice President, NSG Product Engineering, Oracle Corporation, runs the Product Engineering division for Oracle's National Security Group. Prior to his current role overseeing Product Engineering and R&D Innovation for all Oracle technologies, he held positions as Vice President of Oracle's Protected Enterprise & Security Business. A majority of his career was spent within the Oracle Consulting group, driving innovative solutions and enhancing Oracle products.

Since joining Oracle in 1988, Mr. Sack has worked with customer organizations, including the Department of Defense, intelligence agencies, financial services, and a variety of other industries, giving him a broad understanding of key business drivers and processes. His expertise in information security derives from his working knowledge of Oracle products and application of these technologies on customers' projects, including multilevel security.

He specializes in Oracle's Information Assurance technologies, architectures, and solutions. He has been instrumental in driving new security technologies, features, and solutions for customers, such as Database Vault for Compliance. He is the primary architect and founder of many of the advanced security capabilities available in the Oracle Database product offerings, including Oracle Database Vault, Oracle Audit Vault, Oracle Label Security, and fine-grained auditing. He has filed many U.S. patents with Oracle Corporation in the information security category, such as Multiple Database Security Policies, Row-Level Auditing, Database Vault, Mandatory Access Control Base, Dynamic Access Controls, and Auditing and Cross Domain Security.

Mr. Sack understands how critical information and security is to most organizations, asserting that the data must be available, accountable, and accessible. He earned a bachelor's degree in computer science from the State University of New York.

Richard Wark, CISSP, works as a Principal Technologist in Oracle's Enterprise Solutions Group, helping to develop security and identity management solutions, demonstrations, and training since 2004. He is a "retread" at Oracle, having worked briefly for the City of San Antonio from 2002 to 2003 to help manage a large enterprise resource planning (ERP) project implementation. He initially joined Oracle to work as a sales consultant working with Air Force customers across the country in 1996. Since then, he has worked on solutions for banks, airlines, financial institutions, and a host of other customers to protect their data and practice good security.

With more than 15 years of experience with Oracle products, Mr. Wark has worked with customers to build secure database systems in the government, Department of Defense, healthcare industry, and other commercial sectors. As a result of dealing with brilliant colleagues and customers with challenging problems, he has developed a working knowledge and some level of expertise in network security design, security policy creation, business continuity planning, data classification, secure database configuration, and large-scale implementation reality.

Prior to joining Oracle, Mr. Wark worked for Computer Sciences Corporation (CSC) and Science Applications International Corporation (SAIC) on DoD Oracle database projects, starting his professional career in 1991 as a UNIX admin and Informix DBA. He holds a bachelor's degree in information systems from University of Texas, San Antonio.

Bryan Wise is a Business Intelligence Solution Specialist for Oracle's Public Sector division, where he helps customers find secure, innovative ways to use their existing data and run their organizations more efficiently. His career with Oracle technology started in the late 1990s while serving as an officer in the U.S. Navy. He managed all database administration and led application and report development for the Navy's Nuclear Power School.

Over the years, Mr. Wise has been an active participant in the Oracle community, including providing presentations for the Mid Atlantic Association of Oracle Professionals, the Oracle Government Users Group, and the Business Intelligence, Warehousing and Analytics Special Interest Group of the IOUG. He is also a contributing author on the Oracle BI Publisher blog.

In addition to being an Oracle specialist, Mr. Wise has spent most of his career teaching. His teaching assignments include developing and delivering hand's-on Oracle Business Intelligence seminars, teaching mathematics at the Navy's Nuclear Power school and various community colleges, as well as teaching database concepts at the University of Maryland University College. He holds bachelor's and master's degrees in mathematics from Brigham Young University and a master's certificate in e-commerce engineering from Regis University.

About the Technical Editors

Ben Ault is a Business Intelligence Specialist Manager at Oracle, where he has worked since 1995. He has focused on implementing and selling decision support and business intelligence solutions throughout his career. He has spent the last several years concentrating on business intelligence and data warehousing solutions for Oracle's Public Sector customers. Prior to his time at Oracle, he worked as a Decision Support Consultant for IRI Software, where he designed and implemented custom database applications to provide executive-level analysis of sales, marketing, and financial data.

Tammy Bednar has worked in the computer industry for more than 25 years. She started out coding applications in ADA and decided a change was needed. Oracle hired her in the Database Support Organization 14 years ago and she has been involved with database releases since version 6.0.36. She started her Product Management career on the database High Availability team with Recovery Manager (RMAN) and database backup and recovery. High availability and security go hand-in-hand, and Ms. Bednar is currently a member of the Database Security development team, focusing on auditing and Oracle Audit Vault.

Derrick Cameron leads the Business Intelligence team in Solutions Engineering at Oracle. He has worked with Oracle technology for more than 15 years and for Oracle (Canada, and then U.S.) for the past 12 years, initially working in applications consulting and later in sales, supporting data warehousing and business intelligence. He is one of the primary architects of Oracle's internal integrated BI demonstration and training platform (used at Oracle Open World), and is also the build lead for Oracle's external partner BI platform. He works closely with development to build cross-product integration solutions, and he also works with customers in the sales cycle when technical expertise is required. Previously, he worked in financial accounting systems roles in the public sector and a financial institution.

Sergio Leunissen joined Oracle in 1995. Since then, he has worked as a sales engineer, developer, and product manager on technologies including Oracle Application Express, Oracle Database, Linux, and Oracle VM. He was one of the original members of the Oracle Application Express team, helping to develop and bring the product to market. In 2006, he helped launch the Unbreakable Linux support program. He is currently Senior Director, Linux Business Solutions.

Robert Lindsley is a Principal Sales Consultant in Oracle's North American Public Sector organization. He specializes in Oracle's business intelligence, analysis, and data warehousing solutions and has worked in the software industry for more than ten years. Prior to that, Mr. Lindsley was a research scientist, specializing in the analysis of large neuroscience datasets. He has written several publications in the areas of multisensory integration and neuropharmacology.

Mr. Lindsley has a bachelor's degree from Cornell University in Ithaca, New York. He lives in Washington, DC.

Bill Maroulis is a Technical Director in Oracle's National Security group. He has more than 15 years experience in software development, with a primary focus on Oracle database security. He is the lead database engineer for software components and MAC security policies that protect the Oracle Database in a cross-domain environment. Mr. Maroulis also teaches Oracle as an adjunct professor at Strayer University. He has a bachelor's degree in computer science from the North Carolina State University and a master's in software engineering from the University of Maryland University College. He lives in Virginia and enjoys spending time with his wife and daughter.

Raj Mattamal, a co-president at Niantic Systems (www.nianticsystems.com), started developing web applications at Oracle in 1995 with the very same people who came to create Oracle Application Express. During his more than ten years with the company, he helped customers in a wide range of industries to deliver web-based solutions in Oracle Database. In addition to helping customers with their applications, he developed numerous web applications for use internally at Oracle as well. Outside of application development, Mr. Mattamal spent much of his time with Oracle evangelizing the Oracle Application Express development environment. This entailed teaching classes globally, writing articles for *Oracle Magazine*, writing Technotes for the Oracle Technology Network, and assisting with the development of training materials and workshops.

Having earned a bachelor's degrees in decision & information studies as well as marketing from the University of Maryland, Mr. Mattamal continues to apply his knowledge of and passion for technology and business to real-world issues. Since leaving Oracle in 2006, he went on to co-found Niantic Systems, LLC, which offers services and training to customers in a wide range of business lines to help get the most out of their Oracle environments.

Scott Spadafore is a member of the Application Express development team at Oracle Corporation, now in his eighth year with that group. Prior to this, he worked 7 years as an Oracle consultant doing various C/Pro*C custom development projects, DBA work, and security technical architecture/implementation for telco and local government customers throughout the United States. Before joining Oracle, he spent 21 years helping Amdahl Corporation develop mainframe computers in various roles as an engineering aide, MVS/VM systems programmer, C programmer, and software development manager.

Peter Wahl is the Product Manager for Oracle's Advanced Security option. He has a masters' degree from the University of Applied Sciences in Ravensburg/Germany and nearly 20 years of industry experience in product development, marketing, and business development. As a member of the Oracle Database Security development team since the initial release of Transparent Data Encryption (TDE), he has helped numerous enterprise customers deploy TDE to address PCI and other compliance requirements. In addition, he serves as the worldwide contact for partner development and has led the certification of Oracle's E-Business Suite, Peoplesoft, Siebel CRM, and JD Edwards EnterpriseOne Applications with TDE as well as the certification of multiple hardware security modules by partner vendors.

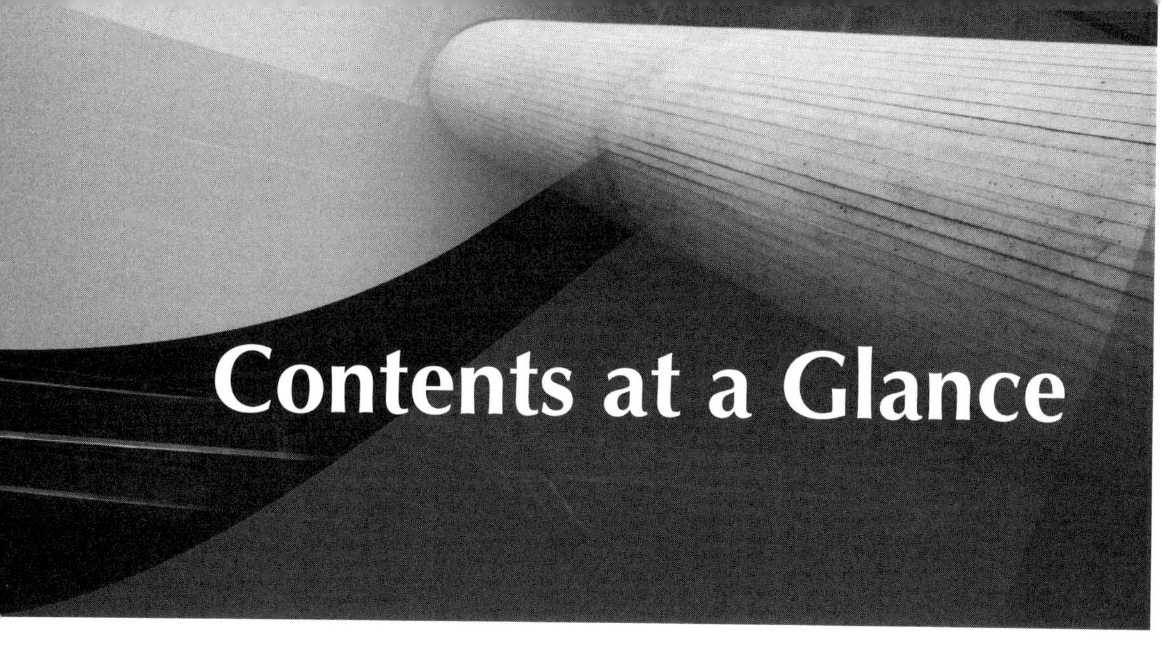

Contents at a Glance

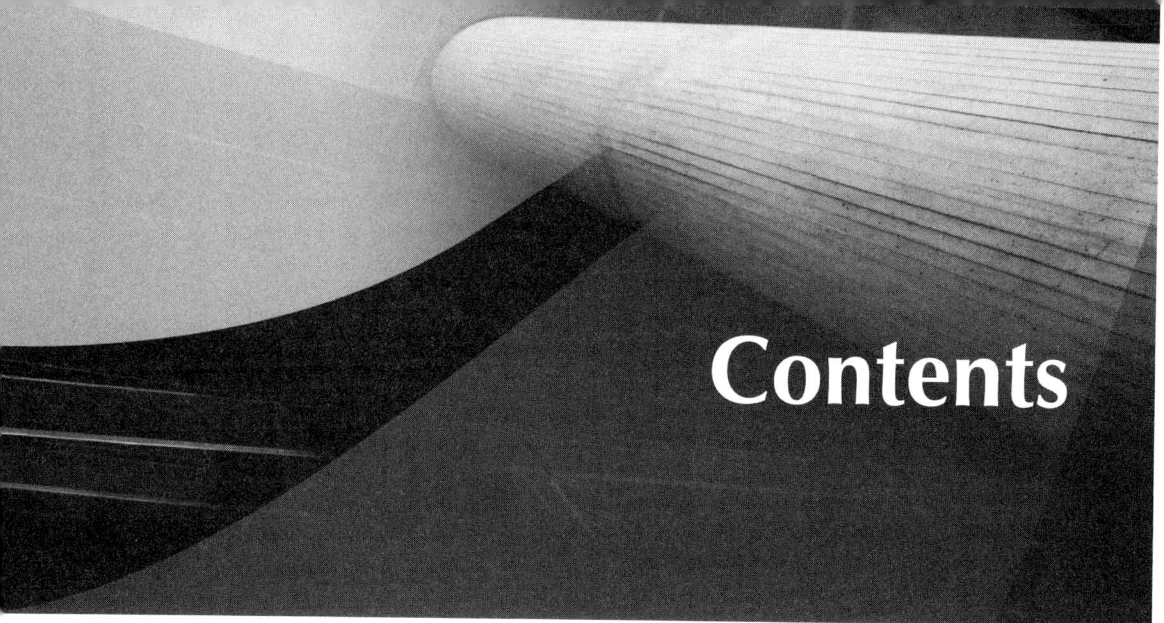

Contents

PART III

Identity Management

PART IV
Applied Security for Oracle APEX and Oracle Business Intelligence

Foreword

racle's business is information: managing it, making it useful, and securing it. As Oracle's Chief Architect, I have always had to ensure that our technologies not only provide business value but also do so in a robust manner. Security is a topic that comes up in practically every Customer Executive Visit and it's no wonder why. Today, security, privacy, and governance are top issues for everyone. These are no longer "nice to have" issues but rather "must have" requirements. As such, people are looking for ways to ensure they have done what they need to do to meet these strenuous requirements.

This book provides the architectural and design scenarios as well as code to help Oracle customers to create and lock down their information security systems. What's most impressive about the book is that it is written by the hands-on experts in Oracle. The authors are the top engineers working with customers every day to bring together security solutions. Many of Oracle's products and technologies have been borne directly from the customer experiences of these very authors.

You will undoubtedly find useful and insightful information in this book. I encourage you to read it cover-to-cover, bookmark items of interest, and most importantly, implement the suggestions presented herein.

—Edward Screven, Chief Corporate Architect
Oracle Corporation

Acknowledgments

I would like to thank the collective team of authors who produced this book. The knowledge they possess in their areas of specialty cannot be surpassed. While I could have written an update on Oracle security, I believe this book is truly the culmination of best practices, topics, ideas, and suggestions from the world's best on the topic of security as it relates to Oracle technologies. I recognize that saying "I am writing a book" and actually writing a book are two vastly different things, and I appreciate the team hanging in until the end and getting the content not only written, but also written very well. Thank you Richard, Pat, Scott, Hamza, Tyler, and Bryan for your hard, hard work and perseverance.

I would also like to thank my peers and management within Oracle. As writing books is not why I was hired, I appreciate their support and encouragement to allow me to capture the knowledge so it can be used by the entire Oracle community. Mark Tatum and Glen Dodson have been especially supportive, and without Edward Screven's support, the book could not have been produced. I would also like to thank my teammates—Ed Montes, Fred Justice, Joe Mazzafro, and Mark Lunny—for tolerating me during the production time for this book. I would also like to acknowledge Vipin Samar and Paul Needham's team for their constant support over the years. Tammy Bednar in particular played a key role in the production of this book.

Lastly, I would like thank my wife, Sandy, and the Knox boys. Sandy, you once again gave me the time and space to do something I said I would never do again (write a book!). I recognize your sacrifice and know that I could not have done it without your support. For the Knox boys, it gave me great pains to tell you that I could not play with you while writing this book. I hope you understand that sometimes daddy has to work but that you are truly the most important thing to me. I love you very much. Now, let's go play! You hide and I'll count. 1-2-3… Ready or not!

—David Knox

Patrick Sack would like to thank Glen Dodson and Ray Prescott for providing an innovative environment, where ideas can materialize, as well as a culture that drives these ideas into solutions that create business value. Thanks Glen and Ray.

Scott Gaetjen would like to recognize that Patrick Sack's strategic vision of what database security should be and his keen awareness of customer security requirements are the primary reasons Database Vault exists today. I want to thank Pat for extending the invitation to work with him on Database Vault and for challenging me every day to reach a higher level of assurance in all that I do.

Patrick Sack would like to offer a special thanks to Scott Gaetjen and William (Bill) Maroulis for their diligence, positive attitude, and professionalism. Scott and William have developed some key solutions around Database Vault concepts that inspired many examples and concepts presented in this book. Special thanks to Scott and Bill.

We would also like to acknowledge the following people for inspiring the idea, clearing the way, or getting the job done to make Database Vault a product: Glen Dodson, Raymond Prescott, Jay Gladney, Jon Bakke, Wendy Delmolino, David Knox, Rusty Austin, Gail Wright, Jack Brinson, Chi Ching Chui (and his team!), Chon Lei, Ben Chang, Vipin Samar, Paul Needham, Daniel Wong, Kamal Tbeileh, Aravind Yalamanchi, Timothy Chorma, Frank Lee, Nina Lewis, Maria Chen, Cindy Li, Matthew Mckerley, Xiaofang Wang, Martin Widjaja, Sumit Jeloka, Patricia Huey, Ernest Chen, James Spiller, Tom Best, Duncan Harris, Howard Smith, Andy Webber, and Jeff Schaumuller.

We would like to recognize the sales and consulting teams of the Oracle National Security Group (NSG) and the Oracle Database Security development teams. These Oracle groups work together to deliver the industry's best security products and solutions to some of the most demanding customers in the information technology field.

—Patrick Sack and Scott Gaetjen

I want to acknowledge all my peer writers for all their hard work and dedication in making this book happen. I would especially like to thank David Knox for his mentorship and friendship at Oracle. I would also like to thank Richard Wark, Pat Davies, Al Kiessel, Matt Piermarini, and Colin Nurse for their help and valuable support in many forms, including long, tasty lunches. Finally, I would like to thank my two older siblings, Javed and Tabassum, for being a constant force in my life to reach for bigger and better things. I am very grateful for their love, guidance, and friendship.

—Hamza Jahangir

I would like to thank David Knox and Scott Spadafore for their leadership in the Oracle Security community. Their work has directly influenced the security awareness of Oracle professionals, both inside and outside of Oracle, and consequently countless applications and products. I would like to express appreciation to Tim Ryan, Ken Currie, and Peter Doolan for fostering an environment of creativity and innovation. I would also like to thank members of the Application Express development team including Mike Hichwa and Joel Kallman, whose pragmatic philosophy, emphasis on performance, and strong work ethic provided an ideal environment for me to hone his skills. I would especially like to thank Tom Kyte for his years of mentoring, encouragement, and lessons in critical thinking. These individuals are some of the best and brightest in the industry and were a major influence in my professional development.

—Tyler Muth

I would like to thank Peter Wahl, product manager for Advanced Security, for his time, friendship, and contributions to the transparent data encryption chapter. For their help, I would like to acknowledge David Knox, Tammy Bednar, Al Kiessel, Hamza Jahangir, Matt Piermarini, Pat Davies, Tom Kyte, and others who have corrected, educated, and debated the finer points of electronic security along the way.

I would like to thank my Mum, family, friends, and co-workers for their support, encouragement, love, and friendship—I am indebted to you all. Special thanks to Melanie Valdez for her editing assistance and to Bridget, Jeff, Brice, Guy, and Joel for helping me blow off steam along the way.

—Richard Wark

Most importantly, I would like to thank Jennifer, my wife, for all of her wonderful support and for the long nights and weekends where she ended up managing the family solo while I typed away. Jennifer was also a tremendous help in developing my illustrations. I would like to thank Alysia, Samantha, and Matthew for putting up with "Dad being in the workshop."

The technical editors, Ben Ault, Robert Lindsley, and Derrick Cameron, have been incredibly helpful, and I owe them a great deal of gratitude. They provided excellent feedback on the material and examples. In addition to his technical feedback, Derrick also did some of the earliest work in integrating Oracle BI with Oracle Database security. This whole process would have been much harder without his work. The rest of my team here at Oracle have also been very helpful. They provided an excellent sounding board and helped me better understand the material presented. In particular, Jerry Conrad provided a great deal of feedback on the initial development of the concepts I presented.

I would also like to thank Michael Yeganeh, Ken Currie, and Peter Doolan for the opportunities they have provided at Oracle over the years. Their encouragement to innovate and integrate as part of my daily job has helped shape both me as a person and the content of this book. I deeply appreciate their support on this project.

Finally, I would like to thank David Knox for inviting me to work on this project and work with this amazing group of people. I also want to thank him for all that he added to the material I contributed to this book. I often learned more from the feedback he provided than I did from researching or writing the subject.

—Bryan Wise

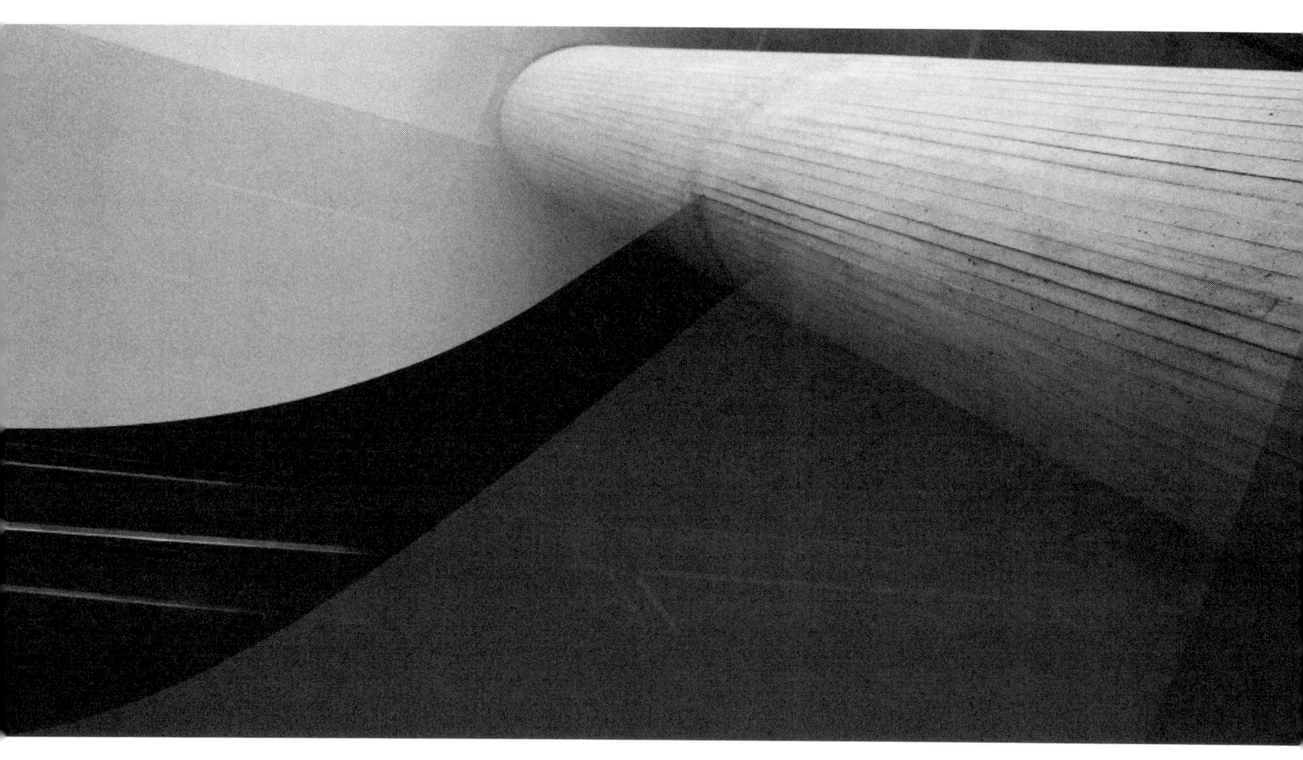

PART I

Oracle Database Security New Features

CHAPTER 1

Security Blueprints and New Thinking

omputer security is a field of study that continues to undergo significant changes at an extremely fast pace. As a result of research combined with increases in computing capacity, computer security has reached what many consider to be "early adulthood." From advances in encryption and encryption devices to identity management and enterprise auditing, the computer security field is as vast and complex as it is sophisticated and powerful.

Database and application security form one end of the computer security field. These two areas are closely aligned because of the heavy and obvious relationship between applications and databases. Along with other areas of security, database and application security continues to evolve rapidly. Creating a sound and secure (database) application is challenging not just because it can be complex, but more so because of the many possible methods that can be used to accomplish it.

While working with the many customers of Oracle Corporation, the authors have noticed two important things with respect to application and database security. First, in the architecture and design phases, complexity exists due to the technology and the various options available to reach an optimal level of security. Second, in the development and deployment phases, most people don't employ full and complete security implementations. Their reasons for this vary, but their obvious lack of knowledge and lack of a set of reference architectures from which to draw upon are key. This not only limits what can be crafted as a viable solution but can also have disastrous effects in cost overruns, project delays, inadequate results, and vulnerable systems. They have not mitigated the risks to an acceptable level.

About This Book

In this book, we have brought together top experts in business intelligence (BI), application development, identity management, and the Oracle Database. We'll show you how to use application security features, the application development environment, and the database itself to create secure database applications. As such, our focus is not simply on studying security features in a stand-alone context. Rather, our intent is to apply security technologies to the art of creating database applications.

We present several patterns for successful security implementations. Our objective is to provide successful security patterns, tips, and tricks that will help you understand what you should do to engineer a secure database application. We identify specific patterns that represent the predominant styles used by application-database interactions and then show you how to engage the features and capabilities in the database, the application server, the identity management platform, and the application itself to build secure and robust applications.

Background Information

This book is purposefully designed as a follow-up to *Effective Oracle Database 10g Security By Design*, published by McGraw-Hill Professional in 2004. In that book, author David Knox, who serves as lead author for this book, takes you from the basics of database security practices and designs to some advanced examples. Included are all the technologies available for the Oracle Database 10*g* Release 1, including secure application roles, virtual private database, Oracle label security, enterprise user security, proxy authentication, auditing, and database encryption using DBMS_CRYPTO. If you are unfamiliar with those technologies or need a better understanding of them, you should read the first book before you read this one.

While an update to that text that added the new options—transparent data encryption, database vault, and audit vault—was certainly a possibility, we decided to create a new book for two main reasons: First, identity and access management advances were needed to form any significant and complete description of security. Second, the goal of this book is to show how you can apply those base database technologies to secure database applications such as the business intelligence and Application Express (APEX) applications. Adding the new options, the identity management sections, and the application examples would have made the book too large for practical purposes.

In summary, the first book explains the basics of Oracle Database 10*g* R1 to help the reader understand what the available security technologies can do, and then it shows how to get them working. This book adds information about new technologies and applies all the security technologies to the task of building secure database applications.

Every attempt has been made to abstain from redundancy with material presented in the first book. Since we did not want to force the reader to refer back to that book too much and too often, parts of that text have been borrowed and placed in the appropriate places to enhance discussions. Our goal was to make this a complete and stand-alone guide that was not too voluminous.

Organization

The book starts with a discussion of the new technologies that were added since the completion of the first book, such as transparent data encryption, audit vault, and database vault. From there, we move out, first to the application server infrastructure and identity and access management. This information is important to understanding what other things an application developer and security administrator need to know when constructing security-conscious applications. We next move out to APEX and finally the Oracle Business Intelligence Suite (OBI).

APEX is a popular platform for developing light-to-medium–weight Oracle Database applications. Its popularity is driven by the fact that it is free to use and is tightly integrated with the database, thereby allowing any DB-knowledgeable person to create powerful and elegant database applications. This is a sweet spot, as many database gurus are not too familiar with other development platforms.

APEX also represents a popular application architecture. It deploys to the Web, and the application developers and users can connect to the database using shared and proxy schemas. APEX also manages much of the application-level security itself. Both of these aspects make APEX a prime case study and valuable aid in understanding how to work with those types of architectures.

OBI is popular and represents a standard way that people interact with Oracle Database. Learning the integration and synchronization points between the BI server and the Oracle Database security technologies proves a valuable, and more importantly, a repeatable lesson in securely connecting applications to the database.

In Chapter 1 we explain our top motivation for writing this book—namely, technology changes have been made to match developer and user behaviors for building and using secure database applications. This is a major theme behind the new technologies discussed.

The discussion then moves to the primary drivers for security. These security motivators are important because they imply what needs to be done to "secure" your database applications. More importantly, they identify the design and business goals that need to be satisfied to ensure that the applications meet an acceptable level of security standards. Put another way, the motivators help you define your business and technical targets. If you cannot reach specific goals, you cannot determine whether you have achieved success. You need to be able to answer the question, Is it secure enough? To do this, you must understand what you need to accomplish and why. Your job is to ensure that the applications and security implementations are aimed at the proper targets and thereby satisfy your business and technical goals.

The security motivators give way to four principles for implementing security correctly. The products, technologies, and blueprints discussed throughout the book are aligned with these principles. The chapter concludes with concrete examples of the architectural evolution of database security. In analyzing applications over the years, we have noted three main blueprints or design patterns that people have employed to varying degrees of success. We examine those patterns and analyze the pros and cons. This serves as a basis for future chapters, where we will build and connect various database applications. You will see the common architectures and best practices for each.

Database Security Today

Database security has changed radically over the years. In some ways, it has outpaced the growth of the general security market. The creation of record-level access via transparent query modifications—aka *virtual private database*—and the ability to perform conditional auditing—aka *fine-grained auditing*—are two examples of these changes. However, there is another side to this discussion, because we have to recognize that many of the design patterns and the Oracle products and technologies are focused on an era about 15 years ago—the mainframe and client-server days.

To achieve the security designs required for today's environment, you must understand not only how things work but also why they work. The intent of a product or technology is the first clue in understanding its usefulness and applicability to your current projects. This book applies (security) technologies to the problems and architectures used today. Before we get into that, though, you need to understand how technology has evolved.

Evolving Technologies

Simple technology models have always been used to explain complex systems, and a model can be used to explain security as well. Security can be described as an understanding of *who* gets access to *what*, from *where*, *when*, and *how*. Physical security and digital security are largely focused on the ability to control all aspects of people and things interacting with people and things.

With this in mind, consider how security has evolved as technology has evolved. Security implications center around two things: user identification for auditing and accountability purposes, and access controls to allow or prevent users from performing specific actions or accessing specific data. In sequence, we tend to think of the security process as identification and authentication—who (authorization and access controls) gets access to what, from where and when; and how (via auditing). Let's translate this into how Oracle technology has evolved over time.

In the early years, much of Oracle's security was based on the concept of a database user, in which the user logs in directly to the database and has a private, dedicated account. As you know, in an Oracle database, a user and a schema are considered one in the same. The reasons for this are numerous, but for the security architect, this can pose a few problems. Access controls and auditing in the Oracle database are optimized for the notion of users connecting directly to database schemas. The problem is, however, that building an application today is different from what it was when many of the baseline security models were designed.

While appropriate at the time, direct database logins have given way to connection pools and middle tier applications running on application servers that in many ways break the direct association of an end user and a database user. Furthermore, as you will see, a significant manageability challenge exists in creating and managing individual database accounts for individual application users who just happen to be accessing an application that uses the database.

Proxy Authentication Addresses Secure, Fast DB Connections

Oracle has slowly acknowledged this pattern over the years, and it has changed its technology as a result. *Proxy authentication* allowed developers to use connection pools and start lightweight database sessions for end users. This solved the challenge of quickly connecting many users to a database.

A problem still persisted, however, because the proxy call required the user to start a session with an existing database account, meaning that while proxy authentication solved a performance challenge presented by the connection pool architecture (and it did so securely by not requiring the connection to maintain the end user's password), it did not address user administration and management issues. That was addressed by enterprise user security, and proxy authentication supported that architecture as well. Manageability is an important principle in achieving an effective security implementation.

Enterprise User Security Addresses Manageability

To adapt the technology to meet the challenges of managing large-scale user populations, Oracle created *Enterprise Users*, a major step forward. The end users (or application users) are managed in a central Lightweight Directory Access Protocol (LDAP) repository. The directory includes an entry for each user that maps the user to a shared database schema. Also included in the user's entry are *role mappings*. This effectively gives us centralized administration and, to some extent, centralized authorizations.

The ability to grant and manage authorizations was not totally complete, however, as database roles in Oracle Procedural Language/Structured Query Language (PL/SQL), or definer's rights, procedures were disabled. Definer's rights procedures still provide the default model and is the prominent mechanism, if not the most popular one, for granting user privileges. As the roles were disabled from within any executing (definer's rights) procedure, any privileges assigned to the roles were unavailable, thereby rendering the roles useless, a less-than-optimal solution for privilege management. While invoker's rights procedures remedied this problem, many applications did not employ them and many architectures today have failed to incorporate them. Nevertheless, centralized user management resolves many of the user manageability challenges and has made Enterprise User Security a very useful architecture.

With enterprise users, identity preservation occurred, but just barely. *Identity preservation* means that you are able to preserve the identity of the end user from source application all the way to the database. You can then implement security and auditing controls on a user level. There are two problems with this, however. First, the DB security and auditing work at a schema level—that is, the identity of the user—is presumed to be the schema. Security is all too often implemented with some reliance on a SELECT USER FROM DUAL. You could, however, write your own fine-grained security via virtual private database, oracle label security, encryption, views, triggers and so forth. (This sentence probably should not say *could write*; it should say *must write*. Otherwise, you have no way of applying different security enforcements for users sharing the same database schema.)

The second issue—and perhaps the more important issue—concerning identity preservation is that security architectures of tomorrow, which to some extent we are already seeing, do not use end user identity as the sole mechanism for access enforcement. These security and control mechanisms will be based on many factors, of which the user's identity may or may not be a relevant piece. End user identity by itself is useful mostly for auditing purposes and not so much for security and access controls.

Security and access controls today and tomorrow will largely be based on authorization models that use roles, group memberships, and data attributes. This is because the users in many situations are unknown not only to the database, but sometimes even to the application! Therefore, no user entry will exist in an application's USERS table (for example), nor will an entry exist in the Oracle Database USER$ table and perhaps not even in the local LDAP directory. With no user entry, you have no access control list (ACL). Without a way to capture users ahead of time, identity is meaningless for security enforcement purposes.

To help you understand a bit better, consider an example that consists of a Web services architecture that federates or makes many calls as part of a single business transaction. Each of these services may be on separate servers, using separate databases, providing separate information for separate and potentially shared purposes. As such, the ability to execute a multi-call transaction requires some way of conveying to all the services, and subsequently the programs that access the databases, that the user is authorized or unauthorized to perform an action. Ideally, this model needs to support an infinite number of users and needs to be as adaptable as the standards on which it relies. The actual user identities will therefore not be stored locally. Authorization information and other aspects about the data and how the information is being accessed or used will be employed to ensure that proper access is controlled. User identities, if properly propagated, will be used only for auditing and accountability reasons.

Hopefully, you now are starting to see the new thinking of today. These highly distributed architectures supporting vast numbers of unknown users are forcing radical changes in architectures and implementations. In addition, another paradigm shift concerns how you address security concerns: What are these concerns? How do you know if your data is secure? What are you protecting and why? You can address all these questions by looking at what motivates the security end of businesses today.

Security Motivators

It used to be that to sell security, you had to *sell* security. That is, other than a few exceptions for a few customers, security was considered a nice-to-have luxury that might be considered at the end of a development cycle when and if enough money and time remained. In fact, most data was not considered sensitive and therefore not worth the effort to secure.

Many people used fear, uncertainty, and doubt (FUD) as primary tools to motivate people to adopt a good security posture. Statistics of insider attacks, network packet sniffing, and computer security hacks could create a level of anxiety sufficient for people to take proactive actions to protect their data. Many times, however, the statistics were insufficient in motivating anyone to do anything. The threat did not seem viable or the examples were irrelevant to the business of the day for that specific organization.

Today's world has radically changed its temperament on security—what it means and how to do it. With service oriented architecture (SOA) representing today's major infrastructure thinking, and business intelligence, collaborative, and social Web 2.0 technologies representing higher order thinking, maintaining a security environment to protect people and assets is just not at the top of the list from an IT viewpoint. But security can be viewed another way, and this has everything to do with the sensitivity of data, the pervasiveness and exposure of data, and the consequences for not sufficiently protecting the data.

Many people now believe that security is more important than ever for two major reasons. First, the primary drivers have shifted, from acting out of fear of direct data theft of hard-to-find and hard-to-obtain information to complying with government and regulatory policies set up to protect information that at one time was not considered sensitive but today is considered highly sensitive. Personally identifiable information is a prime example of such data. The explosion of information and information use has increased the need for security.

The second reason for an increase in the importance of security centers around the results and negative impacts that a compromise or data breach can have on an organization, its reputation, the future employability of those considered accountable, and the always motivating financial penalties and threat of incarceration. A lot of data needs to be protected. This data is shared, transmitted, transferred, analyzed, and integrated, and each action represents an increased risk of compromise. With compromise comes demise. With corporate brands and public perception influencing stock prices and future viability, security is indeed more important now than ever.

Let's explore a little more deeply to clarify this sensitive information and consider how we should protect it.

Sensitive Data Categorization

To satisfy a security requirement properly, you must identify what you are protecting, from whom, and why. By understanding the characteristics and use of the data, you can then understand its vulnerabilities and subsequently derive a plan to protect it.

At a high level, many organizations today break up their data into four top-level categories:

- Personally identifiable information
- Protected health information
- Intellectual property
- Data within the realms of governance

Personally Identifiable Information

The first category, personally identifiable information (PII), includes any information that can be used to obtain or create a false identity. It includes names, addresses, Social Security numbers, and other private information that can be used for nefarious purposes as a way to spoof or pretend to be someone else. The alarming thing about PII is that it is data about people—not just special people such as celebrities and politicians; it is data about essentially everyone. Furthermore, this data is used many times a day to perform the most mundane tasks, such as paying bills, registering for a license, applying for a loan, and applying for a job. These are just a few examples of where highly sensitive personal information can be found.

Identity theft is a growing concern, and organizations are struggling with ways to protect the identities of their customers, employees, and partners. Fortunately, some best practices for how to protect PII are developing, and these will be discussed in later chapters.

Protected Health Information

Protected health information (PHI) is privacy information that deals with a person's health or medical conditions. It is more formerly described and governed in the US Health Insurance Portability and Accountability Act (HIPAA).

PHI pertains not just to healthcare providers (such as hospitals) and healthcare payers (such as health insurance companies). Many organizations collect some PHI, and this data is scattered throughout their IT systems in employee benefit submissions, paid time off, disability insurance, and so forth.

The challenge here is to employ the correct amounts of security to protect the individuals' privacy without hampering the general business flows necessary to operate an organization efficiently. Authorized persons must be able to perform authorized tasks easily, and unauthorized persons should not be able to perform unauthorized tasks easily. The issue regarding ease of use has to do once again with human behavior and incorporating security controls in a transparent or unobtrusive way. This is particularly important in day-to-day tasks and applications that support such things such as HR applications and customer relationship management (CRM) applications.

Intellectual Property

Safe guarding proprietary information in a growing and global economy is more important today than it has ever been. Trade secrets, business transactions, and merger and acquisition strategies are among the top information categories that organizations are struggling to secure.

Often, organizations will (and should) create classifications around the data. Federal governments use classification schemes all the time to help control their information. Confidentiality markings are used to dictate the handling procedures of the data. It may be that some information is not permitted to leave the company, or information can be shared only with a partner who has signed a nondisclosure agreement, and so forth.

What makes this information difficult to secure is that large amounts of information in many forms is distributed to many people for many reasons. As it flows through different media to different people, it becomes increasingly more difficult to control and thus secure. In this book, we will keep our discussions simple while maintaining the point that this category of information is as important as it is large—it concerns lots of data and lots of people.

Governance and Regulations

The biggest challenge that has everyone's attention centers on financial statements in regards to the Sarbanes Oxley (SOX) Act of 2002. As a result of several disastrous events, the legislation holds companies accountable for the precision and authenticity of their financial statements. This is by no means a legal definition, as one is not required here, but suffice it to say that legal penalties can be levied for noncompliance. However, the results of illegal disclosure are often more important outside the legal domain. A publicly traded company's reputation, branding, and public image are constantly at stake. A negative event can have disastrous effects on stock prices and the future viability of a company.

The challenge for this scenario arises from several factors, among them are ensuring the timeliness of reporting the financial information, controlling access to the information, and naturally trying to guarantee that the information is accurate. Once again, this involves a must-have need to manage who gets access to the internal data and under what conditions.

Principles

Regardless of the classification of data and the need to protect it, you can adhere to a few principles when considering a solution to a business problem and contemplating the correct level and appropriateness of security. These principles are adaptations and evolutions of those cited in *Effective Oracle Database 10g Security By Design*. These principles should serve as guidelines to help you drive decisions and effective postures and are echoed throughout the book. Understanding them and why they are important is essential to your understanding the complementary technologies, architectures, and best practices presented herein.

Principles can serve to prove due diligence or, in some cases, negligence. Incorporating security is a delicate balance of preserving ease of use, performance, and manageability. As these factors often compete with security, it is important that you are able to justify and implement a balanced, prudent, and rational solution. Discounting security entirely is rarely, if ever, an option. The point is for you to be able to prove that the correct level of security is being implemented in the correct way. Doing so may assist you in preserving company brand, reputation, and viability and also in protecting your reputation and employability.

Layers of Security

You probably know that dressing in layers of clothing is a prudent approach to staying warm in places where the weather can change quickly and dramatically. Security in layers has an analogous benefit. A removal of one layer—say, by compromise—does not expose the entire system. When you look at how to apply security, you want to look at incorporating multiple layers whenever it makes sense to do so. There is no such thing as being too secure (which should not be confused with too cumbersome a security implementation to be usable).

Of all the things that compete with a security implementation, other security implementations should not be one of them. In fact, quite the opposite is true. The more, the better is the suggestion as long as it does not present a significant cost in money, time, labor, effort, or performance. While that may seem an impossible task, it is not. New technologies such as Transparent Data Encryption (TDE) can add a layer of security, thereby increasing security and keeping coding to a minimum, along with minimal costs, effort, and performance degradation.

Another best practice is to apply a security layer as close to the data as possible. This is an optimization technique in that it allows you to get the biggest return for the effort. If the data can be secured in the database, then do it there. This will ensure that a data security layer is available to anyone accessing the data. Adding security at the middle tier (application server) and within the application itself are the complementary steps advocated in a best practices doctrine.

Manageable Security

As alluded to already, being able to set up, develop, deploy, control, and adapt security is critical to any successful security strategy. You may initially look at these desirable qualities and decide that they are impossible to realize. But you will find ways to move toward effective security management, and you will ultimately achieve a better solution.

In fact, common ways for achieving manageable security have already been realized. Centralization of identities and authorizations—aka identity management—uses this very principle as its selling point. Centralization of security is in fact a major facilitator in managing security efficiently. The problem is that you cannot always consolidate everything into a single, centralized environment. You will see how technology has adapted to this reality and ways in which you can get the benefits of single control with the reality of distributed and autonomous applications and enforcements.

Business Congruency

The next principle to achieving security success is in aligning it with existing business policies and technology architectures. If the business needs analytical tools to investigate the deep meaning and relationships of its data, then the security needs to align with how those tools function and how the users are accustomed to using the application. You will see this incorporated into BI applications.

Another example of this comes from the predominant architecture of the day—SOA. Although this book is not about SOA, we will simply say that the goodness that SOA represents lies in its inherent ability to allow anyone to link into any service, from anywhere, at any time. The security challenge lies in protecting anyone from linking to any service, from anywhere, at any time. The point here is that SOA exists and will continue to exist, and to work securely in it requires an implementation that is congruent with how this architecture is basically employed. You'll see that you can leverage the identity management components and implement techniques that are aligned with many SOA designs.

Transparency

You already know that changing behavior is more difficult than adapting technology. A simple way, then, to employ new technology, and specifically security technology, is to make it transparent. Barring any substantial issues in manageability and performance, transparency will ensure a successful implementation. It practically eliminates the usability issues often associated with an unsuccessful security implementation. Transparency may allow users to continue to behave as always, without your needing to give up the ability to insert enhanced security controls and auditing.

Throughout this book, you will read how many of the technologies have incorporated these principles in their design, creation, and implementation. You should take these concepts and apply them to your thinking, designs, and implementations.

Modeling Secure Schemas

There are many aspects to creating a secure database application. Here we will cover a "jugular" topic that at first seems basic, but is in fact a bit thought-provoking. Our goal here is to answer what seems to be a simple question: When building and deploying an application, which schema do users connect to in the database? As you will see, the answer to this question has the greatest security implications on your overall design.

Two important points need to be made here. First, by understanding these models now, you will save development time in the future, as you will not be agonizing over what is the proper way to set up your application-database connections. If you don't agonize over such decisions today, employing the logic presented here will allow you to create more secure applications—because we have already agonized over the matter.

The second objective is to address the case that you are not architecting a new application but rather installing, maintaining, or securing some other application—that is, a third-party or architected application developed by someone else. The objective here is to provide you with the information you need to ascertain the correct risks in such designs and provide initial guidance on what you might do better to fortify the design.

In later chapters, we will use the information presented here to create or modify our schema models. Defining these models now as a reference will provide consistency for the remaining parts of this book. It will also provide a meaningful baseline to your future design and development endeavors.

Schema Profiles

As mentioned earlier, the Oracle Database does not differentiate between a user and a schema. That is somewhat disappointing, because those two things are remarkably different, especially when security is concerned. In this section, you'll see that this is actually somewhat trivial to overcome once you develop a reference methodology for thinking about your application and database design.

Within the database, you can think of the database users or schemas as serving some distinct purpose. For starters, you can generally separate users from database objects. User accounts are the schemas in which end users connect to the database. Schemas then can be loosely defined as a collection of data, objects, procedures, and so on.

Note that we are not suggesting that only two schemas are involved, only that it is logical to break them into these two broad categories. This argument is based on the design practice that says it's best to separate accounts by purpose and function. This not only simplifies the design logically and intuitively, but it also improves security. It is a basic database design best practice that rationalizes the overall database architecture and simplifies many of the database operations such as backups, version control, and patching.

The security angle to separate database accounts is based on the well-known and well-practiced security tenet that says you should always maintain *least privileges*. This tenet was well described in *Effective Oracle Database 10g Security By Design,* which summarized least privileges as the following: "Least privileges means you give people only the permissions they need to do their job and nothing more: you give them the least amount of privileges." One of the easiest ways to compromise a system is to exploit accounts that have been granted too many privileges.

Using this as your driving factor, you can start to categorize your database accounts into one of the following two:

- **Object owner accounts** The schemas that hold application code, logic, and data structures
- **User access accounts** The schemas to which users connect when they execute application code and query and update application data

Note that for user access accounts, a direct correlation exists between user, function, and security privileges. Users and thus schemas perform some specific function, and each function requires privileges. For simplicity, you can group users/schemas by functional role, which will naturally require a set of security privileges.

Object Owner Accounts

Object owner accounts are the accounts that you typically think of when you think of database *schemas.* The accounts serve as a container for execution code and other database objects such as tables, views, indexes, triggers, and so forth, that are part of an application or database option. The default database accounts that end in "SYS", which includes the schema SYS, are examples of object owner accounts. These accounts are often synonymous with a database option. For example, CTXSYS is the schema for the (Con)Text database option, MDSYS is the schema for the Spatial data option, and SYS is the schema for the database engine itself.

Putting the objects together makes certain tasks such as patching and backup and recovery activities easier to do. It also simplifies some code writing, as object resolution, object creation, and object access can be accomplished without requiring any further privileges—meaning that if you can create a table in your account, then, barring any fine-grained access controls, you can also read from it, write to it, and drop it.

The first practice, then, is to identify and separate the object owner accounts into meaningful yet distinct schemas. Depending on the size and complexity of the application, it may have from one schema to many, many schemas.

The difficult part is deciding at what level to break apart the code and objects into other (related) schemas. At first, keeping everything in a single schema might appear to be the simplest thing to do. However, you might later find this suboptimal for supporting many tasks such as patching, backups, administration, and, for our purposes, providing access and security.

For a single application, for example, it's not uncommon to see base tables in one schema, code in another schema, and metadata or summary data in a third schema. Isolating these might allow procedural code updates to the code schema to be done without significant (if any) impact on the other schemas. Likewise, building new summary data structures would have little impact on the procedural and data schemas. And, finally, backups may be more frequently done on the data schema as the data probably changes more often than do the procedural and code structures.

It's not our intent here to illustrate all the possible ways or possible reasons (barring the security reason) to separate objects into different schemas. Architecture and application design and implementation is as much an art as it is a science. The important point conveyed here is not so much stating the laws on how to organize schemas, but that you should apply a functional and logical organization to your schemas.

Security Concerns

You should understand security implications associated with schemas, as this is critical to ensuring a secure application design and implementation. It's important that we point out that no object-level security within a database schema guards *itself* from *itself*. The schema owner has full access to all the objects within the schema. It may sound a bit ridiculous to say this, because, naturally, that is why you may decide to co-locate the objects, code, and so forth. The obvious interrelationships and interactions among objects that are necessary for the application to work need to exist without security barriers.

It is a fairly common worst practice to allow users—general application users in this reference—to log into the object owner accounts (that is, the schemas where the objects reside). When this is done, the thinking is usually that the application code will protect the objects from any malicious or malevolent user intent. It is most often done to expedite development and minimize execution errors that may arise from an incorrectly or improperly configured database. Unfortunately, there is no way to distinguish between an improper configuration and a genuine security exception until it happens.

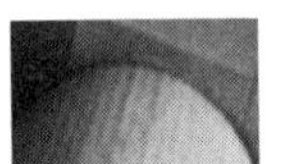

NOTE
It is a bad practice to allow general application users to connect directly to the schema that owns the objects.

This is a bad practice for several reasons. First and foremost, when users are executing within the object owner's schema, no database security will prevent users from having their way with the data or the data structures (recognizing that fine-grained access controls do provide a safety net here, but the point is still valid). Second, as stated earlier, you want layers of security. Turning off the database access security by way of improper design creates a huge risk.

As you can see in Figure 1-1 for a Sales History (SH) schema, you should not allow application users to connect to the database by way of the SH schema. If you do, nothing in the database will prevent users from mutilating the data structures and basically having their way with everything contained within the SH. Obviously, your application would need to provide some sort of security, but even with some security present, allowing user to access the database via the schema is a bad idea.

User Access Accounts

User access accounts are the schemas in which end users connect to the database. These user connections generally occur in one of two ways: The users may be directly connected to the database via a program such as SQL*Plus, or the users may be connected via an application,

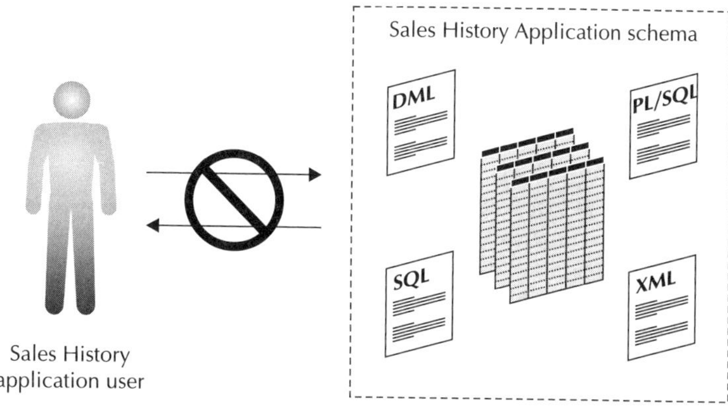

FIGURE 1-1 *A security worst-practice is to allow application users to connect directly to the schema that contains the data structures, objects, and code of the application.*

typically running through an application server that is utilizing some form of connection pool, connection sharing, and/or connection cache. For simplicity, consider only that from the database's perspective, the end user is connected to a schema.

Dedicated Accounts and Shared Accounts

Irrespective of how the users connect, they will be connected either to a dedicated account or a shared account. At the risk of stating the obvious, a dedicated account associates one distinct user with one distinct account. A shared account is used when users share the same functional roles and thus the same sets of privileges.

Security implications center around two things: user identification for auditing and accountability purposes, and access controls to allow or prevent users from performing specific actions or accessing specific data. From a security perspective, the simplest situation occurs when users have dedicated accounts, because the database applies object-level security and auditing controls at the schema level. If the user has logged in directly or used proxy authentication to a dedicated account, maintaining user identity for accountability is accomplished by default. Additionally, you can leverage all the native object-level security controls provided by the database to enforce access controls on a user-by-user basis.

Given all these benefits, you may wonder why everyone doesn't just go with dedicated accounts as the model. The answer to this was presented earlier in our guiding principles. The three reasons for not architecting dedicated user accounts are as follows:

1. User identity may not be known; the database invocation may be done via nested Web services or a federated call, which is unable to convey actual end user identity.
2. User identity alone does not provide enough of a security basis for many security decisions.
3. A one-to-one user-to-account ratio is a management nightmare.

It has long been argued that you should not allow users to share accounts. Whether you agree with this or not, shared accounts happen quite frequently, especially when the users share functions and thus privileges. The scary aspect of shared accounts is that they are often applied to administrator accounts such as root, SYS, or SYSTEM for the database. Shared accounts allow multiple users to access the same account but in doing so, it obfuscates their unique identities. This would therefore limit, if not altogether defeat, any auditing. If someone does something bad, no one knows for sure who did it.

Nevertheless, shared accounts still make sense for manageability reasons, and you can employ such techniques as setting the CLIENT_IDENTIFIER to propagate the real end user's identity. Another prime example on UNIX systems is the use of SUDO, which allows users to execute privileged commands (run as root) while preserving their identity. Notionally, and assuming that the accountability and security privileges are maintained, shared accounts are an ideal way to proceed, which is why it is a popular model used today.

Recall the notion of creating accounts by function. One familiar example of a default account is SYSTEM, the default DBA account for Oracle Database. Using SYSTEM, the DBA can log into this account to conduct most administrative activities. Note that the DBA is not logging into the SYS account unless it is absolutely necessary, as would be the case to grant privileges on a SYS-owned object. Ideally, individual accounts are created for the DBAs, and the DBA role is granted to each of the individual accounts. The authorizations and access controls are then based on the privileges assigned to the DBA role, and each DBA's identity is captured by his or her individual logins.

Note the immediate separation between SYS and SYSTEM. SYS owns the objects; SYSTEM has a functional role as DBA. This separation, which has been established as a precedent by Oracle for many years, serves as the basis on which you should consider your schema designs.

Getting Started

Now you know that you should segment schemas and user accounts. Within user accounts, you need to further divide by function and profile. One effective way to begin these tasks is to divide the user community into four coarse-level groups. These groups are coarse-level and are intended to be such so as to simplify the discussions. This provides the smallest, yet most prevalent, use cases as we discuss security patterns, so the focus can be on the categorizations as opposed to anything else.

We'll use the term *user profiles* to refer to the categories in which user populations are divided. These user profiles allow you to think about the basic requirements and then attach them to an appropriate design pattern. Quite simply, it's a needed first step to designing security correctly. You should be able to use this methodology when you build and design your applications. The intent here is not to solve or complete the design, but to provide a foundation and foundational understanding of what needs to be done and why from a security perspective.

User Profiles

In its simplest form, four categories of user profiles exist:

- Read-only users
- Read-write users
- Application administrators/developers
- Database administrators

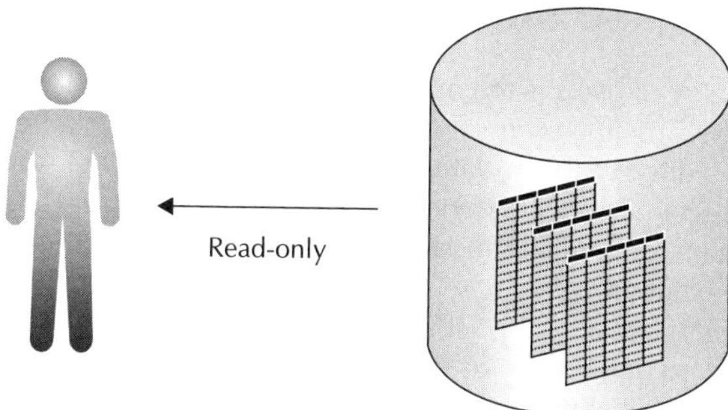

FIGURE 1-2 *Read-only users only consume information.*

The first class of users will be the read-only users (Figure 1-2) who are generally running reports, such as those typically found in BI applications or data viewed via a portal. Since these users do not modify data, their access should be controlled to ensure that they are connected to a read-only account. You don't need to further define the type of data they will be accessing, except to specify that they should not be able to modify any of it. Typically, you would use other access control mechanisms to ensure that these users read only the data that they are supposed to.

You should remember several important security points when building applications for read-only users:

- The security should enforce the fact that the users cannot change the data.
- Users should be confined to the application's data or only the data they need to access to do their job.
- Users should not be able to change the data objects or perform DDL (such as create or drop tables).

The second class of users will be the read-write users (Figure 1-3) who not only read the information but also update, enter, delete, and perform other tasks that can change the data. Typical examples are transaction-based applications and applications that are self-service in nature.

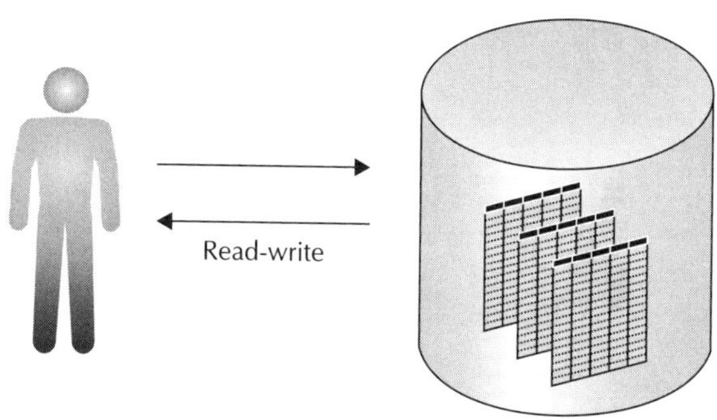

FIGURE 1-3 *Read-write users can read and update information.*

As with read-only users, read-write users should be prevented from accessing information outside of their application. They should also be prevented from manipulating the data objects themselves.

The third category of users is the application administrator or application developer, who are included together because the access they require is generally the same. The administrator/developer (Figure 1-4) will need to create, update, and delete objects as well as data. Configurations and some levels of fine-grained access controls for the application may also be required. This person's job is focused around an application, and they should not necessarily have free access to all information in the database.

Lastly, we want to consider the DBA, As you know, the DBAs are generally concerned about the health and welfare of the database. Due to the enormous amounts of jobs and activities DBAs need to perform, they generally have superuser access that allows them to access any part of the database and do anything necessary.

These four user profiles are meant to serve as a top-level grouping of user accounts. By thinking about the security implications to each of the user profiles, you can immediately decide what risks you will undertake by using dedicated or shared accounts as well as find easy ways to simplify designs and design discussions. Note that if you decide to share accounts, you will want to seriously consider the suggestions in the database vault chapters (Chapters 4 to 7), which will allow you to share accounts securely and maintain accountability.

Schema Naming

A large part of this book is dedicated to conveying best practices and methodologies to assist you in designing and developing secure database applications. To that end, coming up with a predictable and consistent naming convention for your database schemas will prove invaluable. A sound naming convention will allow you to collaborate more easily and mitigate confusion for yourself and others.

A good way to start with naming is to give the database account/schema the same name or abbreviation for the application module in which it serves. For example, the sales history objects could be contained in the SH schema, and the order entry objects could be contained in the OE schema.

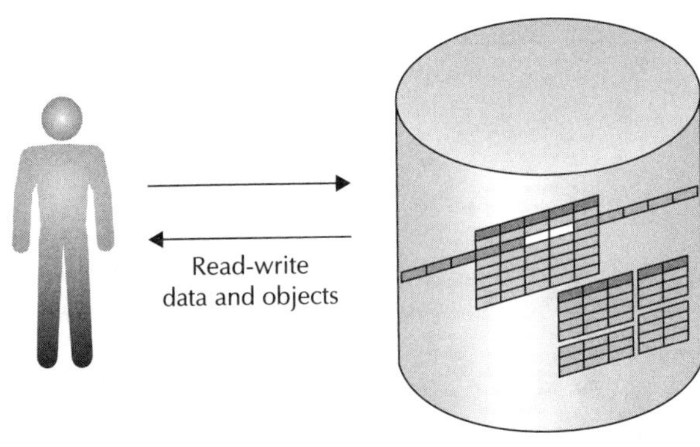

FIGURE 1-4 *Application administrators/developers manipulate objects.*

Another common practice is to create a new schema for each new version of the application. Of course, this makes sense only when the database objects and relationships have been altered as part of the new version. You will often find the new schema with a version number appended to its name. For example, later in this book you will see the Application Express (APEX) examples. We started with Application Express version 3.1.0. This installed itself into a database schema named FLOWS_030100. If you dissect the name, you will see the name of the application is Flows, not APEX. Flows is the Oracle internal project name that later evolved into HTML_DB and now is Application Express. The version naming used groups of three sets of two digits. Therefore, 03 for the major version number of three, 01 for the minor version number of one, and 00 for the initial release. A patched and updated version was released called APEX 3.1.1. As this version contained code modifications only, it stayed in the FLOWS_030100 schema.

The point to naming is not so you can decipher which version of APEX you are using so much as it is to have a consistent and deterministic method for naming your schemas. When you use a naming scheme, you gain the benefits of knowing which application modules (and often which version) are contained within each schema.

Security Architecture Checklist

This chapter has focused on security architecture. With everything stated so far, you might find it useful to create a summarized checklist of questions to think about and answer with respect to your security architecture. Consider the following as a start for a potential checklist that you might need to ensure architectural security. A simple way to start is to consider what happens when the end user clicks something in an application that fetches data from the database.

Consider the following:

- At a high level, how does that user action translate to data access? Can you identify all the modules and connections?
- To which account(s) are users connected?
- What are the privileges on the account(s)? This will begin to tell you what possible things the user could do if application security breaks.
- If the user is supposed to have only a subset of the privileges for the account to which he or she is connected, what mechanisms are in place to ensure least privilege? It's better if this security is declarative and enforced inside the database or application server and not programmed within the application code.
- Are you connected directly to the DB through a private or shared connection? If shared, how can you ensure that no information is leaked between connection threads on the application side?
- Are DB sessions shared? If so, what clears the session cache between users?
- In the DB, can a privilege escalation path be achieved by exploiting procedures?
- Are connections occurring to the schema that owns the objects? That's great for development but not so great for runtime, especially if the desired functionality is read-only reporting.
- How is auditing done? How can it be done in a secure way—that is, not manipulated by the people creating the audit?

You should now understand the security relevance to the interrelationship among schemas, users, and the data and objects with which they interact. Who gets access to what? From where? When? And how? This chapter begins to address these questions. The rest are addressed with technology, tips, and tricks discussed in the upcoming chapters.

Summary

Let's review some key points in this chapter. Computer security continues to change, and technology is moving quickly, so that increased computing capacity has allowed new capabilities as well as exploits. In conjunction with the changes in technology, new thinking about designs and architectures, risks, and requirements have radically changed the security landscape in a short period of time.

Understanding what you are trying to accomplish with an effective security posture is essential to creating a good plan and determining its success. The common security motivators serve as good reference markers for what people are trying to protect and why. Personally identifiable information, protected health information, intellectual property, and an abundance of government regulations are forcing people to think about the pervasiveness of sensitive data and the things they can do to protect this valuable information.

A few guiding principles serve as a practical way to deal with this challenge. We looked at layers of security, manageability, business congruence, and transparency as vital areas that make or break an effective security stance. With all technology—especially security—you need to take a practical approach to implementation. Likewise, manageability is a usability issue for administrators and therefore security must abide by this tenet as well.

You also learned about effective modeling of schemas, which involves comprehension and segmentation according to function. Likewise, connecting users to database accounts must be done with thought and clarity. A lackadaisical approach here can truncate any future successful security designs and worse: it can lead to a disastrous compromise.

In this chapter, we established a baseline from which the rest of the book can refer and which you can use to simplify the real issues around building and deploying a secure database application.

CHAPTER 2

Transparent Data Encryption

ransparent Data Encryption (TDE) is a transparent way to encrypt data in a database. It was introduced in Oracle Database 10*g*. The encryption is transparent because it occurs below the Structured Query Language (SQL) layer. The database engine automatically encrypts and decrypts data as it reads and writes it from the file system. In this chapter, we'll explore how to use TDE and discuss some of the advantages of using it. First, it's important to put TDE in perspective with the various other encryption mechanisms Oracle has and continues to offer.

Oracle has offered some level of cryptographic support for data stored inside a database for many years. In its first release, Oracle developed the DBMS_OBFUSCATION_TOOLKIT for release 8*i*, which gave developers a set of PL/SQL libraries for encrypting data, hashing data, and generating keys in the database. DBMS_OBFUCATION_TOOLKIT, aside from a complex name choice, suffered from several shortcomings and was difficult to use, requiring significant application design changes.

The second generation of encryption technology came with many improvements over its predecessor in the 10*g* release of the DBMS_CRYPTO package. Over a near ten-year period, these packages served as the primary, and really only reasonable method, of encrypting data within the database. DBMS_CRYPTO uses, caveats, and many useful examples are detailed in *Effective Oracle Database 10*g *Security by Design*. Suffice it to say that while DBMS_CRYPTO offered improved algorithms, key generation, and better data type support over the DBMS_OBFUSCATION_TOOLKIT, it still did not manage keys and was programmatic. If you wanted to encrypt and decrypt data, you had to write the PL/SQL functions and send your data through those functions. As with many programmatic approaches, this technology tends be unsupported and difficult to use with many commercial off-the-shelf (COTS) applications. To get the encryption, you have to insert code into the application, thereby altering its structure and most likely breaking the support for it.

TDE, as the third generation of encryption technology offered within the database, is significantly different in many respects from DBMS_CRYPTO. The first difference that you will find is that while DBMS_OBFUCATION_TOOLKIT and DBMS_CRYPTO were features of the database, TDE is a licensed option. TDE is not simply another way to encrypt data; the integration with the database engine and ability to implement encryption through SQL Data Definition Language (DDL) make it unique. Another difference between DBMS_CRYPTO and TDE is that TDE doesn't require significant development effort to implement. Instead, TDE provides a declarative SQL syntax to change the way columns, or entire tablespaces of data, are stored. TDE is a convenient and practical way to resolve many of the challenges introduced by DBMS_CRYPTO.

In this chapter, we highlight those new capabilities. You will hear about several practical uses of TDE, learn details on the mechanics, and see examples of how to get it working for your applications. To accomplish this, you will see examples based on the storage and use of credit card data. Credit card data, like all sensitive data, should be protected from disclosure and misuse, because it can cost both cardholders and credit card issuance companies when it's used in fraudulent transactions. You'll look at examples using credit card data, plus a set of mandates from the Payment Card Industry's Data Security Standard (PCI-DSS), which TDE can help address. As with other security standards, PCI provides a set of guidelines and requirements that help with the classification and protection of data. This will act as the "security target" mentioned in Chapter 1, providing something to work toward.

Encryption 101

Before we jump head first into TDE, let's review the basics of cryptography, otherwise referred to simply as encryption. The following section contains excerpts from the section on encryption from *Effective Oracle Database 10g Security By Design*. If you are familiar with the concepts of encryption, such as public and private keys, key management, encryption algorithms, and most importantly when to use encryption and what problems it solves and does not solve, you can skip forward to the next section.

Goal of Encryption

Encryption has an interesting history. It dates back thousands of years and can even be traced to the Roman Empire. At that time, it was common for Julius Caesar, who was acting president and CEO of the Roman Empire, to send messages to his generals in the field. These sensitive messages gave orders on how to proceed on new military objectives.

The messages were sent by way of a messenger at great risk of capture before the message could be delivered, which would seriously jeopardize the military strategy. Because of this, a simple encryption algorithm was devised and used to encrypt Caesar's messages. Only the generals and Caesar knew how to encrypt and decrypt the messages. If the messenger was captured, bribery, persuasive arguments, or torture were ineffective in divulging the contents of the messages.

This helps to put the use of encryption into proper perspective. It's important that you understand the basic problem that encryption was designed to solve. Encryption provides protection of sensitive data for an unprotected medium. The messages represented sensitive data, and the messengers had to cross unprotected media (land, mountains, water, and so on).

NOTE
Encryption protects sensitive data for an unprotected medium.

In today's interconnected world, encryption is widely used because it clearly meets the criteria for which it was designed: encryption protects sensitive data passing through the unprotected Internet. Many security professionals have extensive experience in the network security realm and a strong understanding of cryptography. This is one reason encryption is so popular today.

Databases and database security are significantly different from networks and network security. This is an important principle because the value of encryption differs when applied to problems outside its original problem definition. This will be your guiding principle for understanding when to use and when not to use encryption within the database.

Today, encryption sits behind every Secure Sockets Layer (SSL) connection and practically every Internet login page and e-commerce site. Many people use it without even knowing it. That's good, and it's called transparency. You will recall that we posited that transparency was one of the key principles to achieving successful security. The fact that SSL is transparently securing user interactions is a major part of what makes it a successful security technology.

The Basics

Encryption is the process of converting plaintext data into an undecipherable form. Once the data has been encrypted, it generally needs to be decrypted. The decryption (the act of unencrypting) of data returns the ciphertext to its original plaintext form. The study of these two processes is called *cryptography*.

A plethora of books are available on the market discussing cryptography (my personal favorite is Bruce Schneier's *Applied Cryptography: Protocols, Algorithms, and Source Code in C,* John Wiley & Sons). The mathematics involved and the issues and nuances of cryptography are staggering in number and complexity and well beyond the scope of this book. Fortunately, you don't need to understand all aspects of encryption. This chapter defines only what you need to know to make the critical decisions about how and when to use encryption within the database.

Encryption Choices

Although data can be encrypted in many ways, there are fewer ways to do it effectively. Many people are inclined to write their own encryption, just as Julius Caesar did. However, unless they are geniuses or very lucky, chances are their encryption will be poor. Today, effective encryption implies the use of standard and proven encryption algorithms. The proven part is important because it ensures that the encryption doesn't have some fatal flaw that would allow an unauthorized person to determine the contents of the sensitive data. Since you want to use standard encryption algorithms, you have quite a few from which to choose. Before you start picking algorithms to use in the database, you need to understand a little more about how encryption works.

The Algorithm and the Key

To encrypt data, two things are required: an encryption algorithm and an encryption key. The high-level description of encrypting data is quite simple: plaintext data is fed into the encryption algorithm. An encryption key is also provided. The algorithm uses the key and very sophisticated logic to encrypt the data. The process of decryption is analogous. It also requires a key and an algorithm.

Figure 2-1 illustrates how basic symmetric key encryption works. A plaintext message, "Applied Oracle Security," is encrypted using an algorithm and a key. To recover the original message, the same key and algorithm must be used.

The overall strength of the encryption is not determined by just the choice of algorithm or the key size. The strength is determined by the combination of the two. A common misconception is that larger keys for one algorithm mean that algorithm is stronger than another algorithm that uses a smaller key size. Some algorithms demand larger keys to make them as strong as other algorithms that use smaller key sizes. However, in some cases, larger keys used within the same algorithm do make the encryption stronger.

By studying Figure 2-1, you may see a challenge to effective encryption. If Caesar is sending General Suchnsuch an encrypted message, the general needs to know both the algorithm and the key that was used to encrypt the message. Studies of cryptography have shown that with today's algorithms, the only thing that needs to remain a secret is the key. Public knowledge of the algorithm doesn't aid the attacker in recovering the sensitive data. Obscuring the algorithm may seem like good security, but it's only a nuisance to a determined attacker.

NOTE

This point can't be overemphasized: Many cycles are wasted on "protecting the algorithm" in the real world. If knowledge of the algorithm is sufficient to break your code, your algorithm isn't an encryption scheme at all.

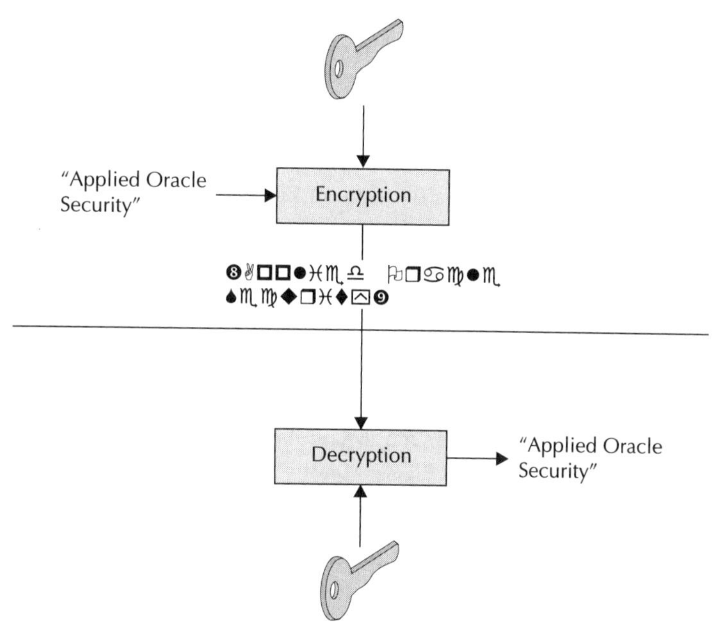

FIGURE 2-1 *Symmetric key encryption requires the use of the same key for both the encryption and decryption processes.*

Symmetric Key Encryption

Two categories of encryption are used today: *symmetric key encryption* and *asymmetric key encryption* or *public key encryption* (*PKE*). The algorithms for symmetric key encryption use the same key for both the encryption and decryption process; they are symmetric! A message encrypted with one key can be decrypted only with that exact same key.

Symmetric key algorithms are very secure and very efficient at encrypting and decrypting data. Some popular examples are RC4, RC5, DES, triple-DES (3DES), and the new Advanced Encryption Standard (AES). Because of their strength and efficiency, these are the algorithms used for "bulk encryption"—they encrypt large amounts of data.

When two people want to use symmetric key encryption, they need to have either a preestablished key or a secure way to transport the key. When two parties already know each other, it's possible that they will both already know the encryption key. For two parties that have never met and that want to share data securely, the problem of getting the key between the two parties becomes the major challenge. You can't leave the key in plaintext because an attacker could see it. If you encrypt the key, you have to do so with another key, which only moves the problem elsewhere. This motivated the development of the second variation of encryption.

Public Key Encryption

With PKE, two keys act in a complementary manner. The PKE algorithms are mathematical inverses: Whatever one key does, the other key undoes. Furthermore, knowing the algorithm and having one of the keys doesn't give the attacker an advantage in determining the other key or in recovering the encrypted data.

With PKE, the two keys are usually called the *private key* and the *public key*.

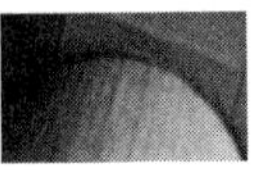

NOTE
Data encrypted with the private key can be decrypted only with the public key, and vice versa.

Private and *public* are used to describe the keys because it is typical for the public key to be accessible to many people. The private key remains a secret known only to the owner. As long as the private key remains private, this option works beautifully.

PKE, therefore, solves the key distribution problem. For two parties to communicate, they need access only to each other's public keys. Figure 2-2 illustrates how PKE can be used to send a secret message between two parties. To ensure that the recipient (the server in the figure) is the only one that receives the message, the message is encrypted with the recipient's public key. As such, only the recipient, the General, will be able to decrypt the message because the only key that can be used is his private key (which only he has). Trying to decrypt the message with an incorrect key yields gibberish. An interloper will be unsuccessful in decrypting the message because he or she will not have the private key. Note that the public key can't be used to decrypt the message that was also encrypted with the public key.

PKE provides another complementary capability. The private key can be used as an authentication method from the sender. As Figure 2-3 illustrates, a sender can encrypt a message with his or her private key. The recipient can use the sender's public key to decrypt the message. If the message decrypts, the sender's identity is authenticated because only the sender has access to his private key and so only he could have encrypted the message. Since our general was able

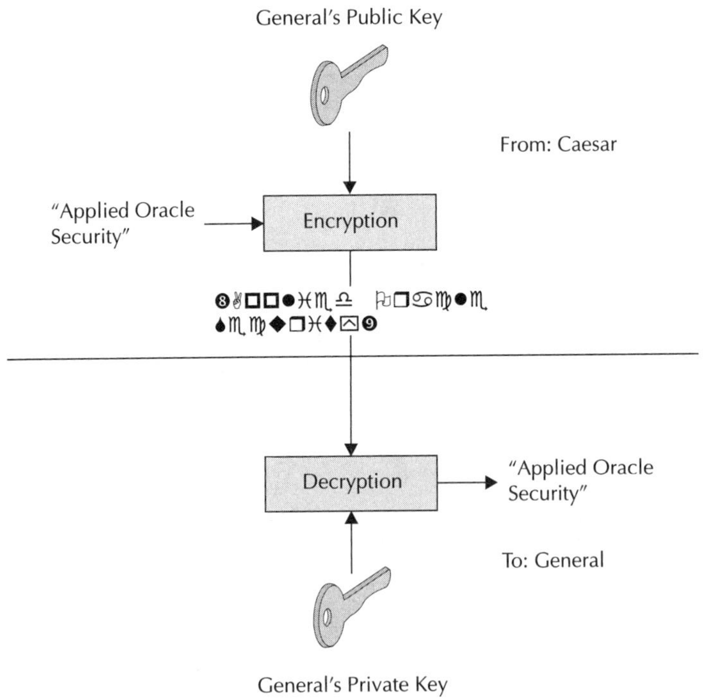

FIGURE 2-2 *PKE uses two complementary keys to pass sensitive data securely.*

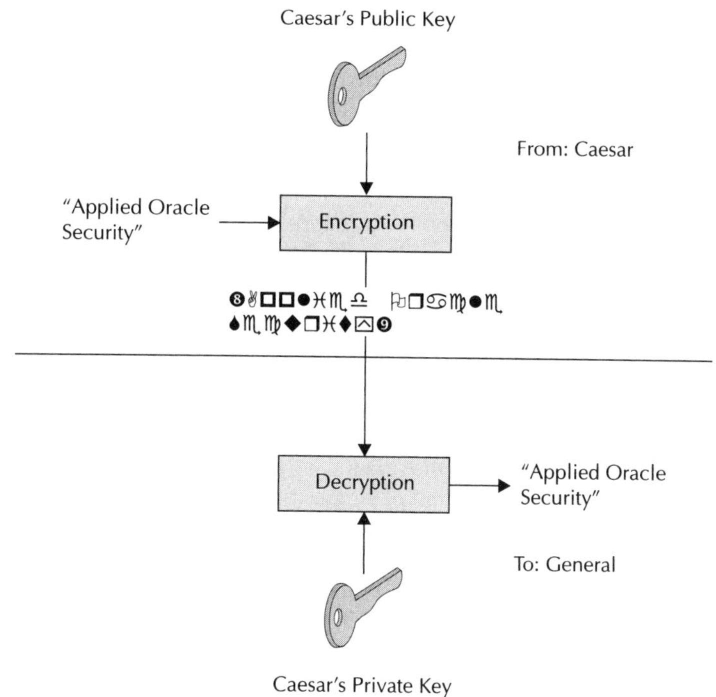

FIGURE 2-3 *PKE can be used to authenticate parties to one another.*

to decrypt Caesar's message using Caesar's public key, then he is assured that the message was sent by Caesar (provided he is keeping his private key private!).

Symmetric Key and Public Key

Unfortunately, the public key algorithms require larger keys to achieve the same strength received from their symmetric key counterparts. Consequently, the public key algorithms perform more slowly and are more computationally expensive.

Today, public key and symmetric key encryption are used together as a part of the standard SSL network protocol. SSL is the de facto standard encryption mechanism for data on the Internet. Due to its superior performance characteristics, symmetric key encryption is used within SSL for bulk data encryption. To transport the symmetric keys securely between the two parties, PKE is used to encrypt the symmetric keys. In Figures 2-2 and 2-3, the secret message is actually the symmetric encryption key.

Public key technology gets more than its fair share of the attention considering that proportionately it actually encrypts a lot less data than symmetric key encryption. This is because the administrators and users have to interface directly with the public key technology. The symmetric key algorithms are neatly concealed and hidden from view.

Understanding and acknowledging the use of public key and symmetric key encryption is important to the Oracle Database because the database supports only symmetric key algorithms. The performance and efficiency of symmetric key algorithms make them a natural choice for the database. Unfortunately, this leaves open the issue of key management, which is addressed later in this chapter.

Encrypting Data Stored in the Database

Understanding that the primary goal of encryption is to protect data in an unprotected medium, you might be wondering if it makes sense to encrypt data in the database at all. As you probably expected, this book emphasizes making the database a *more* secure medium. So, if it is very secure, why encrypt?

It turns out there *are* valid reasons for wanting to encrypt data stored in the database. First, you might be forced to comply with a regulation (legal, industrial, or organizational directive) that states that certain classes of data *must* be stored using encryption. This is the case with PCI for credit card data, and many companies have developed internal rules for what data must be encrypted when stored. In addition, the privacy laws of several states, such as California's SB 1386, remove the requirement for notification of victims of data privacy breaches if the data in question was encrypted. So in some cases, we are told we must encrypt out data, and in others it may be in our best interest in protecting corporate reputation, brand value, and customer relationship.

A second valid requirement for encryption is assurance that data can be protected throughout its life cycle. Think about data storage as a life cycle: data is created, stored, modified, moved, backed up, and deleted over time. At some points in the life cycle, data can be found outside of the protected medium of the database, as data is moved from the database to tape or another system for backup or disaster recovery purposes. Employing encryption in the database provides a level of security that can be maintained throughout the entire storage life cycle. Again, we must think of encryption as one "layer" in a defense-in-depth strategy that has multiple layers of defense. By storing sensitive data in the clear, we have missed a critical part of a comprehensive security strategy.

For example, historically, it might be the case that policy dictates that database administrators (DBAs) must not have access to sensitive data. This is often a requirement when trying to protect privacy-related data and is a valid security concern. Before version 10.2, encryption was the only way to keep data protected from DBAs. Their privileges allowed them to select data from any table and could be controlled only with the use of auditing (a compensation, rather than proactive control). Many organizations used DBMS_CRYPTO to selectively encrypt and store highly-sensitive data in the database, protecting the contents of the encrypted data from the DBA. This was a difficult and costly method to protect data and can now be addressed with the release of Database Vault, which separates the administrative functions data into access realms, as you will learn more about in Chapter 4.

In summary, the two driving requirements for storing data in the database are mandates and protection throughout the data life cycle. Next, you will see the technical vulnerability that's at the root of both requirements.

Where the Data "Sleeps"

To understand why encrypting data stored in the database is important, consider this example. In a table named customer, you store sensitive data—a customer's name and address (both personally identifiable information, or PII), and their credit card's primary account number (protected by the PCI-DSS). In this example, encryption is not used; instead, you will be able to see the data that needs to be protected. To make the example easier to visualize, if you try this at home, you will want to create a small (300K or so) working tablespace for the customer table that has one datafile (named customer_info.dbf in the example that follows).

Data housed within an Oracle database is stored using a proprietary format that makes efficient, high-performance data access possible. Datafiles contain header information, extent details and offset information, and the actual columns of data as they were inserted. It should be noted that while VARCHAR and VARCHAR2 are human-readable within a datafile, some other TDE-supported databases are stored using nonreadable, but reversible, methods such as HEX. Until the release of TDE, no protection mechanism was available from the database to protect the contents of these data structures without your having to write and maintain code, often wreaking havoc on existing applications.

Protecting the Data

Another significant challenge arises for backup files. Backups of large, mission-critical databases are often performed using backup software that writes data from *many* systems over the network to tapes. The centralization of the backup function can increase reliability and reduce the cost of performing backups with economies of scale. As a result, you may find that your database's backup copies of datafiles are on tapes being handled by operators who may not fully understand (or worse yet, do understand) the value of data such as credit card numbers.

As the number of individuals with access to these backup media increases, and as we move these tapes offsite for greater disaster recoverability, our ability to control access to this media is reduced.

Simple Example of the Technical Requirement for Encryption

Let's illustrate the point by looking at an example. We'll base this on the customer table described earlier. You can see the elements that are in need of attention:

```
sh@AOS> desc customer
 Name                                      Null?    Type
 ----------------------------------------- -------- ---------------------
 CUST_ID                                   NOT NULL NUMBER(6)
 CUST_FIRSTNAME                                      VARCHAR2(20)
 CUST_LASTNAME                                       VARCHAR2(20)
 CUST_ADDRESS                                        VARCHAR2(40)
 CUST_CITY                                           VARCHAR2(15)
 CUST_STATE                                          VARCHAR2(2)
 CUST_ZIP                                            VARCHAR2(10)
 CUST_CREDIT_CARD_NO                                 VARCHAR2(19)
 CUST_CREDIT_CARD_EXP                                VARCHAR2(4)

sh@AOS>
```

A look at the table shows the values of the data:

```
1* select * from customer where rownum < 2
sh@AOS> /
   CUST_ID CUST_FIRSTNAME       CUST_LASTNAME        CUST_ADDRESS
---------- -------------------- -------------------- ----------------
CUST_CITY      CU CUST_ZIP   CUST_CREDIT_CARD_NO CUST
--------------- -- ---------- ------------------- ----
      1001 David                Knox                 202 Peachtree Rd.
Reston VA      20190      5466-1112-2233-9342 1008
```

As is shown here, the credit card number and expiration data are clearly visible within the context of the database (as they should through SQL), so we know exactly what we are looking for in the datafile. Look closely at the datafile (customer_info.dbf in the example code) and you can pick out the good bits of data using commonly available editors or with operating system tools such as grep or strings.

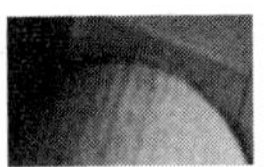

NOTE
While this looks all too easy to accomplish, remember that such access to a datafile requires access to the operating system and read permissions on the datafile itself.

Figure 2-4 shows the datafile (customer_info.dbf) opened in an editor common on nearly every *nix variant, VI.

You can pick out the David Knox record easily; see that 202 Peachtree Rd., Reston, VA 20190 is his address; and even jot down his credit card number and expiration (for later use, of course).

Viewing the Data

You can accomplish this in a variety of ways in addition to using VI. On Windows machines, many text editors or third-party binary editors will allow you to view the datafile. Similarly, on Linux or UNIX machines, the **strings** command lets you strip away nonreadable data and control characters, allowing you to focus on the meaningful data. Using **strings**, you can filter out all the readable ASCII characters and see the data. Unlike opening the datafile in an editor (some editors will not open files that are locked), this technique can also be used against open datafiles without disrupting database operations, making it a handy tool for hackers as well.

```
[oracle@aosdb aos] (aos-db)$ strings customer_info.dbf | more
```

Now that the sample data has been distilled down to readable text, your results will look similar to this:

```
}|{z CUSTOMER_INFO
      @      s
MGMT_SYS_JOB metrics
.
.
.


1209,
David
Knox
202 Peachtree Rd.
Reston
20190
5466-1112-2233-9342
1008<
Richard
.
.
--More--
```

```
jen^M98 Plano Java^FDallas^BTX^E76210^S4488-1112-2233-3764^D1209,^A ^CÂ^K^D^EHamza^HJahangir^P1 District Court^MWas
hington DC^BDC^E20120^S4488-1112-2233-3645^D0109,^A      ^CÂ^K^C^ETyler^DMuth^L11 Apex Blvd^FReston^BVA^E20190^S448
8-1112-2233-7822^D1209,^A     ^CÂ^K^B^EDavid^DKnox^Q202 Peachtree Rd.^FReston^BVA^E20190^S5466-1112-2233-9342^D1008
<^A        ^CÂ^K^H^GRichard^DWark^M511 Cave Lane^KSan Antonio^BTX^E78200^S4488-1112-2233-3998^D1009<^A     ^CÂ^K^G^
```

FIGURE 2-4 *Data in the datafile is human readable.*

Using the **strings** command, you won't see control characters or many "structural" components of the datafile, only the data itself. If a backup tape with company data, such as credit card numbers, were to fall into the hands of someone who shouldn't have it, a simple shell script that parsed through datafiles looking for **strings** of cleartext would expose credit card data (personal account numbers, expiration dates, addresses, and so on). In addition, with the help of regular expressions and utilities included with most operating systems, it would be trivial to script the process of looking for patterns matching, such as credit cards, Social Security numbers or other national identifiers, or other interesting data, or a regular interval.

It is also important to note that the structure of the datafile is not operating system–specific with respect to viewing the underlying data. Windows datafiles are susceptible to the same sort of file-level reads. With access to the datafiles on disk or on tape, data can be viewed on Windows systems with something as simple as Windows Notepad, as shown in Figure 2-5.

Data stored in a tablespace's underlying datafile is readable and potentially exploitable. This is a security risk that must be managed like any other risk, based on the value of the data, the likelihood of someone gaining unauthorized access to the data, and the amount of risk that you and your organization are willing to accept. While your first layer of defense in ensuring that the database's datafiles are well protected and that backup media is maintained using established policies, it becomes apparent that additional controls should be applied to any and all high-value data.

Applied Example

Imagine that your example datafile exists on a physical disk drive in a production system, perhaps in a disk array. Disk arrays provide a great deal of value to organizations by making certain that data is highly available. To do this, disk arrays generally employ RAID (Redundant Arrays of Inexpensive Disks) technology, which allows a single datafile to exist on several physical devices at one time for redundancy. If one copy of the data were lost or corrupt, the overall data availability would be

```
customer_info.dbf - Notepad
File  Edit  Format  View  Help
□1209<□ □Å□□□David□Knox□202 Peachtree Rd.□Reston□VA□20190□5466-1112-2233-9342□1(
```

FIGURE 2-5 *Viewing a datafile with Windows Notepad.*

maintained using the duplicate copies. With many such data storage devices, it is conceivable that a drive could be removed, making data on the drive vulnerable without the database ever being shut down. Another possibility with many of these storage arrays is the hardware sensing that a drive is close to failure (showing errors, and so on). Often, technicians will replace these failing drives with new ones, making it important to know the disposition of the replaced drives since they contain *real,* potentially sensitive data.

Likewise, those who can copy the datafiles to tape or other media could simply walk out of a data center with useable data. As the good custodians of data, we create backup copies of this data in the event of disaster or loss of the data center, often shipping copies of data to remote locations. This means that local and offsite backup media are also potential targets for would-be data thieves. Disaster recovery locations are required by many customers, yet these locations often maintain more copies of your sensitive data that must also be protected by some combination of technology, policy, and procedure.

As has been determined, a database's datafile may sometimes be outside of your security controls, and it may occasionally exist in the unprotected medium so elegantly secured by encryption.

Encrypting in the Database

You know that valid reasons exist for requiring data stored in a database to be encrypted. Now let's look at three approaches to remedy cleartext data being stored in the database's datafiles on a file system, and in subsequent copies used for redundancy or moved to backup media. The choices customers make are influenced by the complexity, cost, performance, openness, and portability of the solutions. You might choose to use an encrypted file system, building a custom encryption strategy or making use of a feature that is built into the database.

When using an encrypted file system, everything that is written to disk undergoes encryption to protect it from unauthorized viewing. This approach deals with the problem of cleartext appearing on disk and backup media by taking a blanket approach—that is, everything gets encrypted. While this approach does work in many situations, encrypted file systems are generally considered to be expensive, proprietary implementations, and you rely completely on the operating system of the host machine to make access control decisions. In fact, the PCI-DSS (as we will discuss later in this chapter) calls out disk encryption specifically, requiring that logical access "be managed independently of native operating system access control mechanisms," which effectively takes most file-system encryption out of the possible solution set.

As another potential solution to this vulnerability, you might choose to encrypt your data programmatically before inserting it into the database (perhaps using DBMS_CRYPTO or by writing your own scheme). When reading the data from the database, you then must decrypt the data to make it available to other applications and users. Programmatic encryption can provide selective encryption at relatively little to moderate costs (for development and testing), but it requires specialized skills and good design. In *Effective Oracle Database 10g Security By Design,* Knox offers some great examples of using DBMS_CRYPTO. With some development effort and use of function-based views, you can make DBMS_CRYPTO fairly transparent to developers, making this an attractive solution in the short term. Look at the longer term impacts of such a solution—issues of character set conversions, potential forced use of RAW datatypes, long-term code maintenance, and key storage make programmatic encryption potentially complex and expensive.

The Transparent Data Encryption Solution

With the shortcomings of other solutions, you need a straightforward, no-code solution to database encryption to protect data throughout the full data life cycle. If you are planning to store the data in an Oracle 10*g* Release 2 or later database, you might consider the Database Security option that includes TDE. TDE provides declarative encryption within the DDL with basic key management. TDE is an implementation of standards-based encryption algorithms built into the database engine, where data stored in a database is encrypted upon write (inserts) and decrypted upon read (select). The cryptographic key that makes this possible, the Master Key, is stored in an Oracle Wallet and can be opened or closed, making it possible to control the decryption of data by essentially flipping a switch. The keys for all tables containing encrypted columns are encrypted using the database Master Key and stored in the data dictionary.

TDE provides a no-code solution to this "cleartext on disk" vulnerability by allowing data architects or DBAs to choose individual columns (introduced in 10*g* R2) or entire tablespaces (introduced in 11*g*) and specify that they be stored in datafiles *after* encrypting the data elements. Since 10*g* TDE applies only to columns and 11*g* broadens support to entire tablespaces, column-level and tablespace-level TDE will be used generically to refer to each feature, with the understanding that tablespace-level TDE was not available in 10*g*.

This proves to be a straightforward, elegant solution, because TDE manages the keys and the implementation of the encryption rather than putting this task on the developer, as other programmatic encryption strategies do. The key management problem is important, because when you want to turn plaintext into ciphertext, you need to use a key. If you then want to decrypt your ciphertext, you must have the key available. *How and where* this key is stored is part of the challenge in developing a programmatic approach or using the DBMS_CRYPTO solution, as are key rotation, key backup, and recoverability.

Key storage is particularly challenging, because if the key were to be stored in the database, it might be vulnerable on the file system or backups just like the data you are protecting. In an attempt to remedy this, you could encrypt the key, but then you are left with the same question: Where do I securely store this key? Transparent data encryption provides the answer to this question by using the Oracle Wallet to store the encryption key.

TDE as Part of the Advanced Security Option

TDE is available with the Enterprise Edition of Oracle Database as the Advanced Security option, or as it's known in 11*g*, Oracle Database 11*g* Advanced Security. The Advanced Security option provides two other security features in addition to TDE: network encryption and strong authentication.

The network encryption provided by the Advanced Security option provides assurance that data is not read or altered between an Oracle .NET client (application, Java Database Connectivity client, and so on) and the database listener of the server, which often makes sense when dealing with any sort of protected data. Network encryption can be configured by adding a couple of lines to the SQLNET.ora file of the client and server, effectively encrypting the entire communication channel between the two.

The third feature provided by Advanced Security, strong authentication, enables the use of smart cards, RADIUS, and certificate-based authentication of the client to the server. Using the strong authentication feature can limit the ability to connect the database to a particular set of machines that have certificate-based authentication configured.

TDE Setup: Oracle 10g

TDE does require a small amount of configuration. The setup basically centers on creating the facilities for the key management. TDE uses the Oracle Wallet Manager to maintain encryption keys. You can think of the Oracle Wallet as secure container used to store authentication and signing credentials. These credentials may take the form of certificates needed for Secure Sockets Layer (SSL), Public Key Infrastructure (PKI) private keys, or a TDE Master Key. When the wallet is used to store the TDE Master Key, it's called an *encryption wallet*. A user with the ALTER SYSTEM privilege must create this wallet. Then you will find it as a file (ewallet.p12) in one of three locations, as specified by the **ENCRYPTION_WALLET_LOCATION** in the SQLNET.ora file. If this is not specified, the wallet creating process will look next to the **WALLET_LOCATION** parameter in SQLNET.ora, and lastly to the default location, <*ORACLEBASE*>/admin/<*SID*>/wallet).

When first configuring TDE, you must specify a value for the **ENCRYPTION_WALLET_LOCATION** parameter, which lives in the SQLNET.ora file—here's an example:

```
ENCRYPTION_WALLET_LOCATION=
  (SOURCE=(METHOD=FILE)(METHOD_DATA=
 (DIRECTORY=c:\<ORACLEBASE\admin\SID\wallet)))
```

Later, we will discuss the options regarding the security, functionality, and location of the wallet; for now, assume the simple case: it exists on the filesystem of our database server in the directory specified earlier.

After including the **ENCRYPTION_WALLET_LOCATION** in the SQLNET.ora file, you can create the wallet and populate it with a generated Master key. You will need the ALTER SYSTEM privilege to issue the following:

```
security_manager@AOS> alter system set key identified by "AppliedOracleSecurity";
```

This command does two things. It physically creates the file that holds the Oracle Wallet used for TDE, and it generates a Master Key that is then stored in the wallet. The wallet itself can be in one of two states, open or closed. The open state means the wallet is accessible to the database and encryption and decryption can be performed. Closed means that the credentials are still locked in the wallet. This is a security measure; to protect the data, the wallet also needs to be protected.

After the creation of a wallet, it is left in an open state until it is closed or the database is restarted. The wallet state can be managed with **ALTER SYSTEM** commands. The following command closes the wallet:

```
security_manager@AOS> ALTER SYSTEM SET WALLET CLOSE;
System altered
```

We can predict that the wallet has been closed by the database and will no longer make the Master Key available to TDE. To check the state of the wallet, check the gv$encryption_wallet view:

```
security_manager@AOS> COL WRL_TYPE format a7
security_manager@AOS> COL WRL_PARAMETER format a55
security_manager@AOS> SELECT WRL_TYPE, WRL_PARAMETER, STATUS FROM
gv$encryption_wallet;
WRL_TYP WRL_PARAMETER                                             STATUS
------- -------------------------------------------------------- ---------
file    /home/oracle/product/11.1.0/admin/aos/encryption_wallet  CLOSED
security_manager@AOS>
```

Note that the process of closing the wallet required only the ALTER SYSTEM privilege and did not require using the wallet password. This should alert you to the fact that ALTER SYSTEM privileges should be granted only to those requiring the permission (see the least privilege discussion in Chapter 1). If a person closes the wallet intentionally or unintentionally, all encryption and decryption halts.

Opening the wallet is accomplished in a similar fashion and requires both the ALTER SYSTEM privilege and the wallet password. Note that the use of keyword **ENCRYPTION** is optional:

```
security_manager@AOS> ALTER SYSTEM SET ENCRYPTION WALLET OPEN IDENTIFIED BY
"AppliedOracleSecurity";
System altered.
```

A quick look back at the wallet status in gv$encryption_wallet provides an updated wallet status:

```
security_manager@AOS> SELECT WRL_TYPE, WRL_PARAMETER, STATUS FROM
gv$encryption_wallet;

WRL_TYP  WRL_PARAMETER                                                   STATUS
------- ------------------------------------------------------------ ---------
file     /home/oracle/product/11.1.0/admin/aos/encryption_wallet OPEN
```

As expected, the wallet is in a open state, making the wallet available for the encryption and decryption of data provided by TDE.

The Oracle Wallet

The Oracle Wallet exists on the filesystem as a PKCS #12, which is a standard key-storage type under Public Key Cryptography Standards. The default filename is ewallet.p12. The file itself is encrypted and must be protected by operating system permissions. The wallet looks like this on the filesystem:

```
oracle@aosdb encryption_wallet] (aos-db)$ pwd
/home/oracle/product/11.1.0/admin/aos/encryption_wallet
oracle@aosdb encryption_wallet] (aos-db)$ ls -lt
-rw-------  1 oracle dba 1694 Aug  2 16:09 ewallet.p12
```

NOTE
Since the encryption wallet stores the Master Key for all encryption carried out by TDE, it is critical that you back it up! It should be backed up often and should not be stored with datafile backups.

The wallet is stored in an encrypted format. To decrypt, you must supply the proper password that releases the encryption key and opens the wallet. Note that the password effectively protects not just the wallet, but all the other credentials inside, such as the other encryption keys and possibly passwords. If the wallet is not open, queries that rely on keys stored in the wallet will fail.

Since TDE stores the Master Key in the Oracle Wallet and encrypts table keys using the Master Key, if the wallet is closed, the Master Key is unavailable and no data may be decrypted. As a result, each time the database is restarted, a security administrator must open the wallet before the database can encrypt and decrypt data using TDE.

Auto Login

With the major emphasis on security and protecting the wallet file and password, you may be surprised to learn that an Auto Login feature is supported. This allows the wallet to remain open—that is, after a reboot of the database or host operating system, the wallet is automatically accessible to the database.

There are good reasons for using Auto Login. Having a security administrator and the separation of duties provided by a separate wallet password is often *not* a requirement in development, testing, and other nonproduction environments. In these situations, an easy way to mirror the production security environment, but still allow for easy restarting of the database and not requiring password entry for the encryption wallet at startup, is to get up the wallet to auto Login. An Auto Login wallet is always open and can be recognized by a second file in the wallet's directory, cwallet.sso. When a wallet has been set to Auto Login, the directory appears as follows:

```
[oracle@aosdb encryption_wallet] (aos-db)$ ls -lt
total 8
-rw-------   1 oracle dba 1722 Aug  2 16:21 cwallet.sso
-rw-------   1 oracle dba 1694 Aug  2 16:21 ewallet.p12
[oracle@aosdb encryption_wallet] (aos-db)$
```

Configuring a wallet to perform the Auto Login function uses Oracle Wallet Manager. To start Wallet Manager, type **owm** at the command line or from Configuration and Administration in the Oracle group from the Windows Start menu.

In Wallet Manager, first choose Wallet | Open to open the wallet. After navigating to the directory that stores the wallet you want, the Auto Login will appear with a checkbox on the Wallet menu, as shown in Figure 2-6. Select the Auto Login checkbox and save the wallet. At this point, the wallet will remain open through database and host restarts.

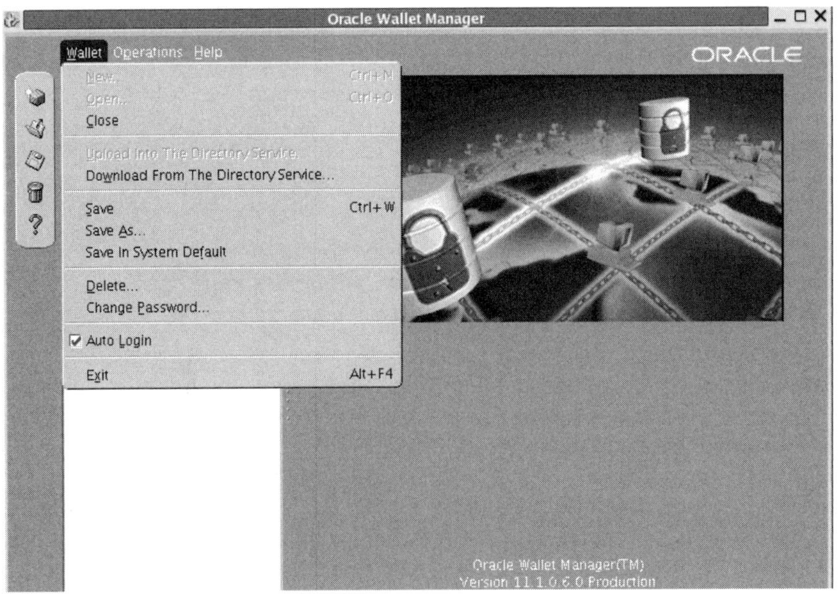

FIGURE 2-6 *Setting Auto Login using the Wallet Manager*

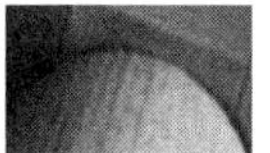

CAUTION
Auto Login is a relatively insecure method of wallet management and its use should be reserved for nonproduction environments. Auto Login creates a wallet that requires no password to open (since it's always open); you should take extra care when using this feature.

TDE's Key Management

The Oracle Wallet stores the Master Key for the database. Rather than using one key to encrypt every table, column-level TDE generates a key for each table with an encrypted column. After generation, this table key is used to encrypt column values. TDE uses symmetric key technology to encrypt and decrypt the data. Symmetric key is the standard approach to performing bulk encryption because of its optimal performance characteristics. As such, the key used to encrypt the data will be the same key used to decrypt the data. Therefore, the key must be stored securely and be available when needed. For tablespace key storage, TDE uses the data dictionary, but it first encrypts the table key using the database Master Key.

Figure 2-7 shows an overview.

TDE uses two cryptographic keys and one password (the wallet password) to encrypt data. Encrypted data stored in an encrypted column in your table, like the credit card numbers in the earlier example, are encrypted using a table key. These table keys are stored in the Oracle data dictionary after first being encrypted using the encryption Master Key. The Master Key is stored in the Oracle Wallet. Access to the Master Key is then controlled by the wallet's password.

This two-key mechanism for storing keys used in TDE provides the additional benefit of allowing for rekeying of data (as is often specified in security guidelines and mandates) without having to decrypt/re-encrypt each column in each row first. By rekeying only the Master Key, only

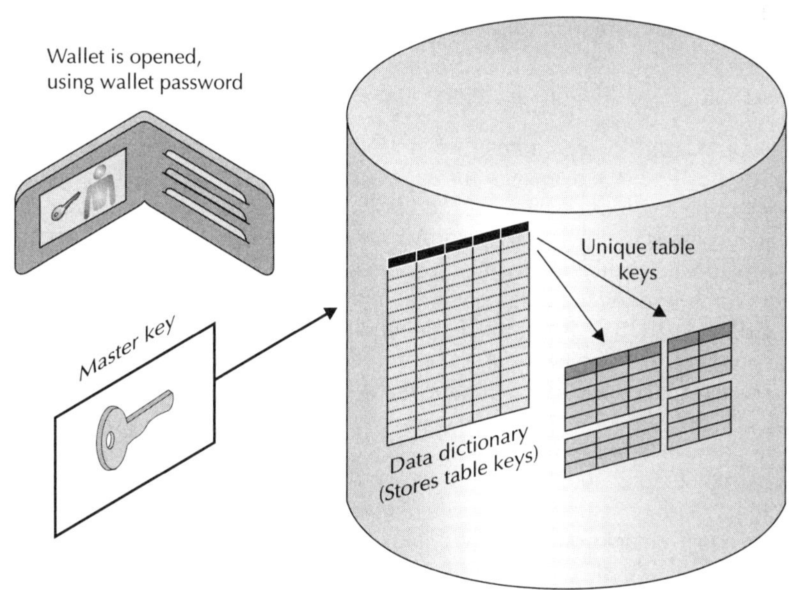

FIGURE 2-7 *Encryption wallet overview*

the table keys must be decrypted and then encrypted with the new Master Key and not the actual data elements. This helps operationally by dramatically reducing the potential number of reads and writes. When a large number of rows are stored in a table, this amounts to a considerable time savings.

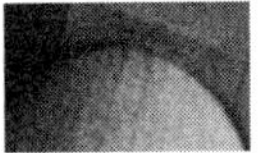

NOTE
With one very large customer, we calculated that decrypting and then reencrypting a credit card number stored in a table with about 7 billion records would take 17 hours when performed on high-end hardware. Using TDE, rekeying the Master Key required that only the table keys be decrypted and reencrypted, with the new Master Key taking only seconds.

Creating an Encrypted Column in a New Table

Let's start with basic column-level encryption. This capability was introduced in the 10*g* R2 release and simply encrypts the contents of a specific column. The general form of SQL to create a new table with an encrypted column is as follows:

```
SQL> CREATE TABLE <table_name> (<column_name> <date_type> ENCRYPT
[algorithm] [nomac] [no salt]);
```

Three elements relating to TDE are relevant to this statement. First, **encrypt [algorithm]** tells the database that you will be encrypting the column using the specified algorithm. The following algorithms in 10*g* R2 are available:

- **3DES168** The 168-bit key length implementation of the Digital Encryption Standard
- **AES128** The 128-bit key length implementation of the Advanced Encryption Standard
- **AES192** The 192-bit key length implementation of the Advanced Encryption Standard (the default if nothing is specified)
- **AES256** The 256-bit key length implementation of the Advanced Encryption Standard

The NOMAC directive/parameter was introduced in 10.2.0.4 and is not available in the original 10*g* R2 (10.2.0.3) release. A message authentication code (MAC) is generated by default when encrypting a column requires an additional 20 bytes of storage for each encrypted value stored. Its purpose is to provide an integrity check for the encrypted data. Certainly, a performance penalty is paid when building the integrity check, as it requires CPU cycles to build and is created for each column inserted into a table with an encrypted column. An obvious storage penalty also results, and while 20 bytes is not much, depending on the volume of data stored in the encrypted table, it could become significant. As is often seen in matters of security, an obvious trade-off exists in performance and the security and integrity of stored data.

Salt

A *salt* is a cryptographic tool that effectively makes any encryption algorithm stronger by introducing a random value—in TDE, 16 bytes—that is concatenated with the plaintext to stop "known text" attacks on encrypted data.

Although valuable for additional security, adding a salt in your definition also somewhat limits the ability to create meaningful indexes on encrypted columns by essentially removing the relationship between values. The use of a salt is required when data is sufficiently sensitive to necessitate the strongest protections possible; it can require that data architects build surrogate keys on tables with naturally occurring keys, making it time-consuming, costly, and detrimental to project schedules.

The DDL for creating a new table with an encrypted column in its most basic form is performed by adding the **ENCRYPT** directive to a **CREATE TABLE** statement:

```
CREATE TABLE foo (columnA datatype, columnB datatype ENCRYPT);
```

This statement defaults to the Advanced Encryption Standard (AES) encryption algorithm, with a key length of 192 bits, a salt, and a MAC of 20 bits. Any column that you might consider a candidate for an index should use the **no salt** directive:

```
CREATE TABLE foo (columnA datatype, columnB datatype ENCRYPT no salt);
```

Applied Example

In 10*g*, you can create a table with an encrypted column by adding the word **encrypt** to the table's **CREATE** DDL. This generates a new table key that's stored in the data dictionary after being encrypted by the database Master Key, and encrypts any data written to that column. Here is an example of the syntax used to encrypt the credit card number from the earlier example using the 192-bit implementation of the AES:

```
system@AOS> CREATE TABLE sh.customer_enc (
        cust_id                      NUMBER(6)    PRIMARY KEY,
        cust_firstname               VARCHAR2(20),
        cust_lastname                VARCHAR2(20),
        cust_address                 VARCHAR2(40),
        cust_city                    VARCHAR2(15),
        cust_state                   VARCHAR2(2),
        cust_zip                     VARCHAR2(10),
        cust_credit_card_no          VARCHAR2(19) encrypt using 'AES192',
        cust_credit_card_exp         VARCHAR2(4)
        )
        TABLESPACE customer_info_protected
        /
```

At this point, by reinserting the data into the newly created table, customer_enc, you can validate that the credit card numbers are protected. If you again use the UNIX command **strings** on the new customer_info_protected datafile, you'll see that no credit card numbers appear in the clear:

```
oracle@aosdb aos]$ strings customer_info_protected.dbf | more
}|{z
CUSTOMER_INFO_PROTECTED
BEGINCREATE
.
.
%oEM
1209,
David
Knox
202 Peachtree Rd.
Reston
```

```
20190
76210D
1008<
Richard
.
.
--More--
```

In the unencrypted example, you were able to see that the credit card number stored for this record in the tablespace's datafile was clearly visible. By encrypting the column used to store this data, as in this example, data stored using the TDE's protection is unreadable from a file system perspective and measurably less vulnerable than it was when stored in its original form.

TDE vs. DBMS_CRYPTO Package

As often happens with technology, there is more to implementing encryption than what appears at first view. Let's examine the details by comparing TDE to DBMS_CRYPTO.

The DBMS_CRYPTO package is used to encrypt values programmatically in PL/SQL that may then be written to the database. To do this, you must give DBMS_CRYPTO the data, an encryption algorithm, and a key to perform the encryption. When the same data is read from the database, it must then be decrypted using the same algorithm and key. Subtle differences can be made by changing padding, modifiers, initialization vectors, and cipher modifiers, but those details are covered sufficiently in the *Effective Oracle Database Security 10g by Design* text.

DBMS_CRYPTO provides one function and two procedures used to encrypt data. The function is built to handle the RAW data type, while the two procedures are large object, or LOB (binary lob object [BLOB] and character large object [CLOB]), centered.

Often, the data type in an existing application is a NUMBER, CHAR, or VARCHAR2, which means that another RAW or LOB column must be added, which is not always possible. The second issue that arises when implementing or planning to implement a strategy with DBMS_CRYPTO is key storage. If the goal is to protect the data, you must protect the keys using very secure methods. Where do you store the keys? Arguably, by storing them in the database with no additional protection, you don't really gain much over storing the data in plaintext as you rely of the Discretionary Access Controls of Oracle Database, so why couldn't you rely on those controls to begin with?

Among the storage options are the following:

- Write the keys to a file system using UTL_FILE or another method; however, the procedure or function that reads/writes this data can be protected only using the same methods of access control used by the database.
- Encrypt the keys with DBMS_CRYPTO (as they are then protected), but then you're left with another key to protect.
- Use a key management appliance, called a hardware security module (HSM), that can then make keys available securely.
- Write a custom solution that manages these keys for you programmatically and provides a secure storage mechanism.

The last option basically describes the basic functionality of TDE, but TDE goes beyond this with its tight integration to the database and the SQL engine of Oracle. The following table provides a side-by-side comparison of the attributes of DBMS_CRYPT and TDE.

Option	DBMS_CRYPTO	TDE
Key management	None, must be developed	Oracle Wallet / HSM
Key storage	None, must be developed	Dual-key Wallet + data dictionary
Implementation	Programmatic	Declarative (DDL)
Algorithms	DES, 3DES, AES, RC4, 3DES_2KEY	3DES168, AES (128, 192, and 256 bit)
Hardware support	None	HSM (via PKCS #11)
Hashing available	Yes (SHA-1)	MAC

Viewing Encrypted Columns

The database dictionary allows administrators and schema owners to see what columns within a particular database or single schema are being stored using encryption and to provide information on the encryption algorithm used in each case. This data is stored in the DBA_ENCRYPTED_COLUMNS view (for administrators) to view details of all encrypted columns with a database. Similarly, the USER_ENCRYPTED_COLUMNS view allows a schema owner access to the details of encrypted column in the objects they own.

```
security_manager@AOS> COL OWNER format a10
security_manager@AOS> COL TABLE_NAME format a25
security_manager@AOS> COL COLUMN_NAME format a25
security_manager@AOS> COL ENCRYPTION_ALG format a18
security_manager@AOS> COL SALT format a5
security_manager@AOS> SELECT owner, table_name, column_name, encryption_alg,
salt FROM dba_encrypted_columns;

OWNER   TABLE_NAME                COLUMN_NAME         ENCRYPTION_ALG     SALT
------- ------------------------- ------------------- ------------------ -----
SH      CUSTOMER_ENC              TABLE_TYPE          AES 192 bits key   YES
```

Encrypting an Existing Column

In many organizations, applications have been running for many years, having been built on an Oracle database or perhaps built on another database subsystem and later migrated to Oracle Database. It certainly makes sense to look at these legacy applications with a critical eye in regard to security and compliance initiatives. It is quite easy to make some minor changes to the underlying schemas of these historical applications to make them more secure in their handling and use of sensitive data.

TDE allows for the modification of existing tables to encrypt columns at rest. The general form for changing an existing column in a table from plaintext to encrypted storage is as follows:

```
SQL> ALTER TABLE <table_name> MODIFY (<column_name> ENCRYPT ['nomac'] [no salt]);
Alter table foo modify (columnA datatype encrypt);
```

You should consider both storage and performance when encrypting an existing column. Earlier, we mentioned that adding a MAC to the encrypted data adds 20 bytes; including a salt will add a few more bytes, and the encryption algorithm itself adds a few bytes per column as it "pads" data to create evenly sized blocks of data to encrypt. As a result of this extra space being added to your plaintext data as it is encrypted, it will no longer fit into the blocks it occupied before encryption. In other words, you encrypted "foo" and now have "@#SK^X", which will no longer fit in the space previously occupied by "foo".

The database handles this additional requirement for more space by chaining the column and storing it out of line in the tablespace's free list. This chaining will not be noticed in many situations, especially those with tables that have a small number of rows (less than 10,000). When the tables you want to encrypt have greater data volumes, the chaining created by the encryption process will increase the load on the database's I/O subsystem by potentially doubling the number of read operations as it first reads the row data and then reads the encrypted column in a separate disk read.

Knowing that the encryption operation can lead to a slightly greater load on the CPU and storage subsystem gives you some specific areas for preproduction testing. Often, a simple reorganization of the table can be the easiest solution to chaining. In very highly available environments with mission-critical applications, online redefinition should be considered because it takes the effected table offline for only an instant.

DBAs will often reorganize a table by first exporting the data (**exp** or **datapump**) to pull data out of the existing table, dropping the old cleartext table, and then creating a new table with the sensitive columns encrypted (usually in a newly created tablespace). Reloading the contents of the export into the newly created secure table resolves the row-chaining problem. This technique also takes care of any unencrypted "artifacts" (unencrypted data left in their original data block while newly encrypted blocks are stored in free space) that may remain in datafiles. The caveat to this approach is that it can require quite a bit of time for large tables, and the table will be unavailable while the process is being carried out.

NOTE
It is definitely a best-practice to reorganize any table that has been modified to include an encrypted column—including tables not originally defined as having an encrypted column and tables with encrypted columns added.

Another technique to use is online redefinition. First introduced with 9*i*, online redefinition allows for reorganization to take place. But instead of the database administrator doing the work of creating the new structure, loading data from the old table into the new, and dropping the old and renaming the new, it instructs the database to handle the whole process and doesn't require a manual process.

To make an in-place, online redefinition of our example table, customer, you would follow these steps to create the table shown in the example:

1. **EXECUTE dbms_redefinition.can_redef_table ('SH', 'CUSTOMER');**
2. **CREATE TABLE sh.customer_stage as SELECT * FROM sh.customer;**
3. **ALTER TABLE sh.customer_stage MODIFY (cust_credit_card_no encrypt);**
4. **EXECUTE dbms_redefinition.start_redef_table ('SH', 'CUSTOMER', 'CUSTOMER_STAGE');**
5. **EXECUTE dbms_redefinition.finish_redef_table ('SH', 'CUSTOMER', 'CUSTOMER_STAGE');**

Example:

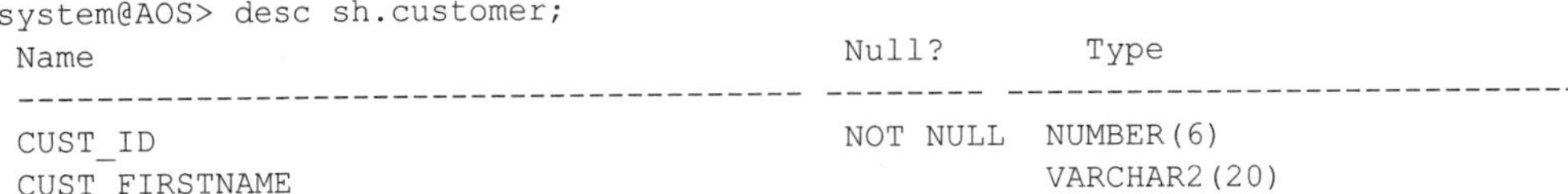

```
system@AOS> desc sh.customer;
 Name                                      Null?    Type
 ----------------------------------------- -------- ----------------------------
 CUST_ID                                   NOT NULL NUMBER(6)
 CUST_FIRSTNAME                                     VARCHAR2(20)
```

```
 CUST_LASTNAME                                       VARCHAR2(20)
 CUST_ADDRESS                                        VARCHAR2(40)
 CUST_CITY                                           VARCHAR2(15)
 CUST_STATE                                          VARCHAR2(2)
 CUST_ZIP                                            VARCHAR2(10)
 CUST_CREDIT_CARD_NO                                 VARCHAR2(19) ENCRYPT
 CUST_CREDIT_CARD_EXP                                VARCHAR2(4)

system@AOS> desc sh.customer;
 Name                                     Null?      Type
 ---------------------------------------- --------   ------------------------------
 CUST_ID                                  NOT NULL   NUMBER(6)
 CUST_FIRSTNAME                                      VARCHAR2(20)
 CUST_LASTNAME                                       VARCHAR2(20)
 CUST_ADDRESS                                        VARCHAR2(40)
 CUST_CITY                                           VARCHAR2(15)
 CUST_STATE                                          VARCHAR2(2)
 CUST_ZIP                                            VARCHAR2(10)
 CUST_CREDIT_CARD_NO                                 VARCHAR2(19)
 CUST_CREDIT_CARD_EXP                                VARCHAR2(4)


system@AOS> EXECUTE dbms_redefinition.can_redef_table ('SH', 'CUSTOMER');
PL/SQL procedure successfully completed.
system@AOS> desc sh.customer_stage;
 Name                                     Null?      Type
 ------------------------------------------------   ----------------------------
 CUST_ID                                  NOT NULL   NUMBER(6)
 CUST_FIRSTNAME                                      VARCHAR2(20)
 CUST_LASTNAME                                       VARCHAR2(20)
 CUST_ADDRESS                                        VARCHAR2(40)
 CUST_CITY                                           VARCHAR2(15)
 CUST_STATE                                          VARCHAR2(2)
 CUST_ZIP                                            VARCHAR2(10)
 CUST_CREDIT_CARD_NO                                 VARCHAR2(19) ENCRYPT
 CUST_CREDIT_CARD_EXP                                VARCHAR2(4)

system@AOS> EXECUTE dbms_redefinition.start_redef_table ('SH', 'CUSTOMER',
'CUSTOMER_STAGE');
PL/SQL procedure successfully completed.
system@AOS> EXECUTE dbms_redefinition.finish_redef_table ('SH', 'CUSTOMER',
'CUSTOMER_STAGE');
PL/SQL procedure successfully completed.
system@AOS> desc sh.customer;
 Name                                     Null?      Type
 ---------------------------------------- -------- ------------------------------
 CUST_ID                                  NOT NULL NUMBER(6)
 CUST_FIRSTNAME                                      VARCHAR2(20)
 CUST_LASTNAME                                       VARCHAR2(20)
 CUST_ADDRESS                                        VARCHAR2(40)
 CUST_CITY                                           VARCHAR2(15)
 CUST_STATE                                          VARCHAR2(2)
 CUST_ZIP                                            VARCHAR2(10)
 CUST_CREDIT_CARD_NO                                 VARCHAR2(19) ENCRYPT
 CUST_CREDIT_CARD_EXP                                VARCHAR2(4)
```

TDE Caveats

Column-level TDE encrypts and decrypts data at the SQL level, making it transparent to the end user. As a result, several database features that access data at the kernel level are incompatible with column-level TDE. Using change data capture (both synchronous and asynchronous), streams (in 10*g*), materialized views, transportable tablespaces, and LOBs are not possible if they include objects containing encrypted columns. These limitations disappear with tablespace encryption available in 11*g*, as you will see in the next section.

Another potential drawback in TDE's column-based encryption is that it cannot be used in certain types of indexes or in the definition of a primary key/foreign key (PK/FK) relationship. Indexes built on encrypted columns are created using the encrypted values stored in the column. As a result, use of an index is possible for an equality match provided that the encryption was defined using the "no salt" option. The index will not be used, however, in queries that do a range scan. In fact, you will not be allowed to create an index on a column encrypted with the salt directive (failing with **ORA-28338:** cannot encrypt indexed column[s] with salt).

In the case of PK/FK relationships, since each table is encrypted using its own table-level key, the keys are different among tables and, therefore, the encrypted values for similar strings are different. In this process, the relationship that existed between the data is lost without first decrypting the column.

While many will argue that natural keys (those that are managed outside of the application, such as SSNs, employee IDs, or stock numbers) are not good candidates as primary keys for establishing uniqueness in a table, the fact is they are and have been used as primary keys and are often found in applications that have, over time, been ported from other database environments. As such, dealing with PK/FK relationships in application that require the protection offered by TDE presents a special problem with column-level TDE. This limitation is addressed in version 11*g* with the introduction of a new capability: tablespace encryption.

Tablespace Encryption: New with Oracle 11*g*

It is obvious that some very real business problems are satisfied by 10*g*'s column-level encryption capability. In a separate subset of use cases, column-level encryptions limitations make it more challenging to encrypt individual data elements to achieve the desired outcome and balance of security and performance.

For instance, many times you might find that an existing application was built to use the most sensitive information as a primary key. Packaged applications often present this problem, and you have little control and limited in-depth knowledge of their data relationships. In such cases, when faced with the challenges of the PCI-DSS or with new privacy legislation such as California's SB 1386 all organizations' healthcare providers must make substantial investments in cataloging, analyzing, and remedying potential leaks for personal health information (PHI) or personally identifiable information (PII).

Consider an insurance company's claims system. Applications use the employee's SSN as the primary key for the insured record. It stands to reason that they would use the insured's SSN as part of the dependant's record foreign key. As application developers and data architects become more security conscious, this situation becomes far less likely, but it still happens. To remedy this in 10*g* would have required a redevelopment effort to create a new, noncanonical, primary key.

Using the tablespace encryption feature of 11*g*, it is possible to move all data considered to be PHI or PII into an encrypted tablespace without needing to redesign the application. Additionally, features such as streams and change data capture are again available when dealing with an encrypted tablespace, making it a good candidate for use in a wider variety of applications than column-level encryption.

Once the tablespace in created, anything stored in it will be encrypted using the algorithm specified at definition time:

```
system@AOS> CREATE TABLESPACE ts_encrypted
  2  DATAFILE '/home/oracle/product/11.1.0/oradata/aos/TSE_encrypted.dbf' size 400K
  3  AUTOEXTEND ON
  4  ENCRYPTION USING 'AES192'
  5* DEFAULT STORAGE(ENCRYPT)
system@AOS> /

Tablespace created.
```

The tablespace TS_ENCRYPTED is then created using the 192-bit AES algorithm. This is confirmed with a look at the v$encrypted_tablespaces view:

```
system@AOS> SELECT TS.name, ET.encryptedts, ET.encryptionalg
  2   FROM v$tablespace TS, v$encrypted_tablespaces ET
  3   WHERE
  4 TS.ts# = ET.ts#;

NAME                           ENC ENCRYPT
------------------------------ --- -------
TS_ENCRYPTED                   YES AES192

system@AOS>
```

Oracle 11*g* Configuration

In addition to tablespace encryption to protect entire collections of tables and their indexes, other enhancements have been included in Oracle Database 11*g*. Support for TDE has been built into Enterprise Manager's database control graphical user interface (GUI), shown in Figure 2-8.

The management of the wallet is now presented with a more intuitive GUI (a bit more intuitive than the SQLPLUS prompt). This allows for creating, opening, closing, and regenerating the TDE Master Key. The option for both closing the wallet and regenerating the Master Key are found under Advanced Options and appear as shown in Figure 2-9.

While the ability to create, open, and close a wallet are still available at the SQLPLUS prompt, you can now accomplish this without ever leaving the database management console.

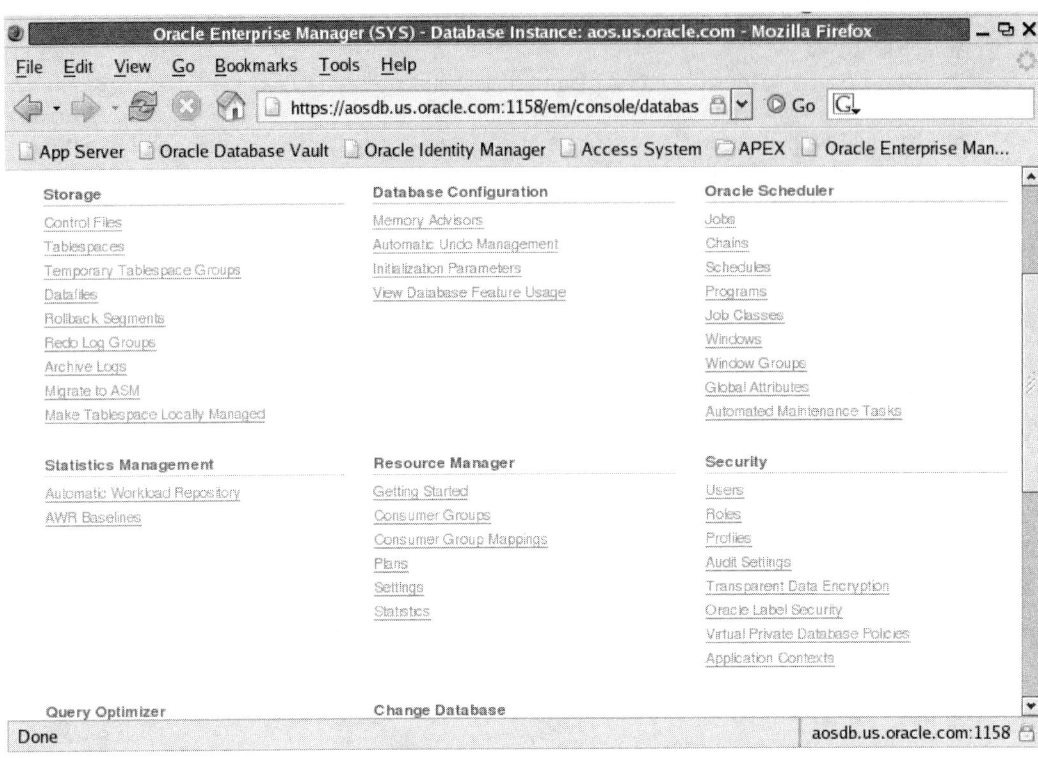

FIGURE 2-8 *Enterprise Manager database control*

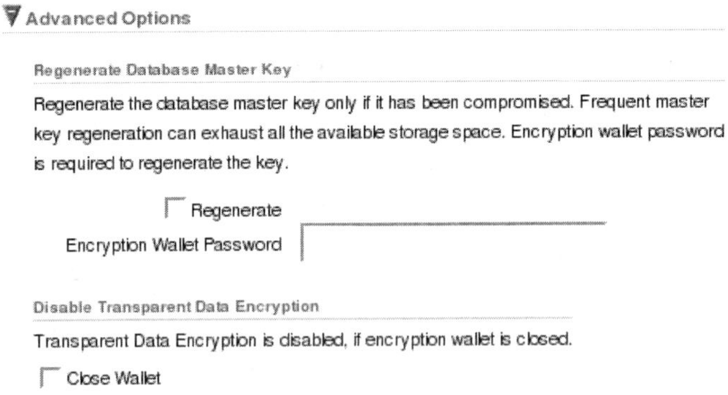

Advanced Options

Regenerate Database Master Key

Regenerate the database master key only if it has been compromised. Frequent master key regeneration can exhaust all the available storage space. Encryption wallet password is required to regenerate the key.

☐ Regenerate

Encryption Wallet Password

Disable Transparent Data Encryption

Transparent Data Encryption is disabled, if encryption wallet is closed.

☐ Close Wallet

FIGURE 2-9 *Closing and rekeying the wallet under Advanced Options*

TDE to Address PCI-DSS

In an effort to thwart the theft and misuse of credit card information (card numbers, cardholder name, and expiration date), major credit card companies have agreed on a set of standards to govern the storage and management of credit card data. The PCI-DSS comprises six control objectives, sets of related requirements. The industry standard is an evolution of the initial Cardholder Information Security Program (CISP) developed by Visa in 2001 to protect cardholder data, wherever it resides. MasterCard's Site Data Protection Program (SDP) was announced in the spring of 2001 to "assist online merchants in defending against Internet hackers."

PCI requires merchants and member service providers (MSPs) who process, store, or transmit cardholder information to adhere to the following control objectives:

- Build and maintain a secure IT network.
- Protect cardholder data.
- Maintain a vulnerability management program.
- Implement strong access control measures.
- Regularly monitor and test networks.
- Maintain an information security policy.

If you use a credit card in your day-to-day business, you are already familiar with the primary data elements involved in the DSS:

- Primary account number (PAN)
- Cardholder's name
- Service code (a three- or four-digit number on the magnetic stripe that specifies the acceptance requirements and limitations for magnetic-stripe read transactions)
- Expiration date

These elements are all permitted to be stored on automated systems under the PCI standard. The primary account number is special when developing a PCI strategy, as only when this account number is stored, processed, or transmitted by an organization does PCI apply. By using the PAN, like most organizations that accept credit cards as a form of payment or authentication of identity, you must comply with the PCI-DSS requirements.

Requirement 3 of the Digital Security Standard for the PCI regulation deals with the storage and protection of cardholder data and is the requirement most directly addressed by the functionality of TDE. Consider the following language in the DSS:

> Requirement 3 of the DSS – Protect Cardholder Data
>
> Encryption is a critical component of cardholder data protection. If an intruder circumvents other network security controls and gains access to encrypted data, without the proper

> cryptographic keys, the data is unreadable and unusable to that person. Other effective methods of protecting stored data should be considered as potential risk mitigation opportunities. For example, methods for minimizing risk include not storing cardholder data unless absolutely necessary, truncating cardholder data if full PAN is not needed, and not sending PAN in unencrypted e-mails.
>
> AND
>
> To minimize risk, store only those data elements needed for business. NEVER store the card verification code or value or PIN verification value data elements.

Section 3.4 of the DSS goes on to advise that the PAN (at a minimum) must be rendered unreadable anywhere it is stored using one of the following approaches:

- Strong one-way hash functions (hashed indexes)
- Truncation
- Index tokens and pads (pads must be securely stored)
- Strong cryptography with associated key management processes and procedures.
- ***The MINIMUM account information that must be rendered unreadable is the PAN.***

Organizations are looking at the available options to protect credit card data as required to maintain day-to-day operations and comply with the DSS. All who accept and store credit card data must comply or lose the ability to accept card transactions—be it an online retailer, a traditional brick-and-mortar store, a local utility that stores credit card data for its monthly ePayment system, or a state's department of transportation storing credit card information for its customers who are billed for toll usage. Luckily, protecting this valuable data can be accomplished in many ways.

The primary benefits of using TDE to help with a PCI-DSS–compliance strategy are threefold. First, implementing the encryption to support PCI doesn't require much, if anything, from the developers regarding changes to the application. The real work, encrypting/decrypting the data and managing the key storage, is handled by the database. The setup requires only a few cycles of a DBA and doesn't necessarily impact day-to-day operations for other administrative staff.

Second, because the encryption occurs within the database engine and not the application, it doesn't matter if multiple applications are accessing the same data—again, since the database handles the process transparently.

Last, if you were to build your own encryption logic into your application, storage of the keys used to encrypt the credit card information must be stored somewhere. Where to store these keys becomes a chicken-or-the-egg paradox, since the keys would need to be stored at a location this is accessible to the applications that need them. If the keys and the encrypted data are colocated, the protection offered by encrypting the credit card information is greatly diminished, since the security of the storage is a main consideration in the first place.

For instance, you may never store Credit Verification Values (CVVs—CVV2 for Visa, CVC2 for MasterCard, and CID for American Express). Those elements that may be stored—card number, expiration date, and cardholder's name—must use protection (such as encryption) to secure the data.

Operational Concerns

TDE, as you know, protects data at rest with a high level of assurance. Data, however, doesn't rest all the time. As organizations use data, other requirements come into play and data gets moved in a variety of ways. Organizations move data from production to development environments, it is loaded into data warehouses from source systems, it gets replicated to offsite disaster recovery locations, it is moved temporarily to make administrative changes to systems, and it must sometimes be moved as a result of hardware changes.

When moving data is a requirement, you cannot simply discard the security you've used to protect your data; instead, you must extend that security to these new processes and procedures. To accomplish the move in a secure fashion, you must think about data security (is it clear or ciphertext?) and communication channel (network, file movement, and so on).

Data Guard with TDE

Oracle Data Guard allows you to maintain a copy of the database at a secondary location that is periodically updated with changes made to the primary database by transmitting redo logs. When used in conjunction with column-level encryption of TDE, both physical and logical standby are possible and any data encrypted in the primary database is also encrypted in the redo log. Since physical standby moves redo logs from the primary to secondary database and then applies them directly, the wallet does not need to be opened because the data in the shipped log files has already been encrypted and can be applied in its encrypted form.

Logical standby moves data from the primary to secondary location in the redo log, but in contrast, it applies the changes to the secondary database using a process called SQL Apply. Since SQL Apply must read the log files before applying the changes at the secondary location, an Oracle Wallet with the same Master Key as the primary must be both present and open.

Performance

Most customers' second question after, "How does TDE work?" is, "What effect will this have on the performance of my database systems?" These are both certainly fair questions. Everyone is trying to maximize their resources, get the most out of their hardware, and keep a user community satisfied with their experience using applications that the database supports. So they are disappointed to hear that while the first question is easy to answer (you've already got a pretty good idea of the mechanics), the answer to the second question usually starts with something like, "It depends…," followed by a less than satisfying conversation.

The truth is, that answer depends on a number of factors—index participation for candidate columns, current system performance, number of tables having encrypted columns, and the raw number of rows in the average transaction having encrypted columns. Once these are understood, it becomes apparent that applications fall into two categories: "minimal effects" or "drastic effects." Most applications fall into the first category, and TDE can be used successfully, especially if an upgrade to 11*g* is an option.

Since arithmetic operations are always used when encrypting and decrypting, and despite the fact that implementations use encryption algorithms designed for efficiency and elegance, they slow system actions by taking processing power from other tasks. When used to encrypt varchar2 data in 10–20 character columns, TDE averages a 5–8 percent performance impact regarding single query performance. Reports of performance degradation can generally be attributed to index build failures after encrypting or to an application using LIKE, BETWEEN, or other functions needing an index to perform well.

Be sure to test applications thoroughly after encrypting any column to gauge the impact of encryption adequately, as you would when making any signification change. Using column-level encryption a 10*g* or 11*g* environment, the following course of action helps minimize risk, if an outage is permissible during the implementation:

1. Identify candidate columns for encryption (credit card number, national identifiers, and so on).
2. Ensure that these are TDE supported datatypes.
3. Ensure that the column doesn't participate in an index.
4. Ensure that the column is not part of a PK/FK relationship.
5. Encrypt the column(s).
6. Reorganize the table.

If an outage is not permissible during the implementation, follow these steps:

1. Identify candidate columns for encryption (credit card number, national identifiers, and so on).
2. Ensure that these are TDE supported datatypes.
3. Ensure that the column doesn't participate in an index,
4. Ensure that the column is not part of a PK/FK relationship.
5. Use online reorganization or modify the table as shown in the "Encrypting an Existing Column" section earlier in this chapter, as it locks the tables (both old and new) for only the period of time it takes to rename the tables.

By creating a very simple test case on a table with 100,000 rows of credit card data, and running a set of timed queries to select values from the columns, we are able to measure the effects of encryption versus a standard unencrypted query. It turns out that the query against encrypted data takes slightly longer than a query on unencrypted data, as long as both are indexed (see Figure 2-10). The difference between queries run on a nonindexed, unencrypted column and those on an indexed, encrypted column are much more significant. This once again highlights the need for good tuning and design of our index strategy for systems requiring quick response times.

Since column-level encryption has the limitations mentioned earlier, not every application is a good fit for its use. This can be due to need for index use such as ranges, PK/FK relationships or nonsupported datatypes. In these cases, tablespace encryption provides good alternative, removing these restrictions and encrypting at course granularity.

The process for migrating to tablespace-level encryption in an Oracle 11*g* environment can be best described as follows:

1. Identify tables containing sensitive columns.
2. Create a new encrypted tablespace.

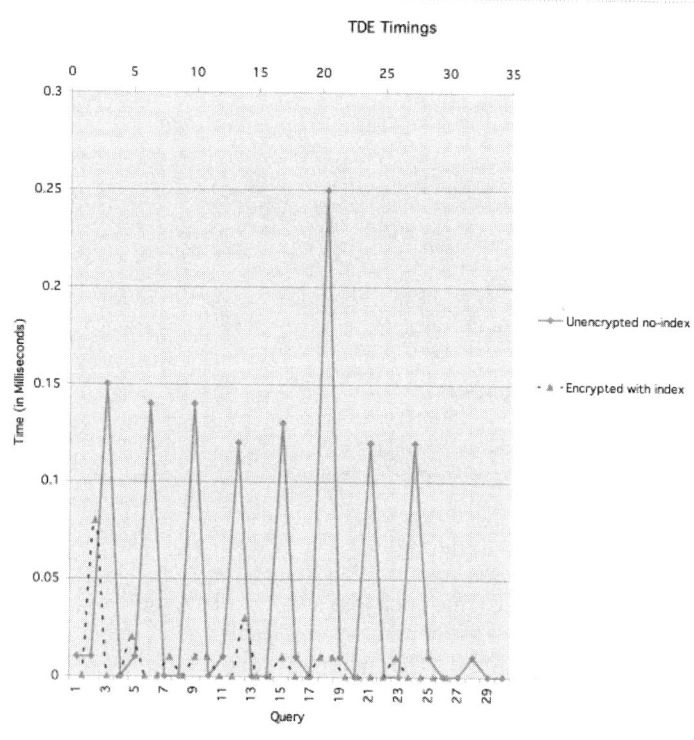

FIGURE 2-10 *TDE timings unencrypted nonindexed versus encrypted with index*

3. Move tables from an unencrypted to encrypted tablespace using **ALTER TABLE customer MOVE TABLESPACE encrypted_customer;**.

The other area of performance to consider is storage. Column-level TDE takes more space for each encrypted column (17–51 bytes per column). This additional space is the result of three things: padding required by the algorithm, Message Authentication Code (20 bytes), and salt (16 bytes). To minimize the amount of additional storage consumed by using TDE, consider using the **NO SALT** and **NOMAC** directives when encrypting columns. When you're dealing with relatively minor sizes (36 bytes seems very small today), it's easy to forget that in cases of large data volumes, these can add up. For a table with one encrypted column and 2 million rows, it is only 68 megabytes, but for customer with large data sets it can become daunting (with 7 billion rows, the additional 240 gigabytes could be an issue). When faced with multiple candidate columns stored in each of multiple tables, large databases must account for storage requirements in planning and testing.

Exporting and Importing Encrypted Data

Moving data out of one system and into another is one of a DBA's many tasks. Generally, tools such as traditional export/import or the newer Data Pump are used to perform this task. Export does not support tables with columns encrypted with TDE. Attempting to export the example customer_enc table shows this incompatibility:

```
[oracle@aosdb ~] (aos-db)$ exp sh/oracle11g tables=customer_enc
Export: Release 11.1.0.6.0 - Production on Sat Aug 23 13:30:19 2008
Copyright (c) 1982, 2007, Oracle.  All rights reserved.
Connected to: Oracle Database 11g Enterprise Edition Release 11.1.0.6.0 - Production
With the Partitioning, Oracle Label Security, OLAP, Data Mining
and Real Application Testing options
Export done in US7ASCII character set and AL16UTF16 NCHAR character set
server uses WE8MSWIN1252 character set (possible charset conversion)

About to export specified tables via Conventional Path ...
EXP-00107: Feature (COLUMN ENCRYPTION) of column CUST_CREDIT_CARD_NO in table
SH.CUSTOMER_ENC is not supported. The table will not be exported.
EXP-00091: Exporting questionable statistics.
Export terminated successfully with warnings.
[oracle@aosdb ~] (aos-db)$
```

Instead, TDE support is built in to Oracle Data Pump. Data Pump, like its predecessor, export/import, allows administrative users to pull data from a table, store that data in a file on the filesystem, and then pull the data from a datafile back into a table (on the same or another system). Data Pump will export data in cleartext, but it can then encrypt (using a new key) the resulting dump file.

Using the Data Pump to export TDE-encrypted table data allows administrators to move data, but you must remember that the data is decrypted by Data Pump and will be stored in the filesystem as cleartext.

```
oracle@aosdb ~] (aos-db)$ expdp system/oracle11g DUMPFILE=exports:customer_enc.dmp tables=sh.
customer_enc
Export: Release 11.1.0.6.0 - Production on Saturday, 23 August, 2008 14:07:01
Copyright (c) 2003, 2007, Oracle.  All rights reserved.

Connected to: Oracle Database 11g Enterprise Edition Release 11.1.0.6.0 - Production
With the Partitioning, Oracle Label Security, OLAP, Data Mining
and Real Application Testing options
Starting "SYSTEM"."SYS_EXPORT_TABLE_01":  system/********
DUMPFILE=exports:customer_enc.dmp tables=sh.customer_enc
Estimate in progress using BLOCKS method...
Processing object type TABLE_EXPORT/TABLE/TABLE_DATA
Total estimation using BLOCKS method: 64 KB
Processing object type TABLE_EXPORT/TABLE/TABLE
Processing object type TABLE_EXPORT/TABLE/CONSTRAINT/CONSTRAINT
Processing object type TABLE_EXPORT/TABLE/INDEX/STATISTICS/INDEX_STATISTICS
Processing object type TABLE_EXPORT/TABLE/STATISTICS/TABLE_STATISTICS
. . exported "SH"."CUSTOMER_ENC"                         8.843 KB       7 rows
ORA-39173: Encrypted data has been stored unencrypted in dump file set.
Master table "SYSTEM"."SYS_EXPORT_TABLE_01" successfully loaded/unloaded
******************************************************************************
Dump file set for SYSTEM.SYS_EXPORT_TABLE_01 is:
  /tmp/exports/customer_enc.dmp
Job "SYSTEM"."SYS_EXPORT_TABLE_01" completed with 1 error(s) at 14:07:12
[oracle@aosdb ~] (aos-db)$
```

Fortunately, Data Pump reminds you that the data is now unprotected with the error message "ORA-39173: Encrypted data has been stored unencrypted in dump file set." This process makes it easy to move data from one system to another without your worrying about having the same Master Key available when importing, but it again puts your data into the "unprotected medium" over which you have little control. Luckily, Data Pump includes a feature that allows you to encrypt the resulting file using the **ENCRYPTION_PASSWORD** option:

```
[oracle@aosdb ~] (aos-db)$ expdp system/oracle11g DUMPFILE=exports:customer_enc_protected.dmp
TABLES=sh.customer_enc ENCRYPTION_PASSWORD='AppliedOracleSecurity'
Export: Release 11.1.0.6.0 - Production on Saturday, 23 August, 2008 14:15:07
Copyright (c) 2003, 2007, Oracle.  All rights reserved.
Connected to: Oracle Database 11g Enterprise Edition Release 11.1.0.6.0 - Production
With the Partitioning, Oracle Label Security, OLAP, Data Mining
and Real Application Testing options
Starting "SYSTEM"."SYS_EXPORT_TABLE_01":  system/********
DUMPFILE=exports:customer_enc_protected.dmp TABLES=sh.customer_enc encryption_password=********
Estimate in progress using BLOCKS method...
Processing object type TABLE_EXPORT/TABLE/TABLE_DATA
Total estimation using BLOCKS method: 64 KB
Processing object type TABLE_EXPORT/TABLE/TABLE
Processing object type TABLE_EXPORT/TABLE/CONSTRAINT/CONSTRAINT
Processing object type TABLE_EXPORT/TABLE/INDEX/STATISTICS/INDEX_STATISTICS
Processing object type TABLE_EXPORT/TABLE/STATISTICS/TABLE_STATISTICS
. . exported "SH"."CUSTOMER_ENC"                          8.851 KB       7 rows
Master table "SYSTEM"."SYS_EXPORT_TABLE_01" successfully loaded/unloaded
******************************************************************************
Dump file set for SYSTEM.SYS_EXPORT_TABLE_01 is:
  /tmp/exports/customer_enc_protected.dmp
Job "SYSTEM"."SYS_EXPORT_TABLE_01" successfully completed at 14:15:14

[oracle@aosdb ~] (aos-db)$
```

The password provided by **ENCRYPTION_PASSWORD** is used to encrypt the resulting file, customer_enc_protected.dmp. It can then be imported only by providing the password.

Integration with Hardware Security Modules

When using TDE functionality, you will in turn be using an Oracle Wallet. As TDE uses the Oracle Wallet to store and generate Master Key values to encrypt table keys and ultimately data, it does so in a simple file-based manner. As mentioned earlier, the generation of the encryption wallet sets the wallet password and generates a Master Key that is then stored in the Oracle Wallet using PKCS #12. Some customers must conform with strict policy or procedural mandates with respect to management of their encryption keys. In very highly protected (professionally paranoid) customer environments, it is considered more secure to manage keys in a hardware device (HSM) rather than on a file system. For those faced with such challenges, Oracle 11*g* TDE introduced the ability to integrated TDE functionality with the Key Management and Key Backup capabilities of an HSM device.

Several third-party vendors produce an Oracle TDE-certified HSM devices, with more being added to the certified list every month. These devices manage several aspects of everyday management of encryption keys. First, they are built to manage the encryption keys inside the device from generation to disposal. This is important, because to keep keys protected, you need to develop good policy and process for backup, restoration, and use of cryptographic keys from all the systems in an organization that use keys. In an HSM device, the keys are processed using specialty hardware that offers speedy cryptographic processing and network access, and handles keys in a tamper-resistant platform that generates keys *within the device,* so file system copies never exist. Keys themselves are never removed from the device in an unencrypted form, and the table keys are sent to the HSM device for decryption over a secure channel. Since such keys are becoming increasingly critical for organizations and are being used in more applications each year, building a key management strategy early in a cryptography program can be a very sound investment.

Secondly, most networked HSM devices provide a central mechanism for managing who has access to which keys. This provides capabilities around separation-of-duties and span-of-control, each examined in any system security audit. Since the keys in question can provide such things as the functionality of TDE and the security for your SSL-protected communications, they provide an extra layer of defense for key storage. Currently supported HSM vendors include the following:

- SafeNet (acquired Ingrian); LUNA SA version 4.2
- Ingrian DataSecure Platform (models i116, i421, and i426, as well as previous models i110, i311, and i321)
- nCipher (acquired certain assets from NeoScale) netHSM 500, 2000; nShield PCI 500, 2000, and 4000
- NetApp OpenKey Client with PKCS#11 API for the LKM-Appliance 'KM-500'
- RSA RKM for the Datacenter Module for Oracle 11*g* TDE
- Thales e-Security (acquired nCipher)
- nuBridges
- Utimaco

Including a vendor-specific library to the host operating system accomplishes the implementation of an HSM device.:

```
/opt/oracle/extapi/32/hsm/<HSM_VENDOR_NAME>/<VERSION>/libpkcs11.so
```

The directory (/opt/oracle) is important: it must exist (create one if it doesn't, and make sure that the file ownership is "oracle" and filesystem permissions allow read and write access to the directory, or set it up as specified by the HSM vendor's guidelines). It will then be possible to configure the database to use this operating system device to store keys in a PKCS #11 keystore. By changing the setting in the SQLNET.ora file, the HSM device can be specified as a **METHOD** for storing the Master Key.

```
# sqlnet.ora Network Configuration File:
/home/oracle/product/11.1.0/db_1/network/admin/sqlnet.ora
# Generated by Oracle configuration tools.

NAMES.DIRECTORY_PATH= (TNSNAMES, EZCONNECT)

ENCRYPTION_WALLET_LOCATION =
 (SOURCE=
   (METHOD=HSM)
```

```
      (METHOD_DATA=
        (DIRECTORY=/home/oracle/product/11.1.0/admin/aos/encryption_wallet)
      )
  )
```

Notice that the directory still points to the file-based encryption wallet. At this point, a security administrator can migrate the Master Keys used for column-based encryption:

```
ALTER SYSTEM SET ENCRYPTION KEY IDENTIFIED BY "HSMusername/HSMpassword"
MIGRATE USING "<existing software wallet password>"
```

This tells the database to reencrypt all TDE column keys with the newly created, HSM-managed, Master Key. As the HSM method is specified in the SQLNET.ora file, communication to the HSM device using the API provided in the vendor-provided library is possible.

Use of an HSM device for Master Key storage is possible only with column-level TDE in the current 11.0.6 release. Tablespace encryption still requires the Master Key to exist in the Oracle Wallet. Using both column-based encryption with keys stored in an HSM device while allowing tablespace encryption is possible, but it uses a file-based Oracle Wallet for tablespace encryption in the 11.0 release by doing the following:

```
"ALTER SYSTEM SET ENCRYPTION KEY IDENTIFIED BY "HSMusername/HSMpassword"
MIGRATE USING "<existing wallet password>".
```

By using the same password for the wallet and the HSM, and not removing the **(DIRECTORY=/home/oracle/product/11.1.0/admin/aos/encryption_wallet)** syntax, an **OPEN WALLET** command will make both the Master Key for columns (stored in the HSM device) and the Master Key for tablespaces (stored in the wallet).

The next release of TDE, 11.0.7, will allow the creation of the tablespace Master Key directly in the HSM (it will not need to be migrated when creating for the first time).

By opening Oracle Wallet Manager using the initial wallet password (from the tablespace encryption example) and then selecting the Auto-Open option, you can re-save the wallet as an auto-open wallet that exists on the filesystem as a cwallet.sso. At this point, you can encrypt moderately sensitive data by storing it in tablespace encrypted using TDE's tablespace feature. Since the wallet is set to auto-open, when the database restarts, any database stored in the tablespaces is available; however, it is still stored in an encrypted form on the drives and any backup media. Very sensitive data (credit card PANs, SSNs, and so on), however, is protected by encrypting the columns, with the keys for this data encrypted using the Master Key stored in the HSM device. A security administrator is then responsible for opening and managing the HSM device-stored keys (**ALTER SYSTEM SET WALLET OPEN IDENTIFIED BY "HSMusername: HSMpassword"**).

Summary

Encryption is quickly moving from the wish list to the must-have list as organizations are faced with tighter internal and external security standards. The ability for organizations to prove that they are doing enough to protect data assets is enhanced with the addition of encryption. Transparent data encryption helps provide greater security for sensitive data throughout the data life cycle by encrypting data as it is written to disk and decrypting it as needed. The Master Key needed to perform encryption/decryption operations may be controlled by a non-DBA user, such as a security officer/administrator. Having this separation of duties is important not only because it is mandated by nearly every security target, but because it helps to ensure that data is protected in such a way that both fraud and collusion must occur to carry out particular actions.

The use of column-level TDE provided in 10*g* R2 provides strong encryption of sensitive columns, but it has limitations regarding datatypes and additional database capabilities. It can use a HSM device to secure the Master Key and generally the performance impact is fairly low. It can provide both encryption capabilities and separates the administrative duties for encryption key management.

Version 11*g* introduced tablespace encryption, which makes it possible to protect entire swaths of data stored in database servers and removes many of the restrictions faced by column-level encryption. Tablespace encryption provides the most transparent mechanism for protecting data in both new and existing applications. The performance impact of either column or tablespace encryption is minimal (average impact is single digits in most test scenarios for non-indexed encrypted values), and implementation can be done as databases are upgraded and tested in the 11*g* environment, which, as you find in future chapters, provides a number of security features that allow you to strengthen the security of your database, applications, and the movement of data between them.

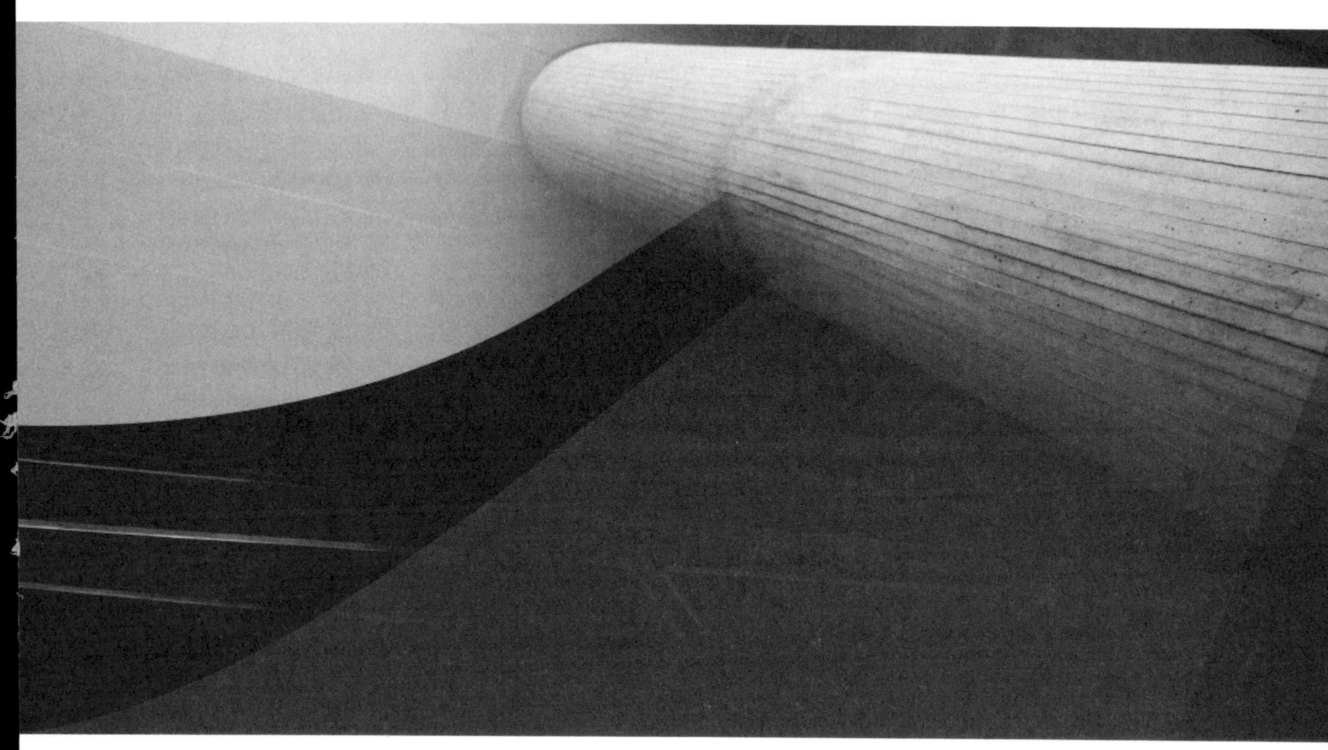

CHAPTER 3

Applied Auditing and Audit Vault

In the security life cycle, we think of the phases as protect, detect, respond, and remediate. Most of the security time and attention is focused on the protect phase. However, we cannot always protect everything from everyone or everyone from everything. This leads us naturally to the detect phase. Sitting squarely at the center of detect is auditing.

If you conducted a survey of security professionals, you would probably find that auditing is considered one of the least exciting areas of security. However, security professionals know they must address auditing at some level, but it rarely gets top attention for several reasons. Some don't know what to audit; some don't know how to audit; some don't know what to do with the audit records once generated; and some believe the auditing is "overhead" and a performance penalty that doesn't justify the additional resources that may be required. While these reasons have some legitimacy, at the end of the day, they are nothing more than excuses for not doing something that should be done.

In this chapter, we look at how to apply effective auditing techniques. The discussion will highlight the value that auditing provides. We also explore Oracle Audit Vault's basic architecture and components and review its various options and capabilities.

An excellent primer for this chapter is in Chapter 8, "Effective Auditing for Accountability," in *Effective Oracle Database 10*g *Security By Design*. That text adequately covers how to enable auditing, and the differences in writing your own auditing, using standard auditing, and using fine-grained auditing. Many concepts and principles described in that book also apply here.

Our goal is to consider auditing beyond a single database instance. The challenge, and to an extent even within a single database, is to join and relate all the information you can capture—SYS operations, Data Definition Language (DDL), Data Manipulation Language (DML), selective auditing, and even the data value changes themselves. You'll see how the audit records will show you the answers to the who, what, where, when, and how of data access. You will see that effective auditing across your databases is not only possible, but invaluable.

An Era of Governance

With the new era of Governance, Risk Management, and Compliance (GRC) firmly upon us, security and auditing excuses are quickly evaporating. As the custodians of data, IT professionals are being asked to protect personally identifiable information (PII), personal health information (PHI), and an assortment of other valuable data such as credit card numbers or bank account information used in electronic banking transactions. We must now comply with the cadre of new legal requirements: Sarbanes-Oxley (SOX), state privacy laws, the Payment Card Industry's Data Security Standard, EU privacy directives, Corporate Law Economic Reform Program Act (CLERP9), and Basel II to name just a few.

In this emerging GRC and privacy era, these requirements are just that—requirements. They are no longer optional and are now part of company business plans. They are not considered extra overhead, or a luxury item—that is, if we have spare time, money, and computing cycles, then we'll audit. Some consider auditing a tax, but as with all taxes, they still have to be paid.

An emerging view of auditing is now gaining popularity, however. From a GRC perspective, auditing provides an additional layer of oversight to existing access and physical controls. You can think of auditing as a safety net that catches things that fall through the protection controls. In these instances, while you cannot prevent a security compromise (because if you could have, you would have), you can detect them when they occur. This allows you to respond to and remediate any data breaches or other negative events. The timeliness of the detection and response is critical and crucial to preserving public image and setting up prevention techniques that will protect against future attacks.

Auditing for Nonsecurity Reasons

In some cases, auditing is set up to detect not only bad things that might occur but to act as an overall system monitor. Auditing can tell us who has accessed what, from where, when, and how. Another benefit of capturing audit data is that we can use this intelligence in considering overall enterprise IT issues such as resource distribution, scalability requirements, and underused and overused resources. This last point is also important to GRC, and many people are starting to understand that auditing offers real value—not only in the event of a security breach but in all cases.

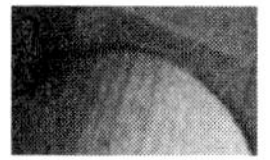

TIP
Effective auditing is not just about security; it has added value for system and application profiling.

You can even use auditing to identify when and if certain business conditions have been reached. For example, you could use audit records to detect and alert you when big financial transactions occur. This would be particularly beneficial when the transaction spans multiple databases or is not part of a single database transaction.

With a consolidated auditing system, aggregate counts and group-by queries on the audit trail can show you patterns of interest. For example, you can identify facts and frequencies on the following:

- Server accesses
- Network paths (client to server)
- Which users are using which databases or a particular database of interest
- Time factors (of year, of week, of day)
- Types of transactions or facts that tell you who is using data (sets) X, Y, and Z

We'll explore these and other examples more thoroughly later in the chapter. Oracle Audit Vault, introduced in Oracle Database 10*g* Release 2, makes major strides toward these goals by allowing you to collect audit data from all Oracle databases within your environment as well as other sources such as DB2 Universal Database (UDB), Sybase ASE, and Microsoft SQL Server (with more sources planned for future releases of Audit Vault.)

The Audit Data Warehouse

In many discussions with customers throughout the years, we have observed a common pattern in the area of auditing. These discussions were not focused on the tactical facets of turning auditing on or off (we refer to that as "micro auditing.") Rather, they concerned the need to have a holistic view about what was going on, from an auditing perspective, everywhere in the enterprise. We call this perspective to auditing "macro auditing." If you looked through all the objectives and requirements, you would conclude that everyone was essentially trying to build the same thing. We found that people were asking for a effective way to build what could be described as an *audit data warehouse.*

Understanding the design intent is always critical to a complete understanding of why you should use it, when you should use it, and how you should use it. With Audit Vault, the design intent was to create a product that captured the requirements of what everyone was already building or trying to build on their own. Note that Oracle security products have largely become "products" through this principle of identifying a common set of customer requirements and then solving those requirements through a professionally developed product.

The benefit to productizing common implementation patterns is that engineering changes to the core products are often required and are essential to meeting the intended requirements. Through the product creation process, those changes can be made. Product optimizations, such as better methods for storing and retrieving metadata, can also be accomplished as well as gaining and sharing best practices. This is precisely what occurred with Audit Vault.

As we explore the needs for an Audit Vault, we must define the requirements in terms of high-level objectives. This is important because technical implementations or technical features may be underutilized or not used at all if these objectives and requirements are not fully understood. Many say a far worse scenario exists when one undergoes the custom buildout of an application that matches an existing product—that is, building an Audit Vault from scratch. Again, this often occurs because of a lack of understanding about how to connect technology features to high-level organizational and application objectives.

Audit Warehouse Objectives

Let's look at the intent and requirements we have considered with respect to macro auditing and creating an audit warehouse.

Consolidated View Across the Enterprise

Our first key objective to explore is how to get a cross-enterprise view of our audits. As you know, GRC is a primary driver, as is looking for ways to optimize the IT infrastructure. If you think about what is required to create a consolidated view, you can map it easily to other systems. For example, organizations typically want to aggregate and analyze key financial data. Organizations also need to aggregate and analyze human resources (HR) information (for example, to be able to answer the question, "How many employees do we have?"). Other operational systems such as sales databases and facility databases (databases that maintain all the building and capital assets) also require that the information be gathered, and analyzed using sophisticated reporting and analysis tools.

This is accomplished today through the multibillion-dollar technology field called Business Intelligence (BI). BI is in fact such a huge value to organizations that the success or failure of an organization is largely dependent on how much insight it can glean from its business operations. Being able to identify suboptimal expenses and operations and then act to rectify them quickly can be the difference between a growing and profitable organization and one that does not grow or profit.

In a gross oversimplification, you could say that doing BI involves two key elements: First, you need to get all the data, and second, you need to analyze it. The multibillion-dollar industry exists because both elements are quite complex and require sophisticated technology to accomplish them correctly and efficiently. As a testament to the maturity and importance of BI, consider that Oracle Corporation has been actively working in the BI field for almost 20 years and has developed and acquired an extensive portfolio of tools and technologies that can be uses to construct a cross-enterprise BI capability.

Two critical points should be noted: BI is essential to the success of every organization and effectively implementing it requires advanced tools, technologies, and techniques. And getting intelligence from the data is nontrivial, and no one should embark on a project to re-create BI tools, technologies, and techniques.

Data Warehouse Recall the first objective of BI is getting all the data, which is commonly accomplished via a data warehouse. A data warehouse is simply a single database that acts as the resting point for all the collected data. "Warehouse" is a very appropriate term, as in many ways a data warehouse has to replicate a real-world warehouse. It must be organized; products or information must be able to flow in and out of the warehouse efficiently; and it generally contains a lot of stuff.

Implementing a data warehouse involves three basic steps: Extract the data. Transform the data. Load the data.

Extracting the data means that you must pull the data from the place in which it resides. For Oracle database auditing, this translates to replicating (in a figurative sense) the audit logs from the databases of interest. Across an enterprise, this would mean finding a way to extract all the auditing and logging data.

Data transformation means the data is put into a form that is consistent in meaning and often in format. From an auditing perspective, this could mean being able to define and identify users, applications, and server consistently s. You can imagine the confusion if something as basic as a user's identity is not represented in a meaningful or consistent way. This would likely result in an inability to correlate audit records from different applications and databases.

Data loading addresses the other end of the data extraction process, which is to load or fill up the warehouse. An infrastructure that allows large amounts of data to be loaded quickly and easily is required. Also required is a data model that includes such things as indexes and partitions. This all must be done using technology that supports the vast amount of data that will ultimately be loaded.

For enterprise auditing, you can now see the huge similarities. You would probably predict that a lot of auditing records would exist across the enterprise. You would also probably predict that an infrastructure would need to be in place to collect all the data across the enterprise. You would also identify the need to transform the data into a common description to understand what is really happening.

Once the information is loaded, you need the second BI element: analysis tools.

BI Tools To some, nothing is scarier than having to create useful and summarized information from terabytes of data. Successfully accomplishing this requires quite a few issues, including the ability to find, correlate, aggregate, and disseminate the information.

Each of these tasks takes time and effort to do well. For auditing, we need to search through the warehouse to find individual users, tables, applications, and so forth. We need to be able to relate the information across the various pieces of the warehouse.

For example, if we want to understand every task a user performed, we may have to correlate their authentication with their application invocation down to the actual database SQL or PL/SQL that resulted from the application interactions. Another valuable piece of information could be derived by simply being able to see what data a user manipulated across several core databases (or by way of association, the applications the user accessed.)

As you may gather, you'll want to be able to obtain quite a few legitimate nuggets of information from the audit data you collect. What we have learned about BI can be applied here once again: You need to know a lot of information and you will need advanced tools to discover, correlate, and present this information. BI products, especially Oracle's BI Suite, offer the off-the-shelf solution for culling the meaningful information from the reams of data you collect.

This is an important fact for you to internalize. Most custom-built BI applications do a tenth of what a commercial product would do, and the overall operations and maintenance costs tend to run ten times that of the product and support fees they would have otherwise paid. Therefore, the best practice for enterprise auditing is to use commercial technologies to perform BI. You'll want to create a data warehouse and then use the analysis tools to find the information of value.

Secure Audit Records

One of the underlying principles to auditing effectively is security—for the auditing itself. For auditing to hold its integrity as an effective mechanism, the audit logs or audit trail have to be secured. This may be a challenge because one of the prime uses of auditing is to detect unauthorized actions conducted by privileged users—that is, you need to secure auditing from the people who have access to the auditing.

This is best explained through the following scenario: A nefarious person conducts a nefarious deed and the audit function captures this. A strong requirement exists to keep the same nefarious person from deleting his malintentioned actions from the audit logs.

Securing Audit at the Source Here's the classic example: Someone accessing a database from a DBA account alters core and critical data. (Note this doesn't have to be the DBA account—just assume it's an account with a few critical system privileges.) The point here in our use case is that the data changes are not authorized. They were allowed to occur—that is, the database was unable to prevent or protect the data because the account used possessed system privileges that allows him to change the data. This is not an uncommon scenario, as you will see in Chapter 4. Many accounts (default and custom) have critical system privileges, and those privileges are required to perform legitimate and authorized work. The problem occurs because the privileges are not technically constrained to include only the *authorized* work (thus the need for an Oracle Database Vault, as discussed in Chapter 4).

If the data is critical, database auditing has been enabled and it will be capturing updates to the data records. This means the changes are captured via the database's auditing functions. Note that this is one of the best use cases for micro auditing: it captures privileged accounts abusing their privileges. Let's assume that the person knows that the database auditing is enabled. In that database, with the proper system privileges, the person who changed the data can now simply go to the audit logs and delete the records that recorded the original data manipulation. This effectively covers his tracks from the scene of the crime.

Note that you can turn on auditing for the audit logs themselves, thus generating an audit indicating that the audit logs were tampered with, but this gets us into a recursive discussion. Also note that, for completeness, you can audit the **NOAUDIT** command as well to detect someone disabling auditing, doing bad things, and then later re-enabling auditing.

How, then, do you secure the audit logs given that you may be auditing to detect unauthorized actions from privileged accounts? The answer is simply to move the audit logs from the database that is being audited to someplace else. This solves the problem based on the assumption that the privileged accounts are accessible only for the database being audited and that the same people do not have access to the audit destination. You can write the audit information to a different location—perhaps the file system—or you can ship the audit trail to a different location, to protect the audit trail.

This was the genesis of the conversation for many Oracle customers. The topic required conversation because the extract process—recall that this is not only a good idea for security but also the first step to data warehousing—is not readily done in Oracle. The audit trail could not be replicated via standard Oracle Advanced Replication technology, because the audit records by default (prior to Oracle Database 10*g* R2) were owned by SYS. To be specific, you cannot create triggers on SYS-owned tables. Triggers, however, are the heart of what makes Oracle Advanced Replication work.

We will not discuss other alternatives to this dilemma here, other than to say that the solution exists with Audit Vault.

Securing Audit at the Warehouse The conversation has now flowed from the need to obtain cross-enterprise awareness to a discussion of how to build a data warehouse and perform analytics of security at the audit source. Both the notion of needing a data warehouse and the need for security have informed us that we want to move the data out of its source and into a single database, where it can be used for reporting and analysis.

With the centralization of important data comes a requirement for increased security for that data. This immediately puts a focus on the security of this audit data warehouse for the following reasons: Although the original user may not have access to the audit data warehouse, someone may still be able to make unauthorized changes to the data. From an auditing perspective, especially when the audits are used for compliance reasons or for possible legal actions, the audit repository itself needs to be hardened. Regardless, in most cases, the desire, if not the requirement, is to have a secure audit system.

It does not make sense to send all of the security audits to an unprotected system. This fact, combined with the need to run advanced reporting and analytics, usually rules out any file system–based approach, even if the files are stored in XML. All of these reasons have driven conversations on how to secure a database in general. In these specific situations, the databases require greater security because they are acting as a centralized auditing data warehouse.

What to Audit and When to Audit

Given you have the capacity to audit, the discussion now moves to what actions should be audited or when should you do the auditing. First, realize that you can't audit everything. To some, auditing everything sounds like a good idea: if you audit everything, you are guaranteed to have audited and thus captured every bad thing that happened.

While this is true theoretically, problems arise for two reasons. The first and most obvious involves performance and resources. Auditing consumes resources, which impacts performance. For selective auditing, the impact may be negligible, but it will occur nonetheless. Auditing everything maximizes the drain on resources. In many cases, auditing or anything analogous (such as logging) is not used on every possible action for this very reason. This leads us to the second logical reason for not auditing everything all the time: data proliferation.

An audit-everything action means that the audit size will grow as rapidly as possible. This is not so much a storage concern as it is a "needle in the haystack" problem. When you audit everything, all the legitimate actions are captured along with those you may be trying to find. The problem is that the legitimate actions create audit records, possibly by the thousands, which conceal the audit records for the things you are most interested in. The goal here is to capture only the needles while letting the hay fall through.

Guiding Principles

When considering *what* to audit, the obvious conclusion is to audit the most critical and sensitive data. For example, if a data table is used for financial reporting, you may want to audit all DML actions on that table. If done correctly, this will later allow you to verify that the numbers used for the financial reporting were not tampered with or manipulated in any unauthorized way by any unauthorized person. In the case of a security breach, you need enough information to prosecute. This information includes who logged in, from where, at what time, and what actions were performed. Taken together, this information can imply malicious intent.

When considering *when* to audit, the guiding principle is to audit whenever something destructive occurs and when critical actions take place. A critical action is admittedly a nebulous term, but here it's meant to imply any action that can have significant impact. For example, consider an application in which the update of a field (column and/or row update) allows a user to join a membership group that then gives her privileges to execute important and sensitive tasks. This would be considered a critical action. Note that it's not the fact that a data field value changed, but what the change in the value meant.

Audit Patterns

As mentioned earlier, auditing offers ever-increasing value. Many organizations are obtaining valuable information from their auditing capabilities because they have figured out how to audit—what to audit and when—and not just from a security perspective.

We call this collection of auditing actions "audit patterns" to signify that a grouping exists and that the grouping occurs frequently. Recognizing the grouping tells us that auditing does not have to be considered at a statement-by-statement or action-by-action level. Aggregating and grouping related statements or actions is a more effective auditing technique, as the actions can be grouped into patterns, which subsequently tell us intent.

Consider this example: You need to audit important information, and you decide to audit the table containing financial data. If you simply look at it from a statement-by-statement level, all you may see in the audit logs are a bunch of INSERT, UPDATE, and DELETE statements. These don't tell you everything, however, and they may not tell you anything insightful. It may be difficult to tell whether an update is OK (from a security policy perspective), since some table updates could be OK and others might be problematic. It all depends on the context of the update.

Now consider auditing from the perspective of a financial transaction. The transaction itself is the item of interest, and it happens to consist of several statements. (This is precisely why you can group Oracle audit records by transaction identifier.) The transaction establishes context for the DML statements that make up the transaction. The order of the statements follows a sequence or pattern. Thus, you can relate the pattern to the transaction and you can begin to consider questions such as "Is this transaction authorized at this time of day and day of the year?"

You can take the lesson learned from aggregating statements into transactions up another level by looking at multiple actions or transactions. This time, you may even want to aggregate and correlate across multiple databases and applications. This would require a single auditing repository in which the cooperating databases and applications all sent their audit data.

Regardless of the motive of level, auditing patterns will exist. You can think about audit patterns in two ways: known audit patterns and unknown audit patterns.

Known Audit Patterns

Known patterns consist of transactions that you understand—a series of actions in a specific order that were used for a specific intent. For example, a bank transfer consists of a debit from one account and credit to another account. It occurs in that order and the intent, as stated, was to transfer money.

Within the enterprise, known audit patterns are derived from known activities. Your job will be to recognize the patterns and when they occur.

We've used the top five patterns as examples. An exhaustive list of known patterns is not possible, if for no other reason than known activities (that is, actions that create audit records) are often unique within an organization.

Privilege Escalation Privilege escalation is a common security "attack vector" or method. It is based on the simple process of using one account or privilege within an account to gain greater and greater privileges. The end goal is usually to escalate the privileges to the point at which something harmful can be done.

To identify this problem, you would typically see a series of privilege grants to a single user or to two users. For example, you might see a grant on the EXECUTE ANY PROCEDURE system privilege. This privilege might be used to execute PL/SQL code that, in the code itself, enabled another privilege or possibly even a secure application role. The pattern we identified was an anomalous grant to a user followed by more grants to or from that user.

This example is a simplification used to help convey the point that it can happen and it is not too difficult to do once given access to an account with some privileges. Unfortunately, this attack can be executed in many ways, which makes stopping it difficult. Therefore, from a security perspective, auditing provides an invaluable tool to help you identify such a problem has occurred or, better yet, is occurring.

High-frequency Logon Failures and Failed Accesses A common attack method consists of repetitive attempts to break into an account using a slightly different approach on each attempt, such as by guessing the password. This would easily manifest itself in audit trails as consecutive logon failures for the same user.

Likewise, consecutive failed access attempts may be a strong indication that someone is trying to gain access to something she is not supposed to access. This is analogous to someone banging on a locked door in desperate efforts to break down the door. You generally want to know when someone is trying to break down your door because, sooner or later, they just might get through. The same holds true with data access attempts. In data security, a malicious hacker is often unsuccessful on his first attempts.

A large set of failed attempts is very suspicious—except when it's not! When is a large set of failed attempts not suspicious? Failed access attempts may also signify that an authorized person is trying to gain legitimate access to something she is supposed to access, but an unfortunate coding or configuration error is preventing her from doing this. The benefit to proactive auditing is that you would be able to see who was trying to access what, and upon further investigation, update the security to allow the person the ability to do what she is supposed to be doing. This could theoretically be accomplished before the trouble ticket is issued.

Default Account Logon Failure One aspect that significantly increases the security risks to a product is the popularity of the product itself. The popularity of the product is believed to draw significantly more attackers, because more people know about the product, more information will be available publicly, and more will know how the product works. The saying goes: The bigger the popularity, the bigger the target.

This holds true for Oracle, and you can see this by searching on simple terms such as "Default Oracle Account Passwords." You will find a list of tools that define the default user accounts and passwords for Oracle databases. Many of these accounts are now locked by default and the passwords have expired. However, people are creatures of habit, and you might be surprised at how many will flip the traditional accounts back to their default passwords to make their jobs easier.

While you cannot see what password a person used when he tried to authenticate (which might help you see if he was using the known default password), you can see that a logon failure occurred. The pattern you are looking for is someone cycling through the default accounts. Your audit logs would show failures for these accounts. The logs may even record several failures for the same account where other well-known passwords (such as the password "manager") may be used.

If you are auditing with Audit Vault, you might even see this on multiple databases. The pattern presents the clear intent of someone trying to hack into your database(s).

Across Databases The preceding point regarding failed logons to known accounts across multiple databases is a good transition into this topic. Many security breaches occur through very indirect access paths. Identifying known patterns is as simple as looking at the audit records from the various systems. Any attack on a single database can often be found across database instances. If you notice a series of failed logons on your Oracle10*g* databases, you should inspect any Oracle 9*i* databases, too, since they are not locked by default. Seeing the attempts on multiple databases may indicate that someone has mapped your network and is jumping from server to server, the same way a burglar might move from door, to window, to window, to door.

One of the true values of an enterprise Audit Vault is its ability to present security attacks that were never visible before, because no one could correlate the information.

Business Use Policies In Chapter 4, we discuss the concept of context-based security. Security access decisions can be based on the context of the action and not just the action itself. For example, the ability to update data may be allowed when the user is accessing data through a secure application, but it may be disallowed otherwise.

A corollary to this occurs in auditing when you factor your business or application use with the actual application use. For example, you may allow a credit verification application access to your core financial data. However, a policy may state that the access can occur only during business hours. This is a very good policy, because generally more people are around watching each other during business hours.

An audit of financial data could indicate that someone was accessing the application data at inappropriate or questionable times. A Sunday access at 5 A.M. could, and possibly should, set off an investigation (unless of course, this is when the batch verification program runs).

Unknown Patterns: Looking for Anomalies

Unknown patterns are repeating sets of events whose intent or function are unknown. Sometimes these patterns are harmless, but sometimes they are harmful. Both types are valuable to your understanding of what's going on in the database. The more familiar you are with your data and the manner in which your users and applications access the data, the better you will become at recognizing things that don't fit.

One effective technique for noticing patterns uses the basics of an audit data warehouse. It is based on the notion of aggregates, averages, and trends. Suppose, for example, that you are collecting information, and all the access and actions you see are authorized and legitimate. Within that data, you notice very important statistics that help you determine the health of your systems. For example, you can calculate the average number of users on a given day, when people log on, what schemas are accessed, what tables are accessed, and at what frequency. All this information establishes a baseline considered "normal use."

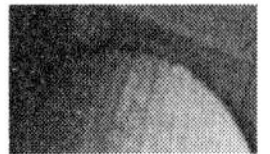

NOTE

In Chapter 7, you'll see how to determine which objects to protect with Database Vault: sensitive objects, users, paths, and privileges information. You will also learn how to establish a baseline for normal database use. Database Vault provides a default audit policy for the best practices mentioned here.

After you have collected this information, you can begin to identify patterns in usage and behavior. For example, you might find that a particular application is used only on Fridays. This turns out to be the activity reporting application, and people log their activities on Friday. You could then set up an alert that notifies you if access occurs any other day of the week.

The three biggest audit factors that stand out as anomalies may be the time of day and day of week that something is accessed, the frequency of access, and the path used for access. The access path is usually a rigid, or static, access path from application server, through a database account to the data. If you find a strong deviation in either one of these factors, you have found something legitimate to investigate. This information can be easily obtained with proper auditing.

Other Audit Action Best Practices

In addition to noticing audit patterns, you should always use several auditing best practices. First on the list of events to audit are logon and access failures, as mentioned earlier in the context of patterning the logons. Frankly, any failed logon as a DBA or analogous account is worthy of an audit inspection. Access failures should also be audited. As with logon failures, an access failure as a single element is worthy of audit inspection because these failures generally mean one of two things: someone is trying to do something he shouldn't, or the code or configuration is broken.

Successful logons are important because they provide a list of eligible suspects. If something bad happens, knowing who was on the system at the time gives you a concrete starting point. Logons are also invaluable in providing information about the normal use of the database or application. When establishing a baseline for your system, the frequency and number of logons are good statistics to note. Any large deviation in the frequency or number of logons may indicate something of significance. For example, a failed server may cause an increased number of logons on your server if your server is the backup. An increase in logons would be an indirect indication that the other server has failed or is unreachable to the clients. This is not necessarily a security issue, but it is an important issue.

Account creations, especially on production systems, may be considered anomalous activities and are worthy of audit and inspection. This could result from a compromised account that has the CREATE USER system privilege. The plan may be to create a new user and then use the new user account for future logons. This would protect someone if the initial account is re-secured.

Part of our message is that auditing is not always a security issue. A new account creation on a production system may not mean that someone is setting up an access account from which to conduct nefarious activities in the future; a new account may simply signal that a new application is being installed. This is good information for you to know, especially if strange things begin to happen shortly after the account is created. It's also not considered unusual for someone to install unapproved applications/products on the production server accidentally, either because the user forgot she was on the production server or forgot she was supposed to get permission to install such an application. Auditing with alerts could proactively detect and notify you of such important events.

You should begin to see the methodology espoused here. You want to look for actions and activities that are considered highly unusual or highly risky. In addition, you can use auditing as a way to indicate that something is broken or working in a suboptimal way. Before we walk through the specifics of Audit Vault, consider the following abbreviated list of audit suggestions:

- **System grants and object grants** The granting of system and object privileges in an already running production system is a huge red flag. Clearly, the only reason this would be done is to fix another problem or patch the system—both of which should be easily confirmable. Something as simple as a **GRANT SELECT** on SH.SALES to SCOTT could be an indication of a privilege escalation attack.

- **DDL in production** If you ask most DBAs whether random DDL changes to a production systems are occurring, chances are you'll get a look of disdain and a quick remark of "absolutely not." Configuration control and the reliability of the system highly depend on the system staying architecturally rigid. Auditing to capture DDL changes is an obvious thing to do.

- **Source code modifications** PL/SQL code in the database can do so much, from integrity to security. No matter what the code is used for, doing anything to it other than executing it is reason for investigation. Viewing the source code and updating the code can be real security issues.

- **System alterations** System changes, often invoked with the **ALTER SYSTEM** command, can have enormous security relevance. Checking to ensure that auditing has not been disabled (**NOAUDIT**) and that other system settings such as O7_DICTIONARY_ACCESSIBLITY, SQL_92_SECURITY, and AUDIT_SYS_OPERATIONS are still operating as planned is critical to ensuring that the system is still acting in a safe and secure state.

- **Resource optimization/usage** Looking at access frequency has huge value in capacity planning and resource optimization. Additionally, unused applications and schemas are security vulnerabilities that provide a potential foothold for nefarious users.

A SQL script that contains many of these settings as well as a few practical others is included in the Audit Vault installation. It can be found at $ORACLE_HOME/demo/secconf.sql.

The Audit Warehouse Becomes the Audit Vault

You may have guessed by now that the best thing you can do to secure your Oracle Database involves the judicious use of Oracle Database Vault. Chapters 4–7 cover the Database Vault in detail. It's mentioned here because Database Vault was needed by the Audit Vault developers to harden the audit data warehouse. This helps you meet many, if not all, security requirements that you desire when considering the use of an audit database for compliance and other important issues.

The notion of customer-built audit data warehouses was transformed into an Oracle-built Audit Vault. Oracle's product is not merely an analogous creation of what people were already doing wrapped up in an Oracle package. Audit Vault almost always undergoes kernel and code changes and various optimizations when it's put to use. Add to that regression testing and support, and the overall cost per functionality could not get lower.

In addition, when you consider the code tweaks and optimizations, the Oracle products are in fact technically superior to those we would create using the base technology, and Oracle Audit Vault is no exception. It is a hardened database that acts a data warehouse for auditing data.

A final important note on Oracle auditing, and Oracle Audit Vault in particular: Auditing is always transparent to the application. As mentioned in Chapter 1, this is one of the critical success factors for an effective security implementation. The good thing about auditing is that the administrator, security administrator, or even the auditor can control what to audit and when. This important separation between auditing and audit policy are important factors for implementing a compliance-based auditing environment.

Throughout the remaining sections, we describe how Oracle Audit Vault meets the auditing requirements described in the first parts of this chapter. A key reference used for this section was the document "Oracle Audit Vault Best Practices," published in 2007 by Oracle Corporation. This document was written by Tammy Bednar with contributions by Paul Needham and Vipul Shah. It is extremely well written, so, with their permission, we have reused some of their graphics and tables here to provide the highest quality content without replicating what has already been done.

Audit Vault Architecture

The Oracle Audit Vault architecture consists of two basic components: the Audit Vault Server and the Audit Vault Collection Agent.

Audit Vault Server

The Audit Vault Server is the audit data warehouse and acts as the consolidated repository of all audit data. It installs with an Oracle Containers for J2EE (OC4J) Audit Vault Console and is integrated with Oracle Enterprise Manager's Database Control.

The Audit Vault Server is built on a hardened Oracle database. The data is transformed in the Audit Vault Server and loaded into a special data warehousing schema that is optimized for reporting and query functions and leverages advanced data warehousing technologies, such as partitioning, that Oracle builds into the database.

Audit Vault Collection Agent

As Figure 3-1 shows, the Audit Vault collection agent consists of the collectors for the relevant audit source. The collectors work to extract the data from the audit source and securely transfer that data to the Audit Vault Server. When login credentials are required, the collection agent also maintains an Audit Vault Wallet that securely stores the credentials for later access to the audit sources.

Audit Vault collection agents are deployed on the each of the database servers from which you intend to collect audit data. Clustering technology, which provides load-balancing and active-active failover, is used along with Data Guard, which provides offsite disaster-recovery capability.

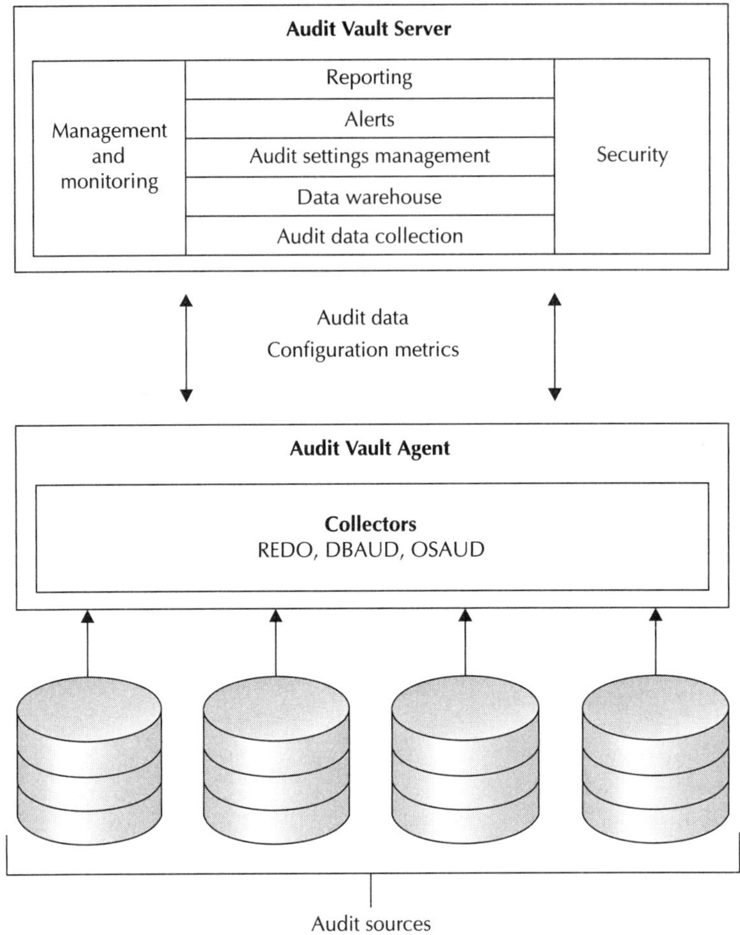

FIGURE 3-1 *Audit Vault architecture overview*

Installation Options

You will consider several factors when deciding how and where to install the Audit Vault Server and the Audit Vault collection agents. In this section, we describe these options. The intent here is not to duplicate the information provided in the installation manuals, but to describe the components and discuss installation from an architectural perspective.

Installing Audit Vault Server

The Audit Vault Server, the data warehouse for the enterprise audit functions, is built on a hardened Oracle database. The schema is optimized for reporting and query functions and leverages the advanced data warehousing technologies, such as partitioning, that Oracle builds into the database for doing these very things. You should install this data warehouse on a server that is built to run this type of application.

The Audit Vault Server stores, manages, and acts upon data that is collected by the Audit Vault collection agents. The Audit Vault Server can use other core Oracle database technologies. For example, to achieve scalability and provide high reliability, Oracle Audit Vault can be deployed to a Real Application Cluster (RAC) architecture. To create a disaster recovery capability, Oracle Audit Vault can be deployed using Data Guard.

Communication channels to and from the Audit Vault Server are protected with network encryption via the Advanced Security option, which helps to ensure the data has not been tampered with or viewed while in transit from one of the audit sources to the server itself.

The availability of Audit Vault is required in both the capture and the analysis of audit data. If the Audit Vault were unavailable for a period of time, data would be collected on the source systems and problems would occur during the collection "catch-up." By including both RAC (for high-availability and standby failover) and Data Guard support (for disaster recovery sites), the architecture can be built to suit the needs of any organization's service level requirements. Note that while using RAC and Data Guard are a best practice, Audit Vault doesn't require their use.

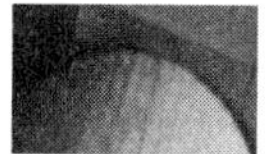

TIP

The Audit Vault Server should be installed on its own host or on a host that contains other repository databases such as Enterprise Manager Grid Control or the Oracle Recovery Manager (RMAN) repository database. You should consider deploying Audit Vault in a RAC configuration with Data Guard enabled for disaster recovery capabilities. By installing the Audit Vault Server separate from the source database servers, you can get better control of the availability, speed, and overall security of the auditing functions. This independence is what makes Audit Vault so appealing.

Installing Audit Vault Collection Agent

The Audit Vault collection agent consists of various collectors for the various sources it supports. As of Audit Vault 10.2.3, audit information can be collected from the following supported database versions:

- Oracle9*i* Database release 2 (9.2)
- Oracle Database 10*g* release 2 (10.2)
- Oracle Database 11*g* release 1 (11.1)
- Microsoft SQL Server 2000
- Microsoft SQL Server 2005
- IBM DB2 UDB 8.2 and 9.5
- Sybase ASE 12.5 and 15.0

Oracle has future plans for an SDK, which would allow you to integrate various audit sources not currently supported. As you might imagine, the actual audit data collected from each source will vary by product.

For Oracle databases, the collection agent can use three different collectors:

- **DBAUD** Grabs data directly from the Oracle database audit trails. It extracts data created from standard auditing, which is stored in SYS.AUD$; it extracts data created from fine-grained auditing, which is stored in SYS.FGA_LOG$; and it extracts data from the Database Vault audit records stored in DVSYS.AUDIT_TRAIL$.
- **OSAUD** Captures Oracle database audit records written to the operating system files (.aud or .xml) or the operating system's syslog daemon.
- **REDO** Extracts data from the database redo log files. This has the benefit of capturing BEFORE and AFTER values and uses the change data capture technology of Oracle Streams, but it is managed centrally in the Audit Vault console.

Figure 3-2 summarizes the three collectors for the Oracle database.

Table 3-1 shows from what, or more specifically from where, the audit information is retrieved for the other supported audit sources.

The Audit Vault collection agent configures the collector processes for each source. It also sets up the configuration and connections from the collectors back to the Audit Vault Server. Later in this chapter, we will look at a collector installation process.

Choosing the Collector Type

Choosing the correct collector has obvious importance in two areas. First, you want to ensure that you collect the right information. Second, you want to do so in a way that does not limit the performance of the audit source. For the non-Oracle audit sources, you don't have a choice on which collector type to choose. For Oracle, however, you can choose among OSAUD, DBAUD, and REDO collections.

Your choice of collector can also be based by logically thinking about Oracle Database auditing. Following is a list of ways you might categorize the types of auditing events that occur

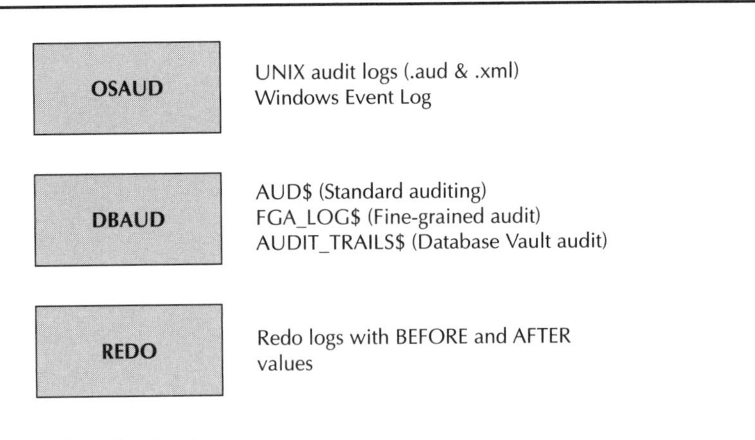

FIGURE 3-2 *Audit Vault agent collectors for the Oracle database*

Database	Collector	Collected Log Location
Microsoft SQL Server	MSSQLDB	C2 audit logs, server-side trace logs, Windows event logs
Sybase ASE	SYBDB	System audit tables (sysaudits_01-08) from the sybsecurity database
IBM DB2	DB2DB	ASCII text file extraction of binary audit log (db2audit.log) located in the security subdirectory of the DB2 database

TABLE 3-1 *Audit Source Collectors for Non-Oracle Databases*

in the database. Using these categories as guidelines, you can decide what to audit based on how the audit events map to your compliance initiatives and security concerns.

- **System and SYS events** Manage settings and initialization parameters. Core changes to the database are included. They are captured only when you audit SYS or use the **ALTER SYSTEM** command. The best practice is to have the audits written to the OS, as whoever generated the audit event may also have the privileges to delete from the database audit tables. This category is often mandatory in compliance settings, because changes to the system imply changes to a standard or baseline configuration.
- **Database DDL and DML events** Track access by any user, operation, or object within the database. The following table depicts some of the basic functions and the specific fields being audited:

Audit Function	Example Audit Fields
User data	DB User, OS User, Client Identifier
Object	Object_Owner, Object_Name, Object_Type
Operation	Action, System Privilege User
Time	Timestamp, Logon, Logoff
Location	Terminal, IP Address
Order of operations	SessionId, EntryId
Transaction	Transaction ID, SCN
SQL request	SQL Text, Bind Variables

- **Database Vault events** Manage the DBV settings, including Realm Audit, Factor Audit, and Rule Audit. This information is stored in DVSYS.AUDIT_TRAIL$.
- **Data access events** Include access to specific table columns, data rows, or data records. This is the primary use of fine-grained auditing (FGA), and the auditing is not enabled through a database event but through invoking the DBMS_FGA package. Auditing is very selective, which allows you to focus precisely on the data fields of interest. The data is stored in SYS.FGA_LOG$.

- **Data changes** The ability to capture data values as they change. The updated values are shown in the redo logs. You therefore must enable Archive Log Mode to ensure that you extract data out of the logs before they are overwritten. Using redo logs saves you from having to capture data value changes yourself (often attempted as a collection of table triggers that copy the **:OLD** and **:NEW** values to custom built application audit tables).

A final point regarding auditing becomes apparent with the preceding parenthetical comment. While the Oracle Audit Vault SDK is not yet available, you can still capture your application audits by turning on auditing for the tables and objects your application manipulates. The auditing functions will pick up changes made by your application. Both OSAUD and DBAUD will capture those changes. REDO will capture the data values that were changed.

Table 3-2 shows three types of Oracle database collectors. An X indicates the actions the auditing will capture.

Collection Agent Location If a collection agent is installed on a separate server (that is, not on the server running the database being audited), then the collectors cannot read any audit files written to the file system. This configuration therefore obviates the OSAUD and REDO collectors. In this case, the audit source will be only the database tables (AUD$, FGA_LOG$, DVSYS .AUDIT_TRAIL$) that can be accessed remotely via Java Database Connectivity (JDBC).

When Oracle RAC is being used, only one instance of the DBAUD and REDO collector is required to collect audit activity. For auditing in a RAC architecture, gathering operating system activity requires an OSAUD collector on each node participating in the cluster to audit operating system activity.

The advantage to installing the collection agent on the audit server is that you end up with a single consolidated environment for your auditing; however, it won't allow collection of OSAUD and REDO. From a performance perspective, Oracle recommends using the OSAUD collector as it has been proven to work much faster than the DBAUD collector.

Audit Operation	OSAUD	DBAUD	REDO
SELECT	X	X	
DML	X	X	X
DDL	X	X	X
FGA	X	X	
DBV audits		X	
Before/after values			X
Success and failure	X	X	
sql text	X (for Sys)	X	
SYS auditing	X		X
Comments	Fast, protected from DBA, managed outside DB	Uses standard auditing tools that run reports based on SQL	Captures before/after values

TABLE 3-2 *Audit Collector Attributes*

Audit Vault Collection Agent Install Recommendation

Architecturally, the Audit Vault collection agent may be installed on the same host as the audit source, the same host as the audit server, or on a separate server altogether. If you are using OS auditing or want access to the redo logs, the Audit Vault collection agent must be installed on the same server as the audit source.

From a best practices perspective, auditing to the OS is the best option, because auditing to database audit tables requires database transactions. This means that insert statements into the database tables occurs and redo information is generated for the audit itself. The redo logs would then show the event that caused the audit to occur and a record of the audit being written about the same event. Depending on how much you audit, your redo logs can get quite full of such redundant audit information. This not only takes up database storage, but it requires extra database resources to perform the audit.

For Audit Vault collection agents, this means the OSAUD, which has two limitations: The REDO Collector is the only way to capture the data changes—that is, the BEFORE and AFTER values that were a result of a database action such as an UPDATE. The other limitation occurs because the DBV audits are not written to OS files.

If you want to capture SYS actions and all DDL, DML, FGA, Database Vault, and BEFORE/AFTER values, all three collectors may be used. Thus guarantees that all SYS actions, standard audits, and FGA audits are captured (via **AUDIT_TRAIL=OS** for standard auditing and XML auditing for FGA); all DBV audits are captured with DBAUD, and the REDO captures the data value changes. The Audit Vault Server brings these otherwise disparate logs together in the warehouse so that you can see who accessed what, when, and how.

Installation Caveats

This section reviews the most important aspects to installing Audit Vault Server and Audit Vault Agent. After careful consideration, we decided that walking you through the step-by-step process of installing Audit Vault would be redundant with the standard installation documents. We highlight a few of the caveats and notes that address the top issues and challenges in getting Audit Vault installed and operational.

An installation plan should use the following model:

1. Prepare the host operating system for Audit Vault Server install (per Install Guide).
2. Install Audit Vault Server.
3. Prepare the source (audit generating) database.
4. Add a new agent to the Audit Vault Server.
5. Add a user to the source database for collection.
6. Install the Agent on source system.
7. Generate audit data.

The collection agent and server install guides provide the detailed installation steps geared toward the server operating system. In general, the following areas tend to catch up first-time Audit Vault users:

- **Not using ARCHIVELOG mode on the source database** Configuring auditing requires some adjustment to standard administration.

- **Using Audit Vault Control (AVCTL)** The Audit Vault Control command line utility is used on both the AV Agent machine and the AV Server machine, but for different purposes. Use AVCTL on the Agent machine to manage the OC4J container in which the collector will run or check the status. Starting and stopping the agents themselves is done on the AV Server, as is administering the AV Server and carrying out warehouse refreshing/purging.
- **Verifying the global database name** This name should be verified from the source database using **SELECT * from GLOBAL_NAME** to ensure that these are unique within the audit environment. The **JOB_QUEUE_INTERVAL** must be set to 1, the **PARALLEL_MAX_SERVERS** must be greater than 20, and **GLOBAL_NAMES** must be true.
- **Adding complexity in Database Vault environments** An additional step is required for Database Vault environments, because the collector user requires access to data dictionary objects protected by the Oracle Data Dictionary realm:

```
dbowner@SOURCE> BEGIN

      dbms_macadm.add_auth_to_realm ('Oracle Data Dictionary',
          'av_collector', NULL, dbms_mactul.g_realm_auth_participant);
END;

/

PL/SQL procedure successfully completed.

dbowner@SOURCE> GRANT dv_secanalyst TO av_collector;

Grant succeeded.
```

Audit Vault Users and Roles

Audit Vault's installation process creates users and roles designed to configure, use, and maintain the audit environment. Separate roles are used to facilitate separation of duty requirements. Two primary users are specified at install time, the Audit Vault Administrative User and the Audit Vault Auditor, which take on the role of AV_ADMIN and AD_AUDITOR, respectively. The Audit Vault Administrator sets up and maintains the servers and processes. The Audit Vault Auditor then has access to the audit data and cannot manipulate the server settings.

Each role and a description are shown in the following tables:

Roles Created at Installation	Description
AV_ADMIN	Configures and manages the Audit Vault system including sources, collection agents, and collectors. May also grant AV_ADMIN or AV_AUDITOR to other administrators.
AV_AUDITOR	Manages Audit Vault's audit settings, alerts, and audit data warehouse.
DV_OWNER	Manages Database Vault configuration and roles.
DV_ACCTMGR	Manages Database Vault user accounts.

Roles Created at Registration	Description
AV_SOURCE	Collector used role for sending audit data to the Audit Vault during runtime.
AV_AGENT	Role used at runtime to grant access to configuration information, created at agent registration.

Installing the Collection Agent

Once Audit Vault Server is installed and running, your next task is to add the definitions for agents you intend to install. In the following example, an agent called aos10g_agent is added and will reside on the machine aosdb.us.oracle.com:

```
[oracle@aosav ~]$ avca add_agent -agentname aos10g_agent -agenthost aosdb.us.oracle.com
AVCA started
Adding agent...
Enter agent user name: aosdb_agent
Enter agent user password:
 Re-enter agent user password:
 Agent added successfully.
```

Next, create a database user who acts as the collector. This user may be called anything you choose, but this person must have roles and privileges assigned depending on the collector type: OSAUD/DBAUD or REDO. In an instance providing both REDO and OSAUD, for example, the following would be used to create the user:

```
sys@SOURCE> CREATE USER av_collector <A>identified by av_collector;
User created.
sys@SOURCE> @/oracle/avagent/av/scripts/streams/source/zarsspriv.sql av_collector SETUP
Granting privileges to AV_COLLECTOR ... Done.
sys@SOURCE> @/oracle/avagent/av/scripts/streams/source/zarsspriv.sql av_collector REDO_COLL;
Granting privileges to AV_COLLECTOR ... Done.
```

NOTE

An additional step is required for Database Vaulted environments, as the collector user requires access to data dictionary objects. This was stated earlier but because it is so often overlooked, we thought mentioning it twice would be beneficial. The following two commands must be executed when using DBV:

```
dbowner@SOURCE> BEGIN
     dbms_macadm.add_auth_to_realm ('Oracle Data Dictionary',
                 'av_collector', NULL, dbms_mactul.g_realm_auth_participant);
END;
/
PL/SQL procedure successfully completed.

dbowner@SOURCE> GRANT dv_secanalyst TO av_collector;
Grant succeeded.
```

After creating the source collector user and granting permissions required to carry out the source collector function, you must verify that the source database is properly configured for gathering audit information:

```
[oracle@aosdb avagent] (avagent)$ $ORACLE_HOME/bin/avorcldb verify -src
aosdb:1521:source -srcusr av_collector/av_collector -colltype ALL
source SOURCE verified for OS File Audit Collector collector
source SOURCE verified for Aud$/FGA_LOG$ Audit Collector collector
parameter _JOB_QUEUE_INTERVAL is not set; recommended value is 1
ERROR: parameter UNDO_RETENTION = 900 is not in required value range [3600 - ANY_VALUE]
ERROR: parameter GLOBAL_NAMES = false is not set to required value true
ERROR: source database must be in ARCHIVELOG mode to use REDO LOG collector
ERROR: global dbname for source database must include domain to use REDO LOG collector
ERROR: set the above init.ora parameters to recommended/required values
[oracle@aosdb avagent] (avagent)$
```

This verification step identifies any parameters that do not conform to Audit Vault source requirements. Perform the required changes to the identified parameters and reverify until an acceptable environment is achieved.

In addition, logging must be started if not in use:

```
sys@SOURCE> ARCHIVE LOG LIST
Database log mode              No Archive Mode
Automatic archival             Disabled
Archive destination            USE_DB_RECOVERY_FILE_DEST
Oldest online log sequence     5
Current log sequence           7
sys@SOURCE> ARCHIVE LOG START
<A>Statement processed.
sys@SOURCE> ALTER DATABASE CLOSE;
sys@SOURCE> CONNECT / AS sysdba
Connected to an idle instance.
sys@SOURCE> STARTUP MOUNT EXCLUSIVE;
ORACLE instance started.

Total System Global Area  397557760 bytes
Fixed Size                  1300184 bytes
Variable Size             180357416 bytes
Database Buffers          209715200 bytes
Redo Buffers                6184960 bytes
Database mounted.
sys@SOURCE>ALTER DATABASE ARCHIVELOG;
Database altered.
sys@SOURCE> ARCHIVE LOG LIST;
Database log mode              Archive Mode
Automatic archival             Enabled
Archive destination            USE_DB_RECOVERY_FILE_DEST
Oldest online log sequence     6
Next log sequence to archive   8
Current log sequence           8
sys@SOURCE>
sys@SOURCE> ALTER DATABASE OPEN;
Database altered.
```

The global name of the database must be in this form:

```
sys@SOURCE> SELECT * FROM global_name;
GLOBAL_NAME
----------------------------------------------------------------------------
SOURCE
sys@SOURCE> ALTER database RENAME global_name TO source.us.oracle.com;
Database altered.

--- add the OS collector ---

[oracle@aosav ~]$ avorcldb add_collector -srcname SOURCE.US.ORACLE.COM -agentname
aos10g_agent -colltype osaud -orclhome /home/oracle/product/11.1.0/db_1
source SOURCE.US.ORACLE.COM verified for OS File Audit Collector collector
Adding collector...
Collector added successfully.
collector successfully added to Audit Vault
remember the following information for use in avctl
Collector name (collname): OSAUD_Collector
[oracle@aosav ~]$
--- add the DB collector ---
[oracle@aosav ~]$ avorcldb add_collector -srcname SOURCE.US.ORACLE.COM -agentname
aos10g_agent -colltype DBAUD
source SOURCE.US.ORACLE.COM verified for Aud$/FGA_LOG$ Audit Collector collectorAd-
ding collector...
Collector added successfully.
collector successfully added to Audit Vault
remember the following information for use in avctl
Collector name (collname): DBAUD_Collector
[oracle@aosav ~]$
```

Reporting

By filling the role of a secure data warehouse with a consolidated view of audit data from a variety of sources, Audit Vault supports the new compliance environment of many enterprises. Figure 3-3 shows the menu page of default reports that are available from the Oracle Audit Vault console.

Note that Audit Vault provides not only the data needed for many standard compliance reports (user login activity, account creation activity, privilege grants), but also reports that are useful in special circumstances. For instance, an organization might find it useful to track data access at critical times during financial reporting periods, or when the enterprise finds itself in the throes of an acquisition. By creating special-use reports with Audit Vault data, these unique situations can be monitored.

After audit data is transferred from the audit sources to the Audit Vault Server, an Oracle DBMS_SCHEDULER job runs to perform the transformation and load processes. This normalizes the raw audit data into the data warehouse. Audit Vault provides statistics of the ETL process to update the warehouse. By using this information, you can estimate how often the job may be run to update the data warehouse infrastructure. The ETL process may be run more often to provide near real-time reporting. Oracle recommends that you complete the previous ETL job before initiating the next ETL job.

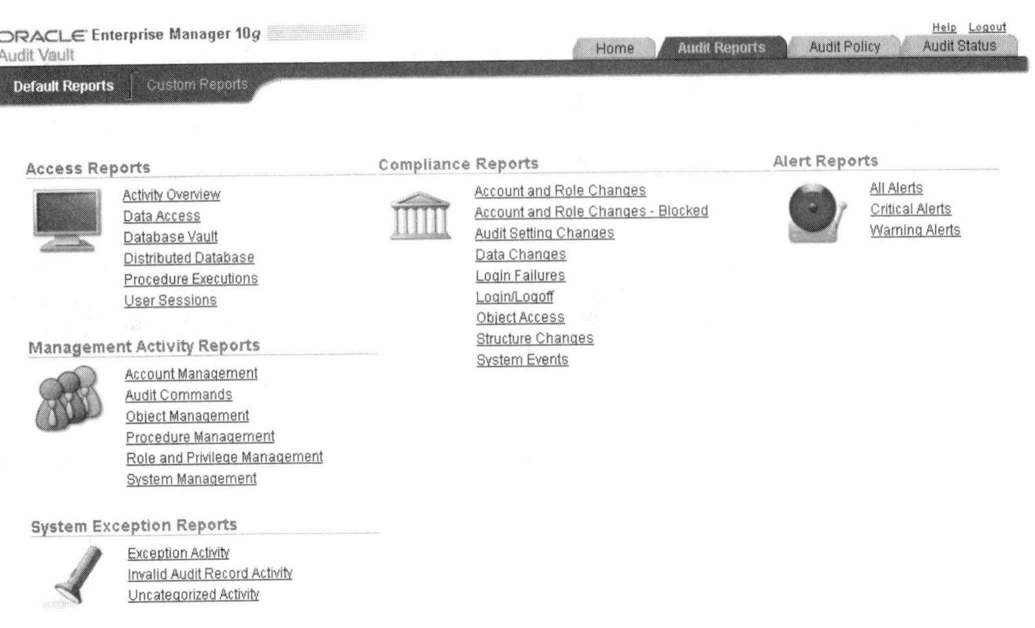

FIGURE 3-3 *Reports are valuable ways to support compliance initiatives.*

The schema in which Audit Vault stores and maintains audit data is accessible, allowing reports to be created using a variety of tools. Audit Vault includes Oracle Application Express (APEX) as the primary reporting tool, but the data warehouse schema is accessible in a nonproprietary way so other reporting tools can also be used for reporting purposes. Chapter 4 of the "Audit Vault Auditor's Guide" details the specifics of the Audit Vault data warehouse schema.

Alerts

Auditing in general is a passive activity. Recall that auditing is considered part of the detect phase of security. After audit records are created, it is up to some auditor to review these records later. How much later is "later"? Unfortunately, passive auditing is not always ideal, especially when the audit records have captured key and critical information. What you really want is a way to be notified of key events automatically so that you can move to the next phase of security after detect—the respond phase.

To this end, Audit Vault supports alerts, which are defined to monitor privacy, compliance, and insider threats across an organization and to help determine when policies have been violated. By monitoring audit data as it arrives from the Audit Vault agents, alerts can be sent to administrative and audit staff that warn of violations of defined internal controls. Alerts are generated when data in a single audit record matches a custom-defined alert rule condition. For example, a rule condition may be defined to raise alerts whenever a privileged user attempts to grant someone access to sensitive data.

Alerts are also defined with a severity level and an event category. As shown in Figure 3-4, the security levels (Informational, Warning, and Critical) help an audit administrator prioritize where to concentrate her efforts.

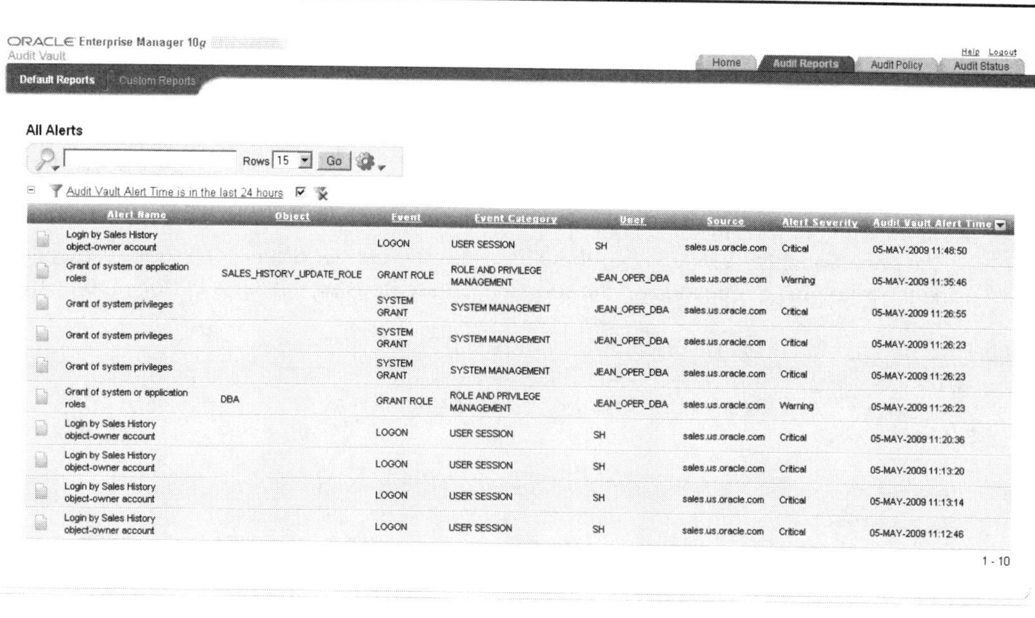

Alert Name	Object	Event	Event Category	User	Source	Alert Severity	Audit Vault Alert Time
Login by Sales History object-owner account		LOGON	USER SESSION	SH	sales.us.oracle.com	Critical	05-MAY-2009 11:48:50
Grant of system or application roles	SALES_HISTORY_UPDATE_ROLE	GRANT ROLE	ROLE AND PRIVILEGE MANAGEMENT	JEAN_OPER_DBA	sales.us.oracle.com	Warning	05-MAY-2009 11:35:46
Grant of system privileges		SYSTEM GRANT	SYSTEM MANAGEMENT	JEAN_OPER_DBA	sales.us.oracle.com	Critical	05-MAY-2009 11:26:55
Grant of system privileges		SYSTEM GRANT	SYSTEM MANAGEMENT	JEAN_OPER_DBA	sales.us.oracle.com	Critical	05-MAY-2009 11:26:23
Grant of system privileges		SYSTEM GRANT	SYSTEM MANAGEMENT	JEAN_OPER_DBA	sales.us.oracle.com	Critical	05-MAY-2009 11:26:23
Grant of system or application roles	DBA	GRANT ROLE	ROLE AND PRIVILEGE MANAGEMENT	JEAN_OPER_DBA	sales.us.oracle.com	Warning	05-MAY-2009 11:26:23
Login by Sales History object-owner account		LOGON	USER SESSION	SH	sales.us.oracle.com	Critical	05-MAY-2009 11:20:36
Login by Sales History object-owner account		LOGON	USER SESSION	SH	sales.us.oracle.com	Critical	05-MAY-2009 11:13:20
Login by Sales History object-owner account		LOGON	USER SESSION	SH	sales.us.oracle.com	Critical	05-MAY-2009 11:13:14
Login by Sales History object-owner account		LOGON	USER SESSION	SH	sales.us.oracle.com	Critical	05-MAY-2009 11:12:46

FIGURE 3-4 *Audit alerts provide proactive notification for critical events.*

Because Audit Vault uses standard Oracle auditing, operating system audit events, and fine-grained auditing, a variety of rules can be defined against this data collection. Many conditions can be potential "policy breakers" and therefore defined as conditions worthy of alert generation. Consider the following policies and the alerts that are defined as potential compensating controls:

- **Policy** The sensitive DBA role must be granted only to administrative users with appropriate approvals.
- **Alert** Audit alert is generated upon any grant of DBA to a database user in any database.
- **Policy** Privileged DBA users should not view information considered to be personally identifiable privacy data.
- **Alert** Audit condition is met on selecting a particular sensitive column (Salary, SSN, Credit card number) using the DBA role.
- **Policy** Existing information may be corrected only by reversing entries to maintain proper auditability, rather than issuing update statements directly against the database.
- **Alert** Updates on any accounting tables generate an alert for any update statement issued against a financial column.

Alerts are shown prominently in the Audit Vault console as graphs, with details made available with a mouse-click. A powerful alerting capability tells the Audit Vault Server to send you e-mail notifying you immediately of any alert(s).

Alert Example

We can demonstrate how to instrument this type of alerting by logging into the Audit Vault console with an account that has the AV_AUDITOR role. Alerts that match our audit patterns of Privilege Escalation and Default Account Logon can be defined under the Alerts tab under the Audit Policy tab. In Figure 3-5, alerts are defined for the granting of roles such as DBA or for a notional application role such as SALES_HISTORY_UPDATE, and these provide object-level access to sensitive data in the Sales History object-owner account SH. An alert for any login attempts by the object-owner account SH is also defined.

An operational DBA may trigger these alerts by attempting to access the objects owned by SH using the following commands on the source database housing the Sales History application:

```
[oracle@aosdb avagent] (avagent)$ sqlplus sh
SQL*Plus: Release 11.1.0.6.0 - Production on Tue May 5 11:48:16 2009
Copyright (c) 1982, 2008, Oracle.  All rights reserved.
Enter password:
ERROR:
ORA-01017: invalid username/password; logon denied
[oracle@aosdb avagent] (avagent)$ sqlplus jean_oper_dba
SQL*Plus: Release 11.1.0.6.0 - Production on Tue May 5 11:48:16 2009
Copyright (c) 1982, 2008, Oracle.  All rights reserved.
Enter password:
Connected to:
Oracle Database 11g Enterprise Edition Release 11.1.0.6.0 - Production
With the Partitioning, Oracle Label Security, OLAP, Data Mining,
Oracle Database Vault and Real Application Testing options
sys@SOURCE>GRANT DBA TO oe;
Grant succeeded.
sys@SOURCE>GRANT EXECUTE ANY PROCEDURE TO oe;
Grant succeeded.
sys@SOURCE>GRANT sales_history_update_role TO jean_oper_dba;
Grant succeeded.
```

The audit records generated as a result of these commands are collected by the Audit Vault collectors on this source database. The audit records trigger the alerts defined in Audit Vault based on the audit pattern concepts discussed. The alerts are summarized on the Home tab's Overview console shown in Figure 3-6. This summary page provides the macro view of auditing that we desire.

If the Audit Vault auditor clicks the Sources With Alerts link under the Summary of Alert Activity pie chart, she can investigate the details of the audit records that generated the alerts. This micro view of auditing is depicted in Figure 3-7. The APEX technology used to generate this alert report can be used to show additional audit record columns, filter the report, sort the report, save the report for customization, and download the report data. These customization features of the APEX technology allow the auditor to generate customized views of the information for a variety of compliance reporting needs.

ORACLE Enterprise Manager 10g
Audit Vault

Help Logout

Home | Audit Reports | Audit Policy | Audit Status

Audit Settings | Alerts

Database Instance: av.us.oracle.com > Alerts

Logged in As AVAUDITOR

Audit Alerts

Audit Source Type

Audit Source

Audit Event Category

Go

Create

Alert Name	Description	Audit Source	Audit Source Type	Audit Event Category	Remove
Grant of system or application roles	Alert on the granting of privileged system roles or application roles	sales.us.oracle.com	ORCLDB	ROLE AND PRIVILEGE MANAGEMENT	
Grant of system privileges	Alert for the GRANT of system ANY privileges	sales.us.oracle.com	ORCLDB	SYSTEM MANAGEMENT	
Login by Sales History object-owner account	Login to object-owner account that is locked and should not be used by administrators or end-users.	sales.us.oracle.com	ORCLDB	USER SESSION	

Home | Audit Reports | **Audit Policy** | Audit Status | Help | Logout

FIGURE 3-5 *Alerts are specific to the organization's policies and compliance objectives.*

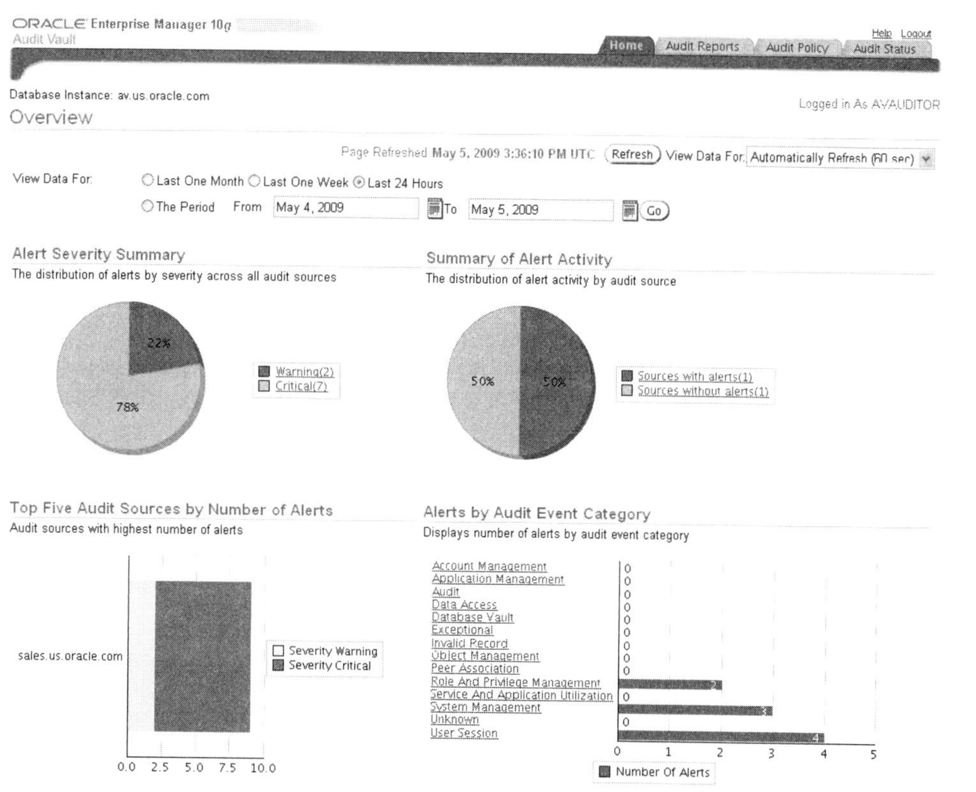

FIGURE 3-6 *The Overview console provides a quick view of the overall enterprise status.*

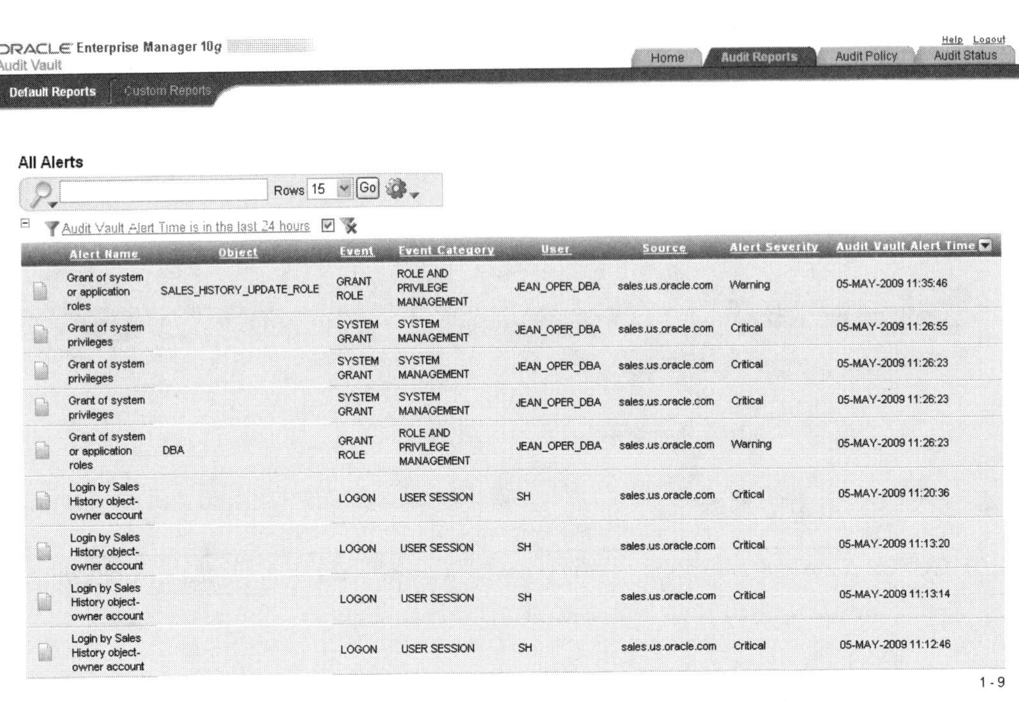

FIGURE 3-7 *Alert drill-downs allow auditors to detect and respondquickly to suspicious activity.*

Customized Alert Handling

You can develop your own alert response mechanism into the Audit Vault alert life cycle by developing an Audit Vault alert subscriber based on the Oracle Java Message Service (JMS) technology. The subscriber can de-queue alerts from the Audit Vault alert queue and respond in a customized manner. This customized response could incorporate existing notification and monitoring capabilities in your organization. The Audit Vault Server installation includes an example Java program that de-queues alerts from the Audit Vault alert queue and sends alert information in an e-mail to a specified user. This example program is described in the file $ORACLE_HOME/av/demo/alert/README.txt of your AV Server installation.

Managing Audit Policy for Source Databases

The Audit Vault console allows the Audit Vault auditor to retrieve the current audit policy (settings) for a source database into the Audit Vault warehouse. Once the baseline version of the audit policy is retrieved, the Audit Vault auditor can augment and refine the policy for any of the following types of audit areas:

- **SQL statements** SELECT, DML, and DDL statements that are not necessarily specific to any individual object in an object-owner account
- **Schema objects** SELECT, DML, AUDIT, and privilege management (GRANT, REVOKE) statements that are specific to individual objects in an object-owner account

- **Privileges** Audit policy options for the use of system ANY privileges, such as **UPDATE ANY TABLE** or security-relevant system privileges such as **ALTER USER**
- **Fine-grained auditing** Audit policy controls that allow you to define specific conditions that must exist for the audit to occur
- **Capture rules** DDL, DML, or both statements from redo log files that occur for any object in a specific object-owner account or a specific object in the account

The AV console also allows you to view summary information of the candidate audit policy and verify the policy for accuracy, as shown in Figure 3-8. Once the audit policy has been defined, verified, and saved in the Audit Vault warehouse, it can be provisioned back to the source database either by generating a SQL file for manual deployment or remotely using the Audit Vault collector account defined for the source database.

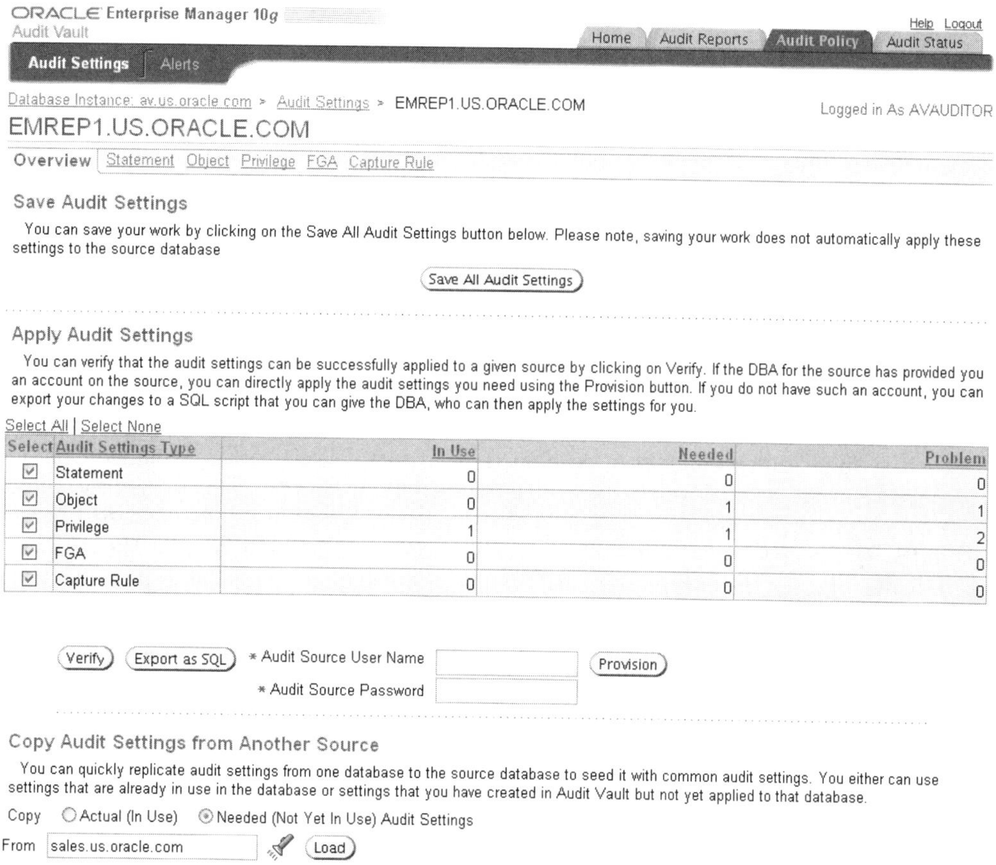

ORACLE Enterprise Manager 10g
Audit Vault

Help Logout

Home | Audit Reports | Audit Policy | Audit Status

Audit Settings | Alerts

Database Instance: av.us.oracle.com > Audit Settings > EMREP1.US.ORACLE.COM

Logged in As AVAUDITOR

EMREP1.US.ORACLE.COM

Overview | Statement | Object | Privilege | FGA | Capture Rule

Save Audit Settings

You can save your work by clicking on the Save All Audit Settings button below. Please note, saving your work does not automatically apply these settings to the source database

(Save All Audit Settings)

Apply Audit Settings

You can verify that the audit settings can be successfully applied to a given source by clicking on Verify. If the DBA for the source has provided you an account on the source, you can directly apply the audit settings you need using the Provision button. If you do not have such an account, you can export your changes to a SQL script that you can give the DBA, who can then apply the settings for you.

Select All | Select None

Select	Audit Settings Type	In Use	Needed	Problem
☑	Statement	0	0	0
☑	Object	0	1	1
☑	Privilege	1	1	2
☑	FGA	0	0	0
☑	Capture Rule	0	0	0

(Verify) (Export as SQL) * Audit Source User Name [ ] (Provision)

* Audit Source Password [ ]

Copy Audit Settings from Another Source

You can quickly replicate audit settings from one database to the source database to seed it with common audit settings. You either can use settings that are already in use in the database or settings that you have created in Audit Vault but not yet applied to that database.

Copy ○ Actual (In Use) ◉ Needed (Not Yet In Use) Audit Settings

From sales.us.oracle.com (Load)

FIGURE 3-8 *Audit policies can be created centrally and then deployed and verified across the enterprise.*

One of the most interesting features of the Audit Vault audit policy management and provisioning features is the ability to copy the audit settings from another source database. This allows you to define one or more nonoperational source databases that have a template audit policy for your production databases. Using this approach and the Audit Vault policy provisioning feature within the console, you can increase your level of assurance that the same version of an audit policy is applied to all of your production databases.

Audit Maintenance Operations

One of the byproducts of auditing is that you collect a lot of data over time. The older the data gets, the less sensitive it is generally and the less valuable it becomes. Oracle Audit Vault includes two primary areas of maintenance: source audit trails and collector audit logs.

One of the events in the life cycle of audit trail records is the archival and purging of older audit records from the source databases. This event is driven not only by audit retention requirements that are common to most compliance regulations, but by integrity and performance requirements as well.

Removing Audit Data from the Database

Over time, the database and operating system can potentially reach a maximum capacity for storing new audit records. If auditing is enabled for some time, the security administrator will want to delete records from the database audit trail to free audit trail space and to facilitate audit trail management. However, it's critical that the administrator not delete data that hasn't yet been transferred to Oracle Audit Vault.

Before deleting audit data from the database, you must determine the last record inserted into Audit Vault Server. You can do this by using Audit Vault's Activity Overview Report. Open the Activity Overview to view the date of the summary data. Remember that Audit Vault report data is displayed based on the last completed ETL warehouse job.

Moving the source audit records off the real-time processing storage area to a secured storage area, possibly with Transparent Data Encryption's tablespace encryption and Oracle Secure Backup of those tablespaces, will not only increase the integrity/safety of the raw data but will allow for improved performance querying the real-time audit records that remain in primary storage.

The Audit Vault product team developed an auxiliary PL/SQL package named DBMS_AUDIT_MGMT that can be deployed to most source databases that are part of your Audit Vault collection environment to perform this function. With this package, you can create database jobs to archive and purge the audit trail data for all the Oracle-supported audit trail formats. The package also provides logic to move the primary/real-time database audit trails to a tablespace that has been optimized for the audit record generation profile your database exhibits.

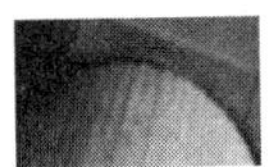

TIP

Refer to Note 731908.1 on Oracle Metalink for details on how you can obtain the PL/SQL package for your OS platform and database release. Refer to Chapter 14 of the "Oracle Audit Vault Administrator's Guide" for details on using this package.

Oracle Audit Vault Utilities Maintenance Periodic maintenance of Audit Vault is important for maintaining optimal performance. Audit Vault generates numerous logs and trace files during normal day-to-day operations. The following information regards the contents of the log files, their purpose, and how and when the files can be removed.

Much like the Oracle Database, the Audit Vault server generates log files that provide current status and diagnostic information. The log files should be monitored and periodically removed to control the amount of disk space used. These files can be found at *<Audit_Vault_Server_Home>/* av/log.

Server Log File	Description
avorcldb.log	Tracks the commands issued by the avorcldb facility used during the initial configuration of audited sources and Audit Vault agents and collectors. It is safe to delete this file at any time.
avca.log	Tracks the creation of collectors and the starting and stopping of Audit Vault agents and collectors. This file may be deleted only after the Audit Vault Server is shut down.

Enterprise Manager stores its logs in the directory *<Audit Vault_Server_Home>/<Host_Name>_<SID>/sysman/log.* The file emdb.nohup in this directory contains a log of activity for the Audit Vault web application, including GUI conversations, requests from the avctl utility, and communication with the various Audit Vault collection agents. This can be used to debug communication issues between the server and the agents.

The Audit Vault collection agent creates several log files and also must be maintained to control the amount of disk space used. These files can be found at *<Audit_Vault_Collection_Agent_Home>*/av/log.

Agent Log File	Description
agent.err	Logs all errors encountered in agent initialization and operation. It is safe to delete this file at any time.
agent.out	Logs all primary agent–related operations and activities. This file may be deleted only after the Audit Vault Collection Agent is shut down.
avca.log	Logs all Audit Vault collection agent commands that have been run and the results of each command. It is safe to delete this file at any time.
avorcldb.log	Logs all AVORCLDB commands that have been run and the results of running each command. It is safe to delete this file at any time.
av_client-%g.log.n	Logs the agent operations and errors returned from those operations. The %g is a generation number that starts from 0 (zero) and increases once the file size reaches the 10MB limit. A concurrent existence of this file is indicated by a *.n* appended to the file type name, such as av_client-%g.log.*n*, where *n* is an integer issued in sequence—for example av_client-0.log.1. The files that contain a *.log.n* extension may be deleted at any time.
<CName><SName><SId>.log CName = Collector Name SName = Source Name SID = Source ID	Logs collection operations for the DBAUD and OSAUD collectors. This file may be deleted only after the Audit Vault collection agent is shut down.

The directory *<Audit_Vault_Collection_Agent_Home>*/oc4j/j2ee/home/log contains the logs generated by the collection agent OC4J. In this directory, the file AVAgent-access.log contains a log of requests the agent receives from the Audit Vault Server. This can be used to debug communication issues between the server and the agent.

Summary

In today's world, auditing is growing in importance and is significant to most IT discussions. We now live in an era of Governance, Risk, and Compliance (GRC) and issues related to data sensitivity are vast. PII, PHI, PCI, and other highly sensitive data are deeply integrated and embedded into existing and new applications. GRC often requires the centralization of both audit policies—what to audit—and the actual audit data—records created to track usage of data. The ability to correlate audit data from multiple sources has been viewed as the holy grail by many security conscious professionals. Databases are viewed as the most important sources because they contain sensitive information. The goal then is to achieve, at an enterprise level, a complete understanding of access to critical databases.

While GRC is a driving factor in executing auditing activities, many organizations are learning that audit data can be more valuable than serving simply as a mandatory checkbox to meet their compliance initiatives. Auditing paints a picture of who is accessing what, from where, when, and potentially how. This intelligence can be used for resource optimization and consolidation issues, hardware sizing discussions, and increasing an organization's stand on cyber security, to name a few.

Auditing in Oracle involves more than just reporting on who works in a certain job or who is a member of a group. In this chapter, we showed that database auditing records provide the who, what, when, where, and how on *actual* information access as opposed to what someone might theoretically be doing or be able to do.

The importance of this style of auditing cannot be overstated. Knowing exactly when a data breach has occurred allows administrators to ask a variety of questions: What resource was accessed? From where was this data/resource accessed? We can often get other useful information about the context of the breach. What networks channels were involved? What users were involved? What was the system state at the time of breach? What SQL statements were issued? What applications were running? All these pieces of information can help you narrow down the execution of a data breach and find both the perpetrator and the vulnerability used to commit the breach.

The audit features of the Oracle Database—standard auditing, extended auditing, and fine-grained auditing—provide the basic mechanics for capturing useable data for a specific database instance. One of the limiting factors of audit data has historically been making it a priority to regularly review and analyze the database being generated by these auditing tools. Since the audit features made available in the database are limited to the scope of that particular database, a holistic audit approach has been difficult to employ.

Audit Vault can best be thought of as a secure data warehouse of audit data. It is secure because it is locked down by Oracle Database Vault. Audit data is first collected at a source database and is based on centrally controlled audit policies. The collection processes are executed by various collection agents that support Oracle databases, SQL Server, Sybase, and IBM. The audit data from these source databases is then transmitted across an encrypted network to the Audit Vault Server.

The Audit Vault Server acts as the data warehouse repository. Audit Vault provides you access to a variety of reports that show system and object access. The reports are neatly organized by categories. The consolidated view provided by Audit Vault Server can provide a variety of reports that can satisfy the requirements of compliance initiatives such as Sarbanes-Oxley, HIPAA, and PCI. As the Audit Vault data warehouse schema is exposed, you can create your own reports using the provided Oracle tools or using your favorite report-writing tools. This will allow you to incorporate application-specific accesses into your enterprise auditing view.

In addition, an administrator can configure Audit Vault Server to implement organizational security policies and generate warnings (called alerts) when these conditions are met. Oracle Audit Vault can generate alerts on specific system or user-defined events, acting as an early warning system against insider threats and helping you detect changes to baseline configurations or activity that could potentially violate compliance. Oracle Audit Vault continuously monitors the audit data collected, evaluating the activities against defined alert conditions. The result is that Oracle Audit Vault provides IT security personnel with the ability to detect and be alerted to suspicious activity, attempts to gain unauthorized access, and abuse of system privileges.

Oracle Audit Vault is important to enterprise security as it fulfills the detect and response phases of the Prevent-Detect-Respond-Remediate security life cycle.

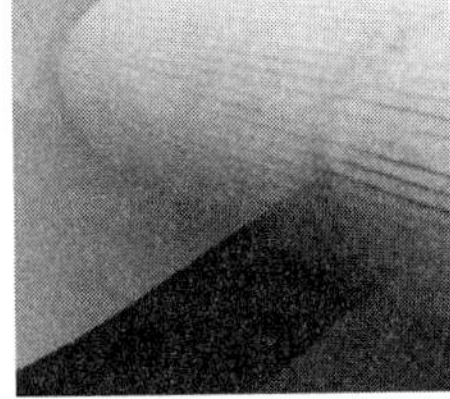

PART II

Oracle Database Vault

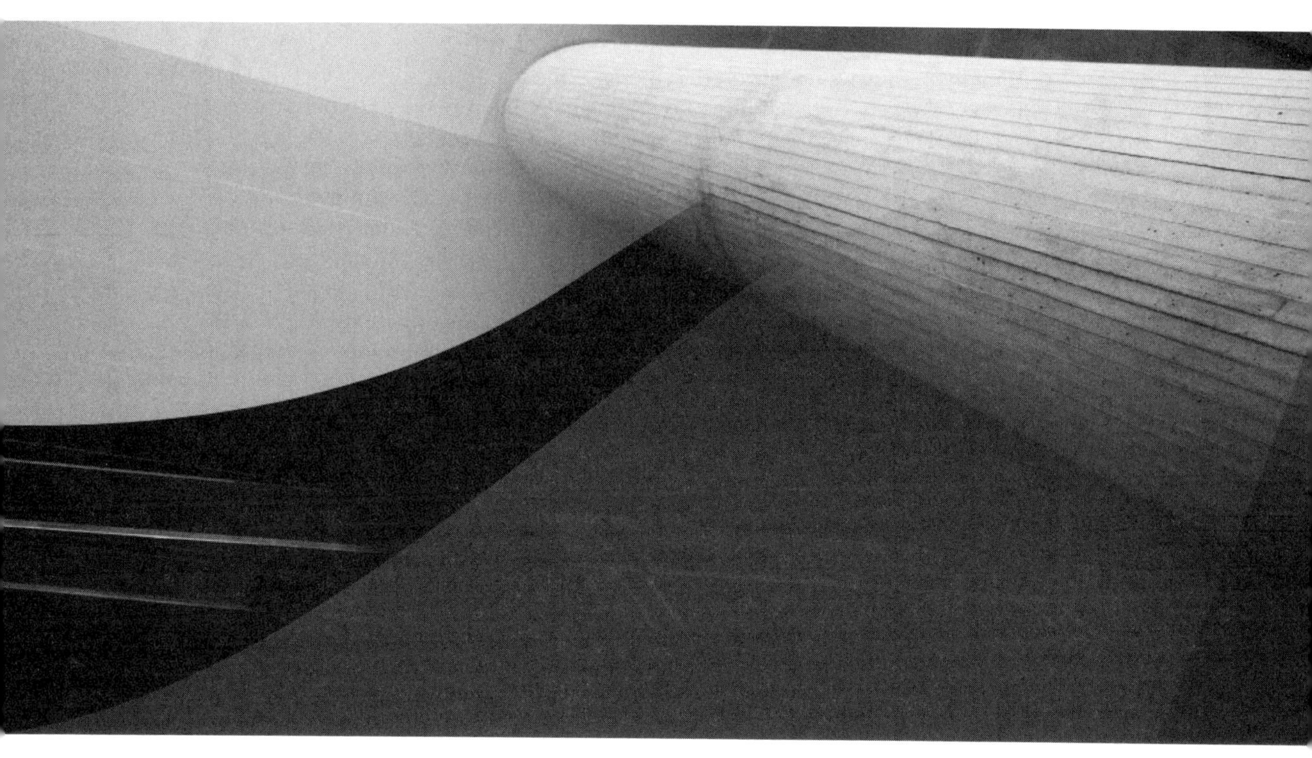

CHAPTER 4

Database Vault Introduction

racle has always endeavored to increase the capabilities of the Oracle Database. Over the years, staggering innovations have been realized in performance, reliability, extensibility, and sheer capability. Oracle Database is the number one database in the world because of these unmatched capabilities. But as robust as Oracle Database is in the database security arena, a few things about the implementation needed to be improved. It may be startling to discover that, until recently, a security gap in Oracle Database desperately needed to be filled. This gap has become wider and more relevant because of the critical security challenges we face with compliance and cyber security today. Oracle Database Vault fills that gap elegantly and innovatively with additional layers of security. And unlike many features of the database, Oracle Database Vault radically changes what you do as a DBA and how you do it. Therefore, you will most certainly want to review this part carefully

In Chapters 4–7, you'll learn about Oracle Database Vault in detail. This chapter discusses the security gap, including the reasons why Database Vault was created. Understanding the design intent can help you understand why you should use it, when you should use it, and how you should use it. That is the goal of this chapter: To understand why Oracle Database Vault is needed and how its core components work the way they work.

Chapter 5 is perhaps the literary equivalent of the military's basic training. This chapter leads you through the basic workings of the product, including the core capabilities and principles that Oracle Database Vault brings to the database.

Chapter 6 puts Oracle Database Vault to work in the context of application building. To appreciate the power of Oracle Database Vault and what it makes possible, the applications used in the examples are somewhat unconstrained—that is, you have the flexibility to modify the application configuration and potentially the code to take advantage of all that the Oracle Database Vault has to offer.

Chapter 7 examines Oracle Database Vault in the context of applications, but this time, for existing applications. We debated how to title Chapter 7 because of what the word "existing" can mean. In this context, existing applications are applications that offer you limited modification options. In fact, modifications are largely configurations. Our approach is that you don't have the luxury of modifying your application's source code, its accounts, or its structure. Anything you do occurs around the application and in a transparent manner.

The Security Gap

Chapter 1 covered important concepts about data categorization, identity management, and database account management. Many of those concepts are important to the information covered in this chapter. Specifically, security issues center on *object owner* accounts or schemas versus *user* accounts—that is, the accounts we want users to log in to.

To understand why you need to use Database Vault, look closely at your core database accounts, including default privileges and their default intent. You may recognize security gaps or suboptimal conditions that can be directly addressed by Oracle Database Vault (DBV).

History of Privileged Accounts

Recall from Chapter 1 the discussion about two of the primary accounts/schemas for Oracle: *SYS*, the object owner of the database engine, and *SYSTEM*, which acts as a DBA user account. Oracle uses metadata tables (aka the data dictionary) to manage many database functions, and the fact that SYS owns these tables accounts for some of Oracle Database's most serious security implications. SYSTEM is the standard account to which DBAs connect to create users, create tablespaces, and perform basic DBA tasks and is covered a bit later in the chapter.

Object owners have all rights on all objects they own. For SYS, this translates to full rights on many of the core database objects, including objects owned by accounts supporting any given application. As you will see, the security discussion goes beyond this simple principle.

The angst around SYS has recently climaxed in part due to the sensitivity of data and data types such as financial records and personally identifiable information (PII). Governance and compliance issues and concepts such as segregation of duty have also focused attention on SYS. The concern is that SYS has the complete and unregulated ability to do absolutely anything and everything in the database. And unlike SYSTEM, SYS doesn't need to be granted privileges to do these things. The privileges are automatic because of the object owner principle and because SYS has to work that way for the database to work at all.

SYS can not only disable security policies (such as Virtual Private Database, or VPD, policies), but can do even more, such as delete data from the audit trail. This means a user logged into the SYS account has the ability to do bad things, and to do them without any record or trace that they were done. In fact, the issue of deleting from the audit tables drove the requirement for operating system auditing for SYS. Although we cannot stop SYS from performing these actions, we must have a way to audit SYS without the risk of SYS deleting or changing the audit logs.

Superuser 0

The all-powerful SYS is not actually intended to be a user. This can be confusing, because you can log into the SYS account with a password, and this process is really no different from the way you would log into any generic database user account. Therefore, it's difficult to discuss the concept of SYS not being a database user with someone unfamiliar with Oracle but very familiar with compliance initiatives.

It turns out that in addition to SYS owning many of the objects that run the database, much of the database code checks to see if the user is specifically SYS. If you query SYS.USER$, you will see a column titled USER#, and for the user SYS, this column has a value of 0 (zero), because SYS is established as the primary owner of the core database objects.

What makes SYS a superuser with unyielding rights has a lot to do with the fact that SYS owns many of the objects that run the database. There are two important points to be made here. First, we know that we must have SYS for the database to function. We need to have a container for core database objects. And we need to be able to log on as SYS to install patches, perform upgrades, conduct backup/recovery operations, and perform other important tasks. Removal of the SYS account is simply not an option.

The second point to be made is that there is a huge security risk in having a super-user account. Security is essentially and intentionally bypassed with SYS, and this is not optimal for many security architects. It is also undesirable if you are trying to conform to compliance guidelines around segregation of duties.

The SYS account's major risks are not necessarily most severe when an actual person has connected to the database as SYSDBA, but rather when the code underneath the user's session is operating in the context of SYS. This can occur through techniques such as privilege escalation and SQL injection code that exploit security vulnerabilities. These techniques, if successful, can allow someone to tamper with the database security controls and/or gain access to very sensitive data. Poorly secured databases are certainly targets, but even well-designed and secured systems can be attacked. But these risks can be significantly reduced by upgrading to DBV and adding a few new DBV concepts to your system. One of the fundamental objectives of DBV is to ensure that the SYS account can be controlled and will not inherently bypass the new security layers it introduces.

Other Privileged Accounts

It wasn't too many versions or years ago that all the core database objects were stored in the SYS account. The first departure occurred with SYSTEM, which was created specifically to address the object owner principle and to separate a user from the database objects. At first, many objects were shared with SYS and SYSTEM, but over time, SYS retained sole ownership and SYSTEM became the intended DBA user account. This allowed us to start controlling who has access to what, because SYSTEM required privileges to perform actions (although giving SYSTEM every possible privilege tends to defeat the intended goal).

As Oracle introduced more options and capabilities, with the release of Oracle 7.3 there came a need and an obvious desire to create separate schemas in which to install these options. Schemas such as MDSYS, which supports spatial data objects, and CTXSYS, which supports Oracle text objects, came to be. These schemas were meant to serve as containers for the objects that made up the options. (In this chapter, we'll refer to them as an "option's schemas" to differentiate them and note their intended role.)

In a similar manner to SYS, administrators—and anyone with the correct password—could log onto the option's schemas. In addition, in combining the object owner principle of SYS and the need to grant many privileges such as SYSTEM, the option's schemas were sometimes considered to be superusers in their own right.

Other accounts of note quickly sprang up as well. Large enterprise applications followed similar models of creating object container schemas with extreme privileges. But this was not isolated to enterprise applications. Many small- to medium-size applications also adopted this architecture. There were good reasons for the apparent excessive privileges, which you will learn more about.

Today's Accounts

Today, lots of accounts can do lots of things: SYS and SYSTEM; every Oracle database option schema; enterprise resource planning (ERP) application schemas and user accounts; customer relationship management (CRM) application schemas and accounts; other back office enterprise application suites; and custom and other third-party software schemas and accounts. There are a lot of schemas, and the implementations are fairly consistent, as described earlier.

It's worth repeating that the security ramifications are enormous. All these accounts have login potential. The object owner principle exists, but, more important, vast privileges—often system *ANY privileges—are in place. This allows the schema or a user logged into that schema to do not only what is required for the application or option, but to do quite a bit more than what was originally intended.

The Security Remedy

Security specialists and best practice recommendations from folks such as the SANS Institute offer a consistent approach to dealing with these security problems: lock and expire the accounts. Other suggestions, such as some made by the authors, have included varying technical Band-Aids such as setting impossible passwords, auditing logons, and sending alerts if someone accesses one of the special schemas.

The thinking is that you don't want people logging into these schemas because they are object owner–intended schemas and not user accounts. In many cases, new requests come in from the security or governance committee, asking if the schemas can be removed altogether. In other cases, such as with the Java Virtual Machine (JVM), removal of the schema can occur, but this is often not a supportable configuration. While the suggestions mentioned here are good security practices, they are still suboptimal.

To resolve the security issues, think about what you need to do to architect this properly. You need to be able to partition schemas to avoid the object owner principle from cross-infecting your applications and data. You also need a way to limit the privileges on those schemas to restrict them to their particular area of responsibility—that is, users should have all privileges only within their application domain.

One More Clarifying Challenge

One final wrinkle that you may recall from Chapter 1 will help you put this discussion in perspective. Recall that many applications span several schemas, often for good design reasons, even outside the security realm. As it turns out, the system privileges—in particular, the system *ANY privileges (such as SELECT **ANY** TABLE, DELETE **ANY** TABLE)—are granted to schemas so that users can access all the tables used by an application regardless of which schema contains the tables.

Many applications include thousands or tens of thousands of objects. Direct object grants are not practical. Logging in to each schema to perform an operation is impractical if not undesirable. The only practical choice is to create new object owner accounts and grant the system *ANY privileges, thereby leaving us with a potpourri of user accounts, schemas, and vast privileges. It is a perplexing dilemma.

The Gap Identified

This last reflection puts a light on the security gap that exists. Before we declare it directly, let's follow the logic of how we identified this the security gap. To illustrate this point, suppose you are building a sales reporting application in which all the historical sales data is stored in a schema called the SH schema. This application requires some helper objects—materialized views, PL/SQL procedures, and other objects—that you naturally create in a different schema called the SHELPER schema.

The administrator for the sales reporting application requires full access to the SH and SHELPER schemas. Logging into one schema does not necessarily do her much good, because object owner rights are limited to the schema in which the admin logs in. (We noted that there are often more than two schemas in most applications.) Logging into every schema is not a practical solution, so the administrator will do one of two things: She will log into one of the schemas directly, such as the SH schema, after having granted system privileges to SH, and she will then use those system privileges to access the SHELPER schema. True user identity is lost in this scenario, however, because it leaves no attribution to the real user who performed the operation.

Option two is to create a new user account that can be associated with a real person (let's call it SR_ADMIN) and grant that user all the system privileges. The good news is that the administrator's identity is preserved because she has a private schema. The bad news with this option is that it creates another user who can do much more than is desirable for security.

You may suggest, as have many, that a new privilege grant or grants are needed to grant all privileges on all objects within a schema to another user. The grant syntax might look something like the following:

```
/* Wouldn't it be nice if
   we could give all privileges
   to everything in the SH schema
   to SR_ADMIN with the following
*/
GRANT ALL ON SH TO SR_ADMIN;
```

```
/* Wouldn't it be nice if
   we could give select every table
   in the SH schema to SR_ADMIN
   with the following
*/
GRANT SELECT ON SHELPER.% TO SR_ADMIN;
```

Now you see the gap. In Oracle, direct object privileges occur at an object by object level—for example, **GRANT SELECT ON SH.SALES TO SR_ADMIN**. System privileges exist for all objects everywhere (barring the data dictionary)—for example, **GRANT SELECT ANY TABLE TO SR_ADMIN**.

You can see the need for a middle ground—a privilege set that allows everything within a certain schema or set of schemas. This last notion of a set of schemas is called a *realm*, and it is one of the new security layers provided by DBV. Before we consider that, and since we are in the mood for improving things in the database, let's look at a few more security should-haves.

Security Should-haves

Over the years, as you've built security into your databases, you have probably come across a few techniques and methods that were extremely useful and effective. As avid security engineers, we, too, have discovered patterns of success not only within the database but also outside of the database. In this section, we'll review a few of these methods or requirements that have found their way into DBV.

Multifactored Authentication

The notion of multifactor authentication is probably a familiar concept. Multifactor authentication involves using more than one item to authenticate a user (or entity) and is usually considered as an alternative to using passwords. Multifactor authentication is considered more secure than single-factor authentication because several authentication mechanisms are far more difficult to compromise, obtain, or spoof than a single form of authentication. Multifactor authentication is required to perform many real-world transactions, such as setting up a new financial account or obtaining a passport.

Our objective is to take the notion of multifactor authentication and bring it to privilege enablement within the database. This is the basis for one of the most loved privilege enablement techniques in the database: Secure Application Roles (SARs).

SARs are enabled from within defined procedural code. The notion is that simply enabling roles either by default or explicitly (via the **SET ROLE** command) was generally not good enough. With SARs, the database validates that the **SET ROLE** call is being made from within the defined procedure code. This complies with multifactor authentication because the code can perform various checks prior to enabling the role. If the checks fail, the role is not enabled. SARs thus gives you a multifactored approach to privilege enablement from within the database.

Conditional Security

While implementing the logic within the SARs procedures, many popular methods and checks would and could be performed to allow us to form some abstractions and classifications:

- **Context-based security** Recognizes that the privilege should be allowed only as part of a specific configuration, fact, function, business flow, or other specific situation. If the situation does not exist, an incongruity exists in the context of what is allowable and supposed to happen, and therefore the privilege should not be enabled. For example, the privilege could be enabled only at a certain time of day or on a certain day of the week.

Alternatively, the privilege can check how the user authenticated, where the user are coming from, and which application the user is using.

- **Adaptive security** The overall security is changing in near real time. The procedural code can detect the current state and loosen or constrain privileges accordingly. For example, an intrusion detection system detects an attack and raises a signal that the procedure reads and then denies a privilege request. The core concept is that the security is not rigid, nor does it rely on human intervention; it is designed to adapt itself to the situation.
- **Separation of duty** An often dreaded phrase, separation of duty prevents (or attempts to prevent) any single person from performing nefarious actions or duties. The separation forces a co-conspirator to play along. Just as a single factor is less secure than multiple factors, a single user is less secure than multiple users. Within the database, many accounts offer privileges that may conflict with a desired regulation. To resolve this, privileges would be enabled sequentially or would be able to validate that a multiple-person action is taking place.
- **Conditional auditing** Auditing is part of the security life cycle, but it suffers many problems similar to those of privilege enablement requirements. Auditing is generally turned on or off. Fine-grained auditing was a major step forward in achieving the desired objective of auditing only when we want to audit. The "when" is based on the contextual basis and adaptive security objectives.

Some of the requirements you derive will probably land in multiple categories. This discussion is meant to serve as a new way of thinking about security—that security can be conditional. It is not rigid like a role with its static set of privileges. It should not be turned either on or off. In deciding whether a user may perform an action can be "it depends." In many ways, conditional security separates the decision-making part of security from the enforcement part.

Practical Implementation Lessons

Many lessons have been learned in the implementation of security and security policies. One that always comes up is transparency, mentioned in Chapter 1 but worth a replay here because it is an essential element of success for many security implementations. Transparency is important for security because it acknowledges that user or application interference for pure security reasons is always undesirable. If you can secure something without causing extra work for the user or code modifications, then that is the way to proceed.

The next lesson learned in effective security implementations is the judicious use of a declarative environment. VPD security is great, but Oracle Label Security (OLS) is better, because OLS is declarative. Having a declarative framework saves coding time, reduces risk, and increases success (assuming that the framework is sound). A declarative framework also facilitates security verification and auditing tasks, as validating settings in the framework is almost always exponentially easier than validating code.

TIP

Move as much of your code as possible into a declarative framework. This saves time, reduces risk, and allows others to validate the implementation more easily.

Securing by Command

A final nice-to-have capability concerns *security by command.* A *command* in this context is any Data Manipulation Language (DML) or Data Definition Language (DDL) SQL statement. SARs help to motivate this discussion, because they suggest that a user must have privileges to execute a command, but the command can be controlled conditionally through another layer of security.

With security by command, the focus shifts from the role to the ability to execute a command. Assigning privileges directly to a user or grouping them in a role and then granting them to the user should not be the only methods that grant users the ability to execute commands. Instead, we can treat the ability to execute a command in a manner analogous to the conditional security mentioned earlier. Consider, for example, a user's direct privileges that are required to perform some action (such as using a **SELECT** on a table), and add another layer that can reject the action if a certain condition is not met.

Recall that the conditional security philosophy says that the answer to deciding whether a user should be able to do something is "it depends." This is not role-dependent. Ultimately, it would be nice for the database to evaluate all commands in a conditional, extensible manner.

Database Vault Components

Now that we have identified a few areas to improve, let's look at how DBV addresses these requirements and security should-haves. The objective is here is simply to impart the natural and intuitive architecture for DBV. Having a fundamental understanding of the DBV components—why they are what they are—will help you to employ DBV in an effective manner.

DBV is built largely around a declarative framework that consists of tables that store information that drives the desired security policy and security enforcement. The framework is manipulated by a set of web-based user interfaces and a set of application programming interface (API) calls to the PL/SQL code.

One of the principles that drove the design of DBV was to provide higher assurance through additional security mechanisms that were separate and distinct from the existing database mechanisms. Risks are not always associated with an actual user's session privileges; they do occur when the code underneath a user's session is operating in the context of a powerful privilege that could be exploited for malicious use.

The High Assurance Principle (HAP) defines a basic security axiom: the use of multiple security mechanisms from different sources provides a higher level of assurance than using multiple security mechanisms from a single source.

NOTE
HAP for database security = 1 DB mechanism + 1 DBV mechanism.

HAP for database security separates the security mechanisms into two sources: core database security (accounts, privileges, roles, VPD and views, PL/SQL, and triggers) and Database Vault security (factors, rules, realms, and command rules).

In addition to making a robust security implementation possible, DBV's declarative nature helps others—auditors, in particular—verify and validate your security policies. We cannot over-emphasize the criticality of this point. When security is buried inside code, it is more difficult to understand, modify, and reuse. To this end, you will see that DBV has built itself around an easily verifiable, yet robust and resilient, security model.

Factors

We'll start at the most elementary place, which for DBV is *factors*. Think back to the discussion about multifactored and conditional security. With conditional security, we are not making security decisions based on whether or not a person has the "privilege" to do something. Security is more dynamic and can involve many factors that are checked at runtime and can be very extensible.

Multiple factors can be considered when you're deciding whether or not to enable a privilege or perform an action—time of day, day of the week, how the user authenticated, whether the request was part of a specific transaction, and so forth. Each, if not all, of those elements can be a factor in the overall security decision—that is, the decision on whether or not to allow an action to take place, and the individual elements can be thought of as security factors.

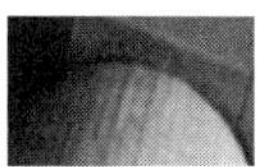

NOTE
For DBV, a factor is simply an item that you decide to use to make security decisions.

Factors are discrete security-related attributes that resolve to a specific value. As you might guess, these factors are generally resolved using PL/SQL expressions. Factors are like application context variables, but you don't have to develop any code to set, audit, and provide event handlers.

Protecting the Security Mechanisms

If you have ever employed SARs or written VPD policies with application context variables, you are quite familiar with the use of factors. Everything from the user's identity, to a client identifier, to an IP address are factors that are commonly used to ensure that the security policies are being upheld. With DBV, factors are declared, named, and stored in tables. This allows factors to be reused, validated, and security enhanced.

Factor security is possible because the entire DBV infrastructure is secured. One of the biggest risks to any security implementation is an attack on the logical implementation itself. If you are using PL/SQL to protect your data, either as part of a SAR, a VPD, or even an API to prevent direct data access, what protects the PL/SQL? Without DBV, nothing protects the security infrastructure other than standard security rights, which, as you have seen, are frequently overridden by system privileges.

DBV ensures that the things that are used to secure the database are also protected. This is an important point: DBV significantly strengthens any security implementation. It cannot be replicated using any other database mechanism.

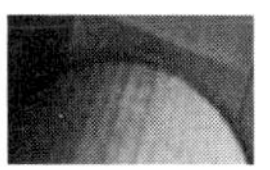

NOTE
DBV protects the things that protect the things.

Rules

If you've written security code, you know that within your security policy or implementation, you construct a set of logical statements. These statements are used to determine whether an action can or should take place. Many statements take the form of Boolean logic that uses logical ANDs and ORs nested inside IF-THEN-ELSE statements. You usually write code that says something analogous to "if this and that, or the user is an administrator, then do choice one, else do choice two." You could say that the security rule determines which choice will occur.

For a simple database example, consider the following logic checks to decide whether a user can SELECT from a table:

- The user authenticated using Secure Sockets Layer (SSL).
- The user's request comes from the application server's known IP address.
- It is currently Monday through Friday.
- The time is not between the hours of midnight and 6:00 A.M.
- The user is a member of the SALES_DEPARTMENT user group.

What you know about these checks is that each is a security factor. In DBV, each will be represented as a factor that, when called, will return the value in a secure way. We are taking the security factors and putting them together in a logical series of ANDs and ORs, which you could call your security rules.

DBV rules are the sequence of factors that you use to determine your security rules. Our five security checks or the factors stated previously could be combined into a rule that is used to determine appropriate access privileges. If all five factors are met, the rule may say, the action can be performed.

DBV Rule Sets

As with factors, rules are stored in the DBV declarative framework. Depending on your experience, you may quickly identify with this best practice. Quite a few implementations use declarative constructs. The security code reads data from the tables and enforces what the data tells it to do. This makes it easy for you to add or modify the security factors or rules. To modify your security, you add or delete a new record in the table. This is also the basis for DBV rules and factors. It is simple, secure, and intuitive.

As DBV was being designed, it became clear that rules were a key component that offered high reusability. Therefore, DBV supports the notion of a library of rule groupings known as *rule sets*, which allow for a large amount of logic reuse that typically governs access for different controls within an application. By aggregating the rules into a rule set, you gain a much simpler and more maintainable security model.

Realms

At the heart of our security gap discussion is an architectural quandary. We have been looking at object owners and user accounts and observing default behaviors, possibilities, and limitations. The quandary concerns the use of implicit and granted privileges on objects based on the schemas in which the objects exist and the schema the user is logged into when attempting to access these objects.

The ideal schema/user design solution is none of the above. In analyzing the basic security requirements, what you are really trying to do is to apply security to a *certain set* of users on a *certain set* of objects. It's not a certain set of users for *all* the objects in the database. The system privileges apply to all objects in the system—that is, the database. Unfortunately, system privileges (especially the ANY privileges) are essential, because our applications access many objects across many schemas.

We need to alter our thinking, then, about how security is supposed to work. Think about the security requirements for only a single application as opposed to security for the entire database. Application security means that you want to ensure that everything that happens to the data for the application is secured. You are not concerned about the other data or applications in the database so long as they don't interfere with your application. Likewise, you want to ensure that any application user or administrator is also prevented from tampering with things outside the application. This is a subtle but important change in thinking for many database experts.

Let's now focus on the simple notion of object grouping, with an emphasis on security. You want to define what your application is with respect to the database. You want to list the objects and schemas and declare those objects to be part of the application. Your ideal security model would then allow you to define the security behavior relevant only to those particular objects without regard to all the other database objects.

This all drives the requirement for DBV *realms,* a new security layer that provides containment and eliminates inadvertent accesses based on system privileges.

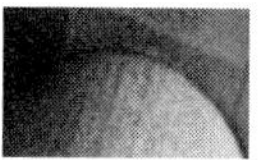

NOTE
Realms are the collection of (application) relevant objects that are grouped together for security reasons.

You can think of realms as marking a set of objects—tables, views, roles, PL/SQL, and so forth—that you want to protect, regardless of which account owns the object. The objects are identified across the various schemas and placed in a realm. Once the objects are placed in a DBV realm, they are instantly protected from users with system ANY privileges.

The sandbox metaphor used to describe how Java applets are secure within a web browser is also relevant here. Each application, when in a realm, can be considered as being in its own security sandbox within the database. System ANY privileges no longer give you access to items protected within a realm. Therefore, putting your application objects in the same protected sandbox or realm allows you to limit very specifically who gets access to what.

Our definition of realms, which used the natural grouping of objects generally associated with applications, helped us explain why you would group objects. However, there is no restriction in DBV for objects to be bound to any application or anything in particular. Realms are purely logical groupings; you define the reason for the grouping.

Realm-isms

Realms can consist of any objects from any schemas. They are not simply subsets of a single schema. This allows you to maintain a database design based on factors other than security while still being able to support security.

Once the objects are in a realm, they are protected from users that have system ANY privileges. Realms can also contain users. The ability to map users to realms works well to support most security policies that define specific application administrators and separation of duty requirements.

You can think of users as realm administrators and realm participants. An administrator can execute privilege management commands (**GRANT**, **REVOKE**) on objects and roles that are protected by the realm, while a participant cannot. The process of setting up a realm is as simple as defining the objects of interest and then adding users to the realm as either administrators or participants. This allows you to keep other users—even SYSTEM and other privileged accounts—from tampering with objects and data in your realm.

Realms generally consist of objects from multiple schemas and are especially important to security relevant information (metadata) such as a table that lists group memberships. Database roles can also be defined as part of a protected realm object in addition to the typical database object types you may identify at first. You can include roles in the realm protections to protect against unauthorized grant (or revoke) operations on the roles. This is where you can see DBV protecting the security infrastructure—that is, securing the components that enforce the security for the database and data itself.

In practice, realms are flexible and transparent. The applications know nothing of the realms. When implemented correctly, the standard security and application capabilities remain functioning. This transparency is essential to an effective implementation so that well-behaved applications won't be negatively affected once the security capabilities are enabled.

Command Rules

Earlier in the chapter, we discussed the idea of applying conditional security to commands to create some context-based or rules-based mechanism for database commands. The commands can be used for objects on which the user has direct object privileges or for system commands, such as **CREATE USER**, that do not apply to a specific object or schema. The notion is similar to the conditional security checks that you would perform for SARs, but this time it's applied to basic commands.

DBV's command rules offer another new security layer that allows the authorization of a database command—such as **SELECT** or **CREATE USER**—for custom-defined rules. The rules may, and often do, use rules and factors. The result is that you derive the same conditional security capabilities that you might otherwise get from enabling a role with SARs. The decision to allow a command to execute is based on an existing privilege and a rule that must be passed.

An important differentiation exists between SARs and command rules. With SARs, the user does not have the privileges to perform the action. The privileges are granted to the role, and when the role is enabled, the user can perform the action. Conditional security was performed to enable the role, thus giving the user privileges.

With command rules, and for DBV in general, the user must already have the base database privileges. DBV acts as an additional security monitor after the basic database privileges have been verified. These privileges can be obtained in one of three ways:

- They may be logged into the schema that owns the objects. We call this the object owner model.
- They may have direct object grants to the object. For example, for a user logged into the SR_ADMIN schema, an appropriate grant can be made to allow the user to access the PRODUCTS table in the SH schema by having the user SH issue a GRANT SELECT ON PRODUCTS to SR_ADMIN, which is a specific object-level privilege.
- They may be able to perform an action based on a system or system ANY privileges.

With command rules, the user must already have the privilege. Command rules pertain to commands that do not need to have relevance to any DBV realms and as such can overrule a command that is allowed by a realm's policy. This makes sense when you consider the many system commands that are irrelevant to any data object (such as **CREATE USER**).

This makes DBV transparent and allows it to work for existing applications. If the existing application security model prevented a user from performing an action, DBV does not and cannot undo the existing security.

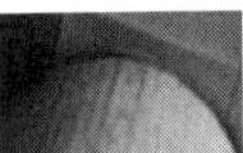

NOTE
DBV adds a layer of security that is called at runtime to mediate actions and access. Access = DB privilege + DBV rule.

Installing Oracle Database Vault

Now that you understand the problems DBV addresses, what it consists of and why, it's time to get started using DBV. This section reviews the DBV installation. We describe and highlight important aspects of the installation process and resulting configuration.

DBV is installed using the Oracle Database Configuration Assistant (DBCA) that comes with Oracle Database Enterprise Edition. During the installation, you will be prompted to create up to two additional end user administration accounts in the database. These accounts will be used to manage DBV policies.

Here is important point number one: The DBV accounts are separate from the traditional Oracle accounts (such as the user SYSTEM) that have similar function. Why? Because traditional accounts use roles and system privileges that will henceforth be constrained, thereby rendering the accounts incapable of managing the policies. The separation of the new DBV accounts also facilitates a separation of duty capability in that you will be able to separate the ability to issue system commands.

Installed DBV Administration Roles

The core administration roles provided with DBV are categorized as follows:

- **Security Policy Administration and Reporting** The DBV install creates three new roles related to DBV policy reporting and administration:
  - **DV_SECANALYST** This role can read (SELECT) from DBV configuration and audit information. It must use the Database Vault Administrator (DVA) web application in a read-only mode.
  - **DV_ADMIN** This role can execute the DVA package, DVSYS.DBMS_MACADM. It also can use the DVA web application to manage DBV security configuration. The DV_ADMIN role is granted the DV_SECANALYST role, so it inherits all of the read privileges from this role.
  - **DV_OWNER** The initial account that is granted to this role at install time can grant the DV_SECANALYST, DV_ADMIN, and DV_OWNER roles to other accounts. This role is granted the DV_ADMIN role, so it inherits the ability to manage security configuration. It also can read the DBV configuration through the privileges obtained via the DV_SECANALYST role, which is granted to the DV_ADMIN role.
- **Account Administration** A single database account administration role, **DV_ACCTMGR**, is created in DBV. After DBV installation, this role has the system privileges and exclusive ability to create, alter, and drop database accounts (Oracle USER object types) as well as database profiles (Oracle PROFILE object types). Note that any account can still change its own password, but the new DV_ACCTMGR role is responsible for password reset responsibilities.

DBV also installs two template roles used for realm administration and realm-based object owning accounts: DV_REALM_OWNER and DV_REALM_RESOURCE. These roles are covered in detail in Chapter 6.

The DBCA prompts you for up to two additional end user administration accounts in the database. The first account name is used to define the initial DBV "owner" who will be granted the DV_OWNER role at the end of the installation. The second account name is optional and is used to define the "account administrator" who will be granted the DV_ACCTMGR role at the end of the installation. If no account administrator account is specified at install time, the owner account specified will be granted both the DV_OWNER and DV_ACCTMGR roles.

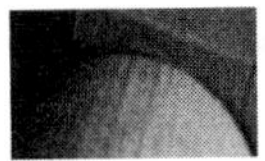

NOTE
For the examples used in this book, the DV_OWNER role was granted to an account named DBVOWNER that was created at install time, so you will see the use of this account for many of the DBV policy configuration examples. The account DBVACCTMGR was created at install time for the account administrator, so this account was granted the DV_ACCTMGR role and will be used for many of the database account management examples in this book.

Managing Oracle DBV Configuration

Configuring DBV policy can be accomplished either by using PL/SQL scripts that leverage the DVSYS.DBMS_MACADM PL/SQL package or by using the DVA web application. The DVSYS.DBMS_MACADM PL/SQL package can be used by any database account that is granted the DV_ADMIN or DV_OWNER role. Most of the DBV policy configuration examples used in this book use the DVSYS.DBMS_MACADM PL/SQL package and the DBVOWNER account that was created during installation.

DVA Web Application

The DVA web application is deployed into an existing Oracle Enterprise Manager Database Console (OEM dbconsole) Oracle Containers for J2EE (OC4J) installation for each database into which the DBV option is installed. You must start the OEM dbconsole software to access the DVA. Before starting the OEM dbconsole, make sure you have set the appropriate environment variables for the installation—for example **PATH**, **LD_LIBRARY_PATH**, **ORACLE_HOME**, and **ORACLE_SID** on UNIX systems—and type the following command:

```
[oracle@node1 ~]$ emctl status dbconsole
Oracle Enterprise Manager 11g Database Control Release 11.1.0.6.0
Copyright (c) 1996, 2007 Oracle Corporation.  All rights reserved.
https://node1.us.oracle.com:1158/em/console/aboutApplication
Oracle Enterprise Manager 11g is not running.
------------------------------------------------------------------
Logs are generated in directory /opt/oracle/db11/node1_aosdb/sysman/log
```

Once the OEM dbconsole is started, you can access the DVA at

https://host:port/dva

The host and port are output from the command **emctl status dbconsole**. As you can see in Figure 4-1, you can log into the DVA with the credentials of the DV_OWNER account—for example, DBVOWNER—and the database connection parameters specific to the environment. The database connection parameters can typically be found in the file $ORACLE_HOME/network/admin/tnsnames.ora for the database being used.

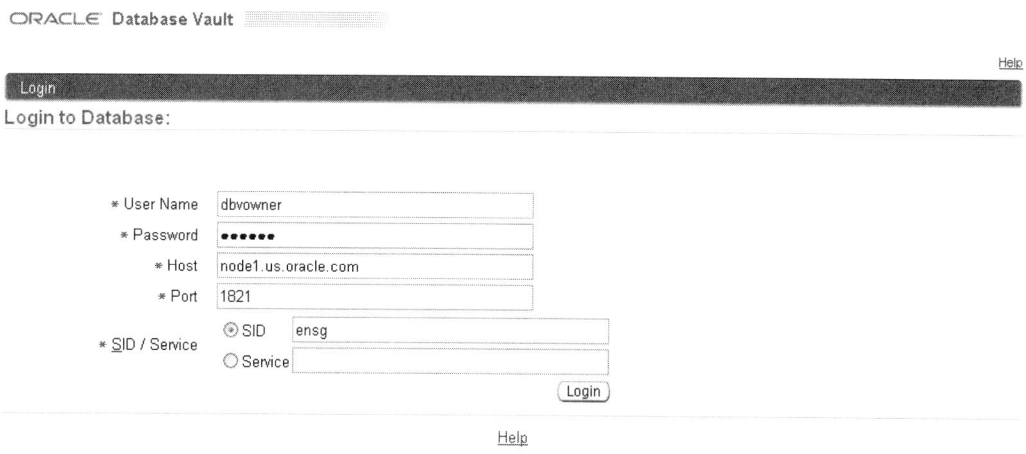

ORACLE Database Vault

Help

Login

Login to Database:

* User Name	dbvowner
* Password	••••••
* Host	node1.us.oracle.com
* Port	1821
* SID / Service	⦿ SID ensg ○ Service

Login

Help

FIGURE 4-1 *DBV administrator login page*

Once the login process is complete, the main menu page for the DVA is displayed. The Administration tab (Figure 4-2) provides navigation links to the pages that allow for the configuration of the core DBV components.

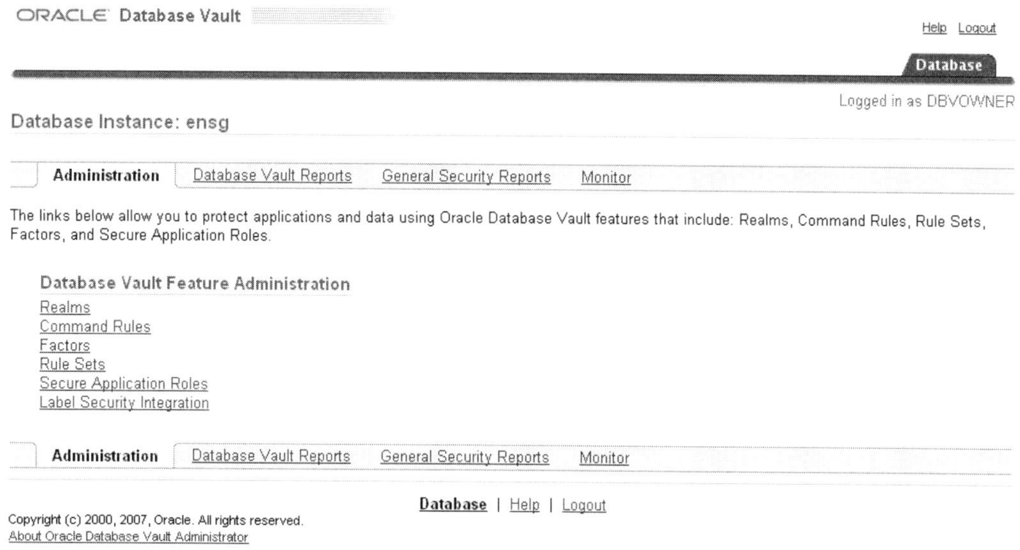

ORACLE Database Vault

Help Logout

Database

Logged in as DBVOWNER

Database Instance: ensg

Administration | Database Vault Reports | General Security Reports | Monitor

The links below allow you to protect applications and data using Oracle Database Vault features that include: Realms, Command Rules, Rule Sets, Factors, and Secure Application Roles.

Database Vault Feature Administration

Realms
Command Rules
Factors
Rule Sets
Secure Application Roles
Label Security Integration

Administration | Database Vault Reports | General Security Reports | Monitor

Database | Help | Logout

Copyright (c) 2000, 2007, Oracle. All rights reserved.
About Oracle Database Vault Administrator

FIGURE 4-2 *DBV Administrator tab*

Accounts that have been granted the DV_OWNER or DV_ADMIN role can make configuration modifications using these navigation links. The DVA uses the DBMS_MACADM PL/SQL package, under the covers, to change the configuration. The Administration tab allows the accounts with the DV_OWNER or DV_ADMIN role to change the configuration for the following DBV components:

- Realms
- Command rules
- Rule sets
- Factors
- Secure application roles
- Oracle Label Security (OLS) integration

Accounts that have been granted the DV_SECANALSYT role can view the DBV configuration of these components but cannot modify the configuration.

The three remaining tabs provide navigation links to the reporting and monitoring features provided by the DVA:

- **Database Vault Reports** These reports can be used to validate the DBV configuration and view the DBV audit trail for each of the core DBV components. The reports are intended to be used to verify the configuration of a DBV-enabled database and to provide a quick mechanism to display recent DBV policy violations.
- **General Security Reports** These reports describe core Oracle database security configurations—for example, in the area of privilege management. These reports are intended for use in compliance reporting and/or reporting against industry standard database hardening profiles.
- **Monitor** This allows the security administrator to monitor for security policy changes, security violations, and database structural changes that have occurred in a recent time frame. The monitor displays recent changes in DBV configuration, OLS configuration, database audit policy, database privilege management, database role management, and database account management with visual charts. You would expect no activity in these areas for a production system. If a change in any one of these configuration areas were to occur, the monitor provides a visual alert to this fact so that the change can be investigated in more detail with the other reports provided by DBV. This feature queries the Oracle RDBMS audit trail for many of the statistics presented and requires the database initialization parameter **AUDIT_TRAIL** to be set to **'DB'** or **'DB, EXTENDED'**.

DBV Administrator PL/SQL Package and Configuration Views

The DVSYS.DBMS_MACADM PL/SQL package allows you to script the DBV configuration for deployment in an automated way and to make changes in an ad hoc manner using a database client tool such SQL*Plus. DBV also includes a number of database views that are owned by the DVSYS account and can be used to query this configuration. Table 4-1 depicts the configuration procedures in the DBMS_MACADM package and associated configuration views organized by their intended configuration usage.

Configuration Usage	DBMS_MACADM Procedure(s)	DVSYS View(s)
Configuring DBV realm name, description, enabled status, and default auditing options	CREATE_REALM RENAME_REALM UPDATE_REALM UPDATE_REALM_AUTH DELETE_REALM DELETE_REALM_CASCADE	DBA_DV_REALM
Configuring DBV realm secured objects and roles	ADD_OBJECT_TO_REALM DELETE_OBJECT_FROM_REALM	DBA_DV_REALM_OBJECT
Configuring DBV realm authorization grantee and authorization rule set	ADD_AUTH_TO_REALM DELETE_AUTH_FROM_REALM	DBA_DV_REALM_AUTH
Configuring DBV command rule command, object owner, object name, rule set, and enabled status	CREATE_COMMAND_RULE UPDATE_COMMAND_RULE DELETE_COMMAND_RULE	DBA_DV_COMMAND_RULE
Configuring DBV rule names and logical expressions	CREATE_RULE RENAME_RULE UPDATE_RULE DELETE_RULE	DBA_DV_RULE
Configuring DBV rule set name, description, enabled status, evaluation option, audit options, failure processing options, and custom handler	CREATE_RULE_SET DELETE_RULE_SET RENAME_RULE_SET UPDATE_RULE_SET	DBA_DV_RULE_SET
Configuring the association of DBV rules to DBV rule sets	ADD_RULE_TO_RULE_SET DELETE_RULE_FROM_RULE_SET	DBA_DV_RULE_SET_RULE
Validating the logical expressions for DBV rules	SYNC_RULES	N/A
Configuring DBV factor types	CREATE_FACTOR_TYPE RENAME_FACTOR_TYPE UPDATE_FACTOR_TYPE DELETE_FACTOR_TYPE	DBA_DV_FACTOR_TYPE

TABLE 4-1 *Configuration Procedures in the DBMS_MACADM Package and Associated Configuration Views*

Configuration Usage	DBMS_MACADM Procedure(s)	DVSYS View(s)
Configuring DBV factor name, description, factor type, identification options, retrieval method, audit options, validation expression, assignment of DBV rule set, and failure options	CREATE_FACTOR RENAME_FACTOR UPDATE_FACTOR DELETE_FACTOR	DBA_DV_FACTOR
Configuring DBV identity value and trust level	CREATE_IDENTITY UPDATE_IDENTITY DELETE_IDENTITY CHANGE_IDENTITY_FACTOR CHANGE_IDENTITY_VALUE	DBA_DV_IDENTITY
Configuring DBV identity maps	CREATE_IDENTITY_MAP DELETE_IDENTITY_MAP ADD_FACTOR_LINK DELETE_FACTOR_LINK	DBA_DV_IDENTITY_MAP DBA_DV_FACTOR_LINK
Configuring DBV Secure Application Role name, enabling DBV Rule Set and enabled status	CREATE_ROLE RENAME_ROLE UPDATE_ROLE DELETE_ROLE	DBA_DV_ROLE
Configuring an OLS policy as integrated with DBV factors	CREATE_MAC_POLICY UPDATE_MAC_POLICY DELETE_MAC_POLICY_CASCADE	DBA_DV_MAC_POLICY
Configuring a DBV factor as linked to an OLS policy	ADD_POLICY_FACTOR DELETE_POLICY_FACTOR	DBA_DV_MAC_POLICY_FACTOR
Configuring the OLS label for a DBV identity	CREATE_POLICY_LABEL DELETE_POLICY_LABEL	DBA_DV_POLICY_LABEL

TABLE 4-1 *Configuration Procedures in the DBMS_MACADM Package and Associated Configuration Views* (continued)

Default Separation of Duty

Once DBV is installed, a number of differences in security policy exist between the database and a standard Oracle database. In the preceding section, we described the new roles that are created for managing the DBV configuration (DV_OWNER and, DV_ADMIN) and for managing database accounts (DV_ACCTMGR). The DBV installation creates a default security configuration for realms and command rules that is also based on separation of duty principles to provide the following responsibilities:

- Security administrator
- Database account administrator
- Operational database administrator

Security Administrator

DBV stores most configuration data for realms, command rules, rule sets, and factors in tables owned by an object owner account named DVSYS. Direct DML (**INSERT**, **UPDATE**, and **DELETE**) against these configuration tables can be done only by the DVSYS account or definer's rights PL/SQL code owned by the DVSYS account. The DVSYS.DBMS_MACADM package is the only means of updating these tables—even the DVA web application uses this package. The ability to execute this package is granted to the DV_ADMIN role (and indirectly to DV_OWNER role) so that when DBV is installed, the account granted the DV_OWNER role is your security administrator. The DBV installation creates a DBV realm called Database Vault (how thoughtful) to enforce the concept of a security administrator responsibility. This realm protects the following database objects:

- **Objects owned by the DVSYS object owner account** Includes the DBV configuration tables and the DBV audit trail, DVSYS.AUDIT_TRAIL$.
- **Objects owned by the DVF object owner account** DVF is an additional object owning account that stores DBV factor PL/SQL functions.
- **Objects owned by the LBACSYS object owner account** LBACSYS contains the OLS option's configuration tables and PL/SQL code.
- **The Oracle VPD administration package (DBMS_RLS)**
- **DBV roles DV_SECANALYST, DV_ADMIN, DV_OWNER, and DV_PUBLIC** DV_PUBLIC is granted privileges to execute utility packages that a database session may use to get DBV factor values or to set a DBV secure application role.
- **The OLS administration role LBAC_DBA**
- **The RDBMS audit trail table SYSTEM.AUD$**

As you can see, security-relevant configuration data for statement-level security (SLS) functionality, such as DBV, and row-level security (RLS) functionality, such as VPD and OLS, are protected by the installed realm. This realm not only protects the DBV audit trail, but it also protects the core RDBMS audit trail. The realm is "owned" by the DV_OWNER role, and only accounts with this role can manage the granting of the roles protected by this realm. This realm offers a secure mechanism to provide and delegate the security administrator responsibilities to other accounts. The installed DBV policy also includes a command rule for both the **GRANT** and **REVOKE** commands on the DBMS_RLS (VPD) administration package that limits these commands to accounts that have been granted the DV_OWNER role. The Database Vault realm and the two DBV command rules enforce the Security administrator concept as the one responsible the security-relevant configuration data and managing the provisioning of additional security administrators.

Database Account Administrator

The DBV installation creates a Database Vault Account Management realm to help enforce the concept of a database account administrator responsibility. This realm protects the DV_ACCTMGR role. This role is also the "owner" of the realm so that accounts with the DV_ACCTMGR role can also manage the delegation of this responsibility to other accounts. The account granted the DV_ACCTMGR role during the DBV installation is therefore the default database account administrator. The installed DBV policy includes a collection of command rules that restrict commands related to database account management and enforces the concept of a database account administrator. DBV command rules restrict the following commands to accounts that have been granted the DV_ACCTMGR role:

- **CREATE USER**
- **ALTER USER**
- **DROP USER**
- **CREATE PROFILE**
- **ALTER PROFILE**
- **DROP PROFILE**

The Database Vault Account Management realm and the six DBV command rules enforce the database account administrator concept as the one responsible for managing not only the initial provisioning of named user accounts to a database but also the locking and unlocking of object-owner accounts and shared accounts, as defined in Chapter 1. The DBV command rules for PROFILE database objects establish this role as the steward for all password policies for the database accounts they manage.

Operational Database Administrator

The database account administrator can perform the initial provisioning (establish or create) a database account, but the operational database administrator is responsible for granting the account the necessary system privileges such as CREATE SESSION, CREATE TABLE, CREATE PROCEDURE, or system ANY privileges, such as CREATE ANY TABLE or SELECT ANY TABLE, for the type of account being created. (See Chapter 1.) Control over the granting of these system privileges depends on the default Oracle Data Dictionary realm that is created during DBV installation. The "owner" of this realm is the only one allowed to grant these types system privileges.

After DBV installation, the SYS account is the only owner of this realm. The database account administrator should create a named user account and the security administrator should modify the DBV realm authorizations to make this named user account the owner of the Oracle Data Dictionary realm to create named accounts for each responsibility. We will present a working example of this type of setup in Chapter 6. The security design concept with this management aspect of system privileges is that one user can create accounts while another user is responsible for granting privileges to execute any commands not automatically available to the Oracle PUBLIC role.

The Oracle Data Dictionary realm protects several standard Oracle database roles, such as DBA and RESOURCE, so this realm owner is responsible for the provisioning and management of these roles as well. Several Oracle database system privileges are affected, including the following:

- BECOME USER
- CREATE ANY JOB
- CREATE EXTERNAL JOB
- DEQUEUE ANY QUEUE
- ENQUEUE ANY QUEUE
- EXECUTE ANY CLASS
- EXECUTE ANY PROGRAM
- MANAGE ANY QUEUE
- MANAGE SCHEDULER
- SELECT ANY TRANSACTION

PL/SQL execute privileges on the Log Miner packages and the UTL_FILE package also operate in a manner that could reduce the assurances offered by this separation of duty model. These system and execution privileges for these packages are revoked from the standard roles such as DBA, IMP_FULL_DATABASE, EXECUTE_CATALOG_ROLE, and SCHEDULER_ADMIN by the DBV installation. If your application requires privileges to create jobs, for example, a more secure design approach would grant the limited privilege CREATE JOB (versus CREATE ANY JOB) to each object owner account that has to create jobs. Operational DBAs should collaborate with application developers to avoid the use of these privileges whenever possible.

The operational DBA is not entirely focused on privilege management, however. The realm also protects the standard Enterprise Edition object owner accounts such as SYS, MDSYS (Spatial), CTXSYS (Text), and many more. The operational DBA is responsible for maintaining the objects and data in these accounts for such procedures as application deployment, patching, and upgrades. The design concept for the operational DBA extends into such areas as storage management (such as tablespaces) and backup/recovery management (such as archive log maintenance). DBV installs a command rule for the **ALTER SYSTEM** command that prevents an operational DBA from modifying security sensitive database initialization parameters, such as disabling the auditing of commands executed by the SYS account or enabling OS authentication, changing the database dump destinations. A complete list of security sensitive database initialization parameters that are protected follows:

- 07_DICTIONARY_ACCESSIBILITY
- _dynamic_rls_policies
- _system_trig_enabled
- audit_file_dest
- audit_sys_operations
- audit_syslog_level
- audit_trail
- background_core_dump
- background_dump_dest
- background_dump_dest
- control_files
- core_dump_dest
- core_dump_dest
- db_create_file_dest
- db_create_online_log_dest_1
- db_create_online_log_dest_2
- db_create_online_log_dest_3
- db_create_online_log_dest_4
- db_create_online_log_dest_5
- db_recovery_file_dest
- job_queue_processes
- max_dump_file_size
- optimizer_secure_view_merging
- os_roles
- plsql_debug
- recyclebin
- remote_os_roles
- shadow_core_dump
- sql92_security
- user_dump_dest
- user_dump_dest
- utl_file_dir

Another control that is installed by DBV is the restriction that a database superuser account cannot modify the DBV policy using the DBMS_MACADM PL/SQL package or even grant the account the roles DV_OWNER or DV_ADMIN to use this package.

```
system@aos>-- attempt to use the DBV administration package
system@aos>-- using SYSTEM, the default Oracle DBA
system@aos>-- to remove the DBV Realm for the database itself
system@aos>BEGIN
 dvsys.dbms_macadm.delete_realm_cascade('Oracle Data Dictionary');
END;
/
 dvsys.dbms_macadm.delete_realm_cascade('Oracle Data Dictionary');
       *
ERROR at line 2:
ORA-06550: line 2, column 8:
PLS-00904: insufficient privilege to access object DVSYS.DBMS_MACADM
ORA-06550: line 2, column 2:
PL/SQL: Statement ignored
system@aos>-- attempt to grant the DBV owner role to SYSTEM which
system@aos>-- would offer control over the DBV policy configuration
system@aos>GRANT dv_owner TO system;
GRANT dv_owner TO system
*
ERROR at line 1:
ORA-00604: error occurred at recursive SQL level 1
ORA-47401: Realm violation for grant role privilege on DV_OWNER.
ORA-06512: at "DVSYS.AUTHORIZE_EVENT", line 55
ORA-06512: at line 31
```

With this triad of database administrators (security, account, and DBA) and the separation of duty that is created with the DBV installation, an enterprise can immediately operate with checks and balances to help meet whatever compliance regulations are required.

Default Audit Policy

The Oracle DBV installation includes a comprehensive database audit policy designed to audit commands and activity related to DBV's DVSYS and DVF accounts and the OLS product account LBACSYS. This policy ensures that any changes (or attempts to change) to the configuration data for these two products is captured. Any subversive commands such as **NOAUDIT**, **REVOKE**, and **RENAME** against these object-owning accounts are also capture by this audit policy. The installation also includes a comprehensive audit policy for the database as a whole that audits the following categories of database activity:

- Session login and logoff
- Privilege management, such as **GRANT** and **REVOKE** commands
- Database Account Management, such as **CREATE**, **ALTER**, and **DROP USER** commands
- Audit Policy, such as **AUDIT** and **NOAUDIT** commands
- Structural Changes, such as tablespace management and object management with command syntax such as **CREATE *<object>***, **ALTER *<object>***, and **DROP *<object>***
- Use of privileged commands including
    - ADMINISTER DATABASE TRIGGER
    - ALTER SESSION
    - ALTER SYSTEM
    - BECOME USER
    - Flashback
    - FORCE ANY TRANSACTION
    - Restricted database sessions
    - Use of system *ANY privileges
    - Table truncation

This audit policy was developed from research conducted by leading government and commercial authorities on computer security that continuously publish up-to-date recommendations on this subject. The protection of the DBV and OLS configuration was then added to this policy to audit these security-relevant features by default.

Default Security-relevant DBV Factors

The DBV installation creates a number of DBV factors that an enterprise may find useful for developing custom DBV rule sets to control DBV command rules, DBV realm authorizations, and DBV secure application roles. The installed factors can be categorized as follows:

- Database and instance information
- Database client network protocol
- Database client language
- Enterprise user information
- Session authentication information

Summary: Database Vault Is Differentiating Security

In our efforts to create a richer summary section, we thought it would be good to place the summary in a discussion context. As with some security capabilities in the past, people will often believe that they have created a security approach that is equal to DBV but that is implemented through some other clever set of (database) technologies. Also similar to historical truth, they are misguided, and it's important to understand this so that you, too, don't try to build your own database vault. To some degree, this is a buy-versus-build discussion. In the next few paragraphs, we'll tell you why DBV is not only unique in what it does, but unique in how it does it. You cannot build an equivalent database vault—even if you could, the costs in doing so would far outweigh the costs of purchasing DBV from Oracle.

One of the early ideas for creating a DBV used triggers. DML triggers, and in particular DDL triggers, can be set to fire for a large number of commands. Conceptually, this is similar to the concept of command rules. The big difference, however, is that DBV is protected from nefarious or unwitting actions even by administrators. Triggers were not designed or intended to be used as security mechanisms. Changing trigger code, disabling a trigger, and dropping a trigger can be performed by any user with the ALTER ANY TRIGGER or ALTER ANY TABLE system privilege.

Although DBV "uses DBV to secure DBV," the security starts before you get to the database tables and PL/SQL code. The security starts in the database kernel, as the DBV exists as a code linked into the Oracle binaries. The importance of binary execution is that, unlike triggers that are implemented in PL/SQL, you are unlikely to see the source code or be able to modify it. The code that is linked into the Oracle binaries supports the numerous commands you will find in the "Oracle SQL Language Reference" and has undergone countless hours of regression testing with each database release. This gives you higher assurance that it has not been tampered with. As you saw when reviewing the installation of DBV, the core DBV controls are in a protected schema. Even SYS is unable to tamper with DBV.

The other differentiators for DBV come with its approach to implementation. The declarative framework is at its core. The invaluable security validation and verification capabilities are possible through the use of the framework. This has been an absolute necessity for getting the security implemented and approved for operational production systems in very secure environments.

Transparency has also enabled DBV to succeed. In Chapter 1, you learned about the importance of transparency, and DBV has enabled this by tapping into the DB kernel. The result is that you can almost always enable DBV for an application and get things working in a more secure manner than ever before. Simply add your objects of interest to a realm, add the right users as realm participants or realm administrators, and you are on the right track. This is simple to do and definitely increases your security with very little or no effort.

Perhaps the most impressive statement about DBV is that it addresses security by taking an innovative approach to governing who gets access to what, where, when, and how. Conditional security can be based on factors chained together in reusable rule sets and allows you to create a myriad of realistic and useful security controls. The factors are based on things you know or can validate. They allow you to ensure that security is happening the way it's supposed to be happening. The ability to use multiple factors significantly increases the security of your access decisions. The adaptive nature of the framework and the rules not only allow extensibility to your security, but they allow it to grow and shrink based on values that can be determined at runtime.

In the next two chapters, you will see several examples of how to apply DBV to applications. You'll not only see how to get it set up and working, but you'll learn how to blend design patterns. This will not only give you a jump start on using the technology, but it will also help you solidify DBV concepts and your understanding of when and how to use it.

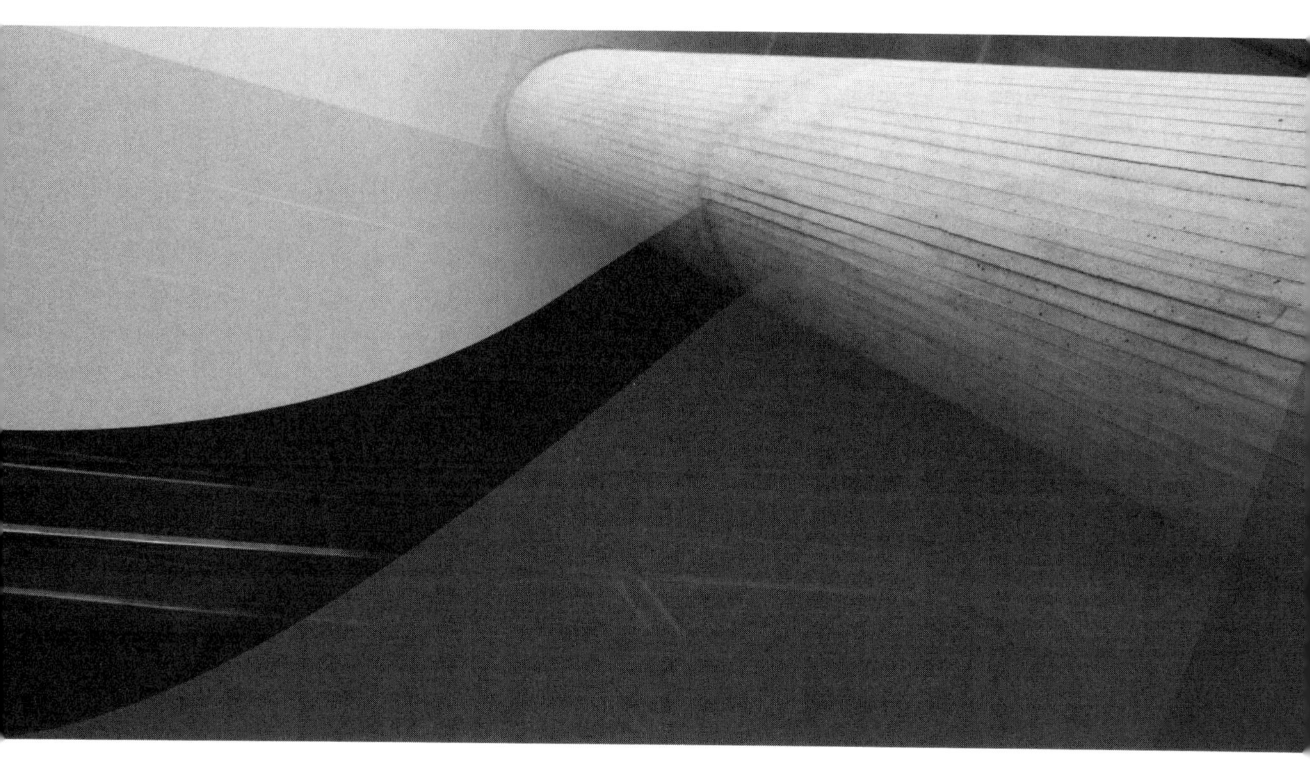

CHAPTER 5

Database Vault Fundamentals

This chapter presents a collection of examples that demonstrate the fundamentals behind how DBV components are configured using the DBMS_MACADM API. The examples are built around the Sales History (SH) object-owner account included with Oracle Database's sample schemas. These examples cover the following component configurations and demonstrate how these components' configurations impact sessions trying to access objects owned by the SH accounts:

- **Realms** Provide boundaries around the use of system ANY privileges that administrators typically have been granted. Realms examples demonstrate how you can meet your organization's compliance and consolidation requirements.
- **Command rules** Protect the use of more than 100 commands in the "Oracle SQL Reference Guide." Command rules allow you to implement security policies based on the business rules maintained by your organization.
- **Rule sets** Serve as the library rules for your security policy engine. We examine the impact of rule evaluation semantics, auditing and how custom event handler mechanisms can be enabled in response to DBV enforcement events.
- **Factors** Fundamental security policy attributes you define that form the building blocks for DBV rule expressions and result in a multifactored security policy. Example of factors linked into policies for Oracle Label Security (OLS) and Oracle Virtual Private Database (VPD) are also presented.
- **Secure application roles** Allow you to control the enablement of the more sensitive privilege sets using business or application rules defined by your organization.

Realms

A realm is a new security layer that provides containment and eliminates inadvertent access based on system ANY privileges. System ANY privileges are required for many application and administration scenarios. These privileges are heavily used in operating a database, but the privileges have no boundaries and therefore must be restricted. The security gap exists between the database objects controlled by object privileges and the system controlled by system ANY privileges. Realms were designed as a security mechanism that establishes boundaries around a set of objects that limit the use of system ANY privileges to authorized realm users or roles. Therefore, any attempt to access a realm protected object by an unauthorized user with system ANY privileges will be blocked and raise a realm violation. Access based on object-level privileges are not considered inadvertent and therefore are not enforced by the realm. Object-level privileges are explicit permissions on individual objects that can be verified through database dictionary views.

Realms are a simple and critical security measure that address many of the issues we face today regarding compliance and separation of duties for different job responsibilities. They also serve as an affective defensive measure for cyber security by limiting the extent to which system privileges can be exploited by an attacker. Therefore, realms not only provide another layer of security, but they add another level of defense. DBAs who are responsible for the health and well-being of production databases should consider the serious nature of realm violations, either legitimate or not. For example, an application needing additional accesses is legitimate and a malicious attempt to access data within the database is not.

In Chapter 4, we suggested that realms could be used to protect the security mechanisms that are protecting your application. We know many customers have leveraged the existing database security technologies and other database mechanisms, such as triggers, views, and PL/SQL, to implement application security within the database. Perhaps you have read David Knox's *Effective Oracle 10g Database Security by Design* that serves as one of the best foundations for implementing good security practices in an Oracle database. Security threats and challenges continue to surface every day and require that you update our security design and implementation on an ongoing basis. Therefore, simply maintaining an existing security approach can lure you into a false sense of security, which effectively decreases your security posture and increases your risk over time.

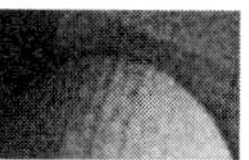

TIP
Realm access = DB ANY privilege + Realm authorization.

Applying realms to existing security approaches increases your security posture and reduces your risk if you perform these simple steps:

1. Protect the data tables by adding them to a realm.
2. Protect security relevant objects by adding them to a realm. This includes PL/SQL procedures for VPD, PL/SQL procedures that perform trusted transactions, and application database roles.

Also consider the intent of any realm violation you encounter. A realm violation will occur if

- A new login session is created or an existing one is highjacked;
- Key privileges are available or new privileges are gained;
- Attempted access of a realm-protected object is determined to be unauthorized.

Without DBV, the attempted access cannot be easily detected or blocked. Realms allow application access paths and profiles to be contained and controlled. It also allows for a system administrator or administrators to be better governed using both a context-based and a data content security model. Realms allow you to govern security by the data semantics themselves. Database administrators should consider the use of realms in production systems to update their database security to meet today's security challenges.

A good example of a need for security is personally identifiable information (PII). Within DBV realms, you can establish boundaries and controls over PII at a either the database schema level or an object level. Likewise, you can segment data as financials, personal health information, Sarbanes Oxley Act (SOX), and so forth across database schemas, so that your realm covers many objects over several database schemas.

With realms for consolidation of IT resources and data, you can meet security for compliance and insider threat concerns, along with data integration for consolidation objectives. Security should not be the primary excuse for not consolidating data into a fewer common databases. Consolidation will clearly add more value to the processing of data that is usually transacted and queried together. Consolidation will reduce operations and maintenance costs associated with multiple systems and offers these primary benefits:

- Increased data availability with a reduction in the labor, power, and storage requirements to increase this availability

- Enhanced and centralized enterprise security that accounts for regulatory compliance controls
- Universal access to data across the enterprise, without inefficient data movement
- Reduced inconsistencies due to fewer instances of data duplication

Simplification of the security management of your Oracle database and applications as centralized policies are not coded into each application. To demonstrate how we meet these objectives for consolidation, consider the sample schemas that are available with Oracle Database. The samples include the following schemas (a partial list):

- Human Resources (HR)
- Order Entry (OE)
- Sales History (SH)

In many enterprises, this type of data is kept in separate databases and on separate servers. This data as shown Figure 5-1.

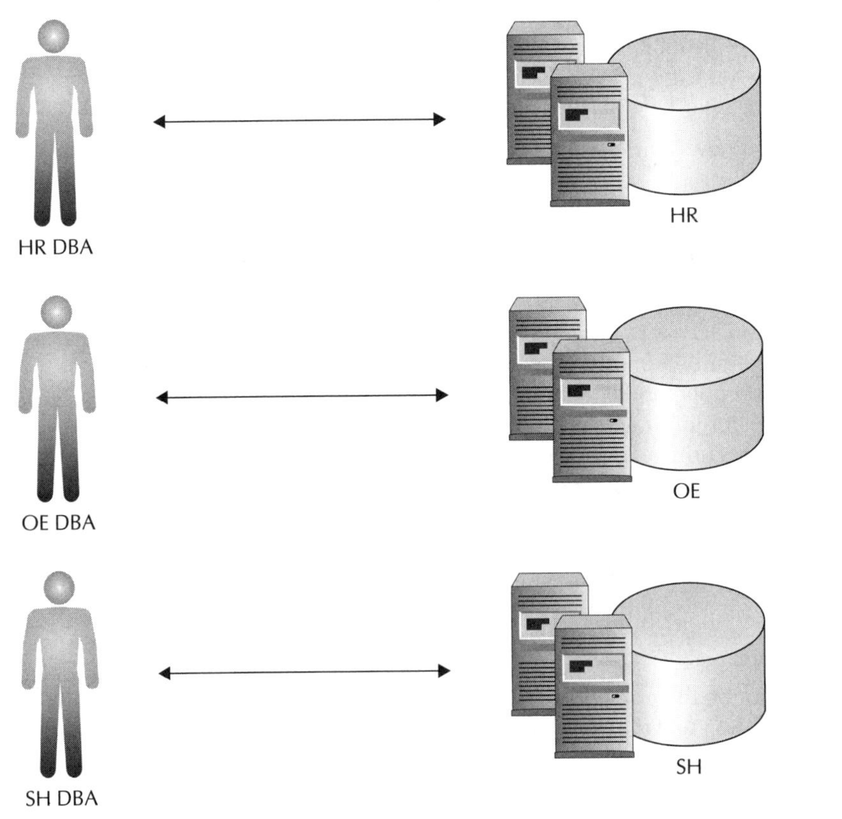

FIGURE 5-1 *Preconsolidation databases*

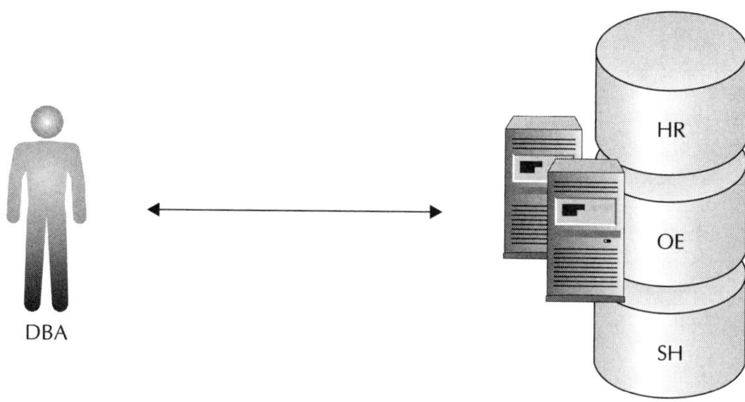

FIGURE 5-2 *Consolidated databases*

When viewed this way, it is easy to see the costs associated with maintaining these databases with respect to the power consumption, hardware costs, labor costs, software license costs, and recurring maintenance fees.

With consolidation efforts in an enterprise, you can reduce the costs by hosting the databases on a shared server platform with a smaller number of administrators, as shown in Figure 5-2.

The challenge in this consolidated database architecture then becomes how to keep database administrators of the Human Resources (HR) data from accessing or manipulating the Sales History (SH) data, or vice versa. To demonstrate, log into the database using the SYSTEM account, a well-known Oracle database account. The SYSTEM account has been granted the powerful DBA role and that role is granted many ANY privileges for TABLE objects:

```
system@aos>-- Display the system (ANY) privileges the account has
system@aos>select privilege name
from session_privs where privilege like '%TABLE%' or
privilege like '%GRANT%' order by 1;

NAME
----------------------------------------
ALTER ANY TABLE
ALTER TABLESPACE
BACKUP ANY TABLE
COMMENT ANY TABLE
CREATE ANY TABLE
CREATE TABLE
CREATE TABLESPACE
DELETE ANY TABLE
DROP ANY TABLE
DROP TABLESPACE
FLASHBACK ANY TABLE

GRANT ANY ROLE
GRANT ANY PRIVILEGE
```

```
GRANT ANY OBJECT PRIVILEGE
INSERT ANY TABLE
LOCK ANY TABLE
MANAGE TABLESPACE
SELECT ANY TABLE
UNDER ANY TABLE
UNLIMITED TABLESPACE
UPDATE ANY TABLE

18 rows selected.
system@aos>-- Attempt to query the sales data using
system@aos>-- the SELECT ANY TABLE privilege
system@aos>select cust_id, amount_sold from sh.sales;

  CUST_ID  AMOUNT_SOLD
---------- -----------
      1258       23.75
      1714       23.75
      1842       23.75
...
system@aos>-- Grant object privileges on the table
system@aos>-- to another account
system@aos>grant select on sh.sales to scott;

Grant succeeded.
system@aos>-- Attempt to query the sales data using direct object
system@aos>-- privileges granted to the account SCOTT
system@aos>connect scott
Enter password:
Connected.
scott@aos>select cust_id, amount_sold from sh.sales;

  CUST_ID  AMOUNT_SOLD
---------- -----------
      1258       23.75
      1714       23.75
      1842       23.75
...
```

As you can see, the SYSTEM account has privileges not only to read or write the Sales History data using privileges such as SELECT ANY TABLE and UPDATE ANY TABLE, but the account can modify the structures in which the data is stored using a privilege such as ALTER ANY TABLE. The same types of system ANY privileges are usually granted to named database administrator accounts, providing the same unbounded access to application data. We must introduce a DBV realm around the SH and HR schemas to enforce the separation of duty and mitigate compliance concerns over unprotected access to PII or the integrity of financial numbers used in an audit.

Realm Protection Patterns

A DBV realm can be defined as a boundary around all the objects in a database schema, a subset of objects in a database schema, or a collection of objects in multiple schemas. These example usages are shown in Figure 5-3.

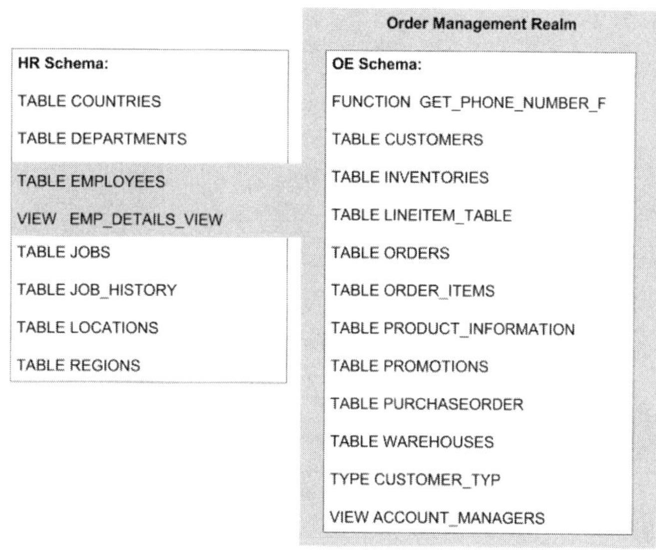

FIGURE 5-3 *Order Management realm (subset of object owner's objects)*

In Figure 5-3, a realm may be defined for objects in several schemas to support the concept of an order management application. The application may use a privileged account to access sensitive customer purchasing information and PII information for employees.

In Figure 5-4, you can see a realm was created for a subset of the HR schema, where tables such as EMPLOYEES and EMP_DETAILS_VIEW can contain PII information and tables such as JOBS and JOB_HISTORY can include personal information such as an employee's salary.

In Figure 5-5, an entire Sales History schema is protected and may contain sensitive information used for SOX compliance and auditing.

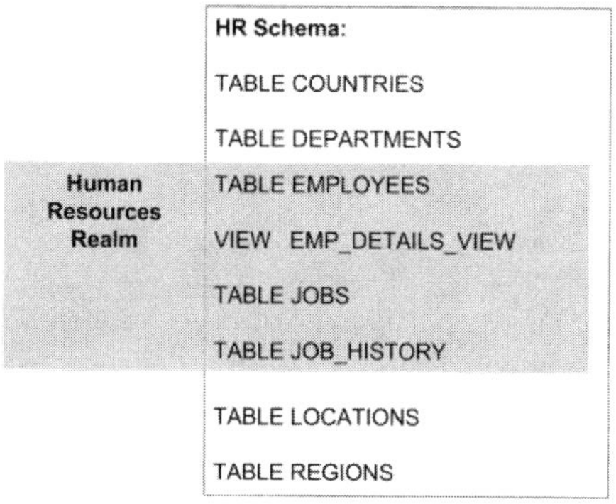

HR Schema:
TABLE COUNTRIES
TABLE DEPARTMENTS
Human Resources Realm
TABLE EMPLOYEES
VIEW EMP_DETAILS_VIEW
TABLE JOBS
TABLE JOB_HISTORY
TABLE LOCATIONS
TABLE REGIONS

FIGURE 5-4 *Human Resources realm (multiple objects, multiple object owners)*

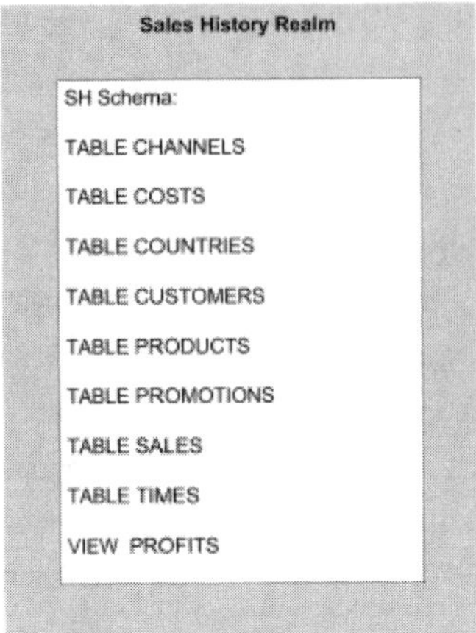

FIGURE 5-5 *Sales History realm (all of one object owner)*

Creating Your First Realm

You can protect and audit access to sensitive financial data in a configuration with a few steps. The protection offers compliance-focused safeguards against insider threats and elevates the integrity posture of the data to avoid accidental or malicious destruction of the data. An example shows how the protection is implemented by the security administrator and not the standard database administrator, demonstrating how DBV satisfies separation of duty requirements.

The first step in naming a realm allows you to identify data boundaries, irrespective of ownership or control, as in the case of the Order Management realm. Realms are also verifiable from audit and compliance perspectives, because you can define the DBV auditing behavior for any commands executed against objects protected by the realm when you define the realm. Realm auditing can be configured for the realm so that audit records are generated if a command is disallowed by the realm's controls (called a realm violation).

Let's look at a simple example creating a realm for the Sales History (SH) schema to remove access to the Sales History data from an account such as SYSTEM and roles such as DBA. First, we log into the database using the DBV owner account named DBVOWNER and create the realm:

```
dbvowner@aos> BEGIN
        dbms_macadm.create_realm(
           realm_name    => 'Sales History'
         , description   =>
'Annual, quarterly, monthly, and weekly sales figures by product'
         , enabled       =>  dbms_macutl.g_yes
         , audit_options =>  dbms_macutl.g_realm_audit_fail
        );
    END;
    /

PL/SQL procedure successfully completed.
```

The DBVOWNER account was specified as the DBV owner during DBV installation and is the initial account that can administer the DBV configuration. DBV realm configuration can be performed using the DVA web application or the DVSYS.DBMS_MACADM administration package discussed in Chapter 4. The PL/SQL package DVSYS.DBMS_MACUTL contains constants and utility functions that are used by DBV. The constants are beneficial when using the DVSYS.DBMS_MACADM package for administration because they avoid the need for you to remember character or numeric values for DBV component configuration procedures. In this example, we have simply created the realm and configured its default auditing behavior, which is to audit when a realm authorization fails. We have not identified the actual objects in the SH schema that will be protected by the realm, but this can be done with one command:

```
dbvowner@aos> BEGIN
     dbms_macadm.add_object_to_realm (
       realm_name    => 'Sales History'
      ,object_owner  => 'SH'
      ,object_name   => '%'
      ,object_type   => '%'
      );
  END;
  /
PL/SQL procedure successfully completed.
```

Accessing Realm-Protected Objects

Once a schema or set of objects is protected by a realm, only the object owning account can issue SELECT, Data Manipulation Language (DML), and EXECUTE statements on the objects. The object owning account is not, however, allowed to execute Data Definition Language (DDL) statements on the protected objects by default. Accounts and roles that have direct object privileges on a realm-protected object can also access the objects protected in a realm for which they have object privileges, shown in the **GRANT SELECT ON sh.sales TO scott** example.

For system ANY privilege usage, realms must have owners and participants established using a realm authorization. One of the most beneficial aspects of realms is that you get security enforcement immediately without needing to perform additional procedures. Another way to look at this is that realms ensure that the ANY privileges are immediately controlled. A realm immediately locks out users who were accessing the objects via the system ANY privileges—even sessions operating with the SYSDBA privilege can no longer access the objects protected in a realm. The DBV security administrator, such as DBVOWNER, must authorize an account or a role in a realm before the account or role can use system ANY privileges against the objects protected in a realm.

At this point, we have defined the logical realm, its auditing characteristics, and the objects that are to be protected in the SH object-owner account. We have not defined any explicit realm authorizations for the Sales History realm. What this means is that any database administrator will be prevented from accessing or manipulating objects in the realm. We can demonstrate this by attempting to read the SH.SALES table again with the SYSTEM account:

```
system@aos>  -- Attempt to query the sales data
system@aos>select cust_id, amount_sold from sh.sales;
select cust_id, amount_sold from sh.sales
                          *
ERROR at line 1:
ORA-01031: insufficient privileges
```

```
system@aos>  -- Attempt to drop the sales data table
system@aos>drop table sh.sales;
drop table sh.sales
*
ERROR at line 1:
ORA-00604: error occurred at recursive SQL level 1
ORA-47401: realm violation for drop table on SH.SALES
ORA-06512: at "DVSYS.AUTHORIZE_EVENT", line 55
ORA-06512: at line 31
system@aos>-- Attempt to grant object privileges on the table to
system@aos>-- another account, which will fail due to realm protections
system@aos>grant select on sh.sales to scott;
grant select on sh.sales to scott
                           *
ERROR at line 1:
ORA-00604: error occurred at recursive SQL level 1
ORA-47401: realm violation for grant object privilege on SH.SALES
ORA-06512: at "DVSYS.AUTHORIZE_EVENT", line 55
ORA-06512: at line 31
system@aos>-- Attempt to query the sales data using direct object
system@aos>-- privileges granted to the account SCOTT.
system@aos>-- This is authorized in the default behavior of a realm
system@aos>connect scott
Enter password:
Connected.
scott@aos>select cust_id, amount_sold from sh.sales;

   CUST_ID  AMOUNT_SOLD
---------- -----------
      1258       23.75
      1714       23.75
      1842       23.75
...
```

Realm Audit Reporting

The DBV owner account DBVOWNER can use the DBA web application to run audit reports on realm violations, as shown in Figure 5-6. The report demonstrates the failed attempts to query and even drop the objects protected in the Sales History realm by the SYSTEM user.

This realm example demonstrates how simple it is to protect sensitive financial data using just two configuration steps with the DBV administration capabilities. With respect to compliance regulations, such as SOX, or an insider threat, you can see how easily we've addressed access controls for privileged users to view financial data and audited attempts to access the data. Furthermore, we've enforced this using a security administrator account (DBVOWNER) versus a database administrator, satisfying our separation of duty requirements. Finally we've prevented a database administrator from accidentally or maliciously destroying this financial data using a privilege such as DROP ANY TABLE. This aspect of DBV protection avoids the need for additional documentation during a compliance audit to describe the catastrophic event and elevates the integrity posture of any system.

ORACLE Database Vault

Help Logout

Database

Database Instance: ensg >

Logged in as DBVOWNER

Report Results: Realm Audit

Page Refreshed Feb 23, 2009 11:42:07 AM

Return To Reports Menu

Violation Attempt	Timestamp	Return Code	Account	User Host	Instance Number	Realm Name	Rule Set	Command
Realm Violation Audit	23-FEB-09 11.33.08 AM	-47401	SYSTEM	NODE1.US.ORACLE.COM	1	Sales History		drop table sh.sales
Realm Violation Audit	23-FEB-09 11.32.59 AM	1031	SYSTEM	NODE1.US.ORACLE.COM	1	Sales History		

Return To Reports Menu

Database | Help | Logout

About Oracle Database Vault Administrator

FIGURE 5-6 *DBV realm violation report*

Realm Components

This is a good jumping off point to delve into the details of the components of a realm and some of the capabilities they provide. Earlier, we presented the creation of a logical realm name and its default auditing characteristics. We will call this the "realm header," and you should note that the APIs used to maintain the realm header can also control the ability to enable and disable the realm, which may be required in situations where database installation, upgrade, or maintenance activities are required.

TIP
Use the disable and enable feature of a realm during installation, upgrade, or maintenance activities.

Realm Objects

Realm configuration can be defined at the schema level, as demonstrated in the SH example, so that all objects, no matter what type they are, will be protected. However, it is also possible to configure the realm to protect specific objects by object type or by object name. Given our SH example, it would be possible to protect only the tables in the SH schema as follows:

```
dbvowner@aos> BEGIN
     dbms_macadm.add_object_to_realm (
       realm_name     => 'Sales History'
      ,object_owner  => 'SH'
      ,object_name   => '%'
      ,object_type   => 'TABLE'
      );
  END;
  /
PL/SQL procedure successfully completed.
```

It is also possible to configure the realm to protect only the SALES table in the SH schema, as follows:

```
dbvowner@aos> BEGIN
     dbms_macadm.add_object_to_realm (
       realm_name    => 'Sales History'
      ,object_owner  => 'SH'
      ,object_name   => 'SALES'
      ,object_type   => 'TABLE'
      );
END;
/
```

The effect of this realm protection is immediate after the configuration step has been executed, in the same way that revoking an object privilege takes effect immediately. Any schema or a specific schema object can belong to multiple realms, so the OE.CUSTOMERS tables could be protected by both the Order Management realm and the Sales History realm.

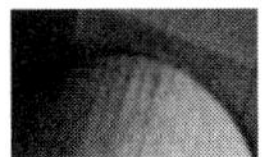

NOTE
An object can be protected by more than one realm to support multiple application scenarios.

The intent here is that an object such as OE.CUSTOMERS may be required for SELECT access by the database administrator of the Sales History realm, but we do not necessarily want to authorize this database administrator in the Order Management realm, which would provide the administrator access to more objects than requirements dictate.

Managing Role Provisioning with Database Vault Realms

In a special case, a database role is protected by a realm. To grant or revoke a role that is protected by a DBV realm, the session user must be authorized as the realm owner of the realm that is protecting the role. If you consider that a database administrator can grant or revoke any role in the database to any other user or role in the database, the need to incorporate protection of realms becomes clear.

Suppose the application developer had defined a database role named SALES_SELECT_ROLE with SELECT privileges on the SH.SALES table and used this role as the only means to authorize access to view this data. A database administrator account could circumvent the Sales History realm controls if he were aware of the role and its privileges:

```
system@aos> -- Display the object privileges defined for the role
system@aos>SELECT grantee, privilege
FROM dba_tab_privs
WHERE owner = 'SH' AND table_name = 'SALES';

GRANTEE                        PRIVILEGE
------------------------------ ----------------------------------------
BI                             SELECT
SALES_SELECT_ROLE              SELECT

system@aos> -- Display the system (ANY) privileges the account has
system@aos> SELECT *
FROM session_privs
WHERE privilege LIKE '%ROLE%'
```

```
ORDER BY 1;

PRIVILEGE
----------------------------------------
ALTER ANY ROLE
CREATE ROLE
DROP ANY ROLE
GRANT ANY ROLE

system@aos> -- Attempt to query sales data, the realm control prevents
system@aos>SELECT cust_id, amount_sold FROM sh.sales;
SELECT cust_id, amount_sold FROM sh.sales
                                    *
ERROR at line 1:
ORA-01031: insufficient privileges


system@aos> -- Grant the role to view the sales data since
system@aos> -- as SYSTEM has the system privilege GRANT ANY ROLE
system@aos> -- through the DBA role
system@aos>GRANT sales_select_role TO system;

Grant succeeded.

system@aos> -- Set the role that allows us to view the sales data
system@aos>SET ROLE SALES_SELECT_ROLE;
Role set.

system@aos>-- Attempt to query the sales data using the
system@aos>-- direct object privileges provided by the role
system@aos>SELECT cust_id, amount_sold FROM sh.sales;

  CUST_ID  AMOUNT_SOLD
---------- -----------
      1258       23.75
      1714       23.75
      1842       23.75
...
```

With DBV, the security administrator can simply add the role as a realm object in the Sales History realm as follows:

```
dbvowner@aos>BEGIN
    dbms_macadm.add_object_to_realm (
      realm_name    => 'Sales History'
     ,object_owner  => 'SH'
     ,object_name   => 'SALES_SELECT_ROLE'
     ,object_type   => 'ROLE'
     );
END;
/
PL/SQL procedure successfully completed.
```

The next time a database administrator, such as SYSTEM, attempts to grant the role to himself or revoke the role from a valid grantee, DBV will prevent the action and audit the event:

```
system@aos>-- Grant the role to view the sales data
system@aos>GRANT sales_select_role TO system;
system@aos>GRANT sales_select_role TO system
*
ERROR at line 1:
ORA-00604: error occurred at recursive SQL level 1
ORA-47401: realm violation for grant role privilege on SALES_SELECT_ROLE.
ORA-06512: at "DVSYS.AUTHORIZE_EVENT", line 55
ORA-06512: at line 31

system@aos> -- Attempt to revoke the role from an existing grantee
system@aos>REVOKE sales_select_role FROM sh;
REVOKE sales_select_role FROM sh *
ERROR at line 1:
ORA-00604: error occurred at recursive SQL level 1
ORA-47401: realm violation for revoke role privilege on SALES_SELECT_ROLE.
ORA-06512: at "DVSYS.AUTHORIZE_EVENT", line 55
ORA-06512: at line 31
```

Realm Authorizations

Realm authorizations define the accounts and roles that can use system ANY privileges on objects protected by a realm. Realm authorizations can be declared as either a realm participant or a realm owner. Both participants and owners can leverage system ANY privileges they have been granted on objects protected by the realm. The difference between a realm participant and a realm owner is that a realm owner can do the following but a participant cannot:

- Grant or revoke object privileges on objects protected by the realm
- Grant or revoke database roles that are protected in the realm

DBV realm authorizations can be configured by accounts with the DV_ADMIN or DV_OWNER roles, like our example DBVOWNER account. Note that realm authorizations do not grant system privileges or even object privileges when configured for a realm. Realm authorizations allow the use of system ANY privileges on objects that are protected by the realm. The underlying system ANY privileges still need to be granted to the account or role being authorized in the realm. In other words, a realm participant needs to be granted the SELECT ANY TABLE privilege explicitly to use a realm authorization, and a realm owner still needs to be granted the GRANT ANY OBJECT PRIVILEGE to use a realm authorization.

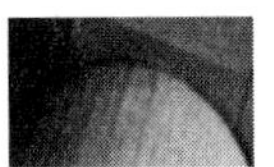

NOTE
Realm authorizations do not implicitly or explicitly grant privileges. They simply authorize the use of system ANY privileges.

The ability to grant system ANY privileges and system privileges is limited once DBV is installed, using an out-of-the box realm called the Oracle Data Dictionary. The default owner of this realm is the SYS account and is the only account capable of granting these privileges because DBV checks to see if the GRANT is performed by the owner of the Oracle Data Dictionary realm.

Realms and Direct Object Privileges

DBV will honor direct object privileges that are already granted (or are granted in the future) for any object protected by the realm. For example, since the account SCOTT had been granted the SELECT privilege on the SH.SALES table, the realm protections are not taken into consideration. The design intent with DBV in this regard was to honor existing application security models, where application developers had the foresight to grant specific object privileges as they were required using a least privilege design. Object-level privileges are verifiable through database dictionary views and extended through DBV privilege reports.

Realms and the DBV Administrators

For security reasons, the DBV roles DV_OWNER, DV_ADMIN, DV_SECANALYST, and DV_ACCTMGR cannot be authorized in customer-defined realms. If this were allowed, the DBV security administrator, such as our example DBVOWNER, would be able to authorize himself in the Sales History realm, grant himself any realm-protected roles, and gain access to the sensitive financial data. The following example helps illustrate this DBV control:

```
dbvowner@aos> -- DBV Security Administrator cannot authorize
dbvowner@aos> -- themselves in a realm
dbvowner@aos>BEGIN
  dbms_macadm.add_auth_to_realm (
      realm_name    =>'Sales History'
    , grantee       => 'DBVOWNER'
    , rule_set_name => NULL
    , auth_options  => dbms_macutl.g_realm_auth_owner );
END;
/
BEGIN
*
ERROR at line 1:
ORA-01031: insufficient privileges
ORA-06512: at "DVSYS.DBMS_MACUTL", line 10
ORA-06512: at "DVSYS.DBMS_MACUTL", line 367
ORA-06512: at "DVSYS.DBMS_MACADM", line 1728
ORA-06512: at line 2
```

Realm Authorizations and Object-owner Accounts

Object-owner accounts, such as SH, are not authorized in a realm by default when the objects they own are protected by a realm. The object-owner accounts do have implicit direct object privileges and DDL privileges for objects they own in the normal Oracle Database security model. The DBV engine provides an implicit realm authorization for SELECT, DML, and EXECUTE, based on the direct object privilege rule, to the object-owner account, but DDL (ALTER, GRANT, AUDIT, and so on) statements are not implicitly authorized. This design allows for existing application code to operate for most environments but maintains a security posture around the structural integrity of the account's objects. Object-owner accounts should have their passwords expired and locked by default. You want to maintain an audit attribution account model, using named administrators, as was discussed in Chapter 1. In this model, there is no expectation that the account would be used directly to manage the objects it owns. The following example shows this default behavior of application schemas being authorized for SELECT, but not being automatically authorized in the realm for DDL:

```
sh@aos>-- Attempt to query the sales data as the object-owner SH
sh@aos>SELECT cust_id, amount_sold FROM sh.sales;

   CUST_ID AMOUNT_SOLD
---------- -----------
      1258       23.75
      1714       23.75
      1842       23.75
...

sh@aos> -- Attempt to modify the SH.SALES table
sh@aos>ALTER TABLE sh.sales ADD extra_column VARCHAR2(100);
ALTER TABLE sh.sales ADD extra_column VARCHAR2 (100)
*
ERROR at line 1:
ORA-00604: error occurred at recursive SQL level 1
ORA-47401: realm violation for alter table on SH.SALES
ORA-06512: at "DVSYS.AUTHORIZE_EVENT", line 55
ORA-06512: at line 31

sh@aos> -- Attempt to grant the realm protected role
sh@aos>GRANT sales_select_role TO system;
GRANT sales_select_role TO system
*
ERROR at line 1:
ORA-00604: error occurred at recursive SQL level 1
ORA-47401: realm violation for grant role privilege on SALES_SELECT_ROLE.
ORA-06512: at "DVSYS.AUTHORIZE_EVENT", line 55
ORA-06512: at line 31
```

To authorize DDL commands for the object-owner account SH in the Sales History realm to perform DDL, the following realm authorization must be configured:

```
dbvowner@aos>BEGIN
  dbms_macadm.add_auth_to_realm (
      realm_name    =>'Sales History'
    , grantee       => 'SH'
    , rule_set_name => NULL
    , auth_options  => dbms_macutl.g_realm_auth_owner );
END;
/
PL/SQL procedure successfully completed.
```

Named Accounts as Application DBAs for Realm Authorizations

To manage the objects in an object-owner account such as SH, it is recommended that you use the application DBA pattern presented in Chapter 1. With this pattern, it would be more appropriate to create a named database account—such as a senior database administrator named MARY—to be the realm owner of the Sales History realm, and a realm participant—such as a junior database administrator named ANTHONY. This forces audit attribution to a named individual (in other words, a real person) for any commands that are executed on objects protected by the realm, regardless of the outcome of those commands.

The first step is to create the accounts. Recall from the DBV policy that is installed that the DBV Account Administrator, DBVACCTMGR, has been granted the only role, DV_ACCTMGR, authorized to use the CREATE USER privilege.

```
-- use the example DBV Account Administrator
-- to create the two new Application DBA accounts
dbvacctmgr@aos>CREATE USER mary IDENTIFIED BY <password>;
User created.
dbvacctmgr@aos>CREATE USER anthony IDENTIFIED BY <password>;
User created.
```

The SYS account is the only account authorized to manage system ANY privileges, such as CREATE ANY TABLE, as well as powerful roles such as DBA that are protected by the default DBV configuration. This SYS account is the realm owner of the Oracle Data Dictionary realm. The SYS account can be used to grant the named accounts, MARY and ANTHONY, the underlying system ANY privileges required to manage the objects protected by the Sales History realm. The DBA role has been granted a number of system ANY privileges that help to demonstrate this approach concisely.

```
dbvacctmgr@aos> -- grant these two new accounts the DBA role so they
dbvacctmgr@aos> -- have the underlying system ANY privileges that allow
dbvacctmgr@aos> -- them to manage objects protected in a realm
dbvacctmgr@aos> connect / as sysdba
Connected.
sys@aos>GRANT dba TO mary;
Grant succeeded.
sys@aos>GRANT dba TO anthony;
Grant succeeded.
```

Finally, we use the example DBV security administrator, DBVOWNER, to authorize the accounts in the Sales History DBV realm as required:

```
sys@aos>CONNECT dbvowner
Enter password:
Connected.
dbvowner@aos> -- configure MARY as the realm owner
dbvowner@aos>BEGIN
  dbms_macadm.add_auth_to_realm (
      realm_name    =>'Sales History'
    , grantee       => 'MARY'
    , rule_set_name => NULL
    , auth_options  => dbms_macutl.g_realm_auth_owner );
END;
/
PL/SQL procedure successfully completed.

dbvowner@aos> -- configure ANTHONY as the realm participant
dbvowner@aos>BEGIN
   dbms_macadm.add_auth_to_realm (
```

```
      realm_name    =>'Sales History'
    , grantee       => 'ANTHONY'
    , rule_set_name => NULL
    , auth_options  => dbms_macutl.g_realm_auth_participant );
END;
/
PL/SQL procedure successfully completed.
```

With the successful authorizations, you can see that MARY and ANTHONY can work in unison to administer the SH application schema, but within the control of their realm authorization:

```
mary@aos> -- Create a table for staging warehouse data
mary@aos>CREATE TABLE sh.sales_staging
    (
      prod_id       NUMBER        NOT NULL
     ,cust_id       NUMBER        NOT NULL
     ,time_id       DATE          NOT NULL
     ,channel_id    NUMBER        NOT NULL
     ,promo_id      NUMBER        NOT NULL
     ,quantity_sold NUMBER(10,2)  NOT NULL
    );

Table created.

mary@aos>   -- As the realm owner, grant access on the new table to OE
mary@aos>GRANT SELECT ON sh.sales_staging TO oe;

Grant succeeded.

mary@aos>  --  As the realm owner, grant a realm protected role
mary@aos>GRANT sales_select_role TO oe;

Grant succeeded.

anthony@aos> -- Anthony can administrator realm protected objects
anthony@aos>ALTER TABLE sh.sales_staging
ADD amount_sold  NUMBER(10,2)  NOT NULL;

Table altered.

anthony@aos>  -- Anthony cannot grant access to the new table
anthony@aos>  -- due to his realm participant status
anthony@aos>GRANT SELECT ON sh.sales_staging TO hr;

GRANT SELECT ON sh.sales_staging TO hr
                   *
ERROR at line 1:
ORA-00604: error occurred at recursive SQL level 1
ORA-47401: realm violation for grant object privilege on
SH.SALES_STAGING
ORA-06512: at "DVSYS.AUTHORIZE_EVENT", line 55
```

```
ORA-06512: at line 31

anthony@aos>  -- Anthony cannot grant access to realm roles
anthony@aos>  -- due to his realm participant status
anthony@aos>GRANT sales_select_role TO hr;

GRANT sales_select_role TO hr
*
ERROR at line 1:
ORA-00604: error occurred at recursive SQL level 1
ORA-47401: realm violation for grant role privilege on
SALES_SELECT_ROLE.
ORA-06512: at "DVSYS.AUTHORIZE_EVENT", line 55
ORA-06512: at line 31
```

Once MARY grants SELECT access on the new table to the OE account, this account can query the table, because realms honor direct object privilege usage:

```
oe@aos> SELECT cust_id, amount_sold, tax_amount FROM sh.sales_staging;

   CUST_ID AMOUNT_SOLD TAX_AMOUNT
---------- ----------- ----------
       987     1232.16      52.37
      1660      616.08      26.18
      1762      410.72      17.46
      1843      308.04      13.09
      1948      246.43      10.47
      2273      205.36       8.73
      2380      176.02       7.48
      2683      154.02       6.55
      2865      136.91       5.82

9 rows selected.
```

Realm Authorizations Controlled with DBV Rule Sets

Realm authorizations can be configured so that authorization is controlled using a DBV rule set that define the conditions (when, where, how) in which a session may leverage system ANY privileges on objects protected by the realm. This feature is extremely important if you want to provide a higher level of assurance that data is accessed or manipulated in the context of its intended usage. The concept of intended usage is crucial to your ability to ensure compliance regulations are met and insider threats are minimized.

We can demonstrate the impact of a DBV rule set on realm authorizations. MARY is the primary database administrator of the objects protected by the Sales History realm and ANTHONY is the alternate database administrator of these objects, possibly while MARY is on vacation or has called in sick. If MARY were out on vacation or were sick, we might expect the company's security system not to have a record of her "badging-in" for the day or the Human Resources system may have a record of her vacation dates. A DBV rule set named CheckPrimaryAdminStatus could be created that integrates into these types of systems to determine whether the primary application DBA MARY is working on a particular day. The rule set can dynamically query these systems to decide whether to "turn off" a realm authorization. This type of integration can be accomplished by updating the realm authorization previously defined for ANTHONY to use the new rule set:

```
dbvowner@aos> -- modify the realm authorization for ANTHONY
dbvowner@aos> -- to be based on the Disabled DBV Rule Set
dbvowner@aos>BEGIN
  dbms_macadm.update_realm_auth (
      realm_name    =>'Sales History'
    , grantee       => 'ANTHONY'
    , rule_set_name => 'CheckPrimaryAdminStatus'
    , auth_options  => dbms_macutl.g_realm_auth_participant );
END;
/
PL/SQL procedure successfully completed.
```

If ANTHONY attempts to leverage his realm authorization after this modification and MARY is at work, the previously successful DDL commands he could issue would be denied.

```
anthony@aos> -- Attempt an ALTER TABLE command that was previously allowed
anthony@aos> ALTER TABLE sh.sales_staging
ADD unit_of_measure  VARCHAR2(10);
ALTER TABLE sh.sales_staging ADD unit_of_measure VARCHAR2(10)
*
ERROR at line 1:
ORA-00604: error occurred at recursive SQL level 1
ORA-47401: realm violation for alter table on SH.SALES_STAGING
ORA-06512: at "DVSYS.AUTHORIZE_EVENT", line 55
ORA-06512: at line 31
```

DBV rule sets powerfully impact realm authorizations in contributing the conditional (when, where, how) aspect of a sound security policies. DBV rule sets also provide critical auditing and error-handling capabilities that we will explore a bit later in the chapter.

Command Rules

In the preceding section, we discussed how DBV realms protect an application schema's objects and database roles from the use of the powerful system ANY privileges that database administrators are typically granted. The DBV product will intercept database commands as they are submitted to the database kernel's SQL engine. Once the command is intercepted, the DBV kernel-resident code will examine the realm protection configuration to determine whether or not to allow the command.

Command rules are a second type of DBV protection and are part of the same enforcement process flow that provides a layer of security within DBV. Statement-level controls are examined and enforced immediately after the realm protections are evaluated. Command rules do not consider whether system ANY privileges or even direct object privileges are used, but focus on the command being used and the object being affected. Command rules are like database triggers, but they were designed as a separate DBV security mechanism in which declarative rules can be applied to the execution of SQL statements and PL/SQL packages, provided a user had some permission to execute the statement. This means a user must have some level of database permission to execute a statement before command rule can be enforced.

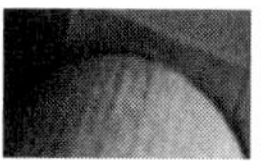

TIP
Statement execution = DB privilege + DBV command rule.

This implies that a realm authorization that would allow for a command to be executed can be overruled by a command rule. Further, an object does not need to be protected by a realm for a command rule to be evaluated. A fundamental difference in the behavior of command rules and realms is that command rules apply both to the use of system ANY privileges and direct object privileges. The following table compares the differences between these two controls:

DBV Control	Direct Object Privileges	System ANY Privileges
DBV realm	Implicitly allowed	Requires that realm authorization and realm authorization rule are set to TRUE (if defined)
DBV command rule	Rule set must be TRUE	Rule set must be TRUE

Let's look at an example to demonstrate the relationship of DBV realms and command rules. An organization's IT policy should have controls on the types of database administration that can occur when critical systems are being used by the general user population. An organization's IT department will typically create system maintenance windows to make system changes in addition to configuration management procedures for validating these changes before they are deployed. Building on the realm examples, we can use DBV command rules to establish controls based on a business rule such as a system maintenance window for the activities of the database administrators who manage the objects protected by the Sales History realm. We first need to identify the rules are a system maintenance window using a DBV rule set:

```
dbvowner@aos>-- First, define the "system maintenance window" rule.
dbvowner@aos>-- The IT department's policy allows for system
dbvowner@aos>-- maintenance on Fridays from 5 p.m. to 11 p.m.
dbvowner@aos>  BEGIN
 dbms_macadm.create_rule(
   rule_name => 'Is Maintenance Timeframe'
 , rule_expr => 'TRIM(TO_CHAR(SYSDATE,''DAY'')) = ''FRIDAY'' AND
TO_CHAR(SYSDATE,''HH24'') BETWEEN 17 AND 23'
 );
 END;
/
PL/SQL procedure successfully completed.
dbvowner@aos>-- We need to define a DBV Rule Set as a container
dbvowner@aos>-- for the 'Is Maintenance Timeframe' rule.
dbvowner@aos>-- This rule set defines the auditing and error handling
dbvowner@aos>-- for any DBV control that uses the Rule Set
dbvowner@aos>BEGIN
    dbms_macadm.create_rule_set(
        rule_set_name => 'Is System Maintenance Allowed',
        description =>
'Checks to determine if the system maintenance is allowed',
        enabled =>dbms_macutl.g_yes,
        eval_options =>dbms_macutl.g_ruleset_eval_all,
        audit_options =>dbms_macutl.g_ruleset_audit_fail,
```

```
        fail_options =>dbms_macutl.g_ruleset_fail_show,
        fail_message =>NULL,
        fail_code =>NULL,
        handler_options =>dbms_macutl.g_ruleset_handler_off,
        handler =>NULL);
END;
/
PL/SQL procedure successfully completed.
dbvowner@aos>-- We can now associate the DBV Rules we want to be true
dbvowner@aos>-- for the DBV Rule Set to evaluate to true
dbvowner@aos>BEGIN
   dbms_macadm.add_rule_to_rule_set (
     rule_set_name => 'Is System Maintenance Allowed'
   , rule_name     => 'Is Maintenance Timeframe'
   );
END;
/
PL/SQL procedure successfully completed.
```

A DBV rule set controls the auditing and error-handling aspects for any DBV component with which it is used. This means that auditing on failure for a DBV rule set will audit when the rule set is used with a DBV command rule or DBV realm authorization. The DBV rule set contains just one DBV rule, 'Is Maintenance Timeframe', but an organization could define additional rules that might be required to match the business rules for system maintenance. Once the DBV rule set is defined, a DBV command rule for a potentially dangerous database command such as **DROP TABLE** can be defined to use this DBV rule set to protect any of the tables in the SH object owner account:

```
dbvowner@aos> BEGIN
  dbms_macadm.create_command_rule (
    command       =>  'DROP TABLE'
    ,rule_set_name => 'Is System Maintenance Allowed'
    ,object_owner  => 'SH'
    ,object_name   => '%'
    ,enabled       => 'Y'
);
END;
/
PL/SQL procedure successfully completed.
```

If the junior database administrator ANTHONY attempts to issue the **DROP TABLE** command outside of this maintenance window time frame on one of the objects protected by the Sales History realm, the command will fail our DBV command rule:

```
anthony@aos>SELECT TO_CHAR(SYSDATE,'DAY') "DAY_OF_WEEK",
        TO_CHAR(SYSDATE,'HH24') "HOUR_OF_DAY"
FROM DUAL;

DAY_OF_WEEK                          HO
------------------------------------ --
MONDAY                               10
```

```
1 row selected.

anthony@aos>DROP TABLE SH.SALES;
DROP TABLE SH.SALES
*
ERROR at line 1:
ORA-00604: error occurred at recursive SQL level 1
ORA-47401: realm violation for drop table on SH.SALES
ORA-06512: at "DVSYS.AUTHORIZE_EVENT", line 55
ORA-06512: at line 31
```

This example shows that DBV realms allow you to meet compliance regulations for separation of duty, and DBV command rules allow you to lay your organization's business rules on top of these compliance regulations.

Command Rule Components

A DBV command rule is configured for a specific database command being controlled by a DBV rule set. The DBV security administrator will define the policy to state the following:

> When this command is attempted, evaluate this rule set to determine whether or not to allow the command.

You cannot define a DBV command rule for a group of database commands. For example, you cannot create a single DBV command rule for a group of DDL commands such as **CREATE TABLE**, **ALTER TABLE**, and **DROP TABLE**. Each individual database command must have a DBV command rule configured as we did for the **DROP TABLE** example earlier. Command rules can be enabled and disabled by the security administrator in the same way realms are enabled and disabled. Command rules can be further qualified by configuring an object owner and/or an object name according to the following options:

1. If the object owner and object name is not specified, the command rule applies to all object owners and object names when the command is issued. An alternative form of the **DROP TABLE** example could have specified the **object_owner** parameter as **'%'**.
2. If a command rule is configured with a specific object owner only and any object name (**'%'**), as demonstrated in the **DROP TABLE** example, if the result set evaluates to TRUE, the command is allowed if the command applies to any object the object owner specified.
3. If a command rule is configured with both an object owner and object name, the command rule evaluation applies to a single object.

It is possible to define multiple command rules for the same database command, such as **DROP TABLE**, where one or more command rules are defined for specific object owners and one command rule is defined for all object owners. For example, the security administrator can define multiple command rules for the **DROP TABLE** database command as follows:

```
dbvowner@aos> -- DROP TABLE for objects owned by SH
  dbms_macadm.create_command_rule (
    command        =>  'DROP TABLE'
    ,rule_set_name => 'Is System Maintenance Allowed'
    ,object_owner  => 'SH'
```

```
    ,object_name    => '%'
    ,enabled        => 'Y'
);
dbvowner@aos> -- DROP TABLE for objects owned by any account
dbvowner@aos> BEGIN
  dbms_macadm.create_command_rule (
    command        =>  'DROP TABLE'
    ,rule_set_name => 'Is System Backup Completed'
    ,object_owner  => '%'
    ,object_name   => '%'
    ,enabled       => 'Y'
);
 PL/SQL procedure successfully completed.
```

In this example, the security administrator has defined the first **DROP TABLE** command rule to check the system maintenance timeframe when the objects are owned by the account SH. The second **DROP TABLE** command rule checks to see if the system backup has completed when the objects are owned by any account. When multiple DBV command rules apply to a database command that is attempted, all the DBV command rules must be authorized for the command to be allowed. With this example, if ANTHONY were to attempt to issue the command **DROP TABLE SH.SALES**, the rule sets Is System Maintenance Allowed and Is System Backup Completed would have to evaluate to TRUE for the command to be allowed.

Certain commands, such as **CREATE TABLESPACE** or **ALTER SYSTEM**, can only be defined with option one because objects such as tablespaces are not defined within an object owner and the concept of an owner does not apply in the Oracle database. In these cases, simply use the percent (**'%'**) parameter for the *object_owner* and *object_name* parameters.

The ability to specify more than one command rule for any given object is an important point, because it allows the security administrator to define specific general access control policies. Many packaged applications for accounting and financials use complex database logic to ensure the integrity of the information that is managed by the application. If database administrators can make direct updates to the tables on which these applications rely, outside of the packaged application code, the guarantee that the compliance regulations are met or insider threats are mitigated is questionable. These packaged applications often perform monthly, quarterly, and yearly closing processes in which summary statistics and financial statements are generated. Once a close process starts, controls should be in place to ensure that data that feeds into these summary statistics and financial statements are not modified during the process.

With DBV command rules, we can enforce the two types of controls. For example, if we consider the Sales History schema, we specify the specific to general policy around the SH.SALES table as follows (and shown in Figure 5-7):

1. **UPDATE** commands are allowed only on the table SH.SALES when executed from the SH.SALES_TRANSACTION package.
2. **UPDATE** commands are not allowed on any table in the SH application schema during the monthly accounting close process.

Let's look at an example of the command rule configuration for part of this example. First we must define the rules and rule set that will establish the conditions in which the command can be executed. The DBV rule will leverage an Oracle PL/SQL package named DBMS_UTILITY that comes with Oracle Database to determine whether we are using the SALES_TRANSACTION package for the SQL UPDATE. The DBMS_UTILITY package has a function named **FORMAT_**

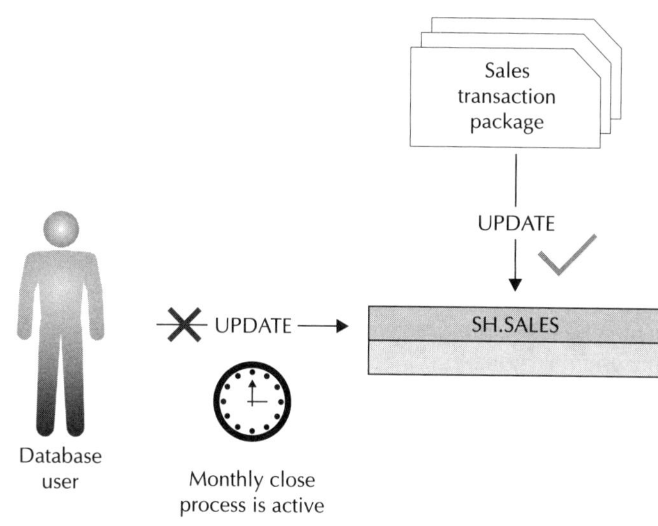

FIGURE 5-7 *DBV command rules support business rules*

CALL_STACK that returns the read-only PL/SQL call stack message that is maintained by (and secured in) the database kernel code. If we embed the DBMS_UTILITY call within our SALES_TRANSACTION procedure, we can see the information the **FORMAT_CALL_STACK** function provides:

```
sh@aos>CREATE OR REPLACE PACKAGE BODY sh.sales_transaction AS
    PROCEDURE update_sales(customer in NUMBER, amount in NUMBER) IS
    BEGIN
        -- show the output of the DBMS_UTILITY function
        DBMS_OUTPUT.PUT_LINE ( DBMS_UTILITY.FORMAT_CALL_STACK  );
        -- perform the SQL UPDATE
        UPDATE sh.sales SET amount_sold = amount
            WHERE cust_id = customer;
    END;
END;
/
Package body created.

sh@aos>-- enable DBMS_OUTPUT tracing
sh@aos>-- SET SERVEROUT ON SIZE 10000
sh@aos>-- execute the procedure to
sh@aos>-- show the DBMS_UTILITY capability
sh@aos>BEGIN
     sh.sales_transaction.update_sales(
          customer => 305
        , amount => 200
     );
END;
/
```

```
----- PL/SQL Call Stack -----
  object      line  object
  handle    number
name
0xa11a3ee0         5  package body SH.SALES_TRANSACTION
0xa1e66428         2
anonymous block

PL/SQL procedure successfully completed.
```

Note that embedding the DBMS_UTILITY call into your own code is not required to enable DBV command rule controls. This was simply added to the trusted package to demonstrate the information maintained by the DBMS_UTILITY package while the trusted package is executing. Armed with this useful information, we can add logic to our DBV rule set to search the read-only call stack information provided by the database kernel for the name of the procedure we trust for SQL UPDATE:

```
dbvowner@aos> -- first lets create the conditional rule that
dbvowner@aos> -- we are using the trusted sales transaction code
dbvowner@aos>BEGIN
         dbms_macadm.create_rule(
         rule_name => 'Called From Sales Transaction Package'
         , rule_expr => 'INSTR(UPPER(DBMS_UTILITY.FORMAT_CALL_STACK),
''PACKAGE BODY SH.SALES_TRANSACTION'') > 0'
    );
    END;
    /

PL/SQL procedure successfully completed.

dbvowner@aos> -- next create a rule set that will group our rules
dbvowner@aos>BEGIN
        dbms_macadm.create_rule_set(
            rule_set_name =>'Using Financials Application',
            description =>'Checks to verify commands
are executed from trusted financials packages',
            enabled =>dbms_macutl.g_yes,
            eval_options =>dbms_macutl.g_ruleset_eval_all,
            audit_options =>dbms_macutl.g_ruleset_audit_fail,
            fail_options =>dbms_macutl.g_ruleset_fail_show,
            fail_message =>NULL,
           fail_code =>NULL,
           handler_options =>dbms_macutl.g_ruleset_handler_off,
           handler =>NULL);
   END;
   /
PL/SQL procedure successfully completed.

dbvowner@aos> -- associate the rule name to the rule set name
dbvowner@aos>BEGIN
   dbms_macadm.add_rule_to_rule_set (
     rule_set_name => 'Using Financials Application'
```

```
    , rule_name      => 'Called From Sales Transaction Package'
    );
END;
/
PL/SQL procedure successfully completed.

dbvowner@aos> -- finally create our Command Rule for UPDATE on SH.SALES
dbvowner@aos>BEGIN
      dbms_macadm.create_command_rule (
        command        =>  'UPDATE'
        ,rule_set_name => 'Using Financials Application'
        ,object_owner  => 'SH'
        ,object_name   => 'SALES'
        ,enabled       => 'Y'
    );
    END;
/
PL/SQL procedure successfully completed.
```

If we test the **UPDATE** command as our Sales History realm owner, MARY, the command will fail unless she is using our trusted sales transaction package:

```
mary@aos> -- attempt the direct table update
mary@aos> UPDATE sh.sales
SET amount_sold = 200
WHERE cust_id = 305;
UPDATE sh.sales
          *
ERROR at line 1:
ORA-01031: insufficient privileges

mary@aos> -- attempt to use the trusted package
mary@aos>BEGIN
     sh.sales_transaction.update_sales(
          customer => 305
        , amount => 200
     );
END;
/
PL/SQL procedure successfully completed.
```

The trusted PL/SQL package code issues the same type of SQL UPDATE statement MARY attempted from the SQL*Plus, but our DBV command rule is designed to allow only the SQL UPDATE statement when it comes from PL/SQL package code. Our example leverages DBV rule sets to provide auditing and error-handling capabilities that we will explore in the next section.

Commands Supported in Command Rules

Database commands within the Oracle database can be categorized as follows:

- **SELECT** A read-only query against a table or view, for example.
- **Data Manipulation Language** Write actions such as **INSERT**, **UPDATE**, or **DELETE** against a table or view, for example, or **EXECUTE** actions on PL/SQL code.

- **Data Definition Language** Database structure related commands that typically have the form **CREATE** *<object type>*, **ALTER** *<object type>*, and **DROP** *<object type>*, such as **CREATE TABLE**, **ALTER TABLE**, and **DROP TABLE**. This category also includes privilege-related commands such as **GRANT** and **REVOKE**, auditing commands such as **AUDIT** and **NOAUDIT**, and data table administration commands such as **ANALYZE**, **COMMENT**, **FLASHBACK**, **PURGE**, **RENAME**, and **TRUNCATE**.
- **System control** Commands such as **ALTER SYSTEM** and **ALTER DATABASE**.
- **Session control** Commands such as **ALTER SESSION** and **SET ROLE**.
- **Transaction control** Commands such as **COMMIT** and **ROLLBACK**.

SELECT and DML commands cannot use **'%'** for both the object owner and object name, and command rules for these commands cannot be applied for the SYS or DVSYS account. DBV does not offer command rules for transaction control commands, as these commands are not security relevant nor do they operate on database objects. By security relevant, we mean the commands do not change session user, change the current user, or give the session user any additional system or object privileges for the session. Command rules cannot be defined on the **ALTER DATABASE** or **ALTER SESSION** commands. The **SET ROLE** command is not directly supported, but the DBV Secure Application Role feature offers a mechanism to control the activation of a database role with a DBV rule set providing the decision point. With the remaining command categories, more than 100 distinct commands can be controlled by the security administrator with DBV command rules.

DBV CONNECT Command Rule

One of the most powerful command rules available controls when accounts that have been granted specific roles can establish connections to the database. This command rule uses a special DBV database operation named **CONNECT** that simply implies a command rule that authorizes a database connection once the standard authentication processing within Oracle has completed. Using this command rule, we can offer higher levels of assurance around when and how (conditions) an account is able to connect to the database.

Let's consider MARY, our senior DBA for Sales History data, in an example. Suppose the IT department wants to tighten the controls around database administrators connecting to the database. The data and applications with which they are working are very sensitive. The first step is to decide under what conditions MARY and other database administrators are allowed to perform administration tasks.

If the IT departments allow MARY VPN access to the corporate network, doesn't that mean she can be sitting in a coffee shop with a laptop viewing sensitive financial data? VPN access is typically much less secure than access at the company's office building because the networks are more open to snooping and the environment is less secure from a physical perspective. Who else has access to her laptop if she walks away from her computer to take a break? Would the customers in the stored in the CUSTOMERS table approve of this access?

With DBV command rules, we can simply define a rule set that resolves whether the database session is being established from a machine that is physically located within the company's building(s). The IT department could establish a policy that mandates the use of a secure authentication method to all sensitive databases. The Oracle Advanced Security option provides authentication methods based on Public Key Infrastructure (PKI)/Secure Sockets Layer (SSL) or Kerberos that could be leveraged. The policy could also dictate that the credential stores used for this authentication could be limited (in deployment) to machines that are located in the company offices. Once the policy is established, a level of trust can be established for all connections to the database. The rule used in the DBV rule set would leverage the Oracle built-in, read-only application context USERENV that stores security-related attributes about the database session. The rule can read the application context values using the PL/SQL function **SYS_CONTEXT** as follows:

```
dbvowner@aos> BEGIN
      dbms_macadm.create_rule(
          rule_name => 'Is Secure Authentication Method'
        , rule_expr => 'SYS_CONTEXT(''USERENV'',
            ''AUTHENTICATION_METHOD'') IN (''SSL'', ''KERBEROS'')'
      );
END;
/
PL/SQL procedure successfully completed.
```

Requiring PKI/SSL or Kerberos is a well-founded requirement because it establishes something a client might have, such as a certificate, and reduces password-based hacking. This increases the assurance that the database access is from a machine physically located at the company. The IT department will also need to account for database administrators working on the console of a database server by inspecting the client IP address of the session. Console-based access to the database implies that the database session was not established through the Oracle database listener that enables remote connectivity to an Oracle database. With remote database clients, the USERENV application context maintains the IP address of the client. The second rule for the DBV rule set is then as follows:

```
dbvowner@aos> BEGIN
      dbms_macadm.create_rule(
          rule_name => 'Is Console Client'
        , rule_expr =>
'SYS_CONTEXT(''USERENV'', ''IP_ADDRESS'') IS NULL'
      );
END;
/
PL/SQL procedure successfully completed.
```

With the rules defined for both remote database clients and console clients, we can configure the DBV rule set required for the DBV CONNECT command rule. DBV includes a predefined DBV rule set named Allow Sessions that is intended for this usage. For this example, we need to reconfigure the **eval_options** parameter of this DBV rule set to return TRUE if either rule is valid (a secure authentication method or a console-based client), and then associate the DBV rules to the DBV rule set. The default configuration of the Allows Sessions DBV rule set is TRUE if all associated rules are valid.

```
dbvowner@aos> -- Reconfigure the "eval_options" parameter to use
dbvowner@aos> -- the "any rule true" algorithm
dbvowner@aos> BEGIN
    dbms_macadm.update_rule_set(
        rule_set_name =>'Allow Sessions',
        description =>'Rule set that controls the ability to create a
session in the database.',
```

```
        enabled =>dbms_macutl.g_yes,
        eval_options =>dbms_macutl.g_ruleset_eval_any,
        audit_options =>dbms_macutl.g_ruleset_audit_fail,
        fail_options =>dbms_macutl.g_ruleset_fail_show,
        fail_message =>NULL,
        fail_code =>NULL,
        handler_options =>dbms_macutl.g_ruleset_handler_off,
        handler =>NULL);
END;
/
PL/SQL procedure successfully completed.

dbvowner@aos> -- Associate the two rules to the rule set
dbvowner@aos> BEGIN
   dbms_macadm.add_rule_to_rule_set (
     rule_set_name => 'Allow Sessions'
   , rule_name     => 'Is Secure Authentication Method'
   );
END;
/
PL/SQL procedure successfully completed.

dbvowner@aos> BEGIN
   dbms_macadm.add_rule_to_rule_set (
     rule_set_name => 'Allow Sessions'
   , rule_name     => 'Is Console Client'
   );
END;
/
PL/SQL procedure successfully completed.
```

Finally, we need to create the DBV CONNECT command rule that uses this DBV rule set. One word of caution here regarding the DBV CONNECT command rule: Make sure you keep a SQL*Plus session open as your DBV security administrator (DBVOWNER) in case you have developed PL/SQL rule expressions that are incomplete, inaccurate, or that produce errors at runtime. You could inadvertently lock out every account from the database, including the DBV security administrator, with these types of problems. Having this SQL*Plus session open allows you to disable or drop the DBV CONNECT command rule if problems arise in the development and testing of the authorization logic.

```
dbvowner@aos> BEGIN
  dbms_macadm.create_command_rule (
    command        =>  'CONNECT'
    ,rule_set_name => 'Allow Sessions'
    ,object_owner  => '%'
    ,object_name   => '%'
    ,enabled       => 'Y'
);
END;
/
PL/SQL procedure successfully completed.
```

At this point, if MARY were to attempt to log into the database from her VPN connection, sitting in the coffee shop, the connection would not be authorized and the session would be terminated immediately by DBV:

```
$ sqlplus mary@aos
SQL*Plus: Release 11.1.0.6.0 - Production on Tue Mar 10 17:04:12 2009
Copyright (c) 1982, 2007, Oracle.  All rights reserved.
Enter password:
ERROR:
ORA-47400: Command Rule violation for CONNECT on LOGON
```

These examples demonstrate the separation of duty for privileged administrators. Using DBV command rules, we can add a layer of control that accounts for business rules and IT policies an organization must support. The access controls provided by DBV realms and DBV command rules are configured in a protected account (DVSYS) with an enforcement mechanism integrated directly into the Oracle database kernel's SQL engine. Application logic that issues SQL to an Oracle database does not need to change to leverage these DBV access controls. The main benefit of this external enforcement point model is that DBV can help cover the gaps in your application's security model so that you can meet compliance regulations without the need to recode or redesign the application.

Rule Sets

A DBV rule is an elementary logic component that is evaluated by DBV. These logic components are written as Oracle PL/SQL expressions to return Boolean results. A simple rule would be **USER != 'SYS'**. This rule uses a standard Oracle PL/SQL function, **USER**, that returns the database account that was logged into and returns a Boolean result of whether or not the account logged into is SYS. Your own DBV rules can use PL/SQL code you have or will develop. A DBV rule can be associated in more than one DBV rule set so that you can develop a library of DBV rules that can be used throughout your DBV security policy.

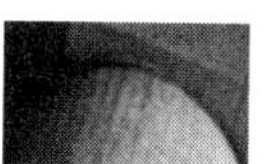

TIP
You can create DBV rules as reusable security policy controls applicable to more than one application.

We have demonstrated example usages of DBV rule sets with the two primary DBV access control components: DBV realms (authorizations) and DBV command rules. DBV rule sets can also control the assignment of DBV factors and the ability to enable DBV Secure Application Roles (SARs). The auditing of these components is controlled by the audit configuration of the DBV rule set. DBV rule sets can be configured to execute custom PL/SQL procedures so that if a DBV command rule is violated, for example, you could pass this information to another system or alert the security administrator in real time.

Rule Set Evaluation Mode

The configuration of DBV Rule sets allows for the association of multiple DBV rules (PL/SQL expressions). DBV rule sets have an evaluation mode that can be configured to require that all associated rules return TRUE, or at least one rule returns TRUE. To help in clarifying the runtime impact of the evaluation mode configuration, consider an example: Suppose we've defined a

DBV rule set, Rule Set #1, depicted in the following table. This DBV rule set has an evaluation mode of ALL TRUE with two DBV rules associated to it. The DBV rule set evaluation result is depicted for the various results returned by the two associated DBV rules.

Rule Set	Evaluation Mode	Rule #1 Result	Rule #2 Result	Rule Set Result
Rule Set #1	ALL TRUE	FALSE	FALSE	FALSE
Rule Set #1	ALL TRUE	TRUE	FALSE	FALSE
Rule Set #1	ALL TRUE	FALSE	TRUE	FALSE
Rule Set #1	ALL TRUE	TRUE	TRUE	TRUE

Now suppose we have a second DBV rule set, Rule Set #2, with an evaluation mode of ANY TRUE. The same two DBV rules are associated with this second DBV rule set. The following table depicts the evaluation results for this configuration of the evaluation mode.

Rule Set	Evaluation Mode	Rule #1 Result	Rule #2 Result	Rule Set Result
Rule Set #2	ANY TRUE	FALSE	FALSE	FALSE
Rule Set #2	ANY TRUE	TRUE	FALSE	TRUE
Rule Set #2	ANY TRUE	FALSE	TRUE	TRUE
Rule Set #2	ANY TRUE	TRUE	TRUE	TRUE

The DBV rule set configuration allows for a DBV rule set to be disabled. The net effect of disabling a DBV rule set is that the DBV rules engine will return TRUE if the rule set is evaluated within the context of its usage—such as a DBV realm authorization or DBV command rule. To clarify the effect of disabling a DBV rule set, consider the example rule set 'Using Financials Application' from the "Command Rules" section earlier in the chapter. If we disable the rule set, then all UPDATE statements on the SH.SALES table will be allowed if the session has direct object privileges or the realm authorization is valid.

Rule Set Auditing

When we configured the rule set 'Using Financials Application' in the DBV command rule example, we used the constant **dbms_macutl.g_ruleset_audit_fail**, which means "audit on failure only" or audit when the DBV rule set evaluation is FALSE. DBV rule set failure can be stated simply as the access control decision points (DBV rules) returned FALSE and the access attempt failed. Let's examine the DBV rule set configuration using the DBV Administrator page, as shown in Figure 5-8.

Auditing on a failed access attempt would be considered a minimum requirement for all DBV rule sets, yet some regulatory requirements may mandate auditing on any data access (in other words, the evaluation result of the DBV rule set). You just need to consider the performance impacts of this level of auditing, given the frequency of evaluation in your production system, as auditing in any software component has some associated overhead.

When we examine the DBV audit trail for the DBV command rule example for an UPDATE on the SH.SALES table (Figure 5-9), we can see the audit trail contains both the DBV rule set and command that triggered the audit. This information can be very useful in developing a policy that can prove your stated security posture.

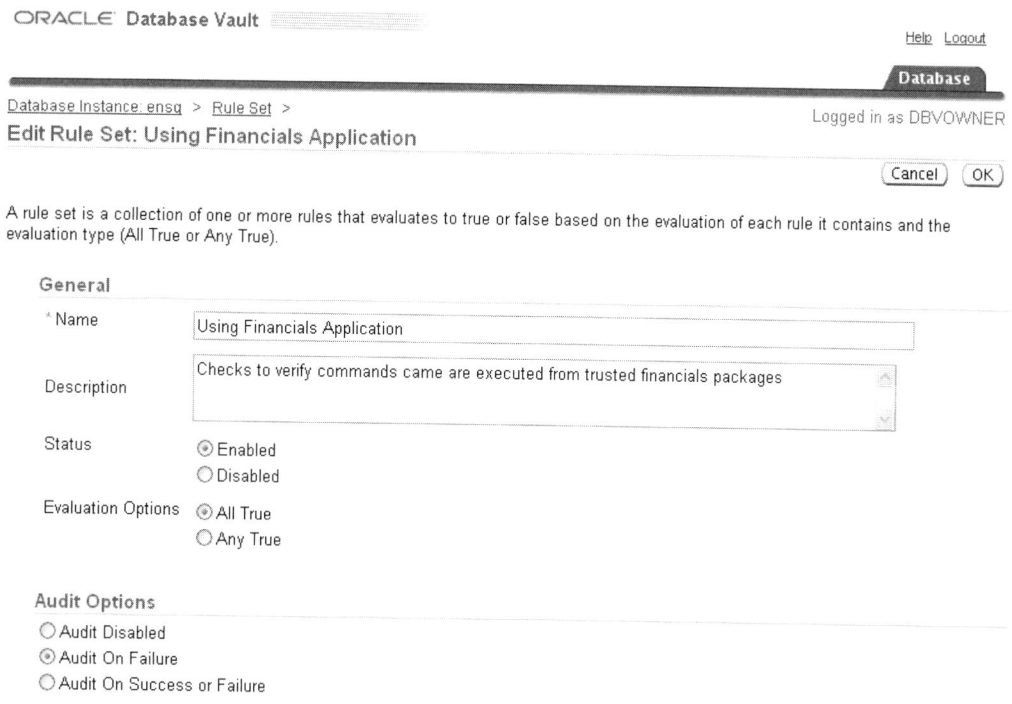

ORACLE Database Vault

Help Logout

Database

Database Instance: ensq > Rule Set >

Logged in as DBVOWNER

Edit Rule Set: Using Financials Application

Cancel OK

A rule set is a collection of one or more rules that evaluates to true or false based on the evaluation of each rule it contains and the evaluation type (All True or Any True).

General

* Name: Using Financials Application

Description: Checks to verify commands came are executed from trusted financials packages

Status: (•) Enabled ( ) Disabled

Evaluation Options: (•) All True ( ) Any True

Audit Options

( ) Audit Disabled
(•) Audit On Failure
( ) Audit On Success or Failure

FIGURE 5-8 *DBV rule set configuration*

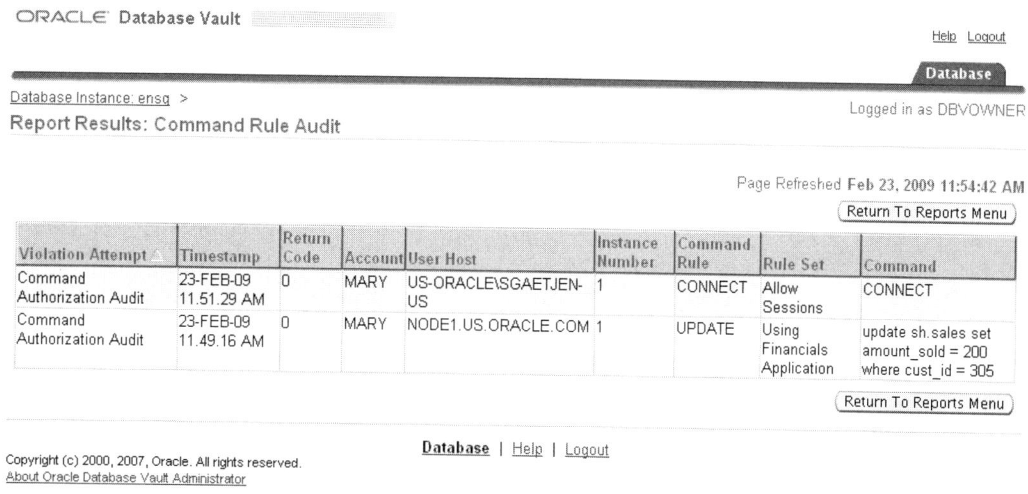

ORACLE Database Vault

Help Logout

Database

Database Instance: ensq >

Logged in as DBVOWNER

Report Results: Command Rule Audit

Page Refreshed Feb 23, 2009 11:54:42 AM

Return To Reports Menu

Violation Attempt	Timestamp	Return Code	Account	User Host	Instance Number	Command Rule	Rule Set	Command
Command Authorization Audit	23-FEB-09 11.51.29 AM	0	MARY	US-ORACLE\SGAETJEN-US	1	CONNECT	Allow Sessions	CONNECT
Command Authorization Audit	23-FEB-09 11.49.16 AM	0	MARY	NODE1.US.ORACLE.COM	1	UPDATE	Using Financials Application	update sh.sales set amount_sold = 200 where cust_id = 305

Return To Reports Menu

Database | Help | Logout

Copyright (c) 2000, 2007, Oracle. All rights reserved.
About Oracle Database Vault Administrator

FIGURE 5-9 *DBV command rule violation report*

Custom Event Handlers

The DBV rule set auditing component can be extended using the custom event handlers feature of the rule set configuration. This feature allows you to integrate DBV with external alerting, systems management, and monitoring systems. Like DBV rule set auditing, this feature can be configured to trigger based on a failure only or on a success and failure. To enable this feature, you need to follow these steps:

1. Define a package procedure or stand-alone procedure that will be triggered when the DBV rule set is evaluated.
2. Grant **EXECUTE** on the procedure to DVSYS. The DVSYS account executes the DBV rules engine and calls the procedure.
3. Configure the DBV rule set to use the custom event handling procedure.

The details of integrating with an external alerting or monitoring system is a bit beyond the scope of this book, so let's just look at a trivial table-based logging example for now:

```
mary@aos> -- First create a table to hold the alerts
mary@aos> create table sh.alerts ( msg varchar2(4000)
, msgdate date default sysdate);

Table created.
mary@aos> -- next create a package to process the alerts
mary@aos> CREATE OR REPLACE package sh.sales_alerts as
PROCEDURE sales_update_alert(ruleset_name IN VARCHAR2,
ruleset_result IN VARCHAR2);
end;
/
Package created.

mary@aos> CREATE OR REPLACE PACKAGE BODY sh.sales_alerts AS
          PROCEDURE sales_update_alert(ruleset_name IN VARCHAR2,
ruleset_result IN VARCHAR2) is
        PRAGMA AUTONOMOUS_TRANSACTION;
    BEGIN
            INSERT into sh.alerts (msg )
VALUES ('Alert for Rule Set:'
|| ruleset_name || ', result is ' || ruleset_result);
            COMMOT;
    END;
END;
/
Package created.

mary@aos> -- GRANT EXECUTE on the handler package to DVSYS
mary@aos> GRANT EXECUTE ON sh.sales_alerts TO dvsys;
Grant succeeded.

mary@aos> -- Update the rule set to use the handler package
mary@aos> -- on rule set failure (failed access attempt)
dbvowner@aos> BEGIN
```

```
    dbms_macadm.update_rule_set(
        rule_set_name =>'Using Financials Application',
        description =>'Checks to verify commands came are
executed from trusted financials packages',
        enabled =>dbms_macutl.g_yes,
        eval_options =>dbms_macutl.g_ruleset_eval_all,
        audit_options =>dbms_macutl.g_ruleset_audit_fail,
        fail_options =>dbms_macutl.g_ruleset_fail_show,
        fail_message =>NULL,
        fail_code =>NULL,
        handler_options =>dbms_macutl.g_ruleset_handler_fail,
        handler =>'sh.sales_alerts.sales_update_alert'
);
END;
/
PL/SQL procedure successfully completed.

mary@aos> -- Attempt to update the table outside the policy
mary@aos> UPDATE sh.sales
SET amount_sold = 200
WHERE cust_id = 305;

UPDATE sh.sales
          *
ERROR at line 1:
ORA-01031: insufficient privileges

mary@aos> -- View our alerts
mary@aos> SELECT * from sh.alerts;

MSG
----------------------------------------------------------------
MSGDATE
---------
Alert for Rule Set:Using Financials Application, result is FALSE
12-JUL-08
```

As you can see, it's a straightforward process to configure your DBV rule set to call custom event handlers. This opens up many possibilities to use e-mail, pagers, systems management tools like Oracle Enterprise Manager Grid Control, and other third-party security monitoring tools for handling notification and monitoring based on security-related events. In Chapter 7, we present a more advanced example custom event handler that will give you full details on the transaction that was involved in DBV violation.

Rule Configuration

The rule expressions used in DBV rule sets must be expressed as a valid PL/SQL expression that evaluates to TRUE or FALSE. This does not imply that you need to return a PL/SQL Boolean data type, but rather you must express the rule as a PL/SQL expression that you could use in an Oracle SQL WHERE clause. The way to test your rule is to run the command in Oracle SQL*Plus or Oracle SQL Developer using this syntax:

```
SELECT COUNT(*) FROM SYS.DUAL WHERE <rule expression>;
```

If the rule expression passes this syntax check, meaning that the above SQL executes without a syntax error, then the rule expression is safe to use.

It is recommended that you use compiled PL/SQL package functions (or stand-alone PL/SQL functions) if your rule expression logic is large or complex or requires PL/SQL components not normally embedded in SQL expressions. Using this approach helps in the following ways:

- The approach helps performance, as the code is precompiled and does not need to be parsed at runtime.
- The approach improves maintenance of the security policy in development, as the code can be changed and tuned when testing for both security and performance begins.
- The approach improves readability of the security policy for auditors, especially if the functions' names are indicative of their purpose.
- You can leverage predefined DBV rule set event functions as parameters to this function.

The process for creating a rule expression involves defining PL/SQL functions that simply return 0 or 1 (for failure and success) and then granting EXECUTE on this function to DVSYS. Using PL/SQL functions is preferable, because you will find that the decision point logic is a nontrivial case-like decision, could involve SQL queries, and over time is easier to maintain and deploy in a compiled procedure. The following example illustrates this point:

```
mary@aos> CREATE OR REPLACE FUNCTION sh.can_perform_sales_summary RETURN NUMBER AS
 l_day  VARCHAR2(10) := TRIM(TO_CHAR(SYSDATE,'DAY'));
 l_hour VARCHAR2(2)  := TO_CHAR(SYSDATE,'HH24');
BEGIN
 -- allow sales summary logic to run on weekends or week nights
 -- weekend
 IF l_day IN ( 'SATURDAY', 'SUNDAY' ) THEN
    RETURN 1;
 -- weekday - business hours
 ELSIF l_hour BETWEEN '08' AND '04' THEN
    RETURN 0;
 -- week night
 ELSE
    RETURN 1;
 END IF;
END;
/
Function created.
mary@aos> GRANT EXECUTE ON sh.can_perform_sales_summary TO dvsys;
Grant succeeded.
```

The logic checks the day of the week and the time of day to return a 0 or 1 that will authorize the execution of a sales summary package during the business nonworking (for some people) hours. We can then use this function in a DBV rule set as follows:

```
dbvowner@aos> -- Create the DBV Rule
BEGIN
     dbms_macadm.create_rule(
        rule_name => 'Is Sales Summary Allowed'
      , rule_expr => 'sh.can_perform_sales_summary = 1'
     );
END;
```

```
/
PL/SQL procedure successfully completed.

dbvowner@aos> -- Create the DBV Rule Set
dbvowner@aos> BEGIN
    dbms_macadm.create_rule_set(
        rule_set_name =>'Can Execute Financials Summary',
        description =>
'Checks to see if summary job for financials can be run.',
        enabled =>dbms_macutl.g_yes,
        eval_options =>dbms_macutl.g_ruleset_eval_all,
        audit_options =>dbms_macutl.g_ruleset_audit_fail,
        fail_options =>dbms_macutl.g_ruleset_fail_show,
        fail_message =>NULL,
        fail_code =>NULL,
        handler_options =>dbms_macutl.g_ruleset_handler_off,
        handler =>NULL);
END;
/
PL/SQL procedure successfully completed.

dbvowner@aos> -- Associate the DBV Rule to the DBV Rule Set
BEGIN
   dbms_macadm.add_rule_to_rule_set (
     rule_set_name => 'Can Execute Financials Summary'
   , rule_name     => 'Is Sales Summary Allowed'
   );
END;
/
PL/SQL procedure successfully completed.
```

Then we can use this DBV rule set in a DBV command rule for EXECUTE on a (notional) Sales History Summary procedure:

```
dbvowner@aos> BEGIN
  dbms_macadm.create_command_rule (
    command       =>  'EXECUTE'
    ,rule_set_name => 'Can Execute Financials Summary'
    ,object_owner  => 'SH'
    ,object_name   => 'SALES_SUMMARY.RUN_SUMMARY'
    ,enabled       => 'Y'
);
END;
/
PL/SQL procedure successfully completed.
```

Validating DBV Rule Syntax and Permission

Development or production deployment changes against underlying PL/SQL logic or database privileges can render DBV rules invalid. Let's look at an example situation that could cause this. Suppose MARY, our Sales History DBA, dropped the function we used in the example just discussed:

```
mary@aos>DROP FUNCTION sh.can_perform_sales_summary;
Function dropped.
```

The DBV rules engine had created DBV rule that references this PL/SQL function. When the function was dropped, the reference was broken along with the underlying GRANT EXECUTE privilege on the function to DVSYS. We can see this problem by attempting to validate the correct syntax of all the DBV rules that are configured. We can perform this validation by issuing the following call as the DBV security administrator (DBVOWNER):

```
dbvowner@aos> exec dbms_macadm.sync_rules;
BEGIN dbms_macadm.sync_rules; END;

*
ERROR at line 1:
ORA-25448: rule DVSYS.DV$5045 has errors
ORA-00904: "SH"."CAN_PERFORM_SALES_SUMMARY": invalid identifier
ORA-06512: at "SYS.DBMS_RULE_ADM", line 188
ORA-06512: at "DVSYS.DBMS_MACADM", line 2794
ORA-06512: at line 1
```

In this example, you can see that one of our rules is invalid, probably because we forgot to GRANT EXECUTE privilege on a function to DVSYS. You can isolate the offending rule by querying the DVSYS.DV$RULE view as follows:

```
dbvowner@aos>SELECT name,rule_expr
from dvsys.dv$rule
WHERE id# = 5045;
NAME                      RULE_EXPR
------------------------- --------------------------------
Is Sales Summary Allowed  sh.can_perform_sales_summary = 1

1 row selected.
```

In this example, the internal rule name is DVSYS.DV$5045. This corresponds to the ID# = 5045 in the view DVSYS.DV$RULE. The DBV security administrator can investigate views such as DBA_TAB_PRIVS and DBA_OBJECTS to determine why the problem exists. In this case, if MARY simply re-creates the function and GRANTs EXECUTE privilege on the function to DVSYS, the DBV security administrator can then reexecute the DBMS_MACADM.SYNC_RULES procedure to recompile the DBV rule.

DBV Rule Set Event Functions

The DBV product installs a collection of PL/SQL functions that can be used in DBV rule expressions to retrieve detailed information about the database command that is being evaluated for realm authorizations and command rules—such as UPDATE on SH.TABLE—as well as the session context in which the command is operating. These PL/SQL functions are called the DBV rule set event functions. Table 5-1 describes these functions.

We can use these event functions directly in our DBV Rule expressions—for example, testing for a list of values:

```
dbvowner@aos> BEGIN
     dbms_macadm.create_rule(
```

```
    rule_name => 'Trusted Sales Administrators'
    , rule_expr => 'DVSYS.DV_LOGIN_USER IN (''ANTHONY'',''MARY'')'
);
END;
/
PL/SQL procedure successfully completed.
```

We can even use SQL subqueries and these event functions directly in our DBV rule expressions. For example, if we want to test to see that the session user is a member of the IT department as defined in the Human Resources schema, we'd use this:

```
dbvowner@aos> BEGIN
    dbms_macadm.create_rule(
    rule_name => 'Works In The IT Department'
    , rule_expr => '(SELECT COUNT(*) FROM hr.employees where email = '
                || ' DVSYS.DV_LOGIN_USER AND department = 60) > 0'
);
END;
/
PL/SQL procedure successfully completed.
```

Rule Set Function	Description
DVSYS.DV_SYSEVENT	Returns the system event firing the rule set, in VARCHAR2 data type; the event name is the same as the syntax found in the SQL statement that is issued, for example, INSERT, CREATE
DVSYS.DV_DICT_OBJ_TYPE	Returns the type of the dictionary object on which the database operation occurred, for example, table, procedure, view; the return type is VARCHAR2
DVSYS.DV_DICT_OBJ_OWNER	Returns the owner of the dictionary object on which the database operation occurred; the return type is VARCHAR2
DVSYS.DV_DICT_OBJ_NAME	Returns the name of the dictionary object on which the database operation occurred; the return type is VARCHAR2
DVSYS.DV_SQL_TEXT	Returns the first 4000 characters of SQL text of the database statement used in the operation; the return type is VARCHAR2
DVSYS.DV_LOGIN_USER	Returns the login user name, in VARCHAR2 data type; returns the same value that SYS_CONTEXT('USERENV', 'SESSION_USER') returns
DVSYS.DV_INSTANCE_NUM	Returns the database instance number, in NUMBER data type
DVSYS.DV_DATABASE_NAME	Returns the database name, in VARCHAR2 data type

TABLE 5-1 *DBV Rule Set Event Functions*

DBV Factors Used in Rule Set Expressions

In the rule examples we've demonstrated so far, most of the logic for the security decisions we've used is implemented in the Sales History schema (SH) for the sake of simplifying the examples. While these are merely examples, we need to think about our rules from the enterprise perspective, so that security controls are maintained outside of the application. This needs to be done not only for security's sake, but also to allow application developers to leverage corporate policies around security. This is also important from the perspective of reuse, because developers and system architects should not have to reinvent or recode the same controls for each application that is being designed.

DBV rules should be based on conditions from a trusted source, whether that source is internal to the database or in an external system. This is where DBV factors play a role. DBV factors are available as PL/SQL functions that have independent access (from the application's perspective) to a method or data for security relevant information. For example, the DBV security administrator can define DBV factors such as User Department and Connection Method. The administrator can then use these factors to create additional factors, such as Sales Staff User or Secure Connection. From a pseudo-code point of view, these may take the following form:

Factor	**Implementation**

User department	`SELECT department`
	`FROM hr.employees`
	`WHERE email =`
	`SYS_CONTEXT('USERENV', 'SESSION_USER')`

Sales staff user	`If DVSYS.GET_FACTOR('User Department') IN`
	`('Retail Sales', 'Government Sales')`
	`Then 'Sales Staff User' is 'TRUE'`
	`Else 'Sales Staff User' is 'FALSE'`

Authentication method	`SYS_CONTEXT('USERENV', 'AUTHENTICATION_METHOD')`

Secure connection	`If DVSYS.GET_FACTOR('Authentication Method')`
	` IN ('SSL', 'KERBEROS')`
	`AND DVSYS.GET_FACTOR('Client IP') LIKE`
	`'192.168.0.%'`
	`Then 'Secure Connection' is 'TRUE'`
	`Else 'Secure Connection' is 'FALSE'`

Application developers do not always need to be concerned about the implementation of the information used to establish the DBV factors. In some cases, you may not want them to know! For example, the User Department could just as easily come from an external LDAP source, such as Oracle Internet Directory (OID) or a web service. Each database application developer or architect should not have to consider how the factor is resolved. They simply need to know what the factor means and how it applies to their applications. The point here is that factors of security-relevant attributes can be shared by more than one application and are maintained by the security administrator, a third party with respect to the application developers and application DBAs. These factors can form the building blocks in DBV rule sets that may be applied to more than one application.

We've discussed how DBV factors provide many advantages to applications, including security controls that can be shared across applications and logic that is maintained outside of application development control. The ability to use them in DBV rule sets provides a more verifiable and readable security policy for compliance. In the next section, we will dig into the details of DBV factor configuration and the component's powerful features that offer information assurance.

Factors

DBV factors are security relevant attributes that help to establish the context for a session to authorize database commands or actions, such as the following (shown in Figure 5-10):

- Connecting to the database, or a session authorization, when used as part of a DBV CONNECT command rule
- Executing a (SQL) command statement on a database object or a statement level authorization when used as part of a DBV command rule or realm authorization
- Filtering data in SELECT and DML statements, or a row-level security (RLS) authorization, when used in Oracle Virtual Private Database (VPD) policy or the Oracle DBV Oracle Label Security (OLS) integration
- Branching in application code, or logic authorizations, when using the DBV factor function or the **GET_FACTOR** function in PL/SQL logic

DBV factors are typically defined and maintained outside of specific database applications. Factors can use information that may be internal or external to the information stored in the database. DBV factors are used primarily to establish the context of the "subject" (who) in your security policy and the "conditions" in your security policy (when, how, where). The context of the subject may include session information on roles granted, group/organizational membership, privileges granted, and even identity management related attributes, such as job title. Conditional attributes may include information such as time of day or month, authentication method used, database client location, or access path (recall the trusted package example) to the enforcement point. The 11.0.6 DBV installation will create 17 factors that may be useful for your organization's security policy.

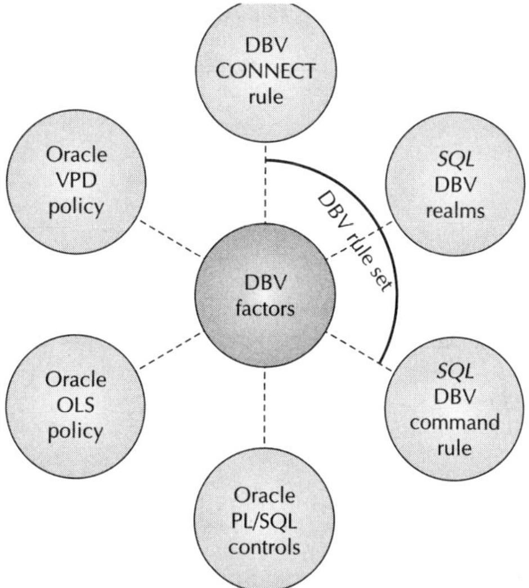

FIGURE 5-10 *DBV factor usage*

Creating Factors

The fundamental configuration of a DBV factor is the factor name and the PL/SQL expression used to retrieve the factor's value, or the factor's *identity* as it is called. One factor that is installed by DBV is Client IP, which is the database client's IP address. The factor uses the PL/SQL expression **UPPER(SYS_CONTEXT('USERENV','IP_ADDRESS'))** to retrieve its identity. To define your own retrieval-based custom factor you would follow these steps:

1. Define the factor's retrieval method using a PL/SQL function.
2. Grant EXECUTE privileges on this PL/SQL function to the DVSYS account.
3. Define the factor definition as the DBV security administrator (DBVOWNER).

Factor Retrieval Method

The factor retrieval method is a PL/SQL expression or SQL SELECT statement that returns a single VARCHAR2 value. PL/SQL expressions can be based on PL/SQL functions or SQL built-in functions defined by the Oracle RDBMS, or they can be based on a custom PL/SQL function that you've built. The key is that the function returns a VARCHAR2 value even if it is NULL, or it returns some data type that can be cast to a VARCHAR2 by typical Oracle data type casting rules. The function's signature can be defined as follows:

```
FUNCTION some_factor RETURN VARCHAR2;
or FUNCTION another_factor(param1 IN data_type1 … paramN IN data_typeN)
          RETURN VARCHAR2;
```

Note in the latter signature that it is possible to pass parameters to your factor function if you need additional information not readily available to the PL/SQL logic inside the function or if you need to integrate existing functions and cannot change the function's signature. Consider the following custom PL/SQL package that retrieves department information for users stored in the Human Resources (HR) object owner account:

```
hr@aos> -- define the package specification
hr@aos> CREATE OR REPLACE PACKAGE hr.employee_utility IS
   FUNCTION get_user_department_id   ( user_name IN
        VARCHAR2 DEFAULT SYS_CONTEXT('USERENV', 'SESSION_USER') ) RETURN NUMBER;
   FUNCTION get_user_department_name ( user_name IN
       VARCHAR2 DEFAULT SYS_CONTEXT('USERENV', 'SESSION_USER') ) RETURN VARCHAR2;
END;
/
Package created.
hr@aos> -- define the package body
hr@aos> CREATE OR REPLACE PACKAGE BODY hr.employee_utility IS
   FUNCTION get_user_department_id   ( user_name IN
        VARCHAR2  ) RETURN NUMBER IS

      l_email    VARCHAR2(120);
      l_dept_id hr.employees.department_id%TYPE;
   BEGIN
      -- input parameter checking
      IF user_name IS NULL OR LENGTH(user_name) > 100 THEN
        RAISE_APPLICATION_ERROR(-20001,
 'Invalid parameter for "user_name"',FALSE);
```

```
      END IF;
      -- database usernames and email names are similar
      l_email := user_name;
      -- query the employee's department assignment
      SELECT department_id
      INTO l_dept_id
      FROM hr.employees
      WHERE email = l_email;
      RETURN l_dept_id;
   EXCEPTION
      WHEN NO_DATA_FOUND THEN
            RETURN NULL;
   END;
   FUNCTION get_user_department_name ( user_name IN
        VARCHAR2  ) RETURN VARCHAR2 IS
      l_dept_id   hr.employees.department_id%TYPE;
      l_dept_name hr.departments.department_name%TYPE;
   BEGIN

      l_dept_id := get_user_department_id(user_name);
      IF l_dept_id IS NULL THEN
        RETURN NULL;
      END IF;
      SELECT department_name
      INTO l_dept_name
      FROM hr.departments
      WHERE department_id = l_dept_id;
      RETURN l_dept_name;
   EXCEPTION
      WHEN NO_DATA_FOUND THEN
            RETURN NULL;
   END;
END;
/
Package created.
```

In these PL/SQL examples, a table named HR.EMPLOYEES and the employees listed in this table may also have database accounts. We can match the database account names to the EMAIL column of the HR.EMPLOYEES table, without the @company suffix. The two functions in this package can retrieve department assignment information, such as the department ID or department name for the employee. To use custom-developed PL/SQL functions in DBV factors, your next step is to GRANT EXECUTE privilege on the package or function to the DVSYS account as follows:

```
hr@aos> GRANT EXECUTE ON hr.employee_utility TO dvsys;
Grant succeeded.
```

When custom-developed PL/SQL functions, such as those defined in the example package, are used as the retrieval method for DBV factors, the function is typically defined with definer's rights, versus invoker's rights. The factor retrieval method may involve the use privileges on database objects or other PL/SQL code. The encapsulation of the factor retrieval methods in PL/SQL packages and their internal functions avoids the need to maintain additional privilege grants to the DVSYS account. With the GRANTS to DVSYS in place, the DBV security administrator can define the factor definitions that make use of the PL/SQL package functions:

```
dbvowner@aos> -- user department identifier
dbvowner@aos> BEGIN
    dbms_macadm.create_factor(
        factor_name      => 'User_Department_Id',
        factor_type_name => 'User',
        description    =>
'The identifier of the department the current user works in.',
        rule_set_name => NULL ,
        get_expr      => 'hr.employee_utility.get_user_department_id',
        validate_expr => NULL,
        identify_by   => dbms_macutl.g_identify_by_method,
        labeled_by    => dbms_macutl.g_labeled_by_self,
        eval_options => dbms_macutl.g_eval_on_access,
        audit_options => dbms_macutl.g_audit_on_get_error,
        fail_options  => dbms_macutl.g_fail_with_message);
END;
/
PL/SQL procedure successfully completed.

dbvowner@aos>-- user department name
dbvowner@aos> BEGIN
    dbms_macadm.create_factor(
        factor_name      => 'User_Department_Name' ,
        factor_type_name => 'User',
        description    =>
'The name of the department the current user works in.',
        rule_set_name => NULL ,
        get_expr      =>
'hr.employee_utility.get_user_department_name',
        validate_expr => NULL,
        identify_by   => dbms_macutl.g_identify_by_method,
        labeled_by    => dbms_macutl.g_labeled_by_self,
        eval_options => dbms_macutl.g_eval_on_access,
        audit_options => dbms_macutl.g_audit_on_get_error,
        fail_options  => dbms_macutl.g_fail_with_message);
END;
/
PL/SQL procedure successfully completed.
```

The DBMS_MACADM package that is used for factor creation allows for the factor retrieval method parameter, **get_expr**, to use a function that returns a VARCHAR2, as is the case with the function **HR.EMPLOYEE_UTILITY.GET_USER_DEPARTMENT_NAME** or a function that can be cast to a VARCHAR2 value, as is the case with the function **HR.EMPLOYEE_UTILITY.GET_USER_DEPARTMENT_ID**.

The following example demonstrates how to use a SQL SELECT statement to retrieve a factor value with a query on the V$DATABASE view for the OS platform on which the database is running:

```
dbvowner@aos> BEGIN
    dbms_macadm.create_factor(
        factor_name      => 'Platform_Name' ,
        factor_type_name => 'Instance',
        description   => 'Retrieves the OS Platform the
 database is running on',
        rule_set_name => NULL ,
        get_expr      => '(SELECT platform_name FROM v$database)',
        validate_expr => null,
        identify_by   => dbms_macutl.g_identify_by_method,
        labeled_by    => dbms_macutl.g_labeled_by_self,
        eval_options => dbms_macutl.g_eval_on_session,
        audit_options => dbms_macutl.g_audit_on_get_error,
        fail_options  => dbms_macutl.g_fail_with_message);
END;
/
PL/SQL procedure successfully completed.
```

When using SQL SELECT statements, you must embed the SELECT statement in parentheses and the DVSYS account must be granted SELECT privileges on the table or view being queried.

Naming Factors

It is important that you name your factors with identifiers that convey the attribute retrieved, in human readable form, to improve the readability of your DBV policy where these factors are used. In other words, using readable factor names such User_Department_Name, compared to the names used for variables or columns, such as USR_DEPT, improves readability of the security policy when a factor is used in a DBV rule set expression. Here's an example:

```
dbvowner@aos> BEGIN
     dbms_macadm.create_rule(
         rule_name => 'Is An Employee of the IT Department'
       , rule_expr =>
          'DVSYS.GET_FACTOR(''User_Department_Name'') = ''IT'''
     );
END;
PL/SQL procedure successfully completed.
```

Scope of Factor Retrieval Method

It is important that you test the factor function by executing it using the DVSYS account and several test accounts to determine whether the factor retrieval method raises exceptions for any database sessions. You must consider whether the session contextual information on which the factor function may rely is defined for each account you test, and you should handle these cases in the code that makes up the factor function. You should deal with these conditions because once factor functions are defined, they are evaluated at session establishment for every session, even those running as part of the Oracle RDBMS product, such as Enterprise Manager Database Control jobs. DBV factors do not currently have a scoping mechanism to limit their evaluation to certain accounts, roles, or session conditions, so if you want to prevent processing in the factor logic for certain types of sessions, you will need to codify this in your PL/SQL factor function. With our department example, Oracle database accounts such as SYS, SYSTEM, and SYSMAN, to name a few, will not exist in the HR table records, so we simply return NULLS to handle these cases.

Factor Evaluation The **eval_options** parameter in the DBMS_MACADM.CREATE_FACTOR procedure controls when the identity of the factor should be resolved by calling the factor retrieval method. A factor identity can be resolved just once, at the time the database session is started, using the constant DBMS_MACUTL.G_EVAL_ON_SESSION. With this constant, the factor retrieval method is called once when the database session is established and cached in the database session context namespace MAC$FACTOR. Subsequent calls to resolve the identity are read from this read-only memory area to improve performance. If the constant DBMS_MACUTL.G_EVAL_ON_ACCESS is used for this parameter, each call to resolve the factor's identity will call the factor's retrieval method. In our examples so far, factors such as AUTHENTICATION_METHOD or CLIENT_IP will not change over the course of a database session, so identity resolution should be configured using DBMS_MACUTL.G_EVAL_ON_SESSION. Factors such as User_Department_Name and User_Department_Id could in fact change during the course of a database session (if the employee were reassigned, for example), so the parameter DBMS_MACUTL.G_EVAL_ON_ACCESS should be used.

TIP
Use the evaluation on access for the factor retrieval method if the values can change over the course of a database session.

Factor Auditing

It is possible that the PL/SQL expression used in the DBV factor's retrieval method (the **get_expr** parameter) can encounter some error in processing or return a NULL value. The DBV factor can be configured to audit these outcomes using the **audit_options** parameter in the DBMS_MACADM.CREATE_FACTOR procedure. The DVA web application allows the DBV security administrator to query these audit records using a standard report that is provided with the application.

Factor Functions

When a factor is created, the DBV product will create a PL/SQL function of the form, **DVF.F$<*FactorName*>**, that can be used in DBV rule set expressions or your own PL/SQL code. When we created the factor User_Department_Name, a function named **DVF.F$USER_DEPARTMENT_NAME** was created. This PL/SQL function is publicly available to all database sessions. The following demonstrates the usage of function for the User_Department_Name factor.

```
anthony@aos>select DVF.F$USER_DEPARTMENT_NAME FROM DUAL;

F$USER_DEPARTMENT_NAME
----------------------
IT
1 row selected.
```

If the name of a the factor that must be used is dynamically resolved, the rule set or application logic can use the function **DVSYS.GET_FACTOR('*FactorName*')** to get the value of the factor, as shown in the following example:

```
anthony@aos>select DVSYS.GET_FACTOR('USER_DEPARTMENT_NAME') FROM DUAL;

DVSYS.GET_FACTOR('USER_DEPARTMENT_NAME')
----------------------------------------
IT
1 row selected.
```

Factor Identities

The term "identity" is typically defined as the unique identifier of a user stored in an identity management repository. In DBV, the term is overloaded to mean the value of a factor. DBV can be configured with many more security-relevant attributes than just the user when you're defining a security policy, so you have many identities to consider. We have identities (values) for the client IP addresses, client machines, the time of day, user departments, and so on. As you have seen with the examples so far, the DBV factor configuration supports the use of a simple PL/SQL expression that uses publicly available PL/SQL functions—for example, **SYS_CONTEXT** or **TO_CHAR(SYSDATE)**—and this can be custom PL/SQL code. When we define a factor in this way, we use the constant DBMS_MACUTL.G_IDENTIFY_BY_METHOD for the parameter **identify_by** and place the PL/SQL expression in the **get_expr** parameter in the call to the DBMS_MACADM.CREATE_FACTOR procedure.

Factor Identity as a Constant

The PL/SQL expression used to establish the factor's identity can also be a constant value. We specify a constant identity using the constant DBMS_MACUTL.G_IDENTIFY_BY_CONSTANT for the parameter **identify_by** and place the constant value in the **get_expr** parameter in the call to the procedure DBMS_MACADM.CREATE_FACTOR. A factor with a constant identity can be useful for IF/THEN/ELSE or CASE/SWITCH logic that you may include in your security policy. For example, you may have a highly restrictive policy in a production database and a less restrictive policy in a development database. We could define a factor such as IS_PRODUCTION to return 0 or 1, or a factor such as ENVIRONMENT_NAME to return a value such as 'DEV', 'TEST', or 'PROD' (separately) in each database to handle this type of scenario.

Factors Identified by Other Factors

We can also identify a factor based on the identity of other factors. Using this method, we can assert the identity of a factor using a declarative DBV construct called *identity maps*. Identity maps allow for a multifactored security capability to be defined in your database and does not require special PL/SQL code. This method of factor resolution requires the use of the constant DBMS_MACUTL.G_IDENTIFY_BY_FACTOR for the parameter **identify_by** in the call to the procedure DBMS_MACADM.CREATE_FACTOR. Multifactored security is really one of the most interesting and powerful security features of DBV. To illustrate this feature, consider the example discussed with the DBV CONNECT command rule, where we placed a greater level of trust in database clients that were either on the database server console itself, and those clients that authenticated to the database using an Oracle Advanced Security Option (ASO) credential mechanism, such as PKI/SSL or Kerberos, from within the corporate network. This example was an all-or-nothing type of authorization that either allowed the database connection or did not allow it. The example did in fact consider multiple factors, the authentication method, and the client's IP address. We can extend this example to use the multifactored approach to classify the database connection as a DBV factor using DBV identity maps. This DBV factor for the connection classification can have more than just TRUE/FALSE identity values that can be used for DBV command rules, DBV realm authorizations, VPD or OLS policies, and even your own PL/SQL logic.

Let's assume the following notional environment conditions:

- We are using ASO's PKI/SSL option for secure connections within the corporate network.
- The corporate network (intranet) is defined by the subnet 192.168.0.

The following table depicts a new DBV factor Connection_Type and its identities. We can define these identities based on these notional environment conditions with the Authentication_Method, Client_IP, and Session_User factors contributing to identify the Connection_Type factor.

Connection_Type Identity	Authentication_Method	Client_IP	Session_User
LOCAL_DBA	OS or PASSWORD	NULL	SYS, SYSTEM
CORPORATE_SSL	SSL	LIKE '192.168.0.%'	%
CORPORATE_PASSWORD	PASSWORD	LIKE '192.168.0.%'	%
OTHER	%	NOT LIKE '192.168.0.%'	%

The approach to identifying factors based on the identity of other factors requires the following steps:

1. Define the factor to be identified by other factors. The factor that is identified by other factors is called the parent factor.
2. Define factor links between the parent and contributing factors. With the DVA web application, this factor linking is done automatically with the underlying DBMS_MACADM APIs.
3. Define the identities for the parent factor.
4. Define factors and identities for all factors that identify the parent factor. The factors that identify the parent factor are called child factors.
5. Define the identity maps that map the identities of the child factors to the parent factor.

First we define the Connection_Type factor, which is our parent factor, with a **get_expr** parameter set to an expression that will resolve to one of our identities for the factor. This is simply a default expression before the other factors are resolved and it should default to our least trusted identity.

```
BEGIN
    dbms_macadm.create_factor(
        factor_name      => 'Connection_Type' ,
        factor_type_name => 'Application',
        description    => 'Categorizes the connection security level.',
        rule_set_name => NULL ,
        get_expr       => 'UPPER(''OTHER'')',
        validate_expr => NULL,
        identify_by    => dbms_macutl.g_identify_by_factor,
        labeled_by     => dbms_macutl.g_labeled_by_self,
        eval_options => dbms_macutl.g_eval_on_session,
        audit_options => dbms_macutl.g_audit_on_get_error,
        fail_options   => dbms_macutl.g_fail_with_message);
END;
/
PL/SQL procedure successfully completed.
```

Next we define factor links that identify all the child factors that could be used in our identity maps (which we will define in a bit) to identify the parent factor. The PL/SQL API should be called for each child factor you plan to use in at least one identity map.

```
dbvowner@aos> -- create a link for the Client IP address
dbvowner@aos> BEGIN
     dbms_macadm.add_factor_link(
parent_factor_name =>'Connection_Type',
        child_factor_name =>'Client_IP',
             label_indicator => 'N');
END;
/
dbvowner@aos> -- create a link for the Authentication Method
dbvowner@aos> BEGIN
     dbms_macadm.add_factor_link(
parent_factor_name =>'Connection_Type',
        child_factor_name =>'Authentication_Method',
             label_indicator => 'N');
END;
/
dbvowner@aos> -- create a link for the Session User
dbvowner@aos> BEGIN
     dbms_macadm.add_factor_link(
parent_factor_name =>'Connection_Type',
        child_factor_name =>'Session_User',
             label_indicator => 'N');
END;
/
PL/SQL procedure successfully completed.
```

The **label_indicator** parameter is required for DBV's integration capability with OLS and should be set to **'N'** (FALSE) by default.

Next we define the identities for the parent factor based on the preceding table. Four possible classifications of the connection are shown next in order of the trust we have in the connection (highest to lowest). The **trust_level** parameter is a number that can be defined at your discretion. The level set for each identity should be indicative the trust you would place on a session that has the identity set relative to sessions with other identities.

```
dbvowner@aos> BEGIN
-- create identity for LOCAL_DBA value
-- or connections on the database console
dbms_macadm.create_identity(factor_name=>'Connection_Type',
     value=>'LOCAL_DBA',trust_level=>4);
-- create identity for CORPORATE_SSL value
-- or connections within the corporate network
-- using PKI/SSL authentication
dbms_macadm.create_identity(factor_name=>'Connection_Type',
     value=>'CORPORATE_SSL',trust_level=>3);
-- create identity for CORPORATE_PASSWORD value
-- or connections within the corporate network
```

```
-- using username/password authentication
dbms_macadm.create_identity(factor_name=>'Connection_Type',
     value=>'CORPORATE_PASSWORD',trust_level=>2);
-- create identity for OTHER value
-- or connections coming from outside the
-- corporate network, such as over a VPN connection
dbms_macadm.create_identity(factor_name=>'Connection_Type',
     value=>'OTHER',trust_level=>1);
END;
/
PL/SQL procedure successfully completed.
```

Next we define the child factors whose identities will be used to resolve the parent factor. The factors that are used in this example are all installed by DBV, so we've saved some time in this case. The Client_IP factor will use the LIKE comparison operator in this example, so we do not need to define identities for this factor. The DBV product installs all the possible identities for the Authentication_Method factor as the following query shows:

```
dbvowner@aos> SELECT factor_name,value
FROM  dvsys.dv$identity
WHERE factor_name = 'Authentication_Method'
ORDER BY factor_name
/
FACTOR_NAME                    VALUE
------------------------------ --------------------
Authentication_Method          DCE
Authentication_Method          KERBEROS
Authentication_Method          NONE
Authentication_Method          OS
Authentication_Method          PASSWORD
Authentication_Method          RADIUS
Authentication_Method          SSL

7 rows selected.
```

The only child factor identities that remain are the trusted accounts we want to define for the database console, SYS and SYSTEM:

```
dbvowner@aos> BEGIN
    dbms_macadm.create_identity(factor_name=>'Session_User',
        value=>'SYS',trust_level=>10);
    dbms_macadm.create_identity(factor_name=>'Session_User',
        value=>'SYSTEM',trust_level=>10);
END;
/
PL/SQL procedure successfully completed.
```

The last set of steps requires us to define a set of identity conditions for the child factors that will resolve each identity of our parent factor. These mappings of child factor identities to the identity of the parent factor are called identity maps. For the LOCAL_DBA identity of the Connection_Type factor, the following identity maps will consider the authentication method, the database client's IP address, and the name of the user:

```
dbvowner@aos> BEGIN
        -- WHEN authenticating by OS, such as / AS SYSDBA,
        -- or by PASSWORD
        dbms_macadm.create_identity_map(
             identity_factor_name => 'Connection_Type'
            , identity_factor_value => 'LOCAL_DBA'
            , parent_factor_name => 'Connection_Type'
            , child_factor_name =>'Authentication_Method'
            , operation => '='
            , operand1 => 'OS'
            , operand2 => NULL               );
        dbms_macadm.create_identity_map(
             identity_factor_name => 'Connection_Type'
            , identity_factor_value => 'LOCAL_DBA'
            , parent_factor_name => 'Connection_Type'
            , child_factor_name =>'Authentication_Method'
            , operation => '='
            , operand1 => 'PASSWORD'
            , operand2 => NULL               );
        -- AND the client IP address is NULL, as is the case
        -- when logging into the database on the console
        -- outside the control of the database listener, or
        -- when the IP address is that of the database server
        -- when coming through the listener.
        dbms_macadm.create_identity_map(
             identity_factor_name => 'Connection_Type'
            , identity_factor_value => 'LOCAL_DBA'
            , parent_factor_name => 'Connection_Type'
            , child_factor_name =>'Client_IP'
            , operation => 'IS NULL'
            , operand1 => 'NULL'
            , operand2 => NULL               );
        dbms_macadm.create_identity_map(
             identity_factor_name => 'Connection_Type'
            , identity_factor_value => 'LOCAL_DBA'
            , parent_factor_name => 'Connection_Type'
            , child_factor_name =>'Client_IP'
            , operation => '='
            , operand1 => '192.168.0.251'
            , operand2 => NULL               );
        -- AND the user is SYS or SYSTEM
        dbms_macadm.create_identity_map(
             identity_factor_name => 'Connection_Type'
            , identity_factor_value => 'LOCAL_DBA'
            , parent_factor_name => 'Connection_Type'
            , child_factor_name =>'Session_User'
            , operation => '='
            , operand1 => 'SYS'
            , operand2 => NULL               );
        dbms_macadm.create_identity_map(
              identity_factor_name => 'Connection_Type'
            , identity_factor_value => 'LOCAL_DBA'
```

```
         , parent_factor_name => 'Connection_Type'
         , child_factor_name =>'Session_User'
         , operation => '='
         , operand1 => 'SYSTEM'
         , operand2 => NULL               );

END;
/
PL/SQL procedure successfully completed.
```

It is important that you understand the processing logic for a DBV identity map that makes use of multiple child factors and more than one factor identity in the map configuration. The preceding map has three child factors that will be evaluated with AND logic. For multiple identities within each child factor, such as the case with the Authentication_Method, Client_IP, and Session_User identities used, the evaluation will use an OR logic within each child factor. In other words, the DBV identity map for the **Connection_Type = 'LOCAL_DBA'** will be TRUE when the following occurs:

```
( Authentication_Method = 'OS' OR Authentication_Method = 'PASSWORD' )
AND ( Client_IP IS NULL OR Client_IP = '192.168.0.251' )
AND (Session_User = 'SYS' OR Session_User = 'SYSTEM')
```

For the CORPORATE_SSL identity, the following identity maps consider the authentication method and the database client's IP address:

```
dbvowner@aos> BEGIN
      -- WHEN the authentication method is PKI/SSL (certificate)
      dbms_macadm.create_identity_map(
           identity_factor_name => 'Connection_Type'
         , identity_factor_value => 'CORPORATE_SSL'
         , parent_factor_name => 'Connection_Type'
         , child_factor_name =>'Authentication_Method'
         , operation => '='
         , operand1 => 'SSL'
         , operand2 => NULL               );
      -- AND the client's IP address is on the corporate network,
      -- which we have defined as the 192.168.0 subnet
      dbms_macadm.create_identity_map(
           identity_factor_name => 'Connection_Type'
         , identity_factor_value => 'CORPORATE_SSL'
         , parent_factor_name => 'Connection_Type'
         , child_factor_name =>'Client_IP'
         , operation => 'LIKE'
         , operand1 => '192.168.0%'
         , operand2 => NULL               );
END;
/
PL/SQL procedure successfully completed.
```

For the CORPORATE_PASSWORD identity, the following identity maps consider the authentication method and the database client's IP address:

```
dbvowner@aos> BEGIN
       -- WHEN the authentication method is PASSWORD
       dbms_macadm.create_identity_map(
            identity_factor_name => 'Connection_Type'
           , identity_factor_value => 'CORPORATE_PASSWORD'
           , parent_factor_name => 'Connection_Type'
           , child_factor_name =>'Authentication_Method'
           , operation => '='
           , operand1 => 'PASSWORD'
           , operand2 => NULL              );
       -- AND the client's IP address is on the corporate network,
       -- which we have defined as the 192.168.0 subnet
       dbms_macadm.create_identity_map(
            identity_factor_name => 'Connection_Type'
           , identity_factor_value => 'CORPORATE_PASSWORD'
           , parent_factor_name => 'Connection_Type'
           , child_factor_name =>'Client_IP'
           , operation => 'LIKE'
           , operand1 => '192.168.0%'
           , operand2 => NULL              );
END;
/
PL/SQL procedure successfully completed.
```

For the OTHER identity, the identity map is simply based on the database client's IP address not being on the 192.168.0 subnet and is coming from some other network:

```
dbvowner@aos> BEGIN
      dbms_macadm.create_identity_map(
            identity_factor_name => 'Connection_Type'
          , identity_factor_value => 'OTHER'
          , parent_factor_name => 'Connection_Type'
          , child_factor_name =>'Client_IP'
          , operation => 'NOT LIKE'
          , operand1 => '192.169.0.%'
          , operand2 => NULL              );
END;
/
PL/SQL procedure successfully completed.

dbvowner@aos>COMMIT;

Commit completed.
```

Now that DBV identity maps are defined, we can test them under various scenarios to understand how they work. If we log in as SYS on the database console, we should expect the Connection_Type factor to resolve to LOCAL_DBA:

```
$ sqlplus / AS SYSDBA
SQL*Plus: Release 11.1.0.6.0 - Production on Sat Feb 21 17:18:04 2009
Copyright (c) 1982, 2007, Oracle.  All rights reserved.
```

```
Connected to:
Oracle Database 11g Enterprise Edition Release 11.1.0.6.0 - 64bit Production
With the Partitioning, Oracle Label Security, OLAP, Data Mining,
Oracle Database Vault and Real Application Testing options
sys@aos> SELECT DVSYS.GET_FACTOR('Connection_Type') Connection_Type
, DVSYS.GET_FACTOR('Authentication_Method') Authentication_Method
, DVSYS.GET_FACTOR('Client_IP') Client_IP
FROM DUAL;

CONNECTION AUTHENTICA CLIENT_IP
---------- ---------- ----------
LOCAL_DBA  OS

1 row selected.
```

If we log in as MARY on the corporate network using password authentication, for example, we should expect the Connection_Type factor to resolve to CORPORATE_PASSWORD:

```
$ sqlplus mary@aos
SQL*Plus: Release 11.1.0.6.0 - Production on Sat Feb 21 17:14:42 2009
Copyright (c) 1982, 2007, Oracle.  All rights reserved.
Enter password:
Connected to:
Oracle Database 11g Enterprise Edition Release 11.1.0.6.0 - 64bit Production
With the Partitioning, Oracle Label Security, OLAP, Data Mining,
Oracle Database Vault and Real Application Testing options
mary@aos>SELECT DVSYS.GET_FACTOR('Connection_Type') Connection_Type
   , DVSYS.GET_FACTOR('Authentication_Method') Authentication_Method
   , DVSYS.GET_FACTOR('Client_IP') Client_IP
   FROM DUAL;

CONNECTION_TYPE      AUTHENTICATION_METHO CLIENT_IP
-------------------- -------------------- --------------------
CORPORATE_PASSWORD   PASSWORD             192.168.0.200

1 row selected.
```

If we log in as MARY over a VPN connection, with an access point external to the corporate network, we should expect the Connection_Type factor to resolve to the value **'OTHER'**:

```
C:\> sqlplus mary@aos
SQL*Plus: Release 11.1.0.6.0 - Production on Sat Feb 21 17:14:42 2009
Copyright (c) 1982, 2007, Oracle.  All rights reserved.
Enter password:
Connected to:
Oracle Database 11g Enterprise Edition Release 11.1.0.6.0 - 64bit Production
With the Partitioning, Oracle Label Security, OLAP, Data Mining,
Oracle Database Vault and Real Application Testing options
mary@aos>SELECT DVSYS.GET_FACTOR('Connection_Type') Connection_Type
   , DVSYS.GET_FACTOR('Authentication_Method') Authentication_Method
   , DVSYS.GET_FACTOR('Client_IP') Client_IP
   FROM DUAL;
```

```
CONNECTION_TYPE      AUTHENTICATION_METHO CLIENT_IP
-------------------- -------------------- --------------------
OTHER                PASSWORD             10.10.10.10

1 row selected.
```

This example demonstrates how to create a security-relevant factor whose foundation is based on multiple (other) factors using a declarative method that required no PL/SQL programming. The factors we used in this example are provided by the database kernel code, but your custom factors could also be used with this approach. You can establish a multifactor security policy when these factors are used DBV rule sets or in your own PL/SQL code.

Consider the DBV CONNECT command rule example presented earlier. In this example, two DBV rules were used to authorize a connection to the database. The rules 'Is Secure Authentication Method' and 'Is Console Client' examined the authentication method and database client's IP address in a manner similar to the way that the Connection_Type factor is identified. We can replace these two DBV rules with a single DBV rule, 'Is Trusted Client', to achieve the same result simply by checking for the factor Connection_Type not being **'OTHER'**, as shown in this example:

```
dbvowner@aos> BEGIN
     dbms_macadm.create_rule(
         rule_name => 'Is Trusted Client'
       , rule_expr =>
     'DVSYS.GET_FACTOR(''Connection_Type'') <> ''OTHER'''
     );
END;
/
PL/SQL procedure successfully completed.
```

To demonstrate multifactor security within PL/SQL, we can create a VPD policy on the CUSTOMERS table in the Sales History (SH) schema. In this policy, we will use the factor in the VPD policy function to provide either column-level or row-level security on the table. First we need to grant a named account the ability to manage VPD policy. The realm owner of the Sales History realm, MARY, is authorized to perform not only administration on objects in the SH object owner account, but she can also perform VPD policy administration on the objects. The only step that is required to enable this VPD administration is to grant MARY execute privileges on the VPD administration package, SYS.DBMS_RLS. This package is protected by the Oracle Database Vault realm and requires the DV_OWNER role to grant the privilege.

```
dbvowner@aos> GRANT EXECUTE ON sys.dbms_rls TO mary;
```

MARY must first create the VPD policy function that will leverage our factor to provide row-level security on the SH.CUSTOMERS table:

```
mary@aos>CREATE OR REPLACE FUNCTION sh.customer_policy_function(
   schema_name IN VARCHAR2
 , table_name IN VARCHAR2 ) RETURN VARCHAR2
AS
BEGIN

    -- prevent access to sensitive customer data
    -- outside of the corporate network
```

```
    IF schema_name = 'SH'
        AND table_name = 'CUSTOMERS' THEN
        -- when the connection type factor is OTHER we know
        -- the database client has not connection from
        -- the corporate network
        IF DVSYS.GET_FACTOR('CONNECTION_TYPE')
                = 'OTHER' THEN
            RETURN '1=0';
        -- for all other connection types allow
        -- access to all rows
        ELSE
            RETURN '1=1';
        END IF;
    END IF;
END;
/
Function created.
```

Next MARY can create a VPD policy using the DBMS_RLS package. In this example policy, we will restrict just the ability to show sensitive columns such as date of birth, marital status, and income outside of the corporate network:

```
mary@aos> BEGIN
    dbms_rls.add_policy(
        object_schema       => 'SH'
        ,object_name        => 'CUSTOMERS'
        ,policy_name        => 'POLICY_CUSTOMERS'
        ,function_schema    => 'SH'
        ,policy_function    => 'CUSTOMER_POLICY_FUNCTION' ||
        ,sec_relevant_cols => 'CUST_GENDER,CUST_YEAR_OF_BIRTH' ||
             ',CUST_MARITAL_STATUS,CUST_INCOME_LEVEL,CUST_CREDIT_LIMIT'
        ,sec_relevant_cols_opt => dbms_rls.all_rows
        );
END;
/
PL/SQL procedure successfully completed.
```

If MARY queries the SH.CUSTOMERS table from within the corporate network, the security sensitive columns are visible:

```
mary@aos> -- show the Connection_Type factor and session context
mary@aos>SELECT DVSYS.GET_FACTOR('Connection_Type') Connection_Type
   , DVSYS.GET_FACTOR('Authentication_Method') Authentication_Method
   , DVSYS.GET_FACTOR('Client_IP') Client_IP
   FROM DUAL;

CONNECTION_TYPE      AUTHENTICATION_METHO CLIENT_IP
-------------------- -------------------- --------------------
CORPORATE_PASSWORD   PASSWORD             192.168.0.200

1 row selected.
```

```
mary@aos> -- query the SH.CUSTOMERS table
mary@aos> SELECT
 cust_last_name
, cust_year_of_birth
, cust_marital_status
, cust_income_level
FROM sh.customers
WHERE cust_state_province = 'TX'
      AND ROWNUM < 10
ORDER BY cust_last_name
/
CUST_LAST_ CUST_YEAR_OF_BIRTH CUST_MARIT CUST_INCOME_LEVEL
---------- ------------------ ---------- -------------------------
Beiers                   1982 single     K: 250,000 - 299,999
Duval                    1981 single     H: 150,000 - 169,999
Greeley                  1977            F: 110,000 - 129,999
Grover                   1970 married    D: 70,000 - 89,999
Hamilton                 1961 single     G: 130,000 - 149,999
Krider                   1967            F: 110,000 - 129,999
Majors                   1948 single     G: 130,000 - 149,999
Rowley                   1969 single     H: 150,000 - 169,999
Stone                    1978 single     I: 170,000 - 189,999
9 rows selected.
```

If MARY queries the SH.CUSTOMERS table from outside the corporate network, the security sensitive columns are not visible and VPD will set them to NULL in the result set returned:

```
mary@aos> -- show the Connection_Type factor and session context
mary@aos>SELECT DVSYS.GET_FACTOR('Connection_Type') Connection_Type
   , DVSYS.GET_FACTOR('Authentication_Method') Authentication_Method
   , DVSYS.GET_FACTOR('Client_IP') Client_IP
   FROM DUAL;

CONNECTION_TYPE      AUTHENTICATION_METHO CLIENT_IP
-------------------- -------------------- --------------------
OTHER                PASSWORD             10.10.10.10

1 row selected.

mary@aos> -- query the SH.CUSTOMERS table
mary@aos> SELECT
 cust_last_name
, cust_year_of_birth
, cust_marital_status
, cust_income_level
FROM sh.customers
WHERE cust_state_province = 'TX'
      AND ROWNUM < 10
ORDER BY cust_last_name
/
```

```
CUST_LAST_ CUST_YEAR_OF_BIRTH CUST_MARIT CUST_INCOME_LEVEL
---------- ------------------ ---------- -------------------------
Beiers
Duval
Greeley
Grover
Hamilton
Krider
Majors
Rowley
Stone
9 rows selected.
```

This example demonstrated column-level security using DBV factors and VPD. It is important to note that you can filter the records (row-level security) on the same table with the same approach. You can do this by omitting the **sec_relevant_cols** and **sec_relevant_cols_opt** parameters to the DBMS_RLS.ADD_POLICY procedure call. With this approach, MARY would not have been able to see any records (no rows selected) when querying the SH.CUSTOMERS tables outside the corporate network.

DBV Factor Integration with OLS

DBV includes a feature that allows you to associate DBV identities with OLS labels. When a specific DBV identity is asserted for a session, the OLS label associated with the identity will be merged with the maximum label that is assigned to the user. The merge operation is controlled by an OLS merge algorithm configured by the DBV security administrator. The merge results in an effective OLS session label that cannot be "upgraded" by the user because of the integrated access control of DBV and OLS. Even if the label assigned to the user exceeds the label of the DBV identity, the effective OLS label could be "downgraded" by the label of the DBV identity. The OLS session label controls the records that a user can SELECT, INSERT, UPDATE, or DELETE when OLS labels are applied to data tables.

To illustrate this integration, suppose we have an OLS policy that defines labels with which we will categorize customer data records (SH.CUSTOMERS) based on their credit limit. We categorized the credit limits as shown in the table:

Credit Limit Category	Credit Limit Range
LOW	Less than $5000
MODERATE	Between $5000 and $9999
HIGH	Greater than or equal to $10,000

We can associate these OLS labels with the DBV identities we defined for the Connection_ Type factor used in the preceding section to establish an effective session label for OLS based on the identity that is set by DBV. We will prevent any session from accessing customer data records labeled as HIGH when the database session has come from outside the corporate network (**Connection_Type = 'OTHER'**). The following table summarizes the rules we will establish:

Connection_Type Identity	Effective Session Label for OLS
LOCAL_DBA	HIGH
CORPORATE_SSL	HIGH
CORPORATE_PASSWORD	HIGH
OTHER	LOW

The steps to achieve this type of integration are as follows:

1. Define the OLS policy's components and labels.
2. Create a column for the OLS label to be stored, and label the data records that will be protected.
3. Apply the OLS policy to the tables to be protected.
4. Assign an OLS label range to the users that require access to the data.
5. Enable the OLS policy within DBV and define the merge algorithm.
6. Define the DBV factors whose identities will be merged with the default OLS session label for a user.
7. Associate OLS labels from the policy to each DBV identity.

We can implement an OLS policy for our example by simply defining three OLS level components and three OLS labels using the LBACSYS account. The LBACSYS account is the object-owner account for the OLS option.

```
lbacsys@aos> -- first create the OLS policy with the
lbacsys@aos> -- name of the column to store the label
lbacsys@aos> -- in and the default access control options
lbacsys@aos> BEGIN
    sa_sysdba.create_policy(
        policy_name     => 'CUSTOMER_POLICY'
      , column_name     => 'CUSTOMER_LABEL'
      , default_options =>'READ_CONTROL,WRITE_CONTROL,CHECK_CONTROL'
      );
END;
/
PL/SQL procedure successfully completed.
lbacsys@aos> -- create the OLS levels for the
lbacsys@aos> -- customer policy
lbacsys@aos> BEGIN
    -- customers with a low credit limit
    sa_components.create_level(
        policy_name=> 'CUSTOMER_POLICY'
      , level_num  => 10
      , short_name => 'LOW'
      , long_name  => 'LOW CREDIT LIMIT'
      );
```

```
    -- customers with a moderate credit limit
    sa_components.create_level(
        policy_name=> 'CUSTOMER_POLICY'
      , level_num  => 20
      , short_name => 'MODERATE'
      , long_name  => 'MODERATE CREDIT LIMIT'
      );
    -- customers with a high credit limit
    sa_components.create_level(
        policy_name=> 'CUSTOMER_POLICY'
      , level_num  => 30
      , short_name => 'HIGH'
      , long_name  => 'HIGH CREDIT LIMIT'
      );
END;
/
PL/SQL procedure successfully completed.
lbacsys@aos> -- create the OLS labels for the
lbacsys@aos> -- customer policy
lbacsys@aos> BEGIN
    -- customers with a low credit limit
    sa_label_admin.create_label(
        policy_name => 'CUSTOMER_POLICY'
      , label_tag   => 10
      , label_value => 'LOW'
      );
    -- customers with a moderate credit limit
    sa_label_admin.create_label(
        policy_name => 'CUSTOMER_POLICY'
      , label_tag   => 20
      , label_value => 'MODERATE'
      );
    -- customers with a high credit limit
    sa_label_admin.create_label(
        policy_name => 'CUSTOMER_POLICY'
      , label_tag   => 30
      , label_value => 'HIGH'
      );
END;
/
PL/SQL procedure successfully completed.
```

Note that OLS compartment and group components work with the DBV/OLS integration, but this example will simply use OLS level components. We can now create a column named CUSTOMER_LABEL in the SH_CUSTOMERS table. This column name was specified in the call to SA_SYSDBA.CREATE_POLICY earlier. This column will hold the OLS label number for each data record and is a requirement for OLS. The label numbers were defined in the calls to SA_LABEL_ADMIN.CREATE_LABEL. We will first remove the VPD policy on SH.CUSTOMERS table that we had created in the preceding example, then add the new label column, and then populate the data records with the appropriate label number. Note that Oracle supports the condition in which multiple VPD and OLS policies exist and interoperate on a single table. We are simply removing the example here to clarify that a single access control policy is active. The DBV realm administrator, MARY, of the Sales History realm can perform these steps.

```
mary@aos> -- remove the VPD example from the previous example
mary@aos> BEGIN
    dbms_rls.drop_policy(
        object_schema      => 'SH'
        ,object_name       => 'CUSTOMERS'
        ,policy_name       => 'POLICY_CUSTOMERS'
        );
END;
/
PL/SQL procedure successfully completed.

mary@aos>-- add the column to the customer table
mary@aos>-- to hold the OLS security label
mary@aos> ALTER TABLE sh.customers ADD customer_label NUMBER;
Table altered.

mary@aos> -- populate the customer_label column with the appropriate
mary@aos> --  data label for LOW credit limit customers
mary@aos> UPDATE sh.customers SET customer_label = 10
WHERE cust_credit_limit < 5000;

19309 rows updated.

mary@aos> -- populate the customer_label column with the appropriate
mary@aos> --  data label for MODERATE credit limit customers
mary@aos> UPDATE sh.customers SET customer_label = 20
WHERE cust_credit_limit BETWEEN 5000 AND 9999;

25451 rows updated.

mary@aos> -- populate the customer_label column with the appropriate
mary@aos> --  data label for HIGH credit limit customers
mary@aos> UPDATE sh.customers SET customer_label = 30
WHERE cust_credit_limit >= 10000;
 10740 rows updated.

mary@aos> -- save the data changes
mary@aos>COMMIT;

Commit complete.
```

The next step is to use the LBACSYS account to apply our OLS policy to the SH.CUSTOMERS. This will provide the label-based access control protection on the table for any subsequent SELECT, INSERT, UPDATE, or DELETE transactions on the table. To perform this step, we must consider that OLS places Oracle database triggers on tables that are being protected. These triggers are used to ensure that labels for new data records are provided and will perform auditing for OLS operations on the protected tables. The SH.CUSTOMERS table is protected by the Sales History realm that will obviously prevent these CREATE TRIGGER statements from completing successfully. The best approach to handling this is to authorize the LBACSYS account in the Sales History realm as a participant rather than disabling the realm altogether.

```
dbvowner@aos> -- authorize LBACSYS in the Sales History realm
dbvowner@aos> BEGIN
  dbms_macadm.add_auth_to_realm (
      realm_name    =>'Sales History'
    , grantee       => 'LBACSYS'
    , rule_set_name => NULL
    , auth_options  => dbms_macutl.g_realm_auth_participant );
END;
/
PL/SQL procedure successfully completed.

dbvowner@aos>connect lbacsys
Enter password:
Connected.

lbacsys@aos> -- apply the OLS policy to the customer
lbacsys@aos> -- table with the table-specific
lbacsys@aos> -- access control options
lbacsys@aos> BEGIN
    sa_policy_admin.apply_table_policy(
        policy_name   => 'CUSTOMER_POLICY'
      , schema_name   => 'SH'
      , table_name    => 'CUSTOMERS'
      , table_options => 'READ_CONTROL,WRITE_CONTROL,CHECK_CONTROL'
      );
END;
/
PL/SQL procedure successfully completed.
```

At this point in the configuration, the DBV Sales History realm administrator, MARY, cannot query data in the SH.CUSTOMERS table.

```
mary@aos> SELECT
 cust_last_name
, cust_year_of_birth
, cust_marital_status
, cust_income_level
FROM sh.customers
WHERE cust_state_province = 'TX'
      AND ROWNUM < 1
ORDER BY cust_last_name
/
no rows selected
```

We have to assign MARY a label range in the OLS policy using the LBACSYS account. We want to provide MARY full access to all records in the SH.CUSTOMERS table so the range that will be assigned to her will be LOW–HIGH.

```
-- assign the labels ranges of data
-- records that MARY can read and write
```

```
BEGIN
    sa_user_admin.set_user_labels(
         policy_name     => 'CUSTOMER_POLICY'
       , user_name       => 'MARY'
       , min_write_label => 'LOW'
       , max_read_label  => 'HIGH'
       , max_write_label => 'HIGH'
       , def_label       => 'HIGH'
       , row_label       => 'HIGH'
       );
END;
/
PL/SQL procedure successfully completed.
```

As a result of this label range assignment, MARY can now access the records in the SH.CUSTOMERS table.

```
mary@aos> -- query the SH.CUSTOMERS table
mary@aos> SELECT
 cust_last_name
, cust_year_of_birth
, cust_marital_status
, cust_income_level
FROM sh.customers
WHERE cust_state_province = 'TX'
      AND ROWNUM < 10
ORDER BY cust_last_name
/
CUST_LAST_ CUST_YEAR_OF_BIRTH CUST_MARIT CUST_INCOME_LEVEL
---------- ------------------ ---------- -------------------------
Beiers                   1982 single     K: 250,000 - 299,999
Duval                    1981 single     H: 150,000 - 169,999
Greeley                  1977            F: 110,000 - 129,999
Grover                   1970 married    D: 70,000 - 89,999
Hamilton                 1961 single     G: 130,000 - 149,999
Krider                   1967            F: 110,000 - 129,999
Majors                   1948 single     G: 130,000 - 149,999
Rowley                   1969 single     H: 150,000 - 169,999
Stone                    1978 single     I: 170,000 - 189,999
9 rows selected.
```

Having defined the OLS policy for the table, we want to protect and authorize the named users in this OLS policy, and we can remove the realm authorization for the LBACSYS account in the Sales History realm. We can also identify this OLS policy as being integrated with DBV using the PL/SQL procedure DBMS_MACADM.CREATE_MAC_POLICY.

```
dbvowner@aos> -- remove the realm authorization for LBACSYS
dbvowner@aos> -- as we've applied the policy on the table
dbvowner@aos> BEGIN
  dbms_macadm.delete_auth_from_realm (
      realm_name    =>'Sales History'
    , grantee       => 'LBACSYS'
    );
```

```
END;
/
PL/SQL procedure successfully completed.

dbvowner@aos> -- enable the OLS policy within DBV and
dbvowner@aos> -- define the merge algorithm
BEGIN
     dbms_macadm.create_mac_policy(
        policy_name => 'CUSTOMER_POLICY'
      , algorithm   => 'LII'
      );
END;
/
PL/SQL procedure successfully completed.
```

The algorithm LII means "Least upper-bound of all levels, Intersection of compartments, Intersection of groups." This algorithm is the most appropriate and most commonly used algorithm in commercial and government systems. This algorithm and others are available with OLS and are described in the "Label Security Administrator's Guide" should you need to research them for your application's needs. In our example, this algorithm basically means that the merging of the label LOW with a label of HIGH will result in LOW, or the least upper-bound of the levels. We now need to configure DBV with the name(s) of the DBV factor(s) whose identities will be merged with the default OLS session label for a user using this algorithm. Here we are simply using one factor, Connection_Type, and will use the PL/SQL procedure DBMS_MACADM.ADD_POLICY_FACTOR to accomplish this.

```
dbvowner@aos> BEGIN
     dbms_macadm.add_policy_factor(
        policy_name => 'CUSTOMER_POLICY'
      , factor_name => 'Connection_Type'
      );
END;
/
PL/SQL procedure successfully completed.
```

Note that the DBV integration with OLS does in fact support the merging of multiple factors with OLS. The final step in our configuration is to associate an OLS label from the policy to each DBV identity for the DBV factor Connection_Type. This can be accomplished using the PL/SQL procedure DBMS_MACADM.CREATE_POLICY_LABEL:

```
dbvowner@aos> -- we will assign the LOCAL_DBA identity
dbvowner@aos> -- an OLS label of HIGH
dbvowner@aos> BEGIN
     dbms_macadm.CREATE_POLICY_LABEL(
        identity_factor_name  =>  'Connection_Type'
      , identity_factor_value => 'LOCAL_DBA'
      , policy_name           => 'CUSTOMER_POLICY'
      , label                 => 'HIGH'
      );
END;
/
PL/SQL procedure successfully completed.
```

```
dbvowner@aos> -- we will assign the CORPORATE_SSL identity
dbvowner@aos> -- an OLS label of HIGH
dbvowner@aos> BEGIN
     dbms_macadm.CREATE_POLICY_LABEL(
        identity_factor_name  =>  'Connection_Type'
      , identity_factor_value => 'CORPORATE_SSL'
      , policy_name           => 'CUSTOMER_POLICY'
      , label                 => 'HIGH'
      );
END;
/
PL/SQL procedure successfully completed.

dbvowner@aos> -- we will assign the CORPORATE_PASSWORD identity
dbvowner@aos> -- an OLS label of HIGH
dbvowner@aos> BEGIN
     dbms_macadm.CREATE_POLICY_LABEL(
        identity_factor_name  =>  'Connection_Type'
      , identity_factor_value => 'CORPORATE_PASSWORD'
      , policy_name           => 'CUSTOMER_POLICY'
      , label                 => 'HIGH'
      );
END;
/
PL/SQL procedure successfully completed.

dbvowner@aos> -- we will assign the OTHER identity
dbvowner@aos> -- an OLS label of LOW
dbvowner@aos> BEGIN
     dbms_macadm.CREATE_POLICY_LABEL(
        identity_factor_name  =>  'Connection_Type'
      , identity_factor_value => 'OTHER'
      , policy_name           => 'CUSTOMER_POLICY'
      , label                 => 'LOW'
      );
END;
/
PL/SQL procedure successfully completed.

dbvowner@aos> COMMIT;
Commit complete.
```

We now want to examine how our policy behaves using the scenario in which MARY is querying the SH.CUSTOMERS table from within the corporate network. In this scenario, we expect MARY to be able to see all customers no matter what their credit limit. In addition, we expect the effective OLS session label to be the maximum label MARY is authorized to see—HIGH.

```
mary@aos> -- show the Connection_Type factor and session context
mary@aos>SELECT DVSYS.GET_FACTOR('Connection_Type') Connection_Type
   , DVSYS.GET_FACTOR('Authentication_Method') Authentication_Method
   , DVSYS.GET_FACTOR('Client_IP') Client_IP
   FROM DUAL;
```

```
CONNECTION_TYPE      AUTHENTICATION_METHO CLIENT_IP
-------------------- -------------------- --------------------
CORPORATE_PASSWORD   PASSWORD             192.168.0.200
1 row selected.

mary@aos> -- query MARY's OLS authorization and
mary@aos> -- the effective OLS session label
mary@aos> SELECT sa_session.label('CUSTOMER_POLICY')
       "EFFECTIVE_SESSION_LABEL"
FROM DUAL;

EFFECTIVE_SESSION_LABEL
-----------------------
HIGH
1 row selected.

mary@aos> -- query the SH.CUSTOMERS table
mary@aos> SELECT
 cust_credit_limit
 , count(*)
FROM sh.customers
GROUP BY cust_credit_limit
ORDER BY cust_credit_limit
/
CUST_CREDIT_LIMIT   COUNT(*)
----------------- ----------
             1500      11334
             3000       7975
             5000       7724
             7000       8634
             9000       9093
            10000       5935
            11000       2935
            15000       1870
8 rows selected.
```

Next we want to examine how our policy behaves when MARY is querying the SH.CUSTOMERS table from outside the corporate network. In this scenario, we expect MARY to be able to see only customers with a credit limit of LOW. In addition, we expect the effective OLS session label to be the maximum label MARY is authorized to see—LOW.

```
mary@aos> -- show the Connection_Type factor and session context
mary@aos>SELECT DVSYS.GET_FACTOR('Connection_Type') Connection_Type
   , DVSYS.GET_FACTOR('Authentication_Method') Authentication_Method
   , DVSYS.GET_FACTOR('Client_IP') Client_IP
   FROM DUAL;

CONNECTION_TYPE      AUTHENTICATION_METHO CLIENT_IP
-------------------- -------------------- --------------------
OTHER                PASSWORD             10.10.10.10
```

```
1 row selected.

mary@aos> -- query MARY's OLS authorization and
mary@aos> -- the effective OLS session label
mary@aos> SELECT sa_session.label('CUSTOMER_POLICY')
      "EFFECTIVE_SESSION_LABEL"
FROM DUAL;

EFFECTIVE_SESSION_LABEL
-----------------------
LOW
1 row selected.

mary@aos> -- query the SH.CUSTOMERS table
mary@aos> SELECT
 cust_credit_limit
 , count(*)
FROM sh.customers
GROUP BY cust_credit_limit
ORDER BY cust_credit_limit
/
CUST_CREDIT_LIMIT   COUNT(*)
----------------- ----------
             1500      11334
             3000       7975
2 rows selected.
```

As you can see, even though MARY is in fact authorized to see data records labeled as HIGH and MODERATE, when she connects to the database from outside the corporate network, the integration of this OLS policy with DBV factors prevents this access. This integration allows us to mediate row-level access controls policies such as OLS with environmental factors such as the network path a client used to connect to the database, the method of authentication, or both. This integration capability truly is multifactored security.

When we started our discussion on the DBV and OLS integration, we made the assertion that the effective OLS session label established by this integration could not be "upgraded" by the user. We can demonstrate this by attempting to set the session label to the maximum label the user is authorized to see using the OLS PL/SQL procedure SA_SESSION.SET_LABEL within the context of the session MARY established outside of the corporate network:

```
mary@aos> -- show the Connection_Type factor and session context
mary@aos>SELECT DVSYS.GET_FACTOR('Connection_Type') Connection_Type
   , DVSYS.GET_FACTOR('Authentication_Method') Authentication_Method
   , DVSYS.GET_FACTOR('Client_IP') Client_IP
   FROM DUAL;

CONNECTION_TYPE      AUTHENTICATION_METHO CLIENT_IP
-------------------- -------------------- --------------------
OTHER                PASSWORD             10.10.10.10

1 row selected.
```

```
mary@aos> -- query MARY's OLS authorization and
mary@aos> -- the effective OLS session label
mary@aos> SELECT sa_session.label('CUSTOMER_POLICY')
      "EFFECTIVE_SESSION_LABEL"
FROM DUAL;

EFFECTIVE_SESSION_LABEL
-----------------------
LOW
1 row selected.

mary@aos> -- attempt to set the session label to HIGH
mary@aos> -- which MARY is in fact authorized but the
mary@aos> -- session, under DBV control, is not
mary@aos> EXECUTE sa_session.set_label('CUSTOMER_POLICY','HIGH');
BEGIN sa_session.set_label('CUSTOMER_POLICY','HIGH'); END;
*
ERROR at line 1:
ORA-47905: OLS policy label HIGH is not allowed for policy CUSTOMER_POLICY
ORA-06512: at "DVSYS.DBMS_MACUTL", line 38
ORA-06512: at "DVSYS.DBMS_MACUTL", line 381
ORA-06512: at "DVSYS.DBMS_MACOLS_SESSION", line 116
ORA-06512: at line 1
ORA-06512: at "LBACSYS.SA_SESSION", line 415
ORA-06512: at "LBACSYS.SA_SESSION", line 426
ORA-06512: at line 1
(2 Factor Assignment
```

DBV factors can be configured to allow the identity to be assigned by a database session at runtime using the procedure DVSYS.SET_FACTOR. This feature may seem a little scary at first glance, as we must use caution designing application security around information provided by the client. The assignment of a DBV factor's identity, if configured, is controlled by a DBV rule set that must be true for the assignment to be authorized.

Accepting client information in an application is a common practice in Oracle database applications. For example, many three-tier systems (client, application server, database server) rely on the use of database connection pools from the application server to the database server. These connection pools use a dedicated database account and need a mechanism to assert information about the client (such as the identity of the user) as discussed in Chapter 1. The organization maintaining the application may not have the option to migrate the application to use Oracle Enterprise User Security (EUS) and Oracle Proxy Authentication, but the audit attribution is still required for any database actions performed on behalf of the user.

The use of techniques such as setting CLIENT_IDENTIFIER through DBMS_SESSION.SET_IDENTIFIER are standards used in many applications where information is accepted from the client to ensure the audit attribution, because this CLIENT_IDENTIFIER information is tracked within the standard Oracle RDMS audit trail. Another common practice in Oracle database applications is for developers to create an Oracle application context, and the associated PL/SQL package, using the **CREATE CONTEXT *<context_name>* USING *<package name>*** command. These application contexts are used to track information through the lifetime of the database session so that a "session variable" can be set at one point in time and accessed at a later point in time in the session. This technique is often used in conjunction with Oracle VPD policy functions.

DBV factor assignment offers the ability to support the CLIENT_IDENTIFIER technique and the requirements of Oracle application contexts with the following benefits:

- The ability to assign the information is controlled by a DBV rule set rather than being an open API. In other words, nothing prevents a database session in SQL*Plus from using DBMS_SESSION.SET_IDENTIFIER to masquerade the session's activity as another end user from the perspective of the audit trail. The use of a DBV rule set provides your security administrator with a mechanism to control the sessions and the conditions that will allow the assignment. The level of trust is specific to your application environment.
- The approach requires less overhead and maintenance because the application developer does not need to create a new application context or supporting PL/SQL package. These database objects are already provided by DBV factors.
- The assignment can leverage DBV factor validation to ensure that the data assigned meets the criteria required by the application.

DBV factor assignment can be audited through the use of the audit configuration of the DBV rule set that controls the assignment. DBV factor assignment can also be audited in the same manner that auditing the execution of DBMS_SESSION or an application context's PL/SQL package, which is to AUDIT EXECUTE ON DVSYS.SET_FACTOR.

To illustrate DBV factor assignment, consider the following scenario (see Figure 5-11). A web-based Sales History application is running on an application server. The application uses a dedicated account for connection pool and the application uses DBMS_SESSION.SET_IDENTIFIER to assert the real end user for audit attribution. To use DBV factor assignment in lieu of DBMS_SESSION.SET_IDENTIFIER, we need to create a DBV factor and determine the conditions that must be met to authorize the assignment of this factor in a DBV rule set. We can use database session context information that is available when ASO PKI/SSL authentication is used from the application server to the database as a basis for these conditions. We can place some level of trust in the session because both the application server and database server must be configured to participate in a PKI trust relationship using Oracle wallets (something we have). If the organization's certificate authority (CA) and PKI controls are sound and the physical access to the machines is controlled, we can place an even greater level of trust in the use of this information. The added benefit of the configuration is that all the network communications between the application server and the database server (in support of database session) are encrypted.

For the sake of brevity, let's assume we have configured ASO PKI/SSL authentication between our application server and database server.

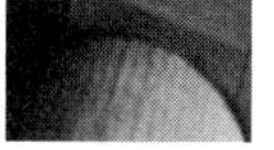

NOTE

If you would like more details on how to set up this type of authentication for the enterprise and a formal CA, read Oracle Metalink note "736510.1 - Step by Step Guide to Configure SSL Authentication". If you want to set up a development capability quickly using self-signed Oracle wallets, refer to Oracle Metalink note "762286.1 - End to End Examples of Using SSL with Oracle's JDBC THIN Driver" or the white paper "SSL With Oracle JDBC Thin Driver" available on the Oracle Technology Network (OTN) at www.oracle.com/technology/tech/java/sqlj_jdbc/pdf/wp-oracle-jdbc_thin_ssl_2007.pdf. These resources will walk you through how the steps to create and configure your Oracle wallets and the Oracle networking files for ASO PKI/SSL authentication.

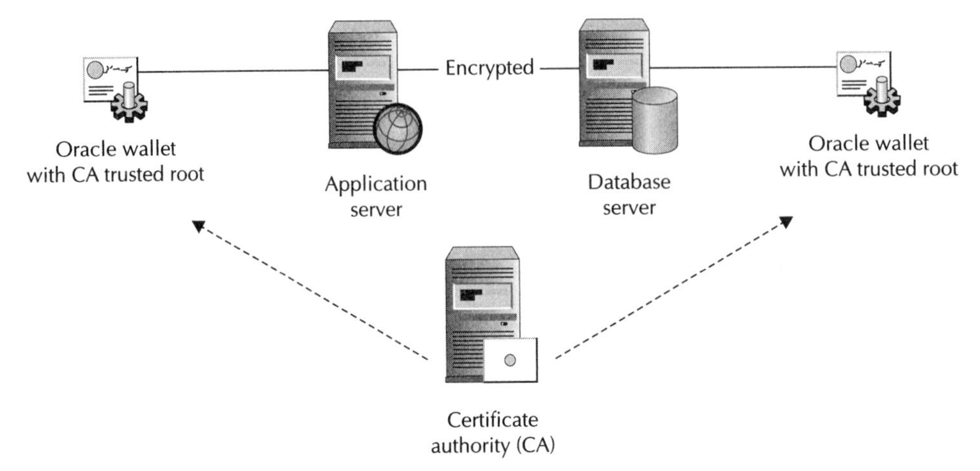

FIGURE 5-11 *Oracle Advanced Security certificate usage*

Once configured, we can create the database account that is identified based on the client's (our application server) wallet credentials as follows:

```
dbvacctmgr@aos> -- create the account
dbvacctmgr@aos> CREATE USER ops$appserver_1
IDENTIFIED EXTERNALLY AS 'CN=appserver_1';
User created.
dbvacctmgr@aos> -- provide the ability to connect to the database
dbvacctmgr@aos> CONNECT / AS SYSDBA
Connected.
sys@aos> GRANT CREATE SESSION TO ops$appserver_1;
Grant succeeded.
```

Creating this type of account requires the database initialization parameter setting **OS_AUTHENT_PREFIX=ops$**, where **ops$** can be customized for the particular environment.

Once we have created this account, we can connect to the database to examine the type of session context information that can be used as conditions in our DBV rule set. Database authentication using ASO/PKI will expose the use of the Oracle Secure Transmission Control Protocol (TCPS), the authentication method, the subject of the certificate, and the context of the X.509 certificate (in HEX2 format) in the session context information.

```
ops$appserver_1@aos>-- query the network protocol
ops$appserver_1@aos>SELECT SYS_CONTEXT('USERENV','NETWORK_PROTOCOL')
"NETWORK PROTCOL" FROM DUAL;

NETWORK PROTCOL
----------------------------------------------------------------------
tcps
1 row selected.

ops$appserver_1@aos>-- query the authentication method
ops$appserver_1@aos>SELECT SYS_CONTEXT('USERENV','AUTHENTICATION_METHOD')
"AUTHENTICATION METHOD" FROM DUAL;
```

```
AUTHENTICATION METHOD
-----------------------------------------------------------------------
SSL
1 row selected.

ops$appserver_1@aos>-- query the subject of the X.509 certificate
ops$appserver_1@aos>SELECT SYS_CONTEXT('USERENV','AUTHENTICATED_IDENTITY') "X.509
ERTIFICATE SUBJECT" FROM DUAL;

X.509 CERTIFICATE SUBJECT
-----------------------------------------------------------------------
CN=appserver_1
1 row selected.

ops$appserver_1@aos>-- query the context of the X.509 certificate
ops$appserver_1@aos>SELECT SYS_CONTEXT('USERENV','AUTHENTICATION_DATA') "X.509 CERTIFICATE
CONTEXT" FROM DUAL;

X.509 CERTIFICATE CONTEXT
-----------------------------------------------------------------------
3082019B3082010402010030 0D06092A864886F70D01010405003016311430120603550403 0C0B61
70707365727665725F31301E170D3039303232353037303231315A170D3139303232333037303231
315A30163114301206035504030C0B6170707365727665725F3130819F300D06092A864886F70D01
0101050003818D00
1 row selected.
```

In reviewing the session context information available under ASO/PKI authentication, we find that the network protocol is set to TCPS versus the typical TCP protocol. In addition, the authentication data that returns the X.509 certificate context will be unique for each wallet issued by our CA, so we can leverage this information to identify a client uniquely with the correct wallet.

Using the network protocol and certificate context is another example of using multiple factors in your database security policy. This policy cannot replace physical security that protects the Oracle wallets from theft and defensive measures such as using the invited nodes feature of the listener to control the machines that can connect to the listener.

The next step is for the DBV security administrator (DBVOWNER) to create a factor for the X.509 certificate context from the read-only session context maintained by the Oracle kernel. DBV is installed with a DBV factor for the network protocol, so we do not need to define it to use it in a DBV rule.

```
dbvowner@aos> BEGIN
    dbms_macadm.create_factor(
        factor_name      => 'Certificate_Context' ,
        factor_type_name => 'Authentication Method',
        description    =>
             'Retrieves the context of the X.509 certificate'
                   ||' when used with the TCPS network protocol.',
        rule_set_name => NULL ,
        get_expr      => 'SUBSTR(SYS_CONTEXT(''USERENV'',''AUTHENTICATION_DATA''),1,255)',
        validate_expr => NULL,
        identify_by   => dbms_macutl.g_identify_by_method,
        labeled_by    => dbms_macutl.g_labeled_by_self,
        eval_options => dbms_macutl.g_eval_on_access,
        audit_options => dbms_macutl.g_audit_on_get_error,
        fail_options  => dbms_macutl.g_fail_with_message);
END;
/
PL/SQL procedure successfully completed.
```

The next step is to create our DBV rule set components that will control the assignment of the factor we create to store the Sales History application end user name. The DBV rules will leverage the DBV factors we've chosen.

```
dbvowner@aos> -- create the rule that checks for an authorized client
dbvowner@aos> -- certificate context
dbvowner@aos> DECLARE
 l_certificate_context VARCHAR2(1024) :=
      '3082019B30820104020100300D06092A864886F'
   || '70D0101040500301631143012060355040300C0B61'
   || '70707365727665725F31301E170D30393032323530'
   || '37303231315A170D313930323233037303231'
   || '315A301631143012060355040300C0B617070736572'
   || '7665725F3130819F300D06092A864886F70D01'
   || '0101050003818D0';
BEGIN
     dbms_macadm.create_rule(
          rule_name => 'Is Valid Certificate'
        , rule_expr => 'NVL(DVF.F$Certificate_Context,''0'') IN ('''
          || l_certificate_context
          || ''')'
        );
END;
/
PL/SQL procedure successfully completed.

dbvowner@aos> -- create a rule that checks for a valid network protocol
dbvowner@aos> BEGIN
     dbms_macadm.create_rule(
          rule_name => 'Is TCPS Protocol'
        , rule_expr => 'NVL(DVF.F$Network_Protocol,''0'') = ''TCPS'''
        );
END;
/
PL/SQL procedure successfully completed.

dbvowner@aos> -- finally create a rule set that will group our rules
dbvowner@aos> -- that allow session assignment. We will audit all
dbvowner@aos> -- evaluations for the rule set for our demonstration
dbvowner@aos> BEGIN
    dbms_macadm.create_rule_set(
        rule_set_name =>'Can Assign Client Identifier',
        description =>
      'Checks to verify that a DBV-based client identifier can be set.',
        enabled =>dbms_macutl.g_yes,
        eval_options =>dbms_macutl.g_ruleset_eval_all,
        audit_options =>dbms_macutl.g_ruleset_audit_fail +
                dbms_macutl.g_ruleset_audit_success,
        fail_options =>dbms_macutl.g_ruleset_fail_show,
        fail_message =>NULL,
```

```
        fail_code =>NULL,
        handler_options =>dbms_macutl.g_ruleset_handler_off,
        handler =>NULL);
END;
/
PL/SQL procedure successfully completed.

dbvowner@aos> -- associate the client certificate rule to the rule set
BEGIN
   dbms_macadm.add_rule_to_rule_set (
     rule_set_name => 'Can Assign Client Identifier'
   , rule_name     => 'Is Valid Certificate'
   );
END;
/
PL/SQL procedure successfully completed.

dbvowner@aos> -- associate the network protocol rule to the rule set
BEGIN
   dbms_macadm.add_rule_to_rule_set (
     rule_set_name => 'Can Assign Client Identifier'
   , rule_name     => 'Is TCPS Protocol'
   );
END;
/
PL/SQL procedure successfully completed.

COMMIT;
Commit complete.
```

Given the fact that wallets can be changed as part of key management and more than one application server would be in use, we would want to store the certificates in a table (protected by a DBV realm). The rule 'Is Valid Certificate' is written for brevity's sake, and it would be more ideal to create PL/SQL function for this rule and query the table of certificates. The goal of our example is to provide an alternative form of the procedure DBMS_SESSION.SET_IDENTIFIER that is based on trust. We cannot implement a separate capability that reproduces the behavior that CLIENT_IDENTIFIER is audited in the core RDBMS audit trail, SYSTEM.AUD$. In fact, we do not have to reproduce it. DBV factors will still let us use the native capability using a feature called factor validation.

Factor Validation

DBV factors can also be configured to allow for the identity of a factor to be validated with a callout to a PL/SQL routine. This PL/SQL routine will be called whenever the function **DVSYS.GET_FACTOR** is called, the **DVF.F$** factor function is called, or the **DVSYS.SET_FACTOR** function is called. With this mechanism, we could establish a "trust but verify" model whereby DBV can verify that the identity is correct with respect to our own rules. In our example, the factor assignment may be authorized but we might also have a requirement to validate the end user value set against a table that contains user names. If the identity fails validation, it will be set to NULL so that other areas of DBV policy, such as subsequent use of the DBV factor in a DBV rule set, can handle this fact. This validation routine could also include all of the logic we might normally place in the PL/SQL package that supports an Oracle application context in use by an organization.

To implement this feature, we simply need to define a PL/SQL function with the following signature:

```
FUNCTION IS_VALID(p_factor_value VARCHAR2) RETURN BOOLEAN
```

The following example code demonstrates how a very simple validation function may be defined for our scenario that uses DBMS_SESSION.SET_IDENTIFIER to preserve the audit behavior it provides:

```
mary@aos> CREATE OR REPLACE FUNCTION sh.valid_client_identifier(
    p_factor_value IN VARCHAR2
    ) RETURN BOOLEAN IS
BEGIN
    -- a simple mechanism to test for a valid factor identity
    IF p_factor_value IS NULL OR
       p_factor_value = '0' THEN
       -- for demonstration let's populate CLIENT IDENTIFIER
       dbms_session.set_identifier('ANONYMOUS SALES HISTORY USER');
       -- returning FALSE clears the factor value (NULL)
       RETURN FALSE;
    ELSE
       -- this logic preserves the audit attribution
       -- capability of the CLIENT IDENTIFIER feature
       -- in Oracle
       dbms_session.set_identifier(p_factor_value);
       -- the logic in this ELSE block could just
       -- as easily check a table for a list of
       -- valid application users or even connect
       -- to an external system to valid the user name
       -- supplied to the function
       -- returning TRUE preserves the factor value
       RETURN TRUE;
    END IF;
END;
/
Function created.
mary@aos> -- execute privileges on the validation routine must
mary@aos> -- be granted to DVSYS
mary@aos> GRANT EXECUTE ON sh.valid_client_identifier TO dvsys;
Grant succeeded.
```

With our DBV rule set for factor assignment in place, as well as a validation routine, we can define the Client_Identifier factor. In this procedure call, we supply the name of the DBV rule set that controls factor assignment in the **rule_set_name** parameter. We supply the object-owning schema and function name of our validation routine in the **validate_expr** parameter.

```
dbvowner@aos> -- create the DBV version of a client identifier
dbvowner@aos> BEGIN
    dbms_macadm.create_factor(
        factor_name      => 'Client_Identifier' ,
        factor_type_name => 'User',
        description    =>
            'Factor that holds the Sales History application end user'
             ||' when used with the TCPS network protocol.'
             ||' Alternative to the CLIENT IDENTIFIER feature.',
        rule_set_name => 'Can Assign Client Identifier',
        get_expr      => 'TO_CHAR(0)',
        validate_expr => 'SH.VALID_CLIENT_IDENTIFIER',
        identify_by   => dbms_macutl.g_identify_by_method,
        labeled_by    => dbms_macutl.g_labeled_by_self,
        eval_options => dbms_macutl.g_eval_on_access,
        audit_options => dbms_macutl.g_audit_on_get_error,
        fail_options  => dbms_macutl.g_fail_with_message);
END;
/
PL/SQL procedure successfully completed.

COMMIT;
Commit complete.
```

We can now test the assignment of this DBV factor with our certificate-based application server account ops$appserver_1 using ASO PKI/SSL authentication to the database:

```
ops$appserver_1@aos> -- the default state of the factor is NULL
ops$appserver_1@aos> -- because our validation routine returned
ops$appserver_1@aos> -- a boolean value of FALSE
ops$appserver_1@aos> SELECT DVF.F$Client_Identifier
      FROM dual;

F$CLIENT_IDENTIFIER
-----------------------------------------------------

1 row selected.
ops$appserver_1@aos>-- the CLIENT IDENTIFIER session context
ops$appserver_1@aos>-- information also demonstrates the execution
ops$appserver_1@aos>-- validation of our routine at session startup
ops$appserver_1@aos> SELECT SYS_CONTEXT('USERENV','CLIENT_IDENTIFIER')
      FROM dual;

SYS_CONTEXT('USERENV','CLIENT_IDENTIFIER')
-----------------------------------------------------
ANONYMOUS SALES HISTORY USER
1 row selected.

ops$appserver_1@aos>-- we can now attempt to set the DBV version of
ops$appserver_1@aos>-- client identifier and it will succeed based
```

```
ops$appserver_1@aos>-- on the correct client certificate being asserted
ops$appserver_1@aos> BEGIN
      dvsys.set_factor('Client_Identifier','jeffrey@mycompany.com');
END;
/
PL/SQL procedure successfully completed.
ops$appserver_1@aos> -- the factor now has the identity supplied
ops$appserver_1@aos> -- set appropriately because our validation
ops$appserver_1@aos> -- routine returned a boolean value of TRUE
ops$appserver_1@aos> SELECT DVF.F$Client_Identifier
      FROM dual;

F$CLIENT_IDENTIFIER
-----------------------------------------------------
jeffrey@mycompany.com

1 row selected.
ops$appserver_1@aos>-- the CLIENT IDENTIFIER session context
ops$appserver_1@aos>-- is also populated as expected based on the code
ops$appserver_1@aos>-- defined in the validation function
ops$appserver_1@aos> SELECTSYS_CONTEXT('USERENV','CLIENT_IDENTIFIER')
       FROM dual;

SYS_CONTEXT('USERENV','CLIENT_IDENTIFIER')
-----------------------------------------------------
jeffrey@mycompany.com
1 row selected.
```

We can also test the ability to perform the assignment of this DBV factor with a certificate-based desktop user account ops$jeffrey using ASO PKI/SSL authentication to the database with a different Oracle wallet than the one we defined as trusted.

```
ops$jeffrey@aos> -- we attempt to set the DBV version of
ops$jeffrey@aos> -- client identifier and it will fail based
ops$jeffrey@aos> -- on an untrusted client certificate being asserted
ops$jeffrey@aos> EXECUTE dvsys.set_factor('Client_Identifier','jeffrey@mycompany.com');
BEGIN dvsys.set_factor('Client_Identifier','jeffrey@mycompany.com'); END;

*
ERROR at line 1:
ORA-47391: attempt to set Factor CLIENT_IDENTIFIER violates Rule Set Can Assign
Client Identifier
ORA-06512: at "DVSYS.DBMS_MACSEC", line 3
ORA-06512: at "DVSYS.DBMS_MACSEC", line 54
ORA-06512: at "DVSYS.SET_FACTOR", line 5
ORA-06512: at line 1
ops$jeffrey@aos> -- the default state of the factor is NULL
ops$jeffrey@aos> -- and preserved when the rule set
ops$jeffrey@aos> -- authorization fails
ops$jeffrey@aos> SELECT DVF.F$Client_Identifier
      FROM dual;

F$CLIENT_IDENTIFIER
-----------------------------------------------------
```

```
1 row selected.
ops$jeffrey@aos> -- the default CLIENT IDENTIFIER session context
ops$jeffrey@aos> -- information is also preserved
ops$jeffrey@aos> SELECT SYS_CONTEXT('USERENV','CLIENT_IDENTIFIER')
      FROM dual;

SYS_CONTEXT('USERENV','CLIENT_IDENTIFIER')
-----------------------------------------------------
ANONYMOUS SALES HISTORY USER
1 row selected.
```

The DBV security administrator can view the DBV audit records for the factor assignment test cases using the DVA web application.

This report (shown in Figure 5-12) queries the table DVSYS.AUDIT_TRAIL$ and the information can be correlated with the standard Oracle RDBMS audit trail stored in the SYSTEM.AUD$ table and exposed through the DBA_AUDIT_TRAIL view. The database administrator can query the DBA_AUDIT_TRAIL view for audit events where the CLIENT_ID column is populated with the successfully assigned factor values from our test.

We had integrated the DBMS_SESSION.SET_IDENTIFIER procedure that populates this CLIENT_ID column within the DBV factor validation method to ensure that our audit attribution capability remains intact. The following query shows audit records that would be created if the Sales History web application issued a DELETE statement on the SH.SALES table when using the connection pool account ops$appserver_1:

```
sys@aos> SELECT username,client_id,action_name,owner,obj_name
FROM dba_audit_trail
WHERE owner = 'SH';

USERNAME          CLIENT_ID              ACTION_NAME  OWNER  OBJ_NAME
----------------- ---------------------- ------------ ------ ----------
OPS$APPSERVER_1   jeffrey@mycompany.com  DELETE       SH     SALES
```

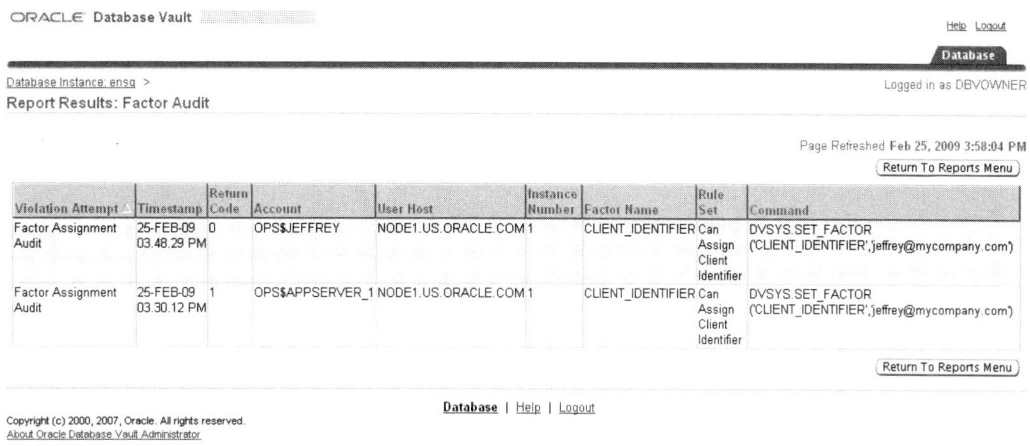

ORACLE Database Vault

Help Logout

Database

Database Instance: ensq >

Logged in as DBVOWNER

Report Results: Factor Audit

Page Refreshed Feb 25, 2009 3:58:04 PM

Return To Reports Menu

Violation Attempt	Timestamp	Return Code	Account	User Host	Instance Number	Factor Name	Rule Set	Command
Factor Assignment Audit	25-FEB-09 03.48.29 PM	0	OPS$JEFFREY	NODE1.US.ORACLE.COM	1	CLIENT_IDENTIFIER	Can Assign Client Identifier	DVSYS.SET_FACTOR ('CLIENT_IDENTIFIER','jeffrey@mycompany.com')
Factor Assignment Audit	25-FEB-09 03.30.12 PM	1	OPS$APPSERVER_1	NODE1.US.ORACLE.COM	1	CLIENT_IDENTIFIER	Can Assign Client Identifier	DVSYS.SET_FACTOR ('CLIENT_IDENTIFIER','jeffrey@mycompany.com')

Return To Reports Menu

Database | Help | Logout

About Oracle Database Vault Administrator

FIGURE 5-12 *Factor audit report*

It is easy to see that DBV factor assignment provides additional access control and validation capabilities when used as a wrapper for traditional methods of asserting client information that use the DBMS_SESSION or DBMS_APPLICATION_INFO packages. The feature provides the same benefits when used in lieu of custom Oracle application context objects and reduces the number of objects that must be maintained. The feature extends the overall auditing capability for these traditional mechanisms while preserving the existing audit capabilities on which applications may rely.

DBV Secure Application Roles

Oracle SARs are database roles that can be enabled only from within a PL/SQL program. The PL/SQL program will typically perform a series of checks to determine whether the conditions are correct for the role to be enabled. DBV provides an integration capability with Oracle SARs that allow you define these conditions using a DBV rule set.

To help illustrate how DBV Secure Application Roles work, consider the DBV Is System Maintenance Allowed rule set presented earlier in the chapter. This rule set allowed system maintenance routines on Fridays from 5 to 11 P.M. We can reuse this rule set to control the ability to set a role that has DELETE privileges on tables protected by the Sales History DBV realm for the purpose of archiving and deleting records that no longer need to be maintained in the table. Privileges that allow for the update or deletion of data are typically considered security-sensitive operations and are perfect candidates for DBV SARs.

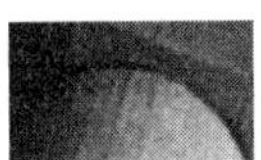

TIP
Use DBV SARs for security-sensitive privilege sets.

The first step in creating this type of capability requires that the DBV security administrator (DBVOWNER) create the DBV SARs using the DBMS_MACADM.CREATE_ROLE PL/SQL procedure. To secure the role from being granted or revoked outside the control of the Sales History realm administrator, MARY, we should also protect the role in the Sales History realm.

```
dbvowner@aos> -- create the DBV Secure Application Role
dbvowner@aos> BEGIN
    dbms_macadm.create_role(
       role_name     => 'SALES_ARCHIVE_ROLE'
     , enabled       => 'Y'
     , rule_set_name => 'Is System Maintenance Allowed'
     );
END;
/
PL/SQL procedure successfully completed.

dbvowner@aos> -- protect the role in the Sales History realm
dbvowner@aos> BEGIN
    dbms_macadm.add_object_to_realm (
      realm_name    => 'Sales History'
     ,object_owner  => 'SH'
     ,object_name   => 'SALES_ARCHIVE_ROLE'
```

```
    ,object_type   => 'ROLE'
    );
END;
/
PL/SQL procedure successfully completed.
```

The created role is a normal Oracle SAR, visible from the DBA_APPLICATION_ROLES view, but the PL/SQL program that can enable the role is defined by DBV itself:

```
sys@aos>SELECT *
FROM dba_application_roles
WHERE role = 'SALES_ARCHIVE_ROLE';
ROLE                 SCHEMA    PACKAGE
-------------------- --------- ------------------
SALES_ARCHIVE_ROLE   DVSYS     DBMS_MACSEC_ROLES

1 row selected.
```

DBV provides a single PL/SQL package procedure named DVSYS.DBMS_MACSEC_ROLES. SET_ROLE that is used to enable the role being protected. This procedure has the invoker's rights definition required for Oracle SARs and will perform the DBV rule set evaluation to determine whether the role should be set. This procedure eliminates the need to create a separate PL/SQL program for each SAR required for your application and offers an increased level of reuse of the DBV rule sets you develop.

The next step is to grant the privileges required by the role to serve its intended purpose. In our example, the SALES_ARCHIVE_ROLE requires DELETE privileges on the tables owned by the SH account. We can also grant this role to a named user account, such as the user SCOTT. The DBV realm administrator, MARY, of the Sales History realm, can perform these steps.

```
mary@aos> -- grant the require object privileges
mary@aos> -- to the DBV Secure Application Role
mary@aos> GRANT DELETE ON sh.channels TO sales_archive_role;
Grant succeeded.
mary@aos> GRANT DELETE ON sh.costs TO sales_archive_role;
Grant succeeded.
mary@aos> GRANT DELETE ON sh.countries TO sales_archive_role;
Grant succeeded.
mary@aos> GRANT DELETE ON sh.customers TO sales_archive_role;
Grant succeeded.
mary@aos> GRANT DELETE ON sh.products TO sales_archive_role;
Grant succeeded.
mary@aos> GRANT DELETE ON sh.promotions TO sales_archive_role;
Grant succeeded.
mary@aos> GRANT DELETE ON sh.sales TO sales_archive_role;
Grant succeeded.
mary@aos> -- grant the DBV Secure Application Role
mary@aos> -- to the account SCOTT
mary@aos> GRANT sales_archive_role TO scott;
Grant succeeded.
```

We now test the use of these privileges and the DBV SAR as the user SCOTT to demonstrate how the configuration works when operating outside of the authorized system maintenance timeframe:

```
scott@aos> -- show the date and time of day factors that affect
scott@aos> -- the DBV Rule Set that controls the role enablement
scott@aos>SELECT TO_CHAR(SYSDATE,'DAY') "DAY_OF_WEEK",
        TO_CHAR(SYSDATE,'HH24') "HOUR_OF_DAY"
FROM DUAL;

DAY_OF_WEEK                          HO
------------------------------------ --
MONDAY                               10

1 row selected.

scott@aos> -- attempt to use the privileges granted to the
scott@aos> -- role to demonstrate the privileges are not enabled
scott@aos> -- by default as with a normal Oracle role.
scott@aos> -- We will test deleting records greater than 10 years old
scott@aos>DELETE sh.sales WHERE time_id < (SYSDATE-(365*10));
DELETE sh.sales WHERE time_id < (SYSDATE-(365*10))
          *
ERROR at line 1:
ORA-01031: insufficient privileges

scott@aos> -- attempt to enable the role outside of the
scott@aos> -- authorized system maintenance timeframe
scott@aos>EXEC dvsys.dbms_macsec_roles.set_role('SALES_ARCHIVE_ROLE');
BEGIN dvsys.dbms_macsec_roles.set_role('SALES_ARCHIVE_ROLE'); END;

*
ERROR at line 1:
ORA-47305: Rule Set violation on SET ROLE (Is System Maintenance Allowed)
ORA-06512: at "DVSYS.DBMS_MACUTL", line 38
ORA-06512: at "DVSYS.DBMS_MACUTL", line 381
ORA-06512: at "DVSYS.DBMS_MACSEC", line 242
ORA-06512: at "DVSYS.ROLE_IS_ENABLED", line 4
ORA-06512: at "DVSYS.DBMS_MACSEC_ROLES", line 24
ORA-06512: at line 1
```

The rule set violation that occurs is audited in the same manner as its usage within any other DBV components. The audit trail records (Figure 5-13) that are created for DBV SAR violations can be queried from the DVA web application as well.

If we fast forward to Friday at 5 P.M., we can demonstrate the success scenario for enabling the DBV SAR and leveraging the privileges the role provides:

```
scott@aos> -- show the date and time of day factors that affect
scott@aos> -- the DBV Rule Set that controls the role enablement

scott@aos>SELECT TO_CHAR(SYSDATE,'DAY') "DAY_OF_WEEK",
        TO_CHAR(SYSDATE,'HH24') "HOUR_OF_DAY"
FROM DUAL;

DAY_OF_WEEK                          HO
------------------------------------ --
FRIDAY                               17

1 row selected.

scott@aos> -- attempt to enable the role, which will succeed
scott@aos>EXEC dvsys.dbms_macsec_roles.set_Role('SALES_ARCHIVE_ROLE');

PL/SQL procedure successfully completed.

scott@aos> -- attempt to use the privileges granted to the
scott@aos> -- role by deleting records greater than 10 years old
scott@aos>DELETE sh.sales WHERE time_id < (SYSDATE-(365*10));

221651 rows deleted.
```

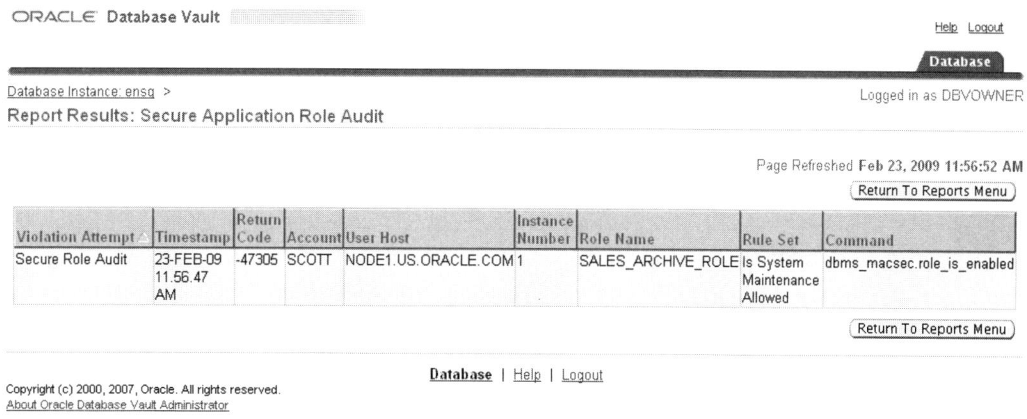
ORACLE Database Vault
Help Logout
Database
Database Instance: ensg >
Logged in as DBVOWNER
Report Results: Secure Application Role Audit
Page Refreshed Feb 23, 2009 11:56:52 AM
Return To Reports Menu
Violation Attempt | Timestamp | Return Code | Account | User Host | Instance Number | Role Name | Rule Set | Command
Secure Role Audit | 23-FEB-09 11.56.47 AM | -47305 | SCOTT | NODE1.US.ORACLE.COM | 1 | SALES_ARCHIVE_ROLE | Is System Maintenance Allowed | dbms_macsec.role_is_enabled
Return To Reports Menu
Database | Help | Logout
Copyright (c) 2000, 2007, Oracle. All rights reserved.
About Oracle Database Vault Administrator

FIGURE 5-13 *Secure Application Role Audit report*

Summary

This chapter presented numerous examples of how to configure the core DBV components to protect an example object-owner account. These examples illustrate the effectiveness of the new DBV security features. Product features such as DBV realms, DBV command rules, and DBV SARs are critical for addressing many of the issues we face today around consolidation, compliance, and separation of duties. These features serve as effective defensive measure for cyber security by limiting the extent to which statements and privileges can be exploited by an attacker.

We demonstrated how DBV realms filled in a gap in the ability to place boundaries around the use of system ANY privileges and how simply defining this realm boundary offers immediate protection against inadvertent access to the objects being protected by the realm. We examined how command rules allow us to implement security policies based on the real business rules we may have defined in our organization. We also demonstrated how DBV SARs can restrict an administrator's or an application's ability to enable sensitive privilege sets. This feature reduces the threat of a privilege set being used outside of the context in which the usage was intended.

Database administrators should consider updating their production databases to DBV to meet current and future security threats and challenges. The declarative policy configuration of the product's security rules, based on multiple factors, helps ensure the appropriateness of an organization's defense against these threats and challenges as they change over time. Once DBV policy is deployed, database security administrators should consider the serious nature of what a violation could mean and question the legitimacy of it. We examined the ability to control policy evaluation semantics, auditing configuration, and custom event handling that allow these administrators to refine policies or respond to these violations when they occur.

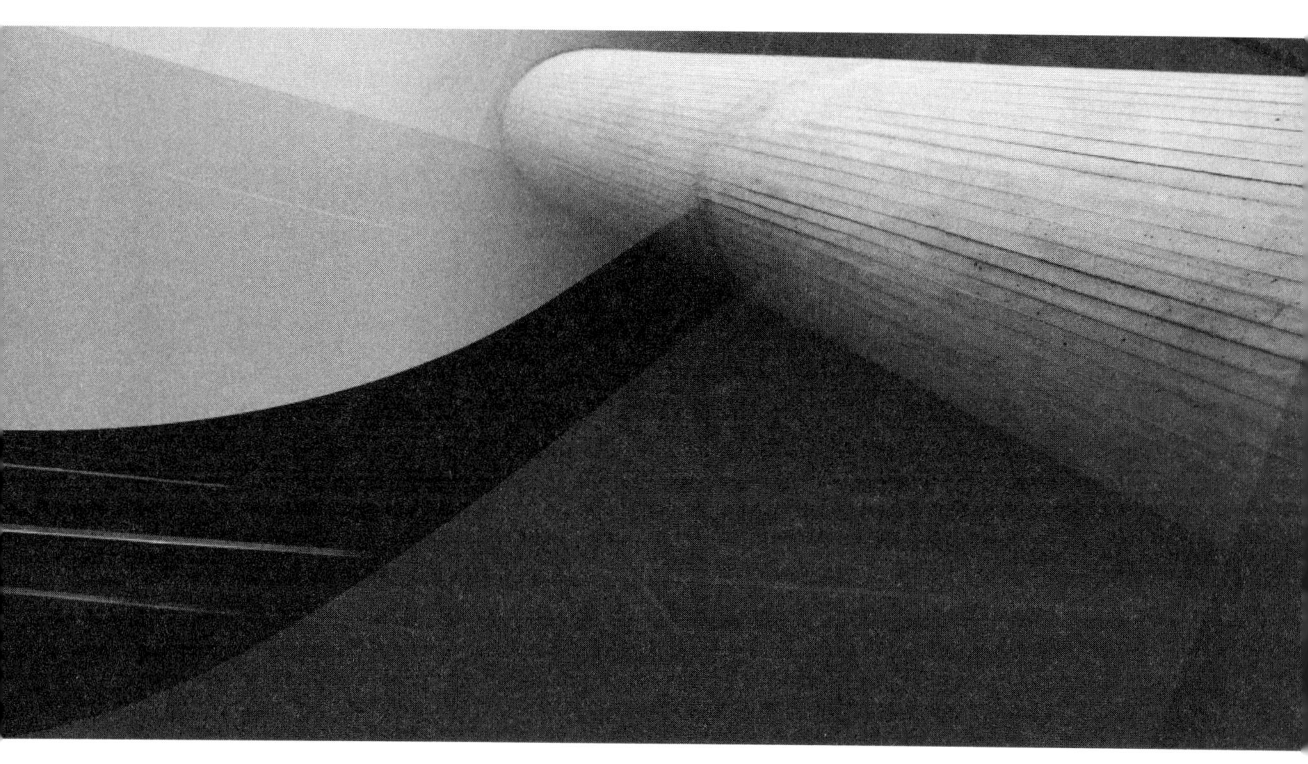

CHAPTER 6

Applied Database Vault for Custom Applications

his chapter introduces design techniques and patterns for DBV security controls that will be incorporated into the process of creating a new application. We first introduce a notional database application environment that is used to describe design techniques for analyzing the applications in this environment. The analysis will uncover opportunities for you to apply DBV security controls. The design techniques include documentation components, rules, and patterns that will be applied during the design phase of new database application.

We encourage you to think about database security at the beginning of the application design phase and understand the importance of considering a DBV security policy at that point. This approach is easier than trying to tack on a security policy at the end of a project development cycle when schedules are tight, budgets are reduced, and code is frozen. Up-front security design allows security policy to be shared among applications covering the same or similar problem domains, such as sales and finance, or those that reside in the same database under an IT consolidation effort.

Much has been written on the subjects of software development methodologies and the software development lifecycle. There is no shortage of words in the IT industry on the steps involved, the artifacts to deliver, or the most efficient processes for developing software. Each software development methodology, be it Agile-based methods, UML-based methods, or classical methods such as Waterfall, share a common set of activities:

- Functional requirements and analysis
- Designs/specifications
- Implementation/coding
- Testing
- Deployment, documentation, and training
- Operations and maintenance

These methodologies differ in ways that dictate how document-centric or prototype-centric each activity should be. These methodologies differ in terms of when each activity is conducted with respect to the overall schedule and who (from a project role perspective) is involved in each activity. We do not present arguments in this chapter on which software development methods are best for you or your organization; instead, we present a generic methodology (practices and procedures) to help you analyze and design your application to take advantage DBV security controls. The goal is to help you increase your application's overall security posture by applying techniques within early stages of the methodology you already use.

Notional Database Applications Environment

A notional sales management database application environment is used to illustrate the security methodology. For this application, the following high-level database applications and functionality are required:

- A web service allows external product reseller applications to query sales history information for the channels in which they participate.

- A web service allows for internal line of business applications to query sales history information from the products they manage.
- A web application allows for the sales managers to administer products, channels, promotions, sales, customers, and the costs of product sales for product lines they manage.
- Batch programs generate sales history information on a scheduled basis.
- Database administrators must be able to back up application data, conduct performance tuning, and perform general database administration functions such as patching and applying upgrades.

Our example of the notional architecture is somewhat contrived because we are aiming to make use of the Oracle Database sample schemas used throughout this book, but it is simple enough to help describe the methodology and has enough variety to help us demonstrate the practices and procedures from more than one example. Figure 6-1 shows a Unified Modeling Language (UML) component diagram that depicts the notional software architecture that is being constructed.

Like a lot of software implementations in the past, the idea for the system probably started on a whiteboard, the back of napkin, or a scrap of paper in a conversation between two executives or a line of business managers. It was much cruder than the illustration in Figure 6-1, but the executives were more concerned about organizational efficiency, return on investment, and other important business matters than security. The next day (or month), they obtained the approvals for a budget and gathered all their functional analysts and technical personnel to begin laying out the

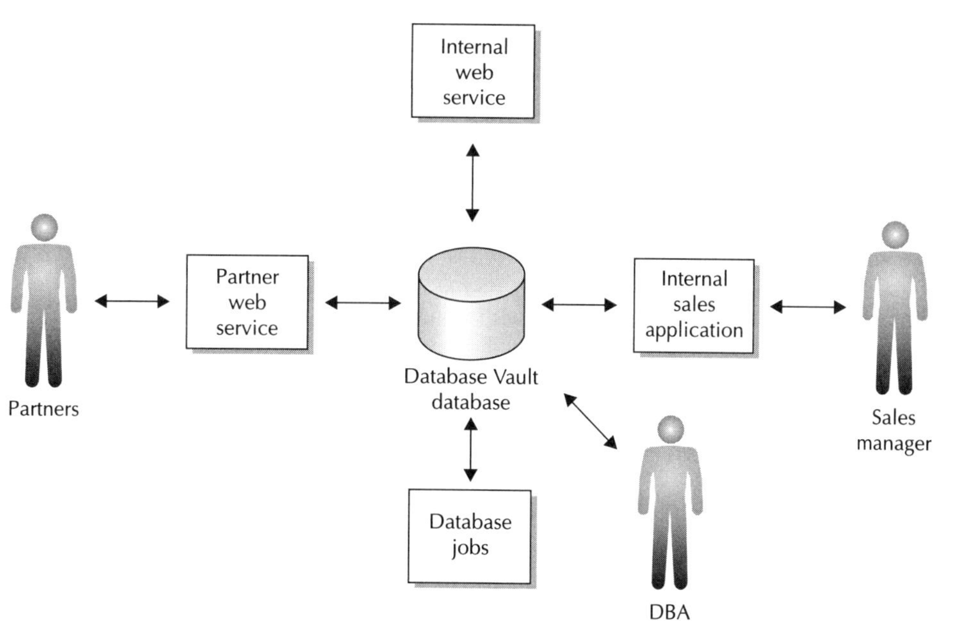

FIGURE 6-1 *Notional database applications*

detailed requirements. From this requirement and analysis exercise and the artifacts this phase produces, we can expose the core elements we will need to develop a security profile for the database applications.

From Requirements to Security Profile Design

The following is a brief outline of the process we will follow to examine the system requirements and build our database security profile. This process is iterative in that we can start with each group of requirements, examine it, move onto the next group of requirements, and revisit completed requirements for more refinement:

- Define or locate requirements documentation, such as use cases.
- Identify coarse-grained "verb object" assertions for the database security profile.
- Identify fine-grained database security profile to include actors and conditions.
- Establish DBV factors based on business or system conditions.
- Identify DBV realms and realm objects from objects.
- Identify accounts, roles, and DBV realm authorizations from actors.
- Establish DBV command rules from conditions.
- Establish DBV Secure Application Roles (SARs) from conditions.

This chapter details requirements analysis techniques that uncover both application security and hidden security requirements that must be considered. These techniques will help you understand the application and its sensitive transactions and privileged operations. Stay focused on the key drivers, such as compliance, cyber security, insider threats, and corporate policy to help you justify these requirements and apply adequate security measures.

Requirements Technique: Use Cases and Scenarios

A popular requirements and analysis technique in use today is the development of use cases and scenarios. *Use cases* are named descriptions of the interaction of an actor (a person or other computer system) within a business process (named business use cases) or with an IT system (named system use cases). System use cases comprise a sequence of steps that outline how the actor achieves a goal using the IT system. For example, "Add Monthly Product Costs" might be a use case with the actor being a sales manager. *Scenarios* are the detailed variations on the sequence of steps or actions that describe how an actor reaches the goal using the primary and alternative paths. Using our example, we may include a path for adding monthly costs for electronic products, including entering the costs of raw materials and manufacturing, and an alternative path for software products, which has inputs of more detailed labor costs. When a use case is formally defined it can include the following sections:

- **Name** A short identifier for the use cause typically of the form *verb noun*, where the verb is a summary of the tasks and the noun is the object being acted upon.
- **Goal** The desired outcome of the use case.

- **Actor(s)** Who is involved in the interaction, typically an end user or another system.
- **Triggers** Events that cause the use case to be initiated.
- **Pre-conditions** Conditions that must be met before the use case can be initiated.
- **Scenario(s)** Primary and alternatives paths through the use case.
- **Business rules** Formal or informal rules associated with an organization and its policies that govern either the pre-conditions, post-conditions, or detailed steps (scenarios) of the use case.
- **Post-conditions** Conditions that are true or state changes in the system once the use case is completed.

While this explanation of use cases and scenarios is intended as an overview, if you look at the context of a use case, it has the components of the security profile language used in security evaluations. Security evaluation conventions related to the evaluation of IT products express rules for testing in the form:

<subject> <verb> <object> <condition(s)>

With use cases, all of the same components are specified:

- **Subjects** The actors
- **Verbs** In the syntax of the name and the actions in scenarios
- **Objects** Expressed in the syntax of the name, goal, and scenarios
- **Conditions** Expressed in the preconditions and post-conditions

Using these similarities, we will demonstrate that we can examine the use cases for a system, or any requirements analysis document for that matter, to identify these components (subjects, verbs, objects, and conditions).

The process of identifying these components allows us to design a security profile for a system if we define the security protection profile within the context of each group of requirements. For the purposes of this book, we try to limit the discussion of the security profile to be applicable to Oracle Database security. It just so happens that with use cases, we can overlay each use case with the appropriate level of detail regarding the security protection profile as it applies to each use case because the syntax/vernacular of both a security protection profile and a use case are similar. This gives us an advantage because we can define a database security policy that will allow operations within the (modeled and documented) context of the intended usage of database objects (the use cases) and prevent unauthorized use of database objects.

Analyzing Requirements: Example Use Case

First let's look at example use case for the notional database applications:

- **Use Case Name** Add Monthly Product Costs
- **Goal** The direct and indirect costs for a given month related to a product the company sells are available to all business processes.

- **Actor(s)** Product Sales Manager
- **Triggers** The representative from the company's Manufacturing, Marketing, and Partner Management departments have all reported their respective monthly costs for the product to the Sales Manager.
- **Pre-conditions**
  - The Sales Manager has authenticated to the Sales Administration application.
  - The Sales Management system is not in the process of summarizing monthly sales data at the time the product costs are being entered.
  - The time the product costs are being entered is not within the weekly maintenance window of the Sales Management system.
- **Scenario (Primary)**
  1. The user opens a browser and accesses the Sales Administration web page.
  2. The system prompts the user for his or her credentials.
  3. The user enters his or her credentials.
  4. The system validates the user's credentials. If the validation fails, the system audits this fact and repeats the prompt for the user's credentials. If the validation succeeds, the appropriate security privilege context based on the user is applied and the system presents the user with the main system menu.
  5. The user selects the Add Monthly Product Costs option.
  6. The system prompts the user to enter a month and year for the product cost.
  7. The user selects the month and year.
  8. The system reads the product list and prompts the user to select a product. The system will present only the products for which the user is responsible.
  9. The user selects the product.
  10. The system reads the channel list and prompts the user to select a (partner) channel.
  11. The user selects the channel.
  12. The system reads the promotion list and prompts the user to select a (marketing) promotion.
  13. The user selects the promotion.
  14. The system prompts the user to enter the costs for the channel and promotion.
  15. The user enters the costs for the channel and promotion.
  16. The system prompts the user to enter another channel and promotion costs.
  17. If the user elects to add another cost, steps 8–16 are repeated.

      Or, if the user selects to finish the transaction, the system presents a summary screen for the cost information entered.

18. If the user elects to cancel the transaction, the information entered is discarded and the system returns the user to the main system menu.
19. If the user elects to save the cost information, the system will
    a) store the information in the database;
    b) audit the transaction;
    c) send the required notifications related to the transaction.

- **Business Rules**
  - Sales managers are the only staff members allowed to maintain overall product costs figures.
  - All product costs figures that are created or updated must be audited for Sarbanes Oxley (SOX) compliance regulations. Company policy related to SOX compliance auditing require the audit record to include the date/time of the transaction, the named user executing the transaction, the system or application that was used to execute the transaction, and the full record of the transaction.
  - The appropriate corporate officers must be notified when product costs figures are created or updated.
  - All system outages, scheduled or accidental, must be recorded for SOX compliance reporting purposes.
- **Post-conditions**
  - The monthly product costs have been stored in the Sales Management system's database.
  - The monthly product costs transaction has been properly audited.
  - Notifications related to the monthly product costs transactions were generated.

Developing use cases for these types of transactions can be also applied to existing systems that can include a user interface or batch product cost upload routine. Don't be afraid to apply the analysis technique in any environment where you are required to apply additional security controls after the fact, as may be the case if you must meet compliance regulations. Two pages' worth of requirements are written into the preceding use case text, but when you apply the process of identifying a security profile to the use case, you will see that a lot more requirements lie "between the lines" when you start design activity.

Identify Coarse-Grained Security Profile

The design technique for defining our database security profile can be applied to just about any requirements document and stems from one of the popular techniques used in object-oriented analysis and design. The Verb Object technique involves identifying nouns (objects) and key verbs to construct an object-oriented class model for the application design needs. This technique is normally applied in designing Java or C++ classes (a domain model) used by the application.

For the database security profile, we want to apply this technique with one slight variation: We first want to identify all "verb objects" facts from the requirements text, as this will be the first pass at the profile itself. Given the example use case from earlier in the chapter, we assert the following "verb objects" facts:

Verb	**Object**
Add	Product Cost
Read	User Credentials
Set	Security Privilege Context
Read	Products
Read	Channels
Read	Promotions
Audit	Product Cost Transaction
Notify	Product Cost Transaction

This table of "verb object" assertions uncovers the basic database operations that will be conducted on either an existing or a new set of tables or views (objects) in the database. So an Add could be an implied INSERT, a Read would be implied SELECT, and so on. This first step in the design process is not only important for defining these database operations (verbs that will be commands), but it also defines the database objects that are involved in the context of the use case (requirements). The resulting value is that the requirements analysis exercise can be used as input the design of database security profiles as well as logical database design efforts.

The actor here is the Sales Manager and is associated to the "subject" of our security profile syntax. We want to state this subject explicitly because the security profile will not be final if we consider each use case or group of requirements in isolation. The process of developing the security will be iterative in nature, so as we examine each use case or group of requirements, we need the subject to be explicitly defined. Note that much of the real code that will be developed (or is developed) operates as the "system" in our use case. However the real "actor" as it relates to the system is the Sales Manager. To this end, we want to ensure that operations available to the session within the system do not overextend their operating privilege model beyond those available to the Sales Manager whenever possible.

Another important component to add to our security profile are conditions that must be presented for each "verb object" pairing to be true. We will uncover other conditions that may need to be added or combined as we work through each section of the requirements analysis. These conditions are often explicitly stated in the scenario, pre-conditions, or business rules. For example, in the scenario of the example use case, step 8 states, "The system reads the product list and prompts the user to select a product. The system will present only the products for which the user is responsible." This is an explicit operational condition based on ownership for the specific product lines the company offers for sale. It may be dictated by the organization's policy that strives to prevent one sales manager from overstepping his or her boundaries or duties.

We should also be looking for opportunities to uncover hidden security requirements or introduce sound security design principles in the context of these conditions. Here are some examples:

- Should all database administrators be able to view (read) the entire product list? The product list may not be sensitive in nature is of less concern.

- Should all of our database administrators be allowed to update the product costs table directly, or should we enforce constraints that all product updates come through a specific application code block? The update operation may be disallowed outside of a trusted code block due to the complex update logic and the notifications required for compliance regulations.

The following questions may help you uncover additional opportunities to improve the overall security profile:

- What are the customer's security standards or conventions? The IT department of your organization probably keeps documented security standards related to the development of IT systems, so make sure you ask about any documentation because it would offer lots of information related to important controls from the customer's perspective.
- What are the customer's privacy requirements? Many organizations are impacted by privacy requirements to protect personally identifiable information (PII), such as Social Security numbers or health care–related information for employees and/or patients. In our example use case, does the "credential validation step" read the storage structures that contain Social Security numbers or salary data? If that is the case, we should limit the privileges or view to this information by the use case.
- Is the customer impacted by the financial compliance regulations such as Sarbanes-Oxley (SOX)? This regulation requires extensive auditing and reporting. You can also uncover opportunities to define preventative security policies that reduce the probability of accidents occurring or malicious intent succeeding.
- What information does the customer consider sensitive or proprietary? Does the system store credit card numbers, financial statements, or engineering documents related to product research efforts?
- Does the customer have well-defined separation of duty requirements? For example, should financial or sales data be administered by a different group than the group that administers human resources data? This is especially important in IT consolidation environments or in highly secure environments in the public sector.

  As we answer these questions, we categorize the conditions as follows:

- **Conditions based on compliance** that typically introduce security policy components for auditing, reporting, and access control.
- **Conditions based on conflict of interest**, a kind of compliance that implies separation of duty (access control) to avoid advanced insider knowledge, theft, or fraud. Publicly traded companies typically use such requirements. Even without these compliance-driven requirements, an enterprise can reduce the risk of accidental or intentional data loss by applying separation of duty controls to the database security policy.
- **Conditions based on organizational policies** that are introduced to reduce risk of loss (data or financial), maintain ownership, or spread control to more than one group/individual.
- **Conditions based on identity management** that typically examine an attribute of the individual or his/her membership in a group.

- **Conditions based on access path or the operational context** that depend on the system access path or method that operation is invoked in the database. The conditions may inspect the network access path or the lack thereof when a client is on the database server's console. The conditions may consider the operational context such as the application call stack or the generic type of SQL command in a given transaction. These types of conditions are typically introduced to prevent data access outside the normal scenario in the same way intrusion detection is applied to network packets.
- **Time-based or Sequential conditions** that can define conditions such as the inside maintenance window, prior to month close, or prior to earnings statements that are designed to limit the timeframe in which a command can be executed or a timeframe in which the command cannot be executed. In a related way, we may want to ensure that sensitive transactions are performed only as part of a trusted sequence of events. For example, if a specific type of DELETE transaction is expected only from a specific application, or the application runs a specific query (SELECT) before the DELETE, can we find evidence of the application authentication step or the SELECT statement being issued?
- **Conditions based on data or events stored externally** ensures that data or conditions stored in external systems are used in the decision-making process. This approach can help enforce separation of duty and/or separation of control but is most beneficial when distributed systems must interoperate to ensure that an overarching business process is followed in the correct sequence.

DBV is extremely valuable in enforcing these types of conditions in your security policy because it is the only declarative database product option that allows you to enforce rule-based decisions at both the statement and role levels. The value comes in being able to codify business rules directly in your database security profile.

Identify Fine-Grained Security Profile

Once we have uncovered the conditions using the process and guidance provided above, we are ready to define our fine-grained security profile. Table 6-1 illustrates a fine-grained version of our security profile that includes the addition of the appropriate subject (actor) and the conditions, both explicitly stated and derived (these are explicitly spelled out as derived), for each "verb object" exercise that was discussed earlier.

Obviously, this list would be substantial as we worked through every use case, but just working on this simple use case gives us plenty to work with. We can build a candidate DBV security policy design for this use case by taking on the task in the following order:

1. Identify DBV factors based on business or system conditions.
2. Identify DBV realms and realm objects based on objects.
3. Identify accounts, roles, and DBV realm authorizations from use case actors.
4. Establish DBV command rules from conditions.
5. Establish DBV secure application roles from conditions.

The following sections describe the steps to take in each of these tasks. We provide advice on how to incorporate DBV security policy and general database security policy in each of these tasks.

Subject	Verb	Object	Conditions
Sales Manager	Add	Product Cost	Add product cost operation can be executed only by a Sales Manager (or higher position) within the sales organization Must not be within the weekly maintenance window Can be created or updated only by the Sales Management package code (derived compliance control)
Sales Manager	Read	User Credentials	Credentials must adhere to organizational password policy requirements (derived corporate IT standards control) May not query employee SS number, salary, or commission data as part of the read operation (derived privacy control)
System	Set	Security Privilege Context	Set only by system-controlled interface (derived compliance control to prevent privilege escalation)
Sales Manager	Read	Products	May query only products for which the manager is responsible
Sales Manager	Read	Channels	No conditions
Sales Manager	Read	Promotions	No conditions
Sales Manager	Audit	Product Cost Transaction	Audit trail cannot be updated or deleted by a database administrator (derived compliance control) Audit trail cannot be read or written to by database clients outside the corporate intranet (derived compliance control) Audit trail must be maintained for a period of seven years (derived compliance control)
Sales Manager	Notify	Product Cost Transaction	Communication of notification details must be encrypted if it leaves the corporate intranet (corporate security policy on sensitive data) A record of all notifications must be maintained (derived compliance control)

TABLE 6-1 *Fine-grained Version of Our Security Profile*

Identify DBV Factors Based on Business or System Conditions

If we examine the conditions in a fine-grained security profile, we can identify a set of DBV factors we'll need to develop by asking: How is each fact in the condition asserted or defined? We can add an extra column to Table 6-1 for the factors we can derive from these conditions.

For readability, we've included the Condition and Candidate DBV Factor(s) columns for a subset of our Subject-Verb-Object-Condition security profile in Table 6-2.

As you can see in Table 6-2 below, we can create factors using the same types of categories we used to identify the conditions of our security policy:

- Factors based on compliance
- Factors based on conflict of interest or separation of duty
- Factors based on organizational policy

Condition	Candidate DBV Factor(s)
Add product cost operation can be executed only by a Sales Manager (or higher position) within the sales organization	**Create factors based on command operational context:** "Product Cost Operation" **Create factors based on traditional identity management concepts such as user attributes or group membership to resolve concept of Sales Manager:** "Job Title" "Department"
Must not be within the weekly maintenance window	**Create factors based on time:** "Day of Week" "Time of Day"
Can be created or updated only by the Sales Management package code	**Create factors based software operational context:** "Sales Management Package"
May not query employee SS number, salary, or commission data as part of the read operation	**Create factors based on command operational context:** "Read Operation"
Set only by system controlled interface	**Create factors based on software operational context:** "Security Management Package"
May query only products for which the manager is responsible	**Create factors based on group membership:** "Department" or further refined "Specific Organization Within Sales" if products sales organizations are aligned by product type, for example. **Create factors based on organizational policy:** "Product Category List", a list of product categories for which the manager is responsible
Audit trail cannot be updated or deleted by a database administrator	**Create factors based on separation of duty:** "Database Role(s)"
Audit trail must be maintained for a period of seven years	**Create factors based on compliance:** "Audit Retention Period"

TABLE 6-2 *Condition and Candidate DVB Factors*

- Factors based on identity management
- Factors based on access or operational context
- Factors based on time or sequential conditions
- Factors based on data or events stored externally

As we discussed in Chapter 5, DBV factors will support conditions when used as part of a DBV rule. We will look at examples of factors for these categories to understand the methods used to create them so they can be applied to an overall enterprise security policy. At a minimum, we want to leverage a common security policy for applications that reside in the same database. To do this, we must have a central location for the PL/SQL routines that will be used for our factor retrieval methods.

Centralizing PL/SQL Routines for DBV Factors and Rules

In Chapter 5, we developed PL/SQL routines that checked for a PL/SQL package on the call stack and routines that maintained the SQL command's event context (SQL text, object owner, object, and so on). At the time, we stored this code in the SH schema to simplify the example and the explanation. Now we find the need for more PL/SQL code to be used as part of our DBV factors. This code will be used not only in DBV factors but in DBV rules as well, as DBV factors are not intended to replace DBV rules. Once you have a scenario in which PL/SQL code needs to be used in both DBV rules and PL/SQL, you can use the PL/SQL code as a function in a DBV factor's retrieval method. This function can simply return a TRUE/FALSE expression such as 1/0.

What we really need is a centralized object-owner account where we can place common security-related PL/SQL code. The DVSYS schema is not the best location for this type of code given its system privileges, direct object privileges on its own security-relevant objects, and its ability to grant the DV-protected roles such as DV_ACCTMGR or DV_OWNER. DBV is installed with another schema named DVF (for Database Vault Factors) that is used to maintain DBV factor functions, and the account is protected by the DBV realm.

The account has only the CREATE PROCEDURE system privilege and no system ANY object privileges that would extend to other object-owner accounts, so it would be a more secure choice. For supportability, we can model a DBV extension account named DBVEXT based on the way the DVF account is set up. In fact, we will grant a few additional system privileges, such as CREATE TABLE, to the DBVEXT account to include custom configuration data and grant SELECT privileges on security-relevant views in the database, such as DBA_ROLE_PRIVS to enable the custom logic. All we need to do is create the DBVEXT account and authorize DBVEXT in the DBV realm to load the code or tables that provide the custom logic required. We can then lock the account when we are done loading these objects.

```
dbvacctmgr@aos>-- create the DBVEXT account and provide the
dbvacctmgr@aos>-- account with storage quotas for tables
dbvacctmgr@aos>CREATE USER dbvext
     IDENTIFIED BY oracle
     DEFAULT TABLESPACE SYSAUX;
User created.
dbvacctmgr@aos>ALTER USER dbvext QUOTA 10M ON SYSAUX;
User altered.
dbvacctmgr@aos>CONNECT dbvowner
```

```
Enter password:
Connected.
dbvowner@aos>-- authorize the DBVEXT account in the DBV Realm
dbvowner@aos>-- so that the account can create PL/SQL programs
dbvowner@aos>-- and grant EXECUTE privileges on these objects
dbvowner@aos>-- to the DVSYS account
dbvowner@aos>BEGIN
  dbms_macadm.add_auth_to_realm (
     realm_name     => 'Oracle Database Vault'
   , grantee        => 'DBVEXT'
   , rule_set_name  => NULL
   , auth_options   => dbms_macutl.g_realm_auth_owner
  );
END;
/
PL/SQL procedure successfully completed.
dbvowner@aos>-- protect the DBVEXT account in the DBV Realm
dbvowner@aos>BEGIN
  dbms_macadm.add_object_to_realm (
      realm_name     => 'Oracle Database Vault'
     ,object_owner   => 'DBVEXT'
     ,object_name    => '%'
     ,object_type    => '%'
  );
END;
/
PL/SQL procedure successfully completed.
dbvowner@aos >CONNECT / AS SYSDBA
Connected.
sys@aos>-- this grant allows the DBVEXT account to
sys@aos>-- connect to the database
sys@aos>GRANT CREATE SESSION TO dbvext;
Grant succeeded.
sys@aos>-- this grant allows the DBVEXT account to
sys@aos>-- create tables in the database
sys@aos>-- we will use this privilege in later
sys@aos>-- examples that require configuration data
sys@aos>GRANT CREATE TABLE TO dbvext;
Grant succeeded.
sys@aos>-- this grant is required by the role check logic
sys@aos>-- we will add to the DBVEXT account
sys@aos>GRANT SELECT ON sys.dba_role_privs TO dbvext;
Grant succeeded.
sys@aos>-- this grant is required by the privilege check logic
sys@aos>-- we will add to the DBVEXT account
sys@aos>GRANT SELECT ON sys.dba_sys_privs TO dbvext;
Grant succeeded.
sys@aos>-- this grant enables the extended rule set
sys@aos>-- event handler demo for Chapter 7
sys@aos>GRANT CREATE ANY CONTEXT TO dbvext;
Grant succeeded.
sys@aos>CONNECT dbvext
```

```
Enter password:
Connected.
dbvext@aos>-- as you can see the DBVEXT account does not have
dbvext@aos>-- roles, e.g. DV_ADMIN or system ANY privileges,
dbvext@aos>-- such as GRANT ANY ROLE, which would cause
dbvext@aos>-- concern for the DBVEXT account being authorized
dbvext@aos>-- as a realm owner in the DBV realm
dbvext@aos>SELECT * FROM session_roles;
ROLE
------------------------------
DV_PUBLIC
dbvext@aos>SELECT * FROM session_privs ORDER BY 1;
PRIVILEGE
----------------------------------------
CREATE ANY CONTEXT
CREATE PROCEDURE
CREATE SESSION
CREATE TABLE
4 rows selected.

dbvext@aos>-- create the DBV extension package and
dbvext@aos>-- grant execute on the package to DVSYS so that it
dbvext@aos>-- can be used in DBV Factor, Rules or Rule Set handlers
dbvext@aos>CREATE OR REPLACE PACKAGE dbvext.dbms_mac_extension AS
  -----------------------------------------------------
  -- used to check software operating context to
  -- determine if a specific PL/SQL package is being executed
  FUNCTION instr_call_stack(object_name IN VARCHAR2
      , object_type IN VARCHAR2 DEFAULT 'PACKAGE BODY') RETURN NUMBER;
  -----------------------------------------------------
  -- used to check if the session user has a specific role
  -- you can send a comma-separated list of roles in the role_name
  -- parameter and if any are granted to the user, a 1 will be returned
  FUNCTION user_has_role(role_name IN VARCHAR2
   ,user_name IN VARCHAR2 DEFAULT SYS_CONTEXT('USERENV','SESSION_USER')
  ) RETURN NUMBER;
  -----------------------------------------------------
  -- used to check if the session user has a specific role
  -- you can send a comma-separated list of privileges in the priv_name
  -- parameter and if any are granted to the user, a 1 will be returned
  FUNCTION user_has_priv(priv_name IN VARCHAR2
  , user_name IN VARCHAR2 DEFAULT SYS_CONTEXT('USERENV','SESSION_USER')
  ) RETURN NUMBER;
  -----------------------------------------------------
  -- used to assert a specific type of SQL command,
  -- e.g. SELECT, INSERT, EXECUTE
  FUNCTION  assert_command(
      check_event     IN VARCHAR2
    , sql_event       IN VARCHAR2
  ) RETURN NUMBER ;
  -----------------------------------------------------
  -- used to assert a specific type of SQL command,
```

```
-- e.g. SELECT, INSERT, EXECUTE
-- on a specific object owner's objects or object
FUNCTION assert_object_command(
    check_event     IN VARCHAR2
  , check_obj_owner IN VARCHAR2
  , check_obj_name  IN VARCHAR2
  , sql_event       IN VARCHAR2
  , sql_obj_owner   IN VARCHAR2
  , sql_obj_name    IN VARCHAR2
) RETURN NUMBER;
-----------------------------------------------------
-- used to assert a specific weekly timeframe is true
FUNCTION weekly_window(
                begin_day      IN VARCHAR2
              , begin_time     IN VARCHAR2
              , end_day        IN VARCHAR2
              , end_timc       IN VARCHAR2
              , time_format    IN VARCHAR2 DEFAULT 'HH24'
              , check_datetime IN DATE DEFAULT SYSDATE
) RETURN NUMBER;
-----------------------------------------------------
-- used to check if a grant or revoke operation is
-- being attempted to the current database session user
FUNCTION grant_or_revoke_to_self RETURN NUMBER;
-----------------------------------------------------
-- used to store the details of a SQL command being
-- executed in an application context so the details
-- can be used in DBV Rule Set custom handlers
PROCEDURE set_event_context(
      command         IN VARCHAR2
    , session_user    IN VARCHAR2
    , instance_num    IN NUMBER
    , database_name   IN VARCHAR2
    , obj_type        IN VARCHAR2
    , obj_owner       IN VARCHAR2
    , obj_name        IN VARCHAR2
    , sql_text        IN VARCHAR2
 ) ;
END dbms_mac_extension;
/
Package created.
dbvext@aos>-- create the package body
dbvext@aos>@@@dbv_ext_body
Package body created.
dbvext@aos>-- grant DVSYS EXECUTE privileges so the code
dbvext@aos>-- can be used in DBV Factors and DBV Rules
dbvext@aos>GRANT EXECUTE ON dbvext.dbms_mac_extension TO dvsys;

Grant succeeded.
dbvext@aos>-- associate the SQL_EVENT application context
dbvext@aos>-- to this package for the Chapter 7 example
dbvext@aos>CREATE OR REPLACE CONTEXT sql_event
```

```
     USING dbvext.dbms_mac_extension ;
Context created.
dbvext@aos>CONNECT / AS SYSDBA
Connected.
sys@aos>-- revoke the ability to connect to
sys@aos>-- the database from DBVEXT
sys@aos>REVOKE CREATE SESSION FROM dbvext;
Revoke succeeded.
dbvowner@aos>CONNECT dbvacctmgr
Enter password:
Connected.
dbvacctmgr@aos>-- lock the account when the database objects
dbvacctmgr@aos>-- owned by DBVEXT have been loaded
dbvacctmgr@aos>ALTER USER dbvext ACCOUNT LOCK PASSWORD EXPIRE;
User altered.
```

We've taken the liberty of scripting this process and creating the DBVEXT.DBMS_MAC_EXTENSION PL/SQL package. The script is named create_dbv_extension.sql in the scripts included with this book. You will need to replace the connection and password DEFINEs at the top of the script with the connection specifics for your environment to load it into your database. The decision to remove the realm authorization for DBVEXT in the DBV can be based on whether or not the code used issues Data Definition Language (DDL) statements on the objects owned by DBVEXT. If the code does not issue DDL, it is OK to remove the authorization as follows:

```
dbvowner@aos>--- remove the realm authorization from
dbvowner@aos>BEGIN
  dbms_macadm.delete_auth_from_realm (
     realm_name      => 'Oracle Database Vault'
   , grantee         =>  'DBVEXT'
  );
END;
/
PL/SQL procedure successfully completed.
```

Even if the code does not issue DDL on DBVEXT objects, you may find it useful to leave the authorization in place for awhile to develop and debug the code stored in the DBVEXT account.

Factors Based on Compliance

DBV factors defined as constants can be used to support compliance regulations in your environment. In our notional example, we have a condition that states that audit trails must be maintained for period of seven years and certain types of administrators are restricted from altering an audit trail. We might also have compliance regulations that dictate the number of days a corporate officer must review internal controls. These conditions for compliance may change over time. DBV factors defined as constants allow for the potential for change and avoid the need to hard code the details of a compliance control in application code. For example, we may define a DBV factor Audit_Retention_Period as follows:

```
dbvowner@aos>BEGIN
    dbms_macadm.create_factor(
        factor_name      => 'Audit_Retention_Period' ,
        factor_type_name => 'Organizational',
```

```
        description   => 'A compliance control that dictates the'
            || 'number of years audit trails must be maintained.',
        rule_set_name => NULL ,
        get_expr      => '7',
        validate_expr => NULL,
        identify_by   => dbms_macutl.g_identify_by_constant,
        labeled_by    => dbms_macutl.g_labeled_by_self,
        eval_options => dbms_macutl.g_eval_on_access,
        audit_options => dbms_macutl.g_audit_on_get_error,
        fail_options  => dbms_macutl.g_fail_with_message);
END;
/
PL/SQL procedure successfully completed.
COMMIT
Commit complete.
```

This factor's function, **DVF.F$Audit_Retention_Period**, could be leveraged in PL/SQL code or Oracle VPD policy to ensure that audit records are not deleted in a manner that would violate the compliance policy. This type of configuration control is available to all applications in the database.

Factors Based on Conflict of Interest or Separation of Duty

To ensure the integrity of audit trails, a separation of duty control was specified to prevent database administrators from updating or deleting them. We can use a DBV factor to define the database administrator roles we want to restrict, such as DBA, OLAP_DBA, or IMP_FULL_DATABASE, and the factor will return an indicator if the current database session has been granted one of these roles:

```
dbvowner@aos>BEGIN
    dbms_macadm.create_factor(
        factor_name      => 'Database_Administrator' ,
        factor_type_name => 'User',
        description   =>
            'The current session has database administrator roles.',
        rule_set_name => NULL,
        get_expr      => 'dbvext.dbms_mac_extension.user_has_role(
                ''DBA,OLAP_DBA,IMP_FULL_DATABASE'')',
        validate_expr => NULL,
        identify_by   => dbms_macutl.g_identify_by_method,
        labeled_by    => dbms_macutl.g_labeled_by_self,
        eval_options => dbms_macutl.g_eval_on_access,
        audit_options => dbms_macutl.g_audit_on_get_error,
        fail_options  => dbms_macutl.g_fail_with_message);
END;
/
PL/SQL procedure successfully completed.
```

Using this approach, we can define factors around sensitive application or database roles that are used in our environment. This factor leverages the DBVEXT.DBMS_MAC_EXTENSION PL/SQL package's **user_has_role** function, which checks the session against the roles to which it has access as defined in the SYS.DBA_ROLE_PRIVS view. It would be straightforward to create a complementary function in this package to leverage the SYS.DBA_SYS_PRIVS view to determine whether a session has access to sensitive system privileges, such as BECOME USER, ADMINISTER DATABASE TRIGGER, or EXEMPT ACCESS POLICY, should your security policy require such checks. The **user_has_priv** function was included with the DBVEXT.DBMS_MAC_EXTENSION PL/SQL package to meet this need. It is important to configure these factors with an **eval_options** parameter set to **dbms_macutl.g_eval_on_access** so that if the conditions change during the course of a database session, the factor's retrieval method is executed to get the most current information available.

Factors Based on Organizational Policy

In our example use case, the organization policy dictates that a Product Manager can query the details only of products for which the manager is responsible. This condition might be based on a small number of product categories or product types in the system. Smaller user-driven lists or user-driven single values defined by organizational policy can be implemented as DBV factors. Consider the SH.PRODUCTS table, for example, and its small number of product categories:

```
sh@aos>SELECT DISTINCT prod_category FROM sh.products ORDER BY 1;

PROD_CATEGORY
--------------------------------------------------
Electronics
Hardware
Peripherals and Accessories
Photo
Software/Other
5 rows selected.
```

If an organization employs a single manager for one or more product categories, we can implement a simple PL/SQL function to return the product categories a logged in user manages and use this function as the retrieval method of a notional factor named Product_Categories_Managed. The advantage of this approach is that the function is called at session startup and available for the remainder of the session as part of a DBV rule or in the PL/SQL that controls Virtual Private Database (VPD) or Oracle Label Security (OLS).

Factors Based on Identity Management

Identity management–related factors such as an end user's job title or department could be resolved using enterprise-specific code that could leverage a human resources system or Lightweight Directory Access Protocol (LDAP) directory such as Oracle Internet Directory (OID). In Chapter 5, we presented an example for a User_Department_Name factor that queried the HR sample schema and used the database end user name as a linking element. This notional example demonstrates how identity management–related factors could be retrieved when the user-specific attributes or group membership information is stored in the database.

A more typical scenario in an enterprise would have the user-specific attributes or group memberships stored in an external HR system or LDAP directory. The Oracle database includes several features and products for remote access such as UTL_TCP, UTL_HTTP, DBMS_LDAP, or Oracle Heterogeneous Services that can be used to access external systems. Oracle Enterprise User Security (EUS) is one technology that allows end users stored in LDAP to authenticate to the database. When this authentication has completed, the database will automatically populate an application context named SYS_LDAP_USER_DEFAULT with non-NULL values of the inetOrgPerson directory object for the user. This inetOrgPerson directory object class includes more than 40 attributes for an end user that can be leveraged with this technology. For example, when an Oracle EUS–based session is started, a DBV factor could be created to query the SESSION_CONTEXT view for specific LDAP attributes from the example context shown here:

```
eus-user@aos>SELECT * FROM session_context
WHERE namespace = 'SYS_LDAP_USER_DEFAULT';

NAMESPACE               ATTRIBUTE        VALUE
----------------------- ---------------- ------------
SYS_LDAP_USER_DEFAULT   UID              eus.user
SYS_LDAP_USER_DEFAULT   TITLE            ANALYST
SYS_LDAP_USER_DEFAULT   MANAGER          eus.manager
SYS_LDAP_USER_DEFAULT   TELEPHONENUMBER  +1 555 456 789
SYS_LDAP_USER_DEFAULT   MAIL             eus.user@mycompany.com
SYS_LDAP_USER_DEFAULT   EMPLOYEETYPE     CONTRACTOR
6 rows selected.
```

The approach defined in Oracle Metalink note 242156.1 "An Example of Using Application Context's Initialized Globally" can also be used with EUS to extend this generic EUS capability to include group membership information or to extend the attributes of an end user that are not available in inetOrgPerson.

Factors Based on Access Path or Operational Context

In Chapter 5, we presented example scenarios for examining the access path to the database and the context of the transaction operation. We demonstrated a fairly complex multifactored approach to identifying the type of connection (a factor) based partially on the IP address (a factor) of the database client to account for the network access path to the database. We also demonstrated DBV rule sets that authorized a specific SQL command only if it had come from a trusted PL/SQL package that was resident on the PL/SQL call stack. In this second scenario, we defined the call stack check logic as a DBV factor using the DBVEXT.DBMS_MAC_EXTENSION PL/SQL package's **INSTR_CALL_STACK** function.

```
dbvowner@aos>BEGIN
    dbms_macadm.create_factor(
        factor_name      => 'In_Sales_Transaction_Package' ,
        factor_type_name => 'Application',
        description    => 'The current transaction was called
                 from the SH.SALES_TRANSACTION package.',
        rule_set_name => NULL ,
        get_expr      =>
      'dbvext.dbms_mac_extension.instr_call_stack(''SH.SALES_TRANSACTION'')',
        validate_expr => NULL,
        identify_by    => dbms_macutl.g_identify_by_method,
        labeled_by     => dbms_macutl.g_labeled_by_self,
        eval_options => dbms_macutl.g_eval_on_access,
        audit_options => dbms_macutl.g_audit_on_get_error,
        fail_options  => dbms_macutl.g_fail_with_message);
END;
/
PL/SQL procedure successfully completed.
```

Our DBV rule definition is updated to leverage this new factor:

```
dbvowner@aos> -- first lets create the conditional rule that
dbvowner@aos> -- we are using the trusted sales transaction code
dbvowner@aos>BEGIN
         dbms_macadm.update_rule(
         rule_name => 'Called From Sales Transaction Package'
         , rule_expr => 'DVF.F$In_Sales_Transaction_Package > 0'
     );
END;
/
PL/SQL procedure successfully completed.
```

Factors Based on Time or Sequential Conditions

In Chapter 5, we presented an example scenario for examining the day of the week and time of day to determine whether a SQL command should be allowed to execute. The IT department's policy allowed for system maintenance to occur on Fridays from 5 to 11 P.M., so this was an organizational policy that used time-based factors.

A word of caution: As you examine time-based factors, consider creating only factors that have meaning to your organization or enterprise. Factors such as Time of Day or Current Date are simply data points that can be resolved using normal PL/SQL routines such as **TO_CHAR** or **SYSTIMESTAMP** and do not provide a tremendous amount of value as DBV factors. You should focus on creating factors for the concept of a maintenance window or other named time windows in which an activity can occur. Creating these types of factors is useful when decisions are made outside of a DBV rule set, such as inside PL/SQL code blocks or in row-level security controls such as Oracle VPD.

The DBVEXT.DBMS_MAC_EXTENSION PL/SQL package includes a utility function called **weekly_window** that can be used to create multiple named time windows. Our example from Chapter 5 could be expressed as a factor in the following way:

```
dbvowner@aos>BEGIN
    dbms_macadm.create_factor(
        factor_name      => 'Is_Maintenance_Window' ,
        factor_type_name => 'Time',
        description   =>
            'Returns an indicator that the system is inside weekly
                 maintenance window.',
        rule_set_name => NULL ,
        get_expr      =>
           'dbvext.dbms_mac_extension.weekly_window(''FRIDAY'',''17:00'','
                || '''FRIDAY'',''22:59'',''HH24:MI'')',
        validate_expr => NULL,
        identify_by   => dbms_macutl.g_identify_by_method,
        labeled_by    => dbms_macutl.g_labeled_by_self,
        eval_options => dbms_macutl.g_eval_on_access,
        audit_options => dbms_macutl.g_audit_on_get_error,
        fail_options  => dbms_macutl.g_fail_with_message);
END;
/
PL/SQL procedure successfully completed.
```

This factor can define a named time window by specifying the starting day of the week and time in the first two parameters and the ending day of the week in the third and fourth parameters. The function's fifth parameter defines the Oracle datetime format model of the time-based parameters. With this factor in place, we return to the example presented in Chapter 5 and define the DBV rule **Is Maintenance Timeframe** as follows:

```
dbvowner@aos>  BEGIN
 dbms_macadm.create_rule(
   rule_name => 'Is Maintenance Timeframe'
 , rule_expr => 'DVF.F$Is_Maintenance_Window = 1'
 );
 END;
/
PL/SQL procedure successfully completed.
```

It is required that you configure time-based factors with an **eval_options** parameter set to **dbms_macutl.g_eval_on_access**, because this information does change during the course of a database session.

Factors Based on Data or Events Stored Externally

DBV factors can be created based on information stored in external systems, as we discussed with the use of Oracle EUS and DBV. The Oracle database includes several features and products for network-based access to external systems. UTL_TCP, UTL_HTTP, DBMS_LDAP, or Oracle Heterogeneous Services can be used for these scenarios. You can also leverage features such as external procedures written in C or Java to interact with the operating system on which the database runs to provide the information for these factors.

Incorporating DBV Factors in Your Application

The following guidelines offer different ways you can leverage DBV factors in your database applications.

Factors in Oracle VPD Policy Functions

Oracle VPD lets you enforce security to a fine level of row-level security (RLS) directly on tables, views, or synonyms with security policies that are attached directly to these objects. When a user directly or indirectly accesses a table, view, or synonym protected with a VPD policy, the server dynamically modifies the SQL statement of the user by adding or modifying the WHERE condition (known as a predicate) returned by a PL/SQL policy function implementing the security policy. VPD policies can be applied to SELECT, INSERT, UPDATE, and DELETE statements. One useful benefit of DBV factor functions being available in PL/SQL is that we can use them in Oracle VPD policy functions, as shown in the following example:

```
CREATE OR REPLACE FUNCTION costs_policy_function(
   schema_name IN VARCHAR2
 , table_name IN VARCHAR2 ) RETURN VARCHAR2
AS
BEGIN
    -- no cost transaction during maintenance window
    IF DVF.F$Is_Maintenance_Window = 1 THEN
```

```
        RETURN '1=0';
    -- filter on costs related to the product categories
    -- the manager is responsible for managing
    ELSE
        RETURN 'EXISTS ( SELECT 1 FROM sh.products '
            || 'WHERE sh.costs.prod_id = sh.products.prod_id '
            || ' AND sh.products.prod_category_id IN ('
            || DVF.F$Product_Categories_Managed || '))' ;
    END IF;
END;
/
```

In this example, we can restrict users from querying or updating any cost-related data during the weekly maintenance window and then use a factor called Product_Categories_Managed that holds the product category list that is maintained by the end user.

Factors in OLS Labeling Functions and SQL Predicates

OLS enables RLS by using Oracle VPD as well. With OLS, a label security administrator defines a set of labels for data and users, along with authorizations for users and program units that govern access to specified protected objects. An OLS policy is nothing more than a name associated with these labels, rules, and authorizations. Oracle OLS controls access to the contents of a record in a table by comparing a row's label with a user's label and privileges. To apply an OLS policy to a table, we would use the package procedure SA_POLICY_ADMIN.APPLY_TABLE_POLICY. This package procedure has the following signature:

```
PROCEDURE APPLY_TABLE_POLICY (
  policy_name       IN VARCHAR2,
  schema_name       IN VARCHAR2,
  table_name        IN VARCHAR2,
  table_options     IN VARCHAR2 DEFAULT NULL,
  label_function    IN VARCHAR2 DEFAULT NULL,
  predicate         IN VARCHAR2 DEFAULT NULL);
```

The **label_function** parameter can be used to declare a PL/SQL function that returns a label value to use as the default label for a record that is created. For example, we could define an OLS PL/SQL label function that uses a notional **Job_Title** factor to increase the sensitivity of product costs records that a vice president can see:

```
CREATE OR REPLACE FUNCTION costs_label RETURN LBACSYS.LBAC_LABEL IS
BEGIN
IF DVF.F$Job_Title = 'VICE PRESIDENT' THEN
      RETURN TO_LBAC_DATA_LABEL('COST_POLICY', 'SENSITIVE');
ELSE
      RETURN TO_LBAC_DATA_LABEL('COST_POLICY', 'CORPORATE');
END;
```

This policy function can then be used in the **label_function** parameter in a SA_POLICY_ADMIN.APPLY_TABLE_POLICY as follows:

```
, label_function => 'sh.costs_label'
```

The **predicate** parameter is an additional SQL predicate that can be combined dynamically, using the AND or the OR logical operator, with the predicated returned from a label function. We can use a predicate similar to the VPD example presented earlier to combine label security with the operational concept of restricting access during the weekly maintenance window as follows:

```
, predicate => ' AND DVF.F$Is_Maintenance_Window = 0'
```

The same type of factor-based policy can be applied to the OLS package procedure SA_POLICY_ADMIN.APPLY_SCHEMA_POLICY. This defines policies at the database schema level so that all existing or new tables in a particular schema can share the same (consistent) policy definition.

Factors in Oracle Fine-Grained Auditing (FGA)

Regular Oracle database auditing allows you to audit commands issued against a database object every time the command is issued. This can typically lead to more audit data than you may want to store when you really just want to audit when certain conditions are met. These conditions may be driven by compliance purposes and can be dynamic in nature.

The Oracle FGA feature is designed to meet the needs of object-level auditing only when certain conditions are met. Consider the Sales History application and the table SH.CUSTOMERS that includes credit limit information for the customer in CUST_CREDIT_LIMIT. Our condition may be that we are interested in auditing only SELECT commands against this table only by users that are not members of the Sales Department and for customers with higher credit limits. Use of these commands may imply suspicious behavior on behalf of a non-sales staff member.

In Chapter 5, we defined a DBV factor that exposes the user's department name so we can leverage this factor in an FGA policy's audit condition as follows:

```
BEGIN
   dbms_fga.add_policy (
        object_schema    =>'SH'
      , object_name      =>'CUSTOMERS'
      , policy_name      =>'SUSPICIOUS_CUSTOMER_ACCESS'
      , audit_column     => 'CUST_GENDER,CUST_YEAR_OF_BIRTH' ||
        ',CUST_MARITAL_STATUS,CUST_INCOME_LEVEL,CUST_CREDIT_LIMIT'
      , audit_condition => 'CUST_CREDIT_LIMIT >= 10000' ||
            ' AND DVF.F$User_Department_Name != ''Sales'''
      , statement_types => 'SELECT'
  );
END;
```

Factors in Views

Another form of RLS that has been used by many applications is to embed filter logic directly in database views. The implementation of factors as PL/SQL functions creates an opportunity to use them directly in view definitions. The following view for sales costs will prevent data being returned during the weekly maintenance window time frame:

```
CREATE OR REPLACE VIEW sh.costs_view AS
SELECT
  products.prod_name
, promotions.promo_name
, channels.channel_desc
, costs.unit_cost
, costs.unit_price
FROM sh.costs, sh.products, sh.promotions,sh.channels
```

```
WHERE products.prod_id = costs.prod_id
AND promotions.promo_id = costs.promo_id
AND channels.channel_id = costs.channel_id
AND DVF.F$Is_Maintenance_Window = 0
/
```

Factors in Application Code (PL/SQL or SQL Statements)

Factors can be used in application code that exists outside the database. The preceding examples show how factors can be embedded within other database objects. It is important to remember that factors are available as PL/SQL functions and can be included within SQL anywhere it may reside. The implementation of factors as PL/SQL functions can be very similar to the view in the preceding paragraph.

The following SQL statement will be defined and executed from the application tier. The query of sales costs will prevent data from being returned during the weekly maintenance window time frame:

```
SELECT
  products.prod_name
, promotions.promo_name
, channels.channel_desc
, costs.unit_cost
, costs.unit_price
FROM sh.costs, sh.products, sh.promotions,sh.channels
WHERE products.prod_id = costs.prod_id
AND promotions.promo_id = costs.promo_id
AND channels.channel_id = costs.channel_id
AND DVF.F$Is_Maintenance_Window = 0
/
```

The factor is resolved when executed within the database. The factor is evaluated and returned to the SQL statement, and then applied as a filter inside the statement itself.

Factor functions are automatically granted to PUBLIC through a special DBV role named DV_PUBLIC. No special work is required to leverage them in PL/SQL code you write as packaged procedures as well as SQL statements that applications or end users issue. You can use the two forms of factor identity retrieval—the DVF schema's **factor** function or the **DVSYS GET_FACTOR** function—as follows:

```
IF DVF.F$Is_Maintenance_Window = 1 THEN
… logic here
END IF;
```

Or equivalently,

```
IF DVSYS.GET_FACTOR('Is_Maintenance_Window') = 1 THEN
… logic here
END IF;
```

This simplifies application logic by reducing the need for common code to be copied or shared among projects and can help performance when the factors are evaluated at session startup (or when proxy authentication sessions start). The result is application code that is more declarative in nature with respect to security. The use of the function **DVSYS.GET_FACTOR** would be preferable when the name of the factor is dynamic depending on your implementation or project.

As you can see, factors can play a significant role in application logic codified in your PL/SQL programs and can be integrated into row-level security mechanisms such as Oracle VPD, Oracle OLS, Oracle FGA, and database views. The implementation of factors as PL/SQL opens up these possibilities and just about any PL/SQL-based database feature such as database triggers or database jobs.

Identify DBV Realms and Realm Objects Based on Objects

The next step in the process of designing the DBV security policy is to examine the objects in our security profile to determine where we may have sensitive information that needs to be protected. We can identify the following objects:

- Product Costs
- Products
- Sales Organization
- Sales Management Package
- User Credentials
- Social Security Number
- Salary
- Commission
- System Security Package
- Products
- Channels
- Promotions
- Audit Trail
- Audit Notifications

Next, we can ask ourselves whether we can categorize the information by the following criteria:

- Application and access requirements
- Content type

This high-level usage analysis can be done using the information in Table 6-3, with requirements documents such as use case scenarios or UML sequence diagrams providing input into the analysis.

Object	Content Type	Application Type	Access Requirement
Product Costs	Sales (SOX compliance)	Sales Management	Read, Write
Products	Sales	Sales Management	Read, Write (Read in this use case)
Channels	Sales	Sales Management	Read, Write (Read in this use case)
Promotions	Sales	Sales Management	Read, Write (Read in this use case)
Sales Management Package	Sales	Sales Management	Read, Write
Sales Organization	Identity Management	Human Resources	Read
User Credentials	Identity Management	Human Resources	Read
Social Security Number	Identity Management (PII compliance)	Human Resources	Prevent Read
Salary	Identity Management (privacy)	Human Resources	Prevent Read
Commission	Identity Management (privacy)	Human Resources	Prevent Read
System Security Package	Identity Management	Human Resources	Read
Audit Trail	System	Database	Write
Audit Notifications	System	Database	Read, Write

TABLE 6-3 *Information for High-level Usage Analysis*

Table 6-3 provides an interesting analysis in that we can clearly see a set of content type or application categories that will provide a nice break-out for our DBV realms. Namely, we want to investigate whether we need to provide DBV realms for the following:

- Sales
- Human Resources
- Database

Yes, database! That seems odd, but the database itself is an application in that it operates in the same manner as custom applications that are loaded into it—tables, indexes, views, and programs are all found. As discussed in Chapter 5, Oracle DBV creates a handful of realms for the Enterprise Edition itself so the concept that the database itself should be protected is built into the product.

We want to consider auditing and auditing notification as a generic application requirement in many customer applications. The Oracle database provides auditing components and features to enable notifications, so we can leverage these capabilities (versus building them) and simply ensure they are properly protected.

Our next step is to determine which database object-owner accounts and objects will be created (or exist) to support the application itself. The use case we are examining is related to Sales Management, so there will certainly be a schema with database objects in it to support this use case. This research will typically be conducted with the assistance of a system or application database administrator, but for this book, we will look at the sample schemas.

We see the Sales History (SH) schema has tables such as COSTS, SALES, PRODUCTS, PROMOTIONS, CHANNELS, and CUSTOMERS. So in simply examining one use case, "Add Monthly Product Costs," we have uncovered new areas of concern related to security and compliance. If the COSTS information is of concern for SOX compliance, we can only assume the SALES information should be treated with the same level of concern. In addition, if we examine the CUSTOMERS table, we can see that privacy related information is being maintained in the organization's databases and includes customer address, phone number, e-mail address, gender, marital status, and income data!

If we examine the candidate realm Human Resources, we have to consider how identity management is handled at the enterprise and application levels. If a corporation is leveraging Oracle technologies such as EUS, it can integrate database authentication with LDAP-based directories, so our concern (at the database level) is more about protecting objects such as database roles used for EUS enterprise roles. We also need to consider that an enterprise may delegate the authentication against directories (or even database tables) to the application tier logic, leaving the database interactions to be based on a shared pool account using a design pattern named "application proxy." For the purposes of this chapter, we will not discuss all the available authentication mechanisms in use across the industry.

For this chapter, we will consider the Human Resources realm to comprise tables in the HR schema, as we can associate database accounts to employee-related records in this schema's tables quite easily to resolve organizational affiliation, such as whether the logged in user works for a Sales Department. We want to address DBV security policy from the perspective of multiple object-owner accounts taking part in the example use case and leave it at that. When we examine the HR schema, we find tables such as EMPLOYEES and DEPARTMENTS that would be used in read operations for the example use case. In the case of the EMPLOYEES table, we have potential PII and privacy concerns, and our security profile even goes so far as to dictate requirements for column-level controls on data related to Social Security numbers, salary, and commission data that might be found in this table.

Configure Standard Object-level Auditing for Realm-protected Objects

At this point, we've uncovered a handful of security-relevant tables based on compliance and privacy criteria. In particular, the SH tables SALES and COSTS and the HR table EMPLOYEES fall into this category. For compliance and privacy concerns, or for mission-critical tables in general, we absolutely want to form a database auditing policy, even for database accounts that are allowed to access or manipulate the data stored in these tables. DBV will allow for the auditing of violations to the realm security policy, but we want to leverage normal/core RDBMS auditing to ensure that a database administrator can provide information sufficient to pass a compliance audit, which will need to include successful transactions as well as unsuccessful transactions. It is recommended that the following audit policy be applied to each sensitive table:

```
AUDIT SELECT  ON <TABLE> BY ACCESS WHENEVER NOT SUCCESSFUL
AUDIT INSERT  ON <TABLE> BY ACCESS
AUDIT DELETE  ON <TABLE> BY ACCESS
AUDIT UPDATE  ON <TABLE> BY ACCESS
AUDIT ALTER   ON <TABLE> BY ACCESS
AUDIT AUDIT   ON <TABLE> BY ACCESS
AUDIT COMMENT ON <TABLE> BY ACCESS
AUDIT GRANT   ON <TABLE> BY ACCESS
AUDIT INDEX   ON <TABLE> BY ACCESS
AUDIT RENAME  ON <TABLE> BY ACCESS
```

This policy provides audit attribution for all write transactions to the sensitive tables as well as any security-relevant operations on the table such as GRANT, REVOKE, AUDIT, and NOAUDIT. Unsuccessful read attempts (SELECT) are captured and offer visibility to potential insider threats. Note that in the policy we do not recommend that you audit all successful SELECT commands against the sensitive table unless your regulations absolutely require each access to be audited. The reason for this omission is that for a heavily loaded system, with a large number of read transactions or a large number of users, the amount of audit data can become quite large. The amount of audit data does not really provide a lot of value unless compliance regulations or audits would need to know about each read transaction. It is important to consider applying this same table-based audit policy to database views as well.

Many packaged database applications leverage PL/SQL stored procedures (packages, procedures, and functions), and you can ensure proper auditing of these program units using a policy similar to the following:

```
AUDIT EXECUTE ON <PROCEDURE> BY ACCESS WHENEVER NOT SUCCESSFUL
AUDIT RENAME  ON <PROCEDURE> BY ACCESS
AUDIT GRANT   ON <PROCEDURE> BY ACCESS
AUDIT AUDIT   ON <PROCEDURE> BY ACCESS
```

We have a situation with auditing successful EXECUTE operations similar to that with SELECTs on tables. We audit the successful EXECUTE operations only if compliance regulations dictate that this be done and the volume of audit data generated does not become unmanageable.

Configure RLS on Realm-protected Objects

As discussed in Chapter 5, Oracle DBV is geared to authorize commands against database objects, or statement-level security (SLS), versus an implementation for row-level security (RLS). As we have done with auditing, we need to examine the security-relevant tables based on compliance and privacy criteria to determine whether any RLS policies are required. Some environments demand absolute requirements for label-based controls, but in many environments, it's up to the database administrators and developers how RLS requirements are defined, designed, and implemented. RLS is the best place to put the data security, because it keeps the security as close to the data as possible. In many cases, RLS requirements are implemented within the application tier and often require additional DBV security. DBV would protect the security-relevant data and packages on which the application relies to enforce the data security from the application. Not adding security is analogous to locking the front door of your house with a dead bolt and leaving your side gate open with the back door unlocked. In addition, if another application comes along that requires access to the same set of tables, you have to copy the existing source code and possibly retool the existing application. Whenever possible, use the advanced RLS features of Oracle Database to implement the security policy within the database.

This analysis for RLS can be based on the conditions from our security profile. As we discussed in the section related to identifying DBV factors, our example security profile presents RLS examples based on the security profile conditions around the concept of "Weekly Maintenance Window" and "Product Ownership/Responsibility." If we dig a little deeper into the conditions and the compliance-driven requirements these conditions impose, we see that controls are required on the visibility of end user Social Security numbers and salary information to the application. Oracle VPD's fine-grained access control for security-relevant column masking meets these compliance-based requirements.

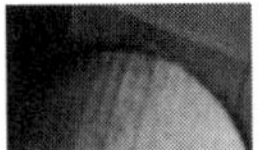

NOTE
Refer to David Knox's Effective Oracle Database 10g Security By Design (McGraw-Hill, 2009) for a comparison between Oracle VPD and Oracle OLS. Oracle OLS is a more intuitive and declarative model to work with initially, while Oracle VPD has the flexibility to create and support more complex PL/SQL function policies that implement row-level security.

Identify Accounts, Roles, and DBV Realm Authorizations from Use Case Actors

If we look at our security profile syntax, we've defined what must be protected (the object), the commands or privileges we need to control (the verb), and how they need be protected (the conditions, based on compliance, application, and business rules), but we haven't spent time describing who (the subject). To define the subject-level aspects of our security profile, we need to consider the entire set of use cases that make up our system and not just the Sales Management–related use case.

If we consider the overall notional software architecture, we find actors such as sales data administrators, database administrators, batch program accounts, internal web service consumers, external (partner) web service consumers, and more subtlety accounts that will own objects and code. In Chapter 1, we introduced the concept of "schema profiles" that include object owner accounts user access accounts. The user access accounts included user profiles with read-only users, read-write users, application administrators/developers, and database administrators.

We need to examine the actors in our use cases and classify them according to the profiles presented in Chapter 1. Next, we'll create database roles and accounts for these actor classifications so we can associate a real database identity to each actor. Once this is done, we can authorize the appropriate role or account in the DBV realms we have identified. To help clarify the process, we will first look at the details of each profile's relationship to DBV roles and concepts. We then present a detailed implementation example that demonstrates how the profiles might be constructed in DBV-enabled database.

Secure Schemas Under DBV

We first want to examine the actors in our notional software architecture to determine how they can be categorized using the profiles presented in the first chapter and understand how DBV may shape the form of those profiles in implementation. As we examine the profiles in more detail, you will discover that DBV helps enable the development of either a coarse-grained and fine-grained separation of duty model for some of the object owner and user access profiles. A fine-grained separation of duty model might be warranted in a system that contains highly sensitive information or when compliance regulations are enforced. Let's examine each profile in more detail to help clarify the approach to constructing these profiles as roles and accounts.

Object-Owner Accounts

In this section, we introduce two types of object-owner accounts: commercial-off-the-shelf (COTS) accounts that may be required by a software product and database application and system accounts that may used in batch (database) processing jobs. We will examine how these two types of object-owner accounts have common privilege models and how you can protect these accounts from being used in a manner in which they were not intended to be used.

Group COTS or Application Account As discussed in Chapter 1, group accounts are installed with vendor commercial off-the-shelf (COTS) products that are rarely accessed by privileged database administrators to perform software maintenance: MDSYS for a spatial or SH account is an example in our use case. As discussed in Chapter 1, the SYS account falls into the category of a group account that is shared by many database administrators through access to an OS account's credentials. Typically, the non-SYS account would be locked with the password expired and controlled by the account administrator as described next. The application account is typically granted a limited set of system privileges that enable the creation and maintenance of tables, views, and PL/SQL objects in its own schema. Note that DBV includes the role DV_REALM_RESOURCE that can be leveraged to create application accounts. The role includes all the system privileges you'd find in the normal RESOURCE role with the addition of the CREATE VIEW and CREATE SYNONYM privileges. This role includes the following system privileges:

- CREATE CLUSTER
- CREATE INDEXTYPE
- CREATE OPERATOR
- CREATE PROCEDURE
- CREATE SEQUENCE
- CREATE SYNONYM
- CREATE TABLE
- CREATE TRIGGER
- CREATE TYPE
- CREATE VIEW
- CREATE SESSION

System Accounts Oracle products and your own applications will leverage accounts that would never really be accessed by a database administrator if you are using the named user account pattern to maintain audit attribution to real end users. For example, Oracle Enterprise Manager (EM) uses the SYSMAN and DBSNMP accounts for statistics collection and runs this collection processing through a database job. Your own applications may have similar accounts that run on a scheduled basis as part of batch processing. This processing might leverage Oracle Secure External Passwords to interact with the database to load or extract database records. These accounts may own data tables, views, PL/SQL programs, and other objects that would be accessed by this account only under normal circumstances. It is a good idea to protect these objects with a DBV realm, in the same way objects owned by the SYSMAN and DBSNMP accounts are protected by the Oracle Enterprise Manager realm.

These system accounts are typically associated with batch programs or database jobs, so the actual database access path is limited to the database servers running the database jobs or crontab processes. Batch programs might also be run from a set of servers that are physically located near the database servers (for example, the same racks), such as a finite set of external application servers. This is a great opportunity to leverage DBV factors as the building blocks for the DBV rule sets that control the realm authorizations or even the DBV CONNECT command rule for these system accounts. This approach can ensure that system accounts are used only under the appropriate conditions.

To help illustrate this concept, consider the fact that the SH account's objects are protected by the Sales History realm. We might create a SH_BATCH account for batch processing on PL/SQL objects owned by the SH account. We can then authorize SH_BATCH as a participant of this realm. You can use DBV factors and DBV rules to control the conditions that allow SH_BATCH to be authorized in this realm so that the authorization is valid only when issued from the database server (defined by the IP Address 192.168.0.251):

```
-- create the batch account
dbvacctmgr@aos>CREATE USER sh_batch IDENTIFIED BY <password>;
User created.

-- grant the appropriate system privileges to the batch account
CONNECT / AS SYSDBA
Connected.
sys@aos>GRANT CREATE SESSION TO sh_batch;
Grant succeeded.
sys@aos>GRANT EXECUTE ANY PROCEDURE TO sh_batch;
Grant succeeded.
-- create the DBV Rule Set that uses DBV Factors to authorize
-- the account in the realm under the conditions we want.
CONNECT dbvowner
Enter password:
Connected.
-- create a rule that we can use to limit
-- realm authorizations to sessions running on
-- the database server
dbvowner@aos>BEGIN
     dbms_macadm.create_rule(
     rule_name => 'Is Client Connection From Database Server'
     , rule_expr =>
           'NVL(DVF.F$Client_IP,''0'') IN (''0'',''192.168.0.251'')'
);
END;
/
PL/SQL procedure successfully completed.
-- create the rule set to associate the rule to
dbvowner@aos>BEGIN
    dbms_macadm.create_rule_set(
        rule_set_name =>'Sales History Batch Allowed',
        description =>
      'Checks to authorize batch commands for the Sales History realm.',
```

```
        enabled =>dbms_macutl.g_yes,
        eval_options =>dbms_macutl.g_ruleset_eval_all,
        audit_options =>dbms_macutl.g_ruleset_audit_fail,
        fail_options =>dbms_macutl.g_ruleset_fail_show,
        fail_message =>NULL,
        fail_code =>NULL,
        handler_options =>dbms_macutl.g_ruleset_handler_off,
        handler =>NULL);
END;
/
PL/SQL procedure successfully completed.
-- associate the rule to the rule set
dbvowner@aos>BEGIN
   dbms_macadm.add_rule_to_rule_set (
     rule_set_name => 'Sales History Batch Allowed'
   , rule_name     => 'Is Client Connection From Database Server'
   );
END;
/
PL/SQL procedure successfully completed.
-- define the realm authorization for this batch account
-- that uses this rule set
dbvowner@aos>BEGIN
  dbms_macadm.add_auth_to_realm (
      realm_name     => 'Sales History'
    , grantee        =>  'SH_BATCH'
    , rule_set_name =>  'Sales History Batch Allowed'
    , auth_options  =>   dbms_macutl.g_realm_auth_participant
  );
END;
/
PL/SQL procedure successfully completed.
```

In this example, we have established these types of rules to ensure that system accounts, such as SH_BATCH, do not issue accounts from database client, such as an application server that hosts a web application. We expect database sessions for enterprise users to be established from these application servers and for them to issue a **SELECT** or **DML** command, but anything else, such as a SH_BATCH session, is an anomaly. Our goal to confine these privileged system accounts to known access paths helps reduce the attack surface of an exploit such as a password-cracking algorithm.

User Access Accounts

In this section, we examine categories for the User Access Accounts that were introduced in Chapter 1. User Access Accounts, which are used by many database applications, can be categorized as follows:

- **System Access Accounts** Enable a real end-user (person) to access database applications without requiring a real database account for each end-user.
- **Read-only or Read-write Application** Users that are dedicated database accounts for each real end-user (person).

- **Database Administrator** The person(s) whose job duties require him or her to connect to the database to maintain the database structure, database security, or the database applications that reside in a database.

This section discusses how to identify these types of accounts within the use-case analysis paradigm we've discussed so far and how the Database Administrator type of account can be broken into a fine-grained separation of duty model. The section serves to lay the groundwork for the detailed separation of duty model example presented in the next section.

System Access Account

Oracle technologies such as proxy authentication and EUS require a real database account to serve as an intermediary between the database and a directory. These accounts are also not typically "directly" logged into but rather are used as part of a connection pool in application servers. The system access accounts are typically granted the privilege sets on objects they do not own and they are a form of the Read-only Application User or Read-write Application User profiles we will discuss next. Similar to the batch-program variety of system accounts, there are access path factors or other conditions that would define the "normal use" of these system accounts. The situation is reverse here, so we allowed database connections and authorized realm activity from the application servers hosting our web applications and disallowed the account usage from the database servers and backend infrastructure.

Our notional database application environment has internal and external web service consumers. Suppose we are using EUS and the same directory server for authentication of employees and partners to these services; we can and should map the different base user trees to different global schemas (the system access account) since the privilege sets for the consumers may be different. Figure 6-2 depicts the mapping defined in the Oracle Enterprise Security Manager (ESM) for internal users to the global schema GLOBAL_INTERNAL.

Figure 6-3 depicts the mapping defined in the ESM for external users to the global schema GLOBAL_EXTERNAL.

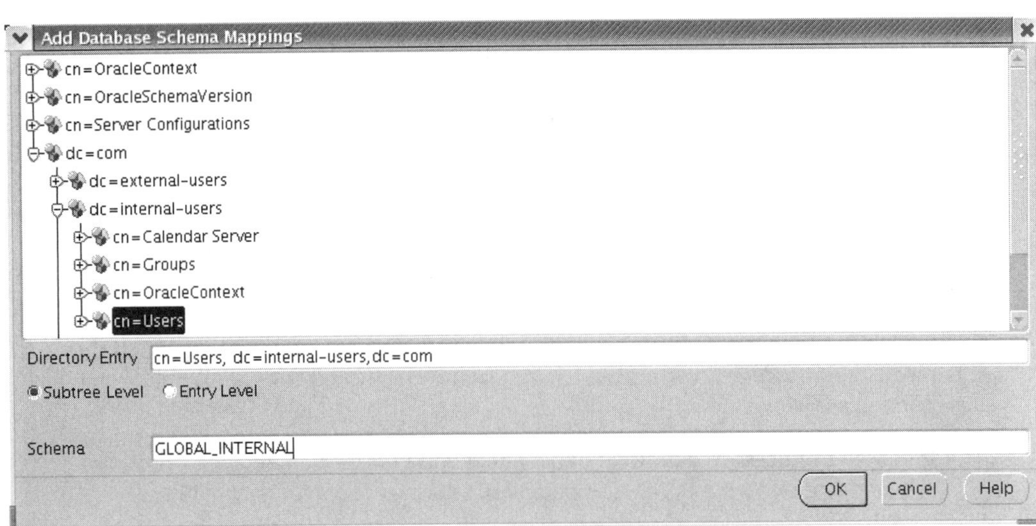

FIGURE 6-2 *Enterprise Security Manager map for internal users*

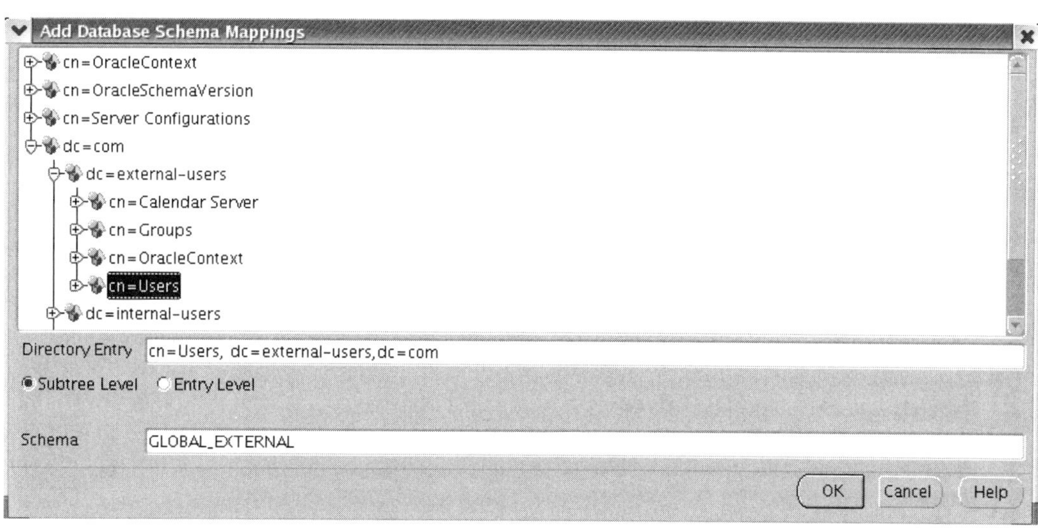

FIGURE 6-3 *Enterprise Security Manager map for external users*

If the application servers that host the web services for the two different sets of users are different, we can then leverage this fact as a DBV factor to fine-tune the authorizations of SQL commands issued by these two global schemas. Suppose the application servers that serve (internal) employees have IP addresses of 192.168.0.100 and 192.168.0.101. The application servers that serve external partners have IP addresses of 192.168.0.50 and 192.168.0.101.51. We can create DBV rules to be used in authorizations for these system access accounts as follows:

```
-- create a rule to authorize commands for an
-- internal global system access account
BEGIN
     dbms_macadm.create_rule(
        rule_name => 'Is Internal Web Service'
      , rule_expr => 'NVL(DVF.F$Client_IP,''0'') IN '
        || '(''192.168.0.100'',''192.168.0.101'')'
        || ' AND DVF.F$Session_User = ''GLOBAL_INTERNAL'''
     );
END;
/
PL/SQL procedure successfully completed.

-- create a rule to authorize commands for an
-- external global system access account
BEGIN
     dbms_macadm.create_rule(
        rule_name => 'Is External Web Service'
      , rule_expr => 'NVL(DVF.F$Client_IP,''0'') IN '
        || '(''192.168.0.50'',''192.168.0.51'')'
        || ' AND DVF.F$Session_User = ''GLOBAL_EXTERNAL'''
     );
```

```
END;
/
PL/SQL procedure successfully completed.
```

These additional identities for the Client_IP and Session_User factors could also be incorporated into the Connection_Type DBV identity map presented in Chapter 5 to establish new connection classifications of INTERNAL_WEB and EXTERNAL_WEB.

Read-only Application Users and Read-write Application Users

Read-only application users are typically found in reporting systems or in a privilege set that is assigned to a "partner" application for a consolidated database with integrated object-owner accounts. For example, we may define an HR read-only role for access to the objects in the HR schema and grant this HR read-only role to the SH schema or a SH-related read-write role. *Read-write application users* are typically found in transactional database systems as they require **INSERT**, **UPDATE**, and **DELETE** commands against objects an application's object-owner account. The users might also have access to execute PL/SQL procedures that are required to participate in the transactional nature of the system, especially in packaged applications for human resources or finance.

The first things to consider before we create the end user access roles are the object access behaviors (the Verb-Object tables discussed earlier) the actors invoke in the use cases we defined for our system. In our notional use case, we've defined SELECT (read) on several objects such as Products, Channels, and Promotions in the SH schema as well as INSERT (write) on the object Product Cost. We also know that additional use cases in our system, such as the internal and external web services, will query Sales History objects.

It becomes evident as we examine the Subject-Verb-Object-Condition tables we create that each use case will exhibit the need for read-only and read-write role pattern from Chapter 1. The difference among the use cases is the objects that are read from or written to. It is perfectly acceptable to define the read-only or read-write roles required for each use case at the start—in other words, a role for each Subject-Verb-Object-Condition table—but we must iterate through each role definition to see where the roles for the use case are the same and can therefore be combined into common roles. We must be careful not to combine them with reckless abandon, as we want to stick with the least privilege principals and avoid exposing sensitive objects to use cases that would lead to compliance issues or policy violation issues. For example, we want to avoid exposing read access to things like the company's balance sheet numbers (compliance) or Social Security numbers of employees (PII) to roles used in a use case such as a Partner Web Service Sales History Query.

Once we've defined the distinct set of read-only and read-write roles we will need, we can establish a basic approach for defining these roles based on the nature of the objects involved. The next topic to consider is how frequently objects are created or destroyed within object-owner accounts over the lifetime of the application(s). We also need to consider whether object-owner accounts are created and destroyed frequently, as this scenario can be found in many applications. If the objects within object-owner accounts are static in nature, the use of a direct object privilege model can be leveraged for the application (read-only and read-write) roles. If object-owner accounts will be dynamic or have dynamically created objects, a system privilege model has to be employed for the application (read-only and read-write) roles.

We are left with a decision to create a finite set of roles for our use cases (or those that we are forced to use) and privilege sets that are based on either direct object privileges or system ANY privileges. The decision is really based on the static or dynamic nature of the objects being protected.

Database Administrator

"Database administrator" is an overloaded term that typically refers to a person who uses a highly privileged database administration account, such as the SYS account with the SYSDBA privilege, the SYSTEM account, or a named account with the DBA role. These administrators can often cut across all application object-owner accounts and security controls to get the job done. What's needed is a methodology to categorize these administrators so that a separation of duty can be achieved. A usable breakout of responsibilities that achieves this separation of duty among various database administrators is presented and demonstrates how DBV enables this separation.

Application Administrator or Developer The application administrator or developer should be granted a limited set of system ANY privileges that would allow him or her to maintain object types and roles that are protected by a DBV realm and are authorized within the appropriate realm. DBV realms are set up to provide separation and areas of responsibility. Different areas of responsibility can be set up when more than one person does the same job but each has responsibilities for different types of data (such as sales or human resources data).

TIP
Define the areas of responsibility for determining realm authorizations.

The administrator would have the system ANY privileges SELECT ANY, INSERT ANY, UPDATE ANY, DELETE ANY, CREATE ANY, ALTER ANY, DROP ANY, EXECUTE ANY (where applicable), and AUDIT ANY (where applicable) on the following object types to read, write, execute, audit, and modify the objects owned by separate object-owner accounts that are protected in the realm:

- CLUSTER
- CONTEXT
- DIMENSION
- INDEX
- INDEXTYPE
- MATERIALIZED VIEW
- OPERATOR
- OUTLINE
- PROCEDURE
- SEQUENCE
- SYNONYM
- TABLE
- TRIGGER
- TYPE
- VIEW

The administrator would also have the following privileges for managing the roles protected by a realm and privileges and objects that are protected by a realm:

- **GRANT ANY OBJECT PRIVILEGE** To grant SELECT, UPDATE, and other direct object privileges on realm protected objects
- **GRANT ANY ROLE** To grant roles protected by the realm to accounts or other roles

This full-featured application database administrator concept is already provided within the DBV product in the DV_REALM_OWNER role and can be used to implement this type of account. You may be concerned about the GRANT privileges, but remember that DBV includes the out-of-the-box realm Oracle Data Dictionary that protects against improper use of the privileges for Oracle COTS roles in the same way the functional application realm would enable the proper use of the privilege among different application realms. At this point, is this full-featured administrator role sufficient? It is sufficient to manage all aspects of the realm, but when viewed another way, it is not sufficient or at least not tolerable. It does not provide for the possibility that some organizations cannot tolerate a highly privileged database administrator within a given application, especially if that application contains sensitive data, where the application administrator could disable auditing of the realm objects while he or she "fixes" the application.

We can create a model for the application administrator role that further breaks this user profile into separate application administrator profiles with distinct and sufficient responsibilities by grouping privilege (sets) granted to the role to perform a specific job.

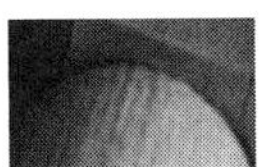

TIP
Break down privilege sets into administrator profiles that define a job.

This method still provides the possibility of combining profiles while maintaining separation of duties. Here's a look at the profile breakout:

- **Application security administrator** This administrator is an application realm owner and can create roles, grant realm-protected roles, or grant realm-protected objects to other accounts or roles. The administrator can also control the audit configuration for the objects protected by the realm. We will demonstrate how to extend this profile to apply OLS policy objects protected by the realm.
- **Application maintenance administrator** This administrator's privileges are limited to performing in the DDL category of commands on the application realm's objects. The administrator is a participant in the application realm but the privileges do not allow for querying or manipulating data protected by the realm, controlling audit configuration for the objects protected in the realm, or granting of realm-protected roles or object privileges to realm-protected objects to other accounts or roles.
- **Application data manager (data steward)** This administrator is a participant in the application realm and the privileges granted are limited to performing queries (read) and DML, or write, commands on the objects protected by the realm. Very simply put, only **SELECT**, **INSERT**, **UPDATE**, **DELETE**, and **EXECUTE** commands are allowed. In certain cases, it may be possible to use the privilege set provided by this profile for read-write end user access profile if we couple it with the Subject-Verb-Object-Condition paradigm presented earlier.

- **Application data analyst** A read-only end user profile whose scope is all objects within a realm. This type of profile is useful for accounts that need direct access to the database outside of an application (such as a web interface) and may use tools such as SQL*Plus or SQL Developer to perform ad hoc queries on the application data. Again, the Subject-Verb-Object-Condition paradigm presented earlier may apply here.

- **Operational database administrator** The operational DBA addresses the concern that an organization too often provides the SYS password to the IT staff members that ensure database integrity, reliability, and performance. This administrator has a wide range of system privileges for SELECT, DDL, DML, and system control commands to perform generic database administration related to storage, database jobs, Oracle COTS group account object maintenance (such as Oracle Spatial or Oracle Text), or performance tuning. The role we create will be granted a subset of the privileges granted to the default Oracle DBA role in the Oracle DBV. The fundamental differences between the operational DBA role and the default DBA role is removal of the following:

  - Account management privileges

  - Administer database-level triggers privileges, and these would be installed on an as-needed basis for applications

  - Oracle Data Change Notification (DCN) and Oracle Flashback privileges to prevent snooping of application realm–protected data

  The operational DBA is not authorized in any application (functional) DBV realms and therefore cannot perform commands that should be executed by the application administrator. However, the operational DBA is authorized as an owner in the Oracle Data Dictionary realm provided with the DBV installation so that named administrator accounts can be established to manage the objects and roles in this "application realm" The DBV policy limits security configuration for this operational DBA role to audit configuration and privilege management (GRANTs, ROLEs) within the Oracle Data Dictionary realm. The operational DBA can grant system privileges, restricted to realm owners of the Oracle Data Dictionary realm. The security controls in place for DBV prevent this role (or the DBA role) from modifying the DBV configuration or row-level security controls such as Oracle VPD or Oracle OLS.

- **Account administrator** This administrator provides separation of duty/controls the ability to create new database accounts or alter existing accounts (especially changing passwords) and database (password) profiles. Many forms of privilege escalation attacks involve creating a new privilege account or modifying the existing privileged accounts. By removing this capability from the operational DBA or SYSDBA, as DBV does out of the box, we reduced the possibility of this form of attack. The DBV product installs a role named DV_ACCTMGR, a DBV account management realm, along with a collection DBV command rules to model this separation-of-duty concept.

- **DBV administrators and analysts** The DBV product includes the roles DV_OWNER and DV_ADMIN and the DBV realm that allow for a named account to manage the DBV policy and authorizations within the overall policy. The responsibility is initially provided to the named account that is granted the DV_OWNER role at the time of the option's installation. This account can create additional DBV administrators, so the use of named accounts versus a group account is the direction we recommend for this administration function. DBV also includes a role named DV_SECANALYST that can query (SELECT) from the DBV configuration tables and the DBV audit trail stored in the table DVSYS.AUDIT_TRAIL$. In a compliance-regulated environment, or during an internal IT security review, you may need to set up named accounts and grant this read-only role to the account.

Figure 6-4 depicts the administrator model along with the types of actions each administrator can perform.

This separation of duty model in the database administrator area may seem overly strict to the typical database administrator. The intent is to demonstrate that a very fine-grained privileged model for administration is possible. The level at which it is broken out can be tailored to any environment based on the unique requirements that exist. The flexibility of DBV, in particular the rules-based approach that is central to the product, would not prevent you from assigning

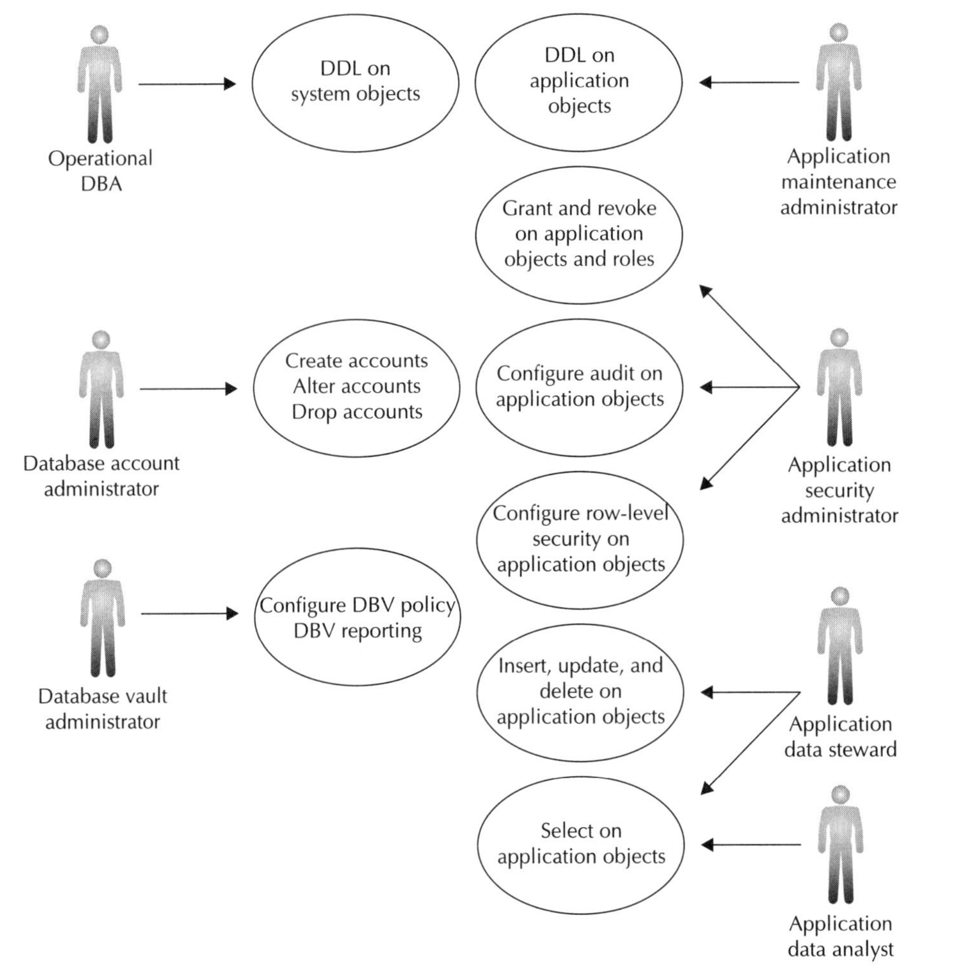

FIGURE 6-4 *Administrators and duties*

multiple administrative duties to a single named account or a new profile that combines application data administrator and application analyst, for example. Instead, the product lets you limit the use of privileges with some externally controlled factor or second person using rules you define and in the business context you desire. Now that we have outlined the content and rules for our model, let's implement it!

Example Implementation of Secure Schemas with DBV

The approach employed to achieve this separation of duties should strive to leverage roles whenever possible as this provides a solution that is the easiest to manage from the perspective of granting system and object privileges. The process presented here includes the code to create these roles and demonstrate how named accounts can be created to leverage these roles within the flow of the overall process. We apply DBV policy as we proceed to help clarify its role in helping control the responsibilities of various actors.

Create Operational Database Administrator Role and Accounts

Recall that our operational DBA is responsible for general database administration tasks such as storage management, job maintenance, performance tuning, and general COTS group account object maintenance related to the Oracle feature set. The implementation of a role for this type of administrator is somewhat lengthy so is included as the script create_oper_dba.sql in the scripts that accompany this book. These scripts can be found on www.OraclePressBooks.com on the Downloads page. We can create this operation DBA role and accounts that require it as follows:

```
sys@aos>-- create the role and grants
sys@aos>@create_oper_dba.sql script.
Role created.
Grant succeeded.
...
Grant succeeded.
sys@aos>-- authorize the role in the Oracle Data Dictionary realm
sys@aos>CONNECT dbvowner
Enter password:
Connected.
dbvowner@aos>BEGIN
  dbms_macadm.add_auth_to_realm (
      realm_name    =>'Oracle Data Dictionary'
    , grantee       => 'OPER_DBA_0101'
    , rule_set_name => NULL
    , auth_options  => dbms_macutl.g_realm_auth_owner );
END;
/
PL/SQL procedure successfully completed.
dbvowner@aos>-- add the role to the Oracle Data Dictionary realm
dbvowner@aos>BEGIN
    dbms_macadm.add_object_to_realm (
      realm_name    => 'Oracle Data Dictionary'
     ,object_owner  => 'SYS'
     ,object_name   => 'OPER_DBA_0101'
     ,object_type   => 'ROLE'
     );
END;
/
```

```
PL/SQL procedure successfully completed.
dbvowner@aos>-- create a new named account who will serve as the Operational
DBA
dbvowner@aos>CONNECT dbvacctmgr
Enter password:
Connected.
dbvacctmgr@aos>CREATE USER jean_oper_dba IDENTIFIED BY <password>;
User created.
dbvacctmgr@aos>-- expire the password for
dbvacctmgr@aos>-- the account so they are forced to
dbvacctmgr@aos>-- change it to something they can control at next login
dbvacctmgr@aos>ALTER USER jean_oper_dba PASSWORD EXPIRE;
User altered.
dbvacctmgr@aos>-- grant the Operational DBA role to new named account
 dbvacctmgr@aos>CONNECT / AS SYSDBA
Connected.
sys@aos>GRANT oper_dba_0101 TO jean_oper_dba
Grant succeeded.
sys@aos>CONNECT jean_oper_dba
Enter password:
ERROR:
ORA-28001: the password has expired
Changing password for jean_oper_dba
New password:
Retype new password:
Password changed
Connected.
jean_oper_dba@aos>-- the account can manage roles as well as system
jean_oper_dba@aos>-- privileges that are protected by
jean_oper_dba@aos>-- the Oracle Data Dictionary
jean_oper_dba@aos>GRANT RESOURCE, CREATE SESSION TO scott;
Grant succeeded.
jean_oper_dba@aos>-- the account can grant object privileges in Oracle
jean_oper_dba@aos>-- COTS account that are protected by the Oracle Data
jean_oper_dba@aos>-- Dictionary realm.
jean_oper_dba@aos>-- CTX_DDL is an object owned by CTXSYS,
jean_oper_dba@aos>-- the Oracle Text feature group account
jean_oper_dba@aos>GRANT EXECUTE ON CTX_DDL TO scott;
Grant succeeded.
jean_oper_dba@aos>-- the account can manage Oracle COTS account objects
jean_oper_dba@aos>-- that are protected by the Oracle Data Dictionary
jean_oper_dba@aos>ALTER PACKAGE CTXSYS.CTX_DDL COMPILE BODY;
Package body altered.
jean_oper_dba@aos>-- the account can perform system level auditing
jean_oper_dba@aos>AUDIT CREATE TABLE BY ACCESS;
Audit succeeded.
jean_oper_dba@aos>-- the account is still subject to
jean_oper_dba@aos>-- application realm protections for SELECT
jean_oper_dba@aos>SELECT * FROM sh.costs WHERE ROWNUM < 6;
SELECT * FROM sh.costs WHERE ROWNUM < 6;
                 *
ERROR at line 1:
```

```
ORA-01031: insufficient privileges
jean_oper_dba@aos>-- the account is still subject
jean_oper_dba@aos>-- to application realm protections for GRANTs
jean_oper_dba@aos>GRANT SELECT ON sh.costs TO oper_dba_0101;
GRANT SELECT ON sh.costs TO oper_dba_0101
                   *
ERROR at line 1:
ORA-00604: error occurred at recursive SQL level 1
ORA-47401: Realm violation for grant object privilege on SH.COSTS
ORA-06512: at "DVSYS.AUTHORIZE_EVENT", line 55
ORA-06512: at line 31
jean_oper_dba@aos>-- the account is still subject
jean_oper_dba@aos>-- to application realm protections for AUDITs
jean_oper_dba@aos>AUDIT INSERT ON sh.costs BY ACCESS;
AUDIT INSERT ON sh.costs BY ACCESS
                   *
ERROR at line 1:
ORA-01031: insufficient privileges
jean_oper_dba@aos>-- tests for privilege escalation
jean_oper_dba@aos>GRANT ADMINISTER DATABASE TRIGGER TO oper_dba_0101;
Grant succeeded.
jean_oper_dba@aos>GRANT ADMINISTER DATABASE TRIGGER TO jean_oper_dba;
Grant succeeded.
```

We don't want the operational DBAs granting themselves privileges we are trying to protect them from using! At the same time, we want them to be able to grant system privileges or roles protected in the Oracle Data Dictionary realm as part of their normal job responsibilities. Sounds like a rule would be in order here—a DBV rule to be precise. The expression that would check for roles being part of the grantee list could be quite complex, if you consider that nested roles could exist. With this complexity, we might not have much luck with this as a simple DBV rule set expression. We will need to create a PL/SQL function to hide the complexity of the logic and need to determine under which object-owner account the PL/SQL should be created.

Centralizing PL/SQL Routines for DBV Rules We want to centralize the PL/SQL routines that we use for DBV rules for the same reasons we centralized PL/SQL code used for DBV factors. We can implement common PL/SQL routines to be used in DBV rule sets in the DBVEXT schema in the same way we did for DBV factors. We've taken the liberty of creating a function named **GRANT_OR_REVOKE_TO_SELF** in the PL/SQL package DBVEXT.DBMS_MAC_EXTENSION. This function is used to indicate whether a grant occurs for the current user or roles they have been granted. This logic can be used to control the realm authorizations we are defining. We added to this package the SQL event context logic and call stack logic that were used in the DBV rule sets examples of Chapter 5.

Protecting Against Privilege Escalation: "NO GRANTS TO THYSELF" We can now revisit the issue where jean_oper_dba was able to GRANT the ADMINISTER DATABASE TRIGGER privilege to the OPER_DBA_0101 role and her own account. Let's revoke the privilege and modify our DBV policy to prevent this in the future:

```
jean_oper_dba@aos>revoke administer database trigger
     FROM oper_dba_0101;
Revoke succeeded.
```

```
jean_oper_dba@aos> revoke administer database trigger
      FROM jean_oper_dba;
Revoke succeeded.
jean_oper_dba@aos>CONNECT dbvowner
Enter password:
Connected.
dbvowner@aos>-- create the rule that checks
dbvowner@aos>-- for grants to one's account or roles
dbvowner@aos>BEGIN
     dbms_macadm.create_rule(
     rule_name => 'Authorized Grant or Revoke'
     , rule_expr =>
      'dbvext.dbms_mac_extension.grant_or_revoke_to_self = 0'
);
END;
/
PL/SQL procedure successfully completed.

dbvowner@aos>-- create a general rule set
dbvowner@aos>-- for operation DBA command authorizations
dbvowner@aos>BEGIN
    dbms_macadm.create_rule_set(
        rule_set_name =>'Authorized Operational DBA Command',
        description =>
'Checks to verify the command is authorized for an Operational DBA',
        enabled =>dbms_macutl.g_yes,
        eval_options =>dbms_macutl.g_ruleset_eval_all,
        audit_options =>dbms_macutl.g_ruleset_audit_fail,
        fail_options =>dbms_macutl.g_ruleset_fail_show,
        fail_message =>NULL,
        fail_code =>NULL,
        handler_options =>dbms_macutl.g_ruleset_handler_off,
        handler =>NULL);
END;
/
PL/SQL procedure successfully completed.
dbvowner@aos>-- add the rule to the rule set
dbvowner@aos>BEGIN
   dbms_macadm.add_rule_to_rule_set(
     rule_set_name => 'Authorized Operational DBA Command'
   , rule_name     => 'Authorized Grant or Revoke'
   );
END;
/
PL/SQL procedure successfully completed.
dbvowner@aos>-- modify the realm authorization to be rules-based
dbvowner@aos>BEGIN
  dbms_macadm.update_realm_auth(
      realm_name    =>'Oracle Data Dictionary'
    , grantee       => 'OPER_DBA_0101'
    , rule_set_name => 'Authorized Operational DBA Command'
    , auth_options  => dbms_macutl.g_realm_auth_owner );
```

```
END;
/
PL/SQL procedure successfully completed.
dbvowner@aos>CONNECT jean_oper_dba
Enter password:
Connected.
jean_oper_dba@aos>-- tests for privilege escalation
jean_oper_dba@aos>grant administer database trigger to oper_dba_0101;
grant administer database trigger to oper_dba_0101
*
ERROR at line 1:
ORA-00604: error occurred at recursive SQL level 1
ORA-47401: Realm violation for grant system privilege on ADMINISTER DATABASE
TRIGGER.
ORA-06512: at "DVSYS.AUTHORIZE_EVENT", line 55
ORA-06512: at line 31
jean_oper_dba@aos>grant administer database trigger to jean_oper_dba;
grant administer database trigger to jean_oper_dba
*
ERROR at line 1:
ORA-00604: error occurred at recursive SQL level 1
ORA-47401: Realm violation for grant system privilege on ADMINISTER DATABASE
TRIGGER.
ORA-06512: at "DVSYS.AUTHORIZE_EVENT", line 55
ORA-06512: at line 31
```

This is much better. We now have a named account with operational DBA privileges that can perform many of the database functions that SYS AS SYSDBA could perform with audit attribution to a named user. We have taken some precautions to prevent privilege escalation for this type of account using standard DBV capabilities and a simple PL/SQL function.

Create (Group) Application Accounts

With DBV installed, creating application accounts and protecting them with a realm is quite simple, as you saw in Chapter 5. We need to present the end-to-end process starting with the creation of an object-owner account for the Sales History application. We will do this with DBV already installed so you can understand the process within this context.

```
dbvacctmgr@aos>-- create the Sales History
dbvacctmgr@aos>-- realm's object-owner account, SH
dbvacctmgr@aos>CREATE USER sh IDENTIFIED BY oracle DEFAULT TABLESPACE SYSAUX;
User created.
dbvacctmgr@aos>-- ensure we establish quotas on object-owner
dbvacctmgr@aos>-- accounts whenever possible
dbvacctmgr@aos>ALTER USER sh QUOTA 500M ON SYSAUX
User created.
dbvacctmgr@aos>CONNECT jean_oper_dba
Enter password:
Connected.
jean_oper_dba@aos>-- grant the DBV role
jean_oper_dba@aos>-- target for object-owner accounts
jean_oper_dba@aos>GRANT dv_realm_resource TO sh;
Grant succeeded.
```

```
jean_oper_dba@aos>GRANT CREATE SESSION TO sh;
Grant succeeded.
jean_oper_dba@aos>-- connect as our object-owner
jean_oper_dba@aos>-- account and create or application's objects
jean_oper_dba@aos>CONNECT sh
Enter password:
Connected.
sh@aos> -- install our application objects
sh@aos> @install_sales_history_objects.sql
Table created.
Table created.
Sequence created.
View created.
…
sh@aos> -- now protect the application's objects in a DBV realm
sh@aos>CONNECT dbvowner
Enter password:
dbvowner@aos>BEGIN
dbms_macadm.create_realm(
  realm_name    => 'Sales History'
, description   =>
'Annual, quarterly, monthly, and weekly sales figures by product'
, enabled       =>  DBMS_MACUTL.G_YES
, audit_options =>  DBMS_MACUTL.G_REALM_AUDIT_FAIL
);
END;
/
PL/SQL procedure successfully completed.

BEGIN
   dbms_macadm.add_object_to_realm<A> (
      realm_name    => 'Sales History'
     ,object_owner  => 'SH'
     ,object_name   => '%'
     ,object_type   => '%'
     );
END;
/
PL/SQL procedure successfully completed.

-- we typically authorize the object-owner account in the realm
-- if application code performs DDL activity on the realm
BEGIN
  dbms_macadm.add_auth_to_realm(
      realm_name    =>'Sales History'
    , grantee       => 'SH'
    , rule_set_name => NULL
    , auth_options  => DBMS_MACUTL.G_REALM_AUTH_OWNER );
END;
/
PL/SQL procedure successfully completed.
```

Create (Realm-based) Application Database Administrators

We mentioned earlier that DBV comes with a predefined role named DV_REALM_OWNER that works nicely with the application database administrator concept. We do not want to grant the DV_REALM_OWNER role directly to the accounts and then authorize the accounts in the realm, as this yields higher maintenance costs on the DBV policy side for account provisioning. We also do not want to authorize the DV_REALM_OWNER role in each realm as this would provide access to all realms for anyone that has been granted this role. The solution is to define an application-centric role name for this administrator for each realm and simply grant this DV_REALM_OWNER role to the application-centric role. We demonstrate with an example for the Sales History realm:

```
jean_oper_dba@aos>-- login as our new
jean_oper_dba@aos>-- Operational DBA for audit attribution
jean_oper_dba@aos>CREATE ROLE sh_dba_role_0101;
Role created.
jean_oper_dba@aos>-- revoke the role from the account
jean_oper_dba@aos>-- that created it or our privilege
jean_oper_dba@aos>-- escalation realm authorization
jean_oper_dba@aos>-- will fail. The Oracle Database
jean_oper_dba@aos>-- performs an implicit and hidden
jean_oper_dba@aos>-- GRANT of the role to the account
jean_oper_dba@aos>-- that creates a role.
jean_oper_dba@aos>REVOKE sh_dba_role_0101 FROM jean_oper_dba;
Revoke succeeded.
jean_oper_dba@aos>-- no we can grant the DBV realm owner role to the
jean_oper_dba@aos>-- application-centric database administrator role
jean_oper_dba@aos>GRANT dv_realm_owner TO sh_dba_role_0101 ;
Grant succeeded.
```

Once this named role is defined, we would authorize the role in the application realm as a realm owner for grantees of the role to manage the roles and object privilege grants that are protected by the realm as follows:

```
dbvowner@aos>BEGIN
  dbms_macadm.add_auth_to_realm(
      realm_name     =>'Sales History'
    , grantee        => 'SH_DBA_ROLE_0101'
    , rule_set_name => NULL
    , auth_options   => DBMS_MACUTL.G_REALM_AUTH_OWNER );
END;
/
PL/SQL procedure successfully completed.
```

Depending on the organization's IT policy or compliance-related security requirements, we may not necessarily want to use the DV_REALM_OWNER role as the base role for any number of reasons, discussed previously. We decided that we could have up to four profiles of application administrators, and we want a design that takes into account the need to maintain privilege sets for these profiles across any number of applications and their respective DBV realms. The system privilege model should be constructed so that it can be used by several applications in a hierarchical fashion. The approach is to start by defining a set of base roles that will be granted the ANY privileges appropriate to profile. We will then create a named application realm role that corresponds to appropriate base role, just as we did earlier. Easy enough; let's implement our four application administrator roles.

Application Security Administrator This administrator can create roles and grant realm-protected roles or realm-protected objects to other accounts or roles. The administrator can also control the audit configuration for the objects protected by the realm. The implementation is as follows:

```
jean_oper_dba@aos> -- create the base role
jean_oper_dba@aos>CREATE ROLE base_sec_admin_0101;
Role created.
jean_oper_dba@aos>REVOKE base_sec_admin_0101 FROM jean_oper_dba;
Revoke succeeded.
jean_oper_dba@aos>-- grant the security-relevant system privileges to this base role
jean_oper_dba@aos>-- this privilege allows the administrator to
jean_oper_dba@aos>-- grant roles to other accounts or roles
jean_oper_dba@aos>GRANT GRANT ANY ROLE TO base_sec_admin_0101;
Grant succeeded.
jean_oper_dba@aos>-- this privilege allows the administrator
jean_oper_dba@aos>-- to create roles for use in the realm
jean_oper_dba@aos>GRANT CREATE ROLE TO base_sec_admin_0101;
Grant succeeded.
jean_oper_dba@aos>-- this privilege allows the administrator
jean_oper_dba@aos>-- to change the authentication mode of the role
jean_oper_dba@aos>GRANT ALTER ANY ROLE TO base_sec_admin_0101;
Grant succeeded.
jean_oper_dba@aos>-- this privilege allows the administrator
jean_oper_dba@aos>-- to remove roles in the event they are
jean_oper_dba@aos>-- no longer required
jean_oper_dba@aos>GRANT DROP ANY ROLE TO base_sec_admin_0101;
Grant succeeded.
jean_oper_dba@aos>-- this privilege allows the administrator to
jean_oper_dba@aos>-- grant object privileges on realm protected
jean_oper_dba@aos>-- objects to roles or other accounts
jean_oper_dba@aos>GRANT GRANT ANY OBJECT PRIVILEGE TO
                 base_sec_admin_0101;
Grant succeeded.
jean_oper_dba@aos>-- this privilege allows the administer to configure
jean_oper_dba@aos>-- audit policy on realm protected objects
jean_oper_dba@aos>GRANT AUDIT ANY TO  base_sec_admin_0101;
Grant succeeded.
jean_oper_dba@aos>-- create the role for the Sales History realm
jean_oper_dba@aos>-- and grant the base role
jean_oper_dba@aos>CREATE ROLE sh_sec_admin_0101;
Role created.
jean_oper_dba@aos>REVOKE sh_sec_admin_0101 FROM jean_oper_dba;
Revoke succeeded.
jean_oper_dba@aos>GRANT base_sec_admin_0101 TO sh_sec_admin_0101;
Grant succeeded.
```

The DROP ANY ROLE privilege is granted to the application security administrator in the event that a role is no longer required. As a matter of safeguarding against human error, DBV command rules around **DROP** commands may be worthy of consideration (for many commands) in your production environments. This forces the **DROP** command to be approved by a second party, namely the DBV administrator, whose approval is the temporary disablement of the command rule or some factor-based modification to the rule that governs it.

We want to create an initial named security administrator account before we protect the role within the DBV realm or we won't be able to grant the first named account the role without disabling the realm. From this point on, we can use the initial named security administrator account to manage grants for all realm-protected roles.

```
dbvacctmgr@aos>CREATE USER sam_sec_mgr IDENTIFIED BY <password>;
User created.
dbvacctmgr@aos>-- expire the password for the account so they are
dbvacctmgr@aos>-- forced to change it to a password
dbvacctmgr@aos>-- they can control at next login
dbvacctmgr@aos>ALTER USER sam_sec_mgr PASSWORD EXPIRE;
User altered.
dbvacctmgr@aos>CONNECT jean_oper_dba
Enter password:
Connected.
jean_oper_dba@aos>GRANT CREATE SESSION TO sam_sec_mgr;
Grant succeeded.
jean_oper_dba@aos>GRANT sh_sec_admin_0101 TO sam_sec_mgr
Grant succeeded.
```

We now protect the base role and application role as realm-secured objects within the appropriate realm and authorize the application administration role in the realm as a realm owner. With the application role, we will also add a realm authorization, keeping an eye on the privilege escalation concerns we demonstrated previously.

```
dbvowner@aos>-- create a new rule set for privilege escalation
dbvowner@aos>-- that is specific to realm application security
dbvowner@aos>BEGIN
    dbms_macadm.create_rule_set(
        rule_set_name =>'Authorized Realm Security Command',
        description => 'Checks to verify the command is authorized for a realm
                    application security administrator',
        enabled =>dbms_macutl.g_yes,
        eval_options =>dbms_macutl.g_ruleset_eval_all,
        audit_options =>dbms_macutl.g_ruleset_audit_fail,
        fail_options =>dbms_macutl.g_ruleset_fail_show,
        fail_message =>NULL,
        fail_code =>NULL,
        handler_options =>dbms_macutl.g_ruleset_handler_off,
        handler =>NULL);
END;
/
PL/SQL procedure successfully completed.
dbvowner@aos>BEGIN
   dbms_macadm.add_rule_to_rule_set(
     rule_set_name => 'Authorized Realm Security Command'
   , rule_name     => 'Authorized Grant or Revoke'
   );
END;
/
```

```
PL/SQL procedure successfully completed.
dbvowner@aos>-- authorize the Sales History realm's
dbvowner@aos>-- application security administrator with this new rule set
dbvowner@aos>BEGIN
  dbms_macadm.add_auth_to_realm (
      realm_name    =>'Sales History'
    , grantee       => 'SH_SEC_ADMIN_0101'
    , rule_set_name => 'Authorized Realm Security Command'
    , auth_options  => dbms_macutl.g_realm_auth_owner );
END;
/
PL/SQL procedure successfully completed.
dbvowner@aos>-- protect the Sales History application
dbvowner@aos>-- security role in the realm
dbvowner@aos>BEGIN
    dbms_macadm.add_object_to_realm (
      realm_name    => 'Sales History'
     ,object_owner  => 'SH'
     ,object_name   => 'SH_SEC_ADMIN_0101'
     ,object_type   => 'ROLE'
     );
END;
/
PL/SQL procedure successfully completed.
dbvowner@aos>-- protect the base application security
dbvowner@aos>-- role in the Oracle Data Dictionary realm
dbvowner@aos>BEGIN
    dbms_macadm.add_object_to_realm (
      realm_name    => 'Oracle Data Dictionary'
     ,object_owner  => 'SYS'
     ,object_name   => 'BASE_SEC_ADMIN_0101'
     ,object_type   => 'ROLE'
     );
END;
/
PL/SQL procedure successfully completed.
```

Finally, we'll examine how this role behaves when our named security administrator account executes commands against realm-protected objects:

```
dbvowner@aos>CONNECT sam_sec_mgr
Password:
ERROR:
ORA-28001: the password has expired
Changing password for sam_sec_mgr
New password:
Retype new password:
Password changed
Connected.
sam_sec_mgr@aos>-- review and confirm the session privileges
sam_sec_mgr@aos>SELECT * FROM session_privs ORDER BY 1;
```

```
PRIVILEGE
----------------------------------------
ALTER ANY ROLE
AUDIT ANY
CREATE ROLE
CREATE SESSION
DROP ANY ROLE
GRANT ANY OBJECT PRIVILEGE
GRANT ANY ROLE

7 rows selected.

sam_sec_mgr@aos>-- review and confirm the session roles
sam_sec_mgr@aos>SELECT * FROM session_roles ORDER BY 1;

ROLE
------------------------------
BASE_SEC_ADMIN_0101
DV_PUBLIC
SH_SEC_ADMIN_0101

sam_sec_mgr@aos>-- the account can see what the Sales History
sam_sec_mgr@aos>-- COSTS table looks like
sam_sec_mgr@aos>DESCRIBE sh.costs
 Name                                      Null?    Type
 ----------------------------------------- -------- ------------------
 PROD_ID                                   NOT NULL NUMBER
 TIME_ID                                   NOT NULL DATE
 PROMO_ID                                  NOT NULL NUMBER
 CHANNEL_ID                                NOT NULL NUMBER
 UNIT_COST                                 NOT NULL NUMBER(10,2)
 UNIT_PRICE                                NOT NULL NUMBER(10,2)

sam_sec_mgr@aos>-- the account cannot see the data in the table
sam_sec_mgr@aos>-- which is what we want, note this is due
sam_sec_mgr@aos>-- to the privileges versus DBV
sam_sec_mgr@aos> SELECT * FROM sh.costs WHERE ROWNUM < 6;
SELECT * FROM sh.costs WHERE ROWNUM < 6;
                *
ERROR at line 1:
ORA-01031: insufficient privileges

sam_sec_mgr@aos>-- the account can create a role
sam_sec_mgr@aos>CREATE ROLE sh_query;
Role created.
sam_sec_mgr@aos>-- the account cannot perform object privileges
sam_sec_mgr@aos>-- just yet as we've added privilege escalation
sam_sec_mgr@aos>-- logic to the realm authorization rule
sam_sec_mgr@aos>-- and the account has the implicit grant on the role
sam_sec_mgr@aos>GRANT SELECT ON sh.costs TO sh_query ;
GRANT SELECT ON sh.costs TO sh_query
```

```
                     *
ERROR at line 1:
ORA-00604: error occurred at recursive SQL level 1
ORA-47401: Realm violation for grant object privilege on SH.COSTS
ORA-06512: at "DVSYS.AUTHORIZE_EVENT", line 55
ORA-06512: at line 31

sam_sec_mgr@aos>-- revoke the role and we are in business
sam_sec_mgr@aos>REVOKE sh_query FROM sam_sec_mgr;
Revoke succeeded.
sam_sec_mgr@aos>GRANT SELECT ON sh.costs TO sh_query ;
Grant succeeded.
-- drop the role as it was just a test
sam_sec_mgr@aos>DROP ROLE sh_query;
Role dropped.
sam_sec_mgr@aos>-- the account can control the audit policy
sam_sec_mgr@aos>-- on the table, which is also what we want to provide
sam_sec_mgr@aos>AUDIT DELETE ON sh.costs;
Audit succeeded.
```

We can also grant these security administrator accounts the privileges required to maintain OLS policies on the tables protected by the realm. If we use the CUSTOMER_POLICY OLS policy from the examples in Chapter 5, we simply grant the OLS component APIs to our security administrator role and the CUSTOMER_POLICY_DBA role to the named account as follows:

```
lbacsys@aos>-- these OLS label APIs can be granted to the
lbacsys@aos>-- security administrator role
lbacsys@aos>GRANT EXECUTE ON sa_components TO sh_sec_admin_0101;
Grant succeeded.
lbacsys@aos>GRANT EXECUTE ON sa_label_admin TO sh_sec_admin_0101;
Grant succeeded.
lbacsys@aos>-- this OLS user-label assignment API can be granted to the
lbacsys@aos>-- security administrator role
lbacsys@aos>GRANT EXECUTE ON sa_user_admin TO sh_sec_admin_0101;
Grant succeeded.
lbacsys@aos>-- in order to use this policy DBA role it
lbacsys@aos>-- must granted directly to a named account
lbacsys@aos>GRANT customer_policy_dba TO sam_sec_mgr  ;
Grant succeeded.
```

We then authorize LBACSYS in the Sales History realm in the same way we did in Chapter 5 to allow the OLS **CREATE TRIGGER** commands to complete:

```
dbvowner@aos>BEGIN
  dbms_macadm.add_auth_to_realm (
      realm_name    =>'Sales History'
    , grantee       => 'LBACSYS'
    , rule_set_name => NULL
    , auth_options  => dbms_macutl.g_realm_auth_participant );
END;
/
PL/SQL procedure successfully completed.
```

The result is that we have a named account, sam_sec_mgr, who can maintain an OLS policy's label components, labels, and user-label assignments for an OLS policy that is specific to data protected in a realm. This account can also maintain enforcement for data tables protected by OLS for row-level security policy.

```
sam_sec_mgr@aos>-- create a new OLS level for this policy
sam_sec_mgr@aos>BEGIN
    sa_components.create_level(
        policy_name=> 'CUSTOMER_POLICY'
      , level_num  => 40
      , short_name => 'VERY_HIGH'
      , long_name  => 'VERY HIGH CREDIT LIMIT'
      );
END;
/
PL/SQL procedure successfully completed.
sam_sec_mgr@aos>-- create a new OLS label for this policy

sam_sec_mgr@aos>BEGIN
    sa_label_admin.create_label(
        policy_name => 'CUSTOMER_POLICY'
      , label_tag   => 40
      , label_value => 'VERY_HIGH'
      );
END;
/
PL/SQL procedure successfully completed.

sam_sec_mgr@aos>-- assign the labels ranges of data
sam_sec_mgr@aos>-- records that ANTHONY can read and write
sam_sec_mgr@aos>BEGIN
    sa_user_admin.set_user_labels(
         policy_name     => 'CUSTOMER_POLICY'
       , user_name       => 'ANTHONY'
       , min_write_label => 'LOW'
       , max_read_label  => 'HIGH'
       , max_write_label => 'HIGH'
       , def_label       => 'HIGH'
       , row_label       => 'HIGH'
       );
END;
/
PL/SQL procedure successfully completed.
sam_sec_mgr@aos>-- simple test to remove the table policy
sam_sec_mgr@aos>BEGIN
    sa_policy_admin.remove_table_policy(
        policy_name    => 'CUSTOMER_POLICY'
      , schema_name    => 'SH'
      , table_name     => 'CUSTOMERS'
      , drop_column    => FALSE
      );
END;
```

```
/
PL/SQL procedure successfully completed.
sam_sec_mgr@aos>-- simple test to add the table policy back
sam_sec_mgr@aos>BEGIN
    sa_policy_admin.remove_table_policy(
        policy_name    => 'CUSTOMER_POLICY'
      , schema_name    => 'SH'
      , table_name     => 'CUSTOMERS'
      , drop_column    => FALSE
      );
END;
/
PL/SQL procedure successfully completed.
```

This OLS policy control, in addition to the object privilege management, role management, and auditing of the objects protected by the realm, make for a complete application security administrator pattern that can be implemented in your environment.

Application Maintenance Administrator This administrator's privileges would be limited to performing in the DDL category of commands on the application realm's objects. The implementation is as follows:

```
jean_oper_dba@aos>-- create the base role
jean_oper_dba@aos>CREATE ROLE base_maint_admin_0101;
Role created.
jean_oper_dba@aos>REVOKE base_maint_admin_0101 FROM jean_oper_dba;
Revoke succeeded.
jean_oper_dba@aos>-- grant the DDL system privileges to this base role
jean_oper_dba@aos>GRANT ALTER ANY CLUSTER TO base_maint_admin_0101;
Grant succeeded.
jean_oper_dba@aos>GRANT ALTER ANY DIMENSION TO base_maint_admin_0101;
Grant succeeded.
jean_oper_dba@aos>GRANT ALTER ANY INDEX TO base_maint_admin_0101;
Grant succeeded.
jean_oper_dba@aos>GRANT ALTER ANY INDEXTYPE TO base_maint_admin_0101;
Grant succeeded.
jean_oper_dba@aos>GRANT ALTER ANY MATERIALIZED VIEW TO base_maint_admin_0101;
Grant succeeded.
jean_oper_dba@aos>GRANT ALTER ANY OPERATOR TO base_maint_admin_0101;
Grant succeeded.
jean_oper_dba@aos>GRANT ALTER ANY OUTLINE TO base_maint_admin_0101;
Grant succeeded.
jean_oper_dba@aos>GRANT ALTER ANY PROCEDURE TO base_maint_admin_0101;
Grant succeeded.
jean_oper_dba@aos>GRANT ALTER ANY SEQUENCE TO base_maint_admin_0101;
Grant succeeded.
jean_oper_dba@aos>GRANT ALTER ANY TABLE TO base_maint_admin_0101;
Grant succeeded.
jean_oper_dba@aos>GRANT ALTER ANY TRIGGER TO base_maint_admin_0101;
Grant succeeded.
jean_oper_dba@aos>GRANT ALTER ANY TYPE TO base_maint_admin_0101;
Grant succeeded.
```

```
jean_oper_dba@aos>GRANT COMMENT ANY TABLE TO base_maint_admin_0101;
Grant succeeded.
jean_oper_dba@aos>GRANT CREATE ANY CLUSTER TO base_maint_admin_0101;
Grant succeeded.
jean_oper_dba@aos>GRANT CREATE ANY CONTEXT TO base_maint_admin_0101;
Grant succeeded.
jean_oper_dba@aos>GRANT CREATE ANY DIMENSION TO base_maint_admin_0101;
Grant succeeded.
jean_oper_dba@aos>GRANT CREATE ANY INDEX TO base_maint_admin_0101;
Grant succeeded.
jean_oper_dba@aos>GRANT CREATE ANY INDEXTYPE TO base_maint_admin_0101;
Grant succeeded.
jean_oper_dba@aos>GRANT CREATE ANY MATERIALIZED VIEW TO base_maint_admin_0101;
Grant succeeded.
jean_oper_dba@aos>GRANT CREATE ANY OPERATOR TO base_maint_admin_0101;
Grant succeeded.
jean_oper_dba@aos>GRANT CREATE ANY OUTLINE TO base_maint_admin_0101;
Grant succeeded.
jean_oper_dba@aos>GRANT CREATE ANY PROCEDURE TO base_maint_admin_0101;
Grant succeeded.
jean_oper_dba@aos>GRANT CREATE ANY SEQUENCE TO base_maint_admin_0101;
Grant succeeded.
jean_oper_dba@aos>GRANT CREATE ANY SYNONYM TO base_maint_admin_0101;
Grant succeeded.
jean_oper_dba@aos>GRANT CREATE ANY TABLE TO base_maint admin_0101;
Grant succeeded.
jean_oper_dba@aos>GRANT CREATE ANY TRIGGER TO base_maint_admin_0101;
Grant succeeded.
jean_oper_dba@aos>GRANT CREATE ANY TYPE TO base_maint_admin_0101;
Grant succeeded.
jean_oper_dba@aos>GRANT CREATE ANY VIEW TO base_maint_admin_0101;
Grant succeeded.
jean_oper_dba@aos>GRANT DROP ANY CLUSTER TO base_maint_admin_0101;
Grant succeeded.
jean_oper_dba@aos>GRANT DROP ANY DIMENSION TO base_maint_admin_0101;
Grant succeeded.
jean_oper_dba@aos>GRANT DROP ANY INDEX TO base_maint_admin_0101;
Grant succeeded.
jean_oper_dba@aos>GRANT DROP ANY INDEXTYPE TO base_maint_admin_0101;
Grant succeeded.
jean_oper_dba@aos>GRANT DROP ANY MATERIALIZED VIEW TO
        base_maint_admin_0101;
Grant succeeded.
jean_oper_dba@aos>GRANT DROP ANY OPERATOR TO base_maint_admin_0101;
Grant succeeded.
jean_oper_dba@aos>GRANT DROP ANY OUTLINE TO base_maint_admin_0101;
Grant succeeded.
jean_oper_dba@aos>GRANT DROP ANY PROCEDURE TO base_maint_admin_0101;
Grant succeeded.
jean_oper_dba@aos>GRANT DROP ANY SEQUENCE TO base_maint_admin_0101;
Grant succeeded.
jean_oper_dba@aos>GRANT DROP ANY SYNONYM TO base_maint_admin_0101;
```

```
Grant succeeded.
jean_oper_dba@aos>GRANT DROP ANY TABLE TO base_maint_admin_0101;
Grant succeeded.
jean_oper_dba@aos>GRANT DROP ANY TRIGGER TO base_maint_admin_0101;
Grant succeeded.
jean_oper_dba@aos>GRANT DROP ANY TYPE TO base_maint_admin_0101;
Grant succeeded.
jean_oper_dba@aos>GRANT DROP ANY VIEW TO base_maint_admin_0101;
Grant succeeded.
jean_oper_dba@aos>-- create the role for the Sales History realm
jean_oper_dba@aos>-- and grant the base role
jean_oper_dba@aos>CREATE ROLE sh_maint_admin_0101;
Role created.
jean_oper_dba@aos>REVOKE sh_maint_admin_0101 FROM jean_oper_dba;
Revoke succeeded.
jean_oper_dba@aos>GRANT base_maint_admin_0101 TO sh_maint_admin_0101;
Grant succeeded.
```

This administrator's privileges basically allow CREATE, ALTER, and DROP of objects that are owned by an application schema and protected by a realm. We now protect the base role and application role as realm-secured objects within the appropriate realm and authorize the application administration role in the realm as a realm participant. We are not concerned about privilege escalation, as this administrator does not have the underlying system privileges to grant privileges or roles.

```
dbvowner@aos>-- authorize the Sales History maintenance
dbvowner@aos>-- administrator role in the realm
dbvowner@aos>BEGIN
  dbms_macadm.add_auth_to_realm (
      realm_name    =>'Sales History'
    , grantee       => 'SH_MAINT_ADMIN_0101'
    , rule_set_name => NULL
    , auth_options  => dbms_macutl.g_realm_auth_participant );
END;
/
PL/SQL procedure successfully completed.

dbvowner@aos>-- protect the Sales History maintenance
dbvowner@aos>-- administrator role in the realm
dbvowner@aos>BEGIN
   dbms_macadm.add_object_to_realm (
     realm_name    => 'Sales History'
    ,object_owner  => 'SH'
    ,object_name   => 'SH_MAINT_ADMIN_0101'
    ,object_type   => 'ROLE'
  );
END;
/
PL/SQL procedure successfully completed.

dbvowner@aos>-- protect the base application maintenance role
dbvowner@aos>-- in the Oracle Data Dictionary realm
```

```
BEGIN
    dbms_macadm.add_object_to_realm (
      realm_name    => 'Oracle Data Dictionary'
     ,object_owner  => 'SYS'
     ,object_name   => 'BASE_MAINT_ADMIN_0101'
     ,object_type   => 'ROLE'
     );
END;
/
PL/SQL procedure successfully completed.
```

Let's examine how we create this type of administrator and how the privileges work:

```
dbvacctmgr@aos>-- create the maintenance administrator account
dbvacctmgr@aos>  CREATE USER mark_maint_mgr IDENTIFIED BY <password>;
User created.
dbvacctmgr@aos>-- expire the password for the account so they are
dbvacctmgr@aos>-- forced to change it to a password
dbvacctmgr@aos>-- they can control at next login
dbvacctmgr@aos>ALTER USER mark_maint_mgr PASSWORD EXPIRE;
User altered.
dbvacctmgr@aos>CONNECT jean_oper_dba
Enter password:
Connected.
jean_oper_dba@aos>-- provide the ability to connect to the database
GRANT CREATE SESSION TO mark_maint_mgr;
jean_oper_dba@aos>
Grant succeeded.
jean_oper_dba@aos>-- this won't work, the role is now protected
GRANT sh_maint_admin_0101 TO mark_maint_mgr;
jean_oper_dba@aos>GRANT sh_maint_admin_0101 TO mark_maint_mgr
*
ERROR at line 1:
ORA-00604: error occurred at recursive SQL level 1
ORA-47401: Realm violation for grant role privilege on SH_MAINT_ADMIN_0101.
ORA-06512: at "DVSYS.AUTHORIZE_EVENT", line 55
ORA-06512: at line 31
jean_oper_dba@aos>-- we have to login as the Sales History Security
jean_oper_dba@aos>-- administrator to perform the grant
jean_oper_dba@aos>CONNECT sam_sec_mgr
Enter password:
Connected.
sam_sec_mgr@aos>GRANT sh_maint_admin_0101 TO mark_maint_mgr;
Grant succeeded.
sam_sec_mgr@aos>-- now connect as the maintenance administrator
sam_sec_mgr@aos>-- and see how it works
sam_sec_mgr@aos>CONNECT mark_maint_mgr
Enter password:
ERROR:
ORA-28001: the password has expired
Changing password for mark_maint_mgr
New password:
```

```
Retype new password:
Password changed
Connected.
mark_maint_mgr@aos>-- the account can see what the Sales History
mark_maint_mgr@aos>-- COSTS table looks like
mark_maint_mgr@aos>DESCRIBE sh.costs;
 Name                                      Null?    Type
 ----------------------------------------- -------- ---------------
 PROD_ID                                   NOT NULL NUMBER
 TIME_ID                                   NOT NULL DATE
 PROMO_ID                                  NOT NULL NUMBER
 CHANNEL_ID                                NOT NULL NUMBER
 UNIT_COST                                 NOT NULL NUMBER(10,2)
 UNIT_PRICE                                NOT NULL NUMBER(10,2)

mark_maint_mgr@aos>-- the account cannot query the COSTS table
mark_maint_mgr@aos>SELECT * FROM sh.costs WHERE ROWNUM < 6;
SELECT * FROM sh.costs WHERE ROWNUM < 6;
                 *
ERROR at line 1:
ORA-01031: insufficient privileges
mark_maint_mgr@aos>-- but the account can manage the
mark_maint_mgr@aos>-- structure of the COSTS table
mark_maint_mgr@aos>ALTER TABLE sh.costs
      MODIFY UNIT_COST NUMBER(10,2) NULL;
Table altered.
```

Application Data Manager (Data Steward) This administrator's privileges are limited to performing queries (SELECT) and DML (**INSERT**, **UPDATE**, **DELETE** and **EXECUTE**) commands on the application realm's objects. The implementation is as follows:

```
jean_oper_dba@aos>-- create the base role
jean_oper_dba@aos>CREATE ROLE base_data_admin_0101;
Role created.
jean_oper_dba@aos>REVOKE base_data_admin_0101 FROM jean_oper_dba;
Revoke succeeded.
jean_oper_dba@aos>-- grant the SELECT, DML and EXECUTE system
jean_oper_dba@aos>-- privileges to this base role
jean_oper_dba@aos>GRANT SELECT ANY SEQUENCE TO base_data_admin_0101;
Grant succeeded.
jean_oper_dba@aos>GRANT SELECT ANY TABLE TO base_data_admin_0101;
Grant succeeded.
jean_oper_dba@aos>GRANT INSERT ANY TABLE TO base_data_admin_0101;
Grant succeeded.
jean_oper_dba@aos>GRANT UPDATE ANY TABLE TO base_data_admin_0101;
Grant succeeded.
jean_oper_dba@aos>GRANT DELETE ANY TABLE TO base_data_admin_0101;
Grant succeeded.
jean_oper_dba@aos>GRANT EXECUTE ANY INDEXTYPE TO base_data_admin_0101;
Grant succeeded.
jean_oper_dba@aos>GRANT EXECUTE ANY OPERATOR TO base_data_admin_0101;
```

```
Grant succeeded.
jean_oper_dba@aos>GRANT EXECUTE ANY PROCEDURE TO base_data_admin_0101;
Grant succeeded.
jean_oper_dba@aos>GRANT EXECUTE ANY TYPE TO base_data_admin_0101;
Grant succeeded.
jean_oper_dba@aos>-- create the role for the Sales History realm
jean_oper_dba@aos>-- and grant the base role
jean_oper_dba@aos>CREATE ROLE sh_data_admin_0101;
Role created.
jean_oper_dba@aos>REVOKE sh_data_admin_0101 FROM jean_oper_dba;
Revoke succeeded.
jean_oper_dba@aos>GRANT base_data_admin_0101 TO sh_data_admin_0101;
Grant succeeded.
```

This administrator's privileges allow for read commands (SELECT), write commands (INSERT, UPDATE, DELETE) and finally execute (EXECUTE) commands on objects that are owned by an application schema and protected by a realm. This provides a named account capability for administrators that are restricted to managing data records, either directly or through an application's PL/SQL APIs—hence the concept of a data steward. The administrator cannot modify the underlying data structures, indexes, or application code and has no control over the realm-protected roles.

We must protect the base role and application role as realm-secured objects within the appropriate realm and authorize the data administration role in the realm as a realm participant. We are not concerned with privilege escalation, as this administrator does not have the underlying system privileges to grant privileges or roles.

```
dbvowner@aos>-- authorize the Sales History data
dbvowner@aos>-- administrator role in the realm
dbvowner@aos>BEGIN
  dbms_macadm.add_auth_to_realm (
      realm_name    =>'Sales History'
    , grantee       => 'SH_DATA_ADMIN_0101'
    , rule_set_name => NULL
    , auth_options  => dbms_macutl.g_realm_auth_participant );
END;
/
PL/SQL procedure successfully completed.

dbvowner@aos>-- protect the Sales History data
dbvowner@aos>-- administrator role in the realm
dbvowner@aos>BEGIN
   dbms_macadm.add_object_to_realm (
     realm_name    => 'Sales History'
    ,object_owner  => 'SH'
    ,object_name   => 'SH_DATA_ADMIN_0101'
    ,object_type   => 'ROLE'
  );
END;
/
PL/SQL procedure successfully completed.

dbvowner@aos>-- protect the base data administrator role
```

```
dbvowner@aos>-- in the Oracle Data Dictionary realm
BEGIN
    dbms_macadm.add_object_to_realm (
      realm_name    => 'Oracle Data Dictionary'
     ,object_owner  => 'SYS'
     ,object_name   => 'BASE_DATA_ADMIN_0101'
     ,object_type   => 'ROLE'
     );
END;
/
PL/SQL procedure successfully completed.
```

Here's how we create this type of administrator and how the privileges work:

```
dbvacctmgr@aos>-- create the data administrator account
dbvacctmgr@aos>CREATE USER deb_data_mgr IDENTIFIED BY <password>;
User created.
dbvacctmgr@aos>-- expire the password for the account so they are
dbvacctmgr@aos>-- forced to change it to a password
dbvacctmgr@aos>-- they can control at next login
dbvacctmgr@aos>ALTER USER deb_data_mgr PASSWORD EXPIRE;
User altered.
dbvacctmgr@aos>CONNECT jean_oper_dba
Enter password:
Connected.
jean_oper_dba@aos>-- provide the ability to connect to the database
GRANT CREATE SESSION TO deb_data_mgr;
Grant succeeded.
jean_oper_dba@aos>-- this won't work, the role is now protected
jean_oper_dba@aos>GRANT sh_data_admin_0101 TO deb_data_mgr;
GRANT sh_data_admin_0101 TO deb_data_mgr
*
ERROR at line 1:
ORA-00604: error occurred at recursive SQL level 1
ORA-47401: Realm violation for grant role privilege on SH_data_admin_0101.
ORA-06512: at "DVSYS.AUTHORIZE_EVENT", line 55
ORA-06512: at line 31
jean_oper_dba@aos>-- we have to login as the Sales History Security
jean_oper_dba@aos>-- administrator to perform the grant
jean_oper_dba@aos>CONNECT sam_sec_mgr
Enter password:
Connected.
sam_sec_mgr@aos>GRANT sh_data_admin_0101 TO deb_data_mgr;
Grant succeeded.
sam_sec_mgr@aos>-- now connect as the data administrator
sam_sec_mgr@aos>-- and see how it works
sam_sec_mgr@aos>CONNECT deb_data_mgr
Enter password:
ERROR:
ORA-28001: the password has expired
Changing password for dba_data_mgr
New password:
```

```
Retype new password:
Password changed
Connected.
deb_data_mgr@aos>-- the account can query the COSTS table
deb_data_mgr@aos>SELECT * FROM sh.costs WHERE ROWNUM < 6;
   PROD_ID TIME_ID     PROMO_ID CHANNEL_ID  UNIT_COST UNIT_PRICE
---------- --------- ---------- ---------- ---------- ----------
        13 20-JAN-98        999          2     793.14    1205.99
        13 30-JAN-98        999          3     783.03    1232.16
        13 21-FEB-98        999          3     813.07    1237.31
        13 25-FEB-98        999          3     798.69    1232.99
        14 19-JAN-98        999          2     886.45    1108.99

5 rows selected.
deb_data_mgr@aos>-- the account can delete the COSTS table
deb_data_mgr@aos>DELETE sh.costs WHERE prod_id = 22;

1221 rows deleted.
deb_data_mgr@aos>ROLLBACK;
Rollback complete.
deb_data_mgr@aos>-- demonstrate the account cannot change the
deb_data_mgr@aos>-- structure of the COSTS table
deb_data_mgr@aos>ALTER TABLE sh.costs MODIFY
      UNIT_COST NUMBER(10,2) NULL;
ALTER TABLE sh.costs MODIFY UNIT_COST NUMBER(10,2) NULL
*
ERROR at line 1:
ORA-01031: insufficient privileges
```

Application Data Analyst This administrator's privileges are simply SELECT with a scope of all objects protected within a realm. The implementation is as follows:

```
jean_oper_dba@aos>-- create the base role
jean_oper_dba@aos>-- grant the SELECT system privilege to this base role
jean_oper_dba@aos>CREATE ROLE base_data_analyst_0101;
Role created.
jean_oper_dba@aos>REVOKE base_data_analyst_0101 FROM jean_oper_dba;
Revoke succeeded.
jean_oper_dba@aos>GRANT SELECT ANY TABLE TO base_data_analyst_0101;
Grant succeeded.
jean_oper_dba@aos>-- create the role for the Sales History realm
jean_oper_dba@aos>-- and grant the base role
jean_oper_dba@aos>CREATE ROLE sh_data_analyst_0101;
Role created.
jean_oper_dba@aos>REVOKE sh_data_analyst_0101 FROM jean_oper_dba;
Revoke succeeded.
jean_oper_dba@aos>GRANT base_data_analyst_0101 TO sh_data_analyst_0101;
Grant succeeded.
```

This administrator's privileges allow for read (SELECT) only on objects that are owned by an application schema and protected by a realm. This provides a named account capability for administrators that are restricted to querying data records. The administrator cannot modify the underlying data, data structures, indexes, or application code and has no control over the realm-protected roles.

We now must protect the base role and application role as realm-secured objects within the appropriate realm and authorize the data analyst role in the realm as a realm participant. We are not concerned with privilege escalation, as this administrator does not have the underlying system privileges to grant privileges or roles.

```
dbvowner@aos>-- authorize the Sales History data
dbvowner@aos>-- analyst role in the realm
dbvowner@aos>BEGIN
  dbms_macadm.add_auth_to_realm (
      realm_name    =>'Sales History'
    , grantee       => 'SH_DATA_ANALYST_0101'
    , rule_set_name => NULL
    , auth_options  => dbms_macutl.g_realm_auth_participant );
END;
/
PL/SQL procedure successfully completed.

dbvowner@aos>-- protect the Sales History data
dbvowner@aos>-- analyst role in the realm
dbvowner@aos>BEGIN
   dbms_macadm.add_object_to_realm (
     realm_name    => 'Sales History'
    ,object_owner  => 'SH'
    ,object_name   => 'SH_DATA_ANALYST_0101'
    ,object_type.  => 'ROLE'
  );
END;
/
PL/SQL procedure successfully completed.

dbvowner@aos>-- protect the base data analyst role
dbvowner@aos>-- in the Oracle Data Dictionary realm
BEGIN
    dbms_macadm.add_object_to_realm (
      realm_name    => 'Oracle Data Dictionary'
     ,object_owner  => 'SYS'
     ,object_name   => 'BASE_DATA_ANALYST_0101'
     ,object_type   => 'ROLE'
     );
END;
/
PL/SQL procedure successfully completed.
```

Here's how we create this type of administrator and how the privileges work:

```
dbvacctmgr@aos>-- create the data analyst account
dbvacctmgr@aos>  CREATE USER alan_analyst IDENTIFIED BY <password>;
User created.
dbvacctmgr@aos>-- expire the password for the account so they are
```

```
dbvacctmgr@aos>-- forced to change it to a password
dbvacctmgr@aos>-- they can control at next login
dbvacctmgr@aos>ALTER USER alan_analyst PASSWORD EXPIRE;
User altered.
dbvacctmgr@aos>CONNECT jean_oper_dba
Enter password:
Connected.
jean_oper_dba@aos>-- provide the ability to connect to the database
GRANT CREATE SESSION TO alan_analyst;
Grant succeeded.
jean_oper_dba@aos>-- this won't work, the role is now protected
GRANT sh_data_analyst_0101 TO alan_analyst;
jean_oper_dba@aos>GRANT sh_data_analyst_0101 TO alan_analyst
*
ERROR at line 1:
ORA-00604: error occurred at recursive SQL level 1
ORA-47401: Realm violation for grant role privilege on sh_data_analyst_0101.
ORA-06512: at "DVSYS.AUTHORIZE_EVENT", line 55
ORA-06512: at line 31
jean_oper_dba@aos>-- we have to login as the Sales History Security
jean_oper_dba@aos>-- administrator to perform the grant
jean_oper_dba@aos>CONNECT sam_sec_mgr
Enter password:
Connected.
sam_sec_mgr@aos>GRANT sh_data_analyst_0101 TO alan_analyst;
Grant succeeded.
sam_sec_mgr@aos>-- now connect as the data analyst
sam_sec_mgr@aos>-- and see how it works
sam_sec_mgr@aos>CONNECT alan_analyst
Enter password:
ERROR:
ORA-28001: the password has expired
Changing password for alan_analyst
New password:
Retype new password:
Password changed
Connected.
alan_analyst@aos>-- the account can query the COSTS table
alan_analyst@aos> SELECT * FROM sh.costs WHERE ROWNUM < 6;
   PROD_ID TIME_ID     PROMO_ID CHANNEL_ID  UNIT_COST UNIT_PRICE
---------- --------- ---------- ---------- ---------- ----------
        13 20-JAN-98        999          2     793.14    1205.99
        13 30-JAN-98        999          3     783.03    1232.16
        13 21-FEB-98        999          3     813.07    1237.31
        13 25-FEB-98        999          3     798.69    1232.99
        14 19-JAN-98        999          2     886.45    1108.99

5 rows selected.
alan_analyst@aos>-- demonstrate the account cannot delete
alan_analyst@aos>-- data in the COSTS table
alan_analyst@aos>DELETE sh.costs WHERE prod_id = 22;
DELETE sh.costs WHERE prod_id = 22
```

```
        *
ERROR at line 1:
ORA-01031: insufficient privileges
```

Create Named Account Administrators

For account administrators, we will leverage the out-of-the-box DBV role DV_ACCTMGR because it has been granted the CREATE/ALTER/DROP USER and CREATE/ALTER/DROP PROFILE system privileges required for this type of administrator. Suppose we want to create a named account administrator, jim_acctmgr. We simply log in as the account that was specified as the DBV account administrator (DBVACCTMGR) at install time and execute the following statements to create this named account. The jim_acctmgr account can be used right away with no additional DBV realm or command rule changes to enforce the rules for this type of administrator.

```
dbvacctmgr@aos>-- create the new account manager account
dbvacctmgr@aos>CREATE USER jim_acctmgr IDENTIFIED BY <password>;
User created.
dbvacctmgr@aos>-- expire the password for the account so they are
dbvacctmgr@aos>-- forced to change it to a password
dbvacctmgr@aos>-- they can control at next login
dbvacctmgr@aos>ALTER USER jim_acctmgr PASSWORD EXPIRE;
User altered.
dbvacctmgr@aos>GRANT DV_ACCTMGR TO jim_acctmgr;
Grant succeeded.
dbvacctmgr@aos>CONNECT jean_oper_dba
Enter password:
Connected.
jean_oper_dba@aos>-- provide the ability to connect to the database
GRANT CREATE SESSION TO jim_acctmgr;
Grant succeeded.
-- test that jim_acctmgr can use his account management privileges
jean_oper_dba@aos>connect jim_acctmgr
Enter password:
ERROR:
ORA-28001: the password has expired
Changing password for jim_acctmgr
New password:
Retype new password:
Password changed
Connected.
jim_acctmgr@aos>CREATE USER jims_test_acct IDENTIFIED BY <password>;
User created.
jim_acctmgr@aos>DROP USER jims_test_acct;
User dropped.
```

Create DBV Administrators and Analysts

In Chapter 5 we discussed the three types of DBV security administrators that are established through the three roles installed with the product: DV_OWNER, DV_ADMIN, and DV_SECANALYST. The DV_OWNER and DV_ADMIN roles have the necessary privileges to modify DBV security configuration, so it is a good idea to follow the same model of creating named user accounts for the individuals who maintain this configuration. This approach ensures audit attribution for DBV configuration changes and separation of duty participants in your configuration management process around activities such as the provisioning of named application administrators we've just described. Creating named user accounts that require read-only access to the DBV configuration, through the DV_SECANALYST role, might be required to meet reporting requirements for a compliance auditing scenario. Most organizations will probably elect to create DBV security administrators based on the DV_OWNER role as its privileges allow for full administration of DBV configuration and the granting and revoking of these DBV roles that would be required in the account provisioning activity. Here's how we create a named account for the DBV security administrator:

```
dbvacctmgr@aos>-- create the data analyst account
dbvacctmgr@aos>CREATE USER diego_dbvmgr IDENTIFIED BY <password>;
User created.
dbvacctmgr@aos>-- expire the password for the account so they are
dbvacctmgr@aos>-- forced to change it to a password
dbvacctmgr@aos>-- they can control at next login
dbvacctmgr@aos>ALTER USER diego_dbvmgr PASSWORD EXPIRE;
User altered.
dbvacctmgr@aos>CONNECT jean_oper_dba
Enter password:
Connected.
jean_oper_dba@aos>-- provide the ability to connect to the database
GRANT CREATE SESSION TO diego_dbvmgr;
Grant succeeded.
jean_oper_dba@aos>-- we have to login as the original DBV Security
jean_oper_dba@aos>-- Administrator to perform the grant of DV_OWNER
jean_oper_dba@aos>CONNECT dbvowner
Enter password:
Connected.
dbvowner@aos>GRANT dv_owner TO diego_dbvmgr;
Grant succeeded.
dbvowner@aos>-- now connect as the DBV Security administrator
dbvowner@aos>-- and see how it works
dbvowner@aos>CONNECT diego_dbvmgr
Enter password:
ERROR:
ORA-28001: the password has expired
Changing password for diego_dbvmgr
New password:
Retype new password:
Password changed
Connected.
diego_dbvmgr@aos>-- the account can modify DBV configuration
diego_dbvmgr@aos>-- immediately to protect a schema like OE
diego_dbvmgr@aos>BEGIN
      dbms_macadm.create_realm(
        realm_name    => 'Order Entry'
      , description   =>
      'Realm to protect the Order Entry (OE) application.'
      , enabled       =>  DBMS_MACUTL.G_YES
      , audit_options =>  DBMS_MACUTL.G_REALM_AUDIT_FAIL
      );
```

```
END;
/
PL/SQL procedure successfully completed.

diego_dbvmgr@aos>BEGIN
    dbms_macadm.add_object_to_realm (
      realm_name     => 'Order Entry'
     ,object_owner   => 'OE'
     ,object_name    => '%'
     ,object_type    => '%'
     );
END;
/
PL/SQL procedure successfully completed.

diego_dbvmgr@aos>BEGIN
  dbms_macadm.add_auth_to_realm (
     realm_name      => 'Order Entry'
    , grantee        =>  'OE'
    , rule_set_name =>  NULL
    , auth_options   =>   dbms_macutl.g_realm_auth_owner
    );
END;
/
PL/SQL procedure successfully completed.

diego_dbvmgr@aos>-- the account is also able to grant the DV_OWNER or
diego_dbvmgr@aos>-- DV_ADMIN role, resulting in a named account that
diego_dbvmgr@aos>-- is able to perform DBV Security administration
diego_dbvmgr@aos>-- as well as delegate that administration
diego_dbvmgr@aos>GRANT dv_owner TO scott;
Grant succeeded.
```

Create Application Read-only, Read-write, and Execute Application Roles for End User Access Accounts

To create read-only, read-write, and execute application roles for end user access accounts we have to understand the static or dynamic nature of the owner-owner accounts and objects being accessed by these accounts. Earlier, we stated that we should create a finite set of roles that use direct object privileges for accounts and objects that are static in nature. These types of roles should also be protected in the same DBV realm that protects the objects to which these roles are granted privileges. The following example demonstrates the use of a direct object privileges granted to the end user access roles for our Sales History schema:

```
jean_oper_dba@aos>-- create the read-only SH application role
jean_oper_dba@aos>CREATE ROLE sh_ro_role_0101;
Role created.
jean_oper_dba@aos>REVOKE sh_ro_role_0101 FROM jean_oper_dba;
Revoke succeeded.
jean_oper_dba@aos>-- create the read-write SH application role
jean_oper_dba@aos>CREATE ROLE sh_rw_role_0101;
Role created.
jean_oper_dba@aos>REVOKE sh_rw_role_0101 FROM jean_oper_dba;
```

```
Revoke succeeded.
jean_oper_dba@aos>-- create the execute SH application role
jean_oper_dba@aos>CREATE ROLE sh_exec_role_0101;
Role created.
jean_oper_dba@aos>REVOKE sh_exec_role_0101 FROM jean_oper_dba;
Revoke succeeded.
jean_oper_dba@aos>-- we have to login as a DBV Security Administrator
jean_oper_dba@aos>-- to protect the roles in the Sales History realm
jean_oper_dba@aos>CONNECT diego_dbvmgr
Enter password:
Connected.
diego_dbvmgr@aos>BEGIN
   dbms_macadm.add_object_to_realm (
     realm_name    => 'Sales History'
    ,object_owner  => 'SH'
    ,object_name   => 'SH_RO_ROLE_0101'
    ,object_type   => 'ROLE'
  );
END;
/
PL/SQL procedure successfully completed.
diego_dbvmgr@aos>BEGIN
   dbms_macadm.add_object_to_realm (
     realm_name    => 'Sales History'
    ,object_owner  => 'SH'
    ,object_name   => 'SH_RW_ROLE_0101'
    ,object_type   => 'ROLE'
  );
END;
/
PL/SQL procedure successfully completed.
diego_dbvmgr@aos>BEGIN
   dbms_macadm.add_object_to_realm (
     realm_name    => 'Sales History'
    ,object_owner  => 'SH'
    ,object_name   => 'SH_EXEC_ROLE_0101'
    ,object_type   => 'ROLE'
  );
END;
/
PL/SQL procedure successfully completed.

jean_oper_dba@aos>-- we have to login as the Sales History Security
jean_oper_dba@aos>-- administrator to perform the object-level grants
jean_oper_dba@aos>CONNECT sam_sec_mgr
Enter password:
Connected.
sam_sec_mgr@aos>GRANT SELECT ON sh.costs
      TO sh_ro_role_0101;
Grant succeeded.
sam_sec_mgr@aos>GRANT SELECT, INSERT, UPDATE, DELETE ON sh.costs
      TO sh_rw_role_0101;
```

```
Grant succeeded.
sam_sec_mgr@aos>GRANT EXECUTE ON sh.sales_transaction
      TO sh_exec_role_0101;
Grant succeeded.
```

We can create and provision an account to use these roles using an approach similar to what we used for the application administrators:

```
dbvacctmgr@aos>-- create the end-user access account
dbvacctmgr@aos>  CREATE USER ellen_enduser IDENTIFIED BY <password>;
User created.
dbvacctmgr@aos>-- expire the password for the account so they are
dbvacctmgr@aos>-- forced to change it to a password
dbvacctmgr@aos>-- they can control at next login
dbvacctmgr@aos>ALTER USER ellen_enduser PASSWORD EXPIRE;
User altered.
dbvacctmgr@aos>CONNECT jean_oper_dba
Enter password:
Connected.
jean_oper_dba@aos>-- provide the ability to connect to the database
GRANT CREATE SESSION TO ellen_enduser;
Grant succeeded.
jean_oper_dba@aos>-- we have to login as the Sales History Security
jean_oper_dba@aos>-- administrator to perform the grants
jean_oper_dba@aos>-- of these end-user access roles
jean_oper_dba@aos>CONNECT sam_sec_mgr
Enter password:
Connected.
sam_sec_mgr@aos>GRANT sh_rw_role_0101 TO ellen_enduser;
Grant succeeded.
sam_sec_mgr@aos>GRANT sh_exec_role_0101 TO ellen_enduser;
Grant succeeded.
sam_sec_mgr@aos>-- now connect as the end-user account
sam_sec_mgr@aos>-- and see how it works
sam_sec_mgr@aos>CONNECT ellen_enduser
Enter password:
ERROR:
ORA-28001: the password has expired
Changing password for ellen_enduser
New password:
Retype new password:
Password changed
Connected.
ellen_enduser@aos>-- the account can query the COSTS table
ellen_enduser@aos>SELECT * FROM sh.costs WHERE ROWNUM < 6;
   PROD_ID TIME_ID     PROMO_ID CHANNEL_ID  UNIT_COST UNIT_PRICE
---------- --------- ---------- ---------- ---------- ----------
        13 20-JAN-98        999          2     793.14    1205.99
        13 30-JAN-98        999          3     783.03    1232.16
        13 21-FEB-98        999          3     813.07    1237.31
        13 25-FEB-98        999          3     798.69    1232.99
        14 19-JAN-98        999          2     886.45    1108.99
```

```
5 rows selected.
ellen_enduser@aos>-- the account can delete the COSTS table
ellen_enduser@aos>DELETE sh.costs WHERE prod_id = 22;
1221 rows deleted.
ellen_enduser@aos>-- undo the transaction as it is only a test!
ellen_enduser@aos>ROLLBACK;
Rollback complete.
```

An important note about the use of Oracle roles here regards the limitation of using object privileges granted through a role. If any application object, such as SH.SALES, must be queried or updated by another application account, such as HR, within a PL/SQL package, we need to perform a direct object privilege grant to the HR account. The read-only and read-write roles defined here are intended for application end user access to specific application object-owner accounts that will issue SQL statements outside of a PL/SQL package.

As we mentioned earlier, if the object-owner accounts that are in use for your applications will be dynamic or have dynamically created objects, then a system privilege model for end user roles is appropriate. This model should be constructed so that it can be used by several applications in a hierarchical fashion. Start by defining a set of base application roles that will be granted the ANY privileges and then creating named application realm roles that correspond to each base application role. This is the same approach we took with the application administrator accounts described earlier and in particular the application data administrator (data steward) and application data analyst roles. The application data administrator role we created, SH_DATA_ADMIN_0101, and the application data analyst role, SH_DATA_ANALYST_0101, will be sufficient for the read-write and read-only end user access account provisioning.

Post-configuration Account Provisioning

Once the core separation of duty roles are created and the DBV policy that accompanies them is defined, the process of creating named accounts (for real end users or administrators) that use these roles can be activated for production use. Here's the general process for this account creation:

1. Log in as the account administrator to create the named end user account with a default password, tablespace, temporary tablespace, and database profile.
2. Expire the password to force the named end user account to change the account password at first login to a password the user can control.
3. Log in as the operational DBA and grant the appropriate system privilege(s), such as CREATE SESSION, to the named end user account.
4. Log in as the realm security administrator and grant the appropriate role(s) to the named end user account.

Establish DBV Command Rules from Conditions

The Add Product Costs example use case has a handful of candidate DBV command rules we can create to meet the requirements documented. These can be discovered by examining the Subject-Verb-Object-Condition table we created at the beginning of the chapter and examined to identify DBV factors. By analyzing this table, we can develop a candidate list of DBV command rules, as shown in Table 6-4, and walk through a process to implement some of them as required.

SQL Command	Owner	Object	Rules
INSERT	SH	COSTS	Only allowed by Sales Managers Outside the weekly maintenance window Only from a trusted Sales Management package
SELECT	HR	EMPLOYEES	Social Security number (SSN), salary, or commission columns are not part of the query
SELECT	SH	PRODUCTS	Return only for products for which the manager is responsible
UPDATE	SYSTEM	AUD$	Not allowed by database administrators
DELETE	SYSTEM	AUD$	Not allowed by database administrators Deletes allowed only for audit data more than seven years old

TABLE 6-4 *List of DBV Command Rules*

The first DBV command rule, INSERT on SH.COSTS, can make use of three categories of DBV factors to provide a multifactored approach to the policy for this operation:

- Factors based on identity management (sales department manager)
- Factors based on access or operational context (sales management package)
- Factors based on time (outside of the weekly maintenance window)

First, we can define a factor to assert whether or not the current user is a sales manager. Consider the following queries that will show us the sales managers defined in the HR object-owner account's tables:

```
hr@aos>-- find the Sales department id
hr@aos>SELECT department_id,department_name
FROM hr.departments
WHERE department_name ='Sales'
/
DEPARTMENT_ID DEPARTMENT_NAME
------------- ------------------------------
           80 Sales
1 row selected.

hr@aos>-- find the Sales department's managers
hr@aos>SELECT employee_id,email,department_id
FROM hr.employees emp
WHERE emp.department_id = 80
 AND EXISTS (
    SELECT 1
    FROM hr.employees reportees
    WHERE reportees.manager_id = emp.employee_id
```

```
        AND reportees.department_id = emp.department_id
 );

EMPLOYEE_ID EMAIL                    DEPARTMENT_ID
----------- ------------------------ -------------
        145 JRUSSEL                             80
        146 KPARTNER                            80
        147 AERRAZUR                            80
        148 GCAMBRAU                            80
        149 EZLOTKEY                            80
5 rows selected.
hr@aos>-- find the Sales employees reporting to JRUSSEL
hr@aos>SELECT employee_id, email FROM employees WHERE manager_id = 145;

EMPLOYEE_ID EMAIL
----------- ------------------------
        150 PTUCKER
        151 DBERNSTE
        152 PHALL
        153 COLSEN
        154 NCAMBRAU
        155 OTUVAULT

6 rows selected.
```

We can extend the HR utility PL/SQL package, HR.EMPLOYEE_UTILITY, used in Chapter 5 to include a function that will return a TRUE/FALSE indicator if the logged-in database user is the manager of the department as follows:

```
hr@aos>CREATE OR REPLACE PACKAGE hr.employee_utility IS
   FUNCTION get_user_department_id   ( user_name IN
         VARCHAR2 DEFAULT SYS_CONTEXT('USERENV', 'SESSION_USER') )
            RETURN NUMBER;
   FUNCTION get_user_department_name ( user_name IN
        VARCHAR2 DEFAULT SYS_CONTEXT('USERENV', 'SESSION_USER') )
            RETURN VARCHAR2;
   FUNCTION is_department_manager (  user_name IN
        VARCHAR2 DEFAULT SYS_CONTEXT('USERENV', 'SESSION_USER') )
            RETURN NUMBER;
END;
/
PL/SQL procedure successfully completed.
```

This function includes a set of queries similar to those we issued above to assert the fact that the logged-in user is a sales department manager. With this function in place, we can create an identity management–related factor for the department manager condition as follows:

```
diego_dbvmgr@aos>BEGIN
    dbms_macadm.create_factor(
        factor_name      => 'Is_Department_Manager' ,
        factor_type_name => 'User',
        description    =>
```

```
'Returns an indicator that the user is a department manager.',
     rule_set_name => NULL ,
     get_expr      => 'hr.employee_utility.is_department_manager',
     validate_expr => NULL,
     identify_by   => dbms_macutl.g_identify_by_method,
     labeled_by    => dbms_macutl.g_labeled_by_self,
     eval_options => dbms_macutl.g_eval_on_access,
     audit_options => dbms_macutl.g_audit_on_get_error,
     fail_options  => dbms_macutl.g_fail_with_message);
END;
/
COMMIT;
Commit complete.
```

Next we can use the example accounts from our operational and application administration model for realm authorizations to create the database access account. We will create one account for a sales manager named JRUSSEL and one account for a sales employee named PTUCKER who reports to JRUSSEL:

```
jim_acctmgr@aos>-- use the DBV Account Administrator to
jim_acctmgr@aos>-- create the account for the Sales Manager JRUSSEL
jim_acctmgr@aos>CREATE USER jrussel IDENTIFIED BY <password>;
User created.

jim_acctmgr@aos>-- expire the password for the account so they are
jim_acctmgr@aos>-- forced to change it to a password
jim_acctmgr@aos>-- they can control at next login
jim_acctmgr@aos>ALTER USER jrussel PASSWORD EXPIRE;
User altered.

jim_acctmgr@aos>-- create the account for the Sales employee PTUCKER
jim_acctmgr@aos>CREATE USER ptucker IDENTIFIED BY <password>;
User created.
jim_acctmgr@aos>-- expire the password for the account so they are
jim_acctmgr@aos>-- forced to change it to a password
jim_acctmgr@aos>-- they can control at next login
jim_acctmgr@aos>ALTER USER ptucker PASSWORD EXPIRE;

jim_acctmgr@aos>-- use the operational DBA to grant these
jim_acctmgr@aos>-- accounts database session privilege
jim_acctmgr@aos>CONNECT jean_oper_dba
Enter password:
Connected.
jean_oper_dba@aos>GRANT CREATE SESSION TO jrussel;
Grant succeeded.

jean_oper_dba@aos>GRANT CREATE SESSION TO ptucker;
Grant succeeded.

jean_oper_dba@aos>-- use the Sales History realms
jean_oper_dba@aos>-- Application Security Administrator sam_sec_mgr
jean_oper_dba@aos>-- to provide DML and EXECUTE privileges
```

```
jean_oper_dba@aos>-- to these accounts for Sales History data and
jean_oper_dba@aos>-- Sales History application code
jean_oper_dba@aos>CONNECT sam_sec_mgr
Enter password:
Connected.
sam_sec_mgr@aos>GRANT sh_data_admin_0101 TO jrussel;
Grant succeeded.
sam_sec_mgr@aos>GRANT sh_data_admin_0101 TO ptucker;
Grant succeeded.
```

We can extend the SH.SALES transaction package from Chapter 5 to include a procedure named **insert_product_cost** that will be our trusted procedure to add new product costs:

```
sh@aos>CREATE OR REPLACE PACKAGE sh.sales_transaction AS
    PROCEDURE update_sales(customer IN NUMBER, amount IN NUMBER);
    PROCEDURE insert_product_cost(
              product    IN VARCHAR2
            , promotion  IN VARCHAR2
            , channel    IN VARCHAR2
            , cost_date  IN DATE
            , cost       IN NUMBER
            , price      IN NUMBER
        );

END;
/
Package created.
```

Both the JRUSSEL and PTUCKER accounts can create new product cost data using standard SQL and the SH.SALES_TRANSACTION package at this point.

```
sh@aos>CONNECT jrussel
Enter password:
ERROR:
ORA-28001: the password has expired
Changing password for jrussel
New password:
Retype new password:
Password changed
Connected.
jrussel@aos>INSERT INTO sh.costs (
        prod_id
      , time_id
      , promo_id
      , channel_id
      , unit_cost
      , unit_price
  )
  SELECT
        prod.prod_id
      , TO_DATE('07-26-2000','MM-DD-YYYY')
      , promo.promo_id
```

```
      , chan.channel_id
      , 15.00
      , 49.95
  FROM
        sh.products prod
      , sh.promotions promo
      , sh.channels chan
  WHERE
          prod_name = 'Smash up Boxing'
      AND channel_desc = 'Direct Sales'
      AND promo_name = 'blowout sale'
  ;

1 row created.
jrussel@aos>BEGIN
  sh.sales_transaction.insert_product_cost(
              product    => '8.3 Minitower Speaker'
            , promotion  =>  'blowout sale'
            , channel    => 'Direct Sales'
            , cost_date  => TO_DATE('07-26-2000','MM-DD-YYYY')
            , cost       => 25.00
            , price      => 99.99
        );
END;
/

PL/SQL procedure successfully completed.

jrussel@aos>CONNECT ptucker
Enter password:
ERROR:
ORA-28001: the password has expired
Changing password for ptucker
New password:
Retype new password:
Password changed
Connected.
ptucker@aos>INSERT INTO sh.costs (
      prod_id
    , time_id
    , promo_id
    , channel_id
    , unit_cost
    , unit_price
)
SELECT
      prod.prod_id
    , TO_DATE('06-15-2002','MM-DD-YYYY')
    , promo.promo_id
    , chan.channel_id
    , 5.00
    , 29.95
```

```
FROM
      sh.products prod
    , sh.promotions promo
    , sh.channels chan
WHERE
        prod_name = 'Adventures with Numbers'
    AND channel_desc = 'Direct Sales'
    AND promo_name = 'everyday low price'
;
1 row created.
ptucker@aos>BEGIN
  sh.sales_transaction.insert_product_cost(
            product    => 'Martial Arts Champions'
          , promotion  =>  'blowout sale'
          , channel    => 'Direct Sales'
          , cost_date  => TO_DATE('06-15-2002','MM-DD-YYYY')
          , cost       => 5.00
          , price      => 19.99
        );
END;
/
PL/SQL procedure successfully completed.
```

We are now ready to create a DBV rule set to control for our example. We will use four of the factors we created in the DBV rules that make up this DBV rule set. Note that we already have a DBV rule named "Called From Sales Transaction Package" defined that uses the In_Sales_Transaction_Package factor so we do not need to redefine this rule.

```
diego_dbvmgr@aos> -- create the Sales department manager rule
diego_dbvmgr@aos>BEGIN
     dbms_macadm.create_rule(
       rule_name => 'Is Sales Department Manager'
     , rule_expr => 'DVF.F$User_Department_Name = ''Sales'''
          || 'AND DVF.F$Is_Department_Manager = 1'
     );
END;
/
PL/SQL procedure successfully completed.

-- create the outside of the system maintenance window rule
BEGIN
     dbms_macadm.create_rule(
       rule_name => 'Outside System Maintenance Window '
     , rule_expr => 'DVF.F$Is_Maintenance_Window = 0'
     );
END;
/
PL/SQL procedure successfully completed.

diego_dbvmgr@aos> -- create the rule set to associate the rules to
diego_dbvmgr@aos> -- using the dbms_macutl.g_ruleset_eval_all value
diego_dbvmgr@aos> -- for the eval_options parameter as we need all
```

```
diego_dbvmgr@aos> -- conditions to be true
diego_dbvmgr@aos>BEGIN
    dbms_macadm.create_rule_set(
        rule_set_name =>'Add Sales Cost Allowed',
        description =>
'Checks to authorize creation of Sales Cost records.',
        enabled =>dbms_macutl.g_yes,
        eval_options =>dbms_macutl.g_ruleset_eval_all,
        audit_options =>dbms_macutl.g_ruleset_audit_fail,
        fail_options =>dbms_macutl.g_ruleset_fail_show,
        fail_message =>NULL,
        fail_code =>NULL,
        handler_options =>dbms_macutl.g_ruleset_handler_off,
        handler =>NULL);
END;
/
PL/SQL procedure successfully completed.

diego_dbvmgr@aos> -- add our Sales department manager rule
diego_dbvmgr@aos>BEGIN
   dbms_macadm.add_rule_to_rule_set (
     rule_set_name => 'Add Sales Cost Allowed'
   , rule_name     => 'Is Sales Department Manager'
   );
END;
/
PL/SQL procedure successfully completed.

diego_dbvmgr@aos> -- add the outside of the system maintenance window rule
diego_dbvmgr@aos>BEGIN
   dbms_macadm.add_rule_to_rule_set (
     rule_set_name => 'Add Sales Cost Allowed'
   , rule_name     => 'Outside System Maintenance Window'
   );
END;
/
PL/SQL procedure successfully completed.

diego_dbvmgr@aos> -- add the Sales management package check rule
diego_dbvmgr@aos>BEGIN
   dbms_macadm.add_rule_to_rule_set (
     rule_set_name => 'Add Sales Cost Allowed'
   , rule_name     => 'Called From Sales Transaction Package'
   );
END;
/
PL/SQL procedure successfully completed.
```

Finally we create our DBV command rule on the INSERT SQL command for the SH.COSTS table and test its effectiveness for both the JRUSSEL and PTUCKER accounts:

```
diego_dbvmgr@aos>BEGIN
  dbms_macadm.create_command_rule (
        command          => 'INSERT'
      , rule_set_name    => 'Add Sales Cost Allowed'
      , object_owner     => 'SH'
      , object_name      => 'COSTS'
      , enabled          => dvsys.dbms_macutl.g_yes
  );
END;
/
PL/SQL procedure successfully completed.

diego_dbvmgr@aos>CONNECT jrussel
Enter password:
Connected.
jrussel@aos> -- direct INSERT on SH.COSTS should fail because it is
jrussel@aos> -- not issued from the sales management package
jrussel@aos> INSERT INTO sh.costs (
        prod_id
      , time_id
      , promo_id
      , channel_id
      , unit_cost
      , unit_price
  )
  SELECT
        prod.prod_id
      , TO_DATE('07-26-2000','MM-DD-YYYY')
      , promo.promo_id
      , chan.channel_id
      , 15.00
      , 49.95
  FROM
        sh.products prod
      , sh.promotions promo
      , sh.channels chan
  WHERE
          prod_name = 'Smash up Boxing'
      AND channel_desc = 'Direct Sales'
      AND promo_name = 'blowout sale'
  ;
INSERT INTO sh.costs (
              *
ERROR at line 1:
ORA-01031: insufficient privileges
jrussel@aos>-- INSERT on SH.COSTS through the sales management package
jrussel@aos>-- should therefore be allowed because JRUSSEL is a Sales
jrussel@aos>-- department manager and we are outside of
jrussel@aos>-- the system maintenance window
jrussel@aos>SELECT DVF.F$User_Department_Name "Department",
```

```
       DVF.F$Is_Department_Manager "Manager"
FROM dual;

Department           Manager
-------------------- ---------
Sales                1

jrussel@aos>SELECT TO_CHAR(SYSDATE,'DAY HH24:MI') "TIMEFRAME"
FROM dual;

TIMEFRAME
----------------------------------------
MONDAY    01:58

jrussel@aos>BEGIN
  sh.sales_transaction.insert_product_cost(
              product    => '8.3 Minitower Speaker'
            , promotion  =>  'blowout sale'
            , channel    => 'Direct Sales'
            , cost_date  => TO_DATE('07-26-2000','MM-DD-YYYY')
            , cost       => 25.00
            , price      => 99.99
        );
END;
/
PL/SQL procedure successfully completed.

jrussel@aos>CONNECT ptucker
Enter password:
Connected.
ptucker@aos>-- PTUCKER is not a Sales department manager so should not
ptucker@aos>-- be able to INSERT data into the SH.COSTS table
ptucker@aos>-- or use the SH.SALES_TRANSACTION package to do so
ptucker@aos>SELECT DVF.F$User_Department_Name "Department",
       DVF.F$Is_Department_Manager "Manager"
FROM dual;
Department           Manager
-------------------- ---------
Sales                0

ptucker@aos>INSERT INTO sh.costs (
      prod_id
    , time_id
    , promo_id
    , channel_id
    , unit_cost
    , unit_price
)
SELECT
      prod.prod_id
    , TO_DATE('06-15-2002','MM-DD-YYYY')
    , promo.promo_id
```

```
     , chan.channel_id
     , 5.00
     , 29.95
FROM
       sh.products prod
     , sh.promotions promo
     , sh.channels chan
WHERE
         prod_name = 'Adventures with Numbers'
     AND channel_desc = 'Direct Sales'
     AND promo_name = 'everyday low price'
;
INSERT INTO sh.costs (
              *
ERROR at line 1:
ORA-01031: insufficient privileges

ptucker@aos>BEGIN
  sh.sales_transaction.insert_product_cost(
              product     => 'Martial Arts Champions'
            , promotion   =>  'blowout sale'
            , channel     => 'Direct Sales'
            , cost_date   => TO_DATE('06-15-2002','MM-DD-YYYY')
            , cost        => 5.00
            , price       => 19.99
        );
END;
/
BEGIN
*
ERROR at line 1:
ORA-01031: insufficient privileges
ORA-06512: at "SH.SALES_TRANSACTION", line 22c
ORA-06512: at line 2
```

We can now consider our remaining candidate DBV command rules in turn to determine how they can be implemented, or if they even should be.

If we look closely at the candidate DBV command rule for SELECT on the HR.EMPLOYEE table, we have to consider that what is being specified is not really a statement-level control. A more appropriate implementation for this requirement is to leverage Oracle's security-relevant column controls, called *masking*, that is part of Oracle VPD. We presented an example of this feature in Chapter 5 and would recommend using this Oracle database feature, possibly with an Oracle DBV factor that helps define the conditions that would allow the visibility of the SSN, salary, and commission information for an employee.

The use of a DBV command rule for requirements on the SELECT of records from the SH.PRODUCT table is not warranted either. In this case, a row-level security control is also being requested that could be implemented using technologies such as Oracle VPD and Oracle OLS. We presented a notional example of meeting this requirement in this manner earlier in this chapter.

The last three candidate DBV command rules concern the write database operations on the standard database audit trail table SYSTEM.AUD$. To meet the requirements defined for these operations, we would create two separate DBV command rules, one for each SQL command. The intent of the UPDATE and DELETE requirements are to protect the integrity of the audit trail both for compliance and conflict of interest concerns. The question to ask is, Who should be able to update (alter) and delete the audit trails in a system? The requirement is written such that the database administrators should not be able to update or delete the audit trail records, but the reality may be that no administrator or end user should have this capability. We can implement this level of protection using the existing DBV rule set Disabled and create the two DBV COMMAND RULES. By default, the Disabled DBV rule set has auditing turned off so we would want to enable auditing on this rule set.

```
diego_dbvmgr@aos>-- enable audit on the Disabled rule set
diego_dbvmgr@aos>BEGIN
    dbms_macadm.update_rule_set(
        rule_set_name =>'Disabled',
        description =>'Convenience rule set to quickly disable system features.',
        enabled =>dbms_macutl.g_yes,
        eval_options =>dbms_macutl.g_ruleset_eval_all,
        audit_options =>dbms_macutl.g_ruleset_audit_fail,
        fail_options =>dbms_macutl.g_ruleset_fail_show,
        fail_message =>NULL,
        fail_code =>NULL,
        handler_options =>dbms_macutl.g_ruleset_handler_off,
        handler =>NULL);
END;
/
PL/SQL procedure successfully completed.

diego_dbvmgr@aos>-- create the command rules for UPDATE and DELETE
diego_dbvmgr@aos>BEGIN
  dbms_macadm.create_command_rule (
          command         => 'DELETE'
        , rule_set_name   => 'Disabled'
        , object_owner    => 'SYSTEM'
        , object_name     => 'AUD$'
        , enabled         => dvsys.dbms_macutl.g_yes
  );
END;
/
PL/SQL procedure successfully completed.

diego_dbvmgr@aos>BEGIN
  dbms_macadm.create_command_rule (
          command         => 'UPDATE'
        , rule_set_name   => 'Disabled'
        , object_owner    => 'SYSTEM'
        , object_name     => 'AUD$'
        , enabled         => dvsys.dbms_macutl.g_yes
  );
END;
/
PL/SQL procedure successfully completed.

diego_dbvmgr@aos>-- test the control by attempting
diego_dbvmgr@aos>-- to delete the audit trail as SYSDBA
```

```
diego_dbvmgr@aos>CONNECT / AS SYSDBA
Connected.
sys@aos>DELETE system.aud$ WHERE ROWNUM < 2;
DELETE system.aud$ WHERE ROWNUM < 2
              *
ERROR at line 1:
ORA-01031: insufficient privileges
```

This simple solution is secure enough, and the overall integrity of the audit trail is still protected via Oracle backup and recovery procedures. We can also extend the policy to meet the row-level security requirement of not deleting records less than seven years old by applying an Oracle VPD policy to the table. This control will offer additional protections for the unintentional deletion of the audit trail records inside the system maintenance window when DBV policy controls might be relaxed.

```
sys@aos>-- create the PL/SQL function used for the DELETE policy
sys@aos>-- on the SYSTEM.AUD$ table
sys@aos>CREATE OR REPLACE FUNCTION system.audit_policy_function(
   schema_name IN VARCHAR2
 , table_name IN VARCHAR2 ) RETURN VARCHAR2
AS
  l_archive_date DATE;
BEGIN
    -- prevent deletion of audit trail records less
    -- than the number of retention years specified
    -- in the DBV Factor Audit_Retention_Period
    l_archive_date := ADD_MONTHS ( SYSDATE ,
                        -1 * (DVF.F$Audit_Retention_Period * 12));
    -- return the SQL predicate that will protect any records
    -- that are still within the retention period
    RETURN 'NTIMESTAMP# <= TO_TIMESTAMP('''
                 || TO_CHAR(l_archive_date,'YYYY/MM/DD HH24:MI:SS')
                 || ''',''YYYY/MM/DD HH24:MI:SS'')';
END;
/
Function created.
sys@aos>-- add the Oracle VPD policy to the audit trail table
sys@aos>BEGIN
    dbms_rls.add_policy(
        object_schema      => 'SYSTEM'
        ,object_name       => 'AUD$'
        ,policy_name       => 'POLICY_AUD$'
        ,function_schema   => 'SYSTEM'
        ,policy_function   => 'AUDIT_POLICY_FUNCTION'
        ,statement_types   => 'DELETE'
        );
END;
/
PL/SQL procedure successfully completed.
```

Depending on the life expectancy of your system, this may be all that is required, and you can simply leave the audit trail records online, even after the audit retention period has passed.

The decision depends on how much the audit trail will grow over time. The retention requirements of seven years will allow you to archive and delete the audit trail at some point if reporting response times started to suffer. The detailed solution for these types of requirement is somewhat beyond the scope of this chapter but might involve the following design approach:

- A PL/SQL package procedure will query the database audit trail for records that are older than the compliance-driven audit retention period. This package procedure could write the resulting records to a file that is backed up to tape media. We could also partition the SYSTEM.AUD$ table by date and simply move this partition to an archive tablespace and take the partition offline for backup to tape.
- This PL/SQL package procedure is scheduled to run as part of an Oracle DBMS_SCHEDULER job every day or month depending on the growth of the audit trail.
- We modify our DBV command rules to account for the PL/SQL package procedure. We can leverage some of the patterns we have discussed so far, in particular an operating context factor that checks for the use of this package. We would also want include a factor that verifies the package is running as part of a database job by calling the standard Oracle function **SYS_CONTEXT('USERENV', 'BG_JOB_ID')** and verifying that the value returned is NOT NULL. In Oracle database jobs this system context value is NOT NULL and for a foreground session (for example, SQL*Plus), the value is NULL.

Configure System-level Auditing

System-level auditing in the database involves auditing the use of privileges that do not affect the data stored in objects maintained in an object-owner account. In our discussion of DBV realms, we stressed the importance of auditing transactions against the data objects stored in object-owner accounts. System-level auditing is closely related to the concept of a DBV command rule as they both affect SQL commands issued in the system, regardless of whether they apply to a data storage object. As discussed in Chapter 5, DBV provides a fairly extensive audit policy for system-level commands that is based on research from industry authorities on the subject. The audit policy provided by DBV for system-level commands is designed to meet most regulations and industry benchmarks for (commercial) compliance and government industries. These types of regulations typically dictate system auditing of the following:

- Session logins and logoffs
- Account management for commands such as **CREATE**, **ALTER**, and **DROP USER**
- Role management for commands such as **CREATE**, **ALTER**, and **DROP ROLE**
- Security policy changes for commands such as **GRANT**, **REVOKE**, **AUDIT**, and **NOAUDIT**
- Structural changes that involve **CREATE**, **ALTER**, or **DROP** of objects stored in the database

When you've concluded the security profile analysis and DBV policy configuration for both realms and command rules, it is a good time to inspect your core database auditing policy and your audit trail through testing. The tests should cover all functional use cases (for example, data altering transaction from applications) and system use cases (such as database account provisioning) to ensure that you capture audit events for all critical transactions. The tests should validate policy changes to Oracle security products and components such as DBV, OLS, VPD, and fine-grained auditing (FGA) where applicable. Resources such as the Center for Internet Security (www.cisecurity.org/) have benchmarks that you can use to validate that the level of auditing you have configured in your database (and on your database servers) complies with a well-respected authority on the subject.

Establish DBV Secure Application Roles from Conditions

DBV SARs can be used when you have operations that are highly sensitive or potentially risky but not used very frequently. Another useful scenario for using DBV SARs are when you have a connection pool account that is used to assert multiple roles with different privileges and want the roles used only under the correction conditions. This approach reduces the risk of an alternative that would require granting several sets of roles directly to the account and creating an over-privileged account.

In Chapter 5 we presented an example of a highly sensitive role that enabled the archiving of sales data only during the system maintenance window. This is an example of a highly sensitive or potentially risky operation that is used infrequently. Creating a DBV secure application role for the oper_dba_0101 role we presented earlier may not make sense if we expect a user such as jean_oper_dba to be managing the database on a daily basis and using these privileges frequently.

If we examine the notional use case for this chapter, we have sales managers using an internal web application to manage sales data such as the product costs presented in the preceding section. It is quite possible that other sales-related web applications such as a query-only sales web service will run from the same set of application servers. We can define a connection pool of database connections using the Java Database Connectivity (JDBC) API on these application servers to support both types of applications and use DBV SARs to switch between the privilege sets required for both applications. The pool account can still leverage the read-write SH_DATA_ADMIN_0101 role for the Sales Manager application and the read-only SH_DATA_ANALYST_0101 for the query-only sales web service. The approach we will take is to create two DBV SARs and grant these multipurpose roles to the SARs. We can leverage the DBV rules we established in Chapter 5 to demonstrate the ability to assign a DBV factor from an application server that had authenticated using Oracle ASO/PKI. Let's create this DBV rule set first:

```
diego_dbvmgr@aos>BEGIN
    dbms_macadm.create_rule_set(
        rule_set_name =>'Can Set Sales Secure Application Role',
        description =>'Rule set to control enabling Sales
            roles from an application server',
        enabled =>dbms_macutl.g_yes,
        eval_options =>dbms_macutl.g_ruleset_eval_all,
        audit_options =>dbms_macutl.g_ruleset_audit_fail,
        fail_options =>dbms_macutl.g_ruleset_fail_show,
        fail_message =>NULL,
        fail_code =>NULL,
        handler_options =>dbms_macutl.g_ruleset_handler_off,
        handler =>NULL);
END;
/
```

```
PL/SQL procedure successfully completed.

diego_dbvmgr@aos>-- associate the valid client certificate
diego_dbvmgr@aos>-- check rule to the rule set
diego_dbvmgr@aos>BEGIN
   dbms_macadm.add_rule_to_rule_set (
     rule_set_name => 'Can Set Sales Secure Application Role'
   , rule_name     => 'Is Valid Certificate'
   );
END;
/
PL/SQL procedure successfully completed.

diego_dbvmgr@aos>-- associate the network protocol rule to the rule set
diego_dbvmgr@aos>BEGIN
   dbms_macadm.add_rule_to_rule_set (
     rule_set_name => 'Can Set Sales Secure Application Role'
   , rule_name     => 'Is TCPS Protocol'
   );
END;
/
PL/SQL procedure successfully completed.
```

The next step is to create the DBV SARs for the two types of applications the pool account will support:

```
diego_dbvmgr@aos>-- create the sales manager application role
diego_dbvmgr@aos>BEGIN
    dbms_macadm.create_role(
       role_name     => 'SALES_MANAGER_APP_ROLE'
     , enabled       => 'Y'
     , rule_set_name => 'Can Set Sales Secure Application Role'
     );
END;
/
PL/SQL procedure successfully completed.

diego_dbvmgr@aos>-- create the sales web service application role
diego_dbvmgr@aos>BEGIN
    dbms_macadm.create_role(
       role_name     => 'SALES_WEB_SERVICE_APP_ROLE'
     , enabled       => 'Y'
     , rule_set_name => 'Can Set Sales Secure Application Role'
     );
END;
/
PL/SQL procedure successfully completed.
```

We must use the application security administrator to grant the realm-protected roles to these DBV SARs:

```
sam_sec_mgr@aos>-- grant the read/write Sales History role to
sam_sec_mgr@aos>-- the sales manager application role
sam_sec_mgr@aos>GRANT sh_data_admin_0101 TO sales_manager_app_role;
Grant succeeded.

sam_sec_mgr@aos>-- grant the read-only Sales History role to
sam_sec_mgr@aos>-- the sales web service application role
sam_sec_mgr@aos>GRANT sh_data_analyst_0101 TO sales_web_service_app_role;
Grant succeeded.
```

We can test the use of these roles from the application server, where we have the valid certificate and demonstrate how to activate the roles:

```
ops$appserver_1@aos>-- notice the roles are not activated at login
ops$appserver_1@aos>SELECT * FROM session_roles;

ROLE
------------------------------
DV_PUBLIC
1 row selected.

ops$appserver_1@aos>-- set the sales manager application role
ops$appserver_1@aos>BEGIN
    dvsys.dbms_macsec_roles.set_role('SALES_MANAGER_APP_ROLE');
END;
/
ops$appserver_1@aos>-- query the current session roles
ops$appserver_1@aos>SELECT * FROM session_roles;

ROLE
------------------------------
SALES_MANAGER_APP_ROLE
SH_DATA_ADMIN_0101
BASE_DATA_ADMIN_0101
3 rows selected.

ops$appserver_1@aos>-- set the sales web service application role
ops$appserver_1@aos>BEGIN
    dvsys.dbms_macsec_roles.set_role('SALES_WEB_SERVICE_APP_ROLE');
END;
/
ops$appserver_1@aos>-- query the current session roles
ops$appserver_1@aos>SELECT * FROM session_roles;
ROLE
------------------------------
SALES_WEB_SERVICE_APP_ROLE
SH_DATA_ANALYST_0101
BASE_DATA_ANALYST_0101
3 rows selected.
```

If the operational DBA were to attempt to set one of these DBV SARs back on the database server, the DBV rule set would return false and the attempt would be blocked based on the lack of a valid certificate for the session and because jean_oper_dba is not a sales department manager.

```
jean_oper_dba@aos>BEGIN
    dvsys.dbms_macsec_roles.set_role('SALES_WEB_SERVICE_APP_ROLE');
END;
/
BEGIN
*
ERROR at line 1:
ORA-47305: Rule Set violation on SET ROLE (Can Set Sales Secure Application Role)
ORA-06512: at "DVSYS.DBMS_MACUTL", line 38
ORA-06512: at "DVSYS.DBMS_MACUTL", line 381
ORA-06512: at "DVSYS.DBMS_MACSEC", line 242
ORA-06512: at "DVSYS.ROLE_IS_ENABLED", line 4
ORA-06512: at "DVSYS.DBMS_MACSEC_ROLES", line 24
ORA-06512: at line 2
```

One final note on the use of DBV SARs follows from this final test. It is important that you ensure that the roles, privileges, and transactions you are attempting to protect with a DBV SAR cannot be accessed through some other means.

Summary

In this chapter we examined the detailed requirements for a new database application to introduce techniques and patterns for determining DBV security controls that could be applied to the design of the new application. The goal of this chapter was to help you increase the overall security posture of a new application by applying these techniques and patterns during the early stages of the development lifecycle no matter which software methodology your organization employs. It is important for you to focus on the key drivers of security for your enterprise and understand the penalty for not applying security. There is a cost for security, there is a cost for not applying security, and there is cost of not applying enough security. Applying security is a risk management process that must evaluate the cost and effort versus the risk of a security incident occurring. The costs of not applying security (or enough of it) can include the following:

- Financial penalties
- Loss of credibility of the organization
- Personal liability
- Loss of stock holder trust
- Loss of customer loyalty

You have seen some techniques and examples within this chapter on how to apply DBV to your application to meet compliance requirements and reduce your risks. The first technique involved decomposing the requirements to discover the application's core data objects and users. This will help you identify DBV realm protections and the associated DBV realm authorizations. Once the objects were identified, we recommended patterns for designing audit policies and row-level security policies to complement the DBV realm protections.

We presented a fine-grained pattern for defining the required database and application administrators that must be authorized in the DBV realms. We urged you to define areas of responsibilities for your application realm administrators and map the privilege sets defined by this fine-grained pattern to each area. The fine-grained pattern that was presented will enable you to meet separation of duty requirements that are part of compliance regulations or a consolidation effort. This pattern can also be collapsed into a more coarse-grained pattern depending on how stringent your compliance regulations are or how constrained you are from a personnel perspective in a consolidation effort.

Decomposing the requirements also helps uncover business rules and conditions that form the basis for DBV command rules and DBV rule sets. We recommend a Subject-Verb-Object-Condition table technique similar to conventions used in the security evaluation of an IT product. This technique was demonstrated with a handful of notional use cases. However, you should consider all of your business application use cases and system use cases (such as upgrades and backup/recovery database administration tasks) when employing this technique. Use cases can be categorized as follows:

- Application transactions (business use cases)
- Application batch processes (business use cases)
- Application reporting (business use cases)
- Database administration (system use cases)
- Database connection rules (business use cases and system use cases)

The business rules and conditions that were uncovered using this technique will also help you identify the DBV factors that can be created and shared among your applications. We presented a collection of patterns for DBV factors that can help you discover and categorize factors as they relate to conflict of interest, separation of duty, organization policy, identity management, operational context, time, and external events. We also presented examples of how you can incorporate these factors in your RLS controls (VPD, OLS, views), PL/SQL code, and FGA policies.

We concluded this chapter with a recommendation to use DBV SARs when operations are highly sensitive or potentially risky but are not used frequently. DBV SARs are also recommended when a connection pool account is used to assert multiple database roles with different privileges based on the operational context of a web-based application.

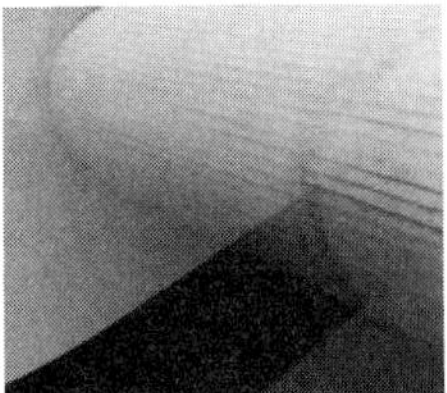

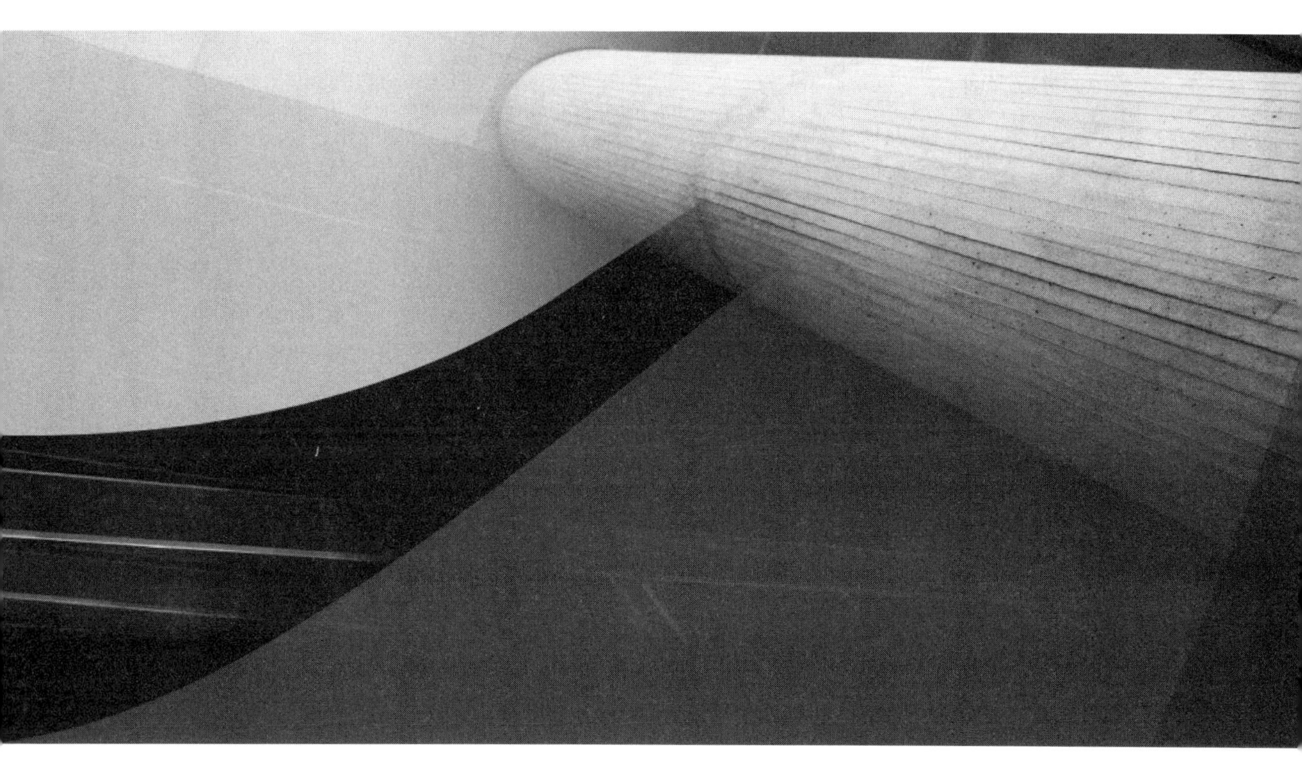

CHAPTER 7

Applied Database Vault for Existing Applications

hapter 6 introduced you to techniques and patterns for designing DBV security controls as part of a custom application development effort. In this chapter, we present several techniques for analyzing existing applications that need additional security controls. This might be the case, for example, for an organization that must comply with regulations and is looking to products such as DBV to help in this effort.

The ability to apply DBV security policy to existing applications is a powerful feature that many customers should consider. It is driven by the fact that DBV enforcement runs within the database kernel and is applied to all SQL commands that are submitted to the database, regardless of the programming language or development product used to write the application. The DBV enforcement engine and its underlying security policy configuration are external to the application and create a unique opportunity to secure applications without changing the underlying application code.

Applying DBV to existing applications is an exercise that involves people, documentation, and technology. The technical experts for an existing application can quickly identify the sensitive mission-critical data managed in the database that would be a candidate for protection by DBV realms. Application experts can identify the accounts/roles used in the database to help determine which DBV realm authorizations and DBV Secure Application Roles (SARs) may be required. These experts can also identify many of the business rules that are embedded in application code or part of the procedures used to manage the system, which can be transformed into DBV command rules. Once business rules and DBV command rules are identified, you can make use of DBV factors for security-related attributes that are commonly used.

If you have access to system engineering or design documentation, you can often shortcut the analysis to determine which object-owner accounts need to be considered for your protection profile. System documentation can be used to help validate the information supplied by the experts or to develop the initial drafts of a DBV policy that can be reviewed by the experts. This is especially helpful when experts have time constraints.

Finally, you can leverage the audit technology and configuration data available in the Oracle database to develop an initial draft of the DBV policy. This chapter focuses on the details of the latter approach as we can provide a generalized mechanism/process of capturing this information that applies to any system. You must first profile usage of system privileges and object privileges using the native Oracle database auditing. You can do this by auditing all accounts in the database or a set of targeted accounts you have identified.

Once you've completed interviews of application experts, reviewed system documentation, and profiled auditing in the database, you can perform the same type of analysis presented in Chapter 6. Specifically, you can develop a fine-grained security profile complete with Subject-Verb-Object-Condition tables for the various system use cases.

Audit Capture Preparation

Connect to the database as SYS and identify the location of the database AUDIT_TRAIL:

```
sys@aos>SHOW PARAMETER audit_trail
NAME                                 TYPE        VALUE
------------------------------------ ----------- ------
audit_trail                          string      DB
```

If the location is DB, DB EXTENDED, XML, or XML,EXTENDED, you are ready to go. If the location is set to NONE, you need to enable auditing by issuing the following command, and then you need to restart the database:

```
sys@aos>ALTER SYSTEM SET audit_trail = DB SCOPE = spfile;
System altered.
```

Once the audit location has been verified or configured, you can enable auditing for all database sessions by issuing the following command:

```
sys@aos>AUDIT ALL BY ACCESS;
Audit succeeded.
```

If you know beforehand which accounts are object-owner accounts and which accounts are connection pool accounts, you can achieve more targeted results that limit the amount of audit data created using the same approach. For example, if you consider the examples presented in this book, you may specify the object-owner accounts SH, HR, and OE and the application server pool account, OPS$APPSERVER_1, in the **AUDIT** command as follows:

```
sys@aos>AUDIT ALL BY sh, hr, oe, ops$appserver_1 BY ACCESS;
Audit succeeded.
```

Once the audit capture process is complete, you can return the audit policy configuration to the original state by issuing the following command when you're auditing all database sessions:

```
sys@aos>NOAUDIT ALL;
Noaudit succeeded.
```

You can return the audit policy configuration to the original state by issuing the following command when auditing only a subset of accounts:

```
sys@aos>NOAUDIT ALL BY sh, hr, oe, ops$appserver_1;
Noaudit succeeded.
```

Capturing Audits

The next step is to exercise all web applications, desktop applications, and batch programs that access the database. You should exercise all possible transactions in the system to ensure that a complete representation of the access paths to the data is captured in the audit trail. These types of tests would exercise the category of use cases known as "business use cases." You should also exercise all system use cases that may include the following:

- Database account management and provisioning processes that include privilege management using **GRANT** and **REVOKE** commands
- Backup/recovery operations
- General database administration tasks such as storage management or performance tuning that occur periodically using tools such as SQL*Plus or Oracle Enterprise Manager
- Application patching or upgrades
- Database patching or upgrades

If your audit capture process includes the use Oracle Real Application Testing workload capture feature, you can replay the workload at a later point in time against your development and deployment systems. This process provides a higher level of assurance that the DBV policy developed does not adversely affect the database applications as the results for a replayed workload would differ from the baseline. We also recommend that you perform the complete testing with Oracle Real Application Testing technology and capture a workload baseline for each category of use cases. You should capture separate workload baselines for each type of use cases—for example, one baseline for web applications, one for batch programs, one for backup/recovery operations, and so on. This improves your efficiency in validating the deployment of the DBV policy as you can just replay the baselines that are adversely affected.

Analyzing the Audit Trail

Now you have captured audit data while the complete transaction profile was run against the database. If your **AUDIT_TRAIL** initialization parameter is set to any of the following values, you can query the view DBA_COMMON_AUDIT_TRAIL for audit data that will help you identify parameters for your candidate DBV policy:

- DB
- DB, EXTENDED
- XML
- XML, EXTENDED

Many queries will use join information from the DBA_COMMON_AUDIT_TRAIL view, the DBA_OBJECTS view, and the AUDIT_ACTIONS table. To simplify the complexity of the queries presented in this section, we've taken the liberty of including a view named AOS_COMMON_AUDIT_TRAIL that already has the required joins. The view definition is as follows:

```
sys@aos> CREATE OR REPLACE VIEW aos_common_audit_trail AS
SELECT
   aud.audit_type
 , aud.session_id
 , aud.proxy_sessionid
 , aud.statementid
 , aud.entryid
 , aud.extended_timestamp
 , aud.global_uid
 , aud.db_user
 , aud.client_id
 , aud.econtext_id
 , aud.ext_name
 , aud.os_user
 , aud.userhost
 , aud.os_process
 , aud.terminal
 , aud.instance_number
```

```
 , aud.object_schema
 , aud.object_name
 , aud.policy_name
 , aud.new_owner
 , aud.new_name
 , aud.action
 , aud.statement_type
 , aud.audit_option
 , aud.transactionid
 , aud.returncode
 , aud.scn
 , aud.comment_text
 , aud.sql_bind
 , aud.sql_text
 , aud.obj_privilege
 , aud.sys_privilege
 , aud.admin_option
 , aud.os_privilege
 , aud.grantee
 , aud.priv_used
 , aud.ses_actions
 , aud.logoff_time
 , aud.logoff_lread
 , aud.logoff_pread
 , aud.logoff_lwrite
 , aud.logoff_dlock
 , aud.session_cpu
 , aud.obj_edition_name
 , act.name action_name
 , obj.subobject_name
 , obj.object_id
 , obj.data_object_id
 , obj.object_type
 , obj.created
 , obj.last_ddl_time
 , obj.timestamp
 , obj.status
 , obj.temporary
 , obj.generated
 , obj.secondary
 , obj.namespace
FROM dba_common_audit_trail aud
  , audit_actions act
  , dba_objects obj
WHERE aud.action = act.action (+)
AND aud.object_schema = obj.owner (+)
AND aud.object_name = obj.object_name (+)
/
View created.
```

DBV Realms from Object-Owner Accounts

The following query will help you narrow the list of object-owner accounts that may own sensitive data that is accessed using a **SELECT**, **DML**, or **EXECUTE** command. The query filters out objects owned by system accounts such as SYS, DVSYS, and LBACSYS.

```
sys@aos>SELECT DISTINCT object_schema
FROM aos_common_audit_trail
WHERE  object_schema NOT IN ( 'SYS','SYSMAN','DVF','DVSYS','LBACSYS','WK_TEST')
AND ( action_name IN (
  'SELECT'
  ,'UPDATE'
  ,'DELETE'
  ,'INSERT'
  ) OR action_name LIKE '%EXECUTE%')
AND object_type NOT LIKE '%PARTITION%'
AND extended_timestamp > sysdate - 1
ORDER BY object_schema;

OBJECT_SCHEMA
---------------
HR
SH
2 rows selected.
```

This query was run against the database we've been leveraging in the examples for the past two chapters and confirms that the query can be used to identify object-owner accounts, as we know both the Sales History (SH) and Human Resources (HR) schemas own objects with sensitive data. The results of the query provide a candidate list for the DBV realms we may need to create.

DBV Realm Secured Objects

We can now identify which objects in each object-owner account may need to be secured by a DBV realm by issuing the following query for the object-owner accounts:

```
sys@aos> SELECT DISTINCT object_schema, object_type, object_name
FROM aos_common_audit_trail
WHERE object_schema IN ('SH', 'HR')
AND ( action_name IN (
  'SELECT'
  ,'UPDATE'
  ,'DELETE'
  ,'INSERT'
  ) OR action_name LIKE '%EXECUTE%')
AND object_type NOT LIKE '%PARTITION%'
AND extended_timestamp > sysdate - 1
ORDER BY object_schema, object_type, object_name;

OBJECT_SCHEMA   OBJECT_TYPE          OBJECT_NAME
--------------- -------------------- ------------------------------
HR              PACKAGE              EMPLOYEE_UTILITY
HR              PACKAGE BODY         EMPLOYEE_UTILITY
SH              PACKAGE              SALES_TRANSCTION
SH              PACKAGE BODY         SALES_TRANSCTION
```

```
SH              TABLE                CHANNELS
SH              TABLE                COSTS
SH              TABLE                CUSTOMERS
SH              TABLE                PRODUCTS
SH              TABLE                PROMOTIONS
SH              TABLE                SALES

10 rows selected.
```

The results of this query can be used to limit the objects that are protected by the candidate DBV realms, or you can choose to protect the entire object-owner schema (OBJECT_SCHEMA) and all the objects owned by the account. This decision depends on the number of objects that are returned for each OBJECT_SCHEMA and the knowledge you have of the other objects that are not returned from the query. If a large number of objects are returned from the query for a given object-owner account, you can protect the all the objects in the account to simplify maintenance of the DBV policy.

Identify Realm Objects Based on Object-level Auditing

We can identify sensitive data objects that should be protected by a DBV realm by examining the existing object-level auditing that is configured in the database. If the database designer or database engineer had the wherewithal to audit an application's table or object, it must be sensitive enough to warrant auditing. The following query helps identify the objects that are being audited in the Oracle database. The query filters out those objects stored in off-the-shelf Oracle object-owner accounts that would not normally be audited by an application.

In this example, you see results for the SH object-owner account based on the audit policy we recommended in Chapter 6. You can also examine the Oracle database configuration to determine whether any Oracle fine-grained auditing (FGA) policies are defined for object-owner accounts. The same argument used earlier to justify querying the core RDBMS object audit policy tables applies to FGA policies:

```
sys@aos>SELECT DISTINCT
 owner
, object_name
, object_type
FROM dba_obj_audit_opts
WHERE owner NOT IN ( 'DVF','DVSYS','LBACSYS','SYS','SYSTEM')
ORDER BY 1,2,3;

OWNER    OBJECT_NAME   OBJECT_TYPE
-------- ------------- --------------------
SH       COSTS         TABLE
SH       SALES         TABLE
2 rows selected.
```

In this example, you can see that an Oracle FGA policy exists on the OE.CUSTOMERS table, and this leads us to believe that the OE object-owner account also contains sensitive objects that require the protection of a DBV realm:

```
sys@aos>SELECT DISTINCT
 object_schema
, object_name
FROM dba_audit_policies;
```

```
OBJECT_SCHEMA                  OBJECT_NAME
------------------------------ ------------------------------
OE                             CUSTOMERS
1 row selected.
```

Identify Realm Objects Based on Row-level Security Policy

The existence of row-level security (RLS) policies on any tables in the database should also serve as an indicator that the table contains sensitive data. If a table is being protected by Oracle VPD policy or Oracle Label Security (OLS) policy, creating DBV realms that protect these tables is also warranted. The following query will help identify those tables that are being protected by either an Oracle VPD policy or an Oracle OLS policy:

```
sys@aos>-- allow LBACSYS to query the VPD configuration table
sys@aos>GRANT SELECT ON sys.dba_policies TO lbacsys;
sys@aos>-- connect as LBACSYS to run the query
sys@aos>CONNECT lbacsys
Enter password:
Connected.
lbacsys/oracle@aos>SELECT 'VPD' policy_type
    , object_owner
    , object_name
  FROM sys.dba_policies
  WHERE object_owner NOT IN ('XDB')
UNION
 SELECT 'OLS' policy_type
    , schema_name object_owner
    , table_name object_name
 FROM
    lbacsys.dba_sa_table_policies
ORDER BY 1,2,3;

POL OBJECT_OWNER                   OBJECT_NAME
--- ------------------------------ ------------------------------
OLS SH                             CUSTOMERS
VPD OE                             PURCHASEORDER
VPD SH                             CUSTOMERS
VPD SYSTEM                         AUD$
4 rows selected.
lbacsys@aos>-- revoke the previous grant used to enable the query
lbacsys@aos>CONNECT / AS SYSDBA
Connected.
sys@aos>REVOKE SELECT ON sys.dba_policies FROM lbacsys;
Revoke succeeded.
```

The Oracle Sample Schemas are installed with a VPD policy on the table OE.PURCHASEORDER. Our example application does not access this table so it was not accessed when we generated the test workload used to populate our audit trail. The configuration queries exposed an additional security policy defined in the database and exposed another sensitive data object we need to account for in the candidate DBV policy.

Identify Roles to Protect as Realm

In many database applications, collections of database roles with direct object privileges are intended to be used to access or manipulate sensitive database objects. It is important to protect these roles in a DBV realm for the same reasons we recommended in Chapter 6 when discussing the security policy for new applications. We can inspect the database privilege configuration view DBA_TAB_PRIVS in conjunction with our captured audit trail to identify these roles:

```
sys@aos> SELECT DISTINCT aud.object_schema , grt.grantee role
FROM aos_common_audit_trail aud
  , dba_tab_privs grt
  , dba_roles rle
WHERE grt.owner = object_schema
AND rle.role = grt.grantee
AND object_schema NOT IN ( 'SYS', 'SYSMAN', 'DVF',
      'DVSYS', 'LBACSYS', 'WK_TEST')
AND ( action_name IN (
  'SELECT'
  ,'UPDATE'
  ,'DELETE'
  ,'INSERT'
  ) OR action_name LIKE '%EXECUTE%')
AND object_type NOT LIKE '%PARTITION%'
AND extended_timestamp > sysdate - 1
ORDER BY object_schema;

OBJECT_SCHEMA                  GRANTEE
------------------------------ ------------------------------
SH                             SALES_ARCHIVE_ROLE
SH                             SALES_SELECT_ROLE
SH                             SH_EXEC_ROLE_0101
SH                             SH_QUERY
SH                             SH_RO_ROLE_0101
SH                             SH_RW_ROLE_0101

6 rows selected.
```

A complimentary strategy for determining which roles are candidates for protection in a DBV realm is to query the audit trail for roles that were recently used in a **GRANT** or **REVOKE** command. The following query will help determine the roles that meet these criteria:

```
sys@aos>SELECT DISTINCT object_name role
FROM aos_common_audit_trail
WHERE action_name IN ('GRANT ROLE','REVOKE ROLE')
AND extended_timestamp > sysdate - 1
ORDER BY object_name;

ROLE
--------------------------
BASE_DATA_ANALYST_0101
CUSTOMER_POLICY_DBA
```

```
DV_ADMIN
DV_OWNER
SALES_SELECT_ROLE
SH_DATA_ADMIN_0101
SH_DATA_ANALYST_0101
SH_EXEC_ROLE_0101
SH_RW_ROLE_0101

9 rows selected.
```

DBV Realm Authorizations

Recall that DBV realm authorizations are intended to allow database administrator accounts to leverage the system ANY privileges (SELECT ANY, CREATE ANY, and so on) on objects that are protected by a realm. The following query on the database audit trail will return the account names that leveraged system ANY privileges to access or manipulate the sensitive data objects in the object-owner accounts we've identified. We can use this query and some additional query logic to identify both the database accounts and database roles that would be candidates for DBV realm authorizations.

```
sys@aos>SELECT DISTINCT db_user, action_name
 , object_schema || '.' || object_name object_name
FROM aos_common_audit_trail
WHERE object_schema IN ('SH', 'HR')
AND priv_used LIKE '%ANY%'
AND object_type NOT LIKE '%PARTITION%'
AND extended_timestamp > sysdate - 1
ORDER BY 1,2,3;

DB_USER          ACTION_NAME           OBJECT_NAME
---------------- --------------------- --------------------
ANTHONY          EXECUTE PROCEDURE     SH.SALES_TRANSCTION
DEB_DATA_MGR     DELETE                SH.COSTS
JRUSSEL          EXECUTE PROCEDURE     SH.SALES_TRANSCTION
JRUSSEL          INSERT                SH.COSTS
JRUSSEL          SELECT                SH.CHANNELS
JRUSSEL          SELECT                SH.PRODUCTS
JRUSSEL          SELECT                SH.PROMOTIONS
MARY             CREATE PACKAGE BODY   SH.SALES_ALERTS
MARY             DELETE                SH.COSTS
MARY             DELETE                SH.SALES
MARY             EXECUTE PROCEDURE     SH.SALES_TRANSCTION
MARY             GRANT OBJECT          SH.SALES_ALERTS
MARY             GRANT OBJECT          SH.SALES_STAGING
MARY             UPDATE                SH.CUSTOMERS
OPS$APPSERVER_1  EXECUTE PROCEDURE     SH.SALES_TRANSCTION
PTUCKER          EXECUTE PROCEDURE     SH.SALES_TRANSCTION
PTUCKER          INSERT                SH.COSTS
PTUCKER          SELECT                SH.CHANNELS
PTUCKER          SELECT                SH.PRODUCTS
PTUCKER          SELECT                SH.PROMOTIONS
SAM_SEC_MGR      ALTER TABLE           SH.CUSTOMERS
```

```
SYSTEM           GRANT OBJECT         SH.SALES
22 rows selected.
```

We know from the DBV examples in Chapter 6 and methodology we've presented so far that many of the account names returned by this query actually leveraged database roles we created for realm administrators. We can leverage this query's results as input into a second query to determine the database roles that may be candidates for DBV realm authorizations as shown here:

```
sys@aos>DECLARE
    l_index NUMBER ;
BEGIN
   FOR c_user IN (
        SELECT DISTINCT db_user, object_schema
        FROM aos_common_audit_trail
        WHERE object_schema IN ( 'SH', 'HR')
        AND priv_used LIKE '%ANY%'
        AND object_type NOT LIKE '%PARTITION%'
        AND extended_timestamp > sysdate - 1
        ORDER BY db_user, object_schema
   ) LOOP
        DBMS_OUTPUT.PUT_LINE (
            'User: '|| c_user.db_user
            || ', Object Owner: ' || c_user.object_schema);
        l_index := 1;
        FOR c_role IN (
            SELECT grant_type,granted_role FROM
            (
                SELECT
                    NULL          grantee
                    ,username      granted_role
                    ,'USER'        grant_type
                    FROM all_users
                    WHERE username = c_user.db_user
                UNION
                    SELECT
                    grantee
                    ,granted_role
                    ,'ROLE'        grant_type
                    FROM dba_role_privs
            )
            WHERE grant_type = 'ROLE'
            START WITH grantee IS NULL
            CONNECT BY grantee = PRIOR granted_role
        ) LOOP
        IF l_index = 1 THEN
            DBMS_OUTPUT.PUT_LINE ( 'Roles:' );
        END IF;
        DBMS_OUTPUT.PUT_LINE ( '----- ' || c_role.granted_role );
        l_index := l_index + 1;
      END LOOP;
  END LOOP;
END;
```

```
/
User: ANTHONY, Object Owner: SH
Roles:
----- DBA
<truncated for brevity>
...

User: DEB_DATA_MGR, Object Owner: SH
Roles:
----- SH_DATA_ADMIN_0101
----- BASE_DATA_ADMIN_0101
User: JRUSSEL, Object Owner: SH
Roles:
----- SH_DATA_ADMIN_0101
----- BASE_DATA_ADMIN_0101
User: MARY, Object Owner: SH
Roles:
----- DBA
<truncated for brevity>
...

User: OPS$APPSERVER_1, Object Owner: SH
User: PTUCKER, Object Owner: SH
Roles:
----- SH_DATA_ADMIN_0101
----- BASE_DATA_ADMIN_0101
User: SAM_SEC_MGR, Object Owner: SH
Roles:
----- CUSTOMER_POLICY_DBA
----- SH_SEC_ADMIN_0101
----- BASE_SEC_ADMIN_0101
User: SYSTEM, Object Owner: SH
Roles:
----- AQ_ADMINISTRATOR_ROLE
----- DBA
<truncated for brevity>
...

----- SALES_SELECT_ROLE
PL/SQL procedure successfully completed.
```

Based on the examples we've presented we know that SH_DATA_ADMIN_0101, SH_SEC_ADMIN_0101, and SALES_SELECT_ROLE are candidate roles for DBV Realm Authorizations. In database applications that are being analyzed for the first time, it is up to you to work with application experts and system documentation identify the functional purpose of the roles you uncover in the query results such as those shown above. Once you've decided which roles should be authorized in the realm, the roles themselves also need to be protected by the realm from unauthorized GRANT/REVOKE commands.

You can map the database roles you discover (or those you should create) to the fine-grained separation of duty model for database administrators presented in Chapter 6. To do this, simply rerun the query above with filters on the privilege used to determine which roles map to the administrator profiles presented in Chapter 6. The filters would be constructed according to the types of privileges granted to each database administrator profile, as shown in the following table:

Administrator Profile	Privilege or Role Filter
Operational database administrator	CREATE/ALTER/DROP TABLESPACE, ALTER DATABASE, ALTER SYSTEM, or the use of the DBA role
Application maintenance administrator	CREATE ANY/ALTER ANY/DROP ANY <object_type>, e.g. INDEX, PROCEDURE, TABLE, VIEW, etc.
Application data manager (data steward)	SELECT ANY SEQUENCE SELECT ANY TABLE INSERT ANY TABLE UPDATE ANY TABLE DELETE ANY TABLE EXECUTE ANY INDEXTYPE EXECUTE ANY OPERATOR EXECUTE ANY PROCEDURE EXECUTE ANY TYPE
Application security administrator	GRANT ANY OBJECT PRIVILEGE GRANT ANY PRIVILEGE GRANT ANY ROLE AUDIT ANY AUDIT SYSTEM
Account administrator	CREATE/ALTER/DROP USER

The following query block determines which accounts or roles could be application data managers (or application proxy accounts) by inspecting the audit records for **SELECT**, **DML**, and **EXECUTE** commands. If we look at the use of system ANY privileges for these types of commands being used, we can identify the candidate accounts and roles.

```
sys@aos>SET SERVEROUT ON
sys@aos> DECLARE
    l_index NUMBER ;
BEGIN
   FOR c_user IN (
        SELECT DISTINCT db_user, object_schema
        FROM aos_common_audit_trail
        WHERE (priv_used IN (
           'SELECT ANY TABLE'
          ,'INSERT ANY TABLE'
          ,'UPDATE ANY TABLE'
          ,'DELETE ANY TABLE'
          ,'EXECUTE ANY PROCEDURE'
          )
          AND object_schema IN ('SH', 'HR'))
        AND object_type NOT LIKE '%PARTITION%'
        AND extended_timestamp > sysdate - 1
        ORDER BY db_user, object_schema
   ) LOOP
```

```
        DBMS_OUTPUT.PUT_LINE (
            'User: '|| c_user.db_user
            || ', Object Owner: ' || c_user.object_schema);
        l_index := 1;
        FOR c_role IN (
            SELECT grant_type,granted_role FROM
            (
                SELECT
                    NULL        grantee
                    ,username    granted_role
                    ,'USER'      grant_type
                    FROM all_users
                    WHERE username = c_user.db_user
                UNION
                    SELECT
                    grantee
                    ,granted_role
                    ,'ROLE'      grant_type
                    FROM dba_role_privs
            )
            WHERE grant_type = 'ROLE'
            START WITH grantee IS NULL
            CONNECT BY grantee = PRIOR granted_role
        ) LOOP
        IF l_index = 1 THEN
            DBMS_OUTPUT.PUT_LINE ( 'Roles:' );
        END IF;
        DBMS_OUTPUT.PUT_LINE ( '----- ' || c_role.granted_role );
        l_index := l_index + 1;
     END LOOP;
  END LOOP;
END;
/
User: ANTHONY, Object Owner: SH
Roles:
----- DBA
<truncated for brevity>
User: DEB_DATA_MGR, Object Owner: SH
Roles:
----- SH_DATA_ADMIN_0101
----- BASE_DATA_ADMIN_0101
User: JRUSSEL, Object Owner: SH
Roles:
----- SH_DATA_ADMIN_0101
----- BASE_DATA_ADMIN_0101
User: MARY, Object Owner: SH
Roles:
----- DBA
<truncated for brevity>
User: OPS$APPSERVER_1, Object Owner: SH
User: PTUCKER, Object Owner: SH
```

```
Roles:
----- SH_DATA_ADMIN_0101
----- BASE_DATA_ADMIN_0101
PL/SQL procedure successfully completed.
```

The query results confirm the fact that accounts such as DEB_DATA_MGR, JRUSSEL, and PTUCKER use a role named SH_DATA_ADMIN_0101 and the role should considered as a DBV realm authorization. While MARY and ANTHONY used the DBA role, we want to avoid using the role in our application-specific realms in favor of the fine-grained administrator roles presented in Chapter 6. One final note regarding why the account OPS$APPSERVER_1 is shown in our results but has no role associated to it. Recall that this account was used in Chapter 6 to demonstrate DBV SARs and the dynamic enablement of a role that was granted the SH_DATA_ADMIN_0101 role. This role is not permanently granted directly or indirectly to the OPS$APPSERVER_1 account so it is not visible within the DBA_ROLE_PRIVS view.

What If System ANY Privileges Are Not Being Used?

It is possible that the preceding queries that filter on the use of system ANY privileges show no results. This condition has a handful of possible implications:

- End user accounts have direct object privileges for **SELECT** and **DML** on the application objects either granted directly to the account or through a database role.
- Applications perform **SELECT** and **DML** commands using the object-owner account.
- Application maintenance for **DDL**, **AUDIT**, **GRANT**, and other database administration commands are performed as the object-owner account.
- End-user accounts have object privileges for **SELECT** and DML through grants to PUBLIC.

Database accounts or roles that have been granted object privileges do not require DBV realm authorizations, so this implication is not a concern. We demonstrated earlier how to discover the roles that fall into this category to protect them within a DBV realm. The worst-case scenario is that your applications do not use database roles and have unnecessary privilege management overhead by keeping all database accounts in synch with the required direct object privileges.

The rest of the implications require more research to determine whether you should be concerned. **SELECT**, **DML**, **DDL**, and other database administration commands performed as the object-owner account could occur if your applications use this account as a connection pool account for **SELECT** and **DML** or database administrators log into the database as this account to perform object maintenance. The problem with this scenario is the loss of audit attribution and the lack of separation of duties. You can verify the existence of this scenario by issuing the following query on the audit trail, which determines whether the database user and object-owner are the same account:

```
sys@aos>SELECT DISTINCT db_user
, action_name || decode(grantee,NULL,'',' TO ' || grantee) action_name
 , object_schema || '.' || object_name object_name
FROM aos_common_audit_trail
WHERE object_schema IN ('SH', 'HR')
AND db_user IN ('SH', 'HR')
AND object_type NOT LIKE '%PARTITION%'
```

```
AND extended_timestamp > sysdate - 1
ORDER BY 1,2,3;

DB_USER ACTION_NAME                         OBJECT_NAME
------- ----------------------------------- --------------------
HR      CREATE PACKAGE                      HR.EMPLOYEE_UTILITY
HR      CREATE PACKAGE BODY                 HR.EMPLOYEE_UTILITY
SH      ALTER TABLE                         SH.SALES
SH      AUDIT OBJECT                        SH.SALES
SH      CREATE PACKAGE                      SH.SALES_TRANSCTION
SH      CREATE PACKAGE BODY                 SH.SALES_RULES
SH      CREATE PACKAGE BODY                 SH.SALES_TRANSCTION
SH      DELETE                              SH.SALES
SH      GRANT OBJECT TO APP_OBJECT_OWNER    SH.CUSTOMERS
SH      GRANT OBJECT TO SH_EXEC_ROLE_0101   SH.SALES_TRANSCTION
SH      GRANT OBJECT TO SH_RO_ROLE_0101     SH.COSTS
SH      GRANT OBJECT TO SH_RW_ROLE_0101     SH.COSTS
SH      SELECT                              SH.SALES

13 rows selected.
```

In these results we find evidence of **SELECT**, **DML**, **DDL**, privilege management, and audit policy commands. For **SELECT**, **DML**, and possibly some Data Definition Language (DDL) commands that are issued from applications, we recommend the use of proxy authentication approach that is covered in great detail in David Knox's book *Effective Oracle Database 10*g *Security by Design*. For DDL, privilege management, and audit policy commands, we recommend implementing the use of the application administrator profiles (roles) for realm authorizations as presented in Chapter 6.

SELECT and DML privileges granted to PUBLIC mean that anyone who can connect to the database can access or manipulate objects owned by your application accounts. You can determine the application account objects that are accessible to PUBLIC with the following query:

```
sys@aos>SELECT
  owner
, table_name
,  privilege
FROM dba_tab_privs
WHERE grantee = 'PUBLIC'
AND owner IN ('SH', 'HR')
ORDER BY 1,2,3;

OWNER  TABLE_NAME                     PRIVILEGE
------ ------------------------------ ----------
HR     COUNTRIES                      SELECT
HR     DEPARTMENTS                    SELECT
HR     LOCATIONS                      SELECT

3 rows selected.
```

If the results of this query for your application accounts cause you concern from a security or compliance perspective, you need to develop a plan to change your security model. This plan should include the creation of database roles with the appropriate direct object privileges for

SELECT and DML on the application objects. Coupled with the use of the proxy authentication feature, these roles would be used with your business applications. For DDL, privilege management, and audit policy commands, we again recommend implementing the use of the application administrator profiles (roles) for realm authorizations, as discussed in Chapter 6.

Externalizing Realm Authorizations

In Chapter 6 we mentioned that we could leverage an external system, such as an Lightweight Directory Access Protocol (LDAP) directory, as the source of information for a realm authorization. We can demonstrate this concept using Oracle Enterprise User Security (EUS) as the mechanism to retrieve information required. To use Oracle EUS, we must first register our database with Oracle Internet Directory (OID) and then configure components such as global schemas and global roles. (Specific details about this registration and these components are also covered in David Knox's book.) For our example, we will create a global schema, GLOBAL_OID_TREE1, to which we'll map our EUS users. We will also create global role that will be used to enable the database privileges required for these users to act as application security administrators.

```
jim_acctmgr@aos>-- create our global schema
jim_acctmgr@aos>CREATE USER global_oid_tree1 IDENTIFIED GLOBALLY ;
User created.
jim_acctmgr@aos>CONNECT jean_oper_dba
Enter password:
Connected.
jean_oper_dba@aos>-- create our global role, we do not need
jean_oper_dba@aos>-- to revoke the role from the operational DBA
jean_oper_dba@aos>-- as these roles cannot be GRANT-ed or
jean_oper_dba@aos>-- REVOKE-ed in the SQL engine
jean_oper_dba@aos>CREATE ROLE sh_data_admin_global IDENTIFIED GLOBALLY;
Role created.
jean_oper_dba@aos>-- allow the global schema to connect
jean_oper_dba@aos>GRANT CREATE SESSION TO global_oid_tree1;
Grant succeeded.
jean_oper_dba@aos>-- grant the Application Data Manager role
jean_oper_dba@aos>-- role to the global role we've created
jean_oper_dba@aos>GRANT base_sec_admin_0101 TO sh_data_admin_global;
Grant succeeded.
```

We use the Oracle 11*g* Database Control to view and configure Oracle EUS in the same way that the Oracle Enterprise Security Manager was used with a 10*g* database. In this example, we've mapped our EUS users to the GLOBAL_OID_TREE1 global schema, as shown in Figure 7-1.

Next we created a EUS enterprise role named SH_DATA_ADMIN_ENTERPRISE that maps to our database global role named SH_DATA_ADMIN_GLOBAL, as shown in Figure 7-2.

We also mapped two EUS accounts, JOE and SALLY, to this EUS enterprise role, as shown in Figure 7-3.

You may already maintain directory groups specific to your organization, under the base group distinguished name (DN) for a specific directory domain, in our example cn=Groups, dc=us,dc=oracle,dc=com. These are called (user defined) enterprise groups in OID. You can grant enterprise roles such SH_DATA_ADMIN_ENTERPRISE to these enterprise groups if they meet your requirements. This may avoid the need to map EUS users, as was done in Figure 7-3, and reduces your overall system maintenance requirements.

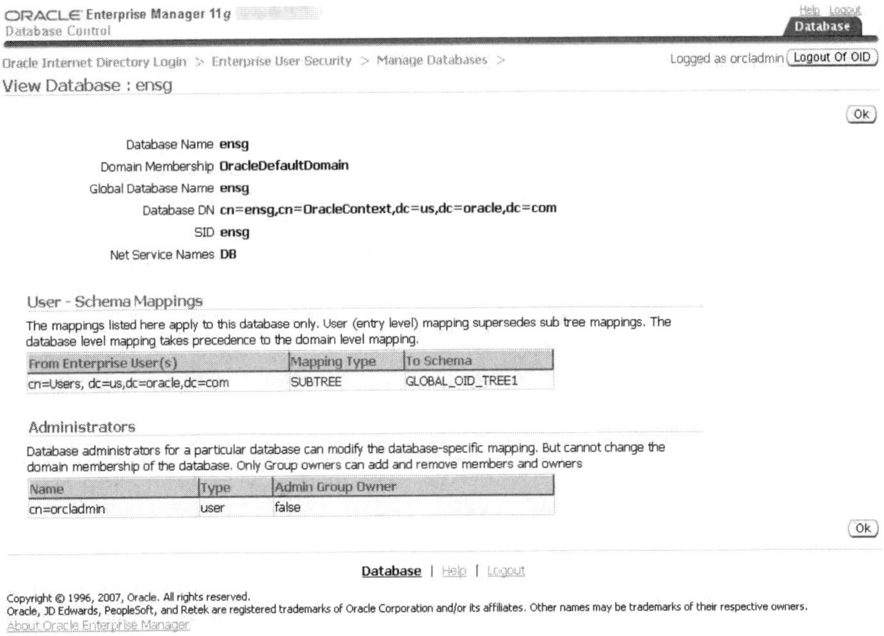

ORACLE Enterprise Manager 11*g*
Database Control

Help Logout
Database

Oracle Internet Directory Login > Enterprise User Security > Manage Databases >

Logged as orcladmin (Logout Of OID)

View Database : ensg

(Ok)

Database Name **ensg**
Domain Membership **OracleDefaultDomain**
Global Database Name **ensg**
Database DN **cn=ensg,cn=OracleContext,dc=us,dc=oracle,dc=com**
SID **ensg**
Net Service Names **DB**

User - Schema Mappings

The mappings listed here apply to this database only. User (entry level) mapping supersedes sub tree mappings. The database level mapping takes precedence to the domain level mapping.

From Enterprise User(s)	Mapping Type	To Schema
cn=Users, dc=us,dc=oracle,dc=com	SUBTREE	GLOBAL_OID_TREE1

Administrators

Database administrators for a particular database can modify the database-specific mapping. But cannot change the domain membership of the database. Only Group owners can add and remove members and owners

Name	Type	Admin Group Owner
cn=orcladmin	user	false

(Ok)

Database | Help | Logout

About Oracle Enterprise Manager

FIGURE 7-1 *EUS global schema mapping*

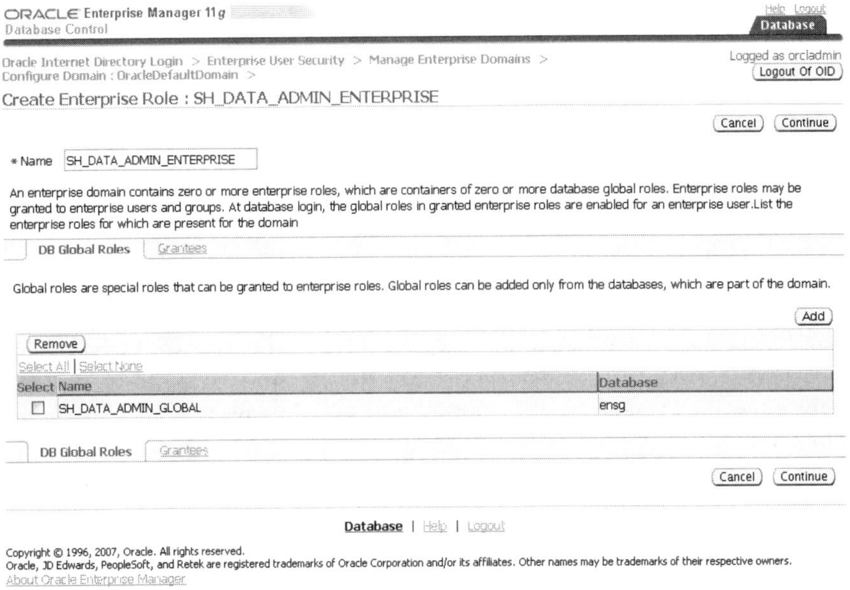

ORACLE Enterprise Manager 11*g*
Database Control

Help Logout
Database

Oracle Internet Directory Login > Enterprise User Security > Manage Enterprise Domains > Configure Domain : OracleDefaultDomain >

Logged as orcladmin
(Logout Of OID)

Create Enterprise Role : SH_DATA_ADMIN_ENTERPRISE

(Cancel) (Continue)

* Name SH_DATA_ADMIN_ENTERPRISE

An enterprise domain contains zero or more enterprise roles, which are containers of zero or more database global roles. Enterprise roles may be granted to enterprise users and groups. At database login, the global roles in granted enterprise roles are enabled for an enterprise user.List the enterprise roles for which are present for the domain

DB Global Roles | Grantees

Global roles are special roles that can be granted to enterprise roles. Global roles can be added only from the databases, which are part of the domain.

(Add)

(Remove)

Select All | Select None

Select	Name	Database
☐	SH_DATA_ADMIN_GLOBAL	ensg

DB Global Roles | Grantees

(Cancel) (Continue)

Database | Help | Logout

About Oracle Enterprise Manager

FIGURE 7-2 *EUS Enterprise role and database global role*

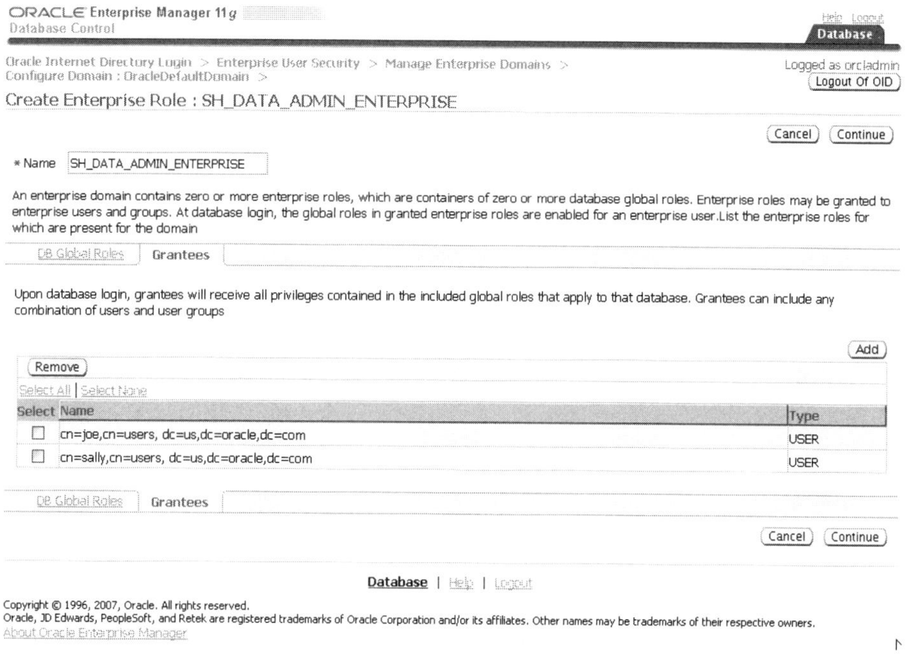

FIGURE 7-3 *EUS-based application security administrators*

Once this configuration is complete, we can immediately leverage externally defined users in the organization as our realm administrators. A key point to this capability is that the membership in the EUS enterprise role SH_DATA_ADMIN_ENTERPRISE, a directory **groupOfUniqueNames** object, is also controlled externally and can be leveraged in more than just a single database in the organization. For example, if we log in as the EUS user JOE, we can see that his database session roles and privileges reflect being the Sales History application data administrator.

```
sam_sec_mgr@aos>CONNECT joe
Enter password:
Connected.
global_oid_tree1@aos>SELECT SYS_CONTEXT('USERENV','EXTERNAL_NAME')
FROM dual;

SYS_CONTEXT('USERENV','EXTERNAL_NAME')
----------------------------------------
cn=joe,cn=users,dc=us,dc=oracle,dc=com
1 row selected.


global_oid_tree1@aos>-- show the session roles that include
global_oid_tree1@aos>-- the SH_DATA_ADMIN_0101 role
```

```
global_oid_tree1@aos>SELECT * FROM session_roles
ORDER BY 1;
ROLE
------------------------------
BASE_DATA_ADMIN_0101
DV_PUBLIC
SH_DATA_ADMIN_0101
SH_DATA_ADMIN_GLOBAL
4 rows selected.

global_oid_tree1@aos>-- show the session privileges
global_oid_tree1@aos>-- that include privileges like AUDIT ANY (object)
global_oid_tree1@aos>SELECT *
FROM session_privs
ORDER BY 1;
PRIVILEGE
----------------------------------------
CREATE SESSION
DELETE ANY TABLE
EXECUTE ANY INDEXTYPE
EXECUTE ANY OPERATOR
EXECUTE ANY PROCEDURE
EXECUTE ANY TYPE
INSERT ANY TABLE
SELECT ANY SEQUENCE
SELECT ANY TABLE
UPDATE ANY TABLE
10 rows selected.

global_oid_tree1@aos>-- attempt to use the SELECT ANY privilege
global_oid_tree1@aos>-- on a table that is protected by the
global_oid_tree1@aos>-- Sales History realm
global_oid_tree1@aos> SELECT
 cust_last_name
, cust_year_of_birth
, cust_marital_status
, cust_income_level
FROM sh.customers
WHERE cust_state_province = 'TX'
      AND ROWNUM < 10
ORDER BY cust_last_name;

CUST_LAST_ CUST_YEAR_OF_BIRTH CUST_MARIT CUST_INCOME_LEVEL
---------- ------------------ ---------- -------------------------
Beiers                   1982 single     K: 250,000 - 299,999
Duval                    1981 single     H: 150,000 - 169,999
Greeley                  1977            F: 110,000 - 129,999
Grover                   1970 married    D: 70,000 - 89,999
Hamilton                 1961 single     G: 130,000 - 149,999
Krider                   1967            F: 110,000 - 129,999
Majors                   1948 single     G: 130,000 - 149,999
Rowley                   1969 single     H: 150,000 - 169,999
Stone                    1978 single     I: 170,000 - 189,999
9 rows selected.
global_oid_tree1@aos>-- attempt to use the SELECT ANY privilege
```

```
global_oid_tree1@aos>-- on a table that is protected by the
global_oid_tree1@aos>-- Order Entry realm
global_oid_tree1@aos>SELECT cust_last_name,
date_of_birth,
marital_status,
income_level
FROM oe.customers;
FROM oe.customers
     *
ERROR at line 2:
ORA-01031: insufficient privileges
```

With Oracle technologies such as Oracle Identity Manager, which is covered in Chapter 9, we could configure self-service workflows that allow a directory user such as JOE to remove himself temporarily from the application data administrator responsibility. The self-service workflow could allow JOE to delegate this function to another directory user. OIM can be configured to update the members of the SH_DATA_ADMIN_ENTERPRISE **groupOfUniqueNames** object with this information so that delegation of realm administration can be achieved. The use of the Oracle Virtual Directory (OVD) will even also allow us to extend the backend directory store for EUS users shown in this example to the Active Directory and Sun Java System Directory Server products. Refer to the OVD home page on the Oracle Technology Network (OTN) at www.oracle.com/technology/products/id_mgmt/ovds/index.html for more details on this type of integration.

We can extend the EUS example we've just presented with user identity attributes in a DBV rule set that controls the DBV realm authorization for the SH_DATA_ADMIN_0101 role. In Chapter 6 we introduced the user identity attributes that are exposed in the EUS session context's SYS_LDAP_USER_DEFAULT namespace. Consider the case where JOE is a permanent employee and SALLY is a contractor. This fact can be stored in the identity attribute **employeeType** that is part of the **inetOrgPerson** directory object as shown in Figure 7-4.

Business rules in the organization may dictate that contractors cannot delete financial data in systems such as the Sales History application. We can define a DBV rule set that leverages the **employeeType** attribute and the type of SQL command issued as follows:

```
diego_dbvmgr@aos>-- create the rule to check for the DELETE
diego_dbvmgr@aos>-- commands and the employeeType attribute
diego_dbvmgr@aos>-- of PERMANENT, or DBA for non-EUS users
diego_dbvmgr@aos>BEGIN
  dbms_macadm.create_rule(
  rule_name => 'DELETE By Permanent Employee Only'
  , rule_expr =>'(INSTR(DVSYS.DV_SQL_TEXT,''DELETE'') = 1 AND ' ||
'NVL(SYS_CONTEXT(''SYS_LDAP_USER_DEFAULT'',''EMPLOYEETYPE''),''DBA'')'
    || '   IN  (''PERMANENT'',''DBA''))'
    || ' OR (INSTR(DVSYS.DV_SQL_TEXT,''DELETE'') = 0)'
  );
END;
/
PL/SQL procedure successfully completed.

diego_dbvmgr@aos>-- create the rule set and add this rule
diego_dbvmgr@aos>BEGIN
    dbms_macadm.create_rule_set(
        rule_set_name =>'Sales History Data Administration Allowed',
```

```
        description =>'Authorizes data administration controls
            commands for the Sales History realm.',
        enabled =>dbms_macutl.g_yes,
        eval_options =>dbms_macutl.g_ruleset_eval_all,
        audit_options =>dbms_macutl.g_ruleset_audit_fail,
        fail_options =>dbms_macutl.g_ruleset_fail_show,
        fail_message =>NULL,
        fail_code =>NULL,
        handler_options =>dbms_macutl.g_ruleset_handler_off,
        handler =>NULL);
END;
/
PL/SQL procedure successfully completed.
diego_dbvmgr@aos>BEGIN
   dbms_macadm.add_rule_to_rule_set (
     rule_set_name => 'Sales History Data Administration Allowed'
   , rule_name     => 'DELETE By Permanent Employee Only'
   );
END;
/
PL/SQL procedure successfully completed.
```

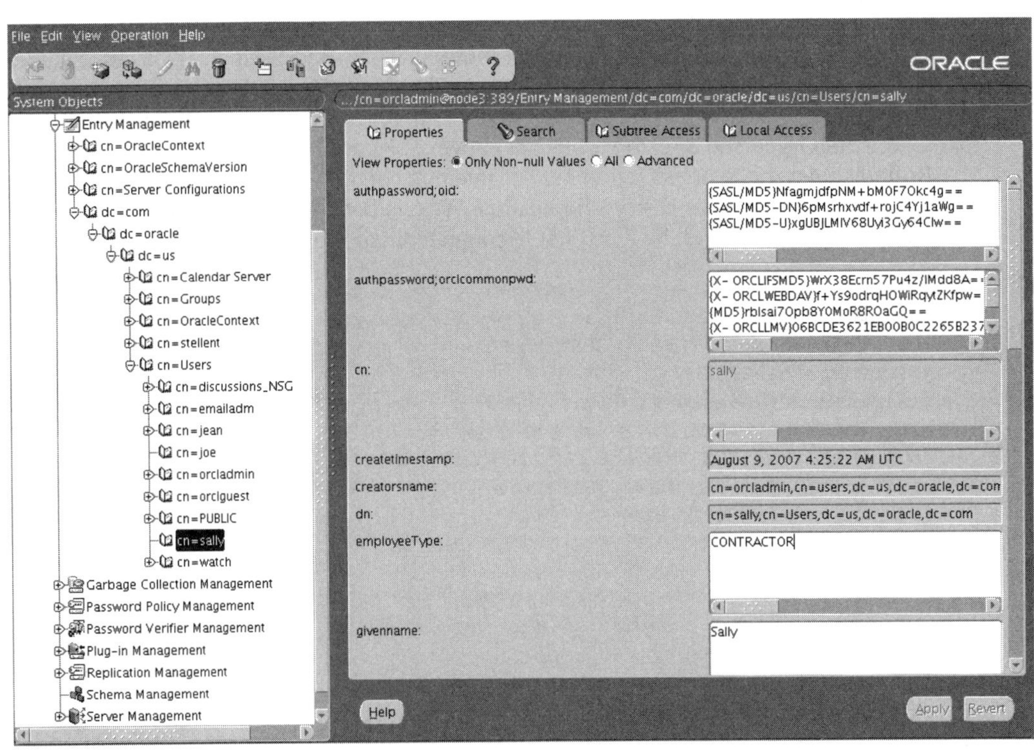

FIGURE 7-4 *Identity attribute employeeType*

Next we would update the realm authorization created for the SH_DATA_ADMIN_0101 role in Chapter 6 to use the new DBV rule set:

```
diego_dbvmgr@aos>BEGIN
   dbms_macadm.update_realm_auth (
    realm_name     => 'Sales History'
    , grantee       => 'SH_DATA_ADMIN_0101'
    , rule_set_name => 'Sales History Data Administration Allowed'
    , auth_options  => dbms_macutl.g_realm_auth_participant
    );
END;
/
PL/SQL procedure successfully completed.
```

Finally, we can test this externally controlled realm authorization using JOE and SALLY as our test accounts for a permanent and contract employee, respectively:

```
diego_dbvmgr@aos>CONNECT joe
Enter password:
Connected.
global_oid_tree1@aos>SELECT
SYS_CONTEXT('SYS_LDAP_USER_DEFAULT','UID') USERNAME
     SYS_CONTEXT('SYS_LDAP_USER_DEFAULT','EMPLOYEETYPE') EMPLOYEETYPE
FROM DUAL;
USERNAME   EMPLOYEETYPE
---------- ---------------
joe        PERMANENT

global_oid_tree1@aos>-- JOE is a permanent employee and therefore
global_oid_tree1@aos>-- is authorized for DELETE commands
global_oid_tree1@aos>DELETE SH.COSTS WHERE ROWNUM < 2;
1 row deleted.
global_oid_tree1@aos>-- next test with SALLY, who is a contractor,
global_oid_tree1@aos>-- and attempt the same DELETE, which will not
global_oid_tree1@aos>-- be authorized according to our DBV Rule
global_oid_tree1@aos>CONNECT sally
Enter password:
Connected.
global_oid_tree1@aos>SELECT
SYS_CONTEXT('SYS_LDAP_USER_DEFAULT','UID') USERNAME
     SYS_CONTEXT('SYS_LDAP_USER_DEFAULT','EMPLOYEETYPE') EMPLOYEETYPE
FROM DUAL;
USERNAME   EMPLOYEETYPE
---------- ---------------
sally      CONTRACTOR
global_oid_tree1@aos>DELETE SH.COSTS WHERE ROWNUM < 2;
DELETE SH.COSTS WHERE ROWNUM < 2
          *
ERROR at line 1:
ORA-01031: insufficient privileges
```

Identify End User Access Accounts and Roles for DBV SARs

To identify end user access accounts, we can examine the query results for the query used to identify roles with direct object privileges for SELECT, DML, or EXECUTE on database objects in an object-owner account. The accounts that have been granted these roles are usually connection pool accounts used for end user access, and the roles themselves may even be used as global enterprise roles with the Oracle EUS technology. Due to the sensitive nature of the data accessed by these accounts and roles, you may want to consider the use of DBV SARs instead of traditional database roles. This approach allows you to apply the multifactored, rule-based control of the enablement of the role (a privilege set on sensitive objects) using some of the techniques we demonstrated with the roles SALES_MANAGER_APP_ROLE and SALES_WEB_SERVICE_APP_ROLE.

We queried the view DBA_TAB_PRIVS earlier in the chapter to show accounts and roles with direct object privileges on an object-owner account's objects. This is a first pass at the roles we need to consider as end user access accounts. We can also identify global schema accounts for EUS and externally identified accounts (for Advanced Security option (ASO)/Public Key Infrastructure (PKI)) using the following query:

```
sys@aos>SELECT username, password
FROM dba_users
WHERE password IN
    ( 'GLOBAL'   -- identified globally
    , 'EXTERNAL' -- identified externally
    ) ;
USERNAME                       PASSWORD
------------------------------ ------------------------------
OPS$JEFFREY                    EXTERNAL
OPS$APPSERVER_1                EXTERNAL
GLOBAL_OID_TREE1               GLOBAL
GLOBAL_OID_TREE2               GLOBAL
4 rows selected.
```

We can identify which accounts may be used for proxy authentication, which is often used with JDBC connection pools and EUS together, using the following query:

```
sys@aos>SELECT proxy, client
FROM proxy_users
ORDER BY 1;
PROXY                          CLIENT
------------------------------ ------------------------------
OID_POOL_1                     GLOBAL_OID_TREE1
OID_POOL_2                     GLOBAL_OID_TREE2
2 rows selected.
```

Finally, we can query the existing SARs in a database if we want to convert the application security logic used to enable these roles into DBV rules as part of any overall effort to consolidate security policies:

```
sys@aos>SELECT *
FROM dba_application_roles
WHERE schema != 'DVSYS'
ORDER BY 1;
```

```
ROLE                           SCHEMA        PACKAGE
------------------------------ ------------- ---------------
CUSTOM_SECAPP_ROLE             SECAPP        ROLE_SECURITY
1 row selected.
```

Identifying DBV Command Rules from Conditions

To identify which commands in a database are candidates for DBV command rules, ask the following questions:

- What are the most sensitive transactions in the database that could affect the organization's ability to meet compliance (or other) regulations?
- Which accounts are authorized to establish connections to the database, and what commands can those accounts perform?
- Under what conditions can each command be performed with respect to time, place, and methods (factors)?

If the database supports a financial system, sensitive transactions may mean transactions related to sales (revenues) and costs (expenses). If the database supports a human resources system, this may mean transactions involving employee Social Security numbers, salaries, and health benefits.

DBV command rules can be applied to these sensitive transactions to ensure that you have the highest level of assurance that they are executed within the appropriate context. The context refers to the category of factors outlined previously and can help validate whether a transaction was executed from the correct client (machines), software programs (such as PL/SQL code), business rules (such as two-person control), and within the appropriate timeframe(s).

One method for determining the most sensitive transactions is to consider the frequency of each transaction with respect to other transactions in the database. In a typical financial system, we would expect "create or update" sales and costs transactions to be executed much more frequently than a "create product category" transaction. We can generate a detailed transaction frequency report that includes the database user and object being accessed in **SELECT**, **DML**, and **EXECUTE** transactions using the audit trail we've captured. This report not only provides an indicator of the most frequently occurring transactions but can also serve as the initial content for a Subject-Verb-Object-Conditions table we can use to develop a fine-grained security profile. The following query on the captured audit trail demonstrates this type of transaction frequency report:

```
sys@aos> SELECT db_user subject, action_name verb,
    object_schema || '.'|| object_name object, COUNT(*)
FROM aos_common_audit_trail
WHERE object_schema NOT IN
 ( 'SYS','SYSMAN','DVF','DVSYS','LBACSYS','WK_TEST')
AND ( action_name IN (
  'SELECT'
  ,'UPDATE'
  ,'DELETE'
  ,'INSERT'
  ) OR action_name LIKE '%EXECUTE%')
AND object_type NOT LIKE '%PARTITION%'
```

```
GROUP BY db_user , action_name ,
    object_schema || '.'|| object_name
ORDER BY db_user , action_name ,
    object_schema || '.'|| object_name
;

SUBJECT              VERB                 OBJECT                 COUNT(*)
-------------------- -------------------- -------------------- ----------
ALAN_ANALYST         DELETE               SH.COSTS                      1
ANTHONY              EXECUTE PROCEDURE    SH.SALES_TRANSCTION           2
DEB_DATA_MGR         DELETE               SH.COSTS                      1
JRUSSEL              EXECUTE PROCEDURE    SH.SALES_TRANSCTION           4
JRUSSEL              INSERT               SH.COSTS                      1
JRUSSEL              SELECT               SH.CHANNELS                   1
JRUSSEL              SELECT               SH.PRODUCTS                   1
JRUSSEL              SELECT               SH.PROMOTIONS                 1
MARY                 DELETE               SH.COSTS                      1
MARY                 DELETE               SH.SALES                      1
MARY                 EXECUTE PROCEDURE    SH.SALES_TRANSCTION           2
MARY                 UPDATE               SH.CUSTOMERS                  1
OPS$APPSERVER_1      DELETE               SH.SALES                      1
OPS$APPSERVER_1      EXECUTE PROCEDURE    SH.SALES_TRANSCTION          26
PTUCKER              EXECUTE PROCEDURE    SH.SALES_TRANSCTION           4
PTUCKER              INSERT               SH.COSTS                      1
PTUCKER              SELECT               SH.CHANNELS                   1
PTUCKER              SELECT               SH.PRODUCTS                   1
PTUCKER              SELECT               SH.PROMOTIONS                 1

20 rows selected.
```

With this initial Subject-Verb-Object-Conditions table in place, we can identify the most important transactions based on the following:

- The frequency of the transactions
- Interviews with application experts to identify transactions that are either critical to the integrity of the system or corporate assets such as a balance sheet

We can start the analysis to determine the conditions that bound each of these important transactions. We can develop DBV command rules for the types of transactions we uncovered in the query results once this final analysis of business conditions is completed.

Limiting the Availability of Extremely Sensitive Transactions

To add a level of security to sensitive transactions, you can use a database feature called Oracle External Tables (OETs). OETs provide a way to limit the ability to execute sensitive transactions to an externally controlled decision point, similar to the directory-based example we used for the realm authorizations earlier. OETs are read-only database tables that are based on information stored in flat files in the operating system. Using an approach based on OETs allows you to create a file that is owned by an OS account (or OS role) other than the Oracle software owner account (oracle). The account needs only read access to the file. The OS file will contain the information that can be used to authorize or deny sensitive transactions. The OS file owner is the only account that can update the file.

To implement this strategy, we use the root OS account to create a directory for the authorization file (/etc/dbv/external_authorize.conf). We will then configure the database to use the directory in the creation of the OET. In addition, we will create a directory (/var/log/dbv) for the logs generated by the OET.

```
[root@node1 ~]# mkdir -p /etc/dbv
[root@node1 ~]# mkdir -p /var/log/dbv
```

Next we will set the permissions on these directories to allow Oracle to read the files that make up the OET and write to the supporting log file directory:

```
[root@node1 ~]# touch /etc/dbv/external_authorize.conf
[root@node1 ~]# chmod -R 750 /etc/dbv
[root@node1 ~]# chown -R root:dba /etc/dbv
[root@node1 ~]# chmod 750 /var/log/dbv
[root@node1 ~]# chown oracle:dba /var/log/dbv
```

The next step is to create the Oracle directories and an OET that will be based on the file. We can use our operational DBA role to create the directories and the DBVEXT account that contains extended DBV security capabilities for the OET object and supporting code:

```
jean_oper_dba@aos>-- create the directories
jean_oper_dba@aos>CREATE OR REPLACE DIRECTORY dbv_dir
      AS '/etc/dbv';
Directory created.

jean_oper_dba@aos>CREATE OR REPLACE DIRECTORY dbv_dir_log
      AS '/var/log/dbv';
Directory created.

jean_oper_dba@aos>-- grant privileges to the DBVEXT user
jean_oper_dba@aos>-- to use the directories

jean_oper_dba@aos>GRANT READ ON DIRECTORY dbv_dir TO dbvext;
Grant succeeded.
jean_oper_dba@aos>GRANT READ, WRITE ON DIRECTORY dbv_dir_log TO dbvext;
Grant succeeded.

jean_oper_dba@aos>-- create an OET under the DBVEXT object-owner account
jean_oper_dba@aos>CONNECT dbvext
Enter password:
Connected.
dvf@aos> CREATE TABLE external_authorize (
     username    VARCHAR2(30)
   , event       VARCHAR2(30)
   , owner       VARCHAR2(30)
   , object      VARCHAR2(130)
   , status      NUMBER
)
```

```
ORGANIZATION EXTERNAL
(TYPE ORACLE_LOADER
 DEFAULT DIRECTORY dbv_dir_log
 ACCESS PARAMETERS
 (
  RECORDS DELIMITED BY NEWLINE
  BADFILE     'dbv_auth.bad'
  DISCARDFILE 'dbv_auth.dis'
  LOGFILE     'dbv_auth.log'
  FIELDS TERMINATED BY ","  OPTIONALLY ENCLOSED BY '"'
  (
     username    CHAR(30)
   , event       CHAR(30)
   , owner       CHAR(30)
   , object      CHAR(130)
   , status      INTEGER EXTERNAL(6)
  )
 )
 LOCATION (DBV_DIR:'external_authorize.conf')
)
REJECT LIMIT UNLIMITED
/
Table created.
```

The decision concept around the OET is that we can model the Subject-Verb-Object portion of a security profile directly in the OET using the USERNAME/EVENT/OWNER and OBJECT columns and use the STATUS column as an indicator of TRUE(1) or FALSE(0) to allow the command. The conditional aspect of our profile is satisfied by the file owner (root, in this example) controlling when the commands are authorized on any given object. The table is empty at this point, but if we populate the underlying comma-separated-values (CSV) file as the root OS account we will see the data in the table.

```
[root@node1 ~] #echo "MARY,DELETE,SH,%,1" >  /etc/dbv/external_authorize.conf
```

In this example we model the concept that the USERNAME MARY is allowed (STATUS=1) to execute a DELETE (EVENT) on any (OBJECT) whose OWNER is SH. If we attempt to update this file with the Oracle OS account, the OS file's permissions prevent the attempt:

```
[oracle@node1 ~]$ echo "ANTHONY,DELETE,SH,%,1" >  /etc/dbv/external_authorize.conf
-bash: /etc/dbv/external_authorize.conf: Permission denied
```

This is a simple example that makes use of the root and Oracle OS accounts. Note that technologies such as fine-grained OS access control lists, based on IEEE's POSIX 1003 standards, would offer a solution that uses a non-root account as the file owner, but for brevity we simply used the root account.

With this file populated, we can now query the external table as the DBVEXT object-owner account and create a PL/SQL package that can be used in DBV rule sets:

```
dvf@aos>-- query the populated OET
dvf@aos>SELECT * FROM dbvext.external_authorize;
```

```
USERNAME EVENT    OWNER    OBJECT       STATUS
-------- -------- -------- -------- ----------
MARY     DELETE   SH       %                 1
1 row selected

dvf@aos>-- create a helper package for DBV Rule Sets that
dvf@aos>-- can query the OET
dvf@aos> CREATE OR REPLACE PACKAGE external_rule AS
   FUNCTION authorized(
          user_name   IN VARCHAR2
        , event_name  IN VARCHAR2
        , owner_name  IN VARCHAR2 DEFAULT '%'
        , object_name IN VARCHAR2 DEFAULT '%'
        ) RETURN NUMBER;
END;
/
Package created.

dvf@aos>CREATE OR REPLACE PACKAGE BODY external_rule AS
   FUNCTION authorized(
          user_name   IN VARCHAR2
        , event_name  IN VARCHAR2
        , owner_name  IN VARCHAR2
        , object_name IN VARCHAR2
   ) RETURN NUMBER
   IS
    BEGIN
        FOR c_rules IN (
            SELECT username
            FROM external_authorize
            WHERE   UPPER(event) = UPPER(event_name)
                AND UPPER(owner) = UPPER(owner_name)
                AND UPPER(object) = UPPER(object_name)
                AND status = 1
        ) LOOP
            IF UPPER(c_rules.username) = UPPER(user_name) THEN
                RETURN 1;
            END IF;
            -- note that we could event use the package procedure
            -- DBVEXT.DBMS_MAC_EXTENSION.USER_HAS_ROLE here to base
            -- the authorization on role names store in CSV file
        END LOOP;
        RETURN 0;
    EXCEPTION
        WHEN OTHERS THEN
          RAISE_APPLICATION_ERROR(-20001, 'external_rule (error):' ||
            SUBSTR(SQLERRM, 1 , 2000) );
          -- RETURN 0;

    END;
```

```
END;
/
Package body created.
dvf@aos>-- grant EXECUTE privilege on the package to DVSYS as always
dvf@aos>GRANT EXECUTE ON dbvext.external_rule TO dvsys;
Grant succeeded.
```

Finally, we create the DBV rule set and an example DBV command rule that uses our OET-based package function.

```
dvf@aos>CONNECT diego_dbvmgr
Enter password:
Connected.
diego_dbvmgr@aos>-- create the DBV Rule for DELETE on an SH objects
diego_dbvmgr@aos>BEGIN
  dbms_macadm.create_rule(
   rule_name => 'Externally Controlled DELETE for Sales History'
   ,rule_expr =>
    'DBVEXT.EXTERNAL_RULE.AUTHORIZED(DVSYS.DV_LOGIN_USER,'
       || '''DELETE'',''SH'',''%'') = 1'
  );
END;
/
PL/SQL procedure successfully completed.

diego_dbvmgr@aos>-- create the DBV Rule Set and
diego_dbvmgr@aos>-- associate our DBV Rule to it
diego_dbvmgr@aos>BEGIN
  dbms_macadm.create_rule_set(
    rule_set_name =>'Sales History DELETE Controls',
    description =>'Authorizes deletes against the
Sales History tables.',
    enabled =>dbms_macutl.g_yes,
    eval_options =>dbms_macutl.g_ruleset_eval_all,
    audit_options =>dbms_macutl.g_ruleset_audit_fail,
    fail_options =>dbms_macutl.g_ruleset_fail_show,
    fail_message =>NULL,
    fail_code =>NULL,
    handler_options =>dbms_macutl.g_ruleset_handler_off,
    handler =>NULL);
END;
/
PL/SQL procedure successfully completed.

diego_dbvmgr@aos>BEGIN
   dbms_macadm.add_rule_to_rule_set (
     rule_set_name => 'Sales History DELETE Controls'
   , rule_name     => 'Externally Controlled DELETE for Sales History'
   );
END;
/
PL/SQL procedure successfully completed.

diego_dbvmgr@aos>-- create the DBV Command Rule that ties into our OET authorizations
```

```
diego_dbvmgr@aos>BEGIN
  dbms_macadm.create_command_rule (
    command       =>  'DELETE'
    ,rule_set_name => 'Sales History DELETE Controls'
    ,object_owner  => 'SH'
    ,object_name   => '%'
    ,enabled       => 'Y'
);
END;
/
PL/SQL procedure successfully completed.
```

We can test the control using the realm administrator account MARY to verify that the **DELETE** command is allowed. We can also verify that the **DELETE** command is not allowed for an EUS-based realm administrator such as JOE, who was authorized to do this based on the earlier realm authorization example.

```
diego_dbvmgr@aos>CONNECT mary
Enter password:
Connected.
mary@aos>DELETE SH.COSTS WHERE ROWNUM < 2;

1 row deleted.
If we change the status
mary@aos>CONNECT joe
Enter password:
Connected.
global_oid_tree1@aos>DELETE SH.COSTS WHERE ROWNUM < 2;
DELETE SH.COSTS WHERE ROWNUM < 2
          *
ERROR at line 1:
ORA-01031: insufficient privileges
```

We can also disable the ability for MARY to perform the sensitive transaction using the root OS account as follows:

```
[root@node1 ~]# echo "MARY,DELETE,SH,%,0" >  /etc/dbv/external_authorize.conf
```

When MARY attempts the same DELETE statement at this point, her attempt is not authorized based on the updated contents of the file:

```
global_oid_tree1@aos>CONNECT mary
Enter password:
Connected.
mary@aos>DELETE SH.COSTS WHERE ROWNUM < 2;
DELETE SH.COSTS WHERE ROWNUM < 2
          *
ERROR at line 1:
ORA-01031: insufficient privileges
```

This example demonstrates how you can create an externally controlled decision point using DBV command rules for sensitive transactions using basic OS and Oracle features. This type of external control is also useful when coupled with the DBV CONNECT command rule to restrict the ability for privileged accounts to log into the database. Privileged accounts such as LBACSYS or object-owner accounts such as SH that house sensitive data can be restricted from login in the foreground. Make sure you account for any database jobs the account may have by adding a check to the PL/SQL package function **DBVEXT.EXTERNAL_RULE.AUTHORIZED** for the value returned from the function

```
SYS_CONTEXT('USERENV', 'BG_JOB_ID')
```

being NOT NULL to authorize these job sessions.

Identifying DBV Factors Based on Business or System Conditions

The DBV rules we develop based on business rules or system conditions can leverage DBV factors as we had demonstrated in Chapter 6. Some types of factors you will develop can be based on the results of the queries we ran previously on the audit and database configuration. You can attempt to have some questions answered by application experts to help uncover these factors.

Factors Based on Compliance

Compliance-related factors are often simple constants that drive system behavior (either in code or in DBV rules) as demonstrated with the audit retention period example in Chapter 6. In addition to time-based constants that have units such as Number of Days, you may seek input from application experts on event-driven controls that can be controlled with a DBV factor. For example, the concept of a "quiet period" may be useful in application controls and depicts a compliance-sensitive stage or event in the context of the business itself, versus the particular application.

Factors Based on Conflict of Interest or Separation of Duty

As you examine the initial Subject-Verb-Object-Condition results created from the preceding sensitive transactions query, you should be asking application experts if a single role or group of accounts is allowed to perform each type of transaction. In our example for creating product costs through the SH.SALES_TRANSACTIONS package, we defined a rule "Is Sales Department Manager" that is a perfect example of a separation of duty control. Once you've identified the roles or accounts for each transaction, you can create factors to support these rules that enforce separation of duty on the transactions. In the examples of Chapter 6, we created factors such as User_Department_Name and Is_Department_Manager to serve this purpose.

Factors Based on Organizational Policy

To understand which organizational policy affects the security in a database application, you need to interview application experts. The types of questions that you need to ask will be related to data ownership, reporting requirements, and timing of key business events. In the example presented in Chapter 6, we looked at the product category to determine the manager who could control sales costs or read detailed product data. Similar data ownership rules may exist within your organization. The controls that enforce these ownership rules can take many forms, such as VPD policy, OLS policy, WHERE conditions in views, PL/SQL application code, and in application code that is external to the database, such as code found in Java or ASP programs.

Factors Based on Time

Factors that are based on time are useful in situations where you want to control the timeframe (WHEN) in which a sensitive transaction can take place. We can examine both the database audit trail's timestamp and schedule for database batch processing (jobs) to derive time-based factors. The following query demonstrates how the audit trail can be examined for time-based factors that could be developed for a sensitive transaction.

```
sys@aos>SELECT db_user subject, action_name verb,
    object_schema || '.'|| object_name object,
    TO_CHAR ( extended_timestamp, 'DAY HH24:MI') "DAY_TIME",
    COUNT(*)
FROM aos_common_audit_trail
WHERE  action_name = 'DELETE'
AND object_schema = 'SH'
AND object_type NOT LIKE '%PARTITION%'
GROUP BY db_user , action_name ,
    object_schema || '.'|| object_name,
    TO_CHAR ( extended_timestamp, 'DAY HH24:MI')
ORDER BY db_user , action_name ,
    object_schema || '.'|| object_name
;
SUBJECT            VERB       OBJECT     DAY_TIME            COUNT(*)
------------------ ---------- ---------- ----------------- ----------
ALAN_ANALYST       DELETE     SH.COSTS   TUESDAY   10:50            1
DEB_DATA_MGR       DELETE     SH.COSTS   TUESDAY   14:39            1
MARY               DELETE     SH.COSTS   SATURDAY  15:36            1
MARY               DELETE     SH.SALES   SATURDAY  15:33            1
OPS$APPSERVER_1    DELETE     SH.SALES   WEDNESDAY 14:07            1
5 rows selected.
```

The DELETE transactions that occurred on TUESDAY and WEDNESDAY may be out of the normal or expected time frame for this type of transaction. This may point to a need to create a factor and rule for the specific time window in which a DELETE is authorized. This type of control is similar to the one we demonstrated with the SYSTEM.AUD$ table in Chapter 6.

We can also identify additional areas for time-based factors by looking at the intervals in which database jobs are executing. The PL/SQL programs that are executing are typically associated with the business events that an application supports, such as the close of a month's financial process. The following query will help you identify the time frame the job intervals in which these types of PL/SQL programs are run:

```
sys@aos>SET SERVEROUTPUT ON
sys@aos>BEGIN
    FOR c_jobs IN (
    SELECT
        cowner owner
        , 'Job #:' || TO_CHAR(job)  job_name
        , interval# repeat_interval
        , what program
```

```
    FROM job$
    UNION
    SELECT
        j.owner
        , job_name
        , decode(j.repeat_interval, NULL,
          decode(s.repeat_interval, NULL,
              w.window_group_name, s.repeat_interval)
                  ,j.repeat_interval) "repeat_interval"
        , decode(j.program_name,NULL
          ,j.job_action,p.owner || '.' || p.program_action) "program"
        FROM dba_scheduler_jobs j
        , dba_scheduler_programs p
        , dba_scheduler_schedules s
        , dba_scheduler_window_groups w
        WHERE
            j.program_owner = p.owner (+)
            AND j.program_name = p.program_name (+)
            AND j.schedule_owner = s.owner (+)
            AND j.schedule_name = s.schedule_name (+)
            AND j.schedule_owner = s.owner (+)
            AND j.schedule_name = w.window_group_name (+)
    ORDER BY 1
        ) LOOP
        DBMS_OUTPUT.PUT_LINE('----------------------');
        DBMS_OUTPUT.PUT_LINE('Job: ' || c_jobs.owner
                  || '.' || c_jobs.job_name );
        DBMS_OUTPUT.PUT_LINE('Interval: ' || c_jobs.repeat_interval );
        DBMS_OUTPUT.PUT_LINE('Program: ' || c_jobs.program );

    END LOOP;
END;
/
----------------------
Job: EXFSYS.RLM$EVTCLEANUP
Interval: FREQ = HOURLY; INTERVAL = 1
Program: begin dbms_rlmgr_dr.cleanup_events; end;
----------------------
Job: EXFSYS.RLM$SCHDNEGACTION
Program: FREQ=MINUTELY;INTERVAL=60
What: begin dbms_rlmgr_dr.execschdactions('RLM$SCHDNEGACTION'); end;
----------------------
Job: FLOWS_030000.Job #:4001
Interval: sysdate + 8/24
Program: wwv_flow_cache.purge_sessions(p_purge_sess_older_then_hrs => 24);
----------------------
Job: FLOWS_030000.Job #:4002
Interval: sysdate + 10/1440
Program: wwv_flow_mail.push_queue(wwv_flow_platform.get_preference('SMTP_HOST_
ADDRESS'),wwv_flow_platform.get_preference('SMTP_HOST_PORT'));
```

```
----------------------
Job: ORACLE_OCM.MGMT_CONFIG_JOB
Interval: MAINTENANCE_WINDOW_GROUP
Program: ORACLE_OCM.MGMT_CONFIG.collect_config

<output truncated for brevity>
```

Factors Based on Identity Management

You can verify whether a database is using Oracle EUS for authentication by issuing the following query:

```
sys@aos>SHOW PARAMETER ldap

      NAME                                 TYPE        VALUE
      ------------------------------------ ----------- --------
      ldap_directory_access                string      PASSWORD
      ldap_directory_sysauth               string      no
```

In this example output, the database is configured to use EUS. If the **LDAP_DIRECTORY_ACCESS** parameter were set to **SSL**, the database would also be configured to use EUS. If the **LDAP_DIRECTORY_ACCESS** parameter were set to **NONE**, the database is not configured to use EUS.

The more difficult question to answer is how a database application is using identity management attributes available in the SYS_LDAP_USER_DEFAULT context namespace that EUS maintains. The difficulty is because SYS_CONTEXT usage is not tracked in the DBA_DEPENDENCIES view and there is no tracking of the namespace usage in an Oracle dictionary view. You can make an educated guess that the application makes use of the techniques outline in Oracle Metalink note 242156.1 "An Example of Using Application Context's Initialized Globally" by querying the DBA_CONTEXT view, as shown next:

```
sys@aos>SELECT namespace
FROM dba_context
WHERE TYPE = 'INITIALIZED GLOBALLY';

NAMESPACE
------------------------------
DBV_POLICY_EXAMPLE

1 row selected.
```

If any namespaces are returned and EUS is configured, there is a good chance that identity management information from EUS is being used within the databases.

Finally, you can attempt to examine PL/SQL source code for usage of the default or custom namespaces to determine where identity management information for EUS is being used. The following query shows how to examine this PL/SQL source code but will work only on source code that has not been wrapped:

```
sys@aos>SELECT DISTINCT owner, name, type
FROM all_source
WHERE
   INSTR (UPPER(text),'SYS_LDAP_USER_DEFAULT') > 0
```

```
OR INSTR (UPPER(text),'<custom namespace from above>') > 0
;

OWNER   NAME      TYPE
------- --------- ------------
SYS     TESTEUS   PROCEDURE

1 row selected.
```

Factors Based on Access Path to the Database

We can determine the network access path used for a given type of transaction by including the USERHOST column in a query against the captured audit trail. The following query shows the access path taken for DELETE transactions on the tables owned by the SH object-owner account. The results of this type of query can help you determine to which database client IP address you'd want to restrict certain sensitive transactions. Convert the hostnames to the appropriate IP address values and use a DBV factor such as Client_IP in your DBV rules.

```
sys@aos>SELECT db_user subject, action_name verb,
    object_schema || '.'|| object_name object, userhost, COUNT(*)
FROM aos_common_audit_trail
WHERE object_schema = 'SH'
AND action_name = 'DELETE'
AND object_type NOT LIKE '%PARTITION%'
GROUP BY db_user , action_name ,
    object_schema || '.'|| object_name,
    userhost
ORDER BY db_user , action_name ,
    object_schema || '.'|| object_name,
    userhost
;
SUBJECT           VERB     OBJECT    USERHOST                  COUNT(*)
----------------- -------- --------- ------------------------ --------
ALAN_ANALYST      DELETE   SH.COSTS  node1.mycompany.com             1
DEB_DATA_MGR      DELETE   SH.COSTS  node1.mycompany.com             1
MARY              DELETE   SH.COSTS  node1.mycompany.com             1
MARY              DELETE   SH.SALES  node1.mycompany.com             1
OPS$APPSERVER_1   DELETE   SH.SALES  appserver1.mycompany.com        1
5 rows selected.
```

Many database environments use the invited nodes feature of Oracle networking to control which IP addresses can connect to the database. If this feature is enabled for your database listener, you will see the following entries in the file $ORACLE_HOME/network/admin/sqlnet.ora:

```
TCP.VALIDNODE_CHECKING=YES
TCP.INVITED_NODES=(192.168.0.251, 192.168.0.252, 192.168.0.200)
```

This list can supplement the queries performed on the captured audit trail as it is a definitive list of the IP addresses for database clients that can actually connect to the database remotely. With this list in hand, you can discuss the requirements for each IP address from the perspective of the database applications that are used and which transactions should be allowed.

Factors Based on Operational Context

The sensitive transactions query results also include several records for EXECUTE transactions on the SH.SALES_TRANSACTION PL/SQL package. We expected this result based on the examples we've created in the past two chapters. As you examine the query results for your own applications, you should ask the application experts whether the PL/SQL programs are the only interfaces (paths) for other more fundament commands such as **INSERT**, **UPDATE**, and **DELETE**. If you find that certain PL/SQL programs fit this classification, you can create command rules for the **INSERT**, **UPDATE**, and **DELETE** commands that enforce the use of the PL/SQL program similar to the examples we created that depend on the DBMS_UTILITY package being part of the PL/SQL call stack.

Factors Based on Transactional Sequence

Another form of operational context that you can mine from your audit trail is related to the sequence of statements that are issued to the database as part of a transaction. If we consider the notional use case presented in Chapter 6 named Add Monthly Product Cost, portions of the audit trail records may look similar to the following:

```
sys@aos>SELECT transactionid
,action_name
,object_schema
,object_name
FROM aos_common_audit_trail
WHERE object_schema = 'SH'
AND action_name IN (
'SELECT'
,'INSERT'
,'UPDATE'
,'DELETE'
)
AND object_type = 'TABLE'
AND extended_timestamp > sysdate - 1
ORDER BY extended_timestamp, transactionid;
TRANSACTIONID    ACTION_NAME   OBJECT_SCHEMA OBJECT_NAME
---------------- ------------- ------------- ---------------
                 SELECT        SH            PRODUCTS
                 SELECT        SH            CHANNELS
                 SELECT        SH            PROMOTIONS
040015004E960000 INSERT        SH            COSTS
040015004E960000 UPDATE        SH            MONTHLY_COST_SUMMARY
                 SELECT        SH            PRODUCTS
                 SELECT        SH            CHANNELS
                 SELECT        SH            PROMOTIONS
0A0014001F950000 INSERT        SH            COSTS
0A0014001F950000 UPDATE        SH            MONTHLY_COST_SUMMARY
                 SELECT        SH            PRODUCTS
                 SELECT        SH            CHANNELS
                 SELECT        SH            PROMOTIONS
03000800FE940000 INSERT        SH            COSTS
03000800FE940000 UPDATE        SH            MONTHLY_COST_SUMMARY

15 rows selected.
```

This audit trail records reveal a pattern that involves three SELECT statements, followed by an INSERT statement, and then an UPDATE statement on tables related to product costs. We can assert that this sequence of statements constitute the normal context of the transaction. You can then develop DBV factors that query the audit trail for the records to validate the correct sequence of statements. It is possible that data other than the audit trail records exists, which you can use to perform this validation. You can use these factors in your DBV rules to prevent direct INSERT or UPDATE statements on the cost-related table unless the proper transactional sequence can be verified. This approach is similar to the types of controls you might find in an intrusion detection system (IDS) that performs pattern matching and anomaly detection.

Factors Based on Data or Events Stored Externally

The use of identity management information, when coupled with Oracle EUS, is one form of a DBV factor that is based on information stored externally. Many Oracle database environments reach out to other systems on the same network to retrieve information for one purpose or another. There is no reason you cannot use these external systems for event information that would be useful to your DBV security policy. This information could be as simple as supplemental data about the current user that is not stored in an identity management infrastructure but is stored in a human resources system. An advanced usage could even query a physical access system used by the company to determine whether the user swiped his or her access badge to get into the building at some point in the business day. We can use several queries to determine whether a database relies on external system for information. First, we can check for the dependency on the following types of PL/SQL routines by custom database application code:

- Oracle file-based APIs (UTL_FILE)
- Oracle network-based APIs (UTL_TCP, UTL_HTTP, DBMS_LDAP)
- Oracle Heterogeneous Services APIs (DBMS_HS_PASSTHROUGH)

We can perform this type of dependency check with the following query, and we see that an application such as HTML DB (APEX) 3.0 has dependencies on these external access APIs:

```
sys@aos>SELECT owner,name,type,referenced_name
FROM dba_dependencies
WHERE referenced_name
    IN ('UTL_FILE', 'UTL_TCP', 'UTL_HTTP',
            'DBMS_LDAP', 'DBMS_HS_PASSTHROUGH')
AND owner NOT IN (
    'SYS'
    ,'PUBLIC'
    ,'OLAPSYS'
    ,'ORDSYS'
    ,'ORDPLUGINS'
    ,'ORACLE_OCM'
    ,'MDSYS'
    ,'SYSMAN'
    ,'XDB'
    ,'WMSYS'
    ,'WKSYS'
)
ORDER BY owner,name,type;
```

```
OWNER        NAME                      TYPE         REFERENCED_NAME
------------ ------------------------- ------------ ---------------
FLOWS_030000 UTL_FILE                  SYNONYM       UTL_FILE
FLOWS_030000 WWV_FLOW_CUSTOM_AUTH_LDAP PACKAGE BODY  DBMS_LDAP
FLOWS_030000 WWV_FLOW_WEB_SERVICES     PACKAGE BODY  UTL_HTTP

3 rows selected.
```

We can also query the Oracle fine-grained access privileges for network services to determine which accounts may have been granted connection privileges to external hosts:

```
sys@aos> SELECT p.principal, p.privilege, h.host, h.lower_port, h.upper_port
FROM dba_network_acl_privileges p,dba_network_acls h
WHERE p.aclid = h.aclid AND p.principal != 'DVSYS'
ORDER BY 1,2;

PRINCIPAL    PRIVILEGE HOST                      LOWER_PORT UPPER_PORT
------------ --------- ------------------------- ---------- ----------
FLOWS_030000 connect   *
SH           connect   hr-system.mycompany.com     8080       8085
SH           connect   badge-system.mycompany.com  2100       2150
SH           resolve   hr-system.mycompany.com     8080       8085
SH           resolve   badge-system.mycompany.com  2100       2150
5 rows selected.
```

Some database applications may use Java stored procedures in the database and the Java socket APIs (versus PL/SQL network APIs) to connect to external systems. We can investigate this case by querying the accounts that may have socket "connect" permissions in the DBA_JAVA_POLICY view as follows:

```
sys@aos>SELECT grantee, action privilege, name host
FROM dba_java_policy
WHERE type_name = 'java.net.SocketPermission'
AND action LIKE '%connect%';

GRANTEE PRIVILEGE         HOST
------- ----------------- -------------------------
SH      connect, resolve  badge-system.mycompany.com
SH      connect, resolve  hr-system.mycompany.com
2 rows selected.
```

In this example, we've created a notional pair of hosts that run the physical access badging system and human resources system to illustrate the point. In a real-world scenario, we could investigate the purpose of these external systems being accessed to determine how those systems might be used to contribute information that can become DBV factors.

Factors Based on Existing PL/SQL Code

As you have seen so far, many opportunities and areas can be researched to uncover attributes that can be used as DBV factors. The process involves the use of queries on database audit trails and configurations as we have shown. For several areas, we may find only that name of a PL/SQL program and the next step is simply to employ a code inspection to determine what exists within the code that we can use as a DBV factor. For example, we used a query on the JOB$ table and

DBA_SCHEDULER views to determine whether any time-based factors existed in the system. This query also provided us insight into the PL/SQL programs that were run. The next step in investigating these jobs would be to research the details of those programs to determine whether security-relevant data attributes or conditions exist that could be used as DBV factors and DBV rules, respectively. Many similar components in the database might be required for detailed research on PL/SQL code as a means to reach the same end result.

The following table provides a short list of database features and the queries that can be used to uncover those PL/SQL program names.

Database Feature or Option	Query
Standard Oracle views and the use of security-relevant conditions in the WHERE clause	SELECT owner , view_name , text FROM dba_views WHERE owner = '<sensitive data object-owner>';
Standard Oracle PL/SQL functions, procedure, or package body	If code is unwrapped in the database: SELECT name, type, text FROM dba_source WHERE owner = '<sensitive data object-owner>' ORDER BY name, type, line;
Oracle VPD's policy function	SELECT object_owner, object_name, pf_owner, package , function FROM dba_policies WHERE pf_owner != 'XDB' ORDER BY 1,2 ;
Oracle OLS and its policy labeling function or SQL predicate clause	SELECT policy_name, schema_name, table_name, function, predicate FROM dba_sa_table_policies WHERE function IS NOT NULL OR predicate IS NOT NULL ORDER BY 1,2,3;
Standard Oracle rules engine	SELECT rule_owner, rule_name, rule_condition FROM dba_rules WHERE rule_owner != 'DVSYS' ORDER BY 1,2;

Refining the DBV Policy Design

Once you've run the queries on the database audit trail, you should capture the results and categorize them using the section headers provided in this chapter. This process yields a draft specification of the DBV policy you want to review with the team of experts and stakeholders with which you are working. Once this policy specification has been reviewed and validated, you can begin writing your PL/SQL scripts with the appropriate DBMS_MACADM procedure calls to implement the policy.

Deploying and Validating the DBV Policy

After you've fleshed out the detailed DBV policy, you can deploy the policy to your existing development environment for unit testing. The next step is to migrate the policy to a formal test environment to perform complete system and load testing. You can use the Oracle Real Application Testing replay feature and the workloads you've captured without DBV enabled on your development and test environments. This will help ensure that the policy does not adversely affect the existing applications under real workload scenarios. Once the change has been officially validated, you will be ready to deploy the DBV policy to your existing production systems.

The most recent version of the Oracle Enterprise Manager Grid Control (OEM GC) product, 10.2.0.5, includes provisioning capabilities for DBV policy to make this deployment process much easier on you. For any DBV-enabled database you've defined in OEM GC, you can select all or parts of the DBV policy and propagate them to the selected databases, as shown in Figure 7-5.

Once you selected the DBV policy components you want to propagate, you can choose the destination database(s) that you want to propagate and the propagate options that control the provisioning of this policy. The OEM GC interface is shown in Figure 7-6.

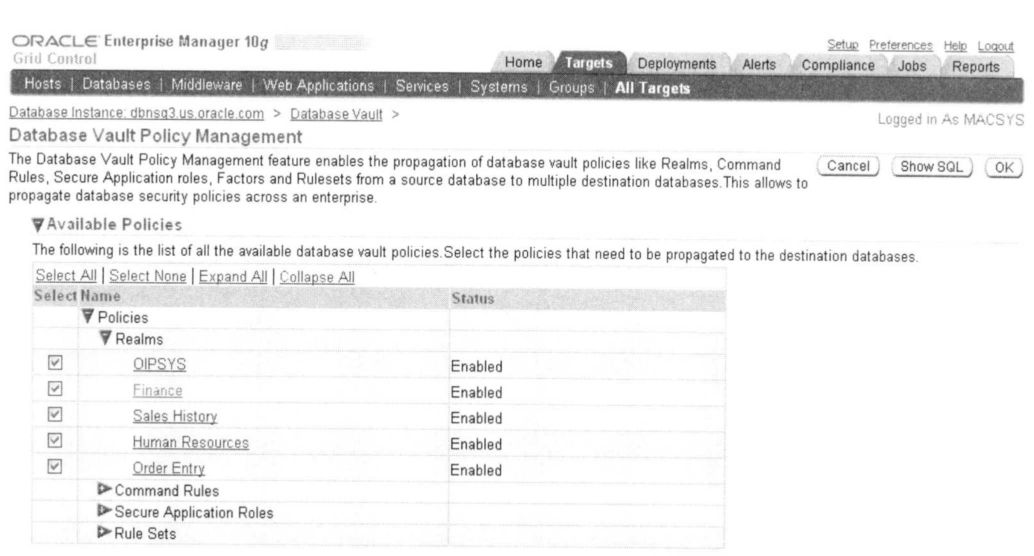

FIGURE 7-5 *Selecting DBV policy components to propagate in OEM GC*

Destination Databases

Select the databases to which these policies need to be applied. Database vault administrator credentials are required for each of the destination databases to successfully propagate the policies.

The table below shows the list of database targets to which these database policies will be applied.

(Add) (Remove)

Select	Database Name	Database Type	Database Vault Administrator User Name	Database Vault Administrator Password
	Add destination databases.			

Propagate Options

☑ Restore on failure.
If policy propagation encounters errors, the original database vault policies on the destination are restored.

☑ Skip propagation if user defined policies exist.
If there are already existing user defined policies, policy propagation would not be attempted.

☑ Propagate Enterprise Manager metric thresholds for database vault metrics.
Database vault related metric thresholds, configured on this database will be propagated to destination databases.

Related Links

Metric and Policy Settings

(Cancel) (Show SQL) (OK)

Home | Targets | Deployments | Alerts | Compliance | Jobs | Reports | Setup | Preferences | Help | Logout

About Oracle Enterprise Manager

FIGURE 7-6 *Selecting destination database and propagation options in OEM GC*

The combination of Oracle Real Application Testing and OEM GC enables full lifecycle deployment and testing for your enterprise, as shown in Figure 7-7.

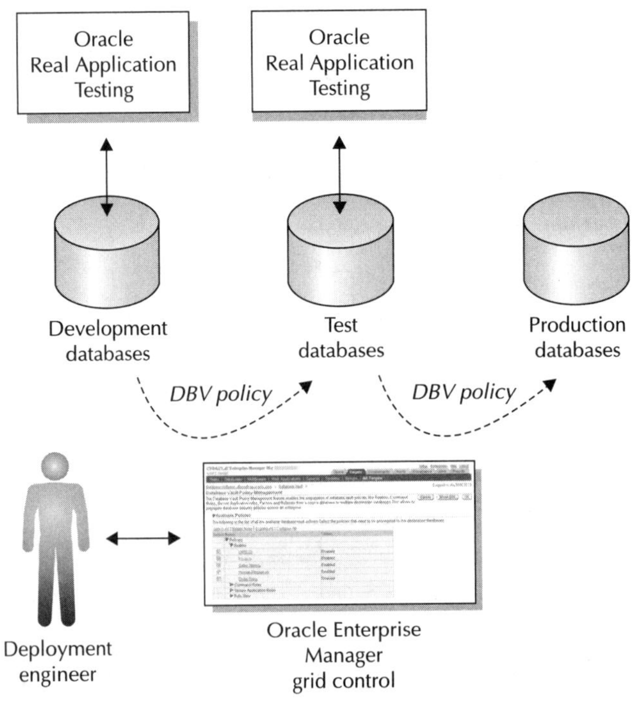

FIGURE 7-7 *DBV policy deployment and testing lifecycle*

This capability not only provides a higher level of assurance that your deployments from development to test and from test to production are successful, but it reduces both deployment risk and deployment time. Refer to Metalink note 760748.1 for more information on how to integrate DBV with OEM GC.

Integrating DBV with Oracle Database Features

We've already presented examples of DBV integration with various security features of the database such as OLS, VPD, and Oracle FGA. The Oracle DBV product leverages the Oracle Data Dictionary realm to protect the object-owner schemas for many of the data processing features, such Oracle Text or Oracle Spatial. We need to account for this realm protection and any application-specific realms you create to ensure the successful use of these features in your applications. DBV components can be integrated with the existing Oracle Database features to add value to the features.

To help illustrate the tricks and techniques presented in this section, in this example, a notional object-owner account for an application is named APP_OBJECT_OWNER. In this object-owner account is a CUSTOMERS table with the following structure:

```
app_object_owner@aos> DESCRIBE customers
 Name                  Null?    Type
 ------------------ -------- ----------------------------
 ID                    NOT NULL NUMBER
 FIRST_NAME            NOT NULL VARCHAR2(20)
 LAST_NAME             NOT NULL VARCHAR2(40)
 GENDER                NOT NULL CHAR(1)
 YEAR_OF_BIRTH         NOT NULL NUMBER(4)
 MARITAL_STATUS                 VARCHAR2(20)
 STREET_ADDRESS        NOT NULL VARCHAR2(40)
 POSTAL_CODE           NOT NULL VARCHAR2(10)
 CITY                  NOT NULL VARCHAR2(30)
 STATE_PROVINCE        NOT NULL VARCHAR2(40)
 MAIN_PHONE_NUMBER     NOT NULL VARCHAR2(25)
 INCOME_LEVEL                   VARCHAR2(30)
 CREDIT_LIMIT                   NUMBER
 EMAIL                          VARCHAR2(30)
 TOTAL                 NOT NULL VARCHAR2(14)
 EFF_FROM                       DATE
 EFF_TO                         DATE
 VALID                          VARCHAR2(1)
 GEO_LOCATION                   MDSYS.SDO_GEOMETRY
 SEARCH_TERMS                   CLOB
```

Oracle Text

Oracle Text is a database feature that uses standard Oracle SQL to store, index, search, and analyze text and documents stored in the Oracle database, in files, and on the Web. Oracle Text can perform linguistic analysis on documents and can search text using a variety of strategies including keyword searching, context queries, pattern matching, thematic queries, and so on. A simple keyword search using Oracle Text against the CUSTOMERS table requires the use of the CONTAINS operator in a traditional SQL WHERE clause. The CONTAINS operator can be combined with normal SQL WHERE clause predicates as shown in the following example:

```
SELECT SCORE(1), first_name, last_name, street_address
FROM app_object_owner.customers
WHERE state_province = 'TX'
  AND CONTAINS(search_terms, 'hospital', 1) > 0
;
```

To provide enterprise-level performance with the CONTAINS operator and the other operators provided with the Oracle Text feature, we can use function-based indexes on the column that is being searched. If we attempt to create (or maintain) an Oracle Text index once DBV is installed, the following error will occur:

```
app_object_owner@aos>CREATE INDEX
app_object_owner.customers_keyword_index
  ON app_object_owner.customers(search_terms)
  INDEXTYPE IS CTXSYS.CONTEXT
  PARAMETERS ('SYNC (ON COMMIT)');
 CREATE INDEX app_object_owner.customers_keyword_index
*
ERROR at line 1:
ORA-29855: error occurred in the execution of ODCIINDEXCREATE routine
ORA-01031: insufficient privileges
ORA-06512: at "CTXSYS.TEXTINDEXMETHODS", line 75
```

This error occurs because the Oracle Data Dictionary realm protects the CTXSYS objects. We can fix this problem by authorizing the APP_OBJECT_OWNER account in the Oracle Data Dictionary realm as a participant. We create an application-specific realm at the same time.

```
app_object_owner@aos>CONNECT diego_dbvmgr
Enter password:
Connected.
diego_dbvmgr@aos>-- authorize the application's object-owner account
diego_dbvmgr@aos>-- in the Oracle Data Dictionary
realm diego_dbvmgr@aos>BEGIN
  dbms_macadm.add_auth_to_realm (
      realm_name    => 'Oracle Data Dictionary'
    , grantee       => 'APP_OBJECT_OWNER'
    , rule_set_name => NULL
    , auth_options  => dbms_macutl.g_realm_auth_participant);
END;
/
PL/SQL procedure successfully completed.
diego_dbvmgr@aos>-- create the realm protections for the
diego_dbvmgr@aos>-- application's object-owner account
diego_dbvmgr@aos>BEGIN
   dbms_macadm.create_realm(
      realm_name    => 'Sample DBV Application'
    , description   => 'Sample to demonstrate feature integration with DBV'
    , enabled       =>  dbms_macutl.g_yes
```

```
    , audit_options =>  dbms_macutl.g_realm_audit_fail
    );
END;
/
PL/SQL procedure successfully completed.

diego_dbvmgr@aos>BEGIN
    dbms_macadm.add_object_to_realm (
      realm_name    => 'Sample DBV Application'
     ,object_owner  => 'APP_OBJECT_OWNER'
     ,object_name   => '%'
     ,object_type   => '%'
     );
END;
/
PL/SQL procedure successfully completed.

diego_dbvmgr@aos>BEGIN
  dbms_macadm.add_auth_to_realm (
      realm_name    => 'Sample DBV Application'
    , grantee       => 'APP_OBJECT_OWNER'
    , rule_set_name => NULL
    , auth_options  => dbms_macutl.g_realm_auth_owner);
END;
/
PL/SQL procedure successfully completed.
```

Authorizing APP_OBJECT_OWNER as a participant in this realm is not a security concern because this account does not have system ANY privileges for SELECT, DML, or DDL that would allow the account to read, write, or modify objects protected by this realm, such as CTXSYS. The account simply has system privileges that enable structural administration for objects that will be owned by the APP_OBJECT_OWNER account.

```
diego_dbvmgr@aos>CONNECT app_object_owner
Enter password:
Connected.
app_object_owner@aos>SELECT * FROM session_privs ORDER BY 1;
PRIVILEGE
----------------------------------------
CREATE CLUSTER
CREATE INDEXTYPE
CREATE OPERATOR
CREATE PROCEDURE
CREATE SEQUENCE
CREATE SESSION
CREATE TABLE
CREATE TRIGGER
CREATE TYPE
9 rows selected.
```

With the realm authorization in place, the object-owner account can now create and maintain the index and query the CUSTOMERS table using Oracle Text CONTAINS clause as follows:

```
app_object_owner@aos>-- remove the invalid index created previously
app_object_owner@aos>DROP INDEX
      app_object_owner.customers_keyword_index;

Index dropped.
app_object_owner@aos>-- create the new valid index
app_object_owner@aos>CREATE INDEX app_object_owner.customers_keyword_index
  ON app_object_owner.customers(search_terms)
  INDEXTYPE IS CTXSYS.CONTEXT
  PARAMETERS ('SYNC (ON COMMIT)');

Index created.

app_object_owner@aos>-- perform the keyword query
app_object_owner@aos>SELECT SCORE(1)
, first_name
, last_name
, street_address
FROM app_object_owner.customers
WHERE state_province = 'TX'
  AND CONTAINS(search_terms, 'hospital', 1) > 0
;
  SCORE(1) FIRST_NAME   LAST_NAME    STREET_ADDRESS
---------- ------------ ------------ ------------------------
        12 Blaine       Fernandez    17 South Hospital Court
        12 Emery        Ryan         37 North Hospital Street
        12 Ian          Tansey       17 South Hospital Court
        12 Chloe        Bishop       37 North Hospital Street
4 rows selected.
```

As you can see, the authorization of the APP_OBJECT_OWNER in the Oracle Data Dictionary realm enables the successful creation of CTXSYS.CONTEXT index types. This approach is also required to enable the creation of CTXSYS.CTXCAT and CTXSYS.CTXRULE index types.

TIP
Enable object-owner accounts in the Oracle Data Dictionary realm when using function-based indexes. Make sure your object-owner accounts are not granted system ANY privileges that would cause a privilege escalation concern.

Oracle Spatial

Oracle Spatial is a database feature in the Oracle Enterprise Edition that provides advanced spatial features to support high-end geographic information system (GIS) and location-based services (LBS). The option can store complex vector-based geographic data such as points, lines, polygons, and even advanced geospatial data types such as raster (bitmap) formats for digital images. Like Oracle Text, Oracle Spatial offers a rich set of Oracle operators to query geographic data to discover spatial relationships, and these operators perform best when used with a special function-based index called a spatial index. In addition to geographic data points, the Oracle Spatial option includes support for the Resource Description Framework (RDF) data standard for storing metadata about relationships between people, places, and objects, known as triples.

Spatial indexes and RDF indexes rely on the extensible indexing capability of the database in the same way Oracle Text indexes do, so attempting to create spatial indexes with DBV installed results in the same type of error we encountered with Oracle Text:

```
app_object_owner@aos>-- attempting to create a spatial index will fail
app_object_owner@aos>-- with the default locked-down DBV policy
app_object_owner@aos> CREATE INDEX app_object_owner.customers_geo_index
   ON app_object_owner.customers (geo_location)
   INDEXTYPE IS MDSYS.SPATIAL_INDEX;
CREATE INDEX app_object_owner.customers_geo_index
*
ERROR at line 1:
ORA-29855: error occurred in the execution of ODCIINDEXCREATE routine
ORA-01031: insufficient privileges
ORA-06512: at "MDSYS.SDO_INDEX_METHOD_10I", line 10
```

To enable index creation with the MDSYS.SPATIAL_INDEX index type, add the application's object-owner account (APP_OBJECT_OWNER) as a participant of the Oracle Data Dictionary realm. This index type supports both vector-based and raster-based geographic formats. This approach is also required for indexes that are created with the MDSYS.SEM_INDEXTYPE index type in support of Oracle RDF capability.

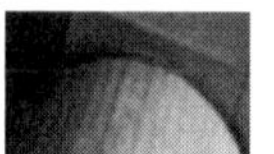

TIP

You will need to drop function-based indexes before issuing a DROP TABLE on a table protected by a realm. The underlying database kernel will issue DROP INDEX statements that will result in realm violations if you do not first remove the indexes.

One interesting integration approach for DBV and Oracle Spatial is centered around the Spatial operator SDO_RELATE and its **mask**, **min_resolution**, and **max_resolution** parameters. These parameters control how many results are returned when used with the operator in a SQL WHERE clause. They can be used as a security control, much like row-level security. We could define a set of DBV factors that assert the values of these parameters for any given session. The actual values of the control factors could be based on other factors such as the Connection_Type example presented in Chapter 5. Using this approach, you might reduce the resolution of imagery or types of geographic intersection matches that are supported when a session has a connection type with less trust (such as OTHER) compared to a session whose connection type has a greater level of trust (such as CORPORATE_SSL).

Expression Filters

An Expression Filter is a feature of the Oracle database that allows you to store rule expressions in a table so that you can compare those expressions against information stored in typical data table. The intent is to compare the rule expressions to the data table so that application code can dynamically respond to matches on those rules without having to hard-code these rules in an application. This might allow a corporation to compare incoming data on solicited customer proposals with rules stored for the sales managers who have the best expertise to respond to the proposal.

Expression Filters use an Oracle operator EVALUATE in a SQL WHERE clause and again rely on function-based indexes for performance. Expression rules use a collection of distinct data attributes (called attribute sets) and Oracle object types. The PL/SQL APIs for creating these attribute sets and mapping them to the tables where the rule expressions will be stored requires two steps: First you must disable the Oracle Data Dictionary realm, and then you must disable the application realm (Sample DBV Application):

```
diego_dbvmgr@aos>-- disable the Data Dictionary realm
diego_dbvmgr@aos>BEGIN
   dbms_macadm.update_realm(
      realm_name    => 'Oracle Data Dictionary'
    , description   =>
            'Defines the realm for the Oracle Catalog'
            || ' schemas, SYS, SYSTEM, SYSMAN,MDSYS, etc.'
            || ' Also controls the ability to grant system'
            || ' privileges and database administrator roles.'
    , enabled       =>  dbms_macutl.g_no
    , audit_options =>  dbms_macutl.g_realm_audit_fail
    );
END;
/
PL/SQL procedure successfully completed.

diego_dbvmgr@aos>-- disable the application realm
diego_dbvmgr@aos>BEGIN
   dbms_macadm.update_realm(
      realm_name    => 'Sample DBV Application'
    , description   => 'Sample to demonstrate feature integration with DBV'
    , enabled       =>  dbms_macutl.g_no
    , audit_options =>  dbms_macutl.g_realm_audit_fail
    );
END;
/
PL/SQL procedure successfully completed.
```

Now we can create our Expression Filter objects for the solicited proposal example:

```
app_object_owner@aos>-- create an Oracle object type of rule attributes
app_object_owner@aos>CREATE OR REPLACE TYPE proposal_type
AS OBJECT (
    industry     VARCHAR2(30)
  , service      VARCHAR2(30)
  , price_limit  NUMBER
);
/
Type created.

app_object_owner@aos>-- create the Expression Filter attribute set
app_object_owner@aos>-- based on the object type
app_object_owner@aos>BEGIN
```

```
  dbms_expfil.create_attribute_set(
      attr_set  => 'proposal_type'
    , from_type => 'YES');
END;
/
PL/SQL procedure successfully completed.

app_object_owner@aos>-- create a table of sales managers
app_object_owner@aos>-- and the rules expression column for
app_object_owner@aos>-- their proposal skills
app_object_owner@aos>CREATE TABLE sales_managers (
      id              NUMBER NOT NULL PRIMARY KEY
    , name            VARCHAR2(30)
    , proposal_skills VARCHAR2(4000)
);
Table created.

app_object_owner@aos>-- map the attribute set to the table
app_object_owner@aos>BEGIN
  dbms_expfil.assign_attribute_set (
                                    attr_set => 'proposal_type',
                                    expr_tab => 'sales_managers',
                                    expr_col => 'proposal_skills');
END;
/
PL/SQL procedure successfully completed.
```

Once the Expression Filter objects are in place, we can re-enable the Oracle Data Dictionary realm and then disable the application realm (Sample DBV Application):

```
diego_dbvmgr@aos>-- disable the Data Dictionary realm
diego_dbvmgr@aos>BEGIN
   dbms_macadm.update_realm(
      realm_name    => 'Oracle Data Dictionary'
    , description   =>
            'Defines the realm for the Oracle Catalog'
            || ' schemas, SYS, SYSTEM, SYSMAN,MDSYS, etc.'
            || ' Also controls the ability to grant system'
            || ' privileges and database administrator roles.'
    , enabled       =>  dbms_macutl.g_yes
    , audit_options =>  dbms_macutl.g_realm_audit_fail
    );
END;
/
PL/SQL procedure successfully completed.

diego_dbvmgr@aos>-- disable the application realm
diego_dbvmgr@aos>BEGIN
   dbms_macadm.update_realm(
      realm_name    => 'Sample DBV Application'
    , description   => 'Sample to demonstrate feature integration with DBV'
    , enabled       =>  dbms_macutl.g_yes
```

```
    , audit_options =>  dbms_macutl.g_realm_audit_fail
    );
END;
/
PL/SQL procedure successfully completed.
```

With the Expression Filters configured and our realm protections back in place, we can populate our rule expressions and use the filters in SQL statements with the **EVALUATE** operator:

```
app_object_owner@aos>-- create a few sales managers
app_object_owner@aos>-- with their proposal skills rules
app_object_owner@aos>INSERT INTO sales_managers VALUES (1, 'Mark',
'industry IN (''Oil'',''Mining'') AND price_limit >= 500000');
1 row created.

app_object_owner@aos>INSERT INTO sales_managers VALUES (2, 'Sandy',
'industry IN (''Retail'',''Food'') AND price_limit >= 500000');
1 row created.

app_object_owner@aos>INSERT INTO sales_managers VALUES (3, 'Roger',
'industry IN (''Retail'',''Food'') AND price_limit < 500000');
1 row created.

COMMIT;
Commit complete.

app_object_owner@aos>-- test the EVALUATE operator
app_object_owner@aos>SELECT id, name
FROM sales_managers
WHERE EVALUATE ( sales_managers.proposal_skills,
   AnyData.convertObject(
        proposal_type('Retail','Marketing',100000)
        )) = 1;

        ID NAME
---------- ------------------------------
         3 Roger

1 row selected.
```

You can also embed DBV factor functions within the PL/SQL functions you create as user-defined functions that are supported in the Expression Filters technology. In the same way that the stored rule expressions for Expression Filters avoid the need to recode applications for new business rules, DBV factors embedded in the user-defined functions feature allow you to integrate security into Expression Filters logic without rewriting code.

Oracle Streams Advanced Queuing

Oracle Streams Advanced Queuing is a database feature that provides message queuing functionality that is integrated directly into the database. Message queuing involves one producer that enqueues (writes) a message into a queue and a consumer(s) that dequeues (reads) the message. This paradigm is typically used to integrate heterogeneous systems or physically remote systems. The message payloads are generally stored in database tables to meet the objectives of message persistence and integrity (through backup/recovery), and to achieve performance goals. Message queue tables can be protected with DBV realms just like any other database object. For example, a new queue table created in the APP_OBJECT_OWNER account is automatically protected with the Sample DBV Application realm we just created:

```
app_object_owner@aos> -- create the message payload objects and tables
app_object_owner@aos> CREATE OR REPLACE TYPE aso_order AS OBJECT(
      order_num NUMBER
    , order_name VARCHAR2(60)
    , order_amount NUMBER
    , order_network VARCHAR2(100) )
/
Type created.

app_object_owner@aos> CREATE OR REPLACE TYPE aso_message AS OBJECT (
      message_id RAW(16)
    , order_objects aso_order
    )
/
Type created.
app_object_owner@aos> CREATE TABLE aso_order_objects
(message_object aso_message)
/
Table created.
app_object_owner@aos>-- create the persistent message queue table
app_object_owner@aos>BEGIN
     dbms_aqadm.create_queue_table(
        queue_table => 'aso_queue_table'
      , queue_payload_type => 'aso_order');
END;
/
PL/SQL procedure successfully completed.

app_object_owner@aos>-- AQ creates tables
app_object_owner@aos>SELECT table_name
FROM user_tables
 WHERE table_name LIKE 'ASO%';

TABLE_NAME
------------------------------
ASO_ORDER_OBJECTS
ASO_QUEUE_TABLE
2 rows selected.
```

If a privileged database administrator account, such as SYSTEM, attempts to access or manipulate these objects, the DBV realm protects these newly added objects:

```
system@aos>SELECT * FROM  app_object_owner.aso_queue_table;
SELECT * FROM  app_object_owner.aso_queue_table
                                *
ERROR at line 1:
```

```
ORA-01031: insufficient privileges

system@aos>DELETE app_object_owner.aso_queue_table;
DELETE app_object_owner.aso_queue_table
                        *
ERROR at line 1:
ORA-01031: insufficient privileges
```

While we have protected the message stored in a queue, how do we add more protections on the consumers that can read the message? One approach is to leverage DBV factors as a form of a shared secret or as a filtering condition so that the information required to dequeue the message must be asserted through a DBV factor. If we consider the factors Certificate_Context and Connection_Type presented in Chapter 5, we might use them as a condition asserted by the message producer on enqueue so that only the appropriate consumers could dequeue the message. The approach is shown in the following code. First, the producer queues a message using a factor as one of the payload attributes:

```
app_object_owner@aos>SELECT
    dvf.f$connection_type connection_type
FROM dual;
CONNECTION_TYPE
--------------------
CORPORATE_SSL

app_object_owner@aos> -- queue the message using this factor
app_object_owner@aos>DECLARE
    message_id number;
    l_msg_handle raw(16);
    l_enqueue_opts dbms_aq.enqueue_options_t;
    l_msg_props dbms_aq.message_properties_t;
    l_msg_object aso_order;
BEGIN
    l_msg_object := aso_order(10
            , 'SUN T5520'
            , 40000.00
            ,DVF.F$CONNECTION_TYPE);
    l_enqueue_opts.VISIBILITY := DBMS_AQ.ON_COMMIT;

    dbms_aq.enqueue (
          queue_name         => 'aso_queue'
        , enqueue_options    => l_enqueue_opts
        , message_properties => l_msg_props
        , payload            => l_msg_object
        , msgid              => l_msg_handle);
    COMMIT;
END;
/
PL/SQL procedure successfully completed.
```

Next, only trusted consumers (such as the notional APP_USER account) can dequeue the message when the factor resolves to the correct value for the consumer's session:

```
app_user@aos>SELECT
    dvf.f$connection_type connection_type
FROM dual;
CONNECTION_TYPE
--------------------
CORPORATE_SSL

app_user@aos>-- dequeue the message using this factor
app_user@aos>SET SERVEROUT ON
app_user@aos>DECLARE
    l_msg_handle raw(16);
    l_dequeue_opts dbms_aq.dequeue_options_t;
    l_msg_props dbms_aq.message_properties_t;
    l_msg_object app_object_owner.aso_order;
BEGIN

    l_dequeue_opts.deq_condition    :=
        'tab.user_data.order_network =
        ''' || DVF.F$CONNECTION_TYPE || '''';
    l_dequeue_opts.dequeue_mode := dbms_aq.remove;
    -- wait for three (3) seconds to demo quickly
    l_dequeue_opts.wait := 3;

    dbms_aq.dequeue (
          queue_name         => 'app_object_owner.aso_queue'
        , dequeue_options    => l_dequeue_opts
        , message_properties => l_msg_props
        , payload            => l_msg_object
        , msgid              => l_msg_handle);

    dbms_output.put_line('Dequeue done');
    dbms_output.put_line('Order id     :' ||
            l_msg_object.order_num);
    dbms_output.put_line('Order name   :' ||
            l_msg_object.order_name);
    dbms_output.put_line('Order amount :' ||
            l_msg_object.order_amount);
    dbms_output.put_line('Order network:' ||
            l_msg_object.order_network);
END;
/
Dequeue done
Order id     :10
Order name   :SUN T5520
Order amount :40000
Order network:CORPORATE_SSL

PL/SQL procedure successfully completed.
```

Untrusted consumers cannot dequeue the message when the factor resolves to the incorrect value for the consumer's session:

```
app_user@aos>SELECT
    dvf.f$connection_type connection_type
FROM dual;
CONNECTION_TYPE
--------------------
OTHER

app_user@aos>-- dequeue the message using this factor
app_user@aos>SET SERVEROUT ON
app_user@aos>DECLARE
    l_msg_handle raw(16);
    l_dequeue_opts dbms_aq.dequeue_options_t;
    l_msg_props dbms_aq.message_properties_t;
    l_msg_object app_object_owner.aso_order;
BEGIN

    l_dequeue_opts.deq_condition     :=
        'tab.user_data.order_network =
''' || DVF.F$CONNECTION_TYPE || '''';
    l_dequeue_opts.dequeue_mode := dbms_aq.remove;
    -- wait for three (3) seconds to demo quickly
    l_dequeue_opts.wait := 3;

    dbms_aq.dequeue (
          queue_name           => 'app_object_owner.aso_queue'
        , dequeue_options      => l_dequeue_opts
        , message_properties => l_msg_props
        , payload              => l_msg_object
        , msgid                => l_msg_handle);

    dbms_output.put_line('Dequeue done');
    dbms_output.put_line('Order id      :' ||
            l_msg_object.order_num);
    dbms_output.put_line('Order name    :' ||
            l_msg_object.order_name);
    dbms_output.put_line('Order amount :' ||
            l_msg_object.order_amount);
    dbms_output.put_line('Order network:' ||
            l_msg_object.order_network);
END;
/
DECLARE
*
ERROR at line 1:
ORA-25228: timeout or end-of-fetch during message dequeue from
APP_OBJECT_OWNER.ASO_QUEUE
ORA-06512: at "SYS.DBMS_AQ", line 335
ORA-06512: at line 15
```

In practice, you would want to wrap the dequeued functionality inside a PL/SQL procedure to hide the algorithm and timeout stack traces, and you'd use standard access controls on the queue. This example demonstrates a mechanism to ensure that data in the queue is dequeued (read) only in the correct context. In this example, the only correct context occurs when clients have a **Connection_Type** of **CORPORATE_SSL**.

Transparent Data Encryption

In Chapter 2 we introduced the encryption feature of the database that protects your data at the storage level so that sensitive information is not accessible using brute-force read methods on Oracle data files. Transparent Data Encryption (TDE) protects your sensitive information from being read at the OS layer. DBV's realms and command rules can provide the same mechanism to prevent information from being read through the database's SQL layer. The natural question to ask next is, why protect your information with DBV without protecting it with TDE?

TIP
If you protect your data with DBV, protect it with TDE as well.

We created the Sample DBV Application realm and protected the objects in the APP_OBJECT_OWNER account by issuing two PL/SQL command blocks. We can encrypt all data in the APP_OBJECT_OWNER.CUSTOMERS table with three commands by creating an encrypted tablespace and moving the table into the tablespace:

```
jean_oper_dba@aos>-- create an encrypted tablespace
jean_oper_dba@aos>CREATE TABLESPACE app_object_owner_ts
  DATAFILE '/opt/app/oracle/oradata/ensg/app_object_owner_encrypted.dbf'
  SIZE 10M
  AUTOEXTEND ON
  ENCRYPTION USING 'AES256'
  DEFAULT STORAGE(ENCRYPT);
Tablespace created.

-- give the APP_OBJECT_OWNER account storage
-- quota on the encrypted tablespace
CONNECT jim_acctmgr
jean_oper_dba@aos>CONNECT jim_acctmgr
Enter password:
Connected.
jim_acctmgr@aos>ALTER USER app_object_owner
      QUOTA UNLIMITED ON app_object_owner_ts;

User altered.

jim_acctmgr@aos>-- move the data table to the encrypted tablespace
jim_acctmgr@aos>CONNECT app_object_owner
Enter password:
Connected.
app_object_owner@aos>ALTER TABLE app_object_owner.customers
      MOVE TABLESPACE app_object_ts;
Table altered.
```

It really is that simple, so why not do it?

Oracle Recovery Manager

Oracle Recovery Manager (RMAN) is the Oracle-preferred method for efficiently backing up and recovering your Oracle database. RMAN is also integrated with the Enterprise Manager–based tools so that it can be instrumented remotely through a web browser. RMAN does not operate on the database for backups through the SQL layer, so it is not subject to DBV realm protections or DBV command rules to maintain integrity. When RMAN is coupled with TDE's ability to encrypt tablespaces, we can ensure that an operational DBA cannot query or manipulate the sensitive data protected by DBV and cannot read the data files holding the sensitive data using TDE. However, the operational DBA can still perform backup and recovery of this data using RMAN, without seeing the data itself.

```
jean_oper_dba@aos>-- attempt to query the data through the SQL layer
jean_oper_dba@aos>SELECT last_name, credit_limit
FROM app_object_owner.customers;
  2  FROM app_object_owner.customers
                      *
ERROR at line 2:
ORA-01031: insufficient privileges
jean_oper_dba@aos>exit
Disconnected from Oracle Database 11g Enterprise Edition Release 11.1.0.7.0 - 64bit
Production
With the Partitioning, Oracle Label Security, OLAP, Data Mining,
Oracle Database Vault and Real Application Testing options

[oracle@node1 ~]$ # Attempt to read the data files at the OS level
[oracle@node1 ~]$ strings /opt/app/oracle/oradata/ensg/app_object_owner_encrypted.dbf
}|{z
ENSG
APP_OBJECT_OWNER_TS

[oracle@node1 ~]$ # backup up the encrypted tablespace with
[oracle@node1 ~]$ # Oracle Recovery Manager
 [oracle@node1 ~]$  rman target jean_oper_dba/oracle
Recovery Manager: Release 11.1.0.7.0 - Production on Thu Apr 23 18:46:16 2009
Copyright (c) 1982, 2007, Oracle.  All rights reserved.
connected to target database: ENSG (DBID=506519968)
RMAN> configure channel device type disk format '/opt/app/oracle/rman/ora_df%t_s%s_
s%p';
using target database control file instead of recovery catalog
old RMAN configuration parameters:
CONFIGURE CHANNEL DEVICE TYPE DISK FORMAT   '/opt/app/oracle/rman/ora_df%t_s%s_s%p';
new RMAN configuration parameters:
CONFIGURE CHANNEL DEVICE TYPE DISK FORMAT   '/opt/app/oracle/rman/ora_df%t_s%s_s%p';
new RMAN configuration parameters are successfully stored
RMAN> backup tablespace app_object_owner_ts ;
Starting backup at 23-APR-09
allocated channel: ORA_DISK_1
channel ORA_DISK_1: SID=137 device type=DISK
channel ORA_DISK_1: starting full datafile backup set
channel ORA_DISK_1: specifying datafile(s) in backup set
input datafile file number=00006 name=/opt/app/oracle/oradata/ensg/app_object_owner_
encrypted.dbf
channel ORA_DISK_1: starting piece 1 at 23-APR-09
```

```
channel ORA_DISK_1: finished piece 1 at 23-APR-09
piece handle=/opt/app/oracle/rman/ora_df684960426_s3_s1
tag=TAG20090423T184706 comment=NONE
channel ORA_DISK_1: backup set complete, elapsed time: 00:00:01
Finished backup at 23-APR-09
RMAN> exit
Recovery Manager complete.

[oracle@node1 ~]$ # anything visible with the backup of the
[oracle@node1 ~]$ #  encrypted tablespace ?
[oracle@node1 ~]$ strings /opt/app/oracle/rman/ora_df684960426_s3_s1
}|{z
ENSG
TAG20090423T184706
ENSG
APP_OBJECT_OWNER_TS
```

Gathering Statistics on Realm-protected Schemas

The Oracle database is installed with a scheduler job named GATHER_STATS_JOB that will iterate over all database accounts to collect optimizer statistics. This ensures that accurate and up-to-date statistics are available to the optimizer. Statistics are collected automatically to provide the best possible performance for your applications without your having to perform the collection manually. On some releases and platforms, you may notice that this statistics collection fails due to realm protections on your database tables. Refer to Metalink document 735167.1 to determine whether a patch for your specific release and platform exists. If a patch is not available, you can request one and implement a work-around in the meantime. To work around this issue, you can set up a scheduler job that runs as the object-owner account to collect statistics using the following sample code block. Just change the **ownname** parameter to the object-owner account (APP_OBJECT_OWNER) for your application.

```
BEGIN
  dbms_stats.gather_schema_stats(
      ownname          => 'APP_OBJECT_OWNER'
    , options          => 'GATHER AUTO'
    , estimate_percent => dbms_stats.auto_sample_size
    , cascade          => TRUE
    );
END;
```

EXPLAIN PLAN on Realm-protected Schemas

When a database session submits SELECT or DML statements to the database, the Oracle database optimizer generates a query execution plan to determine the most efficient method to perform the work. This execution plan will account for performance-enabling features of the database, such as partitions or indexes, that apply to the table(s) involved. The Oracle EXPLAIN PLAN feature allows your database administrator to view this plan in the same way that web-based services for driving directions let you find the quickest path from point A to point B, with turn-by-turn details and mileage between turns. The EXPLAIN PLAN feature might be used by your operational DBA in response to reports of performance issues from application developers or end users. With realm protections on the data tables, the DBA cannot use the AUTOTRACE capability in SQL*Plus.

However, an operational DBA can use EXPLAIN PLAN without being authorized in the realm to determine whether query or storage optimization techniques need to be applied to resolve performance issues.

```
-- an operational DBA cannot query
-- the realm protected data and
-- analyze with AUTOTRACE ON
jean_oper_dba@aos>SET AUTOTRACE ON
jean_oper_dba@aos>SELECT COUNT(*)
FROM app_object_owner.customers
WHERE state_province = 'VA' ;
  2    3  FROM app_object_owner.customers
                        *
ERROR at line 2:
ORA-01031: insufficient privileges

jean_oper_dba@aos>EXPLAIN PLAN FOR
SELECT COUNT(*)
FROM app_object_owner.customers
WHERE state_province = 'VA'
/
Explained.

-- query the EXPLAIN PLAN data to
-- retrieve the diagnostic information
SELECT plan_table_output
FROM TABLE(dbms_xplan.display);
PLAN_TABLE_OUTPUT
-----------------------------------------------------------------------
Plan hash value: 296924608
-----------------------------------------------------------------------
| Id  | Operation           | Name      | Rows  | Bytes | Cost (%CPU)| Time     |
-----------------------------------------------------------------------
|   0 | SELECT STATEMENT    |           |     1 |    11 |   898   (1)| 00:00:11 |
|   1 |  SORT AGGREGATE     |           |     1 |    11 |            |          |
|*  2 |   TABLE ACCESS FULL| CUSTOMERS |   383 |  4213 |   898   (1)| 00:00:11 |
-----------------------------------------------------------------------
Predicate Information (identified by operation id):
PLAN_TABLE_OUTPUT
-----------------------------------------------------------------------
   2 - filter("STATE_PROVINCE"='VA')

14 rows selected.
```

Advanced Monitoring and Alerting with a DBV Database

In this section, we present some exciting new features that are available in the latest version of the OEM GC product. These features offer centralized monitoring, audit reporting, and alerting for all DBV-enabled databases in your enterprise. They also enable the macro-level auditing type view of the enterprise security posture that was first introduced in Chapter 2. We conclude the section with a simple example of how you can extend the DBV Rule Set component to integrate your existing monitoring and alerting systems with context-sensitive information regarding DBV policy violations that occur.

Monitoring and Alerting on DBV with OEM GC

Another useful feature added to OEM GC 10.2.0.5 is the ability to monitor and alert on DBV policy changes, DBV configuration issues, and DBV policy violations in the target databases it monitors. The product defines several metrics in these categories that are collected on an ongoing basis, as shown in Figure 7-8.

When an alert is generated from one of these metrics, it is displayed on the target DBV database's home page in OEM GC providing a real-time, comprehensive view of what may have occurred. This home page display is depicted in Figure 7-9.

For each alert that is presented, the administrators of the systems can choose to acknowledge the alert and add comments related to the research and resolution of the issue. When the alert has been fully resolved, the primary administrator or compliance officer can choose to clear the alert. The alert tracking capability is shown in Figure 7-10.

OEM GC allows you to log into each DBV-enabled database to view summary statistics, charts, and target-specific alerts for the database, as depicted in Figure 7-11.

The target-centric interface also allows you to generate reports using a variety of filter controls to investigate the offending account, SQL commands, and time frame that caused a policy violation as you investigate an alert. This reporting interface is shown in Figure 7-12.

Metrics	Thresholds	Collection Schedule	Upload Interval	Last Upload
Alert Log	All	Every 15 Minutes	Every Collection	-
Alert Log Error Status	All	Every 15 Minutes	Every Collection	-
Archive Area	Some	Every 15 Minutes	Every Collection	-
Database Files	None	Disabled	Every Collection	-
Database Job Status	All	Every 5 Minutes	On Alert	-
Database Limits	Some	Every 5 Minutes	Every Collection	-
Database Services	None	Every 15 Minutes	Every Collection	-
Database Vault Attempted Violations - Command Rules	None	Every 1 Hour	On Alert	-
Database Vault Attempted Violations - Realms	None	Every 1 Hour	On Alert	-
Database Vault Configuration Issues - Command Rules	All	Every 1 Hour	Every Collection	-
Database Vault Configuration Issues - Realms	All	Every 1 Hour	Every Collection	-
Database Vault Policy Changes	All	Every 1 Hour	Every Collection	-
Deferred Transactions	All	Every 5 Minutes	On Alert	-
Dump Area	All	Every 15 Minutes	Every Collection	-
Efficiency	None	Every 5 Minutes	Every Collection	-
Failed Logins	All	Every 30 Minutes	Every Collection	-
Flash Recovery	Not Applicable	Every 15 Minutes	Every Collection	-
Health Check	All	Every 15 Seconds	On Alert	-
Invalid Objects	None	Every 24 Hours	On Alert	-
Invalid Objects by Schema	All	Every 24 Hours	On Alert	-
OCM Instrumentation	All	Every 24 Hours	Every Collection	-
Recovery	All	Every 15 Minutes	Every Collection	-
Recovery Area	Not Applicable	Every 15 Minutes	Every Collection	-

FIGURE 7-8 *DBV metric collection parameters in OEM GC*

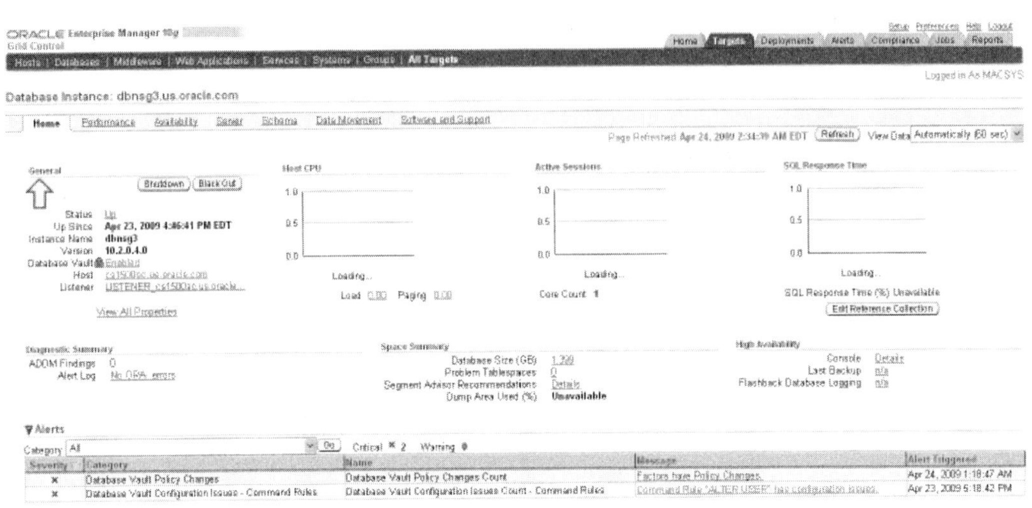

FIGURE 7-9 *Alerts for a DBV database in OEM GC*

ORACLE Enterprise Manager 10g
Grid Control

Setup | Preferences | Help | Logout

Home | Targets | Deployments | Alerts | Compliance | Jobs | Reports

Hosts | Databases | Middleware | Web Applications | Services | Systems | Groups | All Targets

Database Instance: dbnsg3.us.oracle.com > All Metrics > Database Vault Policy Changes Count > Database Vault Policy Changes Category/Database Vault Policy Change Time Object >

Metric Alert : Database Vault Policy Changes Count

Page Refreshed Apr 24, 2009 2:43:11 AM EDT (Refresh)

Alert Details

Metric: Database Vault Policy Changes Count
Database Vault Policy Changes Category: **Factors**
Database Vault Policy Change Time: **2009-04-24 01:18:48**
Severity: × **Critical** (Clear Alert)
Alert Triggered: **Apr 24, 2009 1:18:47 AM**
Last Updated: **Apr 24, 2009 1:18:47 AM**
Acknowledged: **No** (Acknowledge)
Acknowledged By: **n/a**
Message: **Factors have Policy Changes.**

Metric Data

Last Known Value: **Not available**
Last Collection Timestamp: **Not available**

Metric Settings

Warning Threshold: **Not Defined**
Critical Threshold: **0**
Occurrences Before Alert: **1**

Actions

Edit Thresholds

Updates

New Comment (Add Comment)

Timestamp	Type	Administrator	Message
Apr 24, 2009 1:18:47 AM	×	<SYSTEM>	Factors have Policy Changes.

Home | **Targets** | Deployments | Alerts | Compliance | Jobs | Reports | Setup | Preferences | Help | Logout

FIGURE 7-10 *Responding to DBV alerts in OEM GC*

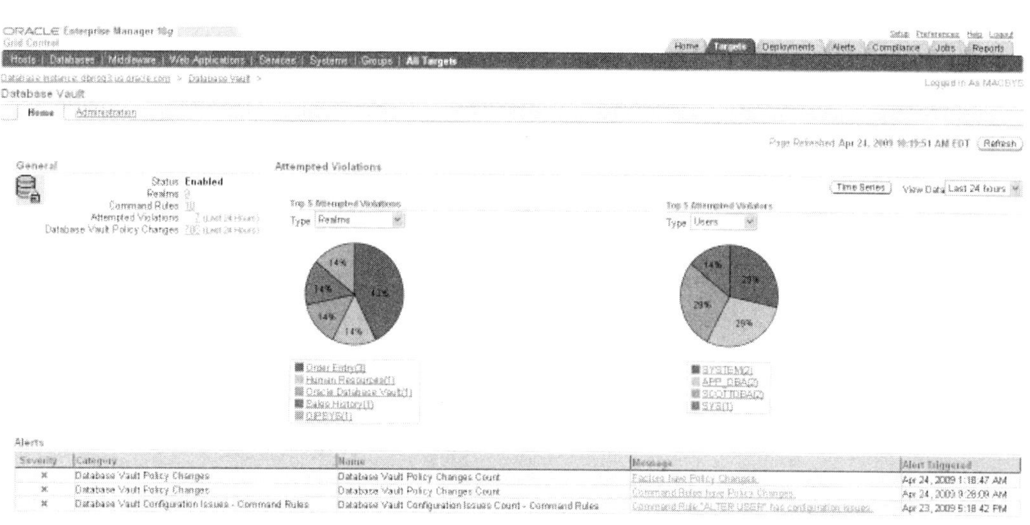

FIGURE 7-11 *Database-specific DBV statistics in OEM GC*

The monitoring and alerting of DBV policy changes, DBV configuration issues, and DBV policy violations in OEM GC provide real-time visibility into potential security issues in your databases. The ability to document the process of responding to these issues provides added value to your compliance reporting needs as OEM GC keeps track of the historical nature of this process.

ORACLE Enterprise Manager 10g
Grid Control

Home | Targets | Deployments | Alerts | Compliance | Jobs | Reports

Hosts | Databases | Middleware | Web Applications | Services | Systems | Groups | All Targets

Logged in As MACSYS

Attempted Violations Report

Displays a report on the Attempted Database Vault Violations

Page Refreshed Apr 24, 2009 10:36:49 AM EDT

Last 24

From Apr 24, 2009 Time 12 0 AM To Apr 24, 2009 Time 11 59 PM

Violation Type All Name %

Database User % Client Host %

Maximum Results 500 Go

Time	Violation Type	Name	Database User	Client Host	Client Host User Name	Action Command
Apr 24, 2009 8:52:06 AM	Realm	Oracle Database Vault	SYSTEM	CS1500SC	ORACLE	GRANT dv_admin to system
Apr 24, 2009 8:53:19 AM	Realm	OIPSYS	APP_DBA	CS1500SC	ORACLE	grant OIP_OWNER to app_dba
Apr 24, 2009 9:18:57 AM	Realm	Sales History	SYS	cs1500sc	oracle	select count(*) from sh.sales
Apr 24, 2009 9:19:31 AM	Realm	Human Resources	APP_DBA	cs1500sc	oracle	update hr.employees set xx = 1
Apr 24, 2009 9:20:02 AM	Realm	Order Entry	SYSTEM	cs1500sc	oracle	select * from oe.orders
Apr 24, 2009 9:21:17 AM	Realm	Order Entry	SCOTTDBA	cs1500sc	oracle	delete oe.orders
Apr 24, 2009 9:21:40 AM	Realm	Order Entry	SCOTTDBA	CS1500SC	ORACLE	alter table oe.orders add yy number

Related Links

View and Manage Transactions

OK

Home | Targets | Deployments | Alerts | Compliance | Jobs | Reports | Setup | Preferences | Help | Logout

FIGURE 7-12 *Fine-grained reporting on DBV policy violations in OEM GC*

Extending the DBV Rule Set Custom Event Handler

Chapter 5 presented a simple example of how you can develop custom PL/SQL handler routines that handle the event that a rule set returns false (or true!) when used as part of a DBV command rule. The DBV command rule allowed only **UPDATE** commands on the SH.SALES table when they came from the PL/SQL package procedure SH.SALES_TRANSACTION. In this example, we wrote a message to the table SH.ALERTS indicating that an event had occurred. An alerting mechanism also needs to have detailed information on the actual security-relevant event that occurred. We can use DBV rule set event functions and application context within the rule expressions used in DBV rule sets to provide this information. The rule will write the details of the security-relevant event based on the data returned from the DBV rule set event functions to an application context namespace as part of the initial evaluation of the rule. We can subsequently read this information from the application context in the rule set's custom event handler procedure.

The first thing we need to do is update our rule definition to pass the DBV rule set event function values into the function we use to authorize the command:

```
diego_dbvmgr@aos>-- update the conditional rule that states
diego_dbvmgr@aos>-- we are using the trusted application code
diego_dbvmgr@aos>-- to pass the event functions, save them in
diego_dbvmgr@aos>-- context so they are accessible from the
diego_dbvmgr@aos>-- custom event handler
diego_dbvmgr@aos>BEGIN
     dbms_macadm.update_rule(
           rule_name => 'Called From Sales Transaction Package'
         , rule_expr =>
             'sh.sales_rules.update_allowed(
                  DVSYS.DV_SYSEVENT'
                  || ',DVSYS.DV_LOGIN_USER'
                  || ',DVSYS.DV_INSTANCE_NUM'
                  || ',DVSYS.DV_DATABASE_NAME'
                  || ',DVSYS.DV_DICT_OBJ_TYPE'
                  || ',DVSYS.DV_DICT_OBJ_OWNER'
                  || ',DVSYS.DV_DICT_OBJ_NAME'
                  || ',DVSYS.DV_SQL_TEXT) > 0'
     );
END;
/
PL/SQL procedure successfully completed.
```

The PL/SQL package DBVEXT.DBMS_MAC_EXTENSION that is part of the example source code provided with this book includes a procedure that can write this information to an application context with the namespace SQL_EVENT. The procedure has the following signature:

```
PROCEDURE set_event_context(
          command         IN VARCHAR2
        , session_user    IN VARCHAR2
        , instance_num    IN NUMBER
        , database_name   IN VARCHAR2
        , obj_type        IN VARCHAR2
        , obj_owner       IN VARCHAR2
        , obj_name        IN VARCHAR2
        , sql_text        IN VARCHAR2
  ) ;
```

DBVEXT must grant execute on this package to the SH for the object-owner account to use the SET_EVENT_CONTEXT procedure that is defined in the package:

```
diego_dbvmgr@aos>CONNECT dbvext
Enter password:
Connected.
dbvext@aos>GRANT EXECUTE ON dbvext.dbms_mac_extension TO sh;
Grant succeeded.
```

The next step is to update the function we use to authorize the command, SH.SALES_RULES.UPDATE_ALLOWED, to have these new parameters passed to it. We will use our Application Maintenance Administrator account from Chapter 6 for this task.

```
dbvext@aos>CONNECT mark_maint_mgr
Enter password:
Connected.
mark_maint_mgr@aos>-- create a rules package procedure
mark_maint_mgr@aos>-- that accepts the event state and
mark_maint_mgr@aos>-- execute rule-specific decisions in one expression
mark_maint_mgr@aos>CREATE OR REPLACE PACKAGE sh.sales_rules AS
    FUNCTION update_allowed(
          command         IN VARCHAR2
        , session_user    IN VARCHAR2
        , instance_num    IN NUMBER
        , database_name   IN VARCHAR2
        , obj_type        IN VARCHAR2
        , obj_owner       IN VARCHAR2
        , obj_name        IN VARCHAR2
        , sql_text        IN VARCHAR2
    ) RETURN NUMBER;
END;
/
Package created.

mark_maint_mgr@aos>-- create a rules package body
mark_maint_mgr@aos>-- that uses the DBVEXT procedure
mark_maint_mgr@aos>-- to save the event state to
mark_maint_mgr@aos>-- the application context SQL_EVENT
mark_maint_mgr@aos>CREATE OR REPLACE PACKAGE BODY sh.sales_rules AS
    FUNCTION update_allowed(
          command         IN VARCHAR2
        , session_user    IN VARCHAR2
        , instance_num    IN NUMBER
        , database_name   IN VARCHAR2
        , obj_type        IN VARCHAR2
        , obj_owner       IN VARCHAR2
        , obj_name        IN VARCHAR2
        , sql_text        IN VARCHAR2
    ) RETURN NUMBER IS

    BEGIN
        -- validate and set event context
```

```
        dbvext.dbms_mac_extension.set_event_context(
          command       => command
        , session_user  => session_user
        , instance_num  => instance_num
        , database_name => database_name
        , obj_type      => obj_type
        , obj_owner     => obj_owner
        , obj_name      => obj_name
            -- ensure we have first 4K only
        , sql_text      => SUBSTR(sql_text,1,4000)
        );
        -- put the original business rules here
        RETURN INSTR(UPPER(DBMS_UTILITY.FORMAT_CALL_STACK),
'PACKAGE BODY SH.SALES_TRANSCTION');
    EXCEPTION
        WHEN OTHERS THEN
            -- ITS A GOOD IDEA TO GIVEN ERROR
            -- CODE FOR ANY EXCEPTION THAT OCCURS
            RETURN -1 * ABS(SQLCODE);
    END;
END;
/
Package body created.
```

The next step is to update our rule set's custom event handler to read the event details from application context and process them. In this example, we will keep it simple and just write them to the SH.ALERTS table:

```
mark_maint_mgr@aos>CREATE OR REPLACE PACKAGE BODY sh.sales_alerts AS
    PROCEDURE sales_update_alert(
              ruleset_name IN VARCHAR2
            , ruleset_result IN VARCHAR2) IS
        PRAGMA AUTONOMOUS_TRANSACTION;
    BEGIN
            INSERT INTO sh.alerts (msg ) VALUES
                 ('Alert for Rule Set:'  || ruleset_name);
            INSERT INTO sh.alerts (msg ) VALUES
                ('result is ' || ruleset_result);
            INSERT INTO sh.alerts (msg ) VALUES
                ('event is '  || sys_context('SQL_EVENT','COMMAND'));
            INSERT INTO sh.alerts (msg ) VALUES
                ('user is '  || sys_context('SQL_EVENT','USER'));
            INSERT INTO sh.alerts (msg ) VALUES
                ('instance is '  ||
                  sys_context('SQL_EVENT','INSTANCE'));
            INSERT INTO sh.alerts (msg ) VALUES
                ('database is '  ||
                  sys_context('SQL_EVENT','DATABASE'));
            INSERT INTO sh.alerts (msg ) VALUES
                ('object type is '  ||
                  sys_context('SQL_EVENT','OBJECT_TYPE'));
            INSERT INTO sh.alerts (msg ) VALUES
```

```
                    ('owner is '  ||  sys_context('SQL_EVENT','OWNER'));
                INSERT INTO sh.alerts (msg ) VALUES
                    ('object name is '  ||
                      sys_context('SQL_EVENT','OBJECT_NAME'));
                INSERT INTO sh.alerts (msg ) VALUES
                    ('SQL text is "'  ||
                      sys_context('SQL_EVENT','SQL_TEXT') || '"');
                COMMIT;
    END;
END;
/
Package body created.
```

The final preparation step is to make sure we revalidate our DBV rule sets as follows:

```
mark_maint_mgr@aos>CONNECT diego_dbvmgr
Enter password:
Connected.
diego_dbvmgr@aos> -- verify the DBV Rule Sets are valid!
diego_dbvmgr@aos> exec dbms_macadm.sync_rules;
PL/SQL procedure successfully completed.
```

We are now ready to test our solution using the realm's Application Data Administrator from Chapter 6 as the trouble-maker!

```
diego_dbvmgr@aos>CONNECT deb_data_mgr
Enter password:
Connected.
deb_data_mgr@aos>-- force the Command Rule violation
deb_data_mgr@aos> UPDATE sh.sales
SET amount_sold = 200
WHERE cust_id = 305;
  2    3   UPDATE sh.sales
           *
ERROR at line 1:
ORA-01031: insufficient privileges

deb_data_mgr@aos>-- view the alert table
deb_data_mgr@aos>SELECT msg
FROM sh.alerts
ORDER BY msgdate;
MSG
-----------------------------------------------
Alert for Rule Set:Using Financials Application
result is FALSE
event is UPDATE
user is DEB_DATA_MGR
SQL text is "UPDATE SH.SALES
SET AMOUNT_SOLD = 200
WHERE CUST_ID = 305"
database is ENSG.US.ORACLE.COM
object type is TABLE
owner is SH
```

```
object name is SALES
instance is 1

10 rows selected.
```

We could perform just about any integration with this handler mechanism when we consider the use of the standard Oracle PL/SQL packages such as UTL_TCP, UTL_HTTP, and UTL_SMTP or features such as external stored procedures and Java stored procedures.

DBV realm authorizations are binary (allow/disallow) control unless coupled with a DBV rule set. We can use the same approach of passing the DBV rule set event function values to a function to provide a fine-grained control of realm authorizations that are based on these values. In other words, we can define an application-specific function for use in a DBV realm authorization's rule set rules as follows:

```
FUNCTION authorize_in_app_realm(
      command          IN VARCHAR2
    , session_user     IN VARCHAR2
    , instance_num     IN NUMBER
    , database_name    IN VARCHAR2
    , obj_type         IN VARCHAR2
    , obj_owner        IN VARCHAR2
    , obj_name         IN VARCHAR2
    , sql_text         IN VARCHAR2
) RETURN NUMBER;
```

This allows us to build case-like statements or table-driven controls in this function that handle command-specific, owner-specific, object-specific, or exception criteria in existing applications once we protect data with a realm.

Summary

In this chapter, we presented techniques for developing DBV policies that can be applied to existing Oracle database applications. DBV policies can be transparently applied to all SQL commands submitted to the database, regardless of the technology used to build the application. This represents an opportunity for you to increase the security posture of your applications without rewriting code. The following might prompt you to add DBV protections to your applications:

- Your organization is striving to meet compliance regulations such as separation of duties or information privacy in the applications.
- Your organization is undergoing a database consolidation effort and security must be applied to achieve separation of control and to reduce the risk of insider threats or external attacks.

The primary technique used in this chapter to identify the candidate DBV policy involves enabling core database auditing for all transactions and then exercising the applications to develop a transaction profile. Once the transaction profile has been created, we demonstrate how you can query it to uncover the candidate DBV policy. We augmented the queries on the transaction profile with additional queries on security-relevant database configuration views to refine the candidate DBV policy.

The transaction profile includes object-owner account names and object names that form the basis of DBV realm protections. You can validate the list of sensitive objects by examining existing audit policies and row-level security policies. Roles associated with a database account are listed as database clients, and the use of system ANY privileges provides insight into which database roles should be authorized in a DBV realm and which database roles should protected by a DBV realm. We included a technique to help you map existing database roles to the Application Administrator roles pattern we recommended in Chapter 6. You can even integrate these Application Administrator roles with an external resource such as OID using the Oracle EUS technology.

The transaction profile can be used to develop the candidate Subject-Verb-Object-Conditions table that we recommended in Chapter 6. This table serves as the basis for candidate DBV command rules and DBV rule sets. Queries presented to develop this table gave you insight into the most sensitive transactions in your database. We've included an example of how to externalize the authorization of these sensitive transactions with a mechanism that was controlled outside of the database.

We concluded the analysis techniques with queries on both the transaction profile and the security-relevant database configuration views to identify DBV factors based on identity management, operational context, time, and external events. Inspecting documentation from existing applications can assist in augmenting analysis, but we recommend that you review your candidate DBV policy with the technical experts of the applications and databases involved. These experts have the greatest knowledge about how a system works and what the impact(s) might be if you add layers of security to an existing application or a database.

We have also demonstrated how the Oracle Real Application Testing feature can be used to validate that your applications continue operating normally under DBV policy control using real-world transactions and workloads. The use of the newly released OEM GC DBV policy provisioning capabilities will reduce the time and risk in deploying the new DBV policy to test and production environments.

Your applications and database may be using any number of existing database features and administration tools, such as Oracle Text, Oracle Spatial, RMAN, and TDE. We included tips and techniques to ensure that these database features and the new Oracle DBV policy controls work together.

Finally, we encourage you to consider the newly released monitoring and alerting features in the OEM GC product for DBV policy changes, DBV configuration issues, and DBV policy violations. These features are critical to tracking and reporting on security-relevant issues that could impact your ability to meet compliance regulations and protect against attacks.

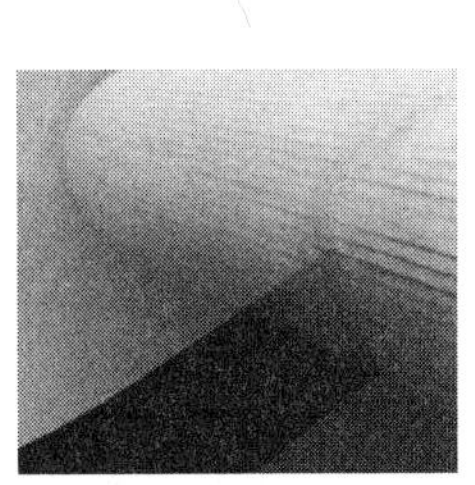

PART III

Identity Management

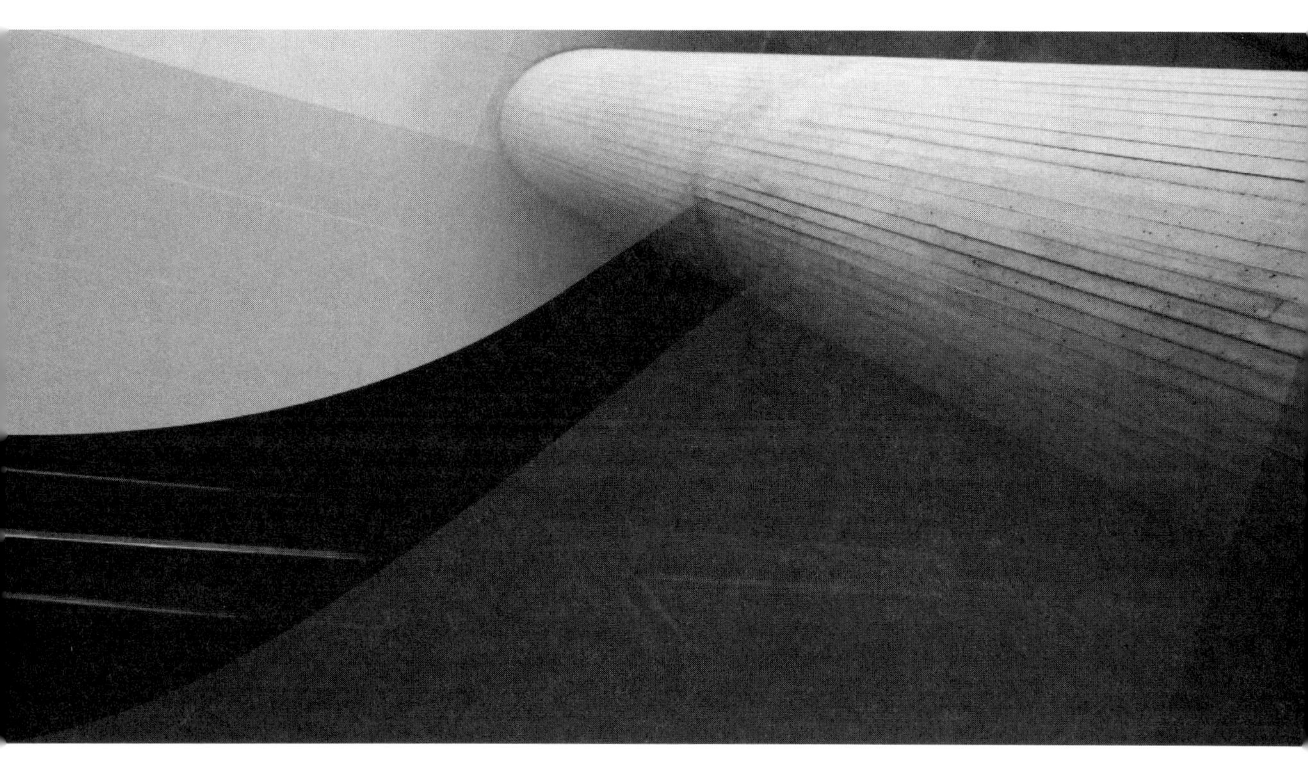

CHAPTER 8

Architecting Identity Management

his chapter discusses the architectural processes and methods used for solving the identity management problems that many enterprises face today when trying to secure access to their applications and information. "Architecting" a solution requires that you understand the functional nature of the problem (such as protecting customer data from privacy threats, and so on) and create a technical solution to address those problems.

Often, as technical people, we can get caught up with possible technological solutions before we fully understand the possible ways of solving the problem from a practical perspective. Subsequently, this chapter covers common techniques and patterns that help you quickly and easily understand the full nature of the challenge surrounding unauthorized access to information applications and a methodical approach to applying appropriate technology solutions to meet those challenges. Keep in mind that this chapter does not intend to cover the comprehensive Oracle Identity Management product portfolio and instead intends to lay out some key products from those offerings in the context of building key identity management solutions.

Understanding the Problem with Identity Management

Recall from Chapter 1 that security can be simply described as understanding who gets access to what, from where, when, and how. In this chapter, we will focus on the first two aspects:

- Who are you?
- What can you access?

In the most fundamental and simplistic view, identity management means managing information for the "who can access what" answer.

You may not realize it, but we are all accustomed to dealing with identity management in almost every aspect of our lives. A classic example for which both the notion of identity and access is used to fulfill a transaction is when you walk into a bank and withdraw money from your checking accounts through an in-person teller. The teller usually requests a proof of identity (such as a driver's license or passport). Once the identity information has been verified—or authenticated, as we like to say in the security world—the teller looks at your account details to see what funds you have access to withdraw. If both the identity and access requests are verified and asserted, the transaction is successful. Essentially, every information transaction scenario follows the model of this bank teller transaction. Before any functional request can be filled, some prerequisite verification of that activity using identity and access information must occur.

Although it's a well-understood and practiced exercise in many parts of our day-to-day business and personal lives, implementing security inside our IT systems can be more challenging. Real-world IT differs from the physical world analogies because of the numerous security models employed and various ways in which applications and programs can represent the users (or the who's) as well as how they authenticate the users, authorize the users, and control access for the users.

Many people consider identity management to be nothing more than a by-product of a generation of application development that was too focused on short-term requirements. After all, it is not a revolutionary concept to authenticate, authorize, and audit user activity inside applications and databases. However, does it make sense to have this infrastructure embedded inside every application? The policies to authenticate, authorize, and audit might vary from application to application, but it does make sense to have them all use a common foundation for making those decisions, and that is precisely the problem identity management solves.

Let's return for a minute to the bank teller example. One of the differences between the bank teller and our electronic information access scenario is the level of trust achieved during a typical transaction. For instance, the bank teller is physically present with the individual making the request, whereas in an electronic scenario, the individual could be literally anywhere in the world. The bank teller is physically receiving the identity document and as such has better assurance that the document was not modified or tampered during the handoff process, whereas in the electronic information access scenario, identity information is presented over a network and therefore is susceptible to tampering during the transmission process. Such differences in the style of a physical bank transaction and the electronic transaction contribute to a basic difference in trust between the server and the client. While this notion of trust is an easy concept to comprehend, it is the hardest to implement in any nonphysical and electronic use case because of three keys limitations in a typical application that does not leverage a centralized identity management architecture: central issuance authority, identity verification, and identity propagation.

Central Issuance Authority

The bank teller has the luxury of being presented with a trusted identity document such as a driver's license or a passport. In the case of a driver's license, the state or a country takes responsibility for issuing such identity documents, which essentially removes the problem of trust between a typical customer and the bank, since both parties implicitly trust that the issuing authority has performed the appropriate identity vetting and issued a document that cannot be easily falsified.

Unfortunately, not all information enterprises can claim such a trusted central authority for issuing identity assertions. The last generation of application development focused on short-term deliverables and local authentication routines with local usernames and passwords at the cost of having a centralized and universally accessible set of identity credentials. The closest we have come to a central issuing authority is Active Directory in enterprises that use it for Windows networking purposes. However, application architects are often reluctant to trust the Active Directory infrastructure to provide a secure set of credentials since it typically does not have the strongest change management processes and therefore could pose a significant risk to the enterprise if credentials are compromised.

Identity Verification

In the bank example, when the customer handed the teller a driver's license or a national passport, the teller can perform some basic verification tasks to validate that identity document by verifying personally identifiable information (such as Social Security numbers, signatures, PIN numbers, and so on). If the transaction requires more sensitivity, the teller can also ask for additional nonstandard identifiers and verifications, such as mother's maiden name or the dollar amount of some recent transactions. These kinds of verifications and cross-verifications allow the teller to build the required level of trust incrementally to help with the customer.

When this scenario is replayed in an electronic format, an information application is typically able to handle the direct and standard verification of the user, most likely using a password; however, few applications natively provide the ability to perform nonstandard cross-verifications. Such advanced authentication needs are usually implemented with a lot of custom coding and added complexity that becomes quite difficult to maintain.

Identity Propagation

The entire bank transaction usually occurs physically in front of the teller, who is most likely sitting inside the bank premises and, therefore, in a somewhat secured context. As a result, when the customer is providing proof of identity, this happens directly from the client to the teller (the server in networking parlance)—in other words, direct identity propagation occurs. This characteristic is challenging to achieve in information applications with intermediate layers (middleware) between the end user application and the backend database. For instance, a typical three-tiered deployment could have end user applications (such as JavaServer Pages [JSP] pages and ASP.NET) communicating with middleware components (such as JavaBeans and Web Services) communicating with other middleware components or data tiers (such as relational databases and file systems).

This kind of multi-layered architecture risks losing identity propagation for reasons including the lack of integration standards and identity formats. I have witnessed many web application deployments in which the end user identity is passed on from an HTML web tier to a Java 2 Platform, Enterprise Edition (J2EE) middle tier but not propagated onto the SQL database that serves as the data tier. The J2EE would simply connect into the database using a shared account that accessed the database for all end users. This is a classic example of how the failure of identity propagation from the middleware to the database can result in low assurance that the right data is being given to the right end user, since the database cannot control access based on the end user's identity.

Identity management exists not because it mimics a bank transaction. It exists because when it is employed it not only adds a central identity authority, identity verification, and identity propagation, but the right identity management solution introduces a platform for security administrators to improve the quality of the security enforcement continuously by improving the policies (such as parameters used to access and control the information). Better policies usually lead to a higher degree of trust, and a higher degree of trust leads to higher adoption of this infrastructure across applications. And a higher degree of adoption usually leads to an overall lowering of the cost of security, since you are able to reuse infrastructure and share efficient enforcement practices across multiple applications. If you compare the cost of implementing the identity management infrastructure, you would see that cost is far less than the cost of building it redundantly everywhere.

Architecting Identity Management

Until recently, identity and access management were not very widely-used terms in a security context. For the most part, identity management was associated with Lightweight Directory Access Protocol (LDAP) directories, such as Novell's eDirectory, and was seen as the means to manage user credentials for operating systems and networks (such as Windows Networking using Active Directory). While that is a perfectly legitimate view of identity management, it should not be limited to those specific contexts. The same basic challenges of user authentication, authorization, and auditing exist in every IT architectural component that involves end user interaction, such as web portals, customer management systems, point-of-sale systems, analysis and reporting tools, online storefronts, content management systems, and so on. As a result, architecturally, we need to realize that we can realize a lot of benefits if we apply the simple LDAP architecture used for basic OS-level authentications to every other user-facing application in the enterprise. As a result, a slightly broader view of identity management can be defined as follows: Identity management is a solution that decouples user management from enforcement of access policies inside applications.

The core challenge of identity management is balancing centralization of management with the decentralization and localization of enforcement. To arrive at the point where we are true to the definition, we need to assess the enterprise's maturity level with respect to security infrastructure. Centralization of identity management requires some basic "IT plumbing" to be in place or be developed before we can truly centralize user management and automate access provisioning. The existence of these key prerequisites of centralization and automation will drive our architectural and implementation choices, since we must often focus first on setting up the basic plumbing, such as integration and storage facilities, before we architect the identity management infrastructure. As a result, we usually start the architecture process at what architects often refer to as the "discovery" phase, when we ask questions to assess and qualify the problem's current state and scope.

Identity Management Discovery

Experience has proven that proper time and attention early in a project reaps tremendous benefits later. Setting up an identity management system certainly follows this tenet. Spending extra time to understand the as-is application security models and their purpose will generally result in a much more effective solution. A simple test to determine whether you are ready to start architecting a security solution for any security problem is to ask yourself the following questions:

- Do I understand the organizational model of the enterprise dealing with the identity management problem? How is authority distributed?
- How are the applications and business processes accessed to perform daily business?
- Do I understand the data that needs protection? Who needs it and how much?

As the questions demonstrate, three areas of discovery must be addressed when trying to solve a typical identity management problem: people, process, and data.

People discovery should focus on identifying the players around a specific application or information repository. These players can be groups, organizations, and roles associated to a specific information access problem. Process discovery should focus on identifying the relationships among people (users, groups, organizations, roles, and so on) and the applications by identifying the steps by the different types of users to carry out a business process inside the application. It should reveal the access privileges required for different users inside each application that is relevant to the business process. Data discovery is similar to process discovery, except it focuses on the relationship between people and the information being accessed. It should identify data ownership, data privacy, and the data storage system. The outputs from this area should form an access privilege model that includes users inside each database (that is, which roles should map to which privileges).

The following sections provide samples questions in each of the three areas and more ideas on how to use the information gathered when answering those questions.

Discovering Identity Management Requirements Around People

At a fundamental level, an identity management problem demands a better and more efficient way to manage information regarding people and their relationships to resources. So it is useful to start by understanding the types of people (users, groups of users, and so on) that are part of the equation.

The approach is a simple one: Try to capture the *Identity Management Organizational Model (IMOM)*. The IMOM is similar to the organizational model that exists in a typical HR system, except IMOM can span from internal employee populations to external user populations, such as customers and partners. The following is a basic list of information elements that are useful to capture when trying to uncover the people-centric data for an identity management problem:

- **Organizations** The logical units that form the entire organization (for example, Oracle North America, Oracle India, Corporate Marketing, Product Development, and so on).
- **Functional roles** An inventory of business roles that are relevant to the application or information (such as Sales, Marketing, Product Development)
- **Authority levels** The categorization of authority and seniority of people in the organization (such as Level 1 Analyst, Senior Manager, Director, Vice President, and so on)
- **User types** The types of users accessing the protected applications and information (for example, Employees, Customers, Contractors, and so on)
- **Identity attributes** Additional identity information used to classify access to information, such as employment status (Full-time, Intern, and so on), physical location, security clearances, and more.

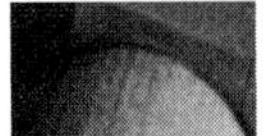

NOTE
The IMOM tries to consolidate all relevant users to the problem including internal users (such as employees and contractors) and external users (such as customers, partners, suppliers, and so on). Discovering the internal user information is usually not too difficult since the HR system is likely to possess most of that information. However, data about external users can be difficult to ascertain and requires additional effort to collect and verify.

The IMOM information can serve as direct inputs to your exercises in defining corresponding objects in the Oracle Identity Manager (OIM) component of your solution, as you will learn in Chapter 9. For instance, if the organization is relatively fluid (that is, reorganized frequently), you might consider keeping the organizations flat and simple in OIM and relying on people's roles and responsibilities to encapsulate their organizational associations. So, for example, if there are frequent reorganizations of who reports to whom in the sales organization, you could use a single "Sales" organizational design in the identity management system with a set of roles or groups (see Chapter 9 for exact definitions of these concepts) to represent either further organization classification (such as geography and product segments) or functional responsibilities (such as Sales Representative, Territory Manager, and Presales Engineer).

External users can be difficult to model since those types of users don't always follow neat organizational hierarchies as internal employees do. So, for example, it is not always obvious how to handle external partners that need to access certain applications. Unfortunately, there are no absolute right answers to many of these organizational design questions, but keeping the litmus test of flexibility is always a good idea. Consider changes in the partner's identity, role, authority, or relationship to the enterprise and see how well your design manages those changes.

You don't need to spend a significant amount of time understanding the organization model because, most likely, you will want to iterate through your design several times before committing to the implementation. Keep this discovery step to a minimum and leverage this information in the next steps of discovery.

Discovering Identity Management Requirements Around Process

Another view of an identity management problem is viewing application security in the context of a business process that executes web services across multiple applications to complete a business function. For instance, a bank customer opening a new online bank account can initiate a business process that subsequently invokes corresponding web services in multiple relevant applications (such as the customer relationship management system, marketing promotions system, and check card management system). Parts of this business process might include direct human interaction (the customer opening the account) and part of this process might be automated (adding a new record into the marketing promotions system). From a security point of view, you need to understand the sensitivity of the different steps in the process and the information that flows through each step. You are not really solving the security problem if all you do is authorize and authenticate the customer to the online banking application and avoid security in the subsequent automated steps. Even if the subsequent steps do not involve direct human interaction, the web services offered by the applications are just as vulnerable to attacks as a user-facing application would be if it didn't have any security checks.

The desired model for web service security should be a seamless and transparent authentication/authorization check before a user or web service client executes the step. To get to that desired model for security for a given business process, you should ask some high-yielding questions:

- What are the end-to-end steps of the business process?
- What is the human interaction workflow in the business process? In other words, explain who (that is, which business roles) can execute which step of the process?
- What information is flowing between each step? What part of that information is sensitive and should be available for display?
- Can a web service be accessed without providing a human user identity?
- Is security being enforced across the business process using the same human identity information? If not, where is the actual end-user's identity propagation ending, and whose identity, if any, is being used in the subsequent process steps?

Ideally, these questions, if answered properly, should illustrate the business process and steps with the highest vulnerability for attacks on your information from unauthorized access. The last two questions usually reveal whether a centralized identity management strategy is in use across multiple applications, especially in enterprise application integration scenarios.

In addition to understanding the security for processes and workflows, you also need to understand processes for security, especially identity management. To uncover the nature of the business processes dealing with identity management, you need to ask some of the following questions:

- What are the steps in the process for provisioning a new identity (for example, employees, customers, contractors, and so on)? What are the approval workflows?
- What are the steps in the process for provisioning a transfer or job change?
- What are the steps in the process for deprovisioning an existing user?
- What are the compliance-mandated attestation processes for information access? This is an artifact of the Sarbanes-Oxley Act of 2002 (refer to Chapter 9 for more information).

These questions should generally cover almost any identity management–related processes in a typical enterprise. Answering these questions should give you a comprehensive view of how identity management is conducted in the current environment and, therefore, should help you prioritize the processes that have the highest complexity and highest risk of authorized access provisioning. For example, automating the deprovisioning process may not drive the highest cost savings but may reduce the risk of having a disgruntled employee with access to mission-critical systems. Understanding and prioritizing these goals will help you identify which problems to solve first.

Discovering Identity Management Requirements Around Information

Every action and investment made in the name of identity management is done for one reason: enforcing that the right person is accessing the right resource (that is, information). Information is an amorphous concept since it exists in so many shapes and forms across the enterprise in so many systems and so many databases. The challenge around information security discovery is knowing what information looks like in each system and knowing who should access what parts of the information.

It is important that you keep a functional/business view and definition of data. For instance, they should be classified by how a business analyst would look at the data (for example, customer data, product data, employee data, supplier data, finance data, facilities data, and so on). Classification should not be driven by their technical characteristics (such as XML, Oracle e-Business Suite 11i, SAP, Business Intelligence, and Austin Data Center). Policies around accessing information should also follow a similar approach and remain as technically neutral as possible, at least at this phase of the project. An example policy around access controlling the finance data could be that a finance analyst can query and read the current quarter earnings data but cannot update or delete that data. Nothing in that policy statement seems to refer to the technical characteristics of the data and, instead, suggests to us that "latest quarterly earnings data" can be read by someone with the finance analyst role but cannot be updated or deleted, regardless of where and how it exists.

To simplify and accelerate the requirements-gathering process around information, you can use the following framework:

1. Inventory all critical systems and applications according to their enterprise name.
2. If those systems are not classified as functional systems (such as HR, Finance, CRM) and instead classified as technical systems (such as Oracle Applications, SAP, Project Nexus Business Intelligence), you need to take some additional time to classify the data that exists in each of those technically-classified systems to reveal what they hold. Often a single system can hold many types of data, usually in a data hub scenario where various data is often combined to provide marketing business intelligence capabilities. The output of this step is to produce a matrix like the one shown in Figure 8-1.
3. Compile a list of functional business roles that exist across the enterprise. This step can be started in parallel with the first step.
4. Map each of those roles to the types of data.
5. For a box that has an X in the mapping (shown in Figure 8-1), map the business roles to local application or system-specific roles that already exists or can be created in that particular application or system.

Applications/Systems

Types of Data

	Project Nexus	PeopleSoft	Oracle Apps 11i	SAP
Employee Data	X	X		
Customer Data	X	X	X	
Product Data	X		X	X

FIGURE 8-1 *Role-to-data mapping*

Through the use of this basic framework, you will reveal the mappings from business roles, to data types, to applications containing that data, to the local application roles that guard the lowest layer of the information architecture. For instance, you could have the following as an example set of mappings:

Marketing Analyst —> Product Data —> Project Nexus —> Viewer

This example illustrates how a functional role (such as Marketing Analyst) can be mapped to a technical Viewer role in the Project Nexus system. The discovery of these mappings will serve as essential input to help you create the access policies around the Marketing Analyst role to the Product information that lives in the Nexus system.

In addition to discovering the rules around access policies for information and applications, you also need to discover and understand the privacy and compliance policies that exist for that information. For example, if financial data exists in a system, it might require that you implement certain auditing policies that track exactly who accessed what record and performed what kind of changes to those records (such as read, write, update, deletes, and so on). In addition to access controlling the data records, additional compliance requirements may exist around the application security model, such as separating the roles of the system administrators of the applications or databases (such as the DBA) and the logical owners of the financial data (such as financial analysts and executives). These kinds of requirements are very common in an enterprise that needs to comply with laws such as Sarbanes-Oxley, Section 404. So, to deal with such compliance or mandate requirements, you could add to your previous framework another set of mappings between the type of data and the compliance requirements and other mandates concerning the information or applications, as shown in Figure 8-2.

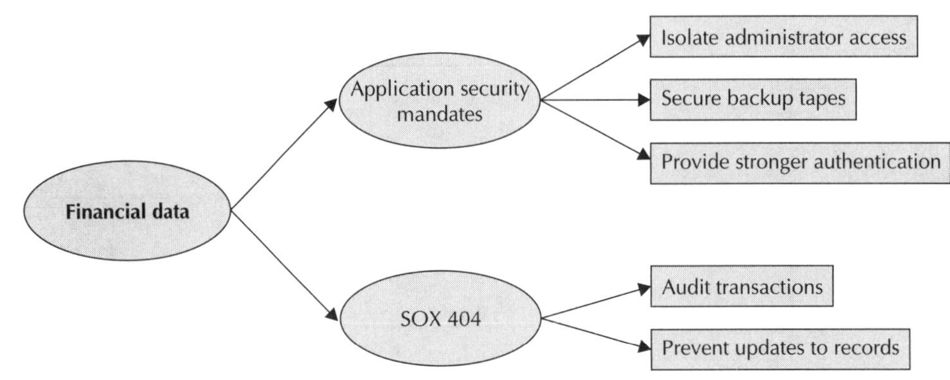

FIGURE 8-2 *Compliance and mandates discovery*

Even though these mini-frameworks are somewhat obvious and simple, they can be useful to an identity management discovery practitioner. They focus on breaking down complex legislative and other compliance mandates to simple requirements that can be mapped to the necessary identity management and security solutions. This is also true of any useful framework in this space. Many people cringe when they hear the word "framework" in any security project. However, over time, creating a framework has become a proven way to gain a better understanding of how solutions are developed and maintained over the long term.

Identity Management Patterns

After you have done a reasonable amount of discovery around the identity management requirements and the enterprise as-is state, you should be at a point at which you can start the "exploration" process for what the solution should look like, given the inputs from the phase discovery and the general experience of an architect in solving these kinds of problems.

To accelerate the process of finding the right solution, you may find it useful to refer to a set of architectural patterns that represent possible solutions for a type of problem (for example, user provisioning, web access control, and so on). The words "reference architectures" and "best practices" are often tossed around with these patterns. However, you should try to refrain from making any value judgments regarding these patterns, since one person's best practice can be another's worst. While reference architectures are useful to "reference," it's not very useful to follow them without understanding the consequences of their implementations. In this chapter, you will read about an approach of placing certain context with every architecture pattern and considering which circumstances are appropriate for keeping them around or replacing them with new ones. These patterns can also serve to provide the architect with a solution baseline that can be tailored to meet specific requirements.

Applying Patterns by Enterprise Maturity

One of the first tasks after the discovery exercise is to use the information gathered about enterprise security architecture to determine the maturity of the organization with regard to security and identity management. An identity management problem is always better solved when you know the limits of the current capabilities, since you can project how well, or if at all, the desired business objectives are going to be met with those existing capabilities and technology

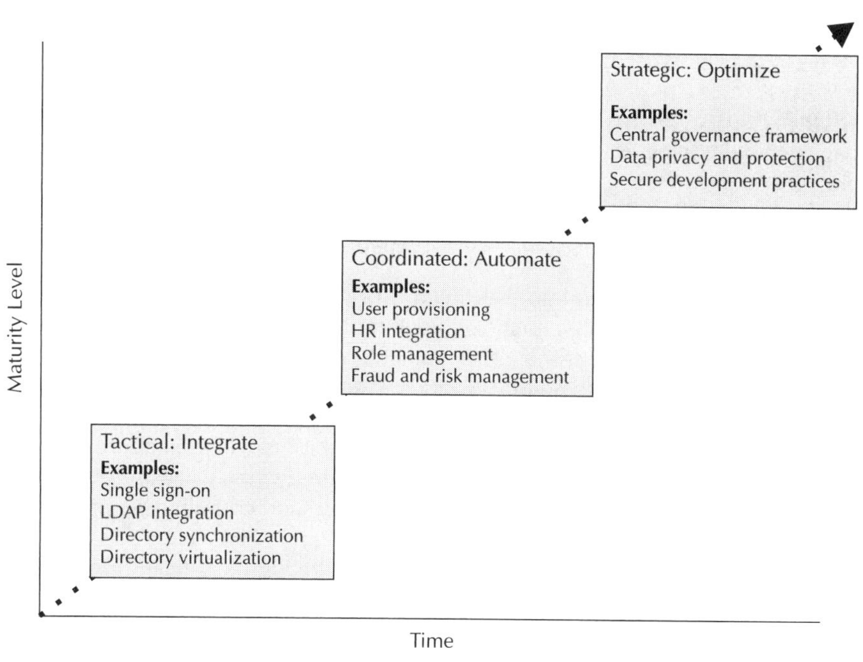

FIGURE 8-3 *Identity management maturity model framework*

investments. If the current capabilities are unable to meet the desired business and enterprise objectives, you can identify the gaps, in terms of the capabilities that need to be developed, and therefore focus your architecture efforts to address those areas.

One tool for illustrating those gaps at a high level is a maturity model framework, shown in Figure 8-3. The job of this maturity model is to categorize any security architecture into a known maturity level, which demonstrates where a particular architecture is in its evolution spectrum.

In each of the boxes shown in the figure, the heading represents the maturity level (tactical, coordinated, or strategic) followed by the main focus of the implementation work (Integration, Automation, or Optimization). The following describes each of the maturity levels and what could lead you to categorize any identity management architecture into any one of those boxes.

Tactical These are relatively simple solutions that focus on key technical pains for the security administrators in the organization. The focus of these solutions is the act of integrating security information and actions across multiple systems and applications. If you are a security architect or engineer facing challenges around integrating identity information among multiple systems or integrating authentication session across applications (for example, a web portal authentication scenario) or dealing with setting up role-based access control of your databases using LDAP servers, you are more of less at a tactical maturity level for your security architecture. Keep in mind that working through these types of pains that come at this level is a prerequisite to solving the problems posed in subsequent maturity levels. Once again, the simple litmus test for categorizing as tactical is in the answer of whether the architects are mainly solving data and system integration problems.

Coordinated This is the next evolutionary step after dealing with tactical security challenges such as identity information integration. In this maturity level, architects try to deliver higher value solutions to the enterprise by automating the processes around identity management. Business processes, such as employee on-boarding, and IT processes, such as password resets, are often convoluted and expensive manual processes that can be automated through the use of identity management technologies. This is the maturity level that most enterprises have been targeting for the past couple of years, and, therefore, the technologies and offerings have focused on these kinds of challenges as well. An enterprise should be categorized in the Coordinated maturity level if the architects are focused on process automation challenges around identities and access.

Strategic This is the final and most evolved category for any security architecture. At this level, the challenges no longer involve tactical integration or identity management automation. Those hurdles have been overcome, so, at this level, enterprises can focus on creating and optimizing governance policies/processes across all systems, applications, and organizations to align security with the operations of the enterprise. Enterprises that have arrived at the strategic maturity level typically have security embedded within their application development process so that any new capability or application service development is required to pass a phase where the applications are secured using standard enterprise-wide governance and compliance guidelines and policies.

Using Different Maturity Models This maturity model is just one approach to breaking down maturity levels. Many similar maturity models are available from many sources, but the model presented here demonstrates how it can be used to navigate successfully through a set of tactical solutions before attempting to solve strategic and enterprise-wide identity management issues. It is a good idea to start with a relatively narrow problem scope since you will inevitably learn key lessons during your tactical implementations that should affect your more strategic initiatives around identity management.

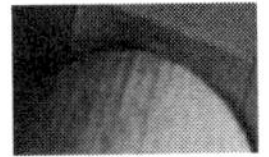

NOTE
The maturity model doesn't necessarily apply only at the enterprise level; it can apply to individual applications as well. For instance, different applications can be at different maturity levels within the same organization, perhaps due to different resources and priorities for security. So you may need to apply the maturity model individually to different applications to apply the appropriate solutions to each application.

Maturity levels can correlate to the kinds of architecture patterns in use. As Figure 8-4 illustrates, the architecture patterns also evolve as an enterprise moves through the maturity levels.

The early days of identity management focused mainly on *point-to-point* directory synchronizations and replications, which then evolved to a *hub-and-spoke* architecture for centralized user administration, and now this space is also heading and orienting itself around the notion of identity and security *services*. Each of these architecture styles is valid and appropriate with respect to the enterprise's current maturity with its security software infrastructure.

It is not a good idea to force an environment to adopt a solution architecture too advanced for the existing infrastructure; this can result in failed implementations. A lot of learning occurs during the process of moving through the different architectural models, such as point-to-point and hub-

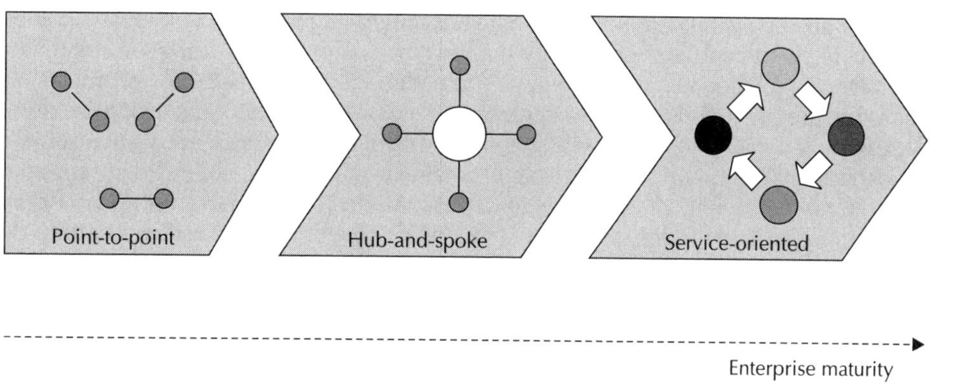

FIGURE 8-4 *Maturing though the patterns of architecture*

and-spoke patterns. At every phase of the architecture's maturity, you can observe the strengths and weaknesses of each architecture pattern and use them through the maturity process. For instance, an enterprise should not aim to build out a service-oriented security platform before solving some basic problems such as centralized user provisioning and directory management. As a rule of thumb, you should try to design an architecture that fits current capabilities rather than trying leapfrog to an advanced maturity level. An organic progression through maturity levels is less risky since it lets you identify the enterprise's strengths and weaknesses around identity management and therefore, tailor your solution to avoid possible pitfalls.

Now that you have a sense of architectural maturity, let's explore each architectural pattern that is typically involved in each of those maturity levels.

Point-to-Point Pattern

A point-to-point architecture is used to solve tactical needs of integration, such as keeping passwords in sync or managing roles and privileges across multiple directories. Basically, it is a solution for synchronizing identity information between application silos. An example of a point-to-point implementation is a directory replication. All major LDAP servers (Oracle, Active Directory, SunOne, and so on) have the notion of replication built into their core products, and we can spread out many instances of each directory over large geographies and still maintain a certain level of consistency of identity information.

Alternatively, you can have point-to-point integrations for synchronizing between heterogeneous applications and environments such as the Oracle and the Microsoft technology stacks. However, the fundamental solution is the same: synchronize user identity from one repository to another without necessarily changing how that user information is managed and administered in each of those systems.

The advantage of a point-to-point architecture is that it is a relatively simple solution to understand and implement. It also does not change the control of the information in any system, since the administrators of the different systems are still as powerful and as free to do as they wish with their data. However, the point-to-point model has significant limitations when the enterprise is looking to centralize management to a single point of control. Also, it adds complexity in terms of managing independent point-to-point integrations of identity and access information between applications. Therefore, if this style of integration starts to grow in an enterprise, the architecture should start to consider the next phase in its evolution, hub-and-spoke.

Hub-and-Spoke Pattern

The hub-and-spoke pattern looks similar to a standard Ethernet switch in today's computer networking landscape. A single device supports many connections using a standard networking interface to allow for all connected parties to communicate. Similarly, an identity management infrastructure, if properly configured, can act as that central hub for managing users and their access into all your enterprise-wide systems and applications. Once every application and system is connected into this hub, users are able to communicate with each other through this standardized and centralized identity management infrastructure. Keep in mind that not all connected applications carry the same weight and influence. Some of the applications connected to this identity management hub may be more influential and may drive the identity management processes in the other applications. For instance, the data from the human resources application (for example, PeopleSoft HCM or SAP HR) can drive the user provisioning policies and processes to the other connected applications (such as ERP systems and LDAP servers).

Identity management hub-and-spoke architecture requires a bit more design and planning than a pure point-to-point implementation, since you need to establish some enterprise-wide ground rules for identity. For instance, if all identities are going to be centralized into a single hub, an enterprise user naming convention must be implemented. While you can continue to use application-centric usernames, the enterprise naming conventions need to map to those local application usernames.

The benefit of this approach is centralization and therefore reduction of the cost and complexity of managing new and existing identities in the enterprise. It can provide some simple but powerful centralized solutions, such as password resets and new account services across all systems. This approach is critical for an enterprise looking for an audit compliance and governance solution. A centralized identity management hub can provide a single view and report on who has access to what systems. It can also provide workflow services so that all those accounts are regularly inspected and attested for continuing authorization, as mandated by laws such as Sarbanes-Oxley. Another key benefit of the hub-and-spoke model is that it allows for a much simpler integration model into heterogeneous packaged applications (for example, Oracle Applications, SAP, Windows Server products, and so on) if you are employing a solution such as Oracle Identity Manager (OIM) that ships with a library of standard prebuilt connectors. (Refer to Chapter 9 for more details on OIM's integration capabilities.)

While a majority of customers and enterprises today are spending most of their investments in ramping up to this hub-and-spoke architectural pattern for identity management, it does have certain limitations. The limitations are especially pronounced when we try to integrate custom-developed applications or services that are being developed inside the enterprise. While it is possible for a custom application to integrate into the centralized hub to leverage existing identity management services (for example, new user provisioning, runtime authorization decisions, runtime auditing, and so on), this is usually a development and maintenance nightmare. Due to the lack of standards around the identity services, it is almost always a one-off integration that cannot be reused and extended over time. The benefit of a centralized Identity management service infrastructure is quickly drowned out by the pains of writing that custom integration code and maintaining it over the lifespan of the application. Such integration limitations in the hub-and-spoke model has given birth to a new generation of architecting security called *service-oriented security (SOS)*, also referred to as *security-as-a-service.*

Service-Oriented Security Pattern

To address the cost and complexity of making changes to existing applications or building security for new applications, many leading-edge enterprises are shifting to the next evolution, SOS. The following is the official Oracle definition of SOS (www.oracle.com/us/corporate/press/015428_EN): Service-Oriented Security decouples hard-coded security features from enterprise applications to create reusable, standards-based security services and protocols which any application can consume. SOS enables organizations to simplify and centralize several critical security processes including authentication, authorization, user administration, role management, identity virtualization and governance, and entitlement management, as well as audit and control.

SOS is a not necessarily an architecture by itself, but a pattern of architectures that advocate the use of standardized services using industry-defined interfaces that provide a complete set of identity management and security capabilities for both home-grown and off-the-shelf applications. SOS relies on standards around Identity management, such as Extensible Access Control Markup Language (XACML), Lightweight Directory Access Protocol (LDAP), and Service Provisioning Markup Language (SPML), which are standardized interfaces for basic security functions such as authorizations, identity data access and provisioning. Another key benefit of SOS-based applications is that they can leverage standards such as XACML to provide much stronger access control with much deeper integrations with the information application.

Application developers are able to leverage and reuse standard security services such as authentication, authorization, user provisioning, role management, identity federation, and auditing. This can be done much more efficiently and without the necessity of knowing the specific implementation details of the security services. The developer of a new application, in a non-SOS environment, will need to write complex and often hard-coded policies dealing with authorization of data inside their applications. With SOS, instead of writing all those policies inside the application, the developer can refer to an externalized service that abstracts and encapsulates all the details of the security policies that are created and maintained by people who better understand that domain (for example the line of business that application will serve). This model is much more efficient since it breaks up the new application development effort and allows people to focus on their core competencies. Also, it is very beneficial in terms of managing changes to security policies or the application itself, since either type of change can occur much more seamlessly.

Under a SOS pattern, you can define standard business access policies that can be reused across any application that needs to enforce those decisions. For instance, you can centrally define an "Exec Management Access" policy in your authorization server that allows access to anyone with a "Vice President" title and above to access certain reports in your financial application. However, if tomorrow you need to lock everyone except the CFO out of that policy, you could make that simple policy change underneath the "Exec Management Access" policy by removing all roles except CFO. This approach does not require any changes to the applications enforcing that decision, since applications rely on the SOS-based authorization service to make the decision.

SOS brings a new way of managing and enforcing identity management policies to the enterprise. However, you should not try to jump to this new style for the sake of being on the cutting-edge. Instead, the progression to SOS should be a natural requirements-driven process that adapts existing infrastructure to working in that new model. SOS, by definition, is a way to reuse existing investments in infrastructure and policies, so ripping and replacing current working components to adopt SOS will fundamentally miss the point of SOS.

Oracle Identity Management Solutions

So far in this chapter, we have discussed identity management architecture from the point of view of problem discovery, environment assessment, and possible architectural patterns. In this section, we will start mapping those problems to solutions available by using Oracle products.

Figure 8-5 represents the typical identity management solutions that you will need to solve the problems discussed so far.

User Provisioning

A user provisioning solution allows you to manage a user's account and access privileges across many enterprise applications from a centralized management engine. The Oracle solution for user provisioning is built using a centralized hub-and-spoke architecture. You can create and manage identities in a single logical place and via an integration solution, corresponding accounts can be created in the appropriate applications that enforce access. The key component in the Oracle solution is the Oracle Identity Manager (OIM), Java-based product with a centralized identity hub and an integration framework that connects that hub to all the applications and systems in which user accounts are to be created. Figure 8-6 illustrates the architecture for an Oracle Identity Manager in a typical enterprise-wide deployment.

As you can see, OIM is typically a centralized hub used for managing and provisioning those identities to all the enterprise systems. However, OIM is not necessarily the "source of truth" and can be driven by an authoritative source, such as an HR application, to provide key events and information about the identity. Once OIM receives such a trigger event, it can then execute provisioning processes to create accounts and privileges in downstream applications based on the access policies predefined in OIM. Just as it can trigger new account creations, it can also trigger changes and revocations of existing accounts if the original event signaled this. You can turn OIM into a central governor of accounts across all applications in the enterprise so that simple business events can have cascading effects on those accounts as appropriate. This style of centralized provisioning can eliminate all the redundant work that would otherwise occur in each individual application.

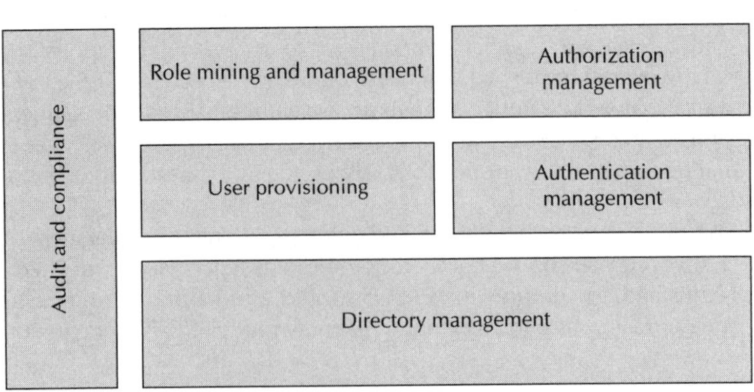

FIGURE 8-5 *Identity management solutions*

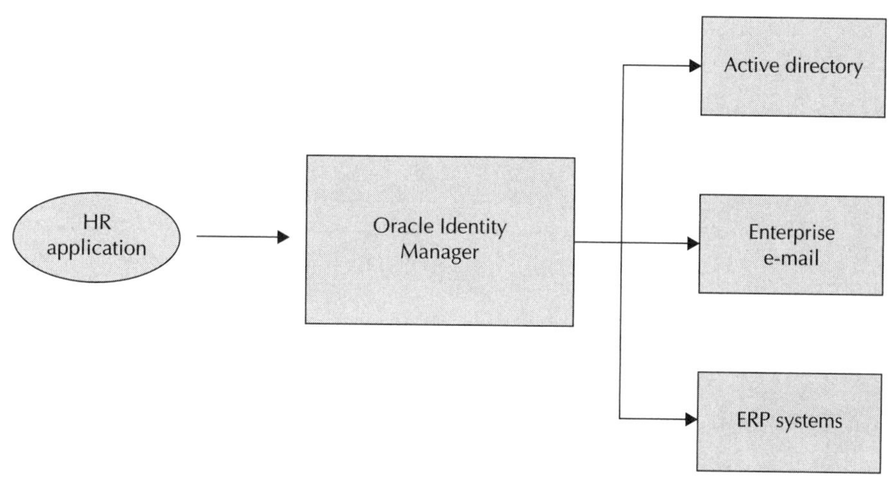

FIGURE 8-6 *OIM user provisioning*

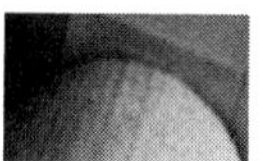

NOTE
Chapter 9 provides much more detail about developing user provisioning solutions using Oracle Identity Manager

Directory Management

A directory management solution offers the enterprise a central, scalable, and efficient user repository, mainly for applications and clients needing to access identity-related data. This solution is one of the basic pillars on which identity management solutions rely for quick and reliable access to identity-related data.

The following are the key capabilities of a directory management solution:

- An LDAP-based directory service offering a fast access to identity information
- A reliable and scalable storage of organized identity data
- A directory integration mechanism that presents data from multiple backend sources

Oracle Directory Management offers all these capabilities, but it packages them according to two styles of directory integration capabilities: meta-directory versus virtualization.

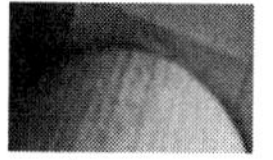

NOTE
Directory virtualization refers to an approach in which identity and access information is integrated at runtime from multiple backend sources and presented as a single record. Virtualization follows a composite service design pattern for identity data.

Oracle offers synchronization (also described as a "meta-directory") functionality within Oracle Internet Directory product to synchronize between OID and other third-party directories so that the information is constantly kept synchronized between multiple LDAP servers. Oracle

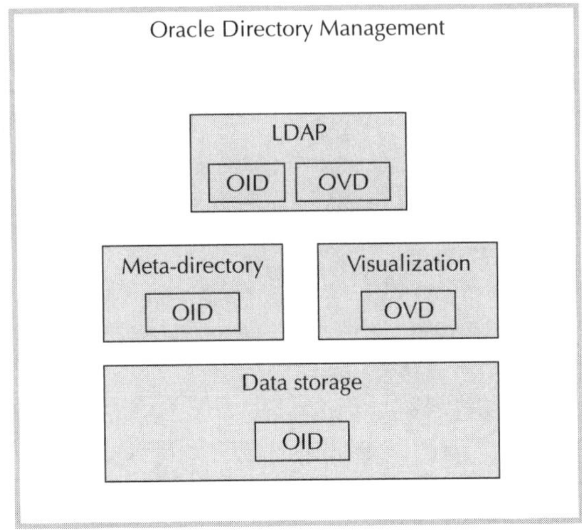

FIGURE 8-7 *Oracle Directory Management*

offers the virtualization within Oracle Virtual Directory (OVD). OVD offers any LDAP clients the ability to query a single LDAP proxy to query many physical LDAP and non-LDAP identity repositories. The technique of directory virtualization is being rapidly adopted over synchronization and meta-directory techniques, since it does not require information to be physically synchronized between servers and so results in a cheaper and faster approach to identity data integration. Oracle Directory Management architecture is shown in Figure 8-7.

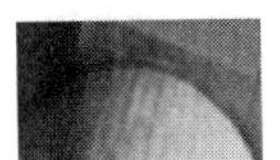

NOTE
Chapter 9 discusses the Oracle Directory Management story in more detail and shows how you can apply OID and OVD together and independently to solve the basic challenges of creating a central logical location for accessing identity information related to any user in your enterprise.

Authentication Management

Authentication management is a category of solutions for identifying and verifying a user's identity. The tactics for the identification process can vary widely, but they always focus on proving that a user is who he or she claims to be. Authentication management does not try to solve the issue of verifying authorizations, which is a separate category altogether. The following types of solutions are included in this category:

- **Single sign-on (SSO)** The ability to reuse an authenticated session in more than one application.
- **Enterprise single sign-on (ESSO)** The ability to integrate an operating system-level authentication or a thick desktop client's authentication with that of your web SSO.

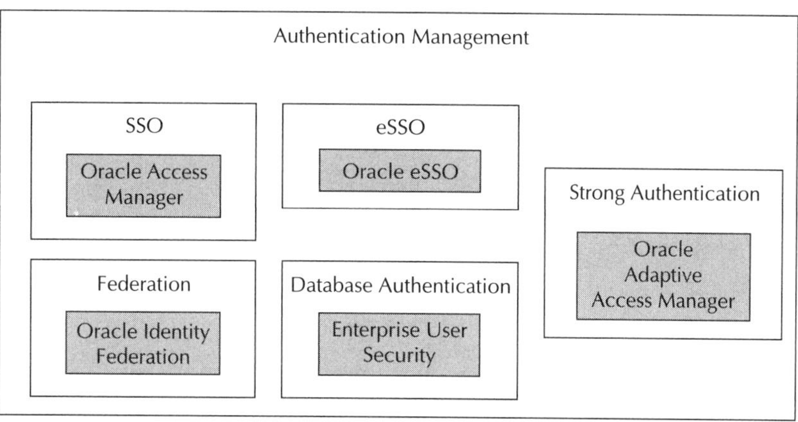

FIGURE 8-8 *Authentication Management*

- **Strong authentication and fraud prevention** The ability to provide stronger levels of authentication and risk analytics to prevent identity fraud.
- **Federation** The ability to integrate web authentication across partnered enterprises.
- **Database authentication** Centralizes the authentications for database repositories to a central user repository (for example, LDAP).

The Oracle Access Management suite offers all these solution both as independent solutions and as an integrated bundle. Figure 8-8 shows the products that support each of these solutions.

Authentication management solutions are part of any access management architecture in which a specific need exists to integrate authentication between one or more applications or technology platforms. For each of these solutions, a server component manages and evaluates the authentication policies and an enforcement agent component is embedded within the application. The specific server and agent architectures are described in the specific authentication solutions that follow.

SSO Using Oracle Access Manager

Since OAM is mainly a web application authentication solution, its components are all designed to protect applications in a typical web/HTTP environment. As illustrated in Figure 8-9, Oracle Access Manager (OAM) has three key components:

- **Policy Manager** The user interface for creating and managing SSO policies for the web applications that need to be protected.
- **Access Server** The component that accepts requests from the enforcement points for access control decisions (for example, password validations) and returns an allow/deny response to the enforcement point.
- **Access Gate** The enforcement component that is embedded in the application, typically as a web server filter where the end user application is deployed.

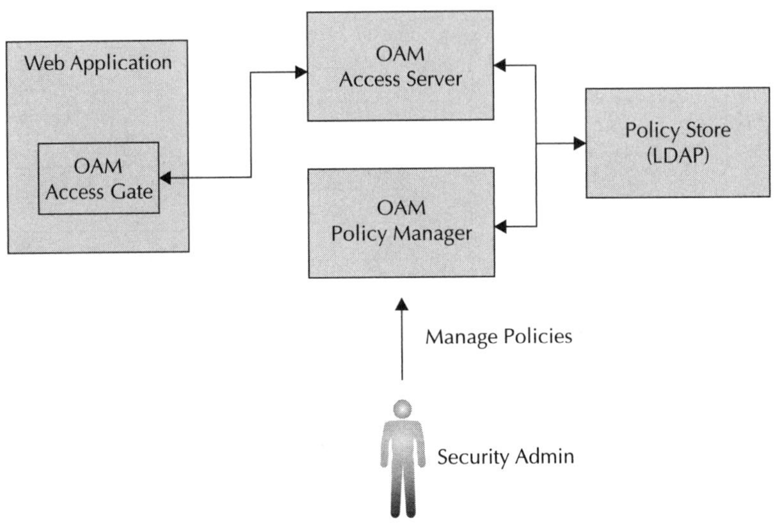

FIGURE 8-9 *OAM Architecture*

Keep in mind that the backend policy store (LDAP) can be a physical LDAP server (for example, OID or Active Directory) or a virtual LDAP directory (for example, Oracle Virtual Directory).

Enterprise SSO Solution Using Oracle eSSO

Enterprise SSO (eSSO), shown in Figure 8-10, is an integration solution between an operating system or a thick client platform, so its components are designed to sit between the desktop and the application. The Oracle eSSO architecture has a component called the Logon Manager which sits on the user's desktop to integrate the OS authentication (such as Windows Domain Authentication) with other desktop client applications or web SSO components such as OAM. Similar to OAM, it provides a management console for administrators to manage the eSSO policies.

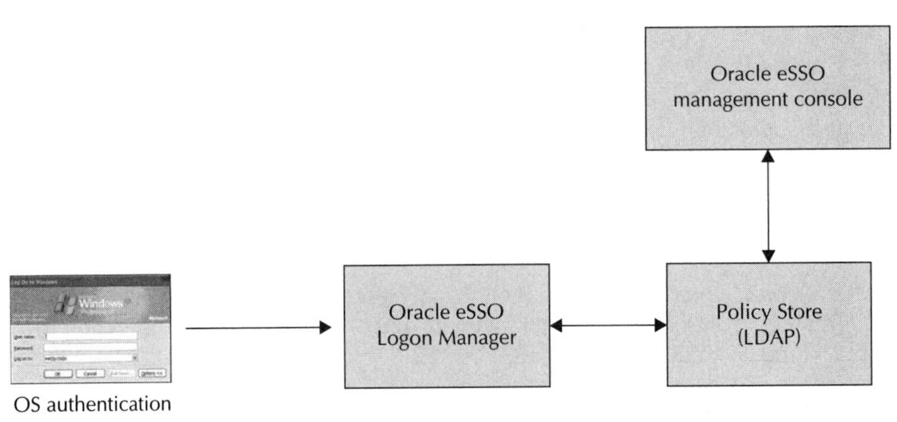

FIGURE 8-10 *Oracle eSSO Architecture*

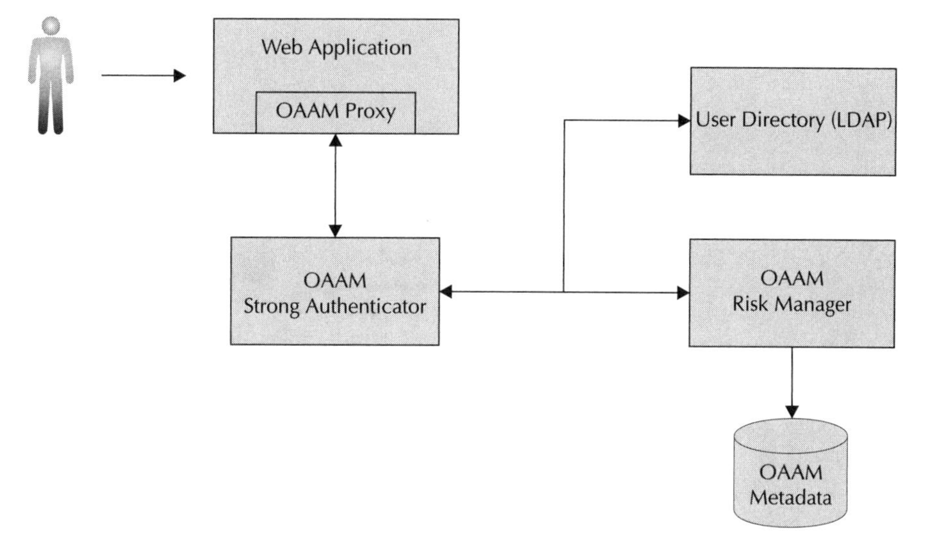

FIGURE 8-11 *OAAM architecture*

Strong Authentication and Fraud Prevention Using Oracle Adaptive Access Manager

To enforce fraud and risk management, an application must be able to detect irregular access behaviors in an application and prevent potential frauds or risky scenarios. This kind of fraud detection is accomplished through intelligent metrics to score for a possible fraud candidate. The Oracle Adaptive Access Manager (OAAM) provides this solution along with strong authentication capabilities.

The combination of strong authentication and fraud/risk management makes OAAM a powerful tool for highly sensitive web applications that have a high degree of exposure to attacks. For instance, OAAM is used by applications that sit on the public Internet and may be exposed to attacks from across the globe. For example, an online banking application can use OAAM and its risk monitoring capabilities to detect irregular and user behaviors and possibly prevent fraudulent transactions from occurring. Figure 8-11 illustrates the OAAM architecture.

Federated Authentication Process Using Oracle Identity Federation

A federation solution focuses on authentication, and in many cases authorization, of information transactions across enterprise boundaries. Figure 8-12 illustrates a sample federation request architecture in which a federation partner in domain A is trying to access information in a web application in domain B through a federated authentication process using Oracle Identity Federation (OIF).

In this scenario, a requestor of information acts as the identity provider (IdP), and a server of information acts as the service provider (SP). The OIF IdP leverages federation standards, such as Security Assertion Markup Language (SAML) and Liberty, to propagate a user's identity to the partner's domain where the OIF SP accepts that request and evaluates the access request to the web application using a local set of federation and access policies. If the requester is a valid user, it allows the access to the federated web application and keeps the HTTP session alive as long as the federation token (for example, SAML token) is valid.

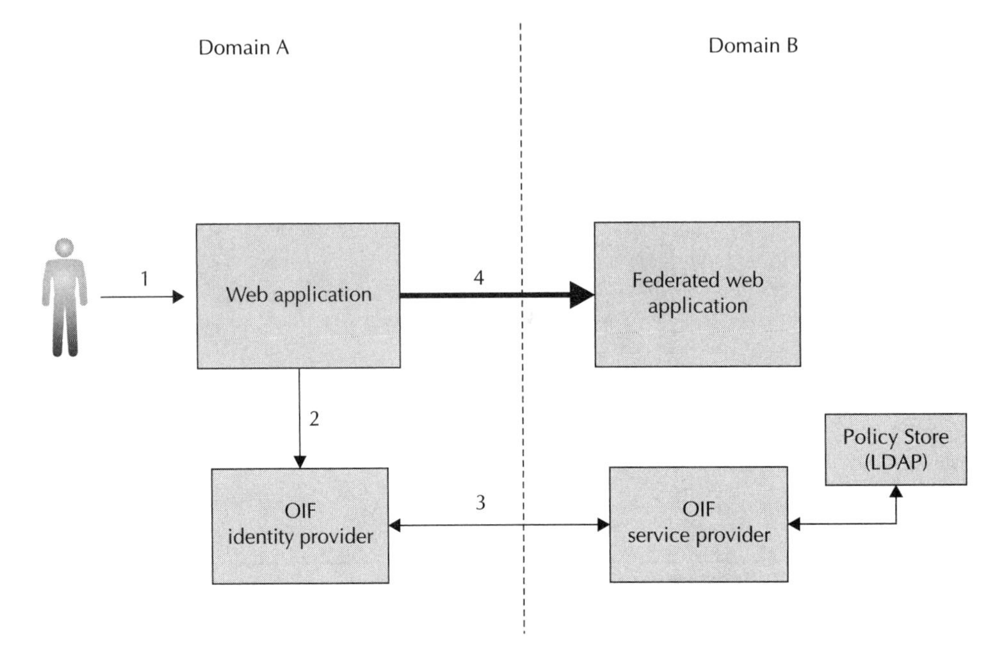

FIGURE 8-12 *Federation architecture*

Centralized Database Authentication Using Oracle Enterprise User Security

Oracle Enterprise User Security (EUS) is a solution offered as part of the Oracle Database (since version 9*i*) that uses an externalized LDAP server, such as Oracle Internet Directory, to externalize database user authentications. In addition to centralizing the authentication to the database, you can also centralize the authorizations for the authenticated sessions by mapping database roles and privileges to centralized LDAP groups. Figure 8-13 shows typical solution when the architecture needs to support end user authentication into the database tier, perhaps for additional access control using database roles/privileges or performing end user auditing on the database objects (tables, views, and so on).

The Oracle products that enable this solution are the LDAP products (OID or OVD) and the EUS feature in the Oracle Database Server. The choice of LDAP product is yours based on your requirements. For instance, if you already have a physical LDAP server, you would simply layer the OVD product on top of the existing repository to make EUS work for your Oracle Database authentications.

Authorization Management

Managing and enforcing proper authorizations in an application are two of the most difficult and growing challenges in identity management. The topic of authorization management could fill an entire book for a comprehensive understanding of the solution. In this section, we will discuss a summary of this class of solution and the basic overview of how Oracle is approaching this space.

As shown in Figure 8-14, two kinds of authorization management solutions exist: *web access management* and *entitlement management*.

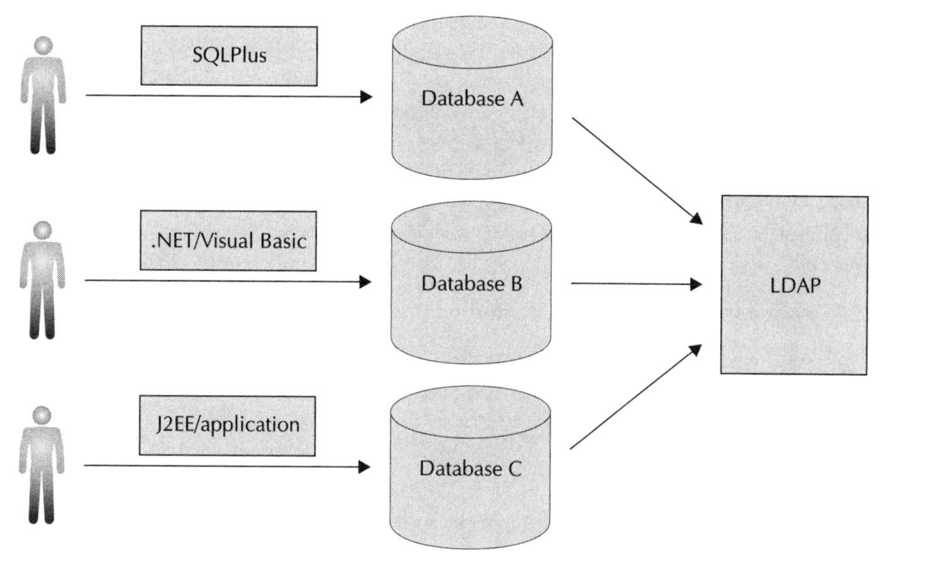

FIGURE 8-13 *Centralized database authentication*

Web access management is a solution to perform authorization checks on resources with a particular URI pattern (for example, xxxx/xxx/xx/pattern.*). This type of authorization is considered coarse-grained and works on web applications that are neatly partitioned using unique URLs, which are then mapped toward roles and privileges in the LDAP server. This solution is useful for protecting application access at high levels, where the policies are adjacent to SSO policies. The Oracle product that allows such coarse-grained authorizations is the same product that provides SSO functionality to web applications: Oracle Access Manager.

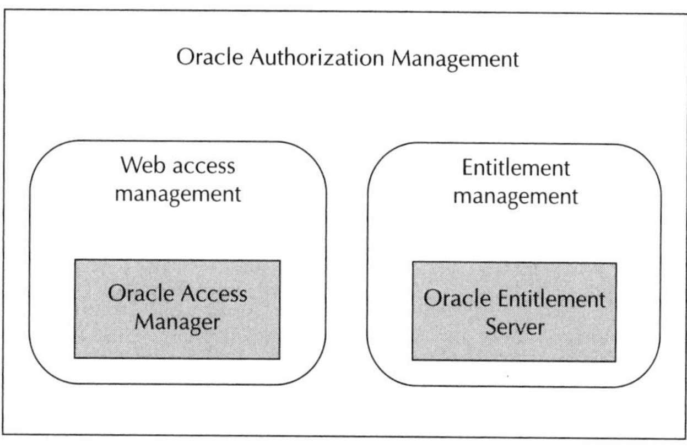

FIGURE 8-14 *Oracle authorization management*

The second kind of authorization management, entitlement management, provides the ability to authorize resources of any kind inside an application. The objects can vary from HTML pages, to Java objects, to Java 2 Platform Enterprise Edition (J2EE) beans, to data records, to user interfaces in middleware applications. This solution provides a much more flexible and sophisticated authorization framework for access control. The Oracle Entitlement Server (OES) provides this kind of fine-grained entitlement (authorization) management solution.

Oracle Entitlement Server Architecture

OES is a Java-based authorization framework that can integrate with Java and non-Java applications. The OES infrastructure comprises five essential components:

- **Policy store** A database holding all the entitlement and authorization policies.
- **Policy administration point (PAP)** The user interface where administrators can define policies around authorizations to resources.
- **Policy information point (PIP)** A provider of policy data to the decision and enforcement points.
- **Policy decision point (PDP)** A policy evaluation engine that decides whether to grant or deny access to a user based on the information it is provided.
- **Policy enforcement point (PEP)** The location where the user is either granted or denied access in the application.

As the architecture shown in Figure 8-15 demonstrates, an application can integrate into the OES authorization decision-making framework in two ways. First, an application can choose to make a direct call from application to the OES PDP for a grant/deny decision for a certain user trying to execute a certain action on a specific resource. This approach requires an out-of-process call every time a protected resource is accessed and therefore can cause application performance degradation. Alternatively, OES offers an embedded policy decision point option for certain types of applications (for example, WebLogic servers, Oracle databases, Microsoft SharePoint servers, and so on) where components known as security modules can embed themselves as part of the application platform and make fast decisions without leaving the boundaries of the application's policy enforcement point. Installing a security module for your application relieves you of the responsibility of knowing how your application communicates with the OES components.

OES is also changing the fundamental shape of access architectures by allowing for the separation of enforcement points from decision points. This separation allows any future application to reuse a huge repository of existing business and information privacy policies and therefore significantly lowers the time and cost of application development. And maintenance is easier since making changes to policies no longer require application code changes.

A Developer's View of OES

Fine-grained access management is definitely on the rise in today's application development space since building this kind of policy enforcement mechanisms into the foundation of any application makes it much more flexible and adaptive to changing enforcement policies. For example, in today's non-OES world, application developers are hard coding statements like this:

```
if (user.memberOf("Manager") {
      changeSalary("..");
}
```

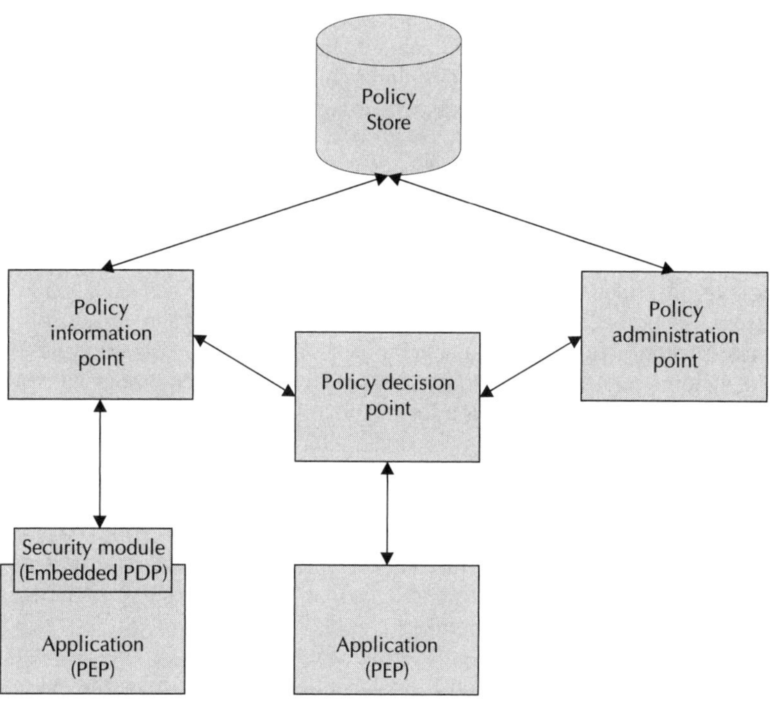

FIGURE 8-15 *OES component architecture*

This is a classic example of embedding an access control decision inside the application. Instead, the method call could have been protected using the following code:

```
if (isAccessAllowed( user, policyId, action )
{
      changeSalary("..");
}
```

The benefit of the second approach is that tomorrow you could make changes to your policy of granting Manager access to calling the **changeSalary()** method. Perhaps you may want to add the Executive role to be able to access that method as well. Using an OES approach, you can offload the actual policies inside OES policies, which can be changed without affecting the application. The only responsibility of the application will be to know the policy identifier to the appropriate policy it wants to enforce. Also, as XACML is being adopted, you can start using declarative policy using the XACML constructs to make requests to the OES server.

Role Mining and Management

Role mining is the ability to introspect and inventory all roles that exist in applications in the enterprise. Once the roles have been mined, they can then be processed, analyzed, and consolidate into a single set of logical business roles that are mapped to enterprise access policies that define the access to different applications based on their business roles.

Role management is another fast-growing space in identity management, since more enterprises are looking to automate identity provisioning policies–based functional business roles that represent their day-to-day responsibilities. The Oracle role management solution is delivered by the Oracle Role Manager (ORM), which is an end-to-end mining, analytics, and management product for all roles across the enterprise. ORM leverages a strong integration with the user provisioning solution (OIM) to execute the provisioning of accounts and roles in different systems based on policies defined within ORM. The functional architecture for ORM is shown in Figure 8-16.

As Figure 8-16 illustrates, ORM is the central rule and policy engine for deciding who belongs to what business roles, which then trigger access provisioning rules in OIM to execute the provisioning processes. From a pure technical perspective, ORM is a type of rules engine that focuses and optimizes business rules around enterprise and technical roles. It can store "static" roles that use a membership list approach to manage assignments to roles. ORM can also use attributes and other identity information to dynamically assign business and technical roles to users. The second approach is more popular since it requires less administrative work to manage role assignments.

Role mining and management is a logical next step after implementing a user provisioning solution for an identity management architecture that is intended to automate processes and reduce risk of noncompliance with governance policies. ORM does allow exceptions and exception handling, which are mechanisms that override the central rules in case of temporary escalations or allowable one-off cases. For example, an exception could be granting administrative privileges to an external contractor, hired to perform critical repair work on a server. However, the number of exceptions should not grow so large that it starts looking like a new rule—in which case, you should probably create a new rule.

In general, ORM projects are data intensive and should be properly planned up front to determine the scope of the implementation. It is unwise to try to mine the entire enterprise for role information at the first phase of the implementation. Instead, taking a more targeted approach, such as mining one application at a time, makes more sense and makes designing the business roles/hierarchies easier to handle. It is reasonable to expect an imperfect role management design

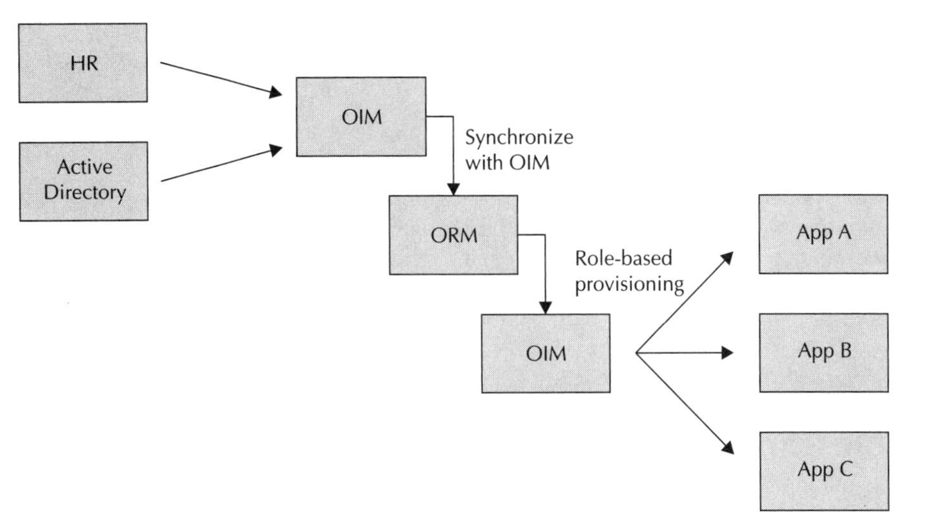

FIGURE 8-16 *ORM functional architecture*

on the first pass of the project, since the ORM architecture factors ongoing changes to design without impacting the applications in a negative manner. As you extend your role management solution to support new applications and new enterprise domains, you will inevitably and continuously refine your roles and hierarchies in ORM.

Summary

One of the main reasons this chapter was written was to emphasize the importance of understanding identity management from the perspective of the problem. As mentioned in the introduction, you may be tempted to jump right into building the solution without fully understanding the consequences of that solution path. Unfortunately, when it comes to identity management problems, the challenge lies not in figuring out a solution to the problem but in deciding which solution to use. As engineers, we can always fit and configure products and technologies to solve short-term and immediate problems. However, this chapter encourages you to put on your architect hats before you start implementing specific solutions, such as User Provisioning or Directory Management, to ensure that your implementation design solves not just your immediate needs, but aligns with a longer term view of managing identities and enforcing application security.

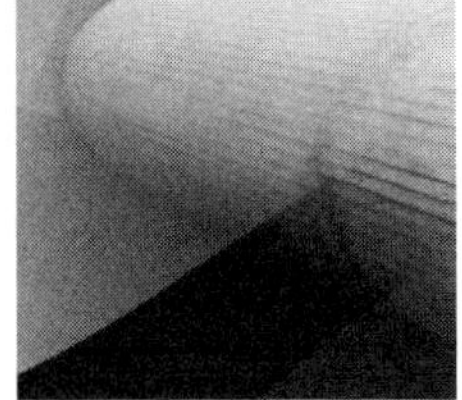

CHAPTER 9

Oracle Identity Manager

This chapter covers Oracle Identity Manager (OIM), which is central to Oracle's identity management strategy. OIM provides a platform for designing provisioning processes for user and access information to solve the challenge of getting the right accounts and privileges automatically set up for users across all applications they need to access. Configuration of such provisioning automation can be done in many ways; we'll show you some examples and best practice implementations of user provisioning. This chapter does not intend to cover the full set of OIM features and functionalities, and instead it highlights those that are used most frequently in solving provisioning problems.

The User Provisioning Challenge

When a new employee joins a company, she needs an office, a computer, office supplies, an e-mail address, access to business applications, and so forth. This process goes by many names—such as on-boarding or hire-to-retire. User provisioning is a subprocess initiated by the on-boarding or hire-to-retire process that deals specifically with giving users access to resources.

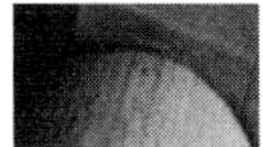

NOTE

"Resource" is a general term that can represent anything from a physical asset (such as computers, phones, offices, cubicles, printers, and so on) to logical assets (such as e-mail, payroll system, expense accounts, and so on). In the context of logical user provisioning, resources typically represent applications, databases, and other systems where accounts and privileges are set up for each user.

User provisioning has become a critical problem for most enterprises looking to lower their administrative burdens of account management while also trying to reduce risk by centralizing the control for granting access to important applications. Instead, with a user provisioning solution, new account creation tasks can execute in a consistent manner, whereby certain approvals and verifications are mandated before access is provided to new users.

The other critical user provisioning challenge is a technical one—system integration. A typical enterprise has a wide-ranging set of applications built on different technologies, standards, and semantics and therefore centralizing the account creation process is often an integration nightmare.

With these three drivers in mind—simpler administration, reduced risk, and easier integration—OIM was added into the Oracle Identity Management product suite with the acquisition of Thor Technologies, a smaller and best-of-breed user provisioning product. Since the acquisition, major development and improvements have been made on the product, but the basic framework and approach of user provisioning is still meant to be one that aligns with the three drivers.

Oracle Identity Manager Overview

OIM is a fundamental building block for an overall identity management solution. Access management, role management, directory services, and entitlement management all depend on having a working user provisioning solution that ensures the right identity data exists in the right location for other solutions to use. And with so many different types of policies, processes, and integrations involved in a typical provisioning problem, the provisioning technology needs to support a high level of flexibility and customization. However, with added flexibility comes complexity, so OIM tries to achieve a balance between supporting customization of provisioning without making the implementation process too difficult.

The OIM product framework is architected in a way that allows the developer to choose the level of complexity to work with. Usually, a higher need for customization introduces higher levels of sophistication in configuration. For example, OIM provides many out-of-the-box standard integration solutions to connect into (in the form of packaged connectors and adapters) that provide basic solutions for OIM to provision into a particular system (such as Active Directory). However, additional requirements, such as approval workflows or custom attributes around provisioning, require that the developer customize the baseline connector to support those requirements. You will learn how to implement many of these requirements using OIM in this chapter.

Overall, OIM remains a sophisticated piece of technology that needs to be well understood before implementation. A good place to start learning about OIM is with some key concepts inside the OIM policy framework for managing user provisioning.

User

As described throughout this book, security entails understanding *who gets access to what* in any context. In OIM, a *user* represents that "who" in context of enterprise user provisioning. An OIM user is application-agnostic and, as such, can be provisioned to accommodate different applications using application-centric representations and data models. An OIM user defines a specific default data model with certain standard identity attributes, such as First Name, Last Name, Employee Type, Title, Organization, and so on, that can be extended as needed. The data model defines the fundamental enterprise-level identity data that drives the user's accounts and privileges in each resource.

User Group

In many applications, users are grouped together based on common functions, organization, job level, and so forth. OIM provides the *user group* object as a mechanism to support organizing users into simple compartments according to certain rules and policies.

A user can be associated to a group in two ways: via direct membership assignments or rule-driven memberships. Direct assignments are the intuitive mechanism with which most people are familiar. Membership is simple, straightforward, intuitive, and easy to understand and validate. Direct assignments are performed in a discretionary manner by another privileged user (such as administrators, managers, and so on), and the memberships are maintained in a static way (memberships are also revoked in a discretionary way). Direct assignment is therefore not a popular approach for certain applications and groupings.

Instead of static group memberships, you can use the notion of *membership rules* to manage group memberships in a more automated manner. Membership rules are simple conditional statements that are evaluated against each user to determine whether or not the user belongs to a group. Figure 9-1 shows a membership rule, "location == San Francisco." This is an example of automating group memberships based a "location" attribute value.

This rule defines its members as users who have a job title of DBA and who work in the San Francisco area. User groups using membership rules are more dynamic in nature and provide significant flexibility for managing *who* belongs to *which* groups and therefore should be granted *what* resources. This mapping is performed inside an access policy (discussed a bit later).

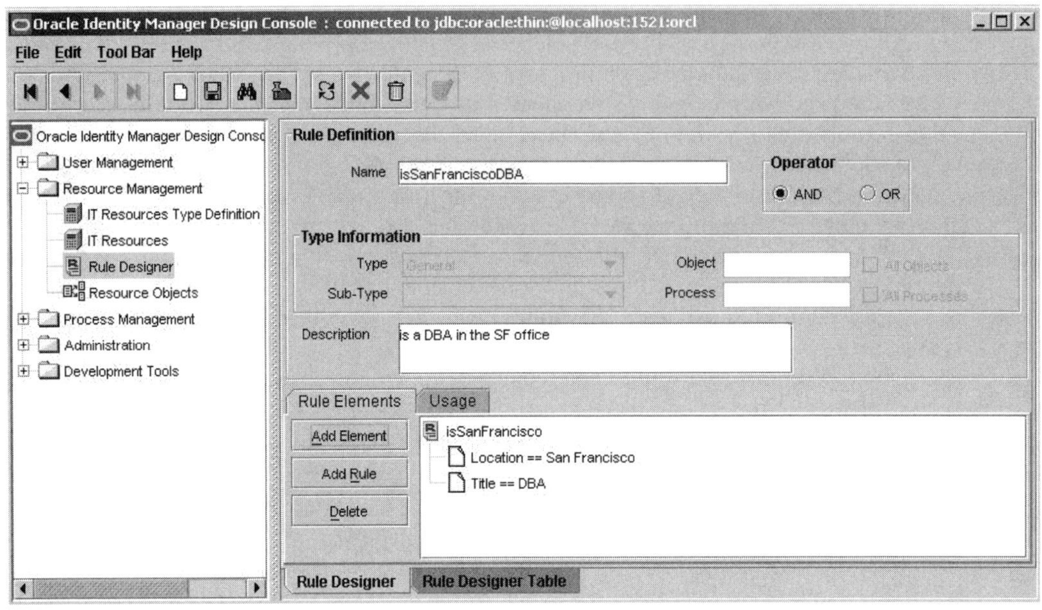

FIGURE 9-1 *Configuring membership rules for user groups*

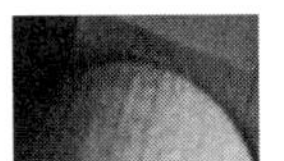

NOTE
User attributes change from time to time and likewise change their group memberships. This removes the task that administrators generally have to perform when making static group assignments.

OIM also offers the organization object to also group users. However, the two objects are meant to organize users with different purposes that are complementary. Typically, user groups partition users based on user attributes that are cross-functional and could exist across the enterprise in any organization or department.

Organization

An OIM *organization* is meant to represent a business function or regional department, such as Sales, Product Development, North America Business Unit, and so on. OIM organization objects can be nested and therefore represent real-world organizational hierarchies.

There are three types of OIM organizations: company, department, and branch. Here is how each type maps common real-world organizational models:

- *Company* objects represent autonomous business units that own multiple business functions typical in any firm (such as Sales, Marketing, Finance, IT, and so on).
- *Departments* exist underneath company objects to represent business functions (such as Sales, Finance, and so on).
- *Branches* exist underneath departments to provide additional groupings of users, typically by geography.

It is not always necessary to divide and model your organizations exactly the way your firm or enterprise is organized, since you may not always need that level of detail. Also, keep in mind that a real-world organizational model can change frequently, so you may not always want to align fully to those models if your provisioning and access policies do not depend on the user's organizational associations.

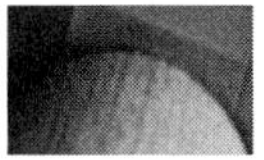

TIP
An organization is different from a user group because a user can have at most one organization, but it can have multiple user group associations at the same time. So if you want to model a matrix organization in which a user belongs to more than one functional department, you can use a user group object to model those relationships instead of the organization objects.

Access Policy

An *access policy* is a way in OIM to map who should have access to what resource. The overall mapping from the user to the resource can be made up of mappings from the user to user groups and from user groups to resources. Figure 9-2 shows an instance of an access policy that can be automated to provision end users to the appropriate resources based on the rules and mappings that are represented by the arrows from each object.

In addition to controlling the resource, you can also control each user's privileges within each resource by associating application-level privileges to user groups in the access policy. For example, suppose two user groups, "Data Analyst" and "Data Administrator," should both be provisioned to access the same database application but with different database roles (such as analyst and DBA). You can set that mapping of user group to database roles inside an access policy.

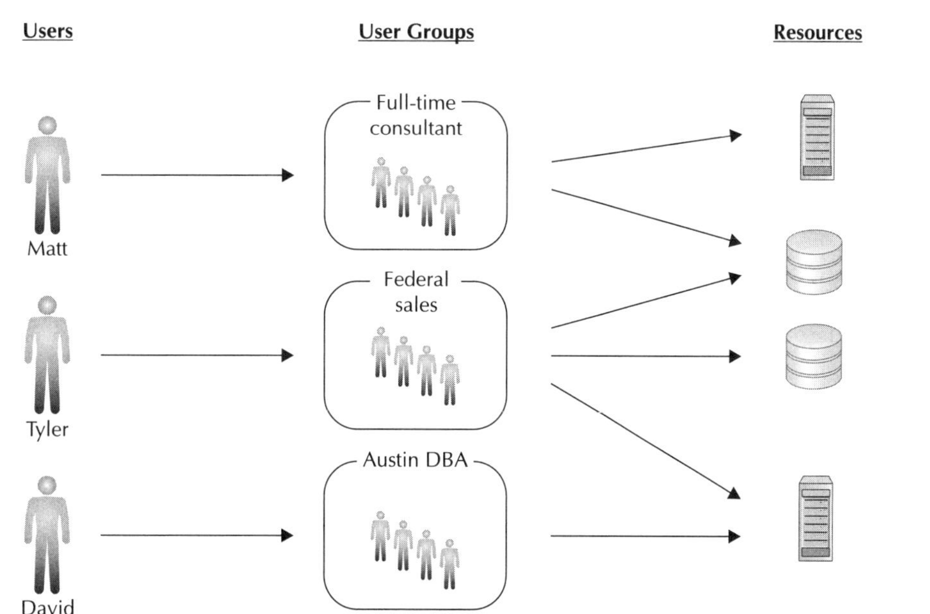

FIGURE 9-2 *Access policies define the mappings for users to groups and groups to resources.*

Resource Object

A *resource object* is an OIM object representing a logical resource for which users need to have accounts created. For instance, you can have OIM resource objects called "e-mail Server" and "Customer Database." A resource object can represent almost anything, from applications, databases, and operating systems, to physical assets and any other entity relevant to provisioning.

A resource object is used to track which users are provisioned to what logical assets. It can report on the current list of users who are provisioned to the E-mail Server resource in our example. Resource objects are also used to design approval workflows and policies around those workflows that are application-centric. So, for example, if a specific person is assigned to approve all new accounts to the e-mail Server system, you can use the resource object to set that condition in your workflow rule.

OIM resource objects do not represent the physical resources themselves and therefore do not contain physical details (such as IP addresses, server hostnames, and so on). For physical server representations and details, OIM provides the concept called IT resources.

IT Resource

An *IT resource* is a physical representation of a logical resource object. It holds all the physical details of the resource for which a new user is provisioned. If, for example, you have a resource object called Customer Database, you need to also define one or more corresponding IT resource objects that represent the physical characteristics of the resource (such as server hostnames, IP addresses, physical locations, and so on). This information is used by the OIM integration engine when it needs to communicate with those servers to complete a provisioning-related task.

The specific set of attributes of an IT resource is highly dependent on the type of system on which the account is being created (relational database IT Resources expect schema names and passwords; LDAP servers IT Resources expect names places and directory information tree details). OIM allows you to define an IT resource type that acts as a template to define a specific data model for certain types of IT resources.

User Provisioning Processes

A user provisioning process looks similar to any other business process. It represents a logical flow of events that deal with creating accounts within enterprise resources to make a new user productive.

Every provisioning process uses some fundamental building blocks, and the following sections provide different levels of sophistication in user provisioning. Your choice of sophistication level should, obviously, depend on the requirement and sensitivity of the particular resource. The level of complexity of a provisioning process is typically related to the level of risk associated with the resource being provisioned for access. For systems or databases holding critically sensitive data, provisioning should enforce a stronger verification process, such as requiring certain user attributes (such as job code or seniority) and management approvals before the user is granted access to an account in that critical system. Traditionally, these advanced provisioning processes were executed manually, but with OIM's process integration capabilities many of these provisioning enforcement tasks can be automated. The following sections provide some configuration solutions for the process-related challenges of user provisioning.

Discretionary Account Provisioning

Discretionary account provisioning is a style of provisioning by which an existing OIM administrator or privileged user can provision a user to an application in a discretionary manner. Inherently, a discretionary method is less consistent and leaves it up to the administrator to know what to do, rather than using a codifying a policy in the provisioning process. By default, this style of provisioning is automatically set up when an OIM is set up with an application using a packaged connector. And typically enterprises use this as a baseline to start designing and implementing their automation rules to make the process less discretionary. To provision a resource to a user in this manner, you'd use the Resource Profile For Users section in the OIM administrative console, shown in Figure 9-3, and click the Provision New Resource button to access the Provision New Resource wizard.

Typically, this style of discretionary provisioning is useful for enterprises that are looking to take the first step from manual provisioning processes to a basic level of automation and centralization. Also, if the enterprise lacks formal governance rules and policies around access

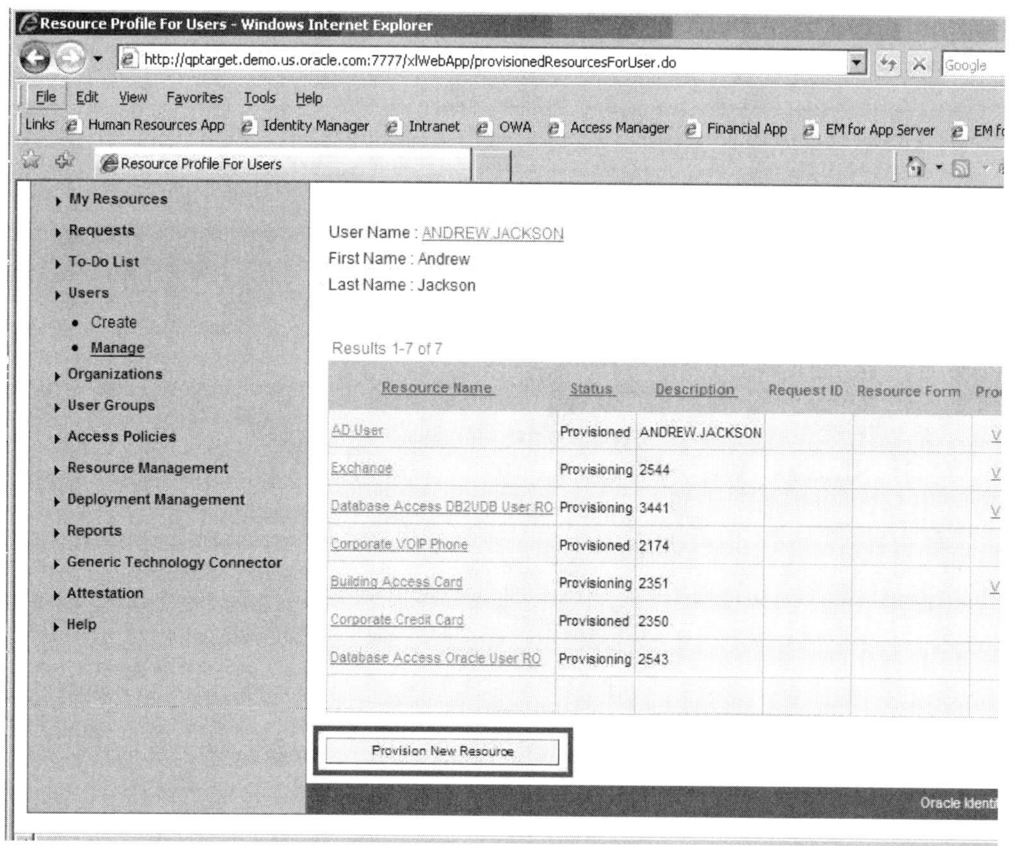

FIGURE 9-3 *Discretionary provisioning of new resources*

to systems and information, handling provisioning requests in a request-based manner might be the inevitable first step. However, if OIM has been put in place, you can accelerate your path to better provisioning automation by leveraging a lot of the built-in features of OIM, such as allowing users to make new requests through OIM and performing basic maintenance tasks such as password resets.

Self-Service Provisioning

The discretionary account provisioning requires an administrator or a privileged user to initiate the provisioning process. In other words, users will still need to make a phone call or send an e-mail to the administrator to request a new account in an application. However, OIM can be easily configured so that users can communicate entirely through the OIM framework when requesting access to new resources. To enable this, you need to set the Self-Service Allowed flag in the resource object for which you want to allow this. Figure 9-4 shows the option in the configuration screen.

Once this configuration has been set for a resource, that resource appears in the list of choices in the Request New Resource section in the OIM administrative console, as shown in Figure 9-5.

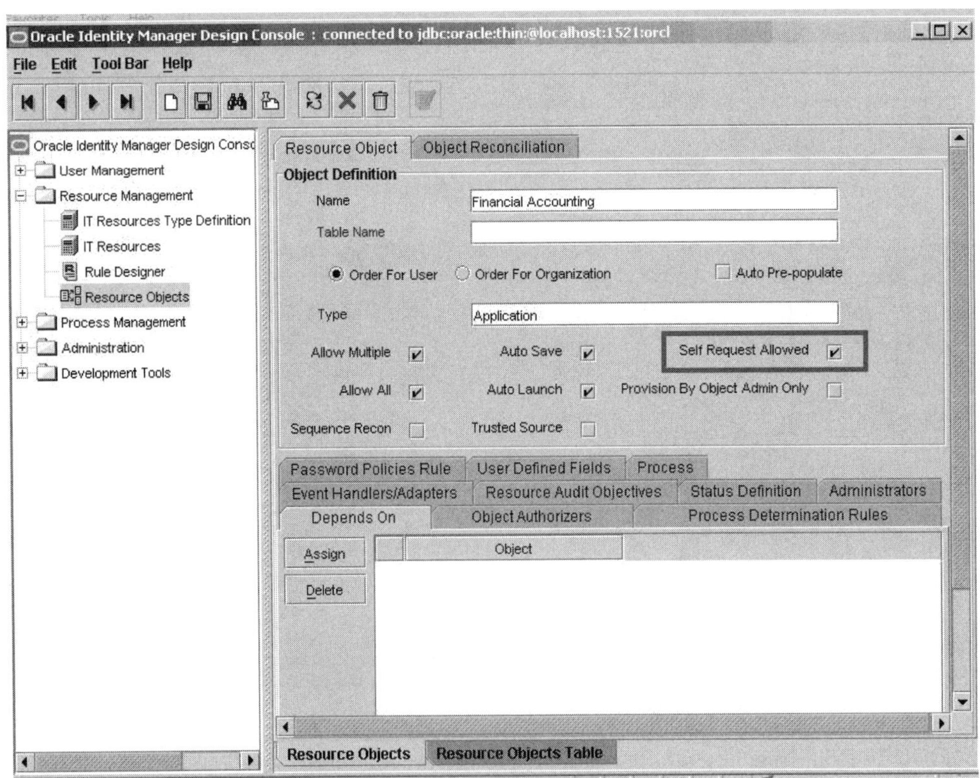

FIGURE 9-4 *Configuring self-service requests on resource objects*

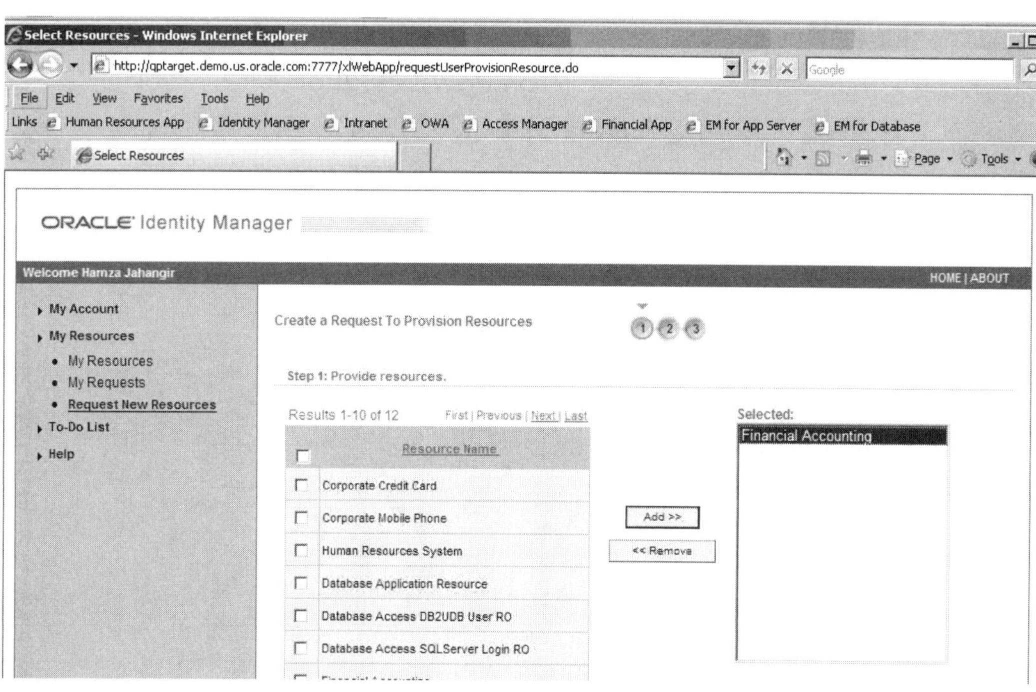

FIGURE 9-5 *Making requests for new self-service–enabled resources*

Over the past few years, self-service user provisioning has been a popular solution especially when delivering simple capabilities such as resetting passwords and requesting accounts in new systems and applications. It can greatly reduce the burden on administrators for performing highly repetitive tasks of manually inputting data from paper forms submitted by an end user. However, enabling the self-service capabilities on resources usually leads to some manual oversight, typically enforced through approval workflows that allow administrators to verify and sign-off on requests from end users. Without such approvals, the resource might as well be a fully public resource.

Workflow-based Provisioning

A workflow-based provisioning process gathers the required approvals from the designated approvers before granting a user access to an application or another resource. For example, the Finance application might require that every new account request be approved by the CFO to maintain tight control of who gets to see sensitive financial information.

To set up approval workflows, you can use the graphical workflow designer in the OIM administrator console, which you can navigate to from the following tabs: Resource Management | Manage | *Resource Name* | Resource Workflows | Create New Workflow

To continue the example from Figure 9-5, we'll create an approval workflow on the "Financial Accounting" resource object that requires two approvals: one from the user's manager and one from the application administrator. The following steps create the workflow:

1. Create a new approval workflow with a descriptive name.
2. Right-click the Workflow Designer and create a new task.

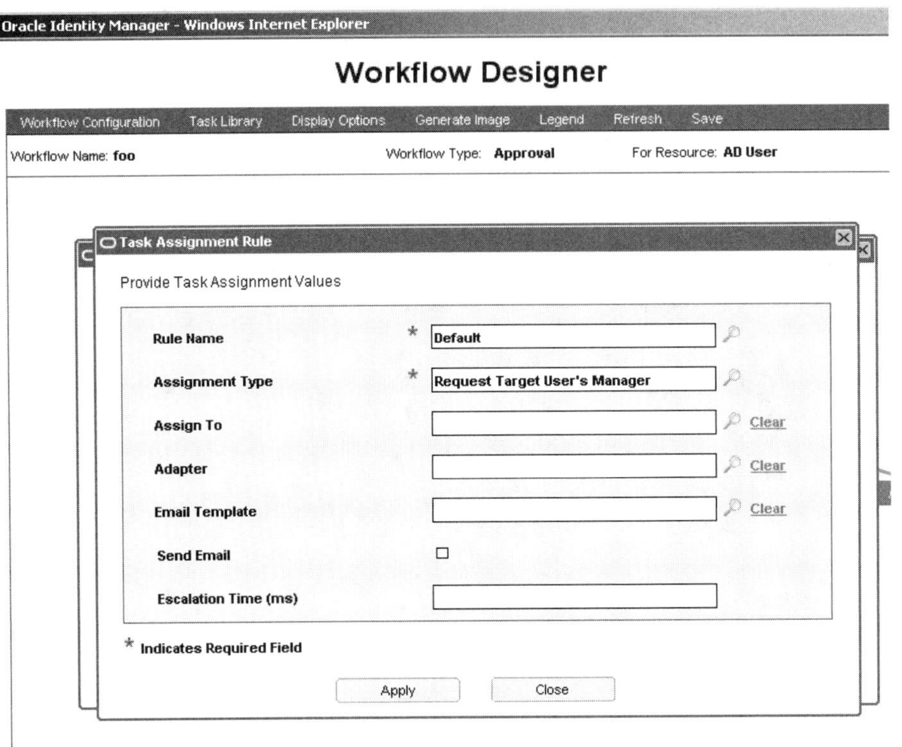

FIGURE 9-6 *Configuring an OIM workflow assignment rule*

3. Double-click the newly created task and go to the Assignment tabs.
4. Edit the Default rule and select the Assignment Type, as shown in Figure 9-6.
5. Select the Request Target User's Manager type, which is configured to route approval through the requesting end user's manager.
6. Once both the tasks are set up and configured appropriately, build the process sequence by right-clicking the Start icon and selecting Add Non-Conditional Task. Then drag the arrow to your first task (Manager Approval).
7. Right-click the Approve box of your first task, select Add Response Generated Task, and drag the arrow to the second task (App Admin Approval) to finish out the workflow. Figure 9-7 (on the next page) illustrates the completed view of this.

Access Policy–driven Provisioning

Recall the two keys questions that drive user provisioning efforts:

- Who *has* access to what resources?
- Who *should have* access to what resources?

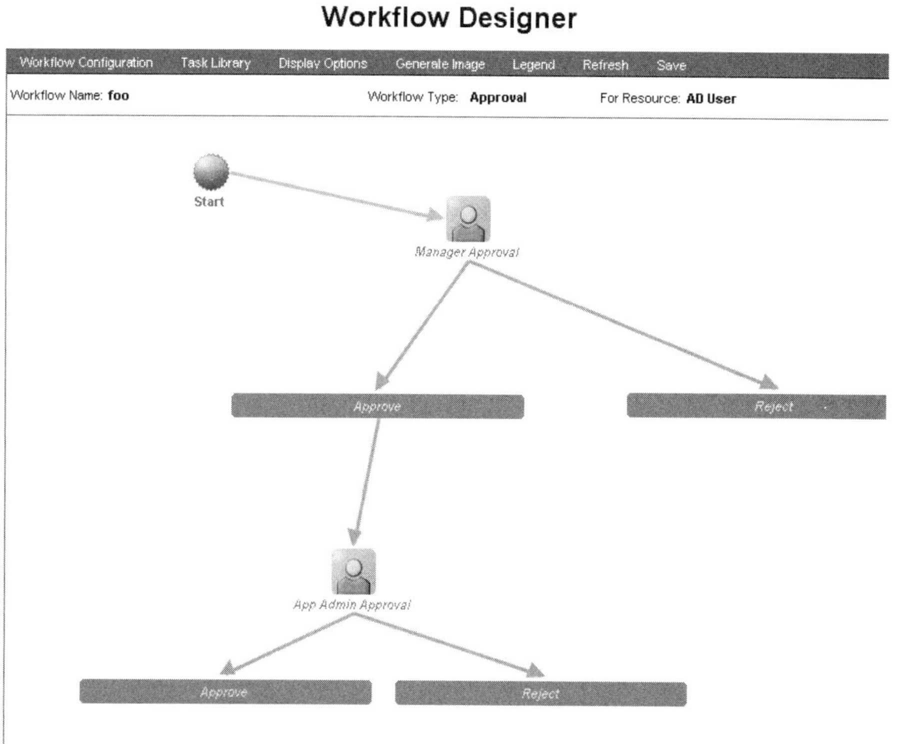

FIGURE 9-7 *OIM Workflow Designer*

Request-driven provisioning certainly helps us answer the first question, since all user provisioning occurs through a centralized process and is therefore tracking who is being provisioned where. However, for the second question, the request-driven style is not taking responsibility for ensuring if a user *should* access a certain resource, since the provisioning occurs in a discretionary manner. To address this issue, corporate security has to lend a hand by providing us a set of access policies that define rules regarding "who should access what." Once those policies are defined, you can implement them very easily in OIM through the web administrative console's Access Policies section.

The following high-level steps are required to set up an access policy:

1. Go to the Create Access Policy section in the OIM administrative console.
2. Select the resource(s) to be provisioned under the chosen access policy, as shown in Figure 9-8.
3. Set the date this for which access needs to be issued.
4. Select the resource(s) that should be denied to the user through this access policy.
5. Select the user groups that apply to this access policy, as shown in Figure 9-9.

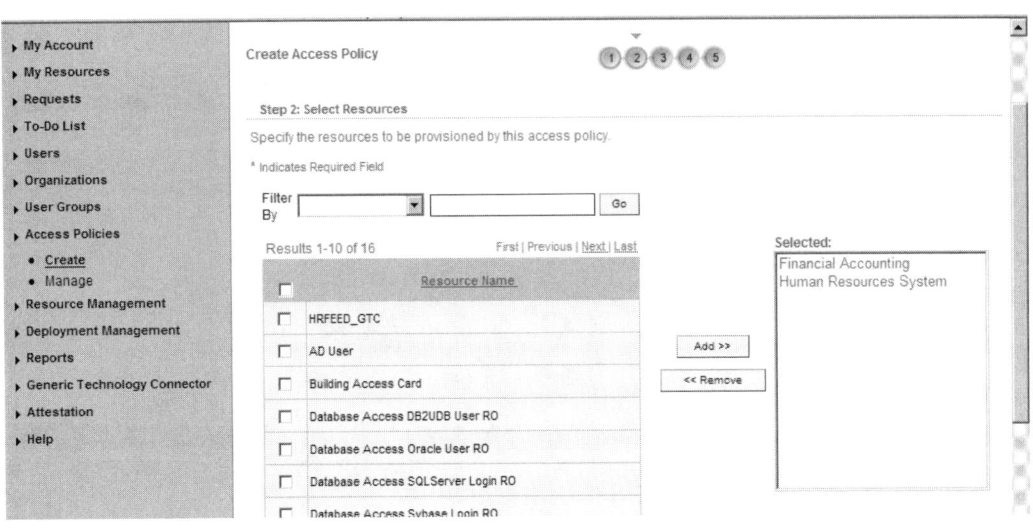

FIGURE 9-8 *Resource selection during access policy configuration*

Once you have defined these four facets of the access policy (what is provisioned, when it is issued, what not to be provisioned, and who this is for), you are ready to automate the majority of your enterprise user provisioning through a collection of these access policies. If you have defined the approval workflows, the access policies will automatically trigger those flows to be routed through the appropriate authorities.

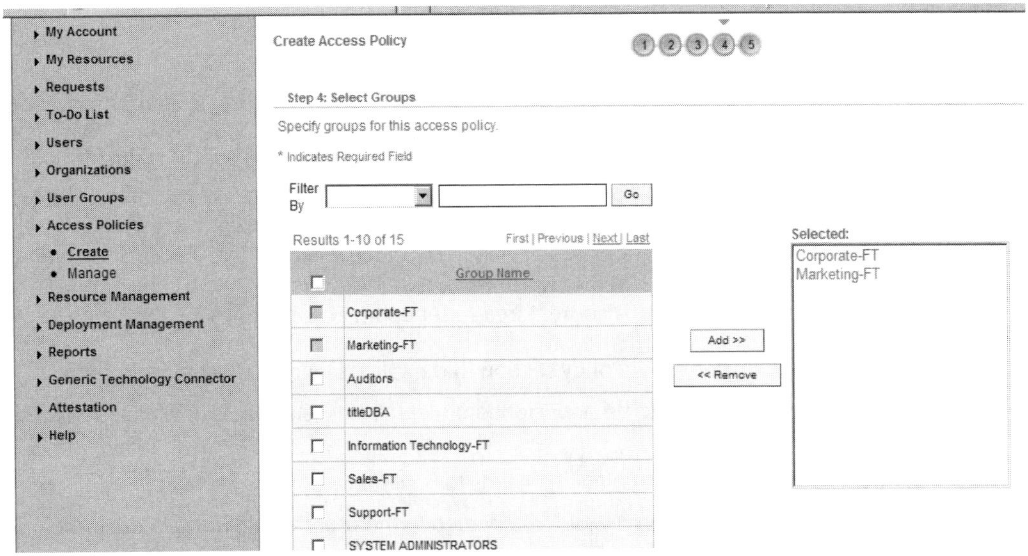

FIGURE 9-9 *User group selection during access policy configuration*

User Provisioning Integrations

One of the key strengths of OIM is the flexibility of its integration platform. However, highly flexible frameworks can often become complex and less usable. As a result, since version 9.1, OIM offers several interaction patterns that allow a user to choose the level of flexibility and sophistication of developing integrations with external systems. I have found that this approach is driven more or less by the 80/20 rule: approximately 80 percent of the use cases are satisfied by 20 percent of the integration types. Those 20 percent integration types are simplified into standard connectors and templates.

Every choice of integration between OIM and an external target systems falls into one of the following categories:

- **Prebuilt connectors** A specific connector implementation for a specific system or application (such as Active Directory, PeopleSoft, SAP, DB2, Oracle Database, and so on).
- **Generic Technology Connector** A connector for commonly-used formats and industry standards (such as flat files, Web Services, and Service Provisioning Markup Language).

Prebuilt Connectors

OIM provides a connector pack that bundles prebuilt and packaged connectors to most third-party systems of all types, including databases, enterprise resource planning (ERP) applications, operating systems, Lightweight Directory Access Protocol (LDAP) servers, and so on. Setting up these connectors in OIM is a fairly straightforward process:

1. Copy the connector files to the OIM server.
2. Import the connector's (XML-based) descriptor file into the OIM repository through the Deployment Manager section in the OIM web console.
3. Define the IT resources associated to this connector,

Through this connector install process, OIM automatically creates the foundational elements of the new resource by creating the necessary resource, IT resource(s), and IT resource type objects associated to the connector. At this point, the environment is ready for basic request-driven provisioning. (See "Discretionary Account Provisioning.")

Generic Technology Connector

One of the first additions Oracle made to the OIM product after its acquisition was the development of the Generic Technology Connector (GTC). Oracle realized that OIM had great capabilities for supporting high-end system integration challenges such as connecting to ERP systems and LDAP servers using prebuilt connectors or developing custom connectors on top of the OIM development framework. However, there was no easy way to perform quick and simple integrations from OIM to smaller scale and perhaps more departmental applications that were built using simpler database technologies such as Application Express or Microsoft Access. As enterprises are looking to automate provisioning to all types of applications (enterprise and departmental), Oracle needed a solution that targeted those applications and systems with a simpler approach to provisioning. This was the genesis of the GTC, introduced in OIM 9.1.

The GTC supports simple integrations to custom-built applications or other systems that rely on simpler data exchange formats such as comma-separated fields. It also supports many industry-standard protocols such as Service Provisioning Markup Language (SPML). The GTC is another example of a packaged integration used for a common set of applications that can read and

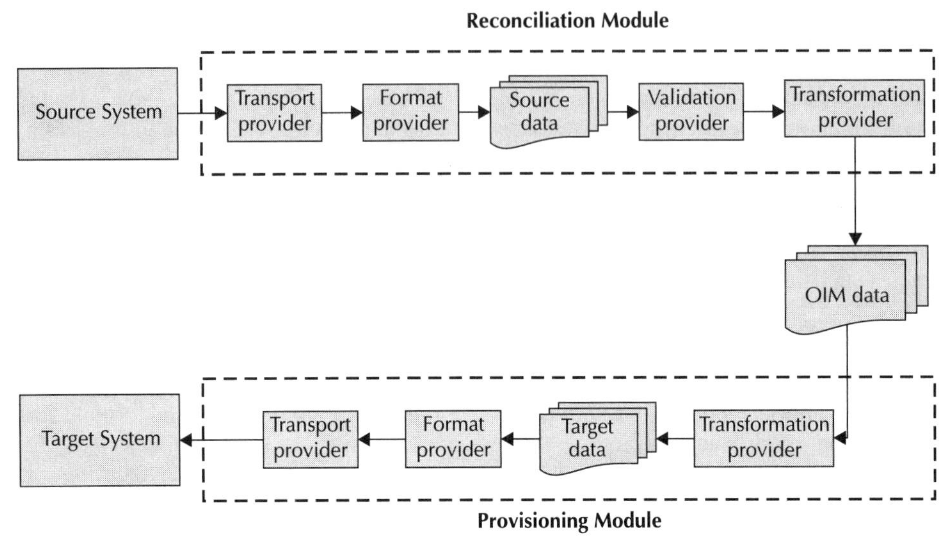

FIGURE 9-10 *The GTC lifecyle*

exchange information in a standard format. While the GTC does not necessarily solve complex integration scenarios, it does provide a quick integration to medium- to low-complexity applications. Figure 9-10 illustrates the provisioning lifecycle of a GTC-based integration.

A GTC-based integration provides a set of packaged functionalities, known as "providers," to perform the different types of actions needed to execute an end-to-end user provisioning process. The process runs starting from identity data reconciliation from a source system to provisioning to a target application.

The GTC is a useful choice whenever you're dealing with applications that can support simpler or standard data exchange formats, such as comma-separated files or the SPML format. The typical cost to set up and maintain a GTC-based integration is much lower than that of other types of OIM integrations. Unlike the prebuilt connectors, the GTC code is shipped with the OIM server so there is no need to install additional software.

Reconciliation Integrations

Two types of system integrations are supported by OIM: *provisioning* and *reconciliation*. Provisioning automates account creation from the OIM server to an application or resource using the data from the OIM repository. Reconciliation automates the creation of an OIM identity record based on an external source of identities (that is, a source of truth). Most often, OIM reconciles from an external human resources application as an authoritative source of employee data and then provisions to business productivity applications, such as email, intranet portals, and other ERP systems.

Reconciliation is often driven by business events such as new hires, new customers, organizational changes, employee transfers, and so on. Since these business events are initiated in an ERP system, most often the Human Resources (HR) system, it makes sense to configure OIM to setup reconciliation with those systems so it can listen for relevant identity events. OIM uses two reconciliation styles: *trusted source reconciliation* and *target resource reconciliation*.

Trusted Source Reconciliation

Trusted source reconciliation (TSR) is used for reconciling information from external authoritative sources (such as HR systems, CRM, and so on) that usually result in creating, modifying, or removing users in the OIM local repository. If the appropriate user groups and access policies are configured, the external reconciliation events can trigger provisioning processes that create or change account data in applications and resources where users are provisioned. For instance, a new employee record entered into the HR application could trigger a record creation in OIM (via reconciliation), which then can subsequently trigger provisioning events (via access policies) to create an e-mail account in the MS Exchange e-mail server.

TSR has two implementation forms:

- **Attribute based** Each trusted source is responsible for reconciling one or more attributes of the user. For instance, the HR system can be the authoritative source that owns the first and last name attributes, whereas the enterprise LDAP server can be the authoritative source for the e-mail address attribute.
- **User-type based** Each trusted source is responsible for reconciling a particular user type in OIM. For instance, the HR system can be the trusted source for employees, whereas the CRM system can be the trusted source for customer user types.

Target Resource Reconciliation

Target resource reconciliation (TRR) is used mainly for reconciling changes to already provisioned users. For instance, if someone changes the phone number of a user in Active Directory without going through the OIM management console, OIM can be configured to reconcile those changes using TRR.

TRR is a very powerful feature in OIM since it can not only choose simple attribute changes from external sources, but it can also be used to identify rogue accounts in external systems quickly. If someone tries to create a privileged account in an external resource (such as Active Directory), TRR can detect that potentially harmful account and take any step that you configure. For example, TRR can configure a policy of automatically disabling rogue accounts until an administrator explicitly re-authorizes the access.

TRR is also useful for reconciling list-of-value fields from target systems (such as LDAP groups, roles, and so on) into OIM so that you can map access policies to actual target system roles and groups.

Compliance Solutions

One of the main drivers of enterprise identity management is the notion of knowing and auditing who has access to what resources. In addition to standard access reporting requirements, compliance mandates often require periodic attestation of users' access to critical applications. Manual attestation of access is an expensive and risky process to enforce, so enterprises are looking to products like OIM to help provide attestation.

Attestation

Attestation requires that a defined approval workflow periodically re-authorizes access to sensitive information (typically financial data) that falls within a particular compliance mandate such as the Sarbanes-Oxley Act (SOX). The person with the authority to re-authorize, also known as the *reviewer*, can have a number of relationships with the user(s) being attested. The reviewer can range from user's direct supervisor, to an application administrator, to the chief operating officer (COO) of the organization. Basically, the reviewer must have the authority and knowledge to answer the question "who should access what resource." This authority can also be delegated to a different reviewer if the first reviewer is unable to answer that question.

OIM provides a fairly simple way of managing attestation by embedding it into the provisioning process framework. In other words, you can wrap any resource with the need for attestation.

Following are the typical steps you need to take to set up an attestation policy that can govern by user type (such as organizations, roles, and so on) and by the resources that require this form of periodic re-authorization:

1. Go the attestation policy manager. In the OIM administrative console, navigate to the Attestation section.
2. Create a new attestation process. Typically it makes good sense to create attestation processes by resource and/or organization.
3. Specify the scope of users for attestation. This lets you partition how you attest different types of users. For instance, the accounting department attestation process could be approved by the user's supervisor, whereas the sales department attestation could be attested by the sales region's vice president.
4. Specify the scope of applications/resources for attestation. This lets you partition your attestation process by different resources. It often makes sense to use the Resource Audit Objective (which is an attribute associated with a resource) to define your attestation process since different audit objectives require different types of attestations.
5. Specify additional attestation process details. Define additional details such as frequency of the attestations, the process owner, and the grace period for completing the process. Keep in mind that a significant delegation of attestations can occur in large organizations, so the grace period should factor that in.

Figure 9-11 shows how a completed attestation process could look.

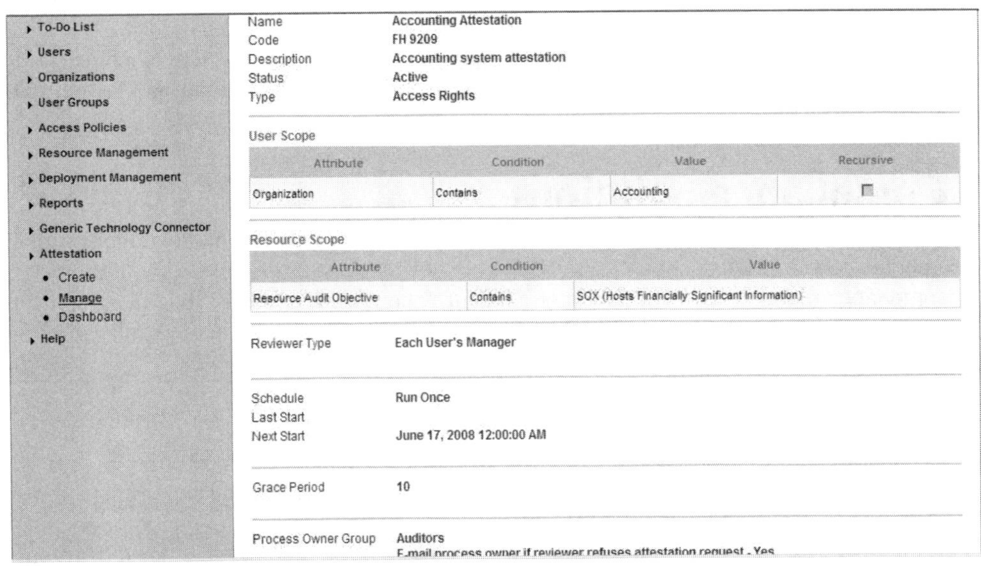

FIGURE 9-11 *Managing an attestation policy in OIM*

Access Reporting

In addition to attestation, another common requirement is to provide compliance and security officers a single consolidated view of who has access to what resources and applications in the enterprise. In other words, officers are looking for a reporting solution around users and their access.

One of the benefits of using a centralized hub-and-spoke architecture (see Chapter 8 for details about this type of architecture) as implemented by a product like OIM is the ability to centralize the identity data into a single repository, which allows you to run reports on top of that data. Access reporting is a key feature of OIM, especially when you need to report on applications that fall under the compliance requirements of SOX and other legislative mandates. Since every new user and modification to existing users is processed through OIM, you can use OIM's reporting infrastructure as a fairly reliable source for asking the question "who *has* access to what" and, occasionally, "who *had* access to what."

Through the web administrative console, OIM offers two types of reporting functionality: *operational* and *historical*. Operational reporting gives the user a snapshot of the current users' access. Historical reporting provides an additional time dimension so that you can view a snapshot in history. A good example that may be driven by SOX requirements is the need to see who had access to the financials application during a certain time period (such as during a corporate quiet period of June 1–30 in 2008). Both types of reports are critical both for compliance and for assuring auditors that the information was under authorized access at all times.

To run either operational or historical reports, navigate to the Reporting section of the OIM administrative UI and click the appropriate report and query with the desired parameters. Figure 9-12 shows a sample report on access to the Financial Accounting application in my environment.

Notice that in Figure 9-12, you can modify parameters to customize your report. You can also export to text-based formats that can be imported into tools such as MS Excel, allowing you to share these reports via e-mail to other parties, such as corporate auditors.

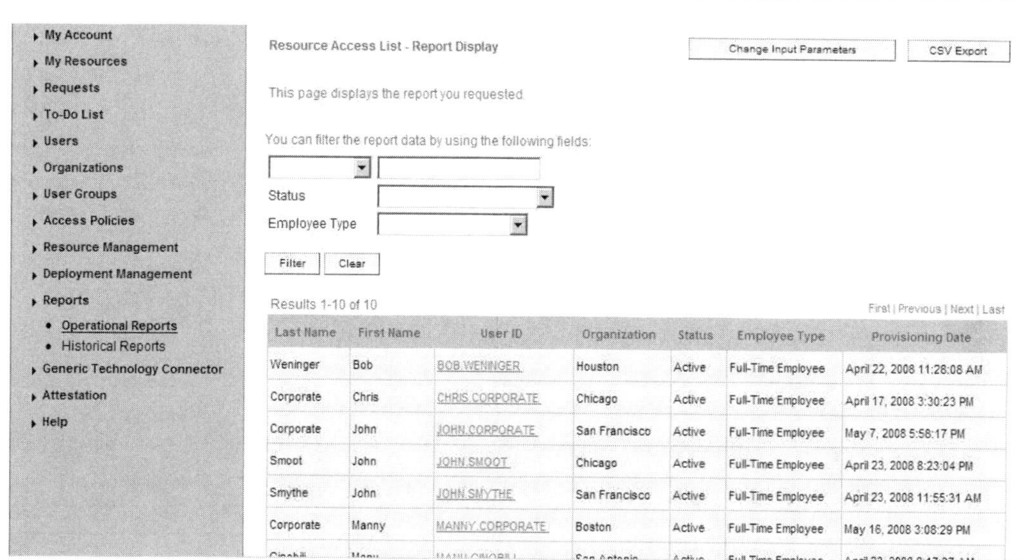

FIGURE 9-12 *Access reporting shows who has access to what and who had access to what.*

OIM Deployment

Every OIM component (design client, web application and core server engine) is written in Java and executes in a multi-tiered deployment model, shown in Figure 9-13.

Client Tier When working with OIM, two types of clients are used: a web-based administrative console and a design-time client. The web administrative console is used mainly for managing users, resources, and all the constructs supporting them. The design-time client is used by the developers of the identity management processes for designing and configuring the core components such as resource objects, IT resources, provisioning processes, and the integration configurations to communicate with the physical applications being provisioned or reconciled. Both types of clients follow a distributed communication model so that you can have many clients from many computers communicating with the same set of policies and objects defined in the OIM business logic tier.

Web Tier This tier exists as a web application container for the OIM administrative user interface. It is a pure Java-based web application environment that uses technologies such as JSP, servlets, Struts, and JavaBeans. By using these standard technologies, the OIM web tier can be deployed in a number of application servers and containers.

Business Logic Tier This tier is the core of the OIM product. In this tier, OIM decides who (the user) to provision where (target resource) and how (the process). This tier is written exclusively in Java and leverages a J2EE design pattern and therefore inherits the core benefits of that combination—platform-neutrality and distributed component architecture. A Java-based

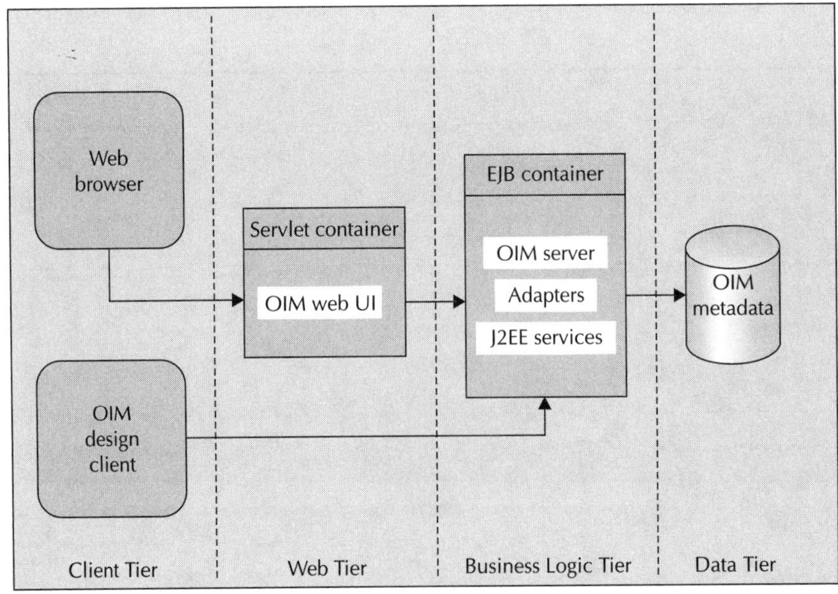

FIGURE 9-13 *OIM deployment architecture*

OIM business tier allows a standard development platform for new integration connectors and adapters. The distributed nature of J2EE allows for the business logic tier to be spread across multiple application server deployments while accessing the common metadata from the data tier.

Data Tier The data tier is a SQL-based relational database that stores all metadata about the identities, accesses, and configurations for the user provisioning platform. The only OIM data that lives outside the database are the JAR (Java Archive) files containing the code to connect to third-party resources and target systems. The data tier is accessed exclusively by the OIM business tier and should not be integrated with any external clients and tools for direct data manipulation. In fact, we recommend that you consider using Oracle database protection technologies, such as Oracle Database Vault and Transparent Data Encryption, to secure and protect the sensitive identity-related metadata stored in the OIM repository. Refer to earlier chapters on TDE and Database Vault for details on how to secure the OIM metadata repository.

Summary

This chapter reviewed the Oracle Identity Manager that addresses the simple to understand but hard to implement area of user provisioning. Provisioning is a mandatory process inside every enterprise, executing constantly either in a manual or an automated manner. As a result, optimizing the processes around provisioning is critical to both achieve operational efficiency and deliver assurance that access policies are not being violated or ignored. Security issues include orphaned accounts that are not de-provisioned. Open, unused accounts are footholds for disgruntled employees and attackers and are at the top of the list of things that compliance auditors look for. As a result, a truly successful user provisioning solution balances building better optimized processes and policies to lower administrative burden with instituting consistency of identity management, in terms of the way it grants and monitors access to information, to result in a higher level of security and protection of all enterprise assets.

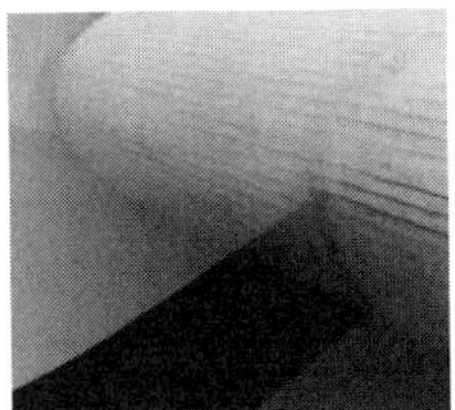

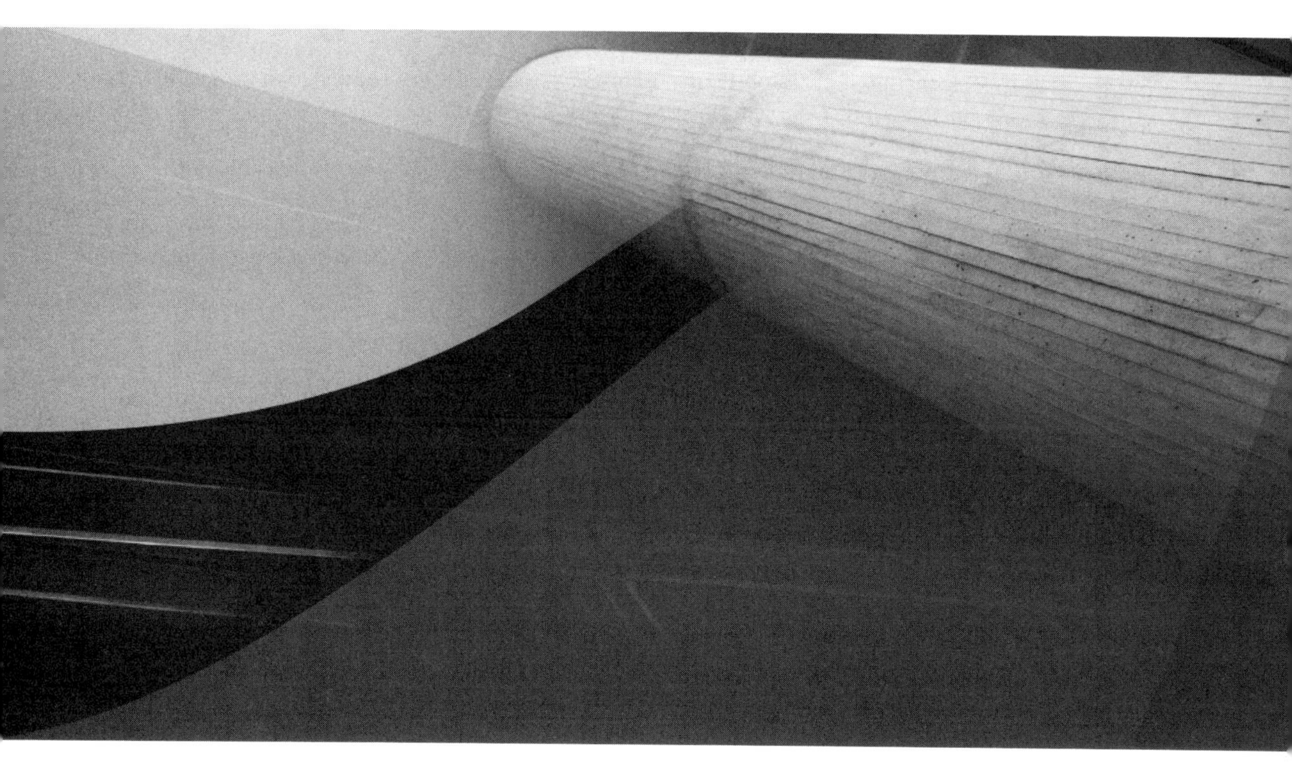

CHAPTER 10

Oracle Directory Services

This chapter focuses on Oracle's approach to solving the challenge of providing fast, reliable, and scalable repository for storing, organizing, and retrieving identity and access information. Oracle's directory strategy relies on the Lightweight Directory Access Protocol (LDAP) standard as the primary interface for exchanging and managing the directory data. The original point of creating the LDAP server was to have an information repository highly optimized for reading data. While Oracle has certainly made its LDAP servers much more capable in handling large transaction (read-write) volumes, optimized reads continues to be the basic driver for using an LDAP server.

Oracle offers two directory products—Oracle Internet Directory (OID) and Oracle Virtual Directory (OVD)—that represent two unique but complementary solutions for managing and exchanging identity and access information via LDAP. In this chapter, we will review these products from the perspective of managing, storing, organizing, and retrieving identity data. Instead of being too focused on the LDAP standard or generic directory design, we focus on how to apply these Oracle products to solve common challenges in this space.

Identity Management and the LDAP Directory

The user directory is a bedrock entity of identity management for storing, managing, organizing, and sharing identity information with applications where those identities are access controlled. LDAP has become the de facto standard in interacting with directory data and is therefore a core part of any identity management product strategy, including that of Oracle. While LDAP provides a standard information access interface and protocol, identity management faces a major issue with the proliferation of directory systems of different types, different data models, and different naming conventions. For example, it is common to see Active Directory being used for the Windows authentication, whereas OID is being used for Oracle databases and web applications. The consequence of having multiple LDAP servers is that the same human user has two, often disparate, records in two separate LDAP repositories. Such fragmented repositories drove Oracle's decision to acquire OctetString in 2005 to add a virtual directory offering for enterprises with a specific need for rationalizing information across multiple physical repositories of identity information.

Today, Oracle caters to a wider set of directory needs by offering OID focused on the physical storage and management, while OVD is focused on tackling integrating data from multiple directories and databases in real-time, to provide applications a single logical LDAP server to query user information pertaining to identity management.

Oracle Internet Directory

OID is a fully compliant LDAP v3 directory server used primarily for storing identity and access information. OID is also often used for managing database instance names and as a lookup service for DBAs who regularly log into different databases using SQL clients. If you already have a basic understanding of LDAP servers, you'll find OID a fairly simple product to understand. The characteristic that separates OID from other directories is its ability to scale to handle very large volumes of identity information quickly, often upwards of 100 million users per implementation. A number of the world's largest LDAP servers use OID as their underlying LDAP repository. The reason it scales in such large numbers is because underneath its covers, OID is an application sitting on top of the highly scalable Oracle Database server. It inherits all of Oracle Database's performance characteristics and can be tuned to scale just like any Oracle Database application.

OID Architecture

As demonstrated in Figure 10-1, the runtime execution of OID flows through three key layers of abstraction: LDAP listeners, LDAP-to-relational mapping, and the backend Oracle Database metadata repository. The listener and mapping layers of OID are middleware components written in Java/J2EE and managed as a component of the Oracle Application Server environment. The backend repository is a specialized metadata repository with a predefined database schema and data model for efficient LDAP data transactions.

A number of packaged configurations of OID allow it to scale rapidly and provide a highly available repository for an enterprise. One such configuration might be leveraging the Oracle Real Application Cluster (RAC) environment for managing the directory metadata. In addition, to optimize the OID server for data reads, you can apply tuning techniques, both at the LDAP server level (for example, adding indexes for LDAP attributes that are frequently used for querying information) and at the database level (for example, tuning the basic kernel parameters and the database I/O parameters). For specific database tuning tips, read Thomas Kyte's *Effective Oracle by Design* (McGraw-Hill Professional, 2003).

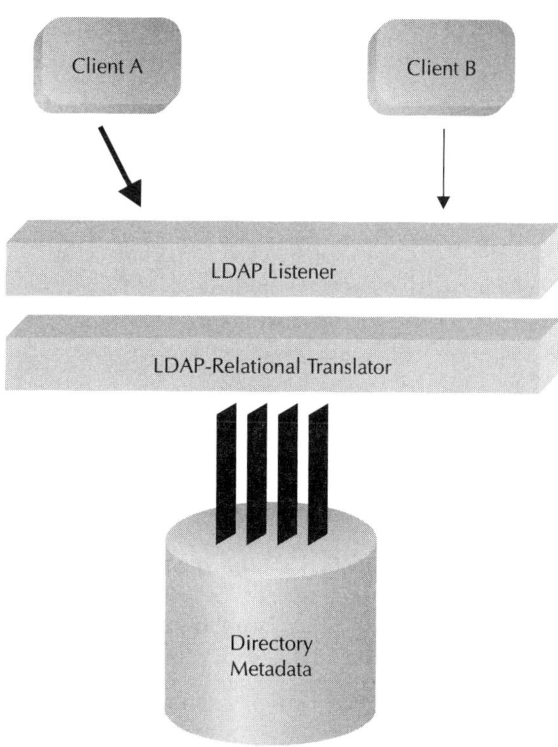

FIGURE 10-1 *Layered view of OID*

OID Synchronizations

One of the key challenges we face today with directories and their deployments is finding the right balance between performance and manageability. We usually need our directories to return queries with subsecond round-trip times. Since the applications rely on the directory constantly to authorize users for access, low latency response is a must.

Two key challenges are apparent in terms of directory data management:

- **Distribution** Since users are often spread all across the country and, increasingly, the globe, a major challenge for directories is to optimize the distance of the directory information from the user. For example, it is very inefficient to authenticate against a centralized LDAP server in the United States when the users in the Tokyo sales office are trying to access the local customer database application.
- **Consistency** Due to proliferation of applications and systems maintaining identity information, it becomes more difficult to keep it all consistent across systems. Inconsistency in the identity data is a major issue from a usability perspective and also a management pain since administrators need to rationalize disparate data records for the same human user.

These challenges have led to the need for directory synchronization, where the core principle is to place the right information in the right location to optimize directory performance, information consistency, and manageability. Several techniques are available for achieving these principles in OID.

Replication

Directory replication is one solution to the cross-enterprise data integrity challenge where data is replicated across two or more LDAP directories. With OID, replication happens at the database level where the replication processes move the LDAP information from one OID database to the other.

Replication is an efficient process for synchronizing large loads of changes from one OID server to another. Keep in mind, however, that replication is not a heterogeneous solution for synchronizing and supports exchanging data only between OID servers. It requires that the following characteristics of the directory be the same:

- **Directory server type** Oracle Internet Directory servers of the same major version (such as 9.*x*, 10.*x*, and so on)
- **Namespace** The hierarchy and namespace in the directory information tree design is identical

As mentioned, this is a recommended approach when the enterprise has standardized on the OID platform and has physical deployments of that standard OID server across geographies serving different populations of users. If you want to implement this kind of replication, the OID administration guide is a good tutorial on the exact configuration steps for setting up replication.

Directory Integration Platform

OID offers an embedded meta-directory solution, called Directory Integration Platform (DIP), for synchronizing identity and access data between OID and other LDAP directories or non-LDAP repositories.

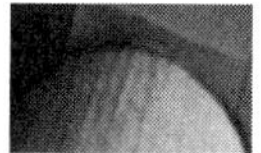

NOTE
Meta-directory is an approach to synchronize directory information by physically moving information among multiple physical repositories. Unlike the replication approach, meta-directory solutions can integrate heterogeneous LDAP and non-LDAP servers (such as OID–Active Directory, OID–Database Tables, and so on) with different information formats (such as asymmetric namespaces, different LDAP schema and naming conventions, and so on).

DIP supports OID and non-OID systems, such as Active Directory, Novell eDirectory, and SunOne, as well as relational tables in Oracle databases. As discussed in Chapter 8, meta-directory solutions such as DIP are usually leveraged for low-level LDAP object synchronization such as user attributes like passwords and group memberships.

Configuring your OID for DIP is adequately covered in the "OID Integration Guide" in the "Directory Integration" section. Setting up a single LDAP for DIP should take no more than a few hours, involving the following high-level steps:

1. Choose a directory synchronization profile that is a predefined template for the different supported systems (such as Active Directory, SunOne and Oracle Relational Database Tables, and so on). For a full list, refer to the "OID Integration Guide."
2. Set up the server connection from the master OID server to the external repository.
3. Set up the namespace and attribute mapping from the source to the destination.
4. Configure the synchronization behavior (such as synchronization frequency, initial information bootstrapping policies, and so on).

While good for certain architectural requirements, directory synchronization has its down side, as discussed in Chapter 8. It is a form of Point-to-Point (P2P) integration, so as the number of systems needing synchronization increase, the effort to manage and maintain these P2P integrations also increase in near linear terms. As a rule of thumb, if you have more than five P2P integrations, you might want to consider alternative integration strategies that lower your management efforts. One such alternative offered by Oracle since 2005, with the introduction of its virtual directory product, is the concept of *directory virtualization.*

Directory Virtualization and Oracle Virtual Directory

Ten years ago, when we didn't have so many online travel web sites like Expedia and Priceline, we used *travel agents.* The travel agent's job was to serve as a proxy between a potential traveler and the airline carrier selling tickets. The traveler could give the travel agent a set of travel parameters (destinations, dates, and so on), and the agent would find the best deal based on those parameters. Alternatively, the travel agent could also create a predefined menu of destination choices and ticket prices from which the traveler could choose. In either scenario, the tickets could come from any carrier (United, American, Lufthansa, Singapore Airlines, and so on), yet the traveler is dealing with only one entity—the travel agent. Directory virtualization is not too different from this travel agent concept. A virtual directory, such as OVD, acts as that single travel agent for any application requesting specific LDAP objects and attributes or simply looking to browse the LDAP tree.

Directory virtualization is emerging as a far more efficient alternative to directory synchronization because, unlike replication and meta-directory technologies, virtual directory products such as OVD do not physically move data between systems. Instead, they rationalize and unify data in real time when an application makes the request. OVD follows a composite access pattern whereby all physical sources are abstracted and "virtualized" as a single LDAP directory. This approach allows the directory architecture to benefit from the following:

- **Loose coupling** A virtual directory decouples LDAP clients from the physical directory, allowing for changes to the underlying repositories without impacting the LDAP clients.
- **Flexible control of data** Allows information to be integrated and joined together without removing control from current administrators of the different repositories.
- **Information semantics normalization** Allows identity information semantics to be normalized across the enterprise. Its data transformation capabilities allow actual physical formats and structures to be mapped to a single unified and normalized data format and definition across the enterprise.

Keep in mind that physical data consolidation is still a good idea and can save maintenance and administration dollars over the long term. However, in some cases, multiple directories are maintained due to product dependency issues or when organizations want to maintain control over their own identity information. Therefore, a virtual directory gives you the flexibility to adapt to those decisions without necessarily compromising your LDAP design principle of having a single logical place for querying identity data.

OVD 101

Oracle Virtual Directory functions much like a database view. In a database view, data from many backend tables and other sources are joined and presented as a single "virtual table" (aka view) to the end user. In a virtual directory, identity data residing in OID, Active Directory, and custom applications can be joined together, at runtime, and presented to the LDAP client as a single LDAP user profile. This is a major advantage over using a meta-directory approach since the information integration is happening only at runtime and doesn't require that the data be moved and updated in systems prior to any application request for the identity profile.

OVD is not meant to replace your existing LDAP servers and other identity repositories, because it has no concept of identity data storage. It does provide some simple ways of storing basic identity attributes, but those types of storage are not meant to replace mass data storage provided by products such as OID. Instead, OVD focuses on the problems around information aggregation and rationalization to present a unified view of data from multiple sources of data (that is, LDAP servers, databases, and so on) to LDAP clients.

OVD Architecture

Before setting up OVD, you need to know architecturally where it resides and how it participates in a typical LDAP request. Figure 10-2 illustrates the end-to-end flow of how an application is access controlled using identity information originating from multiple backend repositories but flowing through a single virtualized LDAP interface to the access controller.

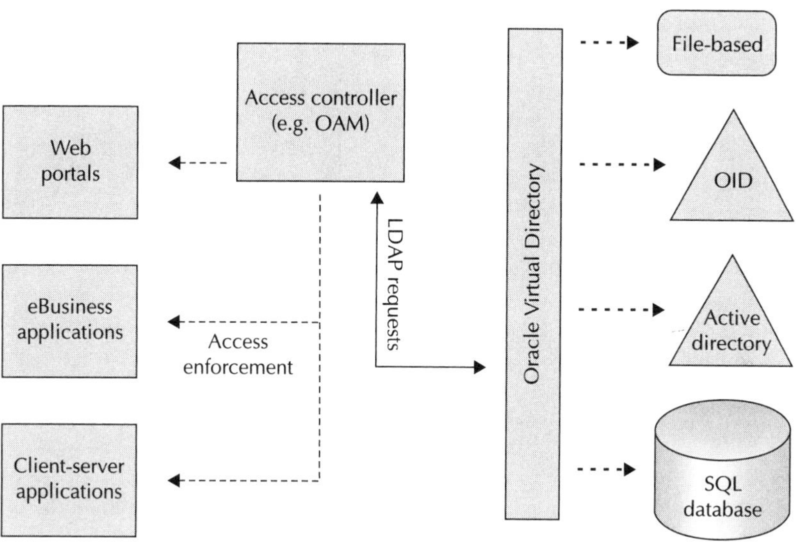

FIGURE 10-2 *OVD in the enterprise*

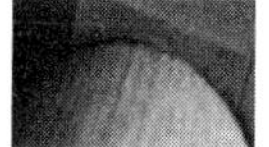

NOTE
Access Controller represents a component in any identity management architecture that is responsible for gathering all the necessary information about access policies and making the decision, on a per-request basis, of whether to allow a user to take a certain action on a particular resource. In Chapter 8, we discussed Oracle Access Manager and Oracle Entitlement Server, which can be characterized as access controllers.

As shown in Figure 10-2, the access controller component (the engine that decides who should and should not access resources) sits in between OVD and the applications. Access controllers can also leverage alternative communication protocols to read the directory data using XML-based formats, such as Directory Services Markup Language (DSML) and HTTP-based communication protocols. The approach of exposing directory APIs as web services is becoming more popular as enterprises are moving toward service-oriented information access architectures. The point of this shift is to make all enterprise information (including identity information) accessible to the consumer applications over a standard integration platform aimed to make it quick and easy for application integration.

OVD Architectural Layers

As implied by Figure 10-3, the core competency of OVD resides in its ability to apply rules to the physical data and change the presentation of that data to the LDAP client.

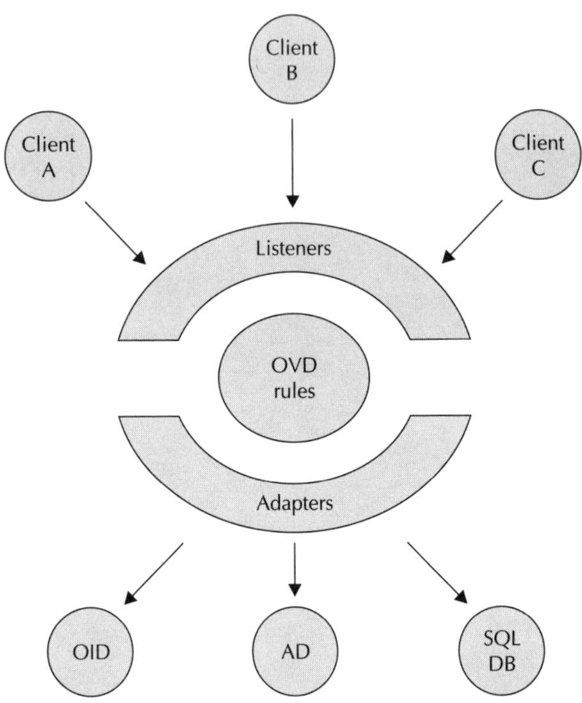

FIGURE 10-3 *Information access to and from Oracle Virtual Directory*

Performing this kind of on-demand transformation and unification of fragmented data requires that the responsibility be split into three specific layers:

- **Listener Interface** Allows the OVD server to share information over multiple communication protocols (such as LDAP or HTTP) and networking choices (such as ports, SSL, and so on).
- **Rules and Mapping** This layer manages the rules and mappings for executing the logic to transform information from the backend repository to the frontend consumer. Consider this the OVD "brain," where you can perform pre- and post-processing of identity information coming from the LDAP servers. In addition to the standard mapping rules and procedures, you can also write any custom code in Python to configure OVD to execute any pre- or post-processing logic that you want executed during an LDAP call. (For example, if I have a policy for which I do not want to share a user's location attribute if he or she belongs to the "Secret" department, I could write and register a simple Python procedure as part of the OVD server, where I make that check and nullify all the location attributes for those users in the "Secret" department.) The Python-based framework in OVD is extremely powerful and can be used for nearly any transformation, verification, or audit type requirement around LDAP information access.
- **Adapter** This layer manages the integration configuration from the OVD server to the backend repositories or other adapters. Many types of adapters have specific setup

and configuration patterns depending on what they are connecting to and what type of information they expect. An adapter is responsible for maintaining two types of configuration:

- The information on how to communicate with the backend identity data source (server host names, ports, protocols, namespaces, and so on)
- A set of join rules and mappings that map the virtual directory tree and definition to the structure and definition of the data in the actual sources

OVD Applied

By now, you should understand Oracle Virtual Directory's architecture and the purpose it serves for solving directory integration challenges without physically synchronizing information. In this section, we work through some common implementation scenarios to give you some more practical knowledge of how to apply OVD in specific directory integration scenarios. The central objective from all the implementation scenarios still remains the same: creating a single unified view of an identity across the enterprise.

OVD Installation

Three key components are involved in installing an OVD: OVD Server, OVD Admin Server, and OVD Manager. The OVD Server component acts as the LDAP process where applications and other LDAP clients connect for directory information. The OVD Admin Server is an administration component that manages all the configurations in the OVD Server. The OVD Manager is a desktop application used by the directory administrator and developers to configure OVD.

When you have a fresh, new install, you need to start the Admin Server and then connect into the Admin Server using the OVD Manager application. Refer to the specific steps of installing the OVD product for your specific O/S platform in the OVD installation guide that comes with the software. This section is meant to give you a quick understanding of what is installed and why.

Creating a New OVD Server

We assume that you now have a working OVD install with a running Admin Server. Now you can start configuring the virtual LDAP server with which applications and clients will interact. All server configurations are performed using the Oracle Virtual Directory Manager (a desktop application that comes with the product). To set up a new OVD server for your enterprise, start the OVD Manager client and follow these steps:

1. Create a directory project for storing all server configurations.
2. Create a Virtual Directory Server under the project and specify the relevant information (name, port, hostname, and so on) for your environment (as shown in Figure 10-4). This step also requires you to verify your OVD administration server credentials, which should have been set up during installation of the software.

If you installed the OVD Admin Server (during the installation process) to be listening on a non-SSL port, you do not need to verify the SSL connection and accept the trusted certificate. However, it is a best practice to run the Admin Server over SSL. At this stage, you are now ready to start integrating OVD with your backend physical repositories.

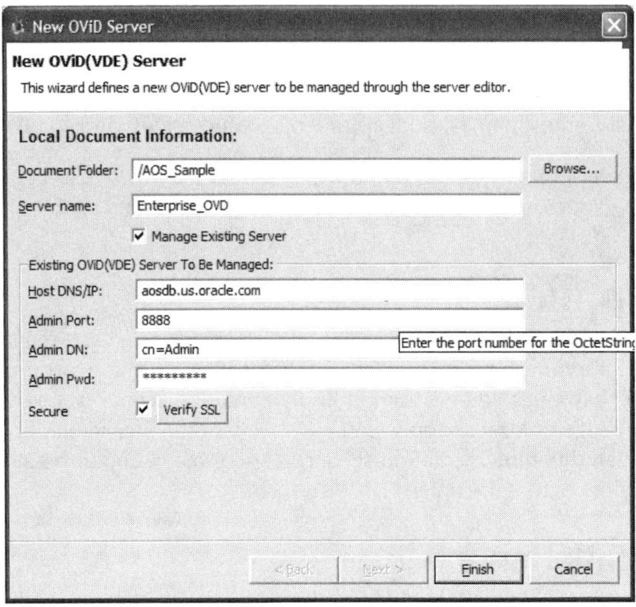

FIGURE 10-4 *Configuring the basic details of the OVD Server*

Initializing the Virtual LDAP Tree Using a Local Store Adapter

Before any physical information is presented through a virtual directory, you need to define and design the directory tree and namespace that organizes all the information across the enterprise. Traditionally, this part of the project can often be a paralyzing step since it requires that people agree on a common namespace. However, OVD supports the notion of a virtual namespace. You are no longer permanently committed to namespaces, and, in fact, you can now host multiple namespaces in the same virtual directory to support two models for organizing the same identity information. However, it is recommended to keep it simple and unified under a common namespace.

In this example, we will use the namespace **dc=oracle,dc=com** as our common unified namespace and integrate data from multiple repositories under a common directory information tree. The easiest way to create the root of the namespace is to use a Local Store Adapter (LSA) in OVD.

An LSA uses a file-based repository to hold a relatively small quantity of information. It is recommended to limit the use of the LSA for only the root node of the directory tree. It is not a good idea to have the LSA store actual users since it is not meant to scale for high volume identity data. Once you define the root node of the tree, you can start integrating the identity repositories that contain the full scale of identity data about all users in the enterprise.

The following example uses a scenario in which different types of identity data is split across Active Directory and OID, you can use the LSA to create a single logical directory tree that can reconcile the two physical directories by integrating that data underneath the namespace defined by the LSA. Figure 10-5 illustrates this design pattern.

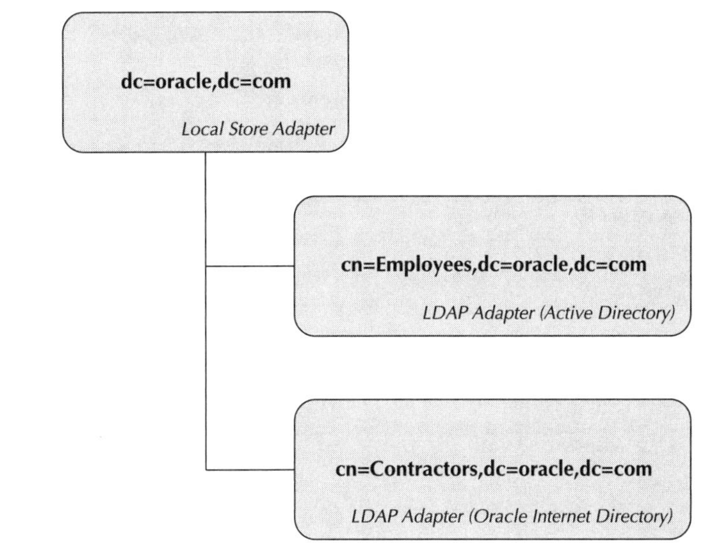

FIGURE 10-5 *Directory tree design using OVD*

Setting up an LSA involves the following steps in the OVD Manager:

1. Right-click the Adapters node under the OVD server you created previously and select a New Local Store Adapter.
2. As shown in Figure 10-6 on the next page, fill in the adapter name, the adapter suffix, and the remaining details as you desire (the defaults values are recommended for testing this integration).

Keep in mind that OVD does not immediately "push" this configuration into the server to take effect. You need to explicitly make that request to upload the configuration change to take effect. The easiest way is to right-click the OVD server and select Save All to Server. To test that your OVD is running on a the configured LDAP port and is exposing a directory tree with the namespace **dc=oracle,dc=com**, you can right-click the OVD Server and select Open Server Browser. This should refresh the Data Browser panel at the bottom with a Client View node.

Expanding the Client View node should show if the directory root was created properly (in our case **dc=oracle,dc=com**), as shown in Figure 10-7 at the bottom of the next page. However, clicking the node should result in an error: "object does not exist." That is expected since you have simply defined the tree's root without any substantive data. The next few sections will show you how to add that substantive data (from the physical sources) to your virtual directory tree.

Integrating OVD with an Active Directory LDAP Server

Now that the root of the tree has been successfully created in the virtual directory, you can start populating the tree with information about users from actual physical repositories, such as the enterprise Active Directory server. The first step of a physical LDAP server integration is to create

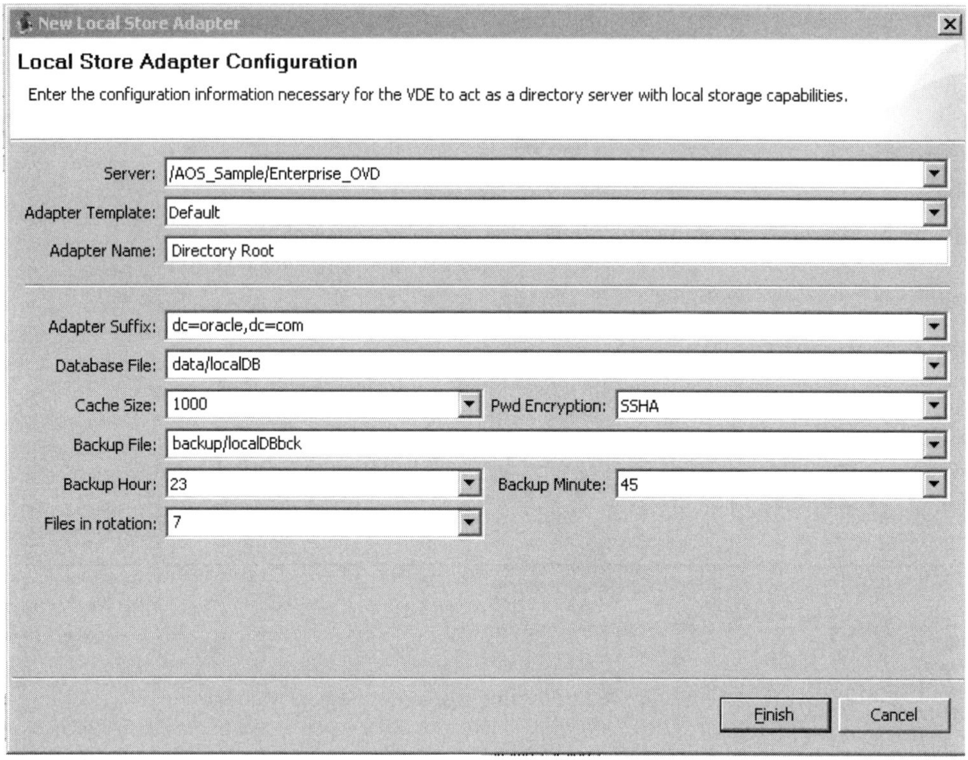

FIGURE 10-6 *Configuring the basic attributes of an LSA*

a new LDAP adapter in the same way you created one for the LSA. However, the configuration information is related to the external LDAP server. Figure 10-8 shows a sample LDAP adapter configuration for Active Directory. In this scenario, a directory of full-time employees is being integrated.

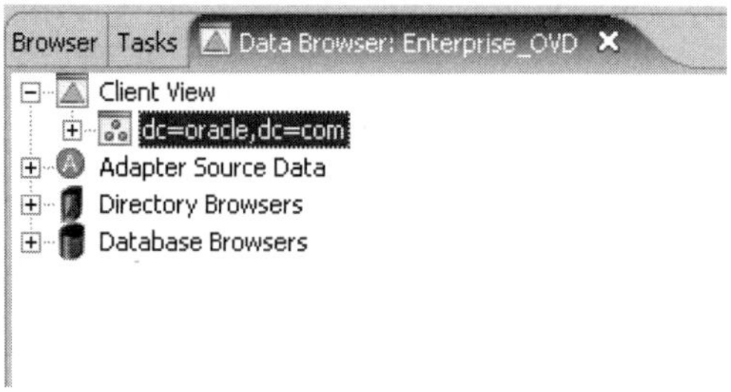

FIGURE 10-7 *Testing whether the new directory tree was created by the LSA*

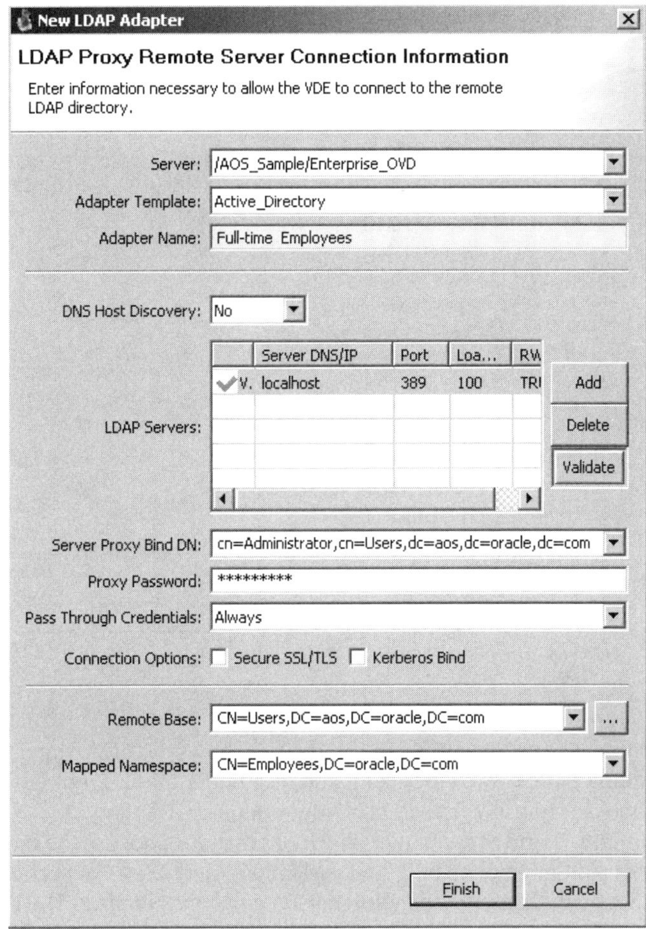

FIGURE 10-8 *Creating an LDAP adapter to integrate with Active Directory*

In Figure 10-8, notice the following details:

- The Active Directory namespace: **CN=Users,DC=aos,DC=oracle,DC=com**
- The OVD namespace mapped to the AD namespace: **CN=Employees,DC=oracle,DC=com**

You can see how the existing AD namespace was easily transformed to look like a global enterprise namespace using a much more functional view of my users rather than a technical system view. At this point, you can go back to the Data Browser panel in the OVD Manager console and test out this integration by right-clicking the Client View node and selecting Refresh Current Node.

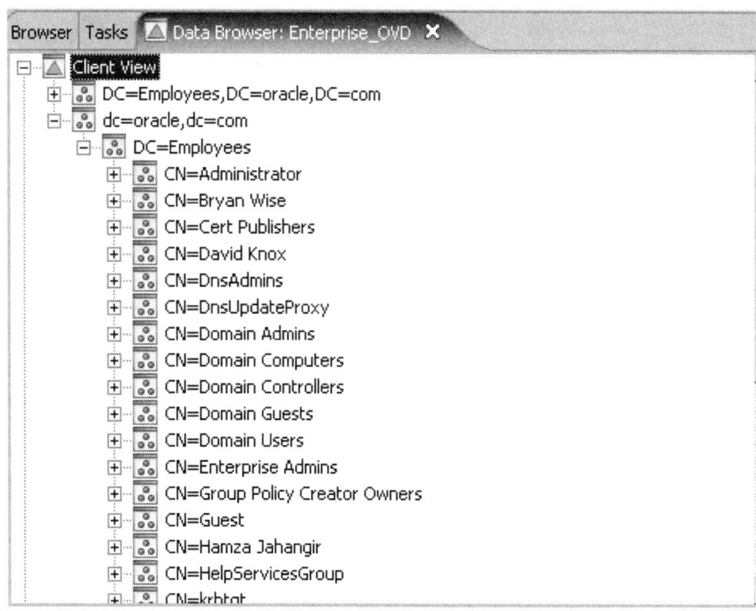

FIGURE 10-9 *The Data Browser is an effective and easy tool to test LDAP integration*

Notice that the Client View node in Figure 10-9 shows the LDAP integration directly at the node **DC=Employees,dc=oracle,dc=com**, and also under the desired root node (created by the LSA) so you can choose where to start your queries.

Active Directory is one of the outlier directories that does not use the **inetorgperson** object class and instead uses a proprietary naming standard for user attributes. For example, Active Directory uses **employeeID** instead of the standard **inetorgperson employeeNumber**. The **inetorgperson** object class has become a widely-used user data model standard in many web and client-server applications, so it makes sense to rationalize and map proprietary naming conventions to the standardized **inetorgperson** using OVD's mapping capabilities. OVD has a prebuilt plug-in called InetAD that provides this normalization between Active Directory and **inetorgperson** as a standard feature.

You can implement this by following these steps:

1. Open the LDAP adapter configuration by double-clicking your Active Directory LDAP Adapter in the OVD console.
2. Select the Plug-in tab and select New Plug-in.
3. In the Plug-In Definition window shown in Figure 10-10, click Select From Server for the class.
4. Select InetAD from the list and then click through Next and Finish to complete adding this plug-in to your AD configuration.

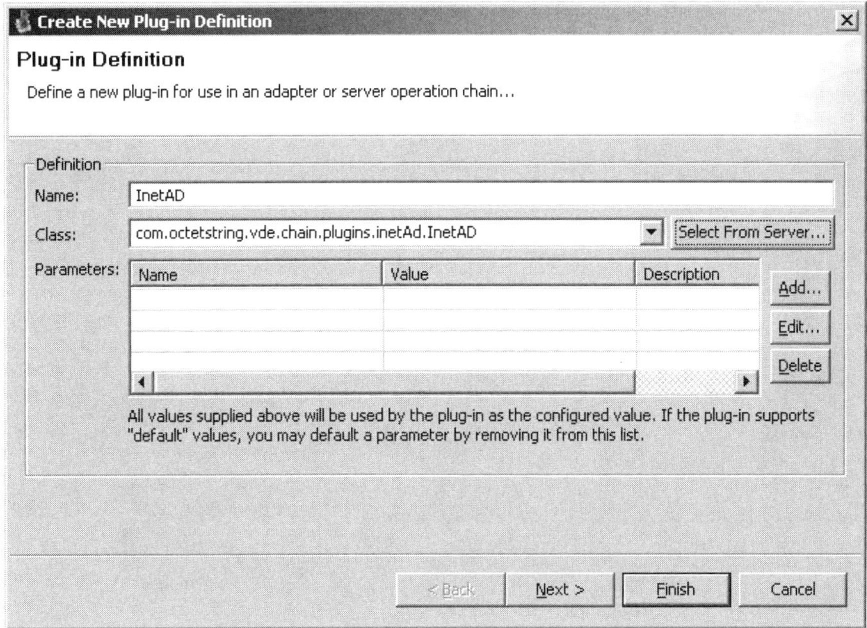

FIGURE 10-10 *Adding a plug-in for Active Directory*

The plug-in is now ready to be fired any time a query is run against the data originating from the Active Directory server. This is one example of how OVD can dynamically transform data to meet certain requirements of the client or the application using this data. You can now test this plug-in by going back to the client view and looking the details of one of your Active Directory users. You should now see the object class **inetorgperson** as part of every AD user.

You just witnessed an example of how OVD integrates existing physical LDAP servers. In the process, data was normalized and changed to a common representation. Next, we will discuss this same idea of integrating more backend sources; however, you will see how you can apply OVD to integrate information from non-LDAP sources, such as relational databases.

Integrating OVD with an Oracle Database

In this section, we explore the possibilities of leveraging more than just LDAP information for making access control decisions. While LDAP servers are the designated place to store and access identity information, it is often insufficient for making very critical access decisions. Often, you need to query additional repositories that may contain key information that helps in making better security decisions. Employment status, security clearances, and external environmental factors are some example types of data that typically do not live in an LDAP server but can live in alternative formats/repositories, such as relational databases. OVD can be applied in such scenarios to tap into that information and expose it via LDAP to all the access decision points while keeping it in its current location (database) and current format (relational).

In this section, we assume that a relational database table contains a user's security clearance level in the enterprise. While this might initially seem like a military or intelligence scenario, businesses are starting to use the idea of security clearance levels to protect their financial records from being accessed inappropriately. So, for now we will assume a table with this simple column structure:

```
SQL> desc user_clearance
 Name                                      Null?    Type
 ----------------------------------------- -------- ------------------------
--
 USER_ID                                                     VARCHAR2(4000)
 CLEARANCE_CODE                                              VARCHAR2(4000)
 CLEARANCE_LEVEL                                             VARCHAR2(4000)
```

The following shows the sample dataset in that table:

```
SQL> select * from user_clearance;

USER_ID    CLEARANCE_CODE CLEARANCE_LEVEL
---------- ---------- --------------------
HJAHANGIR  NC         Not Cleared
PSACK      S          Secret
SGAETJEN   TS         Top Secret
DKNOX      NC         Not Cleared
BWISE      NC         Not Cleared
RWARK      TS         Top Secret
TMUTH      S          Secret

7 rows selected.
```

Before beginning the steps to "virtualize" a relational database table, you need to consider two design decisions that will impact the quality of the virtualization. First, you need to select an attribute that will be used to connect or relate the database records with the records in OVD. This is often the primary key of the database table where the attribute resides. In this case, you will use the USER_ID identifier (similar to an employee identity number in a HR application) that will connect the records.

Next you need to decide where the virtual LDAP entries, originating from the relational database, should be presented in the LDAP tree. Oftentimes, the database records provide only part of an existing user's profile, so the data needs to be joined with an existing LDAP entry that already represents the user. To get that unified user view, we need to do two things:

1. Create a new branch in the LDAP tree for all the user records from the database.
2. Join the new branch with the existing branch (this is covered in the upcoming section, "Joining Information in OVD").

In this example, we intentionally chose a poor namespace (**ou=DB,dc=oracle,dc=com**) to demonstrate how OVD's transformation capabilities can be used to clean up legacy namespace clutter without necessarily undertaking a "rip-and-replace" method. We can also hide the branch from the external LDAP clients, if we choose, by setting a visibility flag for that branch in OVD. The following shows the basic steps for "virtualizing" a database table:

1. Configure the JDBC driver library. Select the appropriate JDBC libraries installed with the Oracle Virtual Directory server using the OVD Library Manager interface, as illustrated in Figure 10-11. In this example, we selected the Oracle database's ojdbc14.jar file for the Oracle-specific JDBC implementation.

   Note that the Library Manager in OVD Manager can be accessed by right-clicking the OVD Server, selecting Manage, and selecting Server Libraries.
2. Create and configure a database adapter in the OVD Manager as a new adapter.

   We will use the Oracle Thin Driver. Once the configuration information is properly entered, click Validate Connection, as shown in Figure 10-12.
3. Map the database table to the directory object by selecting the database table and the LDAP object class.

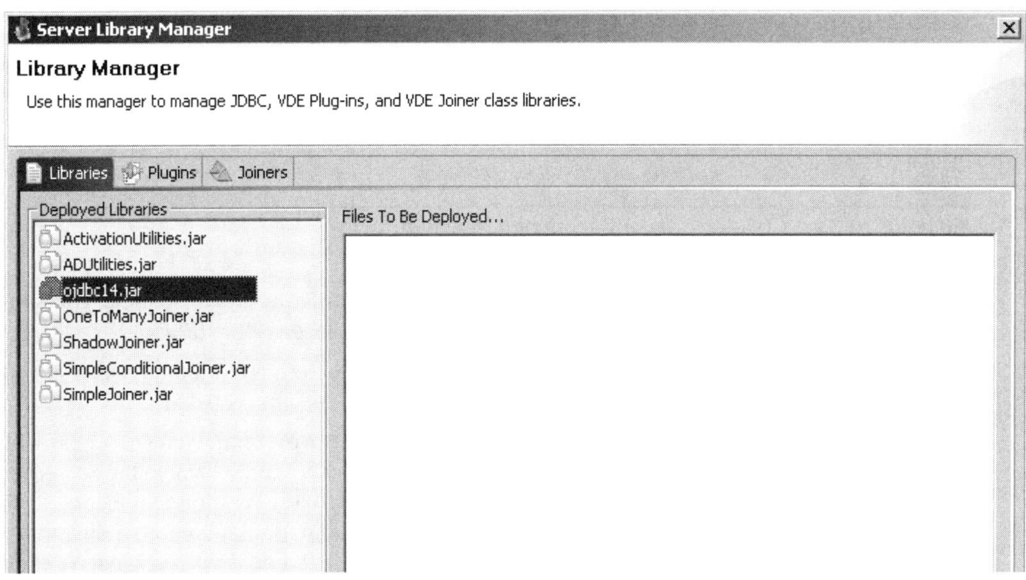

FIGURE 10-11 *Deploying Oracle JDBC drivers to OVD*

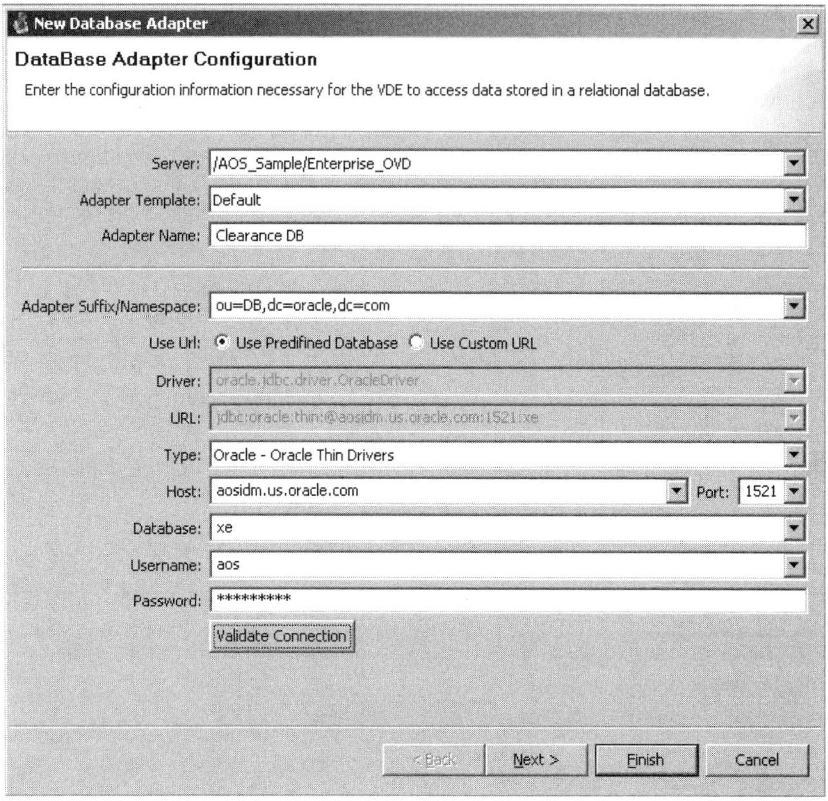

FIGURE 10-12 *Creating a database adapter in OVD*

Note that if these are employees (that is, person records), you choose **inetorgperson** as the object class and **uid** or **cn** as the relative distinguished name (RDN).

4. Map the database columns to attributes of the object class. We map the USER_ID column to the **uid** attribute in the **inetorgperson** object class in Figure 10-13.

At this point, OVD configuration is complete and you will have a virtual directory representation of your identity information from the database. You can test this by going back to the Server Browser panel in OVD Manager and refreshing any node in the Client View, as shown in Figure 10-14.

This exercise illustrates the transformation of a relational database table into a directory tree, where we converted each record in the table to an entry under a certain namespace. While this type of integration can be technically interesting and useful, we are not quite done making the relational data accessible for our identity management purposes, because the new branch we created is in a different part of the directory tree than the rest of the user information that is coming from other LDAP servers. To unify the information from the database and the enterprise LDAP servers, such as OID and Active Directory, we need to apply another OVD function called *joining* using a join view adapter.

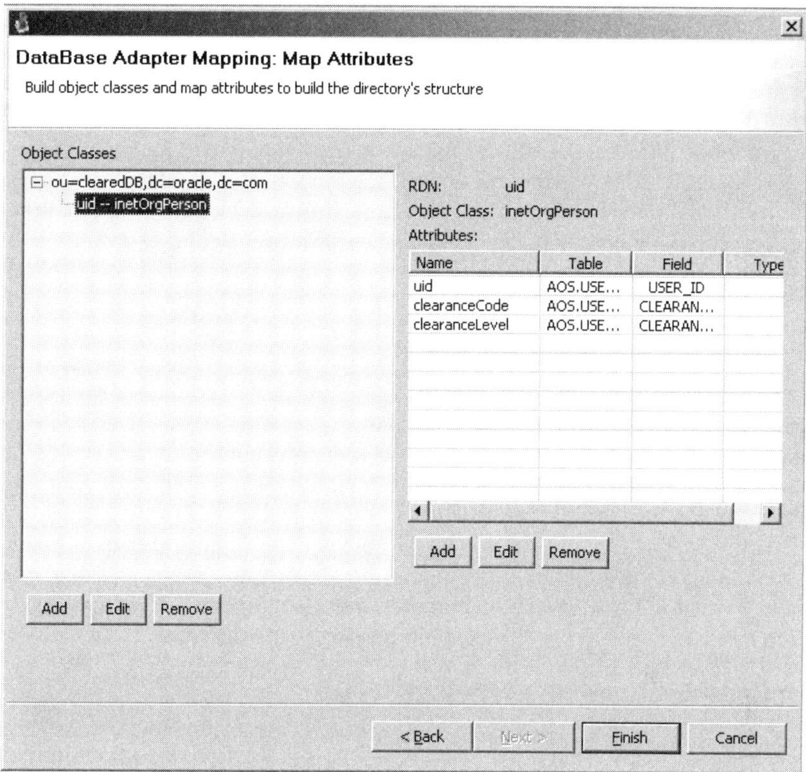

FIGURE 10-13 *Mapping database to OVD*

Browser | Tasks | Data Browser: Enterprise_OVD

Client View
DC=Employees,DC=oracle,DC=com
ou=clearedDB,dc=oracle,dc=com
uid=BWISE
uid=DKNOX
uid=HJAHANGIR
uid=PSACK
uid=RWARK
uid=SGAETJEN
uid=TMUTH
dc=oracle,dc=com
Adapter Source Data
Directory Browsers
Database Browsers

Name	Value
DN	uid=HJAHANGIR,ou=clearedDB,dc=oracle,dc=com
objectclass	inetOrgPerson
objectclass	organizationalPerson
objectclass	person
objectclass	top
clearanceLevel	Not Cleared
clearanceCode	NC
uid	HJAHANGIR

FIGURE 10-14 *Testing the database adapter in OVD*

Joining Information in OVD

A join view is conceptually similar to a database view, where information from other adapters is joined together using some condition, or "joiner." A join view typically has a "primary" source for the user data that is then unified with a "joined" source to create the extended user profile.

Consider this example: An LDAP profile for a user contains the standard LDAP attributes (name, location, contact, and so on). However, you are required to augment the basic user profile with a new attribute called **clearanceCode** for applications that need that piece of user data that lives in an external relational database. This is a great use case for using an OVD join view adapter; you can augment the basic LDAP profile with the additional attribute whose value is stored in the database. Figure 10-15 illustrates use of the join view concept in this scenario.

In OVD, the join view is implemented using a join view adapter that essentially integrates a view on top of the existing adapter integrations to the backend sources of data. In our example, the join view is created over the LDAP adapter integration to Active Directory and the database adapter integration to the Oracle Database. The LDAP adapter will be the "primary" source for the join view since the majority of the data lives in that repository. The additional attributes from the database table will be used to augment the user profile information coming from Active Directory. Figure 10-16 illustrates the relationship between the join view adapter and the other adapters to create that unified view of a user.

It's worth restating that the join view technology is analogous to database views, because the data is maintained in its original location and the view merely provides a single entry point that optionally translates the original data and then merges it together. To achieve a proper unified view, you need to carefully consider certain aspects of the design.

Design Considerations for a Join View

Before we demonstrate the actual steps for creating the join view adapter, we need to decide on certain key characteristics of the joined view—data sources, join conditions, and data presentation. The following sections discuss some options at hand along those three areas of design.

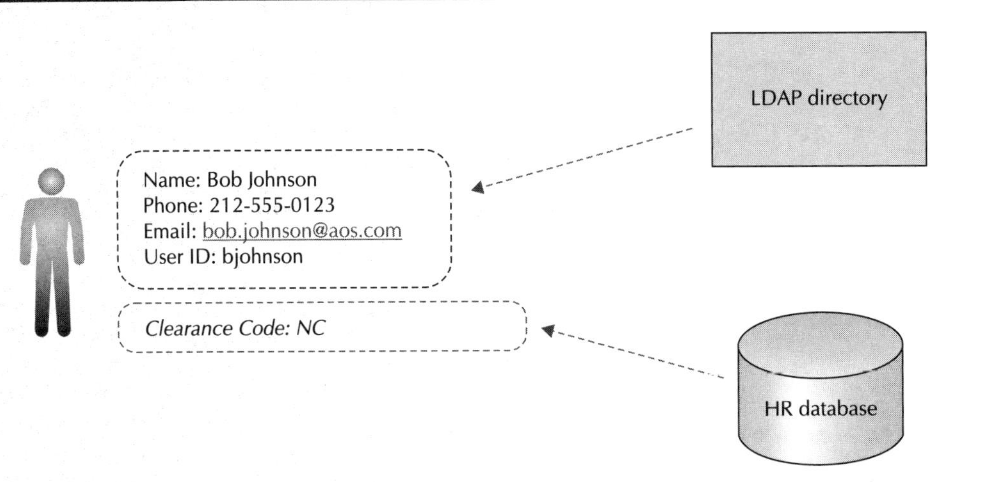

FIGURE 10-15 *Using a join view to unify a user profile from multiple sources of data*

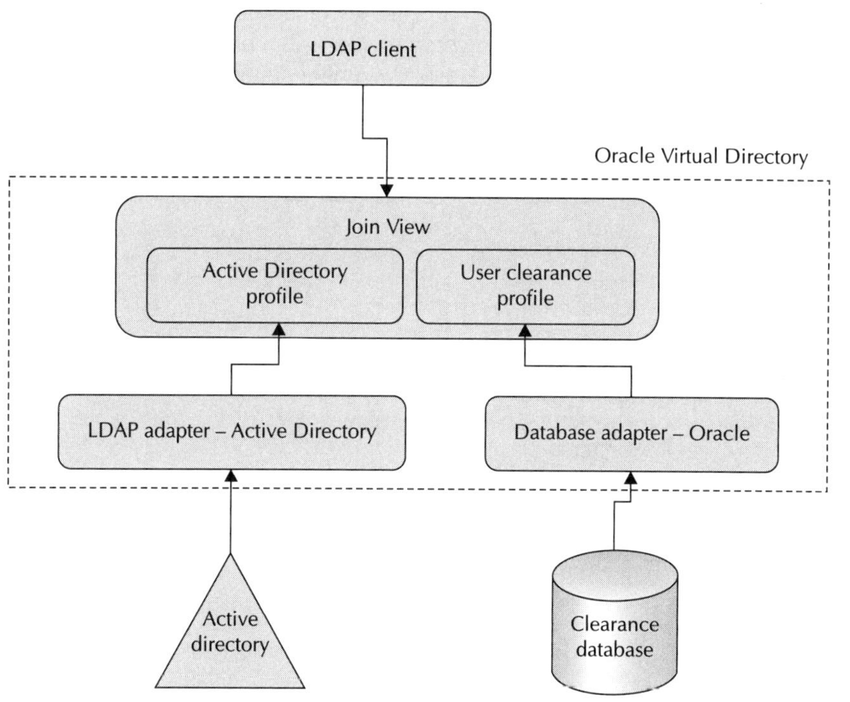

FIGURE 10-16 *Join views used to rationalize the other OVD adapter integrations*

Primary Adapter Our first design decision with regard to a join view adapter is the selection of a primary adapter underneath the join view adapter. The primary adapter is typically the source where the majority of the user profile resides. This is typically the enterprise LDAP server (Active Directory in our example).

Binding Adapter The second design decision is the authoritative source of the authentication attribute (that is, user's password). Any **LDAPBIND** operation request through the virtual LDAP server will route to this adapter to perform user authentications. Typically, this adapter is the same as the Primary adapter. In our example, we will set Active Directory as the binding adapter.

Joiners A joiner is similar to a database foreign key that connects records between two relational tables. In this case, a joiner connects LDAP entries from two existing OVD adapters to look and feel like a single LDAP entry in OVD. Each of the three types of joiners is specialized for a specific scenario:

- **Simple joiner** The simplest form of joining uses an attribute value equality test to join two LDAP entries. A simple joiner supports a rule such as **uid=uid**, where the join adapter can unify all the LDAP entries that share the same value **uid** attribute. This is one of the most common joiners in use for OVD implementations. A simple joiner will take an entry from the primary adapter and join it with the first matching entry in the joined adapter. If more than one entry exists with the matching value, the subsequent entries will be ignored.

- **One-to-many joiner** A one-to-many joiner is identical to a simple joiner, except it can join one entry from the primary adapter with many entries from the joined adapter. This type of adapter is useful when you're trying to join entries with multi-valued attributes that are populated by multiple records from the joined adapter source.

  Consider this example, in which we want to create a new LDAP group called Data Architecture based on a database table that already maintains member information:

```
SQL> select user_id, user_group from user_group_memberships;

USER_ID    USER_GROUP
---------- ----------
BJOHNSON    DATA_ARCHITECTURE
BWISE       DATA_ARCHITECTURE
TMUTH       DATA_ARCHITECTURE
BJOHNSON    DATA_ANALYST
DKNOX       NETWORK_SECURITY
RWARK       ORACLE_DBA

6 rows selected.
```

  Using the one-to-many joiner, you can unify all the group memberships to be presented through the multi-valued **uniqueMember** attribute of the virtual group object in the OVD tree. An **LDAPSEARCH** request on that group object would look like the following from the OVD client's perspective:

```
$ ldapsearch -h hostname -p 389 -b dc=oracle,dc=com "(cn=Data Architecture)"
uniqueMember

dn: uid=Data Architecture,ou=Groups,dc=oracle,dc=com
uniqueMember: uid=bjohnson, ou=Users,dc=oracle,dc=com
uniqueMember: uid=bwise, ou=Users,dc=oracle,dc=com
uniqueMember: uid=tmuth, ou=Users,dc=oracle,dc=com
```

- **Shadow joiner** This type of joiner can augment the standard set of attributes of an LDAP schema with an application-specific set of attributes. If an application wants to maintain a set of custom attributes as part of LDAP entries, a shadow joiner can be used to join the primary user profile with the "shadow" repository where these extended custom attributes are stored. Using this approach, the application writes the attribute to OVD via the LDAP interface; OVD then "quietly" writes this back to the shadow repository without touching the profile in the primary LDAP server. Shadow joiners eliminate the need to extend existing LDAP schema to support custom attributes that are application-centric. This joiner is useful when you're faced with legacy applications that rely on custom attributes, and it provides a way to centralize their directory needs without significant code rewrites.

Adapter Visibility When you set up an adapter in OVD, by default, all the data is public and available to all external LDAP clients. In most circumstances, the purpose of the virtual directory is to rationalize all the data from all the backend sources and present a single view of the directory tree. This means controlling the visibility of each adapter we have setup in OVD and enabling visibility only on the adapter that presents the truly rationalized view.

In our example, we configured integrations to an LDAP server and a relational Oracle table and rationalized those two integrations using the join view adapter. As a result, it makes sense to let the LDAP clients see only the data presented through the Join view.

To enable this, we need to configure the **Visibility** flag of all the adapters we have configured. Three settings are used for **Visibility**:

- **Yes** Adds the adapter data to the directory tree presented to the public
- **No** Completely hides the information from all entities
- **Internal** Hides the information from public access but makes it available for internal plug-ins and adapters

  In our example, we want the following values for each adapter:

- Join view adapter: *Visibility = Yes*
- LDAP adapter: *Visibility = Internal*
- Oracle Database adapter: *Visibility = Internal*

Figure 10-17 illustrates how to set the visibility of an adapter (the full-time employees from Active Directory integration in this scenario).

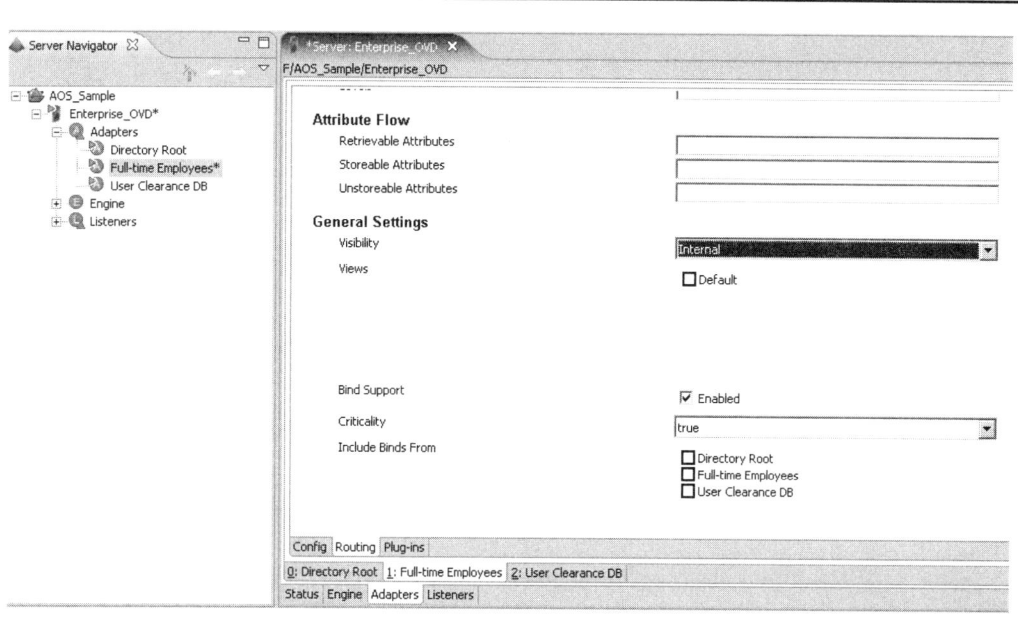

FIGURE 10-17 *Setting OVD adapter visibility*

Creating the Join View Adapter

After thinking through the key design considerations for making a join view of all identity data and therefore creating a truly virtual unified LDAP directory profile, you can take the steps to create the join view adapter itself and implement all those design decisions.

1. Create a new adapter in OVD of type "Join View Adapter" with the following attributes (as shown in Figure 10-18):
   - Adapter Suffix/Namespace: **cn=Employees,dc=oracle,dc=com**
   - Primary Adapter: Full-time Employees
   - Binding Adapter: Full-time Employees

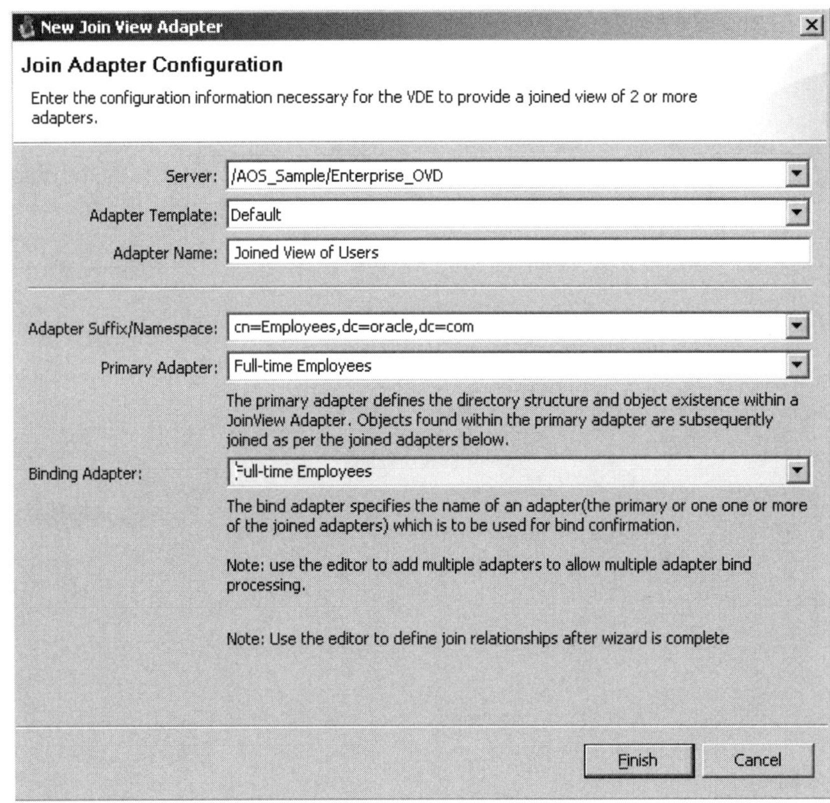

FIGURE 10-18 *Creating join view adapter*

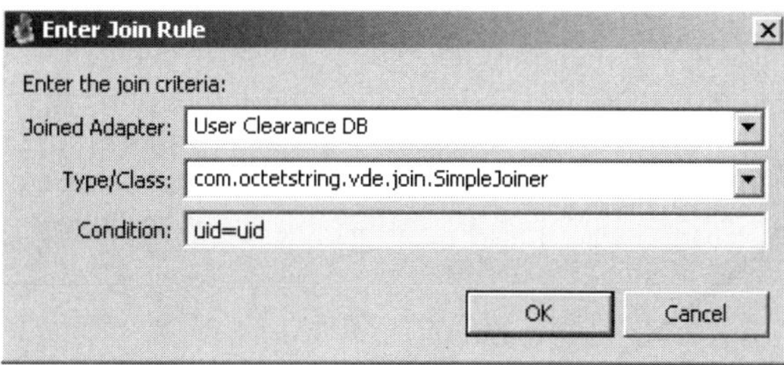

FIGURE 10-19 *Creating a Join Rule*

2. Set up a join rule to map users from the LDAP repository with records in the database table. Inside the configuration panel of the join view, create a new join rule with the following attributes, as shown in Figure 10-19:
   - Joined Adapter: User Clearance DB
   - Type/Class: com.octetstring.vde.join.SimpleJoiner
   - Condition: **uid=uid** (this condition connects LDAP entries and Database records that share the same uid value)
3. Now you can test your newly created join view of users and their information in OVD. Figure 10-20 demonstrates the results.

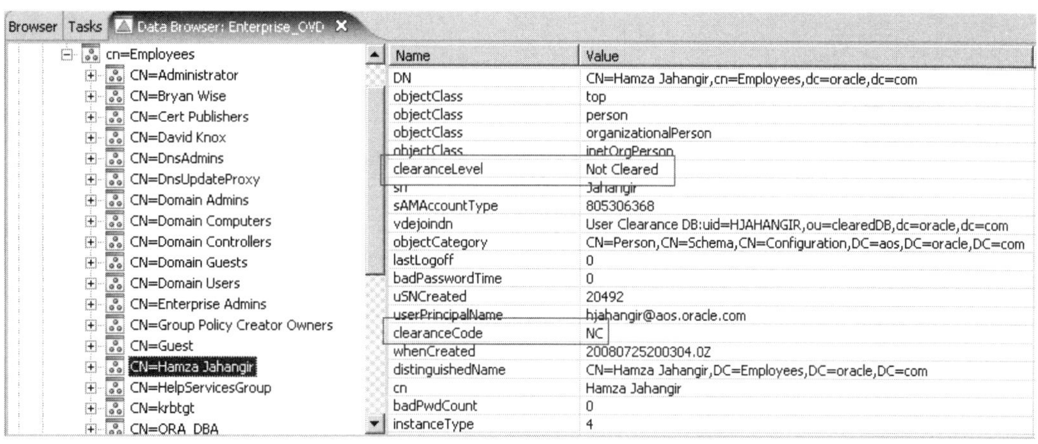

FIGURE 10-20 *Testing the join view*

You can now see that the two additional attributes that we "joined" from the database records (Clearance Level and Clearance Code) are now represented through the LDAP interface as part of the user's overall profile that includes the Active Directory details.

The key point to remember is that throughout this entire process of integrating data from backend source to the OVD server, no data was physically moved or synchronized. The data still lives and is managed using the technologies and processes that existed before OVD was introduced into the picture. However, now all applications and clients have a common interface for querying and viewing that information.

Summary

The key characteristic difference between the directory and a generic user database (such as an HR database) is that an enterprise directory exists for the purpose of providing fast access to user data, mainly for security-related tasks inside applications. This focused scope of the directory's charter should drive all directory design and implementation decisions. Oracle products such as Oracle Internet Directory (OID) and Oracle Virtual Directory (OVD) provide focused capabilities for building that fast and efficient user repository. However, the architects and developers of the directory still need to spend sufficient time and research on answering the key decisions about the data that goes into the directory: scope, source, structure, presentation, and semantics. Those decisions are highly subjective to the organization and can rarely be automated by tools and technologies. Once those decisions have been made, technologies such as OID and OVD, if applied correctly, can make a significant difference in your getting to the end state of having a simple, flexible, and rationalized user directory that any application can leverage for identity management purposes.

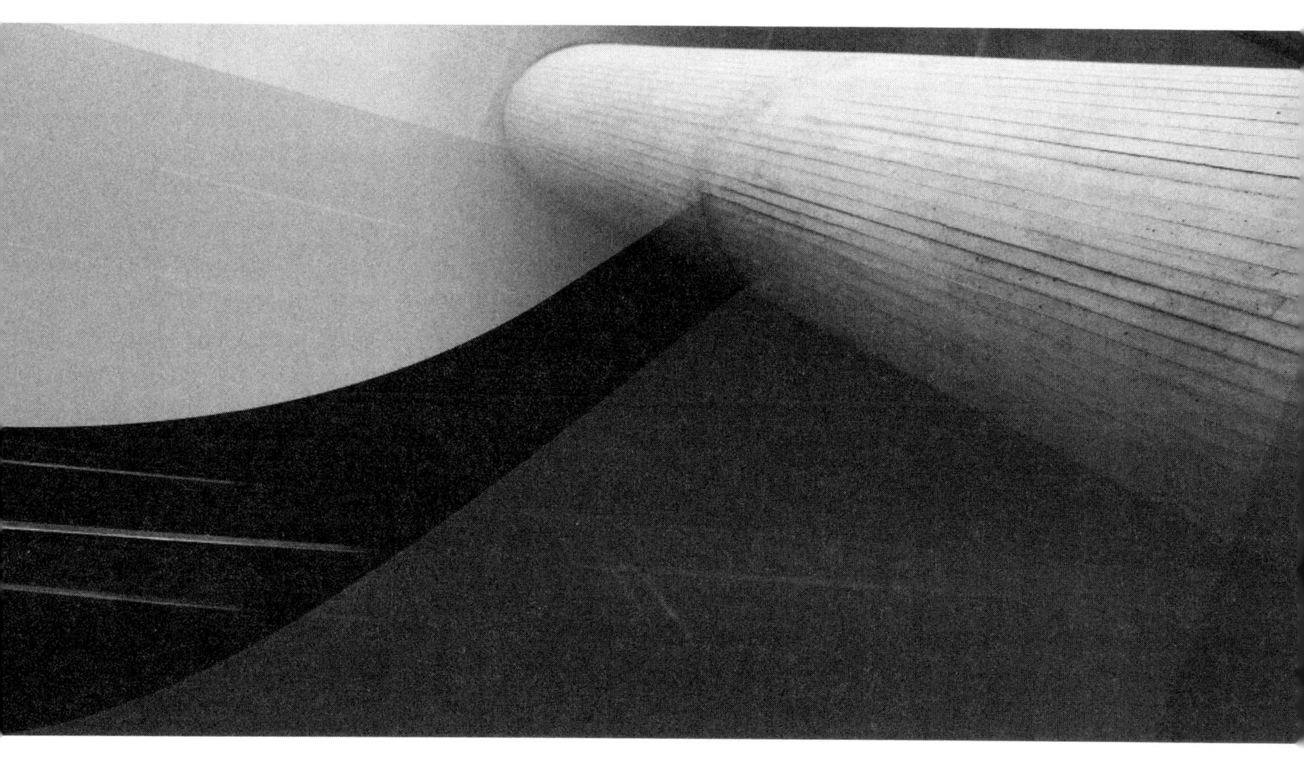

PART IV

Applied Security for Oracle APEX and Oracle Business Intelligence

CHAPTER 11

Web-centric Security in APEX

n this chapter, we look at the Application Express (APEX) architecture and how to configure it securely. This chapter focuses on solutions at the installation and configuration level. The next chapter is dedicated to secure coding practices.

Introduction to the APEX Environment

APEX is a web development environment that lives completely inside the database. Understanding the APEX environment—both development and runtime—is critical to your understanding of how to secure it. Client-server developers have worked in environments in which each user connects to the database as a true database user or schema. Web developers working with technologies such as Java 2 Platform, Enterprise Edition (J2EE) are accustomed to connecting as a single database user and executing all queries and database logic as that user. APEX falls somewhere in between these two approaches, and this causes a great deal of confusion for developers new to the APEX environment.

Components and Configurations

I'm going to make a few assumptions to try and keep the examples in this chapter as simple as possible. All content in this book is based on Application Express 3.2, the most current version at the time of writing. The base architecture has not changed since the first public release of APEX and is unlikely to change in such a way that dramatically affects the concepts. APEX 3.2 offers a number of major enhancements in the area of security and is therefore the minimum version that you should select when you're starting a new project. Some of these enhancements are exposed as documented features or options available to the developer, but many of them are at the core of the APEX engine itself.

Starting with Oracle 10*g* Express Edition and Oracle 11*g* Standard and Enterprise Editions, you can use the Embedded PL/SQL Gateway (EPG) instead of Oracle HTTP Server (OHS). Since this book's focus is security, all examples are based on OHS with mod_plsql, as it is a time-tested solution and offers many options for secure configuration. OHS is based on Apache, which includes mod_plsql and is really a subset of Oracle Application Server (OAS), and APEX can be configured with any version of OAS that includes mod_plsql. Since APEX is a database-centric development tool, and OHS is included on the companion CD of the Oracle Database, the vast majority of APEX deployments use OHS. Consequently, I will refer to OHS only in the APEX chapters of this book to simplify examples and diagrams.

Before you begin configuring OHS, you need to understand which version you are using, because the architecture and configuration is quite different between the two major versions in use today. Two versions of OHS are available for APEX. OHS Version 10*g* Release 2 is based on Apache 1.3 and is included on the Oracle Database 10*g* Release 2 Companion CD. OHS version 10*g* Release 3 is based on Apache 2.0 and is available as an additional component on the Oracle Database 11.1 download page at http://otn.oracle.com/database.

When looking for documentation for either version, keep in mind that OHS is considered a subcomponent of OAS. A stand-alone administrators guide for Oracle HTTP Sever 10*g* Release 2 is available, but the documentation for 10*g* Release 3 is in the OAS administrators guide. This may change over time, but if you are struggling to find documentation on OHS, make sure you look in the OAS documentation. In the context of other OAS components, OHS is considered a middle-tier, not an infrastructure. For any new installations, you should consider OHS 10*g* Release 3 based on Apache 2.0. Apache 2.0 brings significant security and performance enhancements and is indicated as the preferred architecture in the OHS statement of direction.

Architecture

APEX comprises tables and PL/SQL packages installed in three schemas in an Oracle database. The primary schema in APEX 3.2, APEX_030200, is where the majority of the objects are installed. In prior versions, this schema used *FLOWS_* as the prefix, so APEX 3.1 is installed in FLOWS_030100. The FLOWS_FILES schema contains only one table that is used to store any files uploaded through the APEX interface. The third schema, APEX_PUBLIC_USER, is used by OHS to connect to the database. This schema does not own any objects and has a very restricted set of privileges.

Once APEX is installed, you must log into the APEX administration interface and provision a workspace (Figure 11-1), which is a logical grouping of developers, applications, and schemas. Each workspace can have one or more schemas assigned to it. Each application within a workspace has an application-level attribute called Parse-As Schema that defines the schema or user for which all of the code within that application will execute.

To start, let's analyze the sequence of events that occur when an APEX application executes. In doing so, we will cover many of the components in play and see how they interoperate. The following URL will serve as the basis for an example of an APEX page that contains a simple report based on a SQL query: http://apex.oracle.com/pls/apex/f?p=100:3:6789:NO:::P3_DEPTNO:999.

When you enter the URL for this page, your web browser makes a request to the OHS based on Apache. (We'll talk about the embedded PL/SQL Gateway later, but the concepts are similar.) Apache notices that the first part of the URL is */pls/*, so it hands off control to mod_plsql, which looks at the next part of the URL, *apex*, and determines that it should use the APEX Database Access Descriptor (DAD). The definition of the DAD contains a database connect string as well as a username and a password hash. OHS will use this username to connect to the database. By default, this username is APEX_PUBLIC_USER, so if you query the username column from the v$session table in an active APEX environment, you'll see a number of sessions connected as APEX_PUBLIC_USER.

After you connect to the database, mod_plsql tells the database to execute the PL/SQL procedure contained in the URL. APEX uses a public synonym, "f," which points to the "show" procedure in the PL/SQL package wwv_flow owned by APEX_XXXXXX (version 3.2+) or FLOWS_XXXXXX. wwv_flow will then determine the application and page requested base on the colon-delimited parameter string. Each application has a "parse as" attribute that indicates in which database schema the application should operate. APEX then looks at the requested page to find any objects that it should display. Since this page has only a query, the APEX rendering engine then calls the protected system package SYS.WWV_DBMS_SQL to execute the SQL query as the schema specified in the "parse as" attribute. For example, if the parse as schema of your application is HR and the source of your regions is **select * from employees**, that will be parsed and executed with the rights of the HR user (see Figure 11-2).

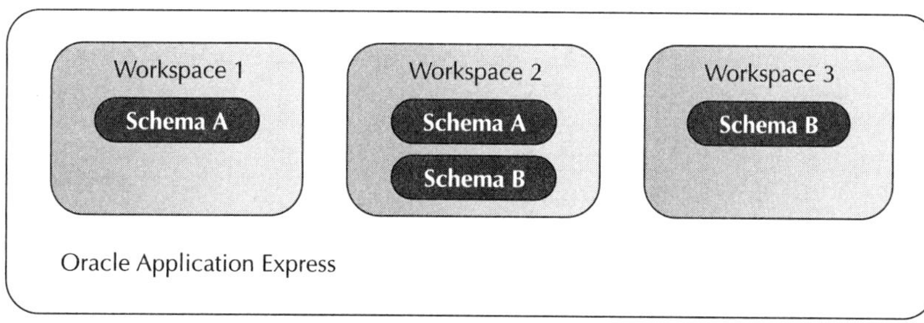

FIGURE 11-1 *Workspace to schema mapping*

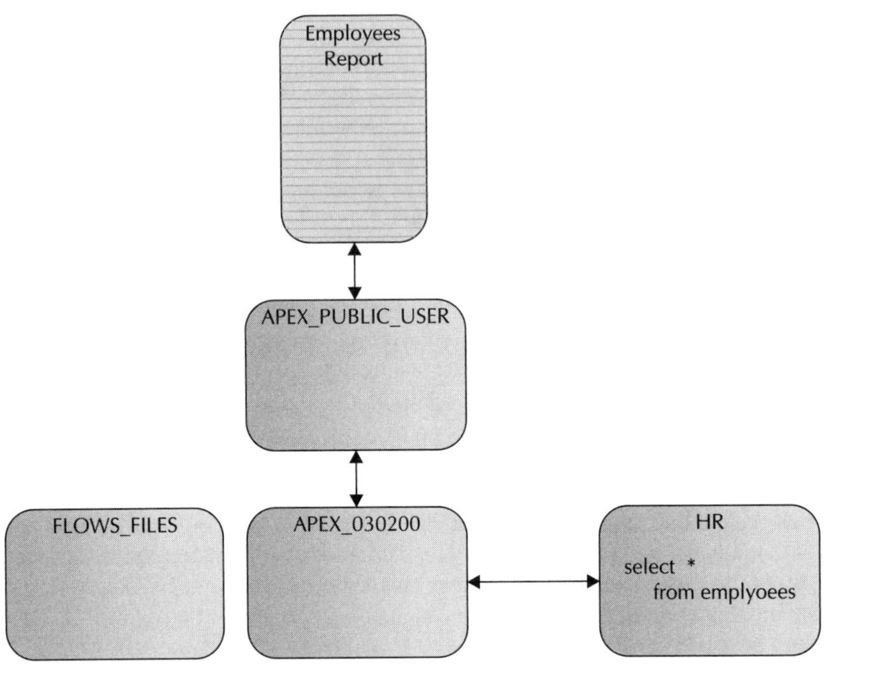

FIGURE 11-2 *APEX and "parse as" schemas*

APEX and Database Connections

APEX uses a number of pre-spawned database sessions between OHS and the database. This technique is called "connection pooling" (see Figure 11-3) and is highly scalable, since creating new database connections is an expensive process that could add significant time to the overall page load time if a new session were created for each request. In addition, each dedicated database session requires a certain amount of Program Global Area (PGA) memory on the database, which could add up to a huge amount of wasted memory for client-server systems with a large number of concurrent users.

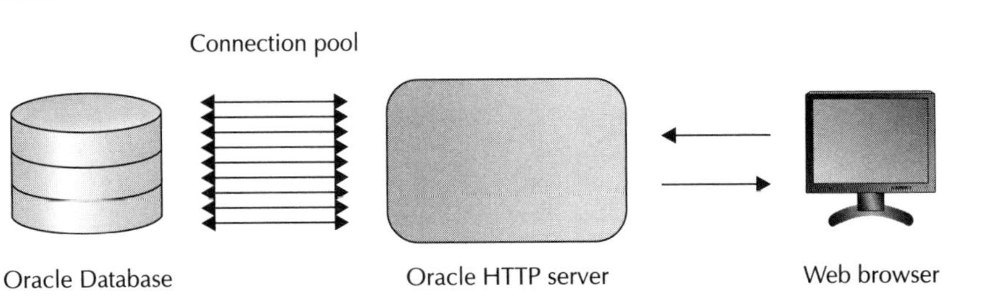

FIGURE 11-3 *Connection pool*

A busy system with hundreds or even thousands of concurrent users may have only 15–30 active database sessions at any given time. These sessions are continually reused by different application users until they reach the time-out period configured in the **PlsqlIdleSessionCleanupInterval** variable located within the plsql.conf file. It defaults to 15 minutes. As an end user navigates from page to page in an APEX application, the user will likely use a different database session for each page view. These sessions are simply reused from the connection pool so a new session is not created for each page view or each new user. This is quite different from a client-server application, where a new database session is created for each user when the client application connects to the database. The same session is typically used as long the client application is running.

Connection pooling also changes a developer's perspective when it comes to security. Traditionally, users of a client-server application, such as Oracle Forms, each connect to a different schema. These schemas are usually a one-to-one mapping with the users. In contrast, all users of an APEX application connect through the same schema.

Another key differentiator between APEX and client-server technologies is the stateless nature of the web. In a client-server environment such as Oracle Forms, a persistent connection exists between the client application and the database. If the network was severed between the application and the database, the database would know it. In a pure web environment such as APEX, the connection is stateless. When an end user requests a page, the request is sent from the web browser to OHS, and then on to the database. The APEX engine will process the request and return the desired page. At that point, a connection between the web browser and OHS or the database no longer exists. In essence, the sequence goes like this: Request, Response, Disconnect. Understanding these concepts is critical to understanding the architecture of APEX and consequently making informed decisions when designing a security strategy.

APEX and Database Roles

Traditional database developers and database administrators are likely accustomed to using database roles to grant privileges on objects. A DBA might grant select on a set of tables to a role, and then grant the role to the database schema used by an application. This scenario will not work in APEX, however, because the underlying packages that APEX used to parse SQL statements as other users did not support roles. The database packages were recently enhanced to support this functionality, so it is only a matter of time before these changes are reflected throughout APEX.

Developers are often troubled by this concept, because they typically test queries or PL/SQL procedures in SQL*Plus or SQL Developer first. The same query or procedure call may fail when executed from an APEX region or process. The reason for this error is that since APEX does not support roles, all privileges on objects must be explicit direct object grants to the parsing schema of an APEX application. Fortunately, a simple command is available in SQL*Plus and SQL Developer to help debug this particular situation. Typing **set role none** and pressing ENTER in SQL*Plus, or pressing F5 in SQL Developer, will remove all roles from your current session and any implicit privileges granted through roles. To illustrate this point, here's a simple example:

```
system@aos> create role hr_viewer;
Role created.
system@aos> grant select on hr.employees to hr_viewer;
Grant succeeded.
system@aos> grant hr_viewer to demo;
Grant succeeded.
system@aos> grant select on hr.departments to demo;
Grant succeeded.
```

This grants SELECT privileges on two tables in the HR schema to the DEMO user. Permissions for SELECT on HR.EMPLOYEES were granted to the role HR_VIEWER. We then granted this role to the DEMO user. In contrast, the last line grants SELECT on HR.DEPARTMENTS to DEMO using a direct object grant. Another way to look at this is that the privileges on EMPLOYEES are implicit, as they are inherited from a role, whereas the privileges on DEPARTMENTS are explicit.

Now let's connect as DEMO to see how this might impact an APEX application:

```
demo@aos> select count(*) from hr.employees;
  COUNT(*)
----------
       107

demo@aos> set role none;
Role set.

demo@aos> select count(*) from hr.employees;
select count(*) from hr.employees
                        *
ERROR at line 1:
ORA-00942: table or view does not exist

demo@aos> select count(*) from hr.departments;
  COUNT(*)
----------
        27
```

Note that once all role-based privileges are removed from the session, DEMO can no longer query HR.EMPLOYEES, yet DEMO can still query HR.DEPARTMENTS.

APEX Sessions

For a developer to understand how to secure APEX, he or she must first understand the relationship between database sessions, APEX sessions, database users, and APEX users. If you simply monitor the common columns in v$session such as USERNAME, SID, and SERIAL#, you might miss a lot of information that APEX provides about the session. As you will see in the next example, APEX uses the MODULE, ACTION, CLIENT_INFO, and CLIENT_IDENTIFIER columns to expose as much information as possible about the APEX session associated with a particular database session. MODULE indicates the APEX application number, ACTION is set to the current page number, CLIENT_IDENTIFIER is the username of the end user logged into the application followed by their APEX session ID, and CLIENT_INFO is the user's username. This concept is called "identity preservation." These four columns are present in many of the SQL tuning views and reports such as V$SQL_AREA, ASH Reports, and ADDM Reports. A number of techniques can use these columns, such as monitoring long-running sessions, fine-grained auditing (FGA) policies, or even part of a Virtual Private Database (VPD) policy. We'll cover detailed examples of these techniques in the next chapter.

To illustrate the relationships between APEX sessions and database sessions, I've constructed an example APEX application with four pages, each with a long-running operation so we have time to capture the database session with a query. Pages one and three use the **DBMS_LOCK.SLEEP()** procedure in a PL/SQL region to cause the page to hang for a specified period of time.

Pages four and five use long-running queries to make sure the session is still active when I switch to SQL*Plus to query V$SESSION.

Note that APEX sessions are very short-lived, typically less than a second, which makes it difficult to capture session values. For this example, I intentionally crafted procedures and queries that would take several minutes to run, thus allowing me to capture the session output for this example. The following is the query and the results while running each of these pages in a new browser session:

```
sys@aos> select username, module, action, client_identifier
  from sys.v$session
 where module like 'APEX:%';
USERNAME           MODULE                ACTION   CLIENT_IDENTIFIER
------------------ --------------------- -------- ----------------------
APEX_PUBLIC_USER   APEX:APPLICATION 119  PAGE 3   DAVID.KNOX:8518310307188154
APEX_PUBLIC_USER   APEX:APPLICATION 119  PAGE 5   BRYAN.WISE:8190266602264378
APEX_PUBLIC_USER   APEX:APPLICATION 119  PAGE 1   RICHARD.
WARK:1019551358185708
APEX_PUBLIC_USER   APEX:APPLICATION 119  PAGE 4   HAMZA.JAHAN-
GIR:6260446272621304
```

The first thing to notice is that all USERNAME's are APEX_PUBLIC_USER. This is the database schema specified in the connection string of the DAD in the dads.conf file for OHS. Further inspection of the first row reveals that this is Application 119 and Page 3. The end user of the application for this database session is DAVID.KNOX. The long number at the end of CLIENT_IDENTIFIER is the APEX session ID that corresponds to the session ID DAVID.KNOX sees in the URL of his browser. To determine the actual database schema used to parse queries for this session, I would need to join to the APEX_WORKSPACE_SESSIONS and APEX_APPLICATIONS views.

Securing an APEX Instance

In this section, you'll learn a few techniques to secure each component in the APEX architecture, including the Oracle Database and OHS. The code and metadata for APEX are installed in a database schema with high-level privileges such as ALTER SYSTEM and ALTER USER, thus making APEX_XXXXXX or FLOWS_XXXXXX schemas a prime target for someone wishing to gain unauthorized access to the database. The front end of APEX is served through OAS or OHS and is often exposed to the Internet, which typically means that a much greater population has access to this tier.

APEX Security Settings

Within the APEX administration interface is a whole section dedicated to security settings. To view or modify these settings, you must have administrator credentials for APEX as whole, not just for a workspace. To access the administration interface, navigate to http://servername:port/pls/apex/apex_admin. If you are using the Embedded PL/SQL Gateway, you can omit */pls* from the URL. If this is a new install, the username is admin and the password must be set using the script apxchpwd.sql found in the APEX installation directory. This script is also used to reset the admin password should it be lost. It's a good practice to create administrator accounts for the people who need them instead of everyone logging in using admin, which provides no accountability. After you are logged into the administrative interface, open the Manage Service tab, shown in Figure 11-4, and click Security in the Manage Environment Settings area.

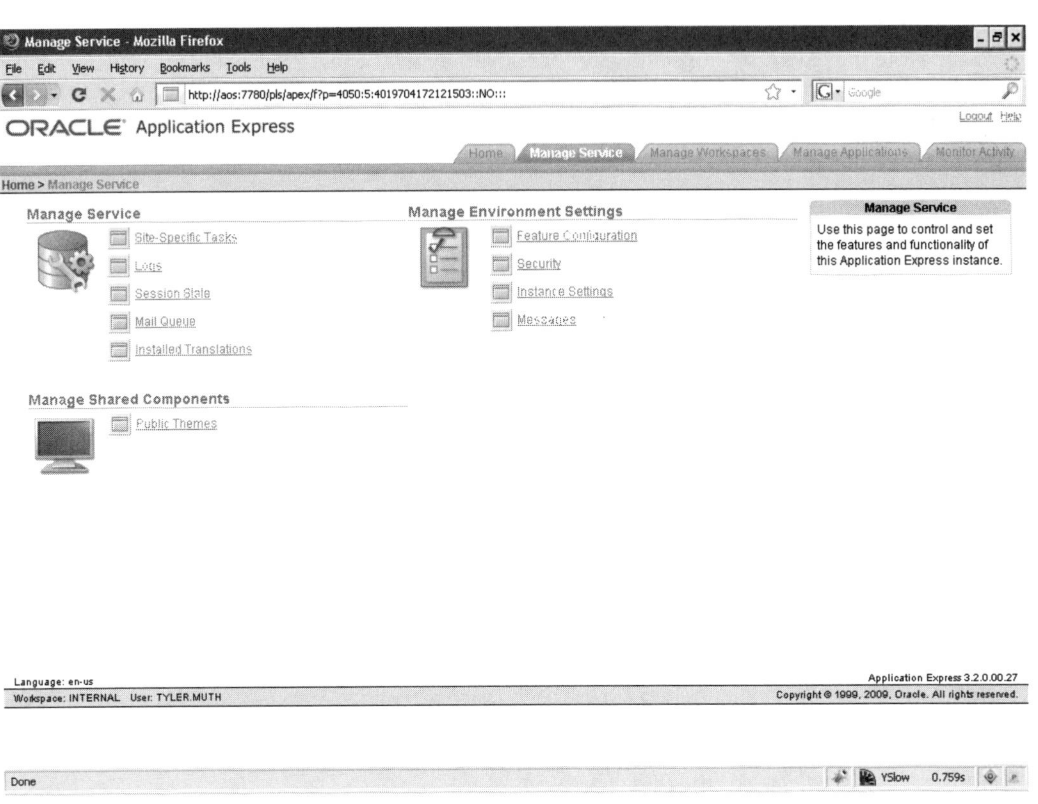

FIGURE 11-4 *Manage Service tab instance settings*

A word of caution before we get into the details of instance level settings: All the settings on this page apply to the whole APEX instance and affect every workspace. Some of the settings can disable the APEX graphical user interface, thus removing your ability to revert the setting. Before we start changing any settings, I will demonstrate the command line interface in case you need to revert any setting that has locked you out of the web interface. Fortunately, you can change all of the settings from a command line interface as long as you have SQL*Plus access to the database and a database account that has been granted the role APEX_ADMINISTRATOR_ROLE. The APEX_INSTANCE_ADMIN package is owned by the APEX schema and is used to set and get the value of any instance-level parameter:

```
APEX_INSTANCE_ADMIN.GET_PARAMETER(
    p_parameter      IN VARCHAR2)
RETURN VARCHAR2;

APEX_INSTANCE_ADMIN.SET_PARAMETER(
    p_parameter      IN VARCHAR2,
    p_value          IN VARCHAR2 DEFAULT 'N');
```

```
The following examples demonstrate the use of APEX_INSTANCE_ADMIN:
$ sqlplus system
Enter password: *******
-- The APEX_030200 schema is locked by default and should remain that way
SQL> alter session set current_schema=APEX_030200;
SQL>
set serveroutput on
declare
    l_value varchar2(4000);
begin
    l_value :=apex_instance_admin.get_parameter('PASSWORD_NOT_LIKE_WORDS');
    dbms_output.put_line('PASSWORD_NOT_LIKE_WORDS: '||l_value);
end;
/

PASSWORD_NOT_LIKE_WORDS: oracle:hello:welcome:guest:user:database
```

The Security page is divided into seven regions with the following parameters:

- **Set Workspace Cookie [YES | NO]** By default, APEX sets a persistent cookie in a developer's browser to remember the last workspace and username used to log into the APEX development environment. This is a convenience to developers, and as long as strong password policy is enforced, the default value of YES represents only a minor decrease in security.

- **Disable Administrator Login [YES | NO]** Warning: Once this parameter is set to YES, the only way to set it back to NO is through the command line API APEX_INSTANCE_ADMIN. This setting disables the APEX administration interface. In some circumstances, this may be desirable, such as in an organization that hosts a lot of workspaces yet needs to allow developers to access the development environment. This would prevent someone from using a brute-force attack to guess an administrator password and gain access to the interface. For production instances, consider using a runtime only installation of APEX.

- **Allow Public File Upload [YES | NO]** This applies only to applications that do not use any type of authentication, so that all users are anonymous. At first glance, file upload into the database seems relatively harmless, since the first threat that comes to mind is someone uploading a file with a virus, yet there is no way to execute a file inside the database that mitigates this risk. However, consider the possibility of someone uploading a bunch of large files. At the very least, this will be very resource intensive. At some point, the tablespace used by the APEX_FILES schema will fill, which is essentially a denial-of-service attack.

- **Restrict Access by IP Address** This parameter allows an administrator to limit the IP addresses that have access to the development environment. The wildcard character (*) can be used only at the end of the string—such as 192.168.1.* or 192.*. It allows you quickly to limit access to a particular subnet, or perhaps internal-only IP address in the case of Internet-facing instances. However, if possible, use other techniques, such as Apache mod_rewrite in addition to this parameter, that are more flexible and will stop traffic at the HTTP server before it reaches the database.

- **Require HTTPS [YES | NO]** Warning: This setting can disable access to APEX. This parameter applies only to the APEX development and administration environment, not to a custom application built with APEX. The default value of NO allows developers to use the APEX development environment and administration interface without the HTTPS protocol. When set to YES, the HTTPS flag is set in the APEX development interface cookie, thus requiring HTTPS to access the development interface. It's important first to configure HTTPS in the HTTP server and verify that it is working properly. If HTTPS is not configured in the HTTP server and this parameter is set to YES, all connections to the APEX development and administration environments will be denied. We discuss how to configure the HTTP Server for HTTPS/SSL later in this chapter.
- **Maximum Session Length in Seconds** This is the total time in seconds a web session is valid regardless of activity. While it does prevent someone, in particular a third party, from attempting to reuse an old session, it can also be a big inconvenience to developers. For most development environments, a value of 8 hours, or 28,800 seconds, is adequate, as the Maximum Session Idle Time in Seconds parameter is more relevant for protecting the environment.
- **Maximum Session Idle Time in Seconds** This parameter defines the maximum time a developer session can sit idle before it times out. In doing this, it addresses a more common security risk in most internal development environments, wherein a developer leaves his or her terminal unlocked and unattended for a long period of time. By setting this parameter to a relatively short time, such as 20 minutes, or 1200 seconds, you can help to mitigate this risk. This leaves a relatively short window of time for someone to find and access an unattended workstation.
- **Domain Must Not Contain** The expected value for this parameter is a colon-delimited list of domains that cannot be used in APEX regions of type URL or web service requests. The primary use case for this feature is to prevent applications developed on hosted environments in a DMZ from access internal sites. For example, suppose all of your internal domain names end in *internal-app.com* and you host an APEX development instance that is accessible outside of your organization. This parameter prevents callouts from the database to any domain named internal-app.com. Keep in mind the callout from a web service or URL region originates from the database and has nothing to do with the HTTP server. While this feature is convenient, it is no substitute for firewall rules defined at the network level to prevent these types of requests.
- **Require User Account Expiration and Locking** By default, each workspace administrator can set this parameter at the workspace level. When this parameter is set to YES at the instance level, it overrides all workspace-level settings.
- **Maximum Login Failures Allowed** Once an end user exceeds the number defined by this parameter, the user's account is locked and can be unlocked only by a workspace administrator. This parameter applies to APEX administrators and developers only. A value between 3 and 5 should allow for the occasional typo, yet not allow enough changes for someone to guess passwords.
- **Account Password Lifetime (Days)** This parameter defines the numbers of days that a developer's password is valid before the password must be changed. If you use Secure Sockets Layer (SSL) and strong passwords, setting this to a larger number is reasonable.

This expiration concept is based on the idea that eventually a password will be guessed or compromised. Therefore, using strong encryption and choosing good passwords tend to obviate the need.

- **Workspace Password Policy** The parameters in this section define a granular password policy that is applied to all administrators, developers, and end users. One important concept to consider is that these password rules do not apply to end user applications using an authentication scheme other than Application Express. For example, if a developer defines an authentication scheme of type LDAP for a particular application, the APEX password policy will not apply to users of that application. However, if the LDAP directory has a password policy, APEX will respect it.
- **Service Administrator Password Policy** This parameter affects only the APEX administration service. The default value is to use the Use Default Strong Password Policy. Changing this parameter to Use Policy Specified In Workspace Password Policy simply applies the custom password policy discussed in the preceding section to the APEX administration service.

Securing the Application Server Tier

The user interface for the APEX development environment is composed of several APEX applications, as APEX is written with itself. These applications are assigned numbers between 4000 and 4999. Consequently, APEX prevents a developer from creating any applications in this range.

The two primary components to the APEX development environment are the Application Builder and the SQL Workshop. The Application Builder allows developers to build web applications. The SQL Workshop provides an interface where developers can browse and modify database objects, as well as execute any SQL or PL/SQL statements. Commands issued from the SQL Workshop are parsed as a particular database schema for both object resolution and database privileges. The schema or schemas available to a developer in the SQL Workshop are defined in the APEX administration interface by mapping a schema to an APEX Workspace.

The idea that a developer doesn't need to install any software is one of the reasons APEX is so easy to use, but this also makes it a particularly tempting target for a hacker as it is a web interface to the database. If a nefarious person gains access to the APEX development environment, he can do a tremendous amount of damage, including exporting sensitive data, adding his own code to the schema or application to intercept and transmit data, and modifying or deleting applications or database objects. Because of this, protecting the APEX development environment against unauthorized users is critical, particularly in production applications.

Preventing Unauthorized Access to the APEX Environment

Prior to Application Express 3.1, the only options for protecting the development environment involved using techniques outside of APEX itself. The most popular technique is using Apache mod_rewrite to redirect all requests to the APEX development environment to a different page. Apache mod_rewrite allows you to chain together additional rules so you can allow access to the APEX development environment from a specific IP subnet or range and only during business hours on Monday through Friday. We'll discuss mod_rewrite in detail later in this chapter in the section "mod_rewrite and APEX," including specific examples.

Application Express 3.1 introduced a new installation option called a Runtime Only installation. A Runtime Only installation includes all of the PL/SQL packages and metadata tables, but all of the 4000 series applications that make up the APEX user interface are removed. The exception to this is application 4155, which allows end users to reset their passwords. It also includes a documented procedure to convert to and from a Runtime Only installation, so you don't have to make this decision at install time. Technically, you could delete these applications in previous versions and achieve the same goal, but then you would be left with no ability to manage any settings within the APEX environment. Since there is no user interface in a Runtime Only installation, all instance configuration changes must occur using the APEX_INSTANCE_ADMIN API discussed earlier.

Oracle SQL Developer 1.2.1 (shown in Figure 11-5) introduced tighter integration with APEX. A developer can now import/export applications and pages and modify application and page-level attributes simply by connecting to a schema associated with an APEX application using SQL Developer, and then right-clicking the application in the APEX tree. These features not only enhance productivity, but they also compliment a Runtime Only installation, as there is no APEX user interface in a Runtime Only installation. Calls to APEX_INSTANCE_ADMIN as well as SQL Developer features can also be tested with full installations of APEX to determine whether or not these interfaces will be acceptable before making the jump to a Runtime Only configuration. Additional security measures, such as removing the APEX administration interface, tend to introduce a level of inconvenience. This solution is a good example of adding security without sacrificing significant functionality or productivity.

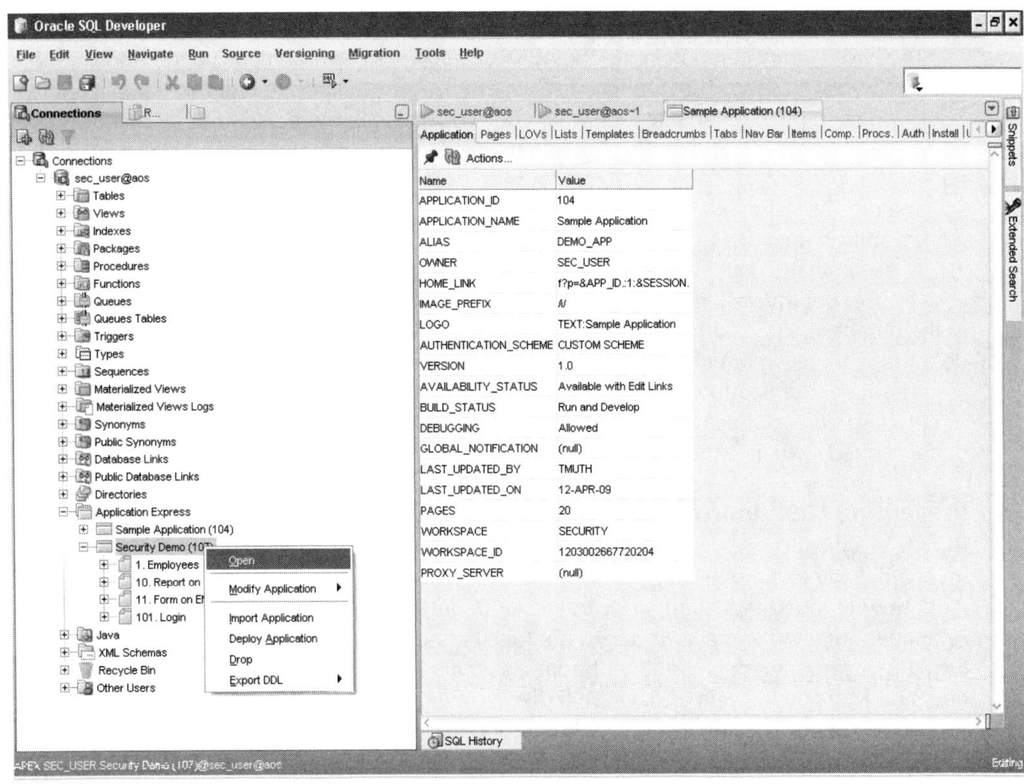

FIGURE 11-5 *Oracle SQL Developer 1.2.1 interface*

Obfuscate the APEX_PUBLIC_USER Password in dads.conf

OHS uses a Database Access Descriptor (DAD), defined in $ORACLE_HOME/ohs/mod_plsql/conf/dads.conf, to connect to the database. Each DAD includes connection information for the database, including the database username and password it should use. By default, the password is stored in clear text, which allows anyone who gains access to the file system to obtain all the information he or she needs to connect to the database using other tools. This security risk is easy to mitigate, but often overlooked. The solution is to use a utility included with OHS to "obfuscate" the password. The result is a hash of the password that only OHS can use to connect to the database. We use the term *hash* loosely as the technique and algorithms used are not public knowledge, but the basic concept is that of a hash. This example will only cover OHS version 10.1.3.3, but the same concepts apply to earlier versions. The obfuscation tool is called dadTool.pl and is located in $ORACLE_HOME/ohs/mod_plsql/conf/ along with its associated dadTool.README. The .README file details the setup of key environment variables, but unfortunately omits a key environment variable, PER5LIB, that will prevent dadTool.pl from working. The following settings are the ones successfully used on Oracle Enterprise Linux 5 for a BASH shell environment:

```
ORACLE_HOME=/opt/oracle/product/ohs_10.1.3.3;export ORACLE_HOME
PATH=$ORACLE_HOME/ohs/modplsql/conf:$PATH;export PATH
PATH=$ORACLE_HOME/perl/bin:$PATH;export PATH
LD_LIBRARY_PATH=$ORACLE_HOME/lib; export LD_LIBRARY_PATH
PERL5LIB=$ORACLE_HOME/perl/lib; export PERL5LIB
```

There are two very important changes to the default instructions to point out. On the second line, the .README indicates that the PATH should be $ORACLE_HOME/Apache/..., when the directory structure is actually $ORACLE_HOME/ohs/.... Depending on the operating system, this line could be different so pay attention to it. The second issue is the PERL5LIB environment variable as shown in the last line. This was never mentioned in the .README and caused an error in every system setup on this particular platform. Once the environment variables are set, simply navigate to $ORACLE_HOME/ohs/modplsql/conf/ and run the following command as indicated in the dadTool.README file:

```
[oracle@aos conf]$ perl dadTool.pl -o
All passwords successfully obfuscated. New obfuscations : 1
```

The following listing shows the "PlsqlDatabasePassword" setting before and after obfuscation:

```
PlsqlDatabasePassword   HelloWorld
...
PlsqlDatabasePassword   @Bq6wJDT7YdtZok0nle12mEj=
```

Network Topology

Another key consideration when installing APEX is the network topology and physical separation of the HTTP server, database, and TNS (Transparent Network Substrate) Listener. It is a security architecture best practice to install the HTTP server on a physical machine that's different from the database, because this topology provides several essential security benefits. The database and TNS Listener should reside completely within the corporate network with no network access exposed to the public Internet. It's not uncommon to place the database behind an additional firewall so that it is not publicly accessible on the corporate intranet. The most common and desirable location for the HTTP server is on a separate server in your networks "demilitarized zone," or DMZ. A DMZ (Figure 11-6) is essentially a network that serves as a buffer zone between an internal private network and the public Internet. Firewall rules can be configured for a DMZ to allow TCP requests only on ports 80 and 443 (HTTP and HTTPS) through to the HTTP server. This type of configuration dramatically reduces the exposure of an APEX system to unauthorized attacks. When combined with the Runtime Only configuration, all external access to sensitive data and systems will be channeled through applications and tightly controlled by security administrators.

One of the most popular topologies in which administrators are concerned about security is a public-facing Internet site connected to a non-public intranet database. Since the machine on which the HTTP server is installed will be directly exposed to the Internet, it is strongly encouraged that this machine be "hardened" as much as possible. While the following is not a comprehensive list, it offers a few suggestions to get you started hardening a Linux-based host:

- This should be a single-purpose server, whose only job is to act as an HTTP server, with the least amount of software installed as possible. Reducing the number of programs installed not only reduces the overall vulnerability of a server, but it also reduces the chance for incompatible versions of software and thus promotes more timely upgrades and patches to the operating system and other essential services on the machine.
- Uninstall or disable all nonessential services, especially network services such as NFS, IMAP/SMTP, and so on. Insecure, legacy services such as telnet, FTP, and VNC should be replaced with modern secure alternatives such as SSH, SCP/sFTP, and FreeNX.
- Disable remote access from common accounts such as root or guest, which are common attack vectors.
- In addition to setting hardware firewall rules at the network level, local firewall software such as iptables on Linux provide an additional layer of OS security.
- Install anti-virus and anti-rootkit software.
- All software, including the operating system, should be regularly patched to include the latest security fixes from various vendors.

Oracle Enterprise Manager can be configured to connect to Oracle Metalink (http://metalink.oracle.com) and to check for updates to all Oracle software and then notify system administrators

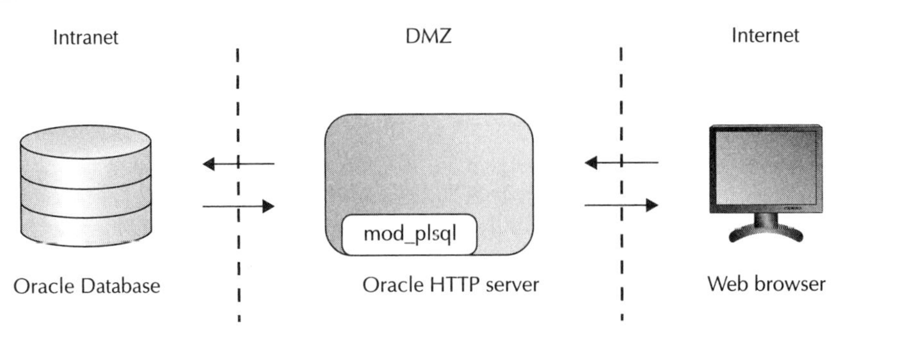

FIGURE 11-6 *DMZ network topology*

that updates are available. Another solution to consider is the Advanced Security option (ASO) of the database as it enables the encryption of the traffic between the HTTP server and the database, thus thwarting any packet inspection techniques that someone might use to view sensitive data. This would also allow internal network traffic from SQL*Plus or SQL Developer connections to be encrypted.

Another topology to consider would be the external HTTP server acting only as a reverse proxy server that forwards all requests to OHS, shown in Figure 11-7. This is a common configuration when an organization has an existing HTTP server in their DMZ that does not have direct access to the database or is an HTTP server other than OHS/OAS that cannot directly render APEX pages. For example, assume that a fictitious company called Acme has a web site at www.acme.com (port 80) running on a vanilla version of Apache (without mod_plsql). The company wants to expose an APEX application to the Internet on port 80 with the same domain name. Apache can be configured to proxy all requests to a particular subdomain or virtual directory on to an additional HTTP server. So, any request to apex.acme.com is then forwarded on to an internal OHS, which in turn connects to the Oracle database. The path is simply reversed when APEX returns a response to the request. This configuration has an additional security benefit in that if the operating system of the external HTTP server is compromised, no Oracle client software is installed on that machine that would allow a hacker to connect directly to the database. Additionally, the TNS Listener and firewall on the database server should be configured to reject all connection attempts from this machine.

mod_rewrite and APEX

OHS is based on Apache, the most used web server on the Internet. Extensions to Apache are done through modules. OHS ships with many common modules already installed. Some of these modules are Oracle-specific, such as mod_plsql and mod_osso, while others are generally available to the Apache community. mod_rewrite is an open-source module that ships with

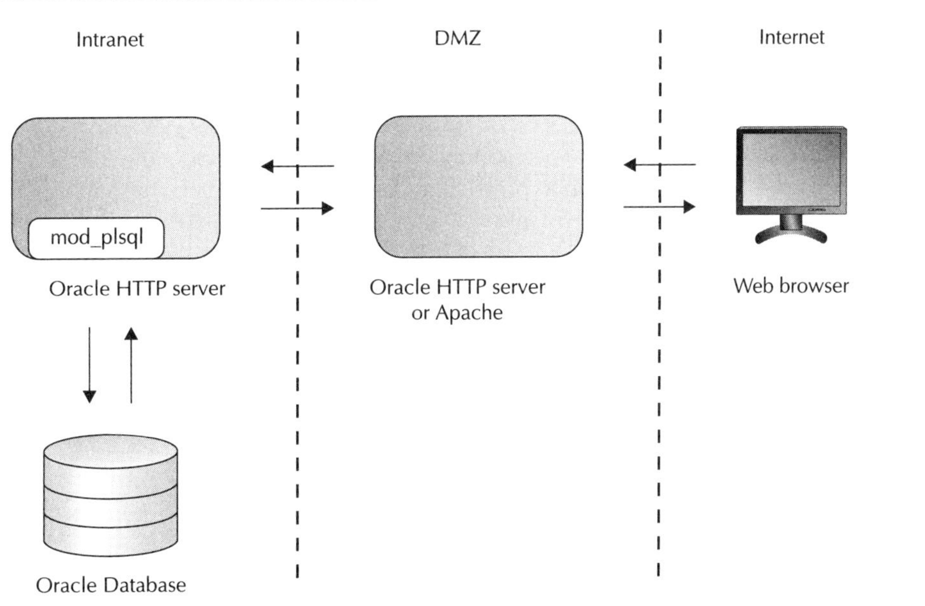

FIGURE 11-7 *Proxy server topology*

OHS and is designed to allow administrators to rewrite, change, and redirect URLs as they are requested from the server. mod_rewrite uses a combination of regular expressions and environment variables to define rules for a particular URL pattern. The most common use of mod_rewrite is to redirect requests to old content that has moved to a new location. The following example redirects all requests for cat.html to dog.html:

```
RewriteEngine on
Options +FollowSymlinks
RewriteRule ^/cat.html /dog.html [R,L]
```

Developing and testing rules for mod_rewrite can be a challenging process since it's difficult to see what rules were actually applied, and each change requires a restart of the HTTP server. Because of these challenges, you should develop and test mod_rewrite on an HTTP server that nobody else is using. You will also want to enable logging so that you can evaluate and verify what rules were applied. The following example enables logging to a file in the \temp (or /tmp) directory:

```
RewriteEngine on
Options +FollowSymlinks

# The following syntax is used for Windows systems.
# RewriteLog "c:\temp\rewrite.log"

RewriteLog "/tmp/rewrite.log"

RewriteLogLevel 3
RewriteRule ^/cat.html /dog.html [R,L]
```

It's also important to note that logging introduces a substantial performance penalty when it is enabled, so you should use it only when testing new rules and certainly not in production environments.

mod_rewrite in Action Now that you have a basic understanding of mod_rewrite, let's do something more useful with it. Earlier in this chapter, we talked about the new Runtime Only option in APEX. Another option to protect the development environment is to use a few mod_rewrite rules. In this case, we will allow access to the APEX development environment from localhost (127.0.0.1) as well as a range of IP addresses:

```
RewriteEngine on

# The following directive is required for mod_rewrite on some platforms,

# even though the concept of a symbolic link does not apply to APEX.
Options +FollowSymlinks

# Make sure the request is NOT for application 4155
RewriteCond %{REQUEST_URI}%{QUERY_STRING} !/pls/(apex|builder)/f?p=4155:.*
# Is the request for an application in the range 4000-4999
RewriteCond %{REQUEST_URI}%{QUERY_STRING} /pls/(apex|builder)/f?p=(4[0-9]{3}:.*)
# Make sure the IP of the requestor is not 127.0.0.1 or 10.11.12.0-255
RewriteCond %{REMOTE_ADDR}        !^(127\.0\.0\.1|10\.11\.12\.[0-9]{1,3})$
# If the previous 3 conditions are true, return HTTP 403 "Forbidden"
RewriteRule /pls/(apex|builder)/ - [F]
```

Let's step through the rules line by line:

1. Application 4155 is a special case in that it allows end users to reset passwords, so we'll exempt it from this policy by using a leading exclamation point that denotes "not" in regular expressions.
2. All applications in the range 4000–4999 match this rule. Notice that **apex | builder** is in parentheses because we have two DADs in this example: **apex** and **builder**. The pipe symbol between them indicates "or" in regular expressions.
3. The environment variable **%{REMOTE_ADDR}** returns the IP address of the client accessing the web server. This rule exempts localhost as well as any IP address in the range 10.11.12.0–255, so they will *not* be redirected.
4. If *all three* of the preceding conditions are met, this rule returns the HTTP 403 "Forbidden" code to the web browser. If any condition fails, the redirect will not occur and the user can access the development environment. It's important to note that rules 1 and 3 use negative logic (!). Also note that the order of the first three rules is not important, since all three must return **true** for the redirect to occur.

Many office networks use a different subnet for each floor or office section, which often creates a convenient way to allow only a certain group of employees access to the APEX development environment. This type of rule also works well for Internet-facing environments in which you want only internal IP addresses to access the development environment. Keep in mind that if your users are going through a proxy server to access your environment, the IP address that mod_rewrite will likely see is the IP address of the proxy server, not the user's actual IP address.

Another option for this solution is to use two HTTP servers, one available only to internal employees and the other in the DMZ that is accessed by Internet users. In this case, you could use the preceding rules on the server in the DMZ and simply omit the line that contains **%{REMOTE_ADDR}**. Developers and administrators can access the development environment using the internal HTTP server that has no restrictions imposed by mod_rewrite, while the rules applied to the Internet-facing HTTP server would prevent anyone from accessing the development environment.

The solutions in this section used the IP address as one of the components of the solution. It's important to note that IP addresses can be spoofed in certain types of attacks, where a direct connection or immediate response is not required. A great example of this is a Denial of Services (DoS) attack, as the goal is to flood the host with requests, yet no response is required for the attack to succeed. The overarching theme of this book is *defense in depth,* and these solutions are merely one, not the only, line of defense.

Prevent Web-based Attacks with mod_security

Chapter 12 covers the concepts of SQL injection and cross-site scripting (XSS) from a programmatic perspective. It is critical that developers understand these concepts in detail and use appropriate coding practices to prevent them. However, in the interest of defense in depth, one instance-level security measure will prevent these types of attacks from getting through to the application code.

SQL injection vulnerabilities occur when an attacker is able to pass full or partial SQL statements, such as **drop table employees**, into the application. XSS attacks are focused on an attacker inserting code, typically JavaScript, that will be executed by another user of the system.

mod_security is an open source Apache module that is analogous to an application firewall. For SQL injection or XSS attacks to succeed, particularly in an APEX environment, nefarious code must pass through the OHS and on to the database. The general syntax for this code is well known within the security community and therefore represents a signature that can indicate an attack. mod_security is designed to look for these types of signatures and stop them from doing any damage. When an HTTP request is made to an Apache-based server with mod_security enabled, mod_security intercepts the request very early in the processing sequence. The request is then run through a series of user-defined directives designed to look for SQL injection or XSS attacks.

Following are a few example directives to illustrate this concept:

```
# Ignore all SQL Injection for the APEX Builder, as a developer must be able
# to enter SQL DML and DDL as well as JavaScript.
# You could comment this out for production.
SecFilterSelective ARG_p_flow_id "^4[0-9]{3}$" allow

# SQL injection attacks - the following directive is all one line
SecFilterSelective "ARGS|COOKIE_VALUES" "((select|grant|delete|insert|drop|alter|
replace|truncate|update|
create|rename|describe)[[:space:]]+[A-Z|a-z|0-9|\*| |\,]+[[:space:]]+(from|into|
table|database|index|view)
[[:space:]]+[A-Z|a-z|0-9|\*| |\,]|UNION SELECT.*\'.*\'.*,[0-9].*INTO.*FROM)"

# XSS attacks
SecFilter "<[[:space:]]*script"

# Mask our server signature
SecServerSignature "Just Some Web Server"
```

The first directive disables mod_security for the APEX development environment, because we must allow developers to submit JavaScript as well as SQL Data Manipulation Language (DML) and Data Definition Language (DDL). The next rule looks for database statements typically associated with SQL injection attacks. These statements are usually encoded in URL strings or submitted in HTML form elements such as text boxes or select lists, and then executed in the database. Obviously, a developer would prefer that the end user population be prevented from issuing arbitrary statements. The third rule blocks all requests containing an HTML **<script ...>** tag, thus preventing a user from posting JavaScript into the application. The final directive serves to mask the signature of the HTTP server, which makes it much harder for an attacker to leverage a specific known vulnerability of the HTTP server.

Thus far, we've looked at mod_security only as a tool to block malicious incoming requests. mod_security also offers the ability to inspect and filter output from web applications. A prime candidate for output filtering is any sensitive data of a particular pattern that could accidentally be "leaked" out to the public through a web application.

For example, think about a web application built on a database that contains Social Security numbers (SSNs). While most developers would never intentionally display this type of data to the public, it's all too easy to enter **select * from table** and accidentally return the SSN column. Since US SSNs and tax identification numbers conform to a very specific and unique pattern of `###-##-####`, it is easy to add a mod_security filter to check for them:

```
SecFilterSelective OUTPUT "[[:digit:]]{3}-[[:digit:]]{2}-[[:digit:]]{4}"
log,deny,status:500
```

Whenever a web application returns a string that conforms to this pattern, mod_security will trap the page and instead return an error page with an HTTP Status of "500 - Internal Server Error."

Another type of output that could be classified as a security risk are Oracle database errors. Error messages can give an attacker additional information about their target such as whether or not a table or column exists. The following directive will trap Oracle errors before they are displayed to end users. Note that this also has the negative side-effect of making it difficult to detect and debug errors.

```
SecFilterSelective OUTPUT "ORA\-[0-9]{5}" log,deny,status:500
```

Beginning with the release of Oracle 11*g*, the version of OHS available on the Database Companion CD is based on Apache 2.0. Prior versions of OHS are based on Apache 1.3. This change is important in the context of this section for two reasons: OHS 11*g* includes mod_security by default. The version is also important if you choose to install mod_security on your own, as it is dependent on the version of Apache. The version of mod_security included with OHS 11*g* is compatible with rules only for mod_security 1.9.3. Consequently, some of the new syntax for mod_security directives is not compatible with OHS 11*g*. If you want to use the latest rule sets, you can install the latest version of mod_security in OHS or install mod_security in another Apache HTTP server and proxy OHS through Apache, as described earlier in this chapter.

SSL/TLS Techniques

The goal of enabling Secure Sockets Layer (SSL) on OHS is to provide assurance that the host server is not being spoofed and to encrypt traffic in and out of the HTTP server. Recall the section "Encryption 101" from Chapter 2, where we discussed public key encryption and symmetric key encryption and mentioned that SSL uses a clever combination of public key and symmetric key encryption to do its thing. Here's a quick review of SSL that will help you understand the purpose of the certificate files used to enable SSL:

1. An SSL encrypted session is initiated by a user's Web browser requesting a URL that uses the HTTPS protocol, as in https://www.oracle.com.
2. The server then responds with some basic information, such as what ciphers it supports. The server also sends its certificate, which includes its public key signed by (the private key) of a known Certificate Authority.
3. The server's certificate allows the client to verify that the server is indeed who it claims to be. If the user requested https://www.oracle.com, then the certificate should claim www.oracle.com to be the name of the server. If the certificate claimed a different name—say, www.orocle.com—a failure, or in the very least, a warning, would appear in the user's browser. The actual validation comes because the user's browser uses the public key of the known Certificate Authority to decrypt and validate the server's information. If the Certificate Authority is unknown, the user would get a warning or the session would be rejected (depending on how the browser is configured). All of this prevents a nefarious person from pretending to be a legitimate site or redirecting a user from one site to another without the user realizing it.
4. The client's browser creates a random symmetric key (or shared secret) that is used later with the symmetric encryption algorithm. It also chooses the symmetric encryption algorithm including key size from the list provided by the server.
5. If the client is not authenticating itself back to the server, the client then encrypts the symmetric key using the server's public key and sends it back to the server.
6. The server then uses its private key to decrypt the symmetric key sent by the client. Since only the server is in possession of its private key, only it can decrypt the symmetric key sent by the user's browser. This prevents an intermediary person from listening in on the conversation.

The first part of the handshake involving the server's public and private keys is called *public key cryptography* and is computationally more expensive than symmetric key cryptography. However, it is the best practical way to encrypt initial communications between the client and server in which a key is not yet shared. Once the handshake is complete and they both posses the same shared key, all communication between the client and server uses symmetric key encryption, which is much less expensive.

Encryption still adds overhead and will reduce the number of concurrent users that a HTTP server can support. The reduction in performance by enabling SSL is difficult to estimate, because it depends on many factors, including number and speed of CPUs, number of concurrent users, size of pages and static content, network latency, and OHS settings. In the optimal configuration of APEX in which the database and HTTP server are on different servers, the machine running OHS is typically incurring a very small load compared to the database server. This is expected, as the bulk of the work of APEX is done inside the database. If this is the case for your environment, enabling SSL is not likely to have an impact on performance as the database server is usually the limiting factor. The initial handshake is expensive and requires a minimum of five network round trips when compared to a non-SSL HTTP request that requires a minimum of two round trips. This could make the first page view substantially slower and is important to consider in environments with high network latency. Since OHS is based on Apache, any of the numerous SSL tuning guides for Apache are directly applicable, and SSL tuning is beyond the scope of this book. If you plan to have a large number of concurrent users, especially if your applications are on the public Internet, you should consider dedicated hardware solutions to offload the work of SSL encryption. For most intranet applications with well defined population of a few thousand users, software-based SSL encryption should be more than adequate.

The two most common scenarios for SSL are either to encrypt all pages in a web application or to encrypt only certain pages. All financial institutions, at least those worthy of your trust, require SSL for all pages. Online retailers such as Amazon and eBay require SSL for login pages as well as any pages associated with the purchase of goods. Web applications that require less security typically use SSL only for login pages. Most popular web-based e-mail applications fall into this category. If your username and password were intercepted, a hacker could take over your e-mail account, so it's import to protect these requests.

Due to the additional performance requirements of SSL, discussed earlier, combined with the massive volume of traffic incurred by the most popular web mail applications, encrypting all pages would require a substantial investment in additional hardware. As with any changes to your architecture, you should benchmark SSL in your environment with your applications to determine whether the performance penalty is significant. Chances are, it won't even be noticeable.

Enable SSL in OHS

The rest of this section will cover configuration topics for OHS 10*g* Release 3. In most cases, these steps are virtually identical to those for OHS 10*g* Release 2, with subtle differences such as directory structure. OHS 10*g* Release 3 includes a default Oracle Wallet with a signed certificate, and SSL is enabled by default. This is fine for testing purposes and allows developers to configure and test different SSL scenarios immediately. The default wallet should be treated like a self-signed certificate—great for testing but never for production. This is because your end users' web browsers will not recognize the signing authority of this certificate and will either display a warning or block access to the site completely. The process of installing a valid certificate is well documented in the OHS and the OAS Administrators Guides, so we won't repeat the details of the process here. However, a quick summary of the process is certainly helpful in understanding the big picture.

The first step is to navigate to $ORACLE_HOME/bin, where $ORACLE_HOME is the HTTP server home. If you are on a Linux or UNIX system, you should do this using a terminal in an X Window session:

1. Run Oracle Wallet Manager (OWM), a GUI tool that also has a command line interface.
2. Create a new wallet.
3. Create a new certificate request. This creates a private/public key pair.
4. Export the certificate request to a file. The certificate you are exporting is your public key. Your private key remains secured in the Oracle Wallet.
5. Send this certificate file to valid Certificate Authority. Choose one of the well-known Certificate Authorities, since its root public key is likely distributed with all modern web browsers.
6. The Certificate Authority will sign your public key using its private key. Typically, it will take steps to verify that you are who you claim to be.
7. The Certificate Authority will then return your signed public key. Since the key was signed by the authority's private key, a client's web browser can use its public key to verify that your public key was signed by a well-known, trusted signing authority, thus establishing a chain of trust.
8. The signed certificate is then imported into the Oracle Wallet.
9. Update ssl.conf to point to the new wallet location.

To test SSL on OHS, we must first determine the port in which it is running. The easiest way to do this is to open the $ORACLE_HOME/ohs/conf/ssl.conf file, where $ORACLE_HOME is the home of OHS, not the Oracle home of the database. ssl.conf contains a directive in the form of "Listen 443", where 443 is the port that is listening for HTTPS requests. It's important to note that this port number is also in the Virtual Hosts section later in ssl.conf. If you change the port number, you must change it in both places. The following code is an excerpt of ssl.conf, with only the lines related to the port number shown:

```
Listen 443
...
## SSL Virtual Host Context
##
<VirtualHost _default_:443>
...
```

Another place to determine which ports are in use by OHS is the portlist.ini file in $ORACLE_HOME/install/. Keep in mind that these port numbers were automatically assigned at installation time. This file will not reflect any changes to port numbers after installation. The following listing is the contents of portlist.ini:

```
[Ports]
Oracle HTTP Server port =  7780
Oracle HTTP Server Listen port = 7780
Oracle HTTP Server SSL port = 4458
Oracle HTTP Server Listen (SSL) port = 4458
Oracle HTTP Server Diagnostic port = 7202
Oracle HTTP Server Listen port = 7780
Oracle HTTP Server Listen (SSL) port = 4458
```

As you can see, the SSL port at the time of install was 4458. I changed this port in ssl.conf to 443, but this change will not show up in portlist.ini. Additionally, if you want to list the ports that OHS is listening on from a bash shell, the following command will show all ports in use by the HTTPD process:

```
$ sudo netstat -tnlp | grep httpd
tcp        0      0 127.0.0.1:7202      0.0.0.0:* LISTEN      5830/httpd
tcp        0      0 :::7780             :::*      LISTEN      5830/httpd
tcp        0      0 :::443              :::*      LISTEN      5830/httpd
```

This does not tell you what type of traffic the ports are listening for, but it is useful for a quick reminder of the ports in use without your having to dig too deep into the file system to find ssl.con. Keep in mind that HTTPD is the process name for Apache-based HTTP servers, so if you're running more than one HTTP server that uses Apache, you will see all the ports from all of the Apache instances.

Now that you know what port to test, let's test an HTTPS connection from a web browser by entering **https://*machine-name*:443/** in a web browser to display the OHS home page (substituting your actual values for *machine-name* and port, which is 443 in this case). If we were using the default wallet, the browser should display a warning that this certificate is not valid. The certificate actually fails all three criteria, in that it is expired, the domain name listed does not match our domain, and it is not signed by a trusted Certificate Authority. For testing purposes, however, this is fine.

SSL and APEX

Now that we have verified that SSL is working correctly, let's configure an APEX application using two different scenarios regarding SSL. The goal of the first scenario is to switch to HTTPS for the login page of an application, and then switch back to HTTP for subsequent requests. We want to encrypt the usernames and passwords sent over the network from the login page, but the company policy allows internal traffic to be unencrypted, so the application will switch back to unencrypted HTTP requests once a user is logged in.

The configuration for this scenario is all done inside our APEX application and requires no additional steps for OHS. We will use two application processes: one to enable HTTPS and one to enable HTTP. The conditions for firing these processes reference page 101, as 101 is the login page of our application. The following is the first application process used to change from the HTTPS protocol to the HTTP protocol for all pages except page 101 (which is shown in Figure 11-8):

```
-- This code goes in the block of an Application Process
htp.init;
owa_util.mime_header('text/html', FALSE);
htp.p('Location: http://'||
  owa_util.get_cgi_env('SERVER_NAME')||
  ':7780'||
  owa_util.get_cgi_env('SCRIPT_NAME') ||
  owa_util.get_cgi_env('PATH_INFO')||'?'||
  owa_util.get_cgi_env('QUERY_STRING'));
owa_util.http_header_close;
-- The following are attributes of the process
-- Sequence: 1
-- Condition Type: PL/SQL Process
-- Condition Text: owa_util.get_cgi_env('REQUEST_PROTOCOL') = 'HTTPS' and :APP_
PAGE_ID != 101
```

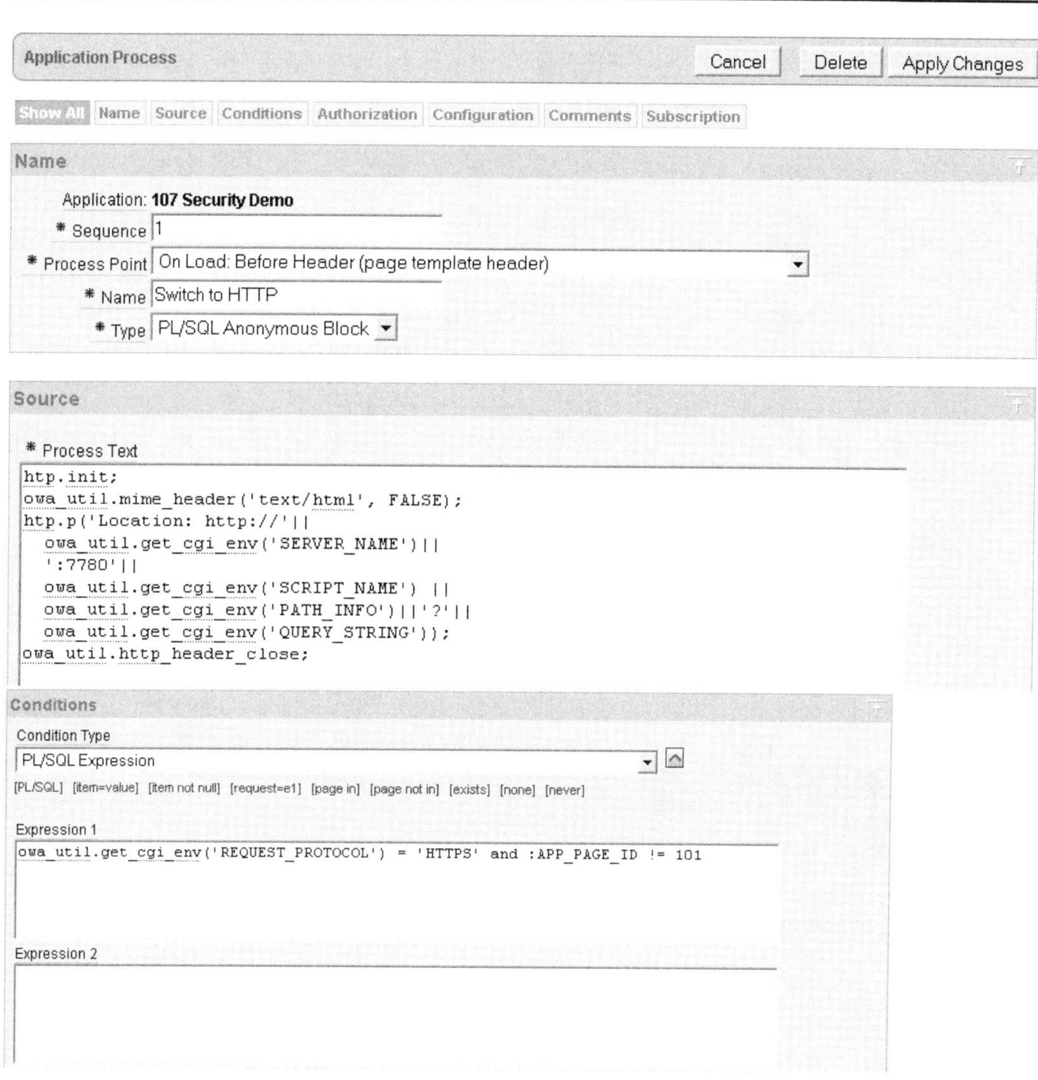

FIGURE 11-8 *Application process to switch to HTTP*

In summary, the process condition checks to see whether the protocol is HTTPS and the page is not 101; it then redirects to the same URL, but substitutes HTTP for HTTPS and appends the non-SSL port to the **SERVER_NAME** variable. You should change the port number, currently 7780, and login page number, currently 101, to reflect the proper values for your environment. The purpose of our next application process is to switch to HTTPS for the login page:

```
-- This code goes in the block of an Application Process
htp.init;
owa_util.mime_header('text/html', FALSE);
htp.p('Location: https://'||
```

```
  owa_util.get_cgi_env('SERVER_NAME')||
  ':443'||
  owa_util.get_cgi_env('SCRIPT_NAME') ||
  owa_util.get_cgi_env('PATH_INFO')||'?'||
  owa_util.get_cgi_env('QUERY_STRING'));
owa_util.http_header_close;
-- The following are attributes of the process
-- Sequence: 2
-- Condition Type: PL/SQL Process
-- Condition Text: owa_util.get_cgi_env('REQUEST_PROTOCOL') = 'HTTP' and :APP_PAGE_
ID = 101
```

Note that our HTTPS port is 443, but your HTTPS port may be different, so make sure you edit this process to match the configuration of your environment. If you are using the default ports of 80 for HTTP and 443 for HTTPS, you can simply omit the line in each process that adds the port.

Now run your application to test it. The login page should seamlessly redirect to HTTPS. Once you log in with valid credentials, you will see the URL change to HTTP and the corresponding HTTP port. This scenario requires that you add these processes to each application.

mod_rewrite and SSL

Apache mod_rewrite is also a powerful tool to conditionally require HTTPS. A word of caution about mod_rewrite: Its directives affect the whole HTTP server. Developing a directive often takes a number of test cases and more than a few tries to get right, and it requires a restart of the HTTP server for each change to take effect. As such, it's not a good idea to test any directives on an HTTP server that is in use by other developers and a terrible idea to test it on a production server. Fortunately it's easy to install another HTTP server and configure it to point at the same APEX installation without impacting other users. The following directive simply redirects all non-HTTPS requests to HTTPS and our HTTPS port:

```
RewriteEngine On
RewriteCond %{HTTPS} !=on
RewriteRule ^.*$ https://%{SERVER_NAME}:443%{REQUEST_URI} [R,L]
```

Another option is to redirect to HTTPS for all applications that are *not* the APEX development environment:

```
RewriteCond %{HTTPS} !=on
RewriteCond %{REQUEST_URI}%{QUERY_STRING} /pls/apex/f?p=.*
RewriteCond %{REQUEST_URI}%{QUERY_STRING} !/pls/apex/f?p=(4[0-9]{3}:.*)
RewriteRule ^.*$ https://%{SERVER_NAME}:443%{REQUEST_URI} [R,L]We can also
enable HTTPS for a specific subset of applications. In the following example
OHS will redirect to HTTPS for applications 111,222,333 and 444.RewriteCond
%{HTTPS} !=on
RewriteCond %{REQUEST_URI}%{QUERY_STRING} /pls/apex/f?p=(111|222|333|444):.*
RewriteRule ^.*$ https://%{SERVER_NAME}:443%{REQUEST_URI} [R,L]
```

Protecting the APEX Database Schemas

As discussed earlier in this chapter, all code and metadata for APEX are installed in two schemas in the database. In versions prior to APEX 3.2 the schemas followed the pattern FLOWS_FILES and FLOWS_XXXXXX (FLOWS_030100 for APEX 3.1). With the introduction of Application Express 3.2, the primary schema now follows the pattern APEX_XXXXXX (APEX_030200 for APEX 3.2).

The primary APEX schema, APEX_XXXXXX, is granted several system-level privileges that could allow an attacker to execute malicious DML and DDL against any other schema in the database. This schema should be treated with the caution that a security-conscious DBA would afford the SYSTEM schema. As such, this schema is locked by default at the end of the APEX installation, and it should always remain locked. A few operations may require that you unlock this account for a very short period of time, such as modifying instance settings from the command line or resetting the admin password. However, most if not all of these operations could be performed by another user account that has been granted the APEX_ADMINISTRATOR_ROLE. We'll discuss Database Vault later in this section, as it provides a much more robust alternative for protecting privileged accounts.

Any periodic security audits conducted against a database where APEX is installed should check to make sure this account is still locked. There is no reason that developers or DBAs should connect to any of the APEX_ or FLOWS_ schemas on a regular basis, as this opens up unnecessary security risks in addition to making it very easy for someone to issue a command accidentally that could irreparably damage an APEX installation. The tables and packages in the FLOWS_ and APEX_ schemas should be treated like any other data dictionary objects—that is, as untouchable.

Companies often employ a segregation of duty policy that may force the separation of the APEX schemas from the data the APEX applications will serve. This is especially true when highly sensitive data or personally identifiable information (PII) is involved. For this reason, some developers choose to install APEX in a database that's different from the database where their sensitive data is stored. This technique does provide physical separation of the data and the development tool, but it is little more than a perfunctory measure that also adds a lot of inconvenience to developers.

For APEX to access data in another database, a database link must be created to allow queries in one database to access tables in another. There are three problems with this solution that typically relegate it to a measure of last resort: The first problem is that in an online transaction processing (OLTP) environment with a lot of subsecond queries, database links can add a tremendous amount of latency to a system, even if both databases are on the same Gigabit network switch. The second problem with database links relates to the APEX development environment. The wizards used to build APEX components such as reports or forms will only work with local database objects, not objects accessed over database links. For these wizards to create APEX controls for objects in remote databases, local synonyms or views must be created for all remote objects. Finally, the creation of the database link effectively creates a bridge between the two databases, thus subverting much of the intended security gain expected by separating them in the first place.

Database Vault and APEX

Oracle Database Vault is the best mechanism for securing the database tier of an APEX instance while still allowing developers to be productive. One of the primary benefits of Database Vault is that it limits the power of overprivileged accounts and mitigates, if not eliminates, privilege abuse. We stated earlier that the privileges associated with the APEX_XXXXXX schema are similar to those for SYSTEM, so Database Vault is a logical choice when looking for a solution to securing this account. APEX cannot be installed in a database when Database Vault is enabled, and it will not run without adding some command rules. Disabling Database Vault requires that you relink the database using specific parameters.

To install APEX in a Database Vault database, do the following:

1. Disable Database Vault.
2. Install or upgrade APEX.

3. Enable Database Vault.
4. Execute command rules to allow APEX to function.

The following code can be used to disable Database Vault:

```
# Disable Database Vault
# Shutdown the Database using SQL*Plus
cd $ORACLE_HOME/rdbms/lib
make -f ins_rdbms.mk dv_off
cd $ORACLE_HOME/bin
relink oracle
# Startup the Database using SQL*Plus
# Install or Upgrade Application Express

# Enable Database Vault
# Shutdown the Database using SQL*Plus
cd $ORACLE_HOME/rdbms/lib
make -f ins_rdbms.mk dv_on
cd $ORACLE_HOME/bin
relink oracle
# Startup the Database using SQL*Plus
```

The following list details the command rules that should be executed once APEX is installed and Database Vault is enabled:

```
-- connect dv_owner
begin
    dbms_macadm.add_auth_to_realm(
             realm_name        => 'Oracle DataDictionary',
             grantee           => 'APEX_PUBLIC_USER',
             rule_set_name     => null,
             auth_options      => dbms_macutl.g_realm_auth_owner);
end;
/
begin
    dbms_macadm.update_command_rule
             (command       => 'CREATE USER',
              rule_set_name => 'Can Maintain Accounts/Profiles',
              object_owner  => '%',
              object_name   => '%',
              enabled       => dbms_macutl.g_yes);
end;
/
begin
    dbms_macadm.update_command_rule
             (command       => 'ALTER USER',
              rule_set_name => 'Can Maintain Own Account',
              object_owner  => '%',
              object_name   => '%',
              enabled       => dbms_macutl.g_yes);
end;
/
```

Once APEX is installed and the database is relinked with Database Vault enabled, APEX can no longer provision new workspaces with a new schema. Create User is a protected role and is limited to the Database Vault Manager account. To provision a new APEX workspace that requires a new schema, do this:

1. Ask the Database Vault Manager to create a new schema.
2. Log into the APEX Administration application.
3. Provision a new workspace using an existing schema.

This separation of duties requires that the Database Vault manager and the APEX administrator coordinate when a new project is started. While this may seem like a barrier to productivity to some, it actually creates a perfect opportunity for the people responsible for the security of the data and the people developing applications that access that data to communicate and ensure that both parties agree on the use of this data. This also prevents the possibility of someone connecting to as the APEX schema, creating another privileged account, and then using that account to gain access to sensitive data.

Summary

APEX is built on a unique architecture that tightly couples the application and the data. Understanding this architecture, including its strengths, weaknesses, and nuances, is essential to deploying APEX in a secure configuration. The APEX development team has gone to great lengths to make it as secure as possible out of the box, as is evidenced by the many security enhancements in APEX 3.2. However, an APEX administrator has many choices to make in the areas of topology and configuration that will ultimately determine the security of the environment. This chapter provided solutions to protect the APEX environment as a whole, before a developer writes a single line of code. Once the environment is secure, the focus can shift to securing the applications built in that environment.

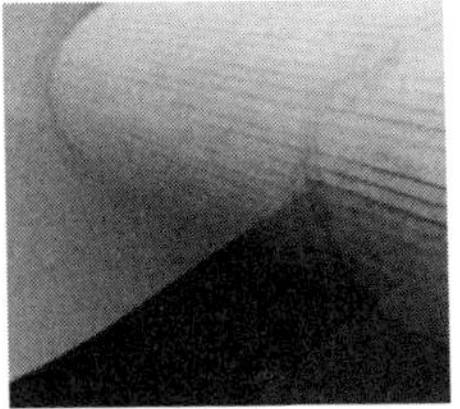

CHAPTER 12

Secure Coding Practices in APEX

This chapter shifts focus from securing the Application Express environment to securing an individual application. The concepts involved in creating a secure application using APEX are very similar to those of other database-centric technologies. Data should be secured at the lowest level possible using techniques such as Virtual Private Database (VPD), Oracle Label Security (OLS), Programmatic Encryption, and Transparent Data Encryption (TDE). End users must be authenticated against some credential store, such as an Lightweight Directory Access Protocol (LDAP) directory or Oracle Access Manager. A user's authorization rights or privileges should also be pulled from a central source such as Oracle Access Manager (OAM).

As discussed in Chapter 11, APEX handles identity preservation out of the box, but it is a developer's responsibility to understand and leverage this feature. Security-conscious developers should also consider other technologies that will access the same data and construct security policies such that the rules are defined and enforced in one place, not spread out across all the systems that access the data. Chapter 11 provided information about APEX's architecture and concepts to lay the foundation for the concepts introduced in this chapter. The more developers understand these technologies, the better prepared they are to secure them.

Authentication and Authorization

Authentication is the process of identifying users and proving they are who they claim to be. In the case of your username and password, the username defines your identity, and the password is the proof that you are who you say you are. Identification can also be verified using other techniques such as certificates or biometric devices.

Once the system authenticates and identifies the user, the process of authorization can occur. Authorization determines what rights and privileges a user has within an application. Database roles are a well know example of authorization, as they are used to define what objects a user can access and what actions the user can perform. Authorization can also be defined in many other places, such as in a database table or an LDAP directory.

Authentication and authorization are both defined as application-level attributes in APEX. The definition of authentication and authorization schemes are decoupled from the individual pages and objects within an APEX application, which makes them easy to redefine as requirements change.

Authentication Schemes

Authentication schemes are declarative constructs in APEX that allow a developer to define how users will authenticate to the application. You can think of them as a way to determine *who* a user is. A typical authentication scheme accepts a username and password and then validate those credentials against an internal or external source. An authentication scheme is defined at the application level, and an application can have only one current authentication scheme. It is common, however, for an application to have several authentication schemes that are used in different environments, such as development and production. A developer can simply change which authentication scheme is current before moving the application from the development environment to production. It is not possible to switch between authentication schemes at runtime, to have more than one current authentication scheme, or to use different authentication schemes for different pages within the same application. In rare cases when it is necessary to authenticate against multiple sources, such as either LDAP or database credentials, this logic must be written into a single custom authentication scheme.

APEX includes several preconfigured authentication schemes including LDAP, Database Credentials, Oracle Single Sign-On (SSO), and APEX Credentials. These are well documented and plenty of examples of these schemes are publicly available. We'll focus on several custom authentication schemes to supplement the built-in authentication schemes.

Custom Table of Usernames and Passwords

One of the most common questions around authentication schemes in the APEX community is how to use a simple table of usernames and passwords for authentication. In general, I strongly advise developers to leverage an identity management solution such as Oracle Access Manager, because it provides many benefits, not the least of which is the ability to authenticate many systems, not just an APEX application. However, this question is asked so often that it is beneficial to provide an example here. It is also a great opportunity to demonstrate the use of the DBMS_CRYPTO package in the context of APEX.

One of the key concepts to take away from this example is this: *Never store passwords in clear text.* Many people use the same password or subset of passwords for all applications. This means it is very likely that at least some of the username/password sets stored in your table could also be used to access a person's online applications, including financial institutions. This scenario was the subject of several high-visibility data breaches and represents a very real security risk. The question is, How do you securely store a password in a database table? The answer: You don't store it at all; you store a cryptographic hash of the password instead. This is exactly how the Oracle Database and APEX authenticate users. Here's how this solution works:

1. A password is run through a one-way hash algorithm and the resulting value is stored in the table. For example, let's say the user's password is *welcome* and the hash of *welcome* is *#H*8F@90.*
2. When a user attempts to log into the application, she enters the password of *elcome.*
3. This password is run through the same one-way hash algorithm. The resulting hash is *Z;&R3!.*
4. We then compare the two hash values. Since they are not equal, authentication fails.
5. The user now enters the correct password of *welcome.*
6. The resulting hash of *welcome* is *#H*8F@90,* which is then compared to the hash stored in the table.
7. Since *#H*8F@90 = #H*8F@90,* the user is now authenticated.

In this example, the term "hash" was used for brevity. The reality is that the hash algorithms included with most software distributions, including the DBMS_CRYPTO package, are well known. As such, an attacker could generate a table of common passwords and their corresponding hash values. If the attacker gains access to a table, he would probably be able to determine one or more passwords by matching the stored hash with his table of hash values. To combat this threat, our example will use a message authentication code (MAC) algorithm. These algorithms also take in a key to generate the hash, so an attacker must know both the algorithm and the key to get access. Using a sufficiently long and random key will all but eliminate this threat. You should store this key in a secure location that is *not* on the server running the database. If this key is compromised, it will be significantly easier for an attacker to generate a hash table and compromise passwords.

For this example, we'll use DBMS_CRYPTO.RANDOMBYTES to generate a 16 byte key:

```
SYSTEM@AOS> grant execute on dbms_crypto to sec_admin;

Grant succeeded.

SEC_ADMIN@AOS> select DBMS_CRYPTO.RANDOMBYTES(16) salt from dual;

SALT
--------------------------------------------------------------------------------
--
231F8E440E65B5C180FA184F94F55B71
```

Now we'll use following table to store usernames and passwords. The user SEC_ADMIN will own this table and related packages.

```
create table application_users(
      id                  raw(16) default sys_guid(),
      user_name           varchar2(255),
      verification        raw(128),
      constraint app_users_pk primary key (id),
      constraint app_users_uq unique(user_name)
      )
/
```

The following package will be used to create and authenticate users. Note the use of **EXECUTE IMMEDIATE** for any queries or DML against the APPLICATION_USERS table. In the event that someone does gain access to our table, he cannot simply query one of the dictionary views such as DBA_DEPENDENCIES to determine the package used to set the password. This is certainly not a foolproof technique, but does make it more challenging to dissect the logic associated with password hashes.

```
create or replace package custom_apex_auth
as
      procedure create_user(
            p_username  in    varchar2,
            p_password  in    varchar2);

      function      validate_user(
            p_username  in    varchar2,
            p_password  in    varchar2)
            return boolean;
end custom_apex_auth;
/

create or replace package body custom_apex_auth
as
      -- key from dbms_crypto.randombytes
g_salt       raw(256) := '231F8E440E65B5C180FA184F94F55B71';

      function get_mac(
            p_password  in varchar2)
```

```
            return raw
      is
      begin
            return dbms_crypto.mac(
                              src  =>    utl_raw.cast_to_raw(p_password),
                              typ  =>    dbms_crypto.hmac_sh1,
                              key =>     utl_raw.cast_to_raw(g_salt));
      end get_mac;

      procedure create_user(
            p_username  in    varchar2,
            p_password  in    varchar2)
      is
            l_mac       raw(128);
      begin
            l_mac := get_mac(p_password);

            execute immediate 'insert into application_users
                                                            (user_name,verification)
                                                values  (:a,:b)'
                                                using       upper(p_username),l_mac;
      end create_user;


      function   validate_user(
            p_username  in    varchar2,
            p_password  in    varchar2)
            return boolean
      is
            l_mac                raw(128);
            l_user_name  varchar2(255) := upper(p_username);
            l_count              pls_integer := 0;
      begin
            l_mac := get_mac(p_password);
            execute immediate
                  'select count(*)
                    from application_users
                   where user_name = :username

                     and verification = :mac ' into l_count  using l_user_
name,l_mac;

            if l_count = 1 then
                  return true;
            else
                  return false;
            end if;
      end validate_user;

end custom_apex_auth;
/
```

Since we are storing the key inside the package, we must note that this code is accessible to anyone with a privileged account that can query data dictionary views such as DBA_SOURCE. To prevent this, we will use the PL/SQL "wrap" utility included with the Oracle Database. This utility obfuscates the code so that it is still functional, yet is not readable by an attacker. Here's the procedure for wrapping this package:

1. Save the package body in a file named custom_apex_auth.pkb.
2. Copy this file to a computer that has the Oracle database installed. You should check for the existence of the wrap executable in $ORACLE_HOME/bin.
3. Make sure $ORACLE_HOME/bin is in your path variable.
4. Execute the following from the command line, where ***iname*** is the name of the input file and ***oname*** is the name of the output file:

   ```
   $ wrap iname=custom_apex_auth.pkb oname=custom_apex_auth.plb
   ```

   If you open the output file in a text editor, you can see that the contents are completely obfuscated:

   ```
   create or replace package body custom_auth wrapped
   a000000
   1
   abcd
   abcd
   abcd
   abcd
   abcd
   abcd
   abcd
   abcd
   abcd
   abcd
   abcd
   abcd
   abcd
   abcd
   abcd
   b
   49b 2fa
   tEQWVnLxdhO2QpYe8q3ImRMGA2UwgzsJMUiDZ47NCjoY+Mlxa55aWhbzjdSGbS0GLgMhQ95d
   CYA14bY3oT+dgofd882EY0pWQou5wW4T05JazzZ4CCtLIqTZc9wBsJtEI0aEcpuUSWtLBEL8
   0Em/y0eLcJoG1+pl7ZBFucjL+pHyucbrlX3UpPAHubK+mMQs9VH5b2XoZlrgpcxN41C8YZMm
   8r3Brr1O2MpAu0azbDgLxlMEnvrgUO3S1XxVTNIyUJVDvvPqiTsJ98/emfxqiET2+TteElAw
   28UNX7ATU3dYGJaAeUfv4l10IVSkggDUh9oyHRsBvemuZTaXyOfD8e/2L1gKGKFGq/E95qtx
   jA1FuNWpKxGjpsM20NTr5TqIMs13icQ2h5et11Rv+WfFROYv6X1EI3xLeJV/JIlLPpcAkWRk
   Bdd71Xj45pCg0rSp37AgdOWFnzqPYiR+QRNXwXabp3muOvMOJNk5A09KshfQXTWK1mzrw7dQ
   qN2IRmIXQBXLXNc0kA1QfkY3/iRNfrFqLvEvoc/puVufDYElGjtRnBIJYv4qURsHG2VvIxjI
   ```

Now create a user to test the code and verify that the password is not stored in clear text, and then verify that the function works as expected:

```
begin
      custom_apex_auth.create_user('tyler','welcome');
end;
/
SQL> select user_name,verification from application_users;

USER_NAME                      VERIFICATION
------------------------------ ----------------------------------------
TYLER                          02F4BB94F2C10F05F51E01B6E8A8A82928E243A8

SEC_ADMIN@AOS> set serveroutput on

declare
  l_result boolean := false;
begin
  l_result :=  custom_apex_auth.validate_user('tyler','welcome');
  if l_result then
    dbms_output.put_line('User Authenticated');
  else
    dbms_output.put_line('Authentication Failed');
  end if;
end;
/

User Authenticated

PL/SQL procedure successfully completed.

declare
  l_result boolean := false;
begin
  l_result :=  custom_apex_auth.validate_user('tyler','hello');
  if l_result then
    dbms_output.put_line('User Authenticated');
  else
    dbms_output.put_line('Authentication Failed');
  end if;
end;
/

Authentication Failed

PL/SQL procedure successfully completed.
```

Before testing this code in APEX, we need to grant execute on this package from the SEC_ADMIN schema to the SEC_USER schema. SEC_ADMIN will own the package, but our APEX application will parse as SEC_USER.

```
SEC_ADMIN@AOS> grant execute on custom_apex_auth to sec_user;

Grant succeeded.
```

Now that all of the code is in place, the final step is to create a new authentication scheme in APEX that leverages this code. To create a new authentication scheme in an application, navigate to Shared Components | Security | Authentication Schemes. Create a new authentication scheme, select From Scratch, and name it **Custom Table-Based**. Edit the newly created authentication scheme and scroll down to the Login Processing section and enter the following code in the Authentication Function attribute (as shown in Figure 12-1):

```
return custom_apex_auth.validate_user
```

The default login page for a new application is page 101. The next two attributes assume that your login page is also 101. If it is not, be sure to substitute the correct value of your login page. Select page 101 for the Session Not Valid attribute and make sure the Session Not Valid URL attribute is blank. Set the Logout URL attribute to the following string:

```
wwv_flow_custom_auth_std.logout?p_this_flow=&APP_ID.&p_next_flow_page_sess=&APP_
ID.:101:&APP_SESSION.
```

Save this authentication scheme. To activate this authentication scheme, click the Change Current tab on the Authentication Schemes page, and then select Custom Table-Based. To test the new authentication scheme, simply run the application and log in with a username of *tyler* and password of *welcome*—or any valid username and password that you created with the CUSTOM_APEX_AUTH package.

Authorization Schemes

APEX authorization schemes offer a powerful and flexible solution to allow or deny access selectively to any component of an application. Their design encourages developers to define the logic for authorization at the application level and then apply that logic where it is needed. The more this code is centralized and reused, the easier it is to review, audit, and change in the event that security requirements change.

To define an authorization scheme, navigate to the Shared Components section of an application. Authorization Schemes are listed in the Security section, just under Authentication Schemes. A developer can create authorization schemes based on values of APEX items, SQL queries, or PL/SQL functions. Once you create an authorization scheme and give it a unique name, this name will appear in the authorization scheme select list attribute of every APEX object that supports this feature. A partial list of APEX objects that support authorization schemes includes applications, pages, regions, report columns, list entries, and page items.

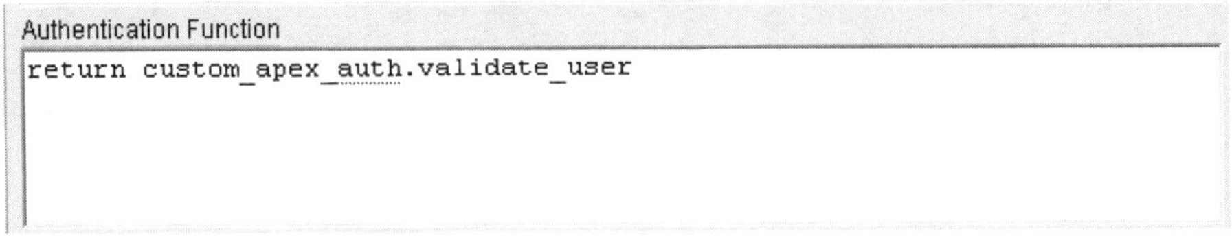

Authentication Function

```
return custom_apex_auth.validate_user
```

FIGURE 12-1 *Custom authentication scheme*

When an authorization scheme fails for a given user, the effect differs, depending on the type of object to which it is applied. For an application or page, APEX will return an error to any user that violates the authorization scheme. All other objects, such as report columns, regions, items, and buttons, will simply not appear on the page for users that do not pass the authorization scheme. This allows you to hide navigational elements or actions that a user cannot perform. Note that simply hiding a list item or tab that links to an administrative page is not enough, however, as the user could simply enter the page in the URL. The authorization scheme should also be applied to the page. If a nefarious user tries to access a page for which she is not authorized, the APEX will display the error message associated with the authorization scheme.

In the following example, we create an Authorization scheme based on a PL/SQL function. This function uses the APEX_LDAP package to query an LDAP directory and return the Organizational Unit of a person. Based on the value of this attribute, we conditionally allow access to certain parts of the application. Two users are involved in this scenario: Kathy Evans (IT Security) and Robert Smith (Human Resources). Here is the code for the authorization scheme (also shown in Figure 12-2):

```
declare
      l_attributes              wwv_flow_global.vc_arr2;
      l_attribute_values        wwv_flow_global.vc_arr2;
begin
      -- "ou" is the attribute we are interested in.
      l_attributes(1)    :=    'ou';

      apex_ldap.get_user_attributes(
            p_username                => :APP_USER, -- APEX User
            p_pass                    => null,
            p_auth_base               => 'ou=people,dc=example,dc=com',
            p_host                    => '127.0.0.1',
            p_port                    => 389,
            p_attributes          => l_attributes,
            p_attribute_values    => l_attribute_values);

      if l_attribute_values(1) = 'Human Resources' then
            return true;
      else
            return false;
      end if;
end;
```

Here's how to implement this code as an authorization scheme:

1. Navigate to the Shared Components section of an application.
2. Select Authorization Schemes.
3. Create a new authorization scheme with the name In HR Org.
4. Under Scheme Type, select PL/SQL Function Body Returning a Boolean.
5. Enter the code in the preceding listing in the Expression 1 attribute.
6. Provide an error message.

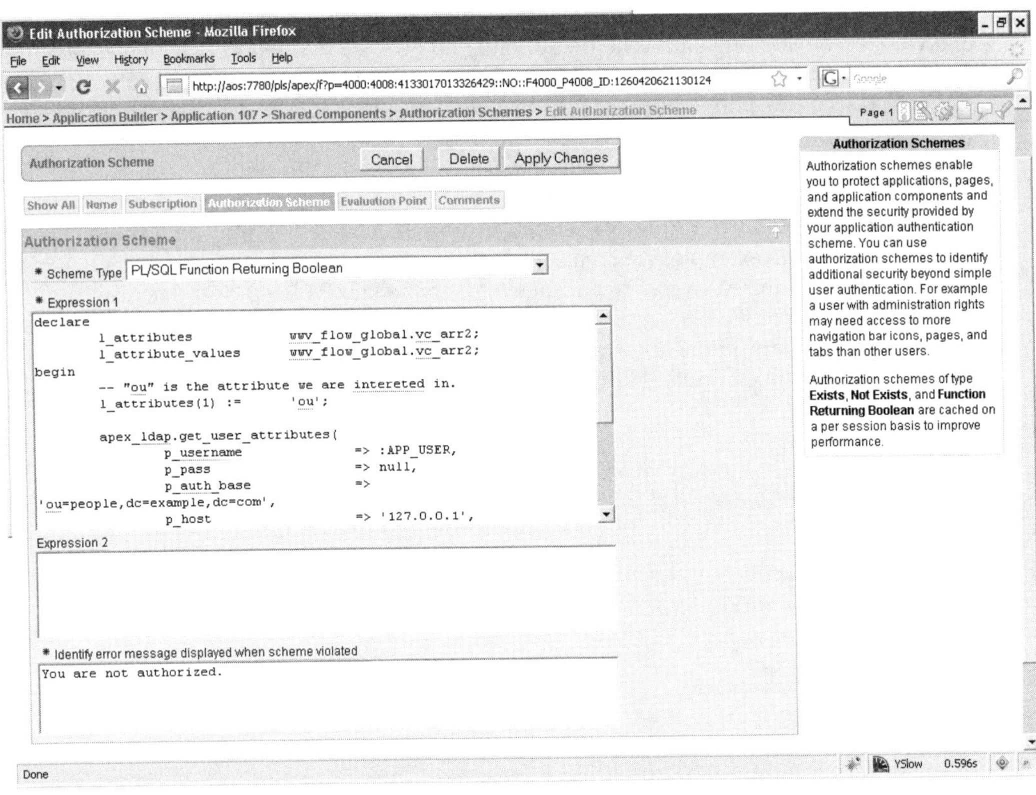

FIGURE 12-2 *In HR Org authorization scheme*

Now that we have created an authorization scheme named In HR Org, that name will appear in the select list of the authorization scheme attribute of almost every APEX object. Figure 12-3 shows this attribute for an APEX button. Note that APEX will also include the opposite of our authorization scheme by including "(Not In HR Org)," as this a common requirement and eliminates the need to implement it in code.

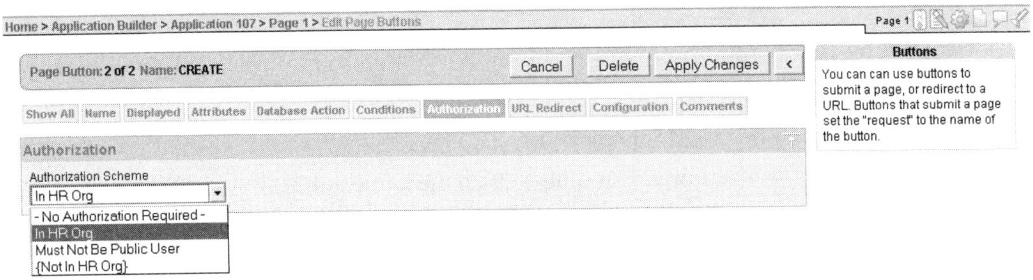

FIGURE 12-3 *Authorization scheme attribute of a button*

Let's use the report on the EMPLOYEES table as an example. Figure 12-4 shows the same page as it appears for two different users. The user Robert Smith passes the authorization scheme, while user Kathy Evans does not. The authorization scheme was applied to the Salary and edit link columns of the report, the Create button, and the Search text box. As you can see, those elements simply do not appear for Kathy Evans.

There are several scenarios in which reusing the logic of an authorization scheme is desirable, yet the declarative attribute is not present. For example, let's say we want to have sensitive items show up as read-only for anyone who is not an administrator. This simply isn't possible with the authorization scheme attribute of an item, as that attribute would completely hide the item for non-administrators, not simply show it as read-only. If the logic for who is considered an administrator is already defined in an authorization scheme, we can leverage that logic by calling the APEX_UTIL.PUBLIC_CHECK_AUTHORIZATION API. This API accepts the case-sensitive name of an authorization scheme and returns a Boolean, true, if the current user passes the authorization scheme, and false if he or she fails the authorization scheme. So, if we have an authorization scheme named IsAdmin, we can set the read-only attribute of one or more items to PL/SQL Function Body Returning a Boolean and enter the following code in the Expression 1 attribute:

```
return apex_util.public_check_authorization('IsAdmin');
```

You can also use this API for certain circumstances in which you want to check more than one authorization scheme. If you need to check more than one authorization scheme in multiple places, it might just be easier and more efficient to code an additional authorization scheme that encompasses the logic of several other schemes.

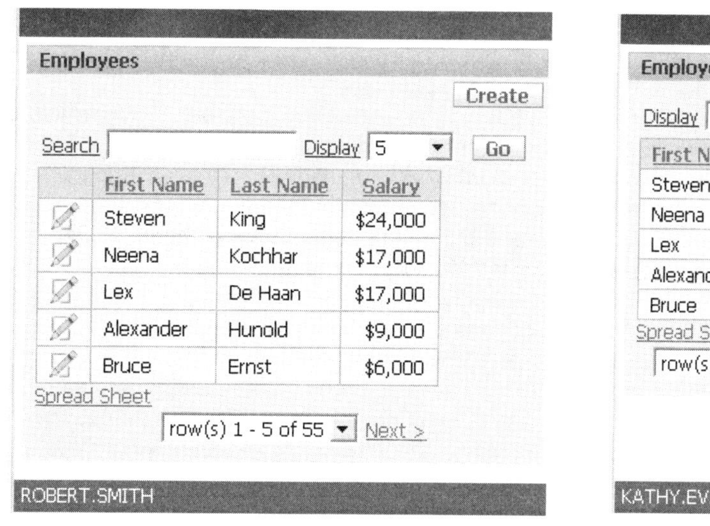

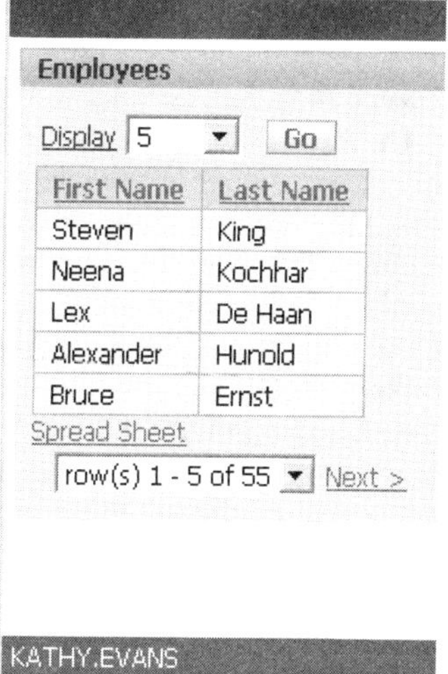

FIGURE 12-4 *Impact of authorization scheme for Robert and Kathy*

SQL Injection

Database-driven web applications are more prevalent than ever. They are no longer relegated to the one-off internal systems of corporations, but have made their way to almost every mainstream web application on the Internet. From photo-sharing sites; to web-based e-mail applications, online auctions, and store-fronts; to content management systems—all have a database behind the scenes. New static HTML sites are now the exception, not the norm. After all, why would anyone choose the management nightmare of a bunch of loosely coupled HTML, CSS, JavaScript, and image files when a content management system can separate the content from the formatting and move the ability of editing content from a few select technologists down to the people actually responsible for the content? A database brings so much power and flexibility to the Web, but it also introduces vulnerabilities.

SQL injection has been around for several years, but few developers know what it is and even fewer know how to prevent it. A SQL injection attack attempts to change the meaning of a predefined SQL query in an application. This type of attack can also change or add Data Manipulation Language (DML) statements, which are any inserts, updates, or deletes. Data Definition Language (DDL) could also be injected.

Most queries that are used inside an application consist of the SQL query and one or more parameters that can be changed at runtime. For example, imagine a web page that lists all employees for a particular department. As a user changes a select list on the web page, the page is submitted and the following query is executed:

```
select first_name,last_name,phone_number
  from employees
 where department_id = || X
```

The only thing that changes between page views is the value of **X** in the predicate. The developer of this application expects that only the value for **DEPARTMENT_ID** will ever be a number. However, a hacker might have very different plans for this predicate, such as returning all rows, or perhaps returning metadata about the database schema to plan an attack.

The key to preventing SQL injection attacks is the use of bind variables. If the structure or semantics of a query can change at runtime, then it is potentially vulnerable to SQL injection. Most of the time, the vulnerability is introduced by concatenating variables within the body of the query. The example in the preceding paragraph shows the variable **X** concatenated with the rest of the query. The query cannot be parsed before this concatenation occurs, and therefore the concatenation can change the structure of the query every time it is run.

For our purposes, we can simplify the Oracle SQL parser a bit and assume that it goes through three phases to run a SQL query: parse, bind, and execute. In the parse phase, the SQL parser checks that the query is syntactically valid and that all the objects that it references are valid, and then it locks in the structure of the query. During the bind phase, the actual values of bind variables are substituted for their placeholders in the query. Again, the bind variables can change the value of the placeholder variables, but they cannot change the structure of the query since that was already established during the parse phase. The final step is for the SQL parser to execute the query. Queries that concatenate, not bind variables, essentially reverse the bind and parse phases. The string is concatenated together, including the values of the variables, and then it is parsed. This reversal of phases allows an attacker to change the semantics of a query completely at runtime.

Example 1: The Wrong Way

To help you better understand the concept of SQL injection, let's construct a procedure that is vulnerable to SQL injection. The following procedure takes in a parameter of **p_last_name**, then outputs all employees that match the parameter. (Note that I am using the "Q quote mechanism" introduced in Oracle Database 10*g* R2 to make the examples easier to read.) The key is that the string is enclosed in the following syntax: **q'! some string!'**. This allows strings to contain single quotes without the need to escape those single quotes.

```
create or replace procedure sql_injection(
  p_last_name in varchar2)
is
  type employee_record is table of employees%ROWTYPE;
  emp_rec employee_record := employee_record();
  x varchar2(32767);
begin
  x := q'!select *
          from employees
         where last_name = '!'||p_last_name||q'!'!';

  execute immediate x bulk collect into emp_rec;

  for i in emp_rec.first..emp_rec.last loop
    dbms_output.put(emp_rec(i).last_name||' - ');
    dbms_output.put_line(emp_rec(i).salary);
  end loop;
  dbms_output.put_line(emp_rec.count||' Rows Returned');
end;
/
```

At first glance, this procedure seems valid, and it would probably run just fine in a production environment. Let's take a look at the first two examples with this procedure. They are semantically the same, though the second procedure uses the **q** quote mechanism.

```
hr@aos> set serveroutput on
hr@aos> exec sql_injection('Grant');
Grant - 2600
Grant - 7000
2 Rows Returned

hr@aos> exec sql_injection(q'!Grant!');
Grant - 2600
Grant - 7000
2 Rows Returned
```

As you can see, the procedure displays both employees with the last name Grant.

Now suppose we want to see all employees, even though the developer of this procedure never intended this functionality:

```
hr@aos> exec sql_injection(q'!Grant' or 1 = 1 --!');
King - 24000
```

```
Kochhar - 17000
De Haan - 17000
Hunold - 9000
Ernst - 6000
Austin - 4800
Pataballa - 4800
...
Gietz - 8300
107 Rows Returned
```

Now we can see all 107 rows! How did this happen?

1. By including the single quote after **Grant**, the where predicate has the correct syntax.
2. Adding **or 1 = 1** essentially negates the where predicate and returns every row since 1 will always equal 1.
3. The **--** at the end of the statement is the comment operator in Oracle SQL, which comments out the trailing single quote that is in the original procedure. Remember that we already closed the quote in step 1.

The addition of this predicate completely changes the result set of the query. Instead of simply passing different last names to the procedure, we are able to construct parameters that will modify the structure of the query.

The more an attacker knows about a system, the more effectively he can plan an attack. In the next example, we will pass a more sophisticated parameter to the same procedure to start investigating the data dictionary views.

```
hr@aos> exec sql_injection(q'!ZZZ' union select null,null,
table_name last_name,null,null,null,null,null,null,null,null
from user_tables --!');
COUNTRIES -
DEPARTMENTS -
EMPLOYEES -
JOBS -
JOB_HISTORY -
LOCATIONS -
REGIONS -
7 Rows Returned
```

Here's the breakdown of this attack:

1. The first part of the parameter is **ZZZ'**. This simply returns no rows from the employees table and closes the first quote. This was intentional since we already have all of the rows in the preceding example.
2. Next, we union in our own query. The syntax of a union operator is such that both queries need to have the same number and type of columns, so an attacker would need to keep adding null columns until he received a result.
3. Once again, we comment out the trailing single quote since we already closed it in step 1.

A variation on this attack might be to query the USER_TAB_COLUMNS table to find all the columns in the employees table. We could then union in our own query of the employees table to select columns that we were not intended to see, such as Social Security Number or Government Identification Number.

Example 2: The Right Way

The fatal flaw with the procedure in the preceding example is that instead of using bind variables, it glues a query together based on values passed in by the user, allowing an attacker to change the structure and the semantics of the query. Bind variables prevent SQL injection by allowing the values of predicates to change at runtime, yet the structure of the query cannot change.

The following example is a modified version of the preceding example implemented using bind variables:

```
create or replace procedure sql_injection_prevented(
  p_last_name in varchar2)
is
  type employee_record is table of employees%ROWTYPE;
  emp_rec employee_record := employee_record();
  x varchar2(32767);
begin
  x := q'!select *
           from employees
          where last_name = :last_name !';

  execute immediate x bulk collect into emp_rec using p_last_name;

  for i in emp_rec.first..emp_rec.last loop
    dbms_output.put(emp_rec(i).last_name||' - ');
    dbms_output.put_line(emp_rec(i).salary);
  end loop;
  dbms_output.put_line(emp_rec.count||' Rows Returned');
end sql_injection_prevented;
/
```

Take a close look at the query string defined in the variable **X**. Because it uses a bind variable, **:last_name**, the query is first parsed without the actual value of **p_last_name** substituted for the bind variable **last_name**. The SQL parser knows during the parse phase that this query has only one predicate and that the only acceptable value for **last_name** is a character string that represents a value. It is impossible to add any structures such as an **OR** predicate that changes structure of the query. To prove this, let's use a few of the tests from our previous example. This procedure works as expected when we call it with a last name:

```
hr@aos> exec sql_injection_prevented(q'!Grant!');
Grant - 2600
Grant - 7000
2 Rows Returned
```

Now let's try one of our SQL injection techniques:

```
hr@aos> exec sql_injection_prevented(q'!Grant' or 1 = 1--!');
BEGIN sql_injection_prevented(q'!Grant' or 1 = 1--!'); END;

*
ERROR at line 1:
```

```
ORA-06502: PL/SQL: numeric or value error
ORA-06512: at "HR.SQL_INJECTION_PREVENTED", line 1
ORA-06512: at line 1
```

This time we receive a "numeric or value error" since the string we passed in is not a valid string when searching for LAST_NAME.

Now that you fully understand the concept of SQL injection, let's talk about how it applies to APEX. Bind variables are remarkably easy to use in APEX since you do not have to write extra code to bind the values of those variables. You can simply reference the APEX items using bind variable syntax. The following examples demonstrate a SQL query and an insert statement as a developer would use them in APEX:

```
-- This query is used in a report region
select first_name,last_name
  from employees
 where instr(upper(last_name),upper(nvl(:P1_SEARCH,last_name))) > 0

 -- This insert statement is used in a page process
insert into employees (first_name,last_name)
                    values (:P2_FIRST_NAME,:P2_LAST_NAME)
  returning employee_id into :P2_NEW_EMPLOYEE_ID;
```

Note that in both examples, bind variable syntax is used to reference items. It is possible to reference APEX items using **&ITEM_NAME.** syntax, which treats them as a string, not a bind variable. For example, in the first query, we could have used **&P1_SEARCH.** instead of **:P1_SEARCH**. In that case, a nefarious user could inject carefully constructed code, through either the URL or the search box, which would modify the semantics of the query at runtime. The documentation, tutorials, and examples used throughout the APEX community encourage bind variable syntax. However, it is still possible for a developer who does not understand the difference to use the wrong syntax. Fortunately, the wrong syntax is substantially more complex than the right syntax when you add in the concatenation operators, so the secure way is actually the easy way.

Cross-site Scripting

Cross-site scripting (XSS) is a type of web exploit that affects every web development technology by attempting to execute client-side code, typically JavaScript, in a user's browser that was not included by the original developers of the application. For example, suppose a JavaScript function was executed on the Accounts page of your online banking application that searched for your account numbers on that page, and then posted those account numbers to some other web server controlled by a hacker. Obviously, the developers of the banking application would never create such a function, but if someone else were able to "inject" this function into your browser session or the page itself, the consequences could be catastrophic.

Of the several different types of XSS attacks, the most obvious one in the context of APEX is called "persistent." The persistent attack takes advantage of applications that have a database backend and that allow end users to save text that includes JavaScript, that will then be displayed by another user (as shown in Figure 12-5). Let's look at another example in an effort to clarify the vulnerability.

Imagine a timecard system or reporting application written in APEX that allowed users to enter the number of hours they worked along with some comments about those hours and a display of their year-to-date earnings. A newly submitted timecard would be routed to a person's manager

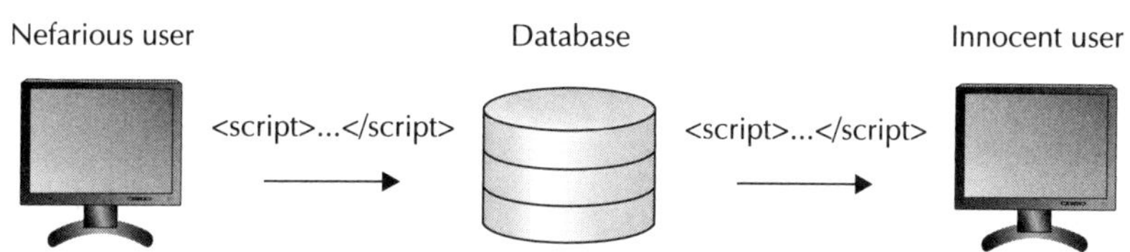

FIGURE 12-5 *Persistent XSS*

for approval. The manager could see all of her employees' hours, comments, and salaries. So far, the application works as intended. Now imagine that in my comments for this week, I include JavaScript that sends all the data displayed on a page to a web server that I control. When my manager views my timecard and my comments, she is unknowingly executing my JavaScript stored in the comments field, which sends the salary of everyone in my group to a server that I control. If I knew that the business rules of the system were such that overtime of more than 20 hours goes up to our group vice president for approval, I could wait for a week when I had more than 20 hours of overtime to inject my code, thus gaining access to the salaries of everyone in the whole organization. Who would have thought that a simple comments field could do so much damage?

Hopefully, you're now asking yourself, What can I do to prevent this? Fortunately, APEX includes features to help developers mitigate the risk of XSS. To summarize, the behavior we are trying to prevent is the ability for one user to submit JavaScript that will be displayed and therefore executed by other users. The most common APEX objects that display data are regions of type Report and APEX page items. When a new Standard Report is created based on a SQL query in APEX 3.2, the default column type for every column is called Standard Column. Unfortunately, this type of column is vulnerable to XSS. To prevent XSS, a developer must change this column type to Display as Text (escape special characters, does not save state). Future versions of APEX will likely change the default column type to the more secure version. The new type of APEX reports, called Interactive Reports, use the secure column type by default.

This same concept applies to APEX page items. If a developer chooses an item of type Display As Text, any JavaScript code that is stored in session state for that item will be executed when the page is displayed. To prevent this, a developer should choose items of type Display As Text (escape special characters, does not save state), as shown in Figure 12-6. In the case of the Report Column type and the APEX page item type, the "escape special characters" aspect is key, because it will send the HTML character codes for the less-than and greater-than signs—**<** and **>**, respectively—to the browser, not the characters < and >. The escaping of such markup-sensitive characters will cause the browser to render the actual characters, rather than interpret them as HTML. Using this technique will prevent data containing **<script>...</script>** from being interpreted as executable JavaScript.

One of the best ways for a developer to understand a security vulnerability is to intentionally create an example that is vulnerable, and then re-create the same example in a secure way. To that end, the following is a simple two-page APEX application that demonstrates the insecure and secure report column types and page item types. The following code, saved in a database table, simply writes a line of text onto a web page. The message is written in Unicode character codes so that it is unreadable unless the JavaScript function is executed:

```
<script type="text/JavaScript">
document.write(String.fromCharCode(88,83,83,32,86,117,108,110,101,114,97,98,108,101));
</script>
```

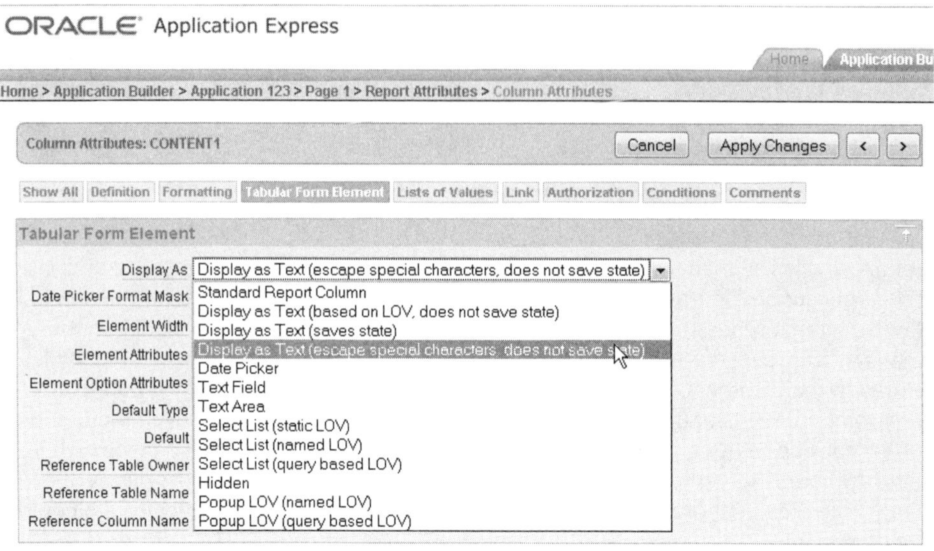

FIGURE 12-6 *Report column types*

The report on the page has two comments columns that display the previous JavaScript function. The first column, Comments - Secure, is set to the secure type of Display as Text (escape special characters, does not save state). The second column, Comments - Insecure, is set to the type Standard Column. As you can see in Figure 12-7, the first column shows the JavaScript function in its entirety, but does not execute it, while the second column is actually executing the JavaScript as you can read the phrase "XSS Vulnerable" in the comments. The developer of this application anticipated that users would enter only comments about an employee. However, it was trivial to add a bit of JavaScript that is now executed by any other user who views the report.

URL Tampering

In the earliest days of the internet web pages were primarily, a static, read-only medium used to share information. The most interaction a user had with a web application was clicking a link. Today, modern web applications have evolved to the point that there is an almost continuous two-way stream of information between a user's web browser and the application server. I'd like to emphasize "almost continuous" because it's important to understand the true nature of the HTTP Protocol as it relates to modern web applications. HTTP is a stateless protocol as a persistent connection is not maintained between the client web browser and the HTTP server. In contrast, traditional client-server applications maintain a persistent connection between the client and the server. The actions of the HTTP protocol are often defined in terms of request, response. I like to add a third term and describe it as request, response, disconnect. The emphasis on "disconnect" helps developers understand the true nature of the technology they are working with. Consider the impact of removing the network connection would have on a web application compared to a client-server application. The stateful client-server application would know immediately if the

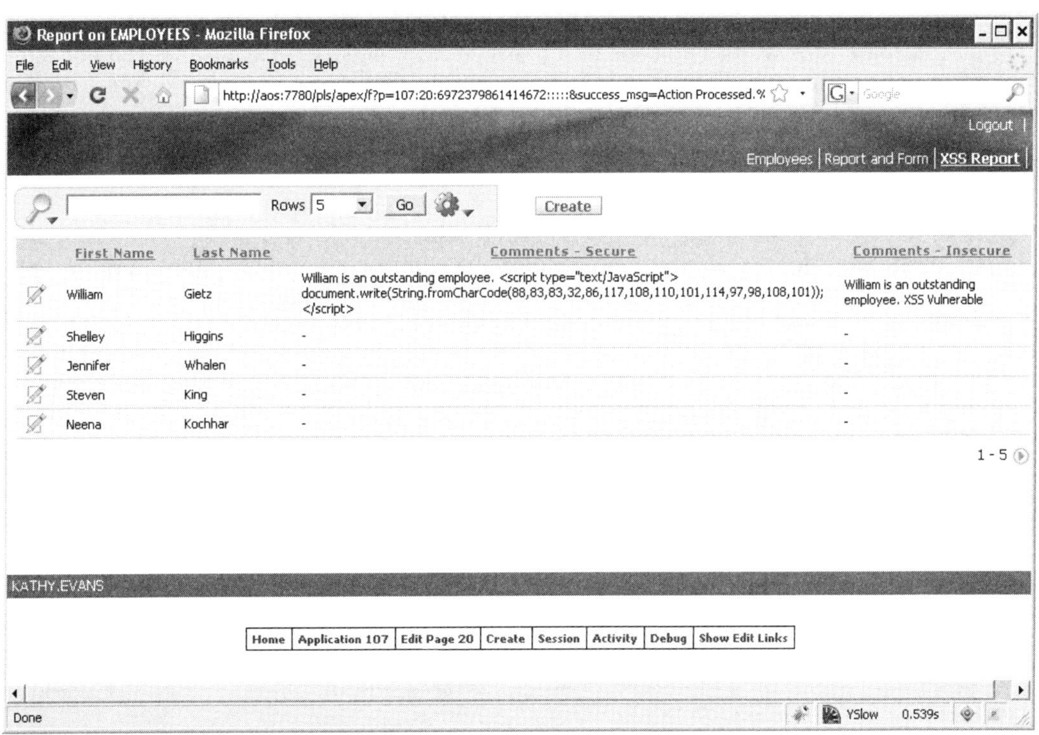

FIGURE 12-7 *XSS example report output*

connection were severed whereas the web application would have no knowledge of this action. Obviously, the end user in the web scenario would know when they clicked a link or posted a form and received no response, but the HTTP Server would have no knowledge of this.

Now that we have a better understanding of the stateless nature of a web application, let's talk about how APEX maintains session state. When a user requests a page from an APEX application, the APEX engine checks to see if this is the first request from this user in this browser session. If it is the first request, APEX assigns a new, unique number for this session. For brevity, we'll refer to this unique user session identifier as the Session ID. When you are using an APEX application, including the APEX Development Environment, notice the third parameter in the colon delimited list in the URL is a long seemingly random number. This number is also stored in a hidden form field on every page called pInstance. APEX also passes variables, such as search criteria, as parameters in the URL when the operation is an HTTP GET. One of the most convenient aspects of APEX for developers is that this session state is automatically managed for them in database tables. Once a value is set for an APEX Page or Application Item, the value of this item is maintained for the duration of the user's session. One simple, yet security-friendly benefit to this is realized when passing data between pages. If you as a developer set the value of an item on page 1, you can refer to it on any other page in the application without the need to constantly pass it through the URL.

A classic example of passing session state through the URL is the "Report and Form on a Table" generated by a wizard within APEX. The wizard builds a report page that shows the rows in a database table with an edit link next to each row. When users click on the edit link they are taken to the form page where they can edit the data in that row, as shown in Figure 12-8. The primary key of the table is passed as a parameter in the URL. The query on the form page uses that primary key as a query predicate to select the desired row.

In our example, what would happen if a user simply changed the value of the primary key in the URL (aka URL tampering)? If the user chose a value that matched another row in the table, that row would appear in the form. This raises an obvious security concern as end users are able to change the value used in the query predicate at will. Imagine now that the developer in this example wanted to limit the rows a user could edit by simply limiting the rows shown on the report page. If there is no row to click, how can a user edit that row? This false assumption by a developer could easily allow a user to gain access to data he or she is not supposed to see.

The first instinct of many developers is to make the request an HTTP **POST** instead of a **GET**, as the value is not passed through the URL. The reality is that this technique is simply "security through obscurity." Many web developer tools are available that allow an end user to view and manipulate post data or simply turn the **POST** into a **GET**. To address these concerns, APEX offers several new features that let developers easily protect their applications against such threats.

Restricted Items

In many scenarios, certain application- or page-level items should never be set by an end user. Suppose, for example, that the end user's role, such as Administrator or Guest, is stored in an application-level item. If an end user can change the value of this item, she could gain access

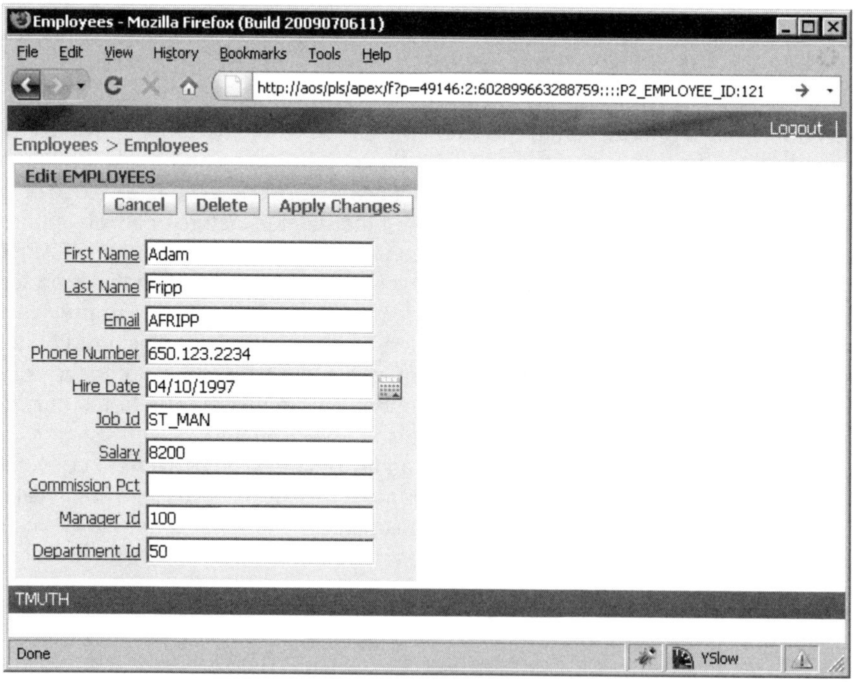

FIGURE 12-8 *Primary Key Passed Through the URL*

to pages or data to which she is not entitled. Each application or page item now has an attribute called Session State Protection. Setting this attribute to Restricted - May Not Be Set From Browser will prevent end users from tampering with the value of the attribute. The only way to change a Restricted... item's value is through constructs inside the application, such as computations or processes at the application or page level. This technique enables the developer to store values in items with the confidence that an end user cannot change their values.

Checksum

Completely blocking the ability to set an item from a URL is the most secure option and works well for application-level roles or attributes that are typically static for the session. However, in many scenarios, this technique simply won't work, such as the "Report and Form on a Table" discussed earlier in this section.

When a user clicks a row, we must have a way of determining which row was clicked to edit the proper row on the form page. The most common technique for this in APEX, as well as many other popular technologies, is to pass the value in the URL. Unfortunately, this gives the end user the opportunity to change the value. In response to this potential security threat, the concept of a URL checksum was built into APEX. When this feature is enabled, APEX uses a cryptographically strong Message Authentication Code or "MAC" to generate a checksum based on the parameters and their values in the URL. APEX then appends this checksum to the URL. This process occurs when APEX generates links to pages that require a checksum. When a link is clicked that sets the value of one or more items, APEX runs the items and values through the same function. Any change of a value in the URL will result in a different checksum when the request is received, thus allowing APEX to detect URL tampering.

A great example of this is the Report and Form on a Table. Once we require a checksum for the ID item on the form page, APEX automatically generates the checksum for each link on the report page. Clicking a link works exactly as it did before, except you will now see a checksum appended to the URL. If you try to change the value of ID in the URL, APEX will simply return an error. If this checksum were a simple hash based on a well-known algorithm, it would be easy to spoof. However, since the algorithm also takes in a key or "salt" that is known only internally to the APEX engine, a nefarious user would need to determine the algorithm or algorithms used as well as the key.

Suggested Session State Protection Scenario

Session State Protection is extensively documented in the APEX Application Builder Users Guide. Many permutations of settings are possible for Session State Protection. Instead of dedicating a large portion of this chapter to all possible scenarios, I'll provide some guidelines that cover the most common ones, which fall into two categories: items that should never be changed by a user, such as an application item storing the user's role, and items that must be set through the URL; however, allowing the user to change item values is a security risk.

Items That Should Never Change To ensure that the value of an item is never set by an end user using URL parameters, set the item-level Session State Protection attribute to Restricted - May Not Be Set From Browser. This is applicable to application- and page-level items.

Sensitive Items Set Through the URL The scenario described earlier using the Report and Form example is a perfect candidate for URL checksums. To enable this feature, navigate to the Application Level Attributes | Security | Session State Protection Section, and click Page. Select the target page of a URL that requires a checksum, in this case the form page. Change the Page Access Protection attribute to Arguments Must Have Checksum. You must also set the session state protection level for key items on the page, typically items that store the primary key of the row. Checksum Required - Session Level is the most secure setting. Application and User Level Checksums are used when sharing URLs or bookmarking is desirable. It is not necessary to require checksums for items that are not passed through the URL, as the values of those items will be overwritten by the process that returns the row into the page items. Figure 12-9 shows an APEX URL in which Session State Protection is enabled. The cs= parameter appended to the URL is the checksum.

Password Items Items of type Password have always obscured the value from appearing on the screen so that someone watching over a user's shoulder cannot read the password. However, password values are stored in the APEX session state table, which is accessible to anyone with a privileged database account. Any login page generated by APEX clears this session state as soon as the user logs in, but that value could persist in online redo log files or archive log files. It is also easy for a developer inadvertently to alter the process that clears session state for the login, leaving the password in the session state table.

To address these situations, two new item types were introduced in APEX 3.2: Password (does not save state) and Password (submits when ENTER pressed, does not save state). Both item types insure that a user's password is never written to a persistent store. Developers who upgrade applications or instances from previous versions of APEX to APEX 3.2 should verify that all password fields use these new item types.

Encrypted Session State

In addition to protecting passwords, a developer may want to protect other sensitive data from system administrators or anyone else who has a privileged account or access to the online redo or archive log files. Even if the data is stored in a table using programmatic or transparent encryption, any data element used in an APEX item is stored in the application session state table in clear text. Starting with APEX 3.2, developers can set an item-level attribute to store session state encrypted.

To illustrate this point, the following example in Figure 12-10 sets the Store Value Encrypted In Session State attribute of the P11_SALARY item to Yes and leaves it set to No for the P11_EMAIL item.

After submitting the page to make sure their values were stored in session state, I queried the WWV_FLOW_DATA table used to store APEX session state:

```
APEX_030200@AOS> select item_name,item_value
                  from wwv_flow_data
                  where flow_instance = 3574272250559947
                    and flow_id = 107
                    and item_name in ('P11_EMAIL','P11_SALARY');

ITEM_NAME                      ITEM_VALUE
------------------------------ --------------------------------
P11_EMAIL                      JWHALEN
P11_SALARY                     948F90BDC554FBB74305B2AFA6E44102
```

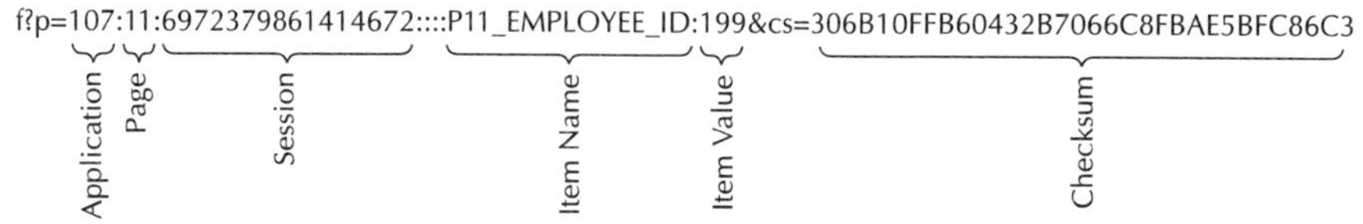

FIGURE 12-9 *Checksum added to URL*

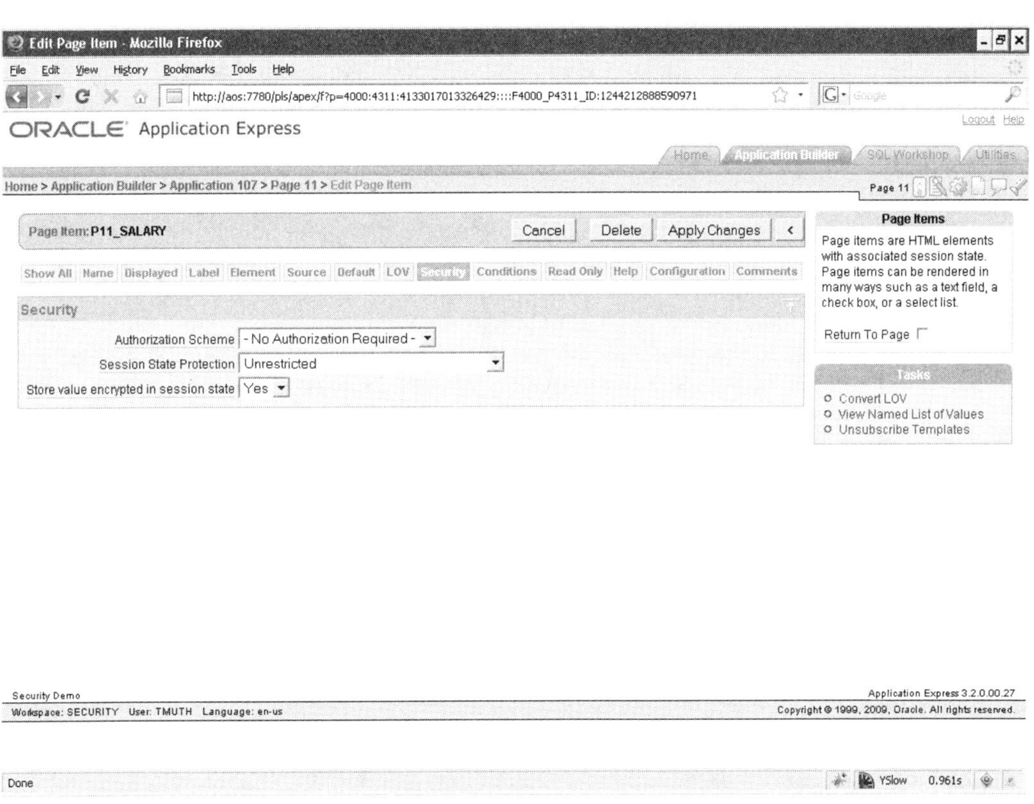

FIGURE 12-10 *Store Value Encrypted In Session State attribute*

As you can see, P11_EMAIL is in clear text, while the value of P11_SALARY that was a four-digit number on screen is now stored in the session state table as an encrypted value. This value can be decrypted only internally by APEX and is thus protected from scenarios such as this. It's very important to note that this setting affects how the data is stored only in APEX session state—it has nothing to do with how the value is stored in application tables. In this example, the value of the EMPLOYEES.SALARY column is not encrypted, only the value stored in the APEX item P11_SALARY. So enabling encryption on this item does not encrypt data in the EMPLOYEES table. It is the developer's responsibility to make sure that the application tables used to store sensitive data do so using technologies such as DBMS_CRYPTO or Transparent Data Encryption at the column or tablespace level.

Leveraging Database Security Features

One key benefit to the APEX architecture is that every database feature is available to APEX developers. In this section, we will explore the integration of VPD to implement row-level security. We'll then leverage fine-grained auditing (FGA) to provide silent alarm for our most sensitive data. Both scenarios take advantage of the context information that APEX provides to better determine who the user is and where they are in a given application.

Virtual Private Database

VPD is one of the best ways to push data security down to the lowest possible level. It's easy to envision scenarios in which all the data security was built into the application layer. When another technology is introduced that needs to access the same data, the semantics of the security policy has to be replicated to the new technology. Obviously, this is difficult to maintain, prone to errors, and easy to subvert, because all a nefarious individual has to do to access the data is connect directly to the database, effectively bypassing the security.

VPD is a critically important solution to protect the data at the source. The classic VPD use case is to set one or more session context variables when an end user logs into an application, and then use those context variables in a VPD policy that determines the rows to which a user has access. This is a fairly straightforward task in client-server environments, where the database session of an end user persists as long as the user is logged into the application. As discussed in Chapter 11, APEX database sessions persist only as long as it takes to process a page request, which is typically less than a second. This is yet another area where the difference between nonpersistent and persistent sessions causes a lot of confusion for developers.

Fortunately, you an integrate VPD with APEX in many ways. One option is to use the Virtual Private Database attribute of an APEX application to call a procedure that sets session context variables. This technique works particularly well with legacy VPD applications that are already using session context variables. Another option is to reference APEX items in the VPD policy, which we will refer to as an *item-based policy*. A third option is to use Oracle Database Global Application Context variables, which were specifically designed for use with stateless applications. Global Application Contexts have a significant drawback in that they offer no built-in way to purge expired sessions. As such, they are not a good solution for APEX and VPD, and are not covered in this book.

APEX Item-based Policy

The easiest approach to implement is to use APEX items. As you might expect, this approach has both advantages and disadvantages.

Following are the advantages of using APEX items:

- APEX items are persistent for the life of the end user's APEX session. If you set the value of an item when a user logs into the application, that value will still be there as long as the user is using the application.
- Because the items are persistent, their values need to be set only once—for example, when a user authenticates. This is especially beneficial if the code used to determine a user's authorization rights is expensive.
- The syntax used to set an APEX item is exceptionally easy.
- APEX items are purged at regular intervals so a developer doesn't need to worry about cleanup procedures.

The disadvantage of using APEX items is that APEX items can be used only with APEX applications. If the VPD policy is to be used in a heterogeneous environment, it will need separate logic for APEX and any other technology that needs to access the data.

In the following example, we will create a simple table to store users and their roles. When a user logs into our APEX application, we will store the role in an APEX item. We will then reference the value of this APEX item in a function used for a VPD policy. If the user's role is ADMINISTRATOR, he will see all rows in the table. If his role is READ, he will see only his own row. All others, such as a user that access this table from a reporting tool, will not see any rows.

```
SYS@AOS> grant create any context to sec_admin;
SYS@AOS> grant execute on sys.dbms_rls to sec_admin;

-- Execute the following DDL as schema SEC_ADMIN
create table sec_admin.user_app_roles(
      id   char(32),
      user_name   varchar2(255),
      role_name   varchar2(255),
      constraint user_app_roles_pk primary key (id),
      constraint user_app_roles_uq unique(user_name,role_name),
      constraint user_app_roles_ck check (role_name in ('ADMINISTRATOR', 'READER'))
)
/

create or replace
trigger  bi_user_app_roles before insert on user_app_roles
for each row
begin
      :new.id := sys_guid();
      :new.user_name := upper(:new.user_name);
      :new.role_name := upper(:new.role_name);
end;
/


insert into user_app_roles (user_name,role_name)
                           values ('DGRANT','ADMINISTRATOR');

insert into user_app_roles (user_name,role_name)
                           values ('JWHALEN','READER');

commit;

grant select on sec_admin.user_app_roles to sec_user;

create or replace function sec_admin.employees_apex_item_fn (
    p_schema  in  varchar2 default null,
    p_object  in  varchar2 default null)
    return varchar2
as
    l_return    varchar2(255) := '1 = 2';-- by default, this will return no rows
      l_role            varchar2(255);
begin
      -- A few basic tests to see if it looks like an APEX Session
      if v('APP_USER') = sys_context('userenv','client_info')
```

```
            and      regexp_instr(sys_context('userenv','module'),
           '^APEX:APPLICATION[[:space:]][0-9]+$') > 0 then
            -- ROLE_NAME is an APEX Application Level Item.  Its value
            -- is set using an APEX Application Process.
            if v('ROLE_NAME') = 'ADMINISTRATOR' then
                  l_return := '1 = 1'; -- all rows
            elsIf v('ROLE_NAME') = 'READER' then
                  l_return := 'email = v('' APP_USER'')'; -- only their own row
            else
                  l_return := '1 = 2'; -- no rows
            end if;
      end if;

    return l_return;
end;
/
-- The following 2 drop statements will drop the policies used in both
-- examples from this section to make sure we have a clean slate.
begin
dbms_rls.drop_policy (object_schema   => 'DATA_OWNER',
                      object_name     => 'EMPLOYEES',
                      policy_name     => 'EMPLOYEES_APEX_ITEM');
end;
/

begin
dbms_rls.drop_policy (object_schema   => 'DATA_OWNER',
                      object_name     => 'EMPLOYEES',
                      policy_name     => 'EMPLOYEES_CONTEXT');
end;
/
begin
    dbms_rls.add_policy
        (object_schema      => 'DATA_OWNER',
         object_name        => 'EMPLOYEES',
         policy_name        => 'EMPLOYEES_APEX_ITEM',
         policy_function    => 'EMPLOYEES_APEX_ITEM_FN');
end;
/
```

This function **EMPLOYEES_APEX_ITEM_FN** references an APEX item named **ROLE_NAME**. Figure 12-11 shows the process that sets this item.

Session Context-based Policy

The next example illustrates the use of a session context variable. This technique is a more traditional approach to VPD and has an advantage in that it is applicable to other technologies such as Oracle Forms. The main disadvantage of this technique when used with APEX is that the function used to set a user's context is called on every page view. If this function is expensive, it could have a negative impact on performance. However, if you are running Oracle Database 11*g*

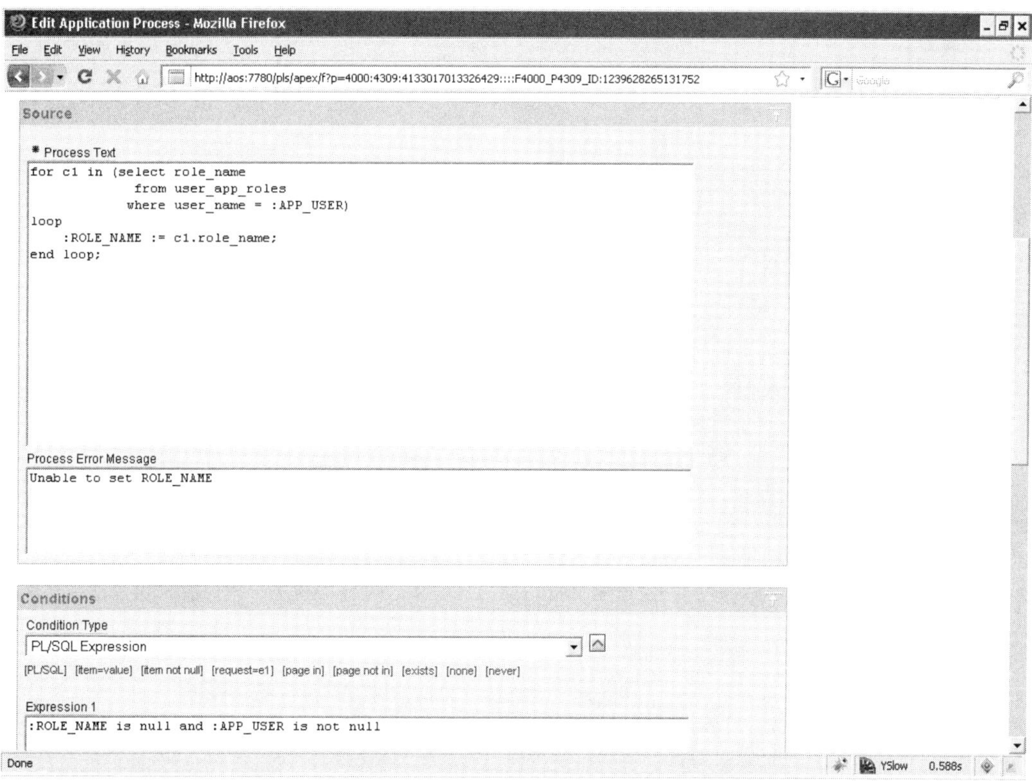

FIGURE 12-11 *Application level, before header process to set the role*

or later, you can use the Function Result Cache feature to cache the results and greatly improve performance.

```
create or replace context sec_admin.employees_context using set_employees_context
/
create or replace procedure sec_admin.set_employees_context
as
begin
      dbms_session.set_context('EMPLOYEES_CONTEXT','ROLE_NAME', null);
      for c1 in (select role_name
                     from sec_admin.user_app_roles
                    where user_name = sys_context('userenv','client_info'))
      loop
            dbms_session.set_context('EMPLOYEES_CONTEXT','ROLE_NAME', c1.role_name);
      end loop;
end;
/
```

```
grant execute on sec_admin.set_employees_context to sec_user;

create or replace function sec_admin.employees_context_fn (
    p_schema  in  varchar2 default null,
    p_object  in  varchar2 default null)
    return varchar2
as
    l_return    varchar2(255) := '1 = 2';-- by default, this will return no rows
      l_role            varchar2(255);
begin
      if sys_context('EMPLOYEES_CONTEXT','ROLE_NAME')  = 'ADMINISTRATOR' then
            l_return := '1 = 1'; -- all rows
      elsIf sys_context('EMPLOYEES_CONTEXT','ROLE_NAME') = 'READER' then
            l_return := 'email = sys_context(''userenv'',''client_info'')'; -- only
their own row
      else
            l_return := '1 = 2'; -- no rows
      end if;
    return l_return;
end;
/

-- The following 2 drop statements will drop the policies used in both
-- examples from this section to make sure we have a clean slate.

begin
dbms_rls.drop_policy (object_schema    => 'DATA_OWNER',
                      object_name      => 'EMPLOYEES',
                      policy_name      => 'EMPLOYEES_APEX_ITEM');
end;
/

begin
dbms_rls.drop_policy (object_schema    => 'DATA_OWNER',
                      object_name      => 'EMPLOYEES',
                      policy_name      => 'EMPLOYEES_CONTEXT');
end;
/

begin
    dbms_rls.add_policy
        (object_schema       => 'DATA_OWNER',
         object_name         => 'EMPLOYEES',
         policy_name         => 'EMPLOYEES_CONTEXT',
         policy_function     => 'EMPLOYEES_CONTEXT_FN');
end;
/

-- APEX Components
```

Keeping in mind that each APEX page view is actually a new database session, you need to set this context with each page view. APEX provides an application-level attribute designed for this exact purpose (shown in Figure 12-12), as it occurs very early in the APEX rendering code. This is to ensure that the context is set before any application code that might need the context is executed.

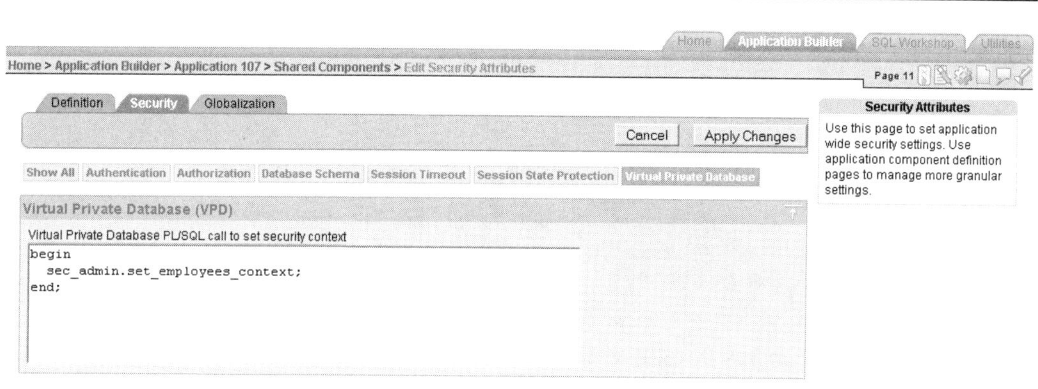

FIGURE 12-12 *VPD application attribute*

Fine-grained Auditing

The balance between security and productivity is often tough to find. Too much security, and people have a hard time doing their jobs. Too little, and you expose your system to a security breach. In many cases, developers are tasked with securing an existing or packaged application, which may limit their ability to change the underlying code or architecture. FGA is a great candidate for these applications because it's a relatively transparent, bolt-on solution to add a layer of defense to your data.

FGA allows a developer to construct an audit policy in PL/SQL and then apply that policy to database tables. Policies have access to all database environment variables of the end user's session, such as **SYS_CONTEXT** variables. These environment variables allow you to define what the signature of an application user should look like, and then trigger audit events for parameters that fall outside of that signature. For example, a FGA policy might check **MODULE**, **ACTION**, **IP ADDRESS**, and time of day. If any of these parameters fall outside those defined by your policy, the audit event is triggered.

As its name implies, this feature is only a way to audit events as they occur, but it won't actually prevent access to the data. Consequently, FGA should be used in conjunction with other security measures that actually protect the data. Think of FGA as the silent alarm of an Oracle database. As a silent alarm, it provides an interesting deterrent to valid users of an application. Unlike techniques that hide data or raise an error, the psychological effect of this invisible tripwire can leave employees with the impression that if they start snooping around where they shouldn't, they could initiate an investigation into their actions. Think about this in the context of a bank robbery. If a thief sets off a loud siren at night, he'll simply run away. However, the fear of triggering a silent alarm and walking out of the bank with bags full of money to a waiting crowd of police officers provides a completely different psychological deterrent.

FGA and APEX

APEX is exceptionally well suited to FGA. As discussed in Chapter 11, APEX sets the environment variables **MODULE** and **ACTION** to the APEX application number and page number. To get an idea of the environment variables available to you in an APEX session, navigate to the APEX SQL Workshop | SQL Commands section and run the following query (shown in Figure 12-13):

```
SELECT sys_context('USERENV', 'MODULE') module,
       sys_context('USERENV', 'ACTION') action ,
       sys_context('USERENV', 'CLIENT_IDENTIFIER') CLIENT_IDENTIFIER,
       sys_context('USERENV', 'CLIENT_INFO') CLIENT_INFO,
       v('APP_USER') app_user,
       sys_context('USERENV', 'CURRENT_SCHEMA') CURRENT_SCHEMA,
       sys_context('USERENV', 'SESSION_USER') SESSION_USER,
       sys_context('USERENV', 'IP_ADDRESS') IP_ADDRESS
  FROM dual;
```

In APEX version 3.2, the SQL Workshop is called Application 4500 and the SQL Commands feature is on page 1200. These numbers will obviously be different when you run the same query in your actual application, but they provide a nice example since the APEX development environment is also a collection of APEX applications. Notice that **CURRENT_SCHEMA** is the parsing schema for the query, as indicated by the select-list control in the upper-right corner of the page. This variable represents the parsing schema of your application. SESSION_USER will always be the schema that the DAD uses to connect to the database. Typically this is APEX_PUBLIC_

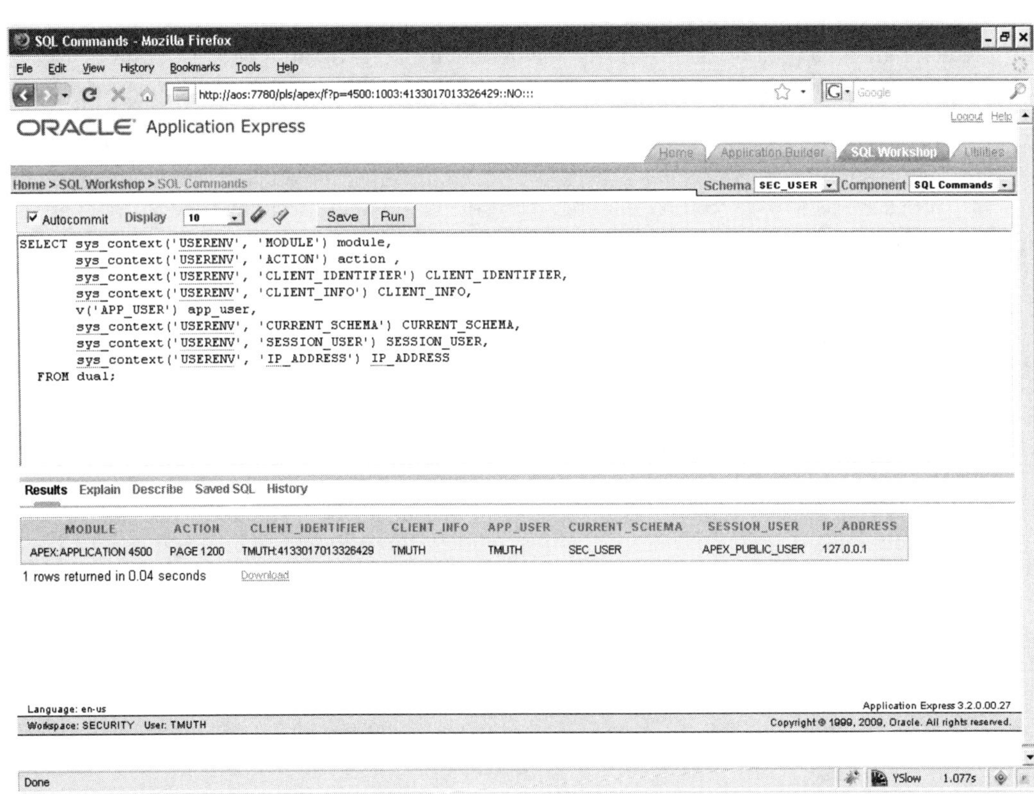

FIGURE 12-13 *Context variable query in the SQL Workshop*

USER for environments using Oracle HTTP Server or ANONYMOUS for environments using the Embedded PL/SQL Gateway. The **IP_ADDRESS** environment variable is the IP address of the client. Most people think this will be the IP address of the end user's machine, but in an APEX environment, the database client is actually the Oracle HTTP server. This concept is useful in the context of a FGA policy designed to allow only APEX access to the data as the IP address should always be the same. However, if someone connects to the database directly with a tool such as SQL*Plus, that session's IP address will be the IP address of the person's PC, not the HTTP server.

FGA Example 1

Now that you have a good idea of what FGA is, let's work through a few examples that get progressively more complex. For the following examples, we'll use two schemas: SEC_USER and SEC_ADMIN. SEC_USER will own the objects we want to audit, and SEC_ADMIN will own the functions and policies used in our auditing examples. Before we can create any policies, we must connect as a DBA and grant SEC_ADMIN execute privileges on the DBMS_FGA package. While we're there, lets also grant select on the sys.dba_fga_audit_trail view to SEC_ADMIN.

```
$ sqlplus / as sysdba

SQL> grant execute on dbms_fga to SEC_ADMIN;

Grant succeeded.

SQL> grant select on sys.dba_fga_audit_trail to sec_admin;

Grant succeeded.
```

The first example uses a function called **IS_APEX_SESSION_ONE** that simply checks to make sure the **SESSION_USER** environment variable is either APEX_PUBLIC_USER or ANONYMOUS, the two most common schemas used for APEX sessions. If the **SESSION_USER** is considered valid, the function returns a *1* (one), or else it returns a *0* (zero). Connect as the SEC_ADMIN user and create the following function:

```
create or replace function is_apex_session_one
  return number
  authid definer
as
begin
  if sys_context('userenv','session_user') in ('ANONYMOUS','APEX_PUBLIC_USER') then
    return 1;
  else
    return 0;
  end if;
end is_apex_session_one;
/
```

Right now, this function is just a traditional function and is in no way associated with a FGA policy or a table. Execute the following code as the SEC_ADMIN user to create the policy that will tie the previous function to the table we want to audit:

```
begin
  dbmS_FGA.add_policy
    (object_schema       => 'SEC_USER',
     object_name         => 'EMPLOYEES',
```

```
    policy_name          => 'IS_FROM_APEX_POLICY',
    audit_condition      => 'SEC_ADMIN.IS_APEX_SESSION_ONE = 0',
    audit_column         => null,
    statement_types      => 'INSERT,UPDATE,DELETE,SELECT',
    enable               => true);
end;
/
```

In simple terms, an audit policy named IS_FROM_APEX_POLICY has been applied to the SEC_USER.EMPLOYEES table. This policy is enforced on all columns and all **INSERT**, **UPDATE**, **DELETE**, and **SELECT** statements. An audit event is triggered whenever the function **IS_APEX_SESSION_ONE** returns a *0* (zero).

Since the goal of this policy is to audit any queries not originating from APEX, let's first test this by querying the EMPLOYEES table from the APEX SQL Workshop. The SQL Workshop is itself an APEX application and thus falls within the allowed parameters of our policy.

```
-- Executed in the Application Express SQL Workshop
select * from employees;
```

By querying the DBA_FGA_AUDIT_TRAIL, we can determine whether or not the previous query triggered an audit event:

```
SQL> select timestamp,db_user, client_id, object_schema,object_name,
            policy_name, scn, sql_text from sys.dba_fga_audit_trail;

no rows selected
```

As expected, no audit event was logged. Now, let's run the same query once again from SQL*Plus:

```
SQL> select * from employees;
```

Now connect as a privileged user and query the Audit Trail table:

```
SQL> select timestamp,db_user, policy_name, scn, sql_text from sys.dba_fga_audit_trail;
TIMESTAMP DB_USER    POLICY_NAME         SCN      SQL_TEXT
--------- ---------- ------------------- -------- -----------------------
08-MAR-09 SEC_USER   IS_FROM_APEX_POLICY 4638186  select * from employees
```

FGA Example 2

For our next FGA example, we'll leverage more session context information to narrow the allowed parameters of the audit condition a bit. This time, we will use **MODULE** to check that the query is coming from a specific APEX application. We can also use the **SYS_CONTEXT** function to determine the IP address of the client that issued the query. In this case, the expected client is our HTTP server; any other IP address indicates the query might be coming from another client such as a SQL*Plus connection from an unauthorized workstation.

```
create or replace
function is_apex_session_two
  return number
  authid definer
as
begin
```

```
  if sys_context('userenv','session_user') in ('ANONYMOUS','APEX_PUBLIC_USER')
  and sys_context('userenv','module') = 'APEX:APPLICATION 123'
  and sys_context('userenv','ip_address') = '192.168.1.123'
  then
    return 1;
  else
    return 0;
  end if;
end is_apex_session_two;
/
```

Before creating a new audit policy to associate this function with a table, we will drop the policy created in the preceding example:

```
BEGIN
  DBMS_FGA.DROP_POLICY
    (object_schema        => 'SEC_USER',
     object_name          => 'EMPLOYEES',
     policy_name          => 'IS_FROM_APEX_POLICY');
END;
/
```

Now we can create a new policy for this function:

```
begin
  dbmS_FGA.add_policy
    (object_schema        => 'SEC_USER',
     object_name          => 'EMPLOYEES',
     policy_name          => 'IS_FROM_APEX_POLICY_TWO',
     audit_condition      => 'SEC_ADMIN.IS_APEX_SESSION_TWO = 0',
     audit_column         => null,
     statement_types      => 'INSERT,UPDATE,DELETE,SELECT',
     enable               => true);
end;
/
```

As you will recall, the SQL Workshop is Application 4500 and our policy is checking to make sure the query is coming from Application 123. Querying the EMPLOYEES table from the SQL Workshop should trigger an audit event:

```
-- Executed in the Application Express SQL Workshop
select * from employees where 1 = 1;
```

I added the predicate **1 = 1** to show that the full SQL text is captured in the audit trail. Now query the audit trail to verify that a new event was logged:

```
SQL> select timestamp,db_user, client_id, scn, sql_text from sys.dba_fga_audit_trail;

DB_USER    CLIENT_ID              SCN     SQL_TEXT
---------- ---------------------- ------- -----------------------------------
SEC_USER                          4638186 select * from employees
ANONYMOUS  TMUTH:3528968924651999 6009443 select * from employees where 1 = 1
```

Note that the new row in the audit trail was issued by the database user ANONYMOUS, which typically means it's coming from APEX using the Embedded PL/SQL Gateway. Also note that APEX sets CLIENT_ID to the APEX User and APEX Session ID number that is captured in the audit trail.

You might wonder why I included SCN (System Change Number) as a column in this example. My goal was to hint at a powerful concept that is a bit beyond the scope of this chapter, and that is to combine FGA with the Oracle database Flashback feature and, new in 11*g*, Flashback Data Archive. Flashback is designed to retain historical data for short periods—say, a week or less—which provides DBAs many more options for data recovery. Flashback is also a great compliment to FGA in that it allows you to put your session back in time. Since the audit trail provides both the SCN and the query, we could put our session back to that time and run the same query to see exactly what data was displayed in a security breach. Flashback Data Archive extends this concept as it is designed to retain data for much longer periods, measured in months or years. The following code is a quick example of how the code is used for this scenario:

```
exec DBMS_FLASHBACK.ENABLE_AT_SYSTEM_CHANGE_NUMBER(6009443);
select * from employees where 1 = 1;
```

FGA Example 3

One parameter of **DBMS_FGA.ADD_POLICY** we haven't explored yet is **HANDLER_MODULE**. While this parameter is not directly related to APEX, the functionality it provides is significant enough to deserve an example. **HANDLER_MODULE** is designed to be able to send alerts when an audit event occurs. Without the ability to send alerts, a security administrator needs to review the audit logs on a regular basis to detect suspicious events. **HANDLER_MODULE** allows you to define a PL/SQL procedure that is called every time an audit event occurs. The PL/SQL procedure must conform to the following signature:

```
procedure_name(
      object_schema in VARCHAR2,
      object_name in VARCHAR2,
      policy_name in VARCHAR2);
```

Our example procedure will use the database package UTL_MAIL. In 11*g*, this package is not installed by default. Installation instructions for this package are detailed in the "Oracle Database PL/SQL Packages and Types Reference." You will also need to set the initialization parameter **SMTP_OUT_SERVER** and grant execute on **UTL_MAIL** to **SEC_ADMIN**.

The following procedure is an example handler module that collects as much information as possible about the session that triggered the audit event and e-mails that information to one or more security administrators.:

```
create or replace procedure fga_notify (
       schema_name in varchar2,
       table_name  in varchar2,
       policy_name in varchar2)
as
    l_msg   varchar2(32767);
      -- the t_row function accepts name / value pairs and returns them
      -- as an HTML table row with 2 cells
    function t_row(
        p_label     in varchar2,
        p_data      in varchar2)
```

```
    return varchar2
    is
    begin
        return '<tr><td style="text-align:right;">'||p_label||'</td>'||
               '    <td style="font-weight:bold;">'||p_data||'</td></tr>'||utl_tcp.
crlf;
    end t_row;
begin
    l_msg := '<html><head><style type="text/css">body{font-family:helvetica}</
style></head><body>'||
             '<table style="border:0px;">'||
             t_row('Schema',schema_name)||
             t_row('Table',table_name)||
             t_row('Policy',policy_name)||
             t_row('User',user)||
             t_row('Client Info',sys_context('userenv', 'client_info'))||
             t_row('Client Identifier',sys_context('userenv', 'client_identifier'))||
             t_row('IP Address',sys_context('userenv', 'ip_address'))||
             t_row('Auth Type',sys_context('userenv', 'authentication_type'))||
             t_row('Session ID',sys_context('userenv', 'sessionid'))||
             t_row('DB Name',sys_context('userenv', 'db_name'))||
             t_row('Host',sys_context('userenv', 'host'))||
             t_row('OS User',sys_context('userenv', 'os_user'))||
             t_row('External Name',sys_context('userenv', ' external_name'))||
             t_row('Current SQL', '<pre> '||sys_context('userenv', 'current_
sql')||'</pre>')||
             '</table></body></html>';

    utl_mail.send(
        SENDER      => 'sec_admin@mycompany.com',
        RECIPIENTS  => 'security_admin@mycompany.com,dba@mycompany.com',
        SUBJECT     => 'Policy Violation',
        MESSAGE     => l_msg,
        MIME_TYPE   => 'text/html',
        PRIORITY    => 1);
end fga_notify;
/
```

To demonstrate the use of this procedure we will use the Audit Function defined in the first example. Note that the last parameter is new.

```
begin
  dbms_fga.add_policy
    (object_schema       => 'SEC_USER',
     object_name         => 'EMPLOYEES',
     policy_name         => 'IS_FROM_APEX_POLICY',
     audit_condition     => 'SEC_ADMIN.IS_APEX_SESSION_ONE = 0',
     audit_column        => null,
     statement_types     => 'INSERT,UPDATE,DELETE,SELECT',
     enable              => true,
     handler_module      => SEC_ADMIN.FGA_NOTIFY);
end;
/
```

Now let's issue a query from SQL*Plus to trigger an audit event:

```
SQL> select * from employees;
```

This solution notifies administrators within seconds of an attempted data breach, enabling them to take proactive measures to prevent further data loss. Since it does not require any schema or code changes, this solution is an excellent addition to any system dealing with sensitive data.

Summary

APEX encourages secure coding practices by providing developers with the right tools and examples. As with any security-focused solution, there is no magic button labeled "Secure My Code." Security is developed through knowledge and awareness. The goal of this chapter is to raise your level of awareness and to provide examples to steer developers in the right direction. It is a developer's responsibility to apply these techniques in their day-to-day development and, more important, to open a dialogue with their colleagues to help raise everyone's level of awareness.

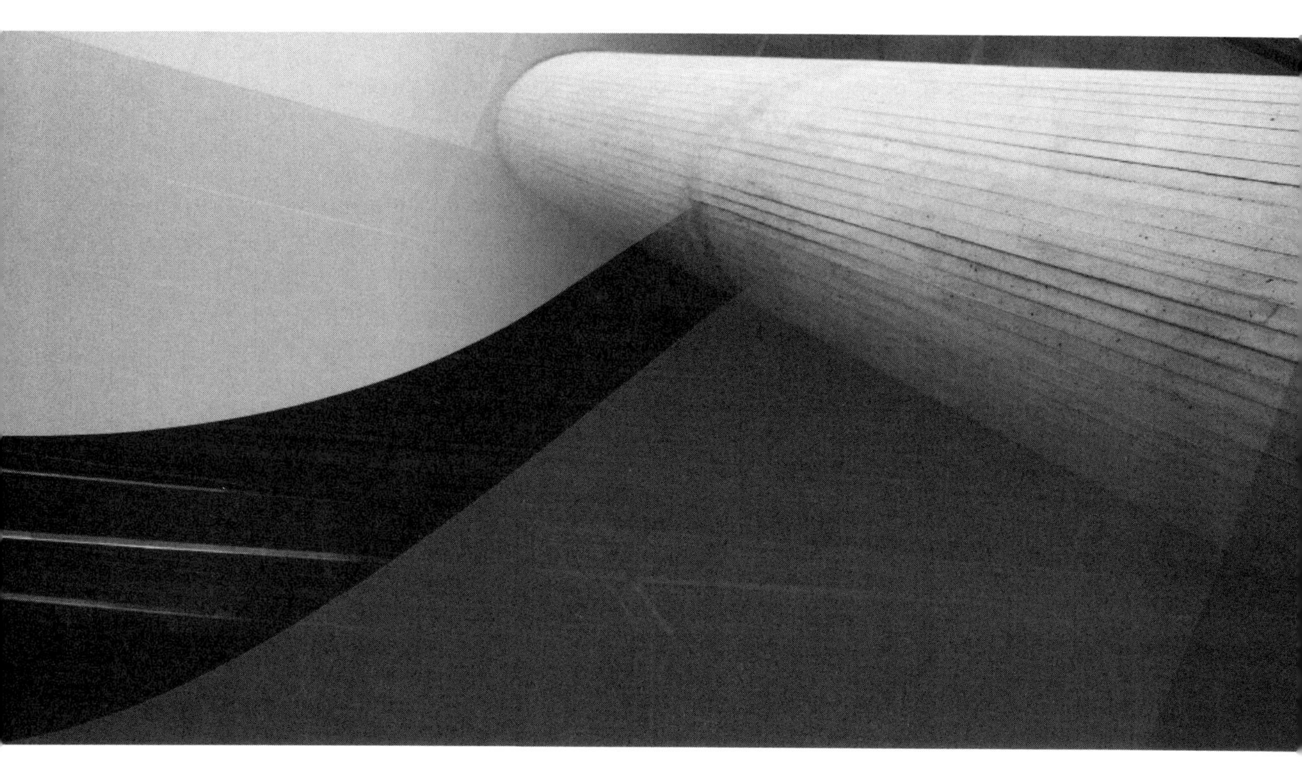

CHAPTER 13

Securing Access to Oracle BI

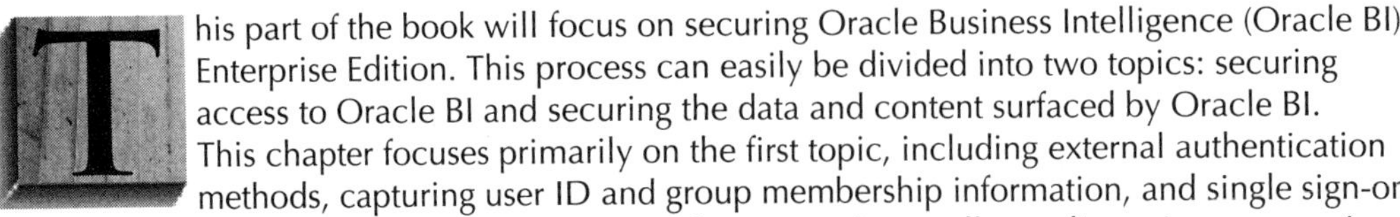

This part of the book will focus on securing Oracle Business Intelligence (Oracle BI) Enterprise Edition. This process can easily be divided into two topics: securing access to Oracle BI and securing the data and content surfaced by Oracle BI. This chapter focuses primarily on the first topic, including external authentication methods, capturing user ID and group membership information, and single sign-on (SSO) integration. Some prerequisite topics are also covered, as well as a discussion on securing communication between components in an Oracle BI system.

The next chapter will focus on securing of Oracle BI content (dashboards, ad hoc requests, and reports) as well as row- and column-level security. To finish off the section, the topic of auditing will be discussed.

The official name of the Oracle product is Oracle Business Intelligence Suite Enterprise Edition Plus. The "Plus" refers to the Hyperion BI components that were added to the suite after Oracle acquired Hyperion. This book does not discuss the Hyperion components of the suite. Instead, it focuses on the following components (hereafter referred to as Oracle BI):

- Oracle BI Server
- Oracle BI Interactive Dashboards
- Oracle BI Answers
- Oracle BI Delivers
- Oracle BI Publisher

Several examples of each of these components are provided in this text. All examples can be downloaded from the Downloads page at www.OraclePressBooks.com.

In this chapter, several authentication schemes are discussed. An Oracle BI repository is provided for each authentication method covered. The Oracle BI metadata, contained in a file with a .rpd extension, is often referred to as the RPD. The data model in each RPD is identical and is designed to run off the Sales History (SH) sample schema provided with the Oracle Database. A collection of reports and dashboards are also provided. The definitions of the reports and dashboards are stored in a web catalog. The sample web catalog provided with this book consists of three dashboards:

- The SH dashboard illustrates how data can be protected.
- The Utilities dashboard offers some tools for accessing variables and testing security settings.
- The Audit dashboard is a combination of the database auditing discussed in Chapter 14 and the usage tracking reports provided with Oracle BI.

See the appendix for instructions on setting up and running these examples.

These examples were all developed on Oracle BI Enterprise Edition 10.1.3.4. Oracle Virtual Directory (OVD) and Oracle Access Manager (OAM) were used as the Lightweight Directory Access Protocol (LDAP)and SSO systems, version 10.1.4. The Oracle Database-specific examples—Virtual Private Database (VPD), DBMS_LDAP, and auditing—were all tested on both Oracle 10*g* R2 and 11*g* R1.

The Challenge in Securing BI

The whole point of a BI system is to give people better access to information—and get the right information to the right people at the right time. BI systems often bring together data from separate systems. The data might be stored in a different fashion for speed of retrieval. Changes to the data might include demoralization, aggregation, and cleansing processes. These factors provide some interesting challenges to the BI administrator in terms of security. In fact, often the desires of the information consumers seem to be at odds with the mandates of the people charged with protecting the data. However, with an effective BI tool, you can provide easier access to data while still maintaining the necessary security for that data. To look at some of these challenges, consider an example of a school district and some of the challenges such an organization might face while deploying a BI system.

Why a school district? First, it's something a little different from the typical example of protecting credit card information or financial information. Second, I've worked with a number of school districts and have seen the interesting security challenges that they encounter as they try to create data warehouses, longitudinal data systems (systems that track students across multiple schools over multiple years), and "No Child Left Behind" reporting systems. Third, if you are reading this, you have likely been to school and have a basic familiarity with the concepts discussed. Finally, the same issues challenging school districts in securing a BI system can be applied to a number of other industries.

System Users

One of the first interesting challenges you'll encounter when securing a BI system concerns the types of users. Again, a goal of a BI system is to give more people access to the information they need. The people seeing the data are no longer just the people who key in the data. In fact, there are many more information consumers than producers.

Let's look at our school district example. A school district has a number of information consumers: superintendents, school board members, local government, state school boards and governments, the federal government, administrators, research departments, principals, teachers, guidance counselors, parents, students, and tax-paying citizens. This list includes an incredibly diverse set of users: from public users to internal users, from very technical users to nontechnical users, and from highly privileged users to restricted users. The research department, for example, will often have access to large amounts of data, and potentially sensitive data, often combining demographic information with performance. Students or parents might be accessing the same data warehouse or BI system, but their information will normally be limited to their own data at the detail level (the student's own standardized test results, for example) and all data at the aggregate level (how a child's school performs compared to other schools in the district). Each type of user must be carefully evaluated, and significant care must be taken to make sure they are given access only to the type of data they *should* see.

Security in the Warehouse vs. the Transactional System

Another security challenge lies in the fundamental difference between a BI system and the transactional systems that feed the warehouse of the BI system. Security in transactional systems is often determined by the business process that the transactional system was designed to address.

For example, if you have a grade entry system, it's fairly easy to define security requirements. Here's a simple list of requirements to start with:

- Only teachers can enter grades.
- Teachers can enter grades for their students only.
- Grades can be entered only at certain times.

Obviously, some special cases would need to be addressed, but by and large the requirements are fairly straightforward.

When you consider grades in the context of a data warehouse, things get much more complicated. Many different types of users are now going after the same information, and different users will have different security requirements. Students want to see details of their grades and possibly class averages. Teachers may look across years. Principals may compare different teachers of the same subject. Research analysts may be investigating whether the lottery-sponsored scholarship program has impacted grade inflation across the state. Also, grade entry is always done at the detail level (this student got this particular grade on this particular exam on this date); however, grade analysis can be done at multiple levels. What started as a simple security problem of entering grades has become exponentially more complex when we start looking at the data for reporting purposes.

As you can tell from these examples, one of the keys to implementing robust security successfully within in a BI system is flexibility. For a transactional system, the security requirements are often easily defined and fairly static; you know exactly who can do what to the data and that normally doesn't change. In a BI system, this just isn't true. Lots of different groups will all be trying to access the same information, and each group will need to have its own security policy in place. In addition, you'll typically see things change significantly over time. Special projects, new requirements, and changing environments will necessitate changes in the user population and what type of access they need.

One last difference between transactional system and BI systems is that transactional systems require read-write permissions and BI systems are generally read-only. At first, this seems like a simple case of selecting the proper user profile, as we discussed in Chapter 1. In reality, putting a read-only policy in place for users of a BI system is only the first step. The question is more about what data users can see than it is about read-write versus read-only access. Ensuring that users see only data they are supposed to see is the focus of this chapter and the next.

Consolidated Data Creates More Interesting Problems

One of the main reasons for implementing a data warehouse is that it allows you to bring together data from multiple systems. This creates a number of interesting security requirements. Each system from which data was pulled will have its own set of security requirements. When you gather all of the data together, these requirements may be different. At the very least, you will need to reconcile the security requirements from each system.

Let's revisit the grades example again. While performing grade entry, teachers probably look only at a small data set. They probably see a student's name and grade for a particular test. However, once the data is consolidated in a data warehouse, different sets of data are combined to yield interesting, but sensitive information. For example, consolidating data from the free lunch program with grade data may provide interesting information for the research department, but this data probably shouldn't be available to the general public. Similarly, providing demographic information together with grade data makes the data more sensitive, because you can now do grade analysis by race, gender, or socioeconomic status (politically charged data, to say the least).

Inferring Information from Lack of Data

Let's continue the example a bit further. School districts often publish information about how students perform, broken out by various demographic indicators at the aggregate level. For example, information might be published on what percentage of students from each race achieved a "Proficient" score on a statewide assessment. That's all well and good, unless a particular racial group is a very small part of the student population. At this point, aggregate data starts to become personal data. Because of this, I've worked with several school districts that have security requirements that data should not be shown if the population size is below a certain amount. This is another example of security requirements that are quite unique to BI systems.

Inheriting Security from Packaged Applications

We discussed the fact that the BI system often has different security requirements from the transactional system. However, that doesn't mean you have to start from scratch in defining security requirements for a BI system. Often, the transactional system has a good set of roles or groups that can be reused in the BI system. The ability to leverage these roles and the already defined membership in these roles can help you jump start the process of setting up BI security. In addition, if you want to provide users the ability to navigate from the BI system back to the transactional system, it is important that you have their security context properly set up in the BI system.

A good example of this can be seen in the Oracle BI Applications, which are prebuilt data warehouses and BI systems designed to be placed on top of major transactional systems (Siebel, PeopleSoft, Oracle, and SAP). With these applications, you can leverage the security model and roles defined in transactional systems. To start with, these BI applications have security groups that map to the roles (PeopleSoft) or responsibilities (Siebel and Oracle) of the source transactional system. They also leverage transactional system information such as Operating Unit Organization or Inventory Organization to provide data-level security. This allows the BI applications to limit the rows returned in queries based on the organization of which the user is a member. This gives you a great starting place in defining the security model for your BI system.

What Needs To Be Secured

Securing a BI system can involve several tasks:

- Securing access to the BI system itself
- Securing the data presented via the BI system
- Securing access to content created with the BI system
- Securing functionality of the BI system

Securing the BI system includes both authentication and authorization. You can authenticate with Oracle BI using externalizing authentication so that you can leverage existing security infrastructure. The SSO server can authenticate the user and provide a coarse level of authorization (for example, this person's credentials check out and he or she is allowed to access the BI system).

We also discuss group membership within Oracle BI for few different reasons. First, with security administration externalized, this topic requires some special attention. Second, it is a critical prerequisite to setting up SSO. Finally, it sets the stage for Chapter 14 and all the other steps required in securing a BI system. Securing data and content and establishing privileges are all based on group membership.

As mentioned, BI systems often bring together an organization's most important data and present it in an analytically friendly way. This data consolidation is great for people who are supposed to have access to the data, but if the data is not properly secured, people can exploit data they shouldn't be allowed to access. We look at ways to provide both coarse- and fine-grained data protection. Coarse permissions are fairly easy to define ("only group A should have access to a certain type of data"), so we focus most of our attention on the fine-grained securing of data, including both row- and column-level security. We will consider two methods of providing row-level security and will compare and contrast these methods.

Next, we look at how web catalog content can be protected. We focus on the mechanisms in Oracle BI used to organize and secure all BI content (dashboards, reports, ad hoc requests, and alerts). Protection means controlling who has access to the definitions of these objects and who can manipulate these definitions.

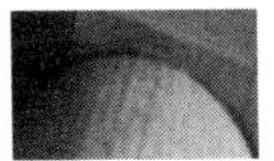

NOTE
In order for a user to run a report successfully, that user must have access both to the definition of the report and the data presented in the report.

Finally, we look at the privileges that need to be granted to different users of the system. We focus on privileges that require specific care. Oracle BI offers some advanced features that should be granted only after careful consideration. Users should have access to these features only if they have been trained in how to use them. Some of these features allow users to impact data and functionality for other users. It is important that you know exactly what you are allowing users to do when you give them access to a specific feature.

Mechanics of Accessing Data with Oracle BI

Before getting into the details of how to secure Oracle BI, let's review the mechanics of accessing data using Oracle BI, including a review of Oracle BI's architecture, primarily from a security perspective.

Architecture

Your understanding of the BI server is critical to understanding the information presented in this chapter and the following one. For example, when we talk about authenticating with Oracle BI, we're referring to the BI server, which you must be logged into. In Chapter 14, when we focus on data security, this again centers on the BI server.

Let's start with what happens when a user tries to access Oracle BI. We'll examine the interaction from end-to-end.

First, the user's browser communicates with the web tier of Oracle BI, a plug-in that is deployed to Internet Information Services (IIS) or a J2EE container. This plug-in handles communication with the Oracle BI presentation server in the middle tier. The presentation server, in turn, talks to the Oracle BI server, another middle-tier component, which handles all communication with the underlying databases. This architecture is depicted in the following illustration.

Oracle BI Architecture

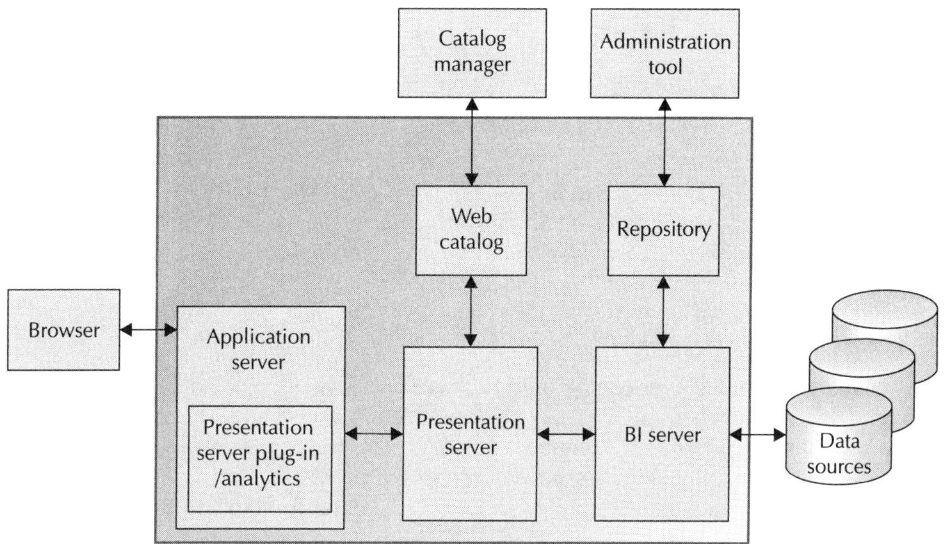

To help you understand the authentication process, let's first examine this process for simple, out-of-the-box, internal authentication. When attempting to access Oracle BI, users will be presented with a login screen. Credentials are captured, passed to the presentation server, and sent to the BI server for validation. With internal authentication, the usernames and passwords are stored in the BI server metadata (the RPD file). So, in this case, the BI server actually validates the credentials and performs the authentication.

After the user is authenticated, a session must be established. Setting up the session properly includes populating a variety of session variables. These session variables are at the core of securing Oracle BI and will be discussed in greater detail later in this section. Once the user is authenticated and a session is established, the Oracle BI server will issue queries to the database on behalf of the end user.

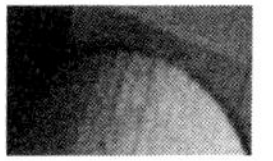

NOTE

This is just a brief introduction to one way of performing authentication with Oracle BI. We will discuss the details of other methods of performing authentication in the next section.

While reviewing the architecture of Oracle BI, you'll find it worthwhile to examine the mechanics of running a report and retrieving data. Let's take a simple ad hoc request. In the Answers component of Oracle BI, you would create a query: deciding what fields to include, filters to be applied, and functions to be evaluated. The presentation server evaluates this request and then creates a logical SQL statement that is sent to the BI server. The BI server analyzes the logical SQL to see what can be satisfied via cache. Oracle BI uses a shared cache mechanism to increase performance. (The security implications of this cache are discussed in detail in Chapter 14.) If the cache cannot be used to satisfy the request, the BI server will use the metadata defined in the RPD to construct a physical SQL statement (in the case of a relational database source) to be issued to the underlying data sources.

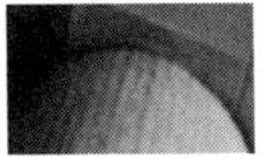

NOTE
Oracle BI does support a variety of data sources, including XML, relational databases, and several multidimensional databases. It also supports multiple data sources in a single request. For simplicity, the examples provided with this book will often refer to data sources as "the database," even though it could be much more than just a database.

Connection Pools

As mentioned, the BI server can be used to query a variety of backend data sources. To set up communication between the BI server and these data sources, you use *connection pools* in the Administration tool. The name "connection pools" can sometimes be misleading. Sometimes these connections really act like connection pools, a cache of database connections. At other times, these connection pools represent a location of data. To help you understand this, let's look at several examples.

Connection Pools by Data Source Type

Connection pools are set up for different types of data sources. Consider, for example, relational databases. The first thing you need to do is decide on a call interface. For Oracle databases, you should always use Oracle Call Interface (OCI). Next, you decide on the maximum number of connections that this pool should allow. The BI server uses the connection pools in the order in which they are listed in the Administration tool. When you attempt to query a data source, the BI server will use the first connection pool that you have permission to access and that has an open connection available.

As shown in Figure 13-1, you must configure several options when setting up a connection pool. The documentation covers these in detail, so we will mention only a few of them.

The Enable Connection Pooling checkbox in the middle of the dialog determines whether this connection pool will really act like a connection pool. The Require Fully Qualified Table Names checkbox is important when setting up a subject area that accesses multiple database schemas. Depending on how you import the metadata into the administration tool, these schemas might actually end up in different databases (meaning different databases in the Administration tool). You most likely do not want that. If your two schemas end up in two databases in the Administration tool, this will force the BI server to use two connections to access the data, and any joins between objects in these schemas will occur at the BI server level. This could really hamper performance. To make the join happen in the database, the data from both schemas needs to be accessed via a single connection. Each schema should be listed under a single database in the Administration tool, the connection pool should connect the database using a user that has permissions to access both schemas, and the Require Fully Qualified Table Names checkbox should be selected. Finally, the Connection Scripts tab is where you run scripts on connections, before or after queries, or on disconnect. This will be very important in Chapter 14.

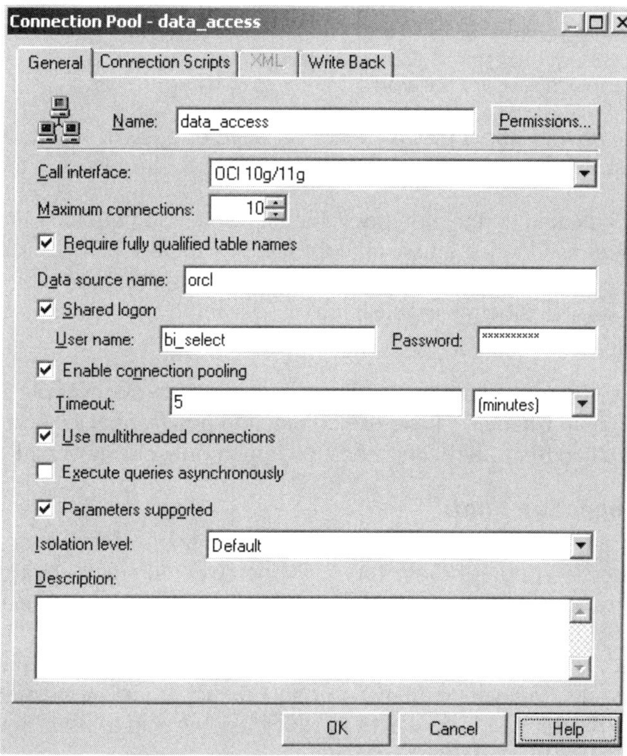

FIGURE 13-1 *Connection pool setup*

Connections to multidimensional data sources are accomplished using XML for Analysis (XMLA). The definition of your connection pool will look quite different. You will use a URL to the XMLA provider for your source. The Use Sessions option in the Connection Pool dialog determines whether a shared connection to the multidimensional data source should be used for all connections.

For XML data sources, the connection pool is merely a pointer to the physical location of the XML data source. With XML data sources, you will notice that the XML tab in the connection pool definition dialog is now available and contains settings specific to XML data sources. These settings include timeout settings and the ability to specify XPath or Extensible Stylesheet Language Transformations (XLST) transformations.

Connection Pool by Function

The documentation recommends that you create connection pools for specific functions. In particular, it lists out the following scenarios:

- Data access
- Authentication

- Authorization
- Populating session variables
- Populating repository variables

Although many of these topics have not yet been discussed, you should understand that you will want to use separate connection pools for each of these scenarios for two reasons:

- First, dedicated connection pools for each scenario help to control performance. The resources used to log a user onto Oracle BI will be separated from the resources used by users actually querying databases. As you will see, many things can happen while a user's session is being established. You'll want to take care to make that logon as fast as possible.
- Second, you may want to run different connection pool scripts in different scenarios. For example, in Chapter 14, we use connection pool scripts to persist the end user's identity to the database. Often, this needs to happen only during actual data access.

Multiple Connection Pools

We just discussed one reason for multiple connection pools: different connection pools based on what that connection pool is doing. You might also want to create multiple connection pools for data access. This allows you to control the maximum number of connections per pool, and it allows you to perform resource management.

Suppose, for example, that you wanted to give one group of users more database resources than another group. You can create two connection pools and set them up to use different shared logons. On the database, it is now easy to isolate each group of users and assign the appropriate resources. In Oracle BI, you can control which group of users uses which connection pool by setting permissions on the connection pool. For example, group A has permission to use connection pool A, and the database applies a certain resource policy to those connections. Group B has permissions to use connection pool B, and the database can apply a different resource policy to these users.

It is worth summarizing how Oracle BI decides which connection pool to use. For everything but data access, you will be able to state explicitly which connection pool you want to use. For example, in the upcoming sections, we will use a feature called "initialization blocks" to set up authentication. In the initialization block, you get to specify the exact connection pool you want to use. For data access, you do not get to specify the connection pool you use. When you define connection pools for a database in the Administration tool, the order is important. For data access, the BI server uses the first connection pool that you have permission to use and that has open connections available.

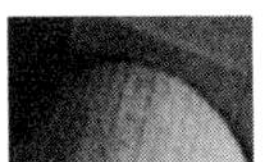

TIP
Make sure your data access connection pools are always listed first in the list of connection pools.

Variables

As mentioned, understanding session variables is a crucial part of securing Oracle BI. Setting up session variables is in fact a prerequisite step to securing Oracle BI. In this section, we will cover all types of Oracle BI variables: server, presentation, and session variables.

Server and Presentation Variables

Server variables are either *static* variables or *dynamic* variables, and they work as their names imply. Static variables are set when the BI server starts, and dynamic variables are refreshed on a periodic basis. The examples used in this book and the metadata that ships with the Oracle BI (SampleSales.rpd) use a static server variable called **BI_EE_HOME**. This holds the value of where you installed Oracle BI and is used in the connection pool for the Sample Sales database to point to the XML data source. (You'll notice in the appendix that you will need to set this variable before the examples can be used.)

An example of a dynamic server variable is also included in the examples for this book. This variable in the example is called **CURRENT_YEAR**. The value of this variable is set to be refreshed every night at midnight (although it will change only once per year). This variable could be used to create a rolling window filter, and it makes it extremely easy for you to create a report that always shows the current year.

Server variables are managed in the BI server metadata using the Administrator tool. Use the Manage Variables screen to create these variables. An initialization block is used to define how the variable is populated and the refresh frequency. Figure 13-2 shows an example server variable that stores the current year.

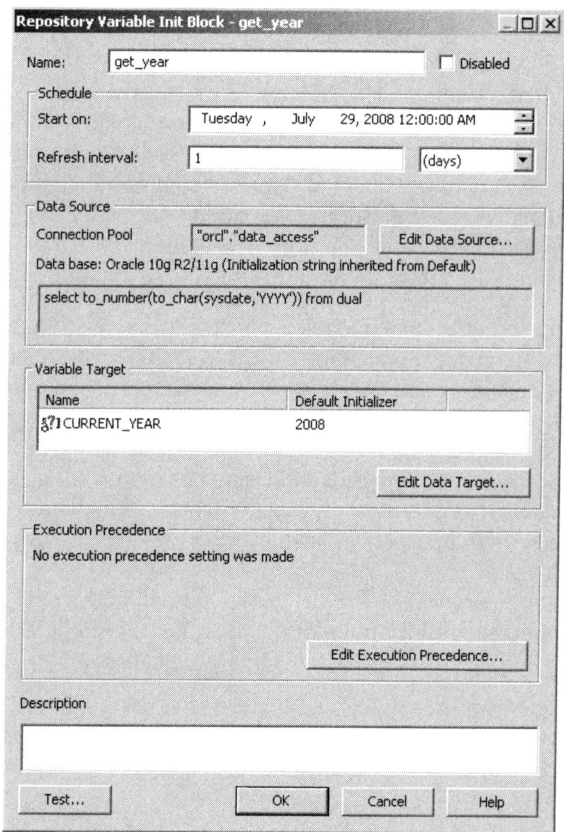

FIGURE 13-2 *Server variables*

Presentation variables are defined and used in the dashboard. These are great to use for such things as allowing the user to set user-defined thresholds on the fly. However, they are not normally used for security purposes and not discussed in detail in this book.

Session Variables

That leaves us with session variables, which are extremely useful for security purposes. They get populated as a session is created. Initialization blocks are used to populate session variables. Initialization blocks have three parts: the data source, the variable target, and the execution precedence.

The data source can be a database, LDAP, or a custom authenticator. If the data you need to establish a session is in a database, you will use a standard SQL query to retrieve that information. If your data is in an LDAP data source, you just specify the LDAP attributes that need to be retrieved by the initialization block. Custom authenticators are actually OS-level programs that you write to obtain session information. Examples of each type of data source will be used in the upcoming section "Authentication and Authorization."

The variable target defines where the initialization block will put the data that it retrieves. A single initialization block can populate one or more variable, each with one or more values. If the initialization block returns single values for each variable, then a simple mapping of column or attribute to variable name is done in the variable target section of the initialization block definition. If the initialization block returns more than one value for a variable, then a feature called "row-wise initialization" is used to populate the variable. (This is discussed in full detail with an example in the next section.)

The third and final part of the initialization block is the execution precedence. The execution precedence determines the order in which initialization blocks are run. This is very important if the value returned in one initialization block is to be used as a parameter in a second initialization block and is extremely common. For example, it is common to first populate the **USER** session variable. After you know who the user is, you can look up other session information such as group membership. For this case, it is important that the initialization block that populates the **USER** session variable runs before the initialization block that populates group membership.

Row-wise Initialization As mentioned, it is possible to return more than one value into a variable. For example, if you are using initialization blocks to assign group membership dynamically (discussed in more detail shortly), a user may belong to more than one group. Each group to which the user belongs will be assigned to the **GROUP** variable separated by semicolons. To return more than one value to a variable, you mark the variable target as row-wise initialization. Row-wise initialization actually does two things: It creates one or more variables, and it assigns one or more values to each variable that it created. Row-wise initialization works only for variables that use databases as a data source. This fact will be important when we look at dynamic group membership and LDAP authentication.

In an example RPD provided with this book, you will find an initialization block called **get_products**. This initialization block populates a variable called **PRODUCT** with the products that a given product manager is allowed to see. Here's the data source:

```
SELECT 'PRODUCT' variable_name,
  product variable_value
FROM bi_tables.product_managers
WHERE user_name = ':USER'
```

You'll notice a couple of things about this SQL statement: When using row-wise initialization, the query must return the variable name in the first column and the value of the variable in the second column. Essentially, you end up with an array of name-value pairs. You should also notice the use of the bind variable **:USER**. This is specifically referring to the **USER** session variable. Running the query for the user biproduct2 yields two rows: one for each product that this user manages. Figure 13-3 shows these results.

The BI server will take the results of this query and populate the **PRODUCT** session variable with the value **Portable PCs; Desktop PCs**. Notice how the multirow result set is automatically transformed into the semicolon-delimited list. If the first column had contained more than one value, then one session variable would be created for each distinct value returned in the first column of the query. For example, if you wanted to populate the **CHANNEL** and **PRODUCT** variables in a single initialization block, your SQL might look something like this:

```
SELECT 'PRODUCT' variable_name,
  product variable_value
FROM bi_tables.product_managers
WHERE user_name = 'biproduct2'
UNION ALL
SELECT 'CHANNEL' variable_name, channel_desc variable_value
FROM sh.channels
```

In the next section, we use session variables to establish group membership. This will require that you use session variables in the BI server metadata. It is also possible to use session variables in reports and dashboards. We will use this to verify that our session variables are working as designed. In Chapter 14, we will use session variable values to implement business model filters and to make Oracle BI work with the Oracle Virtual Private Database feature.

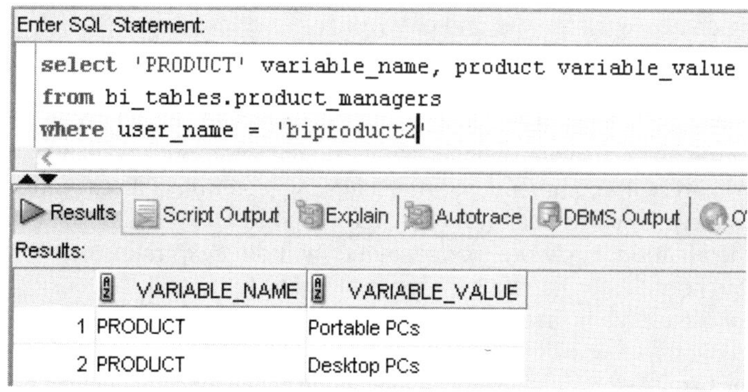

FIGURE 13-3 *Row-wise initialization query*

Authentication and Authorization

Several methods of authentication are available in Oracle BI. Here, we focus on the ways you can externalize authentication; hopefully, enabling you to reuse an existing identity management infrastructure. After detailing how these different methods of external authentication work, we focus on how to handle group membership when using external identity stores.

Authentication Options

You can authenticate with Oracle BI in six ways: built-in, LDAP, database table, database authentication using RPD and database users, database authentication using only database users, and custom authentication. We will explore all of these methods of authentication in this section.

Built-in Authentication

When using built-in authentication, users and groups are defined in the RPD metadata. This method is great for demonstration purposes and test systems but should not be considered for production systems. It lacks many of the capabilities required for strong password policies such as support for password complexity rules, password expirations, self-service password resets, and delegated administration.

Another reason for avoiding built-in authentication is the complexity of the provisioning process. In the "Types of Groups" section, we cover the concepts of groups and web groups. When you provision a user, the user must be properly assigned both to groups and web groups. When using built-in authentication, you cannot assign a user to a web group until that user has logged on to the system. This means that the user must logon to Oracle BI in the middle of the provisioning process and before authorization has been completely set up.

Database Authentication Using RPD and Database Users

There are two ways to set up database authentication: using RPD and database users or using only database users. The first method is described in this section, and detailed setup steps are included in the documentation. The second method is detailed in the "External Authentication Methods" section. Database authentication using RPD and database users allows end users to use their existing database usernames and passwords to authenticate to Oracle BI. This authentication method requires that the user account exist in both the RPD and the database. At the database, the user account must be completely setup including a valid password. In the RPD, an account with the same username must be created, but the password should not be set. The validation of the username and password will happen at the database. At first glance, this might not seem much better than built-in authentication, because you still have to create users in the RPD. However, as the passwords need not be stored in the RPD, it does provide advantages over built-in authentication. Password management, including expirations, resetting of passwords, and password complexity, can be handled external to Oracle BI.

The database username and password being used to authenticate to Oracle BI are not necessarily the same credentials that will be used to access the data in the backend databases. This username and password are used only to establish an Oracle BI session. Connections from the BI server to the backend databases use the credentials defined in the data access connection pool for the respective databases.

External Authentication Methods

The next four methods of authentication are all similar and are referred to as "external authentication." One might argue that the section "Database Authentication Using RPD and Database Users" should be included in this category. I exclude it for few reasons. First, because the users must still be created in the RPD, database authentication does not completely externalize authentication. Second, it does not follow the pattern of authentication you will see in the next four sections. Finally, using the pattern of authentication outlined in the following discussion, you'll find it possible to revisit database authentication using database users only and set it up in such a way that usernames are not stored in the RPD.

For external authentication to work, two things must happen: The username and password must be validated, and the **USER** session variable must be populated with the BI user's username. Remember that our discussion focuses on authentication. To provision a user properly, you must also establish authorization, which is discussed later in the section "Authorization." Authorization is covered in a separate section for two reasons: for clarity and organization, and because your method of authentication does not dictate your method of authorization. You may, for example, choose to use LDAP authentication and table-based authorization.

Table-based Authentication Table-based authentication requires that a list of usernames and passwords be stored in a table in a database. In this section, we are again using a database for authentication. However, this time we are not using database accounts for authentication. Instead, we are using the database to store usernames and password in a table. It is always a good idea to hash stored passwords. The Oracle BI documentation gives an example of setting up table based authentication with plaintext passwords. The example RPD aos_table.rpd provided with this book follows this method but includes a method to hash the passwords. Notice that the hashing process occurs on the database and the password will be passed over the network in plaintext. It is recommended that you encrypt communication between the BI server and the backend database (for example, by using the advanced security option for Oracle).

The first step in setting up table-based authentication is to create the table required to hold the usernames and passwords. An example schema with the necessary tables is included with this book, and the appendix details the specifics of this schema. Here's a function to simplify the hashing of the passwords that uses the DBMS_CRYPTO package of the database:

```
CREATE OR REPLACE
  FUNCTION hash_password
    (
      p_password IN VARCHAR2)
    RETURN VARCHAR2
  AS
    v_hash_algorithm pls_integer;
    v_return VARCHAR2(4000);
  BEGIN
    v_hash_algorithm := dbms_crypto.hash_sh1;
    SELECT dbms_crypto.hash(to_clob(p_password), v_hash_algorithm)
    INTO v_return
    FROM dual;
    RETURN v_return;
  END;
```

Next, I created an initialization block to verify the username and password. Here is the code that the initialization block executes:

```
SELECT user_name
FROM bi_security_tables.bi_users
WHERE upper(':USER')= upper(user_name)
NQS_PASSWORD_CLAUSE(AND hash_password(':PASSWORD') =
   user_password)NQS_PASSWORD_CLAUSE
```

Notice that row-wise initialization is not used here because the query is expected to return a single value. In this case, the value of the **USER** session variable is returned and the variable target section of the initialization block is used to specify that the result of the query be assigned to the **USER** session variable.

The other important thing to notice about this query is the use of **NQS_PASSWORD_CLAUSE**. To help you understand why this is important, you need to understand the notion of "proxy authentication." You can log onto the BI server as one user and tell the BI server to run everything as another user. This technique is used in SSO and is discussed later in the chapter. Oracle BI also uses this feature for interprocess communication. For example, if the scheduler service needs to run a scheduled job for a user called BIUSER, it will log onto the BI server as the user Administrator and tell the BI server to run everything as BIUSER. Oracle BI Publisher also uses proxy authentication when communicating with the BI server.

When the BI server gets a proxy authentication request, it first authenticates the proxy user, Administrator in this example. Then it runs all the initialization blocks for the target user, BIUSER in this example. This is exactly what you want to happen, because then you know that BIUSER's session is properly set up. The only problem with this is that the scheduler service does not know BIUSER's password. The authentication initialization block would fail, then, because it requires both the username and password to be correct. **NQS_PASSWORD_CLAUSE** fixes this problem. When the BI server is performing a proxy authentication, it strips the **NQS_PASSWORD_CLAUSE** out of the authentication initialization block.

LDAP Authentication The Oracle BI documentation mentions two ways that an LDAP server can be used. It discusses importing LDAP users and groups into Oracle BI and using LDAP as an external authentication method. The import capability is really just a quick way to load users into the RPD and actually uses internal authentication. This should be used only for testing purposes and should not be confused with LDAP authentication. If you already have an LDAP set up, you should not import the users from LDAP, but use the LDAP server as an external authentication method instead.

As with external table authentication, two basic steps are required to perform LDAP authentication, as shown in the next illustration. First, the BI server must verify that the user's password is correct. Then it assigns a value to the **USER** session variable.

LDAP Authentication

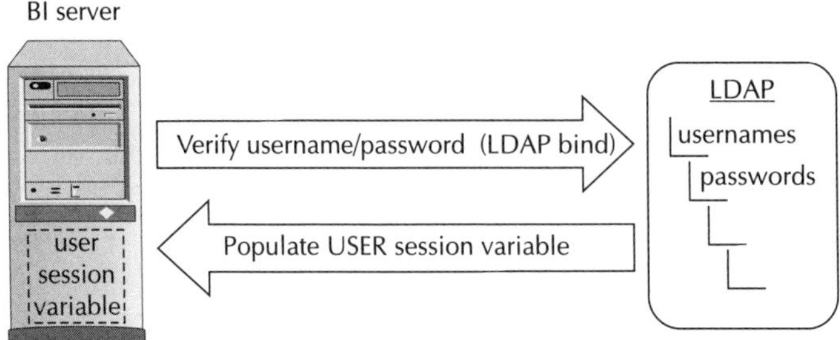

When setting up LDAP authentication, you first define an LDAP server in your BI server metadata, the RPD. This is done in the Security Manager of the Administration tool. Figure 13-4 shows the process of setting up an LDAP server.

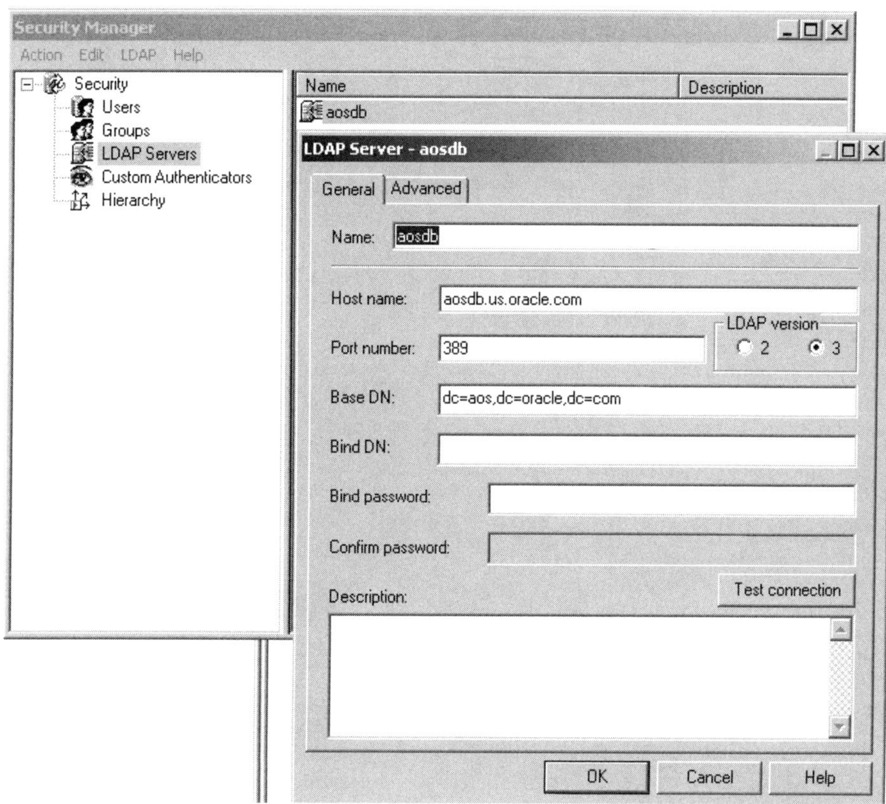

FIGURE 13-4 *LDAP server setup*

If your LDAP server accepts anonymous binds, you can leave the Bind DN and Bind Password fields blank. On the Advanced tab is an option to use SSL connections to the LDAP server. Use of SSL is highly recommended, as passwords are passed over the network in plaintext when using LDAP authentication.

Next, create an initialization block to populate the **USER** session variable. This initialization block will perform the LDAP bind to test the validity of the username and password and can return any LDAP attribute. At a minimum, the username (**uid**) needs to be returned and placed in the **USER** session variable.

Figure 13-5 shows a completed initialization block for LDAP authentication. At this point, you could try logging into Oracle BI using your LDAP credentials. It is important that you remember that authorization still needs to be set up (and is covered in the appropriate section a bit later in the chapter).

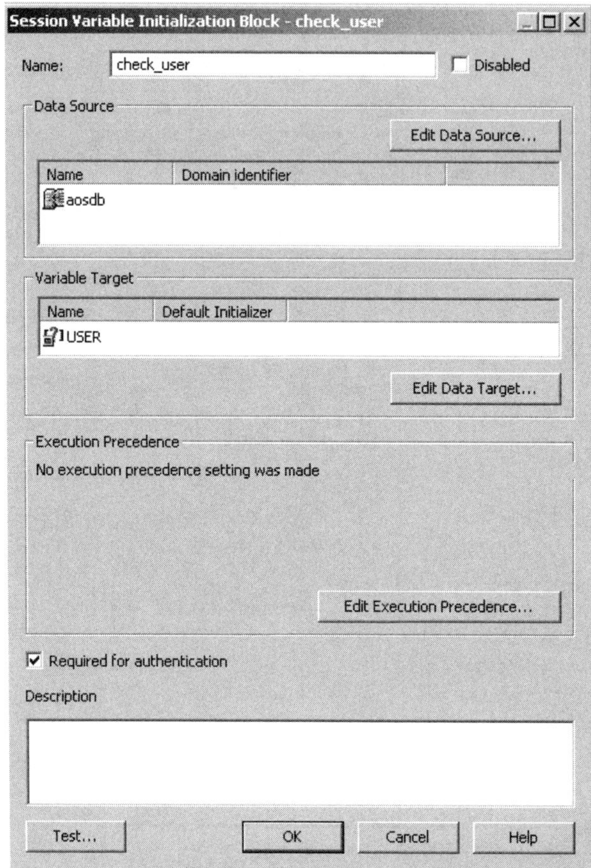

FIGURE 13-5 *LDAP authentication initialization block*

Database Authentication Using Only Database Users As mentioned, using database authentication as documented has several drawbacks. These can be avoided if database authentication is handled more like external table authentication or LDAP authentication. To do this, we just follow the basic principles of external authentication: validate the username and password, and populate the USER session variable.

1. In the database that actually contains the database users, create a connection pool that will be used solely for authentication.
2. For the username and password, use these values: **USER** and **:PASSWORD**, respectively. These are the values the user entered into the logon screen and the presentation service is forwarding them to the BI server. The BI server will attempt to connect to the database using these values.

3. Create an initialization block that executes the following simple query: **SELECT USER FROM dual**. Put the results of that query into the **USER** session variable. The initialization block should use the connection pool defined in step 1.
4. Remember to check the box Required For Authentication.

When a user attempts to log into the system, the BI server will execute this initialization block. If a valid username and password are entered, the use of the connection pool will succeed, the query will be executed, and the **USER** session variable will be populated. If the username and password are not valid, the attempt to run the query will fail because the BI server will be unable to log into the database to execute the query.

Custom Authentication Oracle BI also supports the notion of custom authentication, which allows you to create your own program to authenticate users and then integrate that with Oracle BI. To accomplish this, you must write your own program to authenticate users: a .dll on windows or a .so on UNIX/Linux. The API to which your program must conform is documented in Appendix B of the *Oracle BI Server Administration Guide*. An example custom authentication program also ships with Oracle BI (versions 10.1.3.4 and later). This custom authentication program is designed to allow the Oracle BI Server to use Hyperion Shared Services as the security infrastructure for Oracle BI. This integrated security model is required if you want to integrate Oracle BI with Oracle Hyperion Workspace, a component of the Oracle BI Suite Enterprise Edition Plus product set.

Fallback Authentication

A fallback authentication mechanism is available for each of these methods of authentication. This means that if the first method of authentication fails, Oracle BI will attempt to authenticate using the internal authentication mechanism. For example, if you have set up LDAP authentication and the username and password you entered fails LDAP authentication, Oracle BI will attempt to authenticate using the internal security mechanisms. The most common case of this is the user called Administrator. This user gets created automatically in every RPD but most likely doesn't exist in your LDAP. If you try to log in as Administrator, the LDAP authentication will fail, but the RPD authentication will succeed and you will be considered authenticated.

You may be wondering why you would have both internally defined users and externally defined users. For your primary user community, end users, you will want to externalize your users for the reasons that we have discussed in this section. For your RPD developers, you will need to have accounts created in the RPD for them to use. When editing the RPD, they will need to have an internally defined username and password with which they can log into the RPD.

Oracle BI Publisher Authentication

Oracle BI Publisher can be used as a stand-alone reporting tool or as an integrated component of the Oracle BI suite. Because it can be used in a completely stand-alone fashion, it needs to have its own authentication and authorization infrastructure. Oracle BI Publisher supports the following authentication schemes:

- Internal BI Publisher security
- LDAP
- Oracle E-Business Suite

- Oracle BI Server
- Oracle Database
- Oracle Hyperion Shared Services

Several of these security schemes are designed specifically for situations in which BI Publisher is integrated with other Oracle products. The *Oracle BI Publisher Administrator's and Developer's Guide* covers the process of setting up each of these authentication schemes. The important thing to point out in the context of this book is that if you want to use Oracle BI Publisher as an integral component of Oracle BI Enterprise Edition, you should use the Oracle BI Server security scheme. When this is set up, Oracle BI Publisher delegates authentication and authorization to the Oracle BI server. This is true even when Oracle BI is set up to use external authentication. For example, if Oracle BI is set up to use LDAP authentication, it would seem that you have two choices for BI Publisher security configuration: You could set it up to use Oracle BI Server authentication or LDAP authentication; however, Oracle's recommendation is that you use Oracle BI Server authentication whenever you are using Oracle BI Publisher as an integrated component of Oracle BI Enterprise Edition.

Authorization

After the user is authenticated, you need to make sure that the user has the proper authorization. Authorization happens at two distinct levels in Oracle BI: at the BI server and at the presentation server. This gives the Oracle BI administrator a lot of flexibility. For example, suppose you have a project management dashboard, and one set of users can view these dashboards, while another set can view and edit the dashboards. In both cases, the users need to be able to query the same set of data. The permission to query the data is controlled at the BI server level, because the BI server handles issuing the actual queries to the database. The permission to view or edit the dashboard definition is handled by the presentation server.

This section covers authorization at both the BI server level and the presentation server level. In both cases, managing authorization is accomplished completely by managing user to group assignments.

Types of Groups

Oracle BI has two types of groups that support authorization at two distinct levels: BI server groups (often referred to as just groups) and web catalog groups (often referred to as webgroups).

A BI server group is defined in the BI server metadata (the RPD). These groups are used to control access to data. For example, you might limit what subject areas a user can access based on the user's group membership. You may also use group membership to apply row-level filters to the data. These types of row-level filters are known as *business model filters*. In addition to creating business model filters based on group membership, you can also define filters based on other variables. For example, during the authentication process, you may query the user's organization from a database application. You can then apply business model filters based on the organization value. Business model filters will be explored in great detail in Chapter 14.

A webgroup is defined in the presentation server metadata (the web catalog). Webgroups are used to control access to web catalog objects, such as dashboard definitions, report definitions, and scheduled job definitions. Webgroups are also used to control access to various system permissions, such as the ability to create ad hoc requests or use web services to access Oracle BI. Controlling access to both web catalog content and system permissions is covered in detail in Chapter 14.

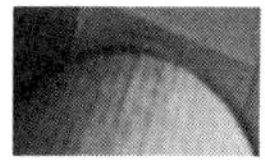

NOTE
BI server groups control access to RPD objects (data) and web catalog groups control access to web catalog objects (dashboard definitions, request definitions, and scheduled jobs).

Sometimes the groupings you would use to control access to data are the same groupings that would control access to web content. If this is the case, just name your webgroups, which control the UI components from the presentation server, exactly the same names used for your BI server groups, which control access to the underlying data elements. When you do this, webgroup membership will automatically be inherited from group membership.

The examples provided with this text include a group called SH Users. I wanted membership in this group to control access to both BI server metadata and web content. To accomplish this, I created a group called SH Users in the RPD and a webgroup also called SH Users in the web catalog. Any user that is a member of the group SH Users will also be a member of the webgroup SH Users. Giving groups and webgroups the same name simplifies the administration process, because you need to manage group membership only at the BI sever level, and group membership at the presentation server level will be inherited automatically.

Internal and External Group Membership

As mentioned, managing authorization is actually an exercise in managing group memberships. You've already read about several different methods of authorization. Some of these require that the users be defined internal to the BI server metadata. Others methods externalize the identity storage. Groups are handled a bit differently. In every case, the groups must be defined in the Oracle BI metadata. BI server groups will be defined in the BI server metadata and web catalog groups will be defined in the web catalog. The group must exist in the metadata so that object-to-group relationships can be defined in the metadata.

Groups must also be defined wherever the users are defined. We can break this into two cases:

- *Users are defined in the BI Server metadata:* built-in authentication or database authentication using RPD and database users
- *Users are defined external to the BI Server metadata:* table-based authentication, LDAP authentication, database authentication using only database users, or custom authentication

In the first case, the user-to-group assignments must be stored in the Oracle BI metadata. Group membership is assigned in the BI server in with the Administration tool using the Security Manager, and webgroup membership is assigned in the presentation server using the Manage Users and Groups screen of the web interface.

In the second case, the user-to-group assignments are defined outside the Oracle BI metadata. While a session is being created, the BI server will dynamically retrieve information about a user's group membership from wherever that information is stored. The location of authorization information need not be the same as the location of authentication information. For example, usernames and passwords might be stored in an LDAP, while user-to-group membership might be defined in database tables. The only restriction is that if you are using internal authentication, you must use internal authorization, and if you are using external authentication, you must use external authorization.

Dynamic group membership is defined using variables and initialization blocks. The session variable **GROUP** is used for BI server group membership and the variable **WEBGROUPS** is used for web catalog group membership. If a user belongs to multiple groups, you will still populate the **GROUP** session variable, but you will use row-wise initialization to populate the **GROUP** session variable. In the examples included with this book, the user *biadmin* belongs to two groups (Administrators and XMLP_ADMIN) and one webgroup (Presentation Server Administrators). When *biadmin* logs on using external authentication, the **GROUP** variable should be set to the value **Administrators;XMLP_ADMIN** and the **WEBGROUPS** variable should be set to **Presentation Server Administrators**. Another user, *biproduct1*, is a member of the SH Users group and the Product Managers group. In this case, the **GROUP** variable needs to be populated with the value **SH Users;Product Managers**. Recall that variables set using row-wise initialization automatically get created as a semicolon-delimited list of values.

Dynamic Group Membership Using Tables

When authorization information is stored in database tables, an initialization block with a database query is used to set the **GROUP** and **WEBGROUPS** variables with values obtained from a database table. This method is implemented in the aos_database_security.rpd and aos_table_security.rpd repositories included with this book, and either of these can be used to test or examine this method. The Variables page on the Utilities dashboard example also included with this book is useful for testing purposes. The appendix details how to use these repositories and the sample dashboard.

In these examples, three tables in the BI_SECURITY_TABLES schema contain all the required information: **BI_USERS**, **BI_GROUPS**, and **BI_USER_GROUPS**. Here is the query used in the **get_groups** initialization block:

```
SELECT g.group_type variable_name,
  g.group_name variable_value
FROM bi_security_tables.bi_groups g,
  bi_security_tables.bi_user_groups ug
WHERE g.group_name = ug.group_name
AND ug.user_name   = ':USER'
```

When setting up the initialization block that will execute this query and populate the **GROUP** and **WEBGROUPS** session variable, you should notice a few things. First, we have set the variable target to row-wise initialization, because a user may belong to multiple groups or web catalog groups. Second, this initialization block is set to execute after the **check_user** initialization block. This ensures that the **USER** session variable is set properly before executing the query to retrieve the group information. Lastly, the initialization block is marked as "required for authentication." If this initialization block fails, the user will not be authenticated and will be denied access to Oracle BI. Figure 13-6 shows the setup for this initialization block.

To summarize, when biadmin logs in, the **check_user** initialization block runs first to authenticate biadmin. Then the **get_groups** initialization block will run with biadmin substituted for **:USER**. The results when the query is run for biadmin in SQL Developer is shown in Figure 13-7.

After the session is established, these session variables can be checked on the Session Variables page of the Utilities dashboard, as shown in Figure 13-8.

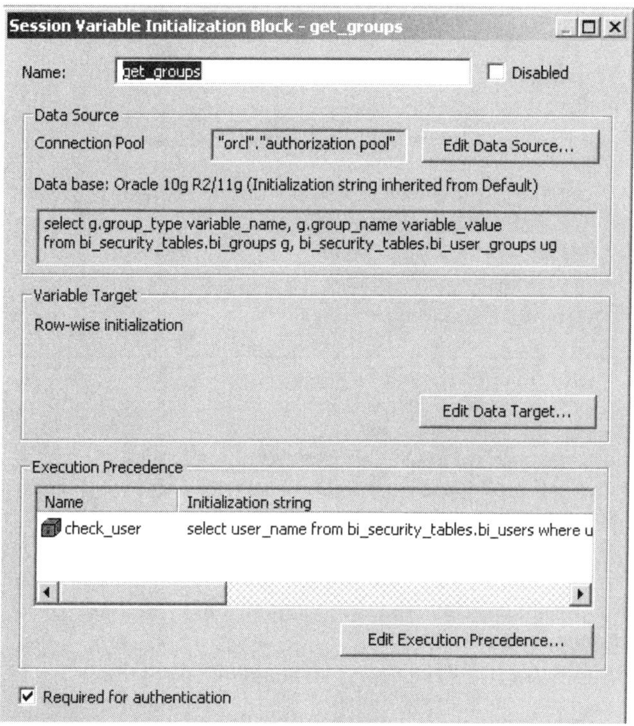

FIGURE 13-6 *Initialization block for dynamic group membership*

Enter SQL Statement:

```
select g.group_type variable_name, g.group_name variable_value
from bi_security_tables.bi_groups g, bi_security_tables.bi_user_groups ug
where g.group_name = ug.group_name
and ug.user_name = 'biadmin'
```

Results | Script Output | Explain | Autotrace | DBMS Output | OWA Output

Results:

	VARIABLE_NAME	VARIABLE_VALUE
1	GROUP	Administrators
2	WEBGROUPS	Presentation Server Administrators
3	GROUP	XMLP_ADMIN

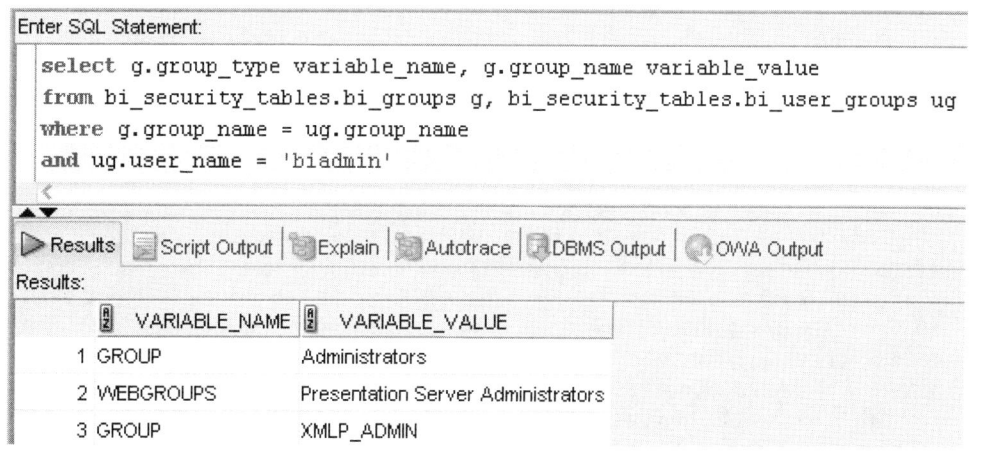

FIGURE 13-7 *Query to populate group membership*

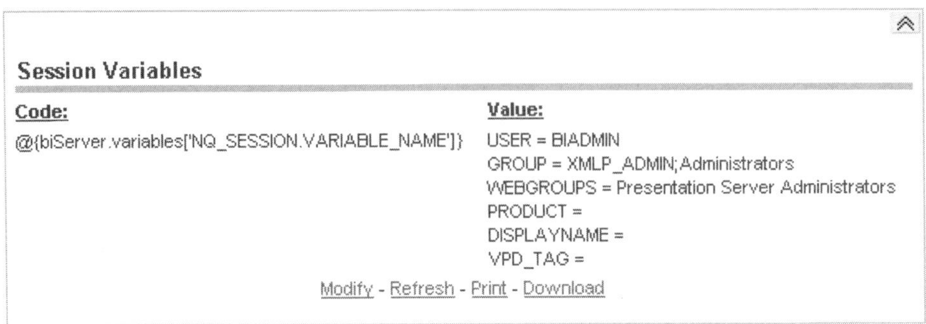

FIGURE 13-8 *Session variables validation test*

In this section, we used database tables to set up group membership dynamically. As mentioned, this type of authorization can be used with any type of external authentication method (database, table, or LDAP). In the examples provided with this book, this method of table-based authorization is used with both the database and table-based authentication examples. Up to this point, our discussion of variables, initialization blocks, authentication, and authorization has been somewhat fragmented. We have now covered enough information to put everything together.

The basic process for using database tables as a method of authorization is as follows:

- Create users in the appropriate place for the method of external authentication that you are using (database, table, or LDAP).
- Create groups in the RPD using the Administrator tool.
- Create web groups in the web catalog using the web interface to Oracle BI.
- Create and populate tables that store user-to-group assignments.
- Authenticate the user and set the **USER** session variable using an initialization block.
- Set the **GROUP** and **WEBGROUPS** session variables using a row-wise initialization block.

Dynamic Group Membership Using LDAP Directly

When using LDAP authentication, it seems natural to assume that group membership information should be obtained from LDAP. This would provide a single location to create users, create groups, and manage group membership. Oracle BI, however, cannot retrieve multiple records from an LDAP server during authentication. When returning multiple records from a database table via an initialization block, you can use the row-wise initialization feature to handle multiple records. Oracle BI does not have an equivalent feature for LDAP servers. You can attack this problem in two ways: The first way requires storing group membership in a unique way in LDAP; the second way involves using Oracle's DBMS_LDAP package and is discussed in the next section.

When retrieving group membership directly from LDAP, Oracle BI needs to group membership information stored in a particular format. There needs to be a single LDAP attribute for each user that contains a semicolon-delimited list of groups to which the user belongs. If group membership can be stored in this fashion, Oracle BI can use an initialization block to retrieve this attribute containing the group membership information. In this setup, it is possible to populate both the **USER** and **GROUP** session variables. Oracle BI will then be able to authentication and authorize the user properly. However, this is a rather unorthodox way to store group membership in an LDAP.

Dynamic Group Membership Using LDAP Indirectly

Using the Oracle database's LDAP functionality and pipelined table functions, it's possible to expose LDAP information through the Oracle database. This allows Oracle BI to think that it's getting its information from a database when the information is really coming from LDAP.

Recall from earlier in the chapter that the authentication initialization block handles retrieving the user's identity from LDAP and populating the **USER** session variable. In the case of Active Directory, the *sAMAccountName* is returned into the **USER** session variable. In the case of Oracle Internet Directory, the *UID* would be returned into the **USER** session variable. In either case, this actually represents the user's common name (**cn**). To look up group membership from the LDAP, we will need to get the **USER**'s distinguished name (**dn**). Let's outline the process required to get group information:

1. Oracle BI has the user's **cn** (**cn=biadmin**). This was obtained via the authentication initialization block.
2. Search the LDAP to get the user's **dn** (**cn=biadmin,cn=Users,dc=aos,dc=oracle,dc=com**).
3. Find all the groups of which biadmin is a member. When we program this, the query will actually return the **dn**s of all the groups to which biadmin belongs (**cn=BI-Administrators, cn=Groups,dc=aos,dc=oracle,dc=com**).
4. Convert the **dn** back to a **cn**. The BI server does not need the full **dn** (**cn=BI-Administrators**).

Following is sample code that implements this outline. This code creates a function that takes as input a username and returns a table of group names. Using the pipelined table function feature of the Oracle database, we will be able to query this function as if it were a table. This allows the BI server to return LDAP information by simply executing a query against the database.

```
CREATE OR REPLACE type bi_security_select.array
AS
  TABLE OF VARCHAR2(255);
  /
CREATE OR REPLACE
FUNCTION bi_security_select.get_groups
  (
    p_username IN VARCHAR2)
  RETURN bi_security_select.array pipelined
AS
  --You must set these variables for your own environment
 ldap_host VARCHAR2(256):= 'aosdb.us.oracle.com' ;
  --Recommend using SSL
  ldap_port PLS_INTEGER  := '389';
  ldap_user VARCHAR2(256):= 'cn=orcladmin';
  --If your LDAP is setup to allow anonymous binds, use null for a password
  --Otherwise, you need to specify a password here
  ldap_password VARCHAR2(256):= NULL;
  group_base    VARCHAR2(256):= 'cn=Groups,dc=aos,dc=oracle,dc=com';
  user_base     VARCHAR2(256):= 'cn=Users,dc=aos,dc=oracle,dc=com';
  retval PLS_INTEGER;
```

```
  my_session DBMS_LDAP.session;
  my_pset_coll DBMS_LDAP_UTL.PROPERTY_SET_COLLECTION;
  my_property_names DBMS_LDAP.STRING_COLLECTION;
  my_property_values DBMS_LDAP.STRING_COLLECTION;
  group_handle DBMS_LDAP_UTL.HANDLE;
  user_dn VARCHAR2(2000);
  group_type PLS_INTEGER := DBMS_LDAP_UTL.TYPE_DN;
  my_mod_pset DBMS_LDAP_UTL.MOD_PROPERTY_SET;
  my_attrs DBMS_LDAP.STRING_COLLECTION;
  group_cn VARCHAR2(2000);
  j        NUMBER;
  my_message DBMS_LDAP.message;
  my_entry DBMS_LDAP.message;
  entry_index PLS_INTEGER;
  my_dn       VARCHAR2(256);
  my_attr_name VARCHAR2(256);
  my_ber_elmt DBMS_LDAP.ber_element;
  attr_index PLS_INTEGER;
  i PLS_INTEGER;
  my_vals DBMS_LDAP.STRING_COLLECTION ;
  subscriber_handle DBMS_LDAP_UTL.HANDLE;
  user_handle DBMS_LDAP_UTL.HANDLE;
  user_type PLS_INTEGER;
BEGIN
  user_type               :=DBMS_LDAP_UTL.TYPE_NICKNAME;
  retval                  := -1;
  DBMS_LDAP.USE_EXCEPTION := TRUE;
  --establish and LDAP session
  my_session := DBMS_LDAP.init(ldap_host,ldap_port);
  retval     := DBMS_LDAP.simple_bind_s(my_session,ldap_user, ldap_password);
  --Define Attributes for the search
  my_attrs(1) := 'dn';
  -- Search User to retrieve full DN
  -- Oracle BI only has the uid
  -- Need to get the DN to search for group membership
  retval := DBMS_LDAP.search_s(my_session, user_base, DBMS_LDAP.SCOPE_SUBTREE,
'uid='||p_username, my_attrs, 0, my_message);
  --Get First Entry of the results
  --put the dn into the user_dn variable
  my_entry := DBMS_LDAP.first_entry(my_session, my_message);
  user_dn  := DBMS_LDAP.get_dn(my_session, my_entry);
  --Search for all the groups that have the user's DN as a UNIQUEMEMBER
  retval := DBMS_LDAP.search_s(my_session, group_base, DBMS_LDAP.SCOPE_SUBTREE,
'uniquemember='||user_dn, my_attrs, 0, my_message);
  -- count the number of entries returned
  retval      := DBMS_LDAP.count_entries(my_session, my_message);
  my_entry    := DBMS_LDAP.first_entry(my_session, my_message);
  entry_index := 1;
  --Loop through the results
  WHILE my_entry IS NOT NULL
  LOOP
    my_dn := DBMS_LDAP.get_dn(my_session, my_entry);
    --Trip the extra info from the DN to get just the group name
    group_cn:=SUBSTR( my_dn, (instr(my_dn,'=')       +1));
```

```
    group_cn:=SUBSTR( group_cn,0,(instr(group_cn,',')-1));
    --push the name of the group onto the output pipe
    pipe row(group_cn);
    my_entry    := DBMS_LDAP.next_entry(my_session, my_entry);
    entry_index := entry_index+1;
  END LOOP;
  --Close the connection
  retval := DBMS_LDAP.unbind_s(my_session);
END;
/
```

We will now use this function in exactly the same way we did when getting group information from a table. Here is the query to put in the initialization block:

```
SELECT 'GROUP' variable_name,
  SUBSTR(column_value,4) variable_value
FROM TABLE(get_groups(':USER'))
WHERE column_value LIKE 'BI-%'
UNION ALL
SELECT 'WEBGROUPS' variable_name,
  SUBSTR(column_value,7) variable_value
FROM TABLE(get_groups(':USER'))
WHERE column_value LIKE 'BIweb-%'
```

A couple of things are worth noticing in this query. First is the use of the pipelined table function: **select * from table(get_groups(':USER'))**. This lets you select from a function just as if it were a table while passing in a parameter. The second thing to notice is the complexity surrounding the substring process. Let's examine that now.

If you recall, Oracle BI uses two types of groups: BI server groups and web catalog groups. In the LDAP, I had just one type of group. To solve this problem, I decided to use a naming scheme to differentiate between BI server groups and web catalog groups. All BI server groups are named *BI-** and all web catalog groups are named *BIweb-**. Looking at biadmin in the LDAP, I see that biadmin is a member of the **BI-Administrator**, **BI-XMLP_ADMIN**, and **BIweb-Presentation Server Administrators** groups. This initialization block will put biadmin in the Administrators and XMLP_ADMIN BI Server groups and the Presentation Server Administrators web group. As is usually the case when writing code, there are many ways to solve this problem of needing to distinguish between BI server groups and web catalog groups when retrieving group information from LDAP. This method of naming schemes seemed like a fairly simple way to solve the problem. Other ways might include using a specific structure in the LDAP or using group attributes to distinguish between groups and webgroups.

To summarize, when using an LDAP indirectly to obtain group membership, you would follow these steps:

1. Populate users and groups in the LDAP.
2. Set up LDAP authentication.
3. Create a pipelined table function to return group information from the LDAP.
4. Create a row-wise initialization block that queries the table function to get group information (similar to what was done in the "Dynamic Group Membership Using Tables").

Oracle BI Publisher Authorization

As mentioned, Oracle BI Publisher supports several security models. When Oracle BI Publisher is being used as an integrated component of Oracle BI, it should be set up to use Oracle BI Server security. In this situation, Oracle BI Publisher groups and group membership is inherited directly from the BI server groups. All BI server groups will show up automatically in Oracle BI Publisher and can be used to restrict access to reports and data sources. No management of groups in BI Publisher is required. All management of groups and group membership for BI Publisher is done wherever you are managing BI server groups and group memberships.

Authorization Summary

We have covered several methods of authorization, which represents a crucial step in the process of creating a session for a user attempting to user Oracle BI. After authenticating the user and authorizing the user, your final step would be to populate any other necessary session variables. In Chapter 14, we will populate session variables as a step in setting up row-level security.

As you have seen, the session creation process in Oracle BI is quite flexible. You can perform any number of steps to set up a user's session. Remember that each step in the session creation process is going to take time, and you do not want the login process to take too long. For example, in the "Dynamic Group Membership Using LDAP Indirectly" section, to place a user in a group, the BI server had to make a connection to the database and the database had to make a connection to the LDAP server. If you could find a way to replicate the group information from the LDAP server into a database you could speed up and greatly simplify the authorization process.

Single Sign-On

When Oracle BI is not protected by a SSO server, the login screen is generated by the presentation server. The presentation server accepts the credentials and passes them to the BI server for authentication. This is handled differently in an SSO environment, however. When a user attempts to access Oracle BI, the SSO server will intercept that request and redirect the user to a login screen generated by the SSO server. The SSO server handles the authentication process and sends a token back to Oracle BI, letting Oracle BI know that the user has been properly authenticated. While Oracle BI has delegated authentication to the SSO server, the BI server will still handle the authorization process.

SSO Options

Oracle BI takes a very flexible approach to SSO options. Several SSO servers are officially certified. In addition to that, Oracle BI supports an SSO server that meets certain basic prerequisites. The key requirement is that the SSO server be able to send the username of the end user to the BI presentation server in the form of a cookie or a HTTP header variable.

SSO Setup Cautions

Several steps must be accomplished before you attempt to enable SSO. Skipping any of these steps can result in some frustrating configurations, including making it impossible to log in as an administrator.

The first step is to set up LDAP authentication. In some situations, you will need to authenticate with Oracle BI without going through a web browser. SSO authentication will work only if you have attempted to log into Oracle BI via a web browser. A good example of this is the Oracle BI Office plug-in. With this plug-in to Microsoft Office, you can log into Oracle BI from within Office and update Oracle BI content embedded in the Office document. This plug-in uses web services to communicate with Oracle BI, and it needs to be able to authenticate directly with Oracle BI.

The second step concerns how Oracle BI is deployed. If you do a Basic install of the product (one of the options in the installation process), you will end up with the presentation server plug-in deployed to a stand-alone Oracle Containers for J2EE (OC4J) container. This stand-alone OC4J container has a lightweight embedded HTTP server. This makes it very easy to do a quick install of Oracle BI; however, this situation is not well suited for SSO. SSO servers are designed to protect web servers, but not the lightweight embedded HTTP server provided with the stand-alone OC4J container. So, in order to integrate Oracle BI with an SSO server, you must frontend the OC4J container with a web server that can be protected by the SSO server. One way to do this is with an Oracle Application Server, which will deploy the Oracle HTTP server (based on Apache) together with OC4J, and the Oracle HTTP server can be protected by a variety of SSO servers.

The third requirement is that dynamic group membership must be set up, and you must have an LDAP user that can log in as an Oracle BI Administrator. Skipping this step will result in an Oracle BI system in which it is impossible to log in as an administrator. It is worth examining this scenario in detail.

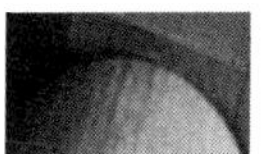

CAUTION
External authorization must be working before SSO is enabled.

By default, every BI server always has an internal user defined with the username Administrator. Let's assume you configure LDAP authentication but skip the step of setting up dynamic group membership, and a user named Administrator does not exist in the LDAP server. If you stop here, you can still log in as Administrator and have full administrative privileges because of fallback authentication. The attempt to authenticate with LDAP will fail, however, the Oracle BI server will fallback to the internal authentication process. Once you turn on SSO, fallback administration no longer works because the BI server is no longer handling authentication. So if you try to log in as Administrator, SSO authentication will fail, and you will not even be allowed to access the Oracle BI URL. If you log in as any other user, you will not be an administrator, because you haven't set up dynamic group membership yet. To reiterate, *before enabling SSO, enable dynamic group membership and set up a user in the LDAP that will get assigned to the BI server Administrators group and the web catalog Presentation Server Administrators group.*

TIP
Make sure you create at least one LDAP user with presentation server administrator privileges. Once SSO is enabled, you will no longer be able to log in as the RPD user Administrator.

SSO Using Oracle Access Manager

While Oracle BI supports multiple SSO servers, we'll focus on using Oracle Access Manager (OAM). This section will cover the necessary steps to get OAM and Oracle BI working together. We'll start by configuring a policy in OAM to protect access to the Oracle BI web site. Then we'll configure Oracle BI to use OAM as an authentication provider.

Set Up a Policy in Oracle Access Manager

In this section, we will create a policy to protect the URL used to access the Oracle BI web site. This policy will define the rules for who can access the URL and under what circumstances the URL can be accessed. It will also provide the necessary information to Oracle BI so that the end user can be logged into the system.

Before we begin configuring OAM, let's review the prerequisites. Oracle BI must be deployed to an application server protected by OAM. Let's start by deploying Oracle BI to Oracle Application Server 10.1.3.2 and then we'll install and configure an OAM access gate on this application server instance. Once the access gate is working, we are ready to being our configuration.

Next, we will create a policy to protect the URL to access Oracle BI. This is done in the Resource section of the policy definition. The URL for Oracle BI takes the form http://server:port/analytics. Here we just enter **/analytics** as the URL to be protected. Next, we specify the authentication method that OAM will use. We select the Basic Over LDAP option.

Finally, we must create an authorization rule. In this rule, we specify that the user attempting to log in must be a member of the BIUsers LDAP group. This group lists all users that are allowed to access Oracle BI. This group is different from the BI server groups and web catalog groups that we discussed earlier. They control access to features, content, and data inside Oracle BI. This BIUsers group is a little more general: users in the group can have access to the URL; users not in the group cannot even access the URL.

Also as part of this rule, we will create an "On Success" action. This action must set a header variable or a cookie with the username of the person who has been authenticated by OAM. Recall that the SSO solution must do two things for Oracle BI: it must authenticate the user and it must tell Oracle BI the username of the user who was just authenticated using either an HTTP header variable or a cookie. The Oracle BI documentation specifies how to use HTTP Header Variables. Here, we'll configure OAM to set a cookie variable. The name of the variable can be set to anything (we'll use this name when configuring the presentation server). We'll call the variable **BI_USER**. In the Return Attribute field, we type in **uid**. This will put the user's UID into the variable called **BI_USER**. (It might be tempting to use the return value. However, that is used to return a specific, hard-coded value in to the variable.) Figure 13-9 shows what our final policy might look like.

To summarize, when a user attempts to access Oracle BI, the following will happen:

1. OAM requests credentials from the end user.
2. OAM verifies the credentials and verifies that the user is a member of the LDAP group BIUsers.
3. OAM creates a cookie with a variable called **BI_USER** and populates it with the user's UID.

At this point, we are not finished with the configuration, but we could attempt to log into Oracle BI. We would find that we have configured OAM to protect the URL for Oracle BI, but we have not configured Auto Login to Oracle BI. When we attempted to access Oracle BI, OAM would prompt us for a login and then allow us to see the Oracle BI login screen. We will configure the Auto Login part of the process next.

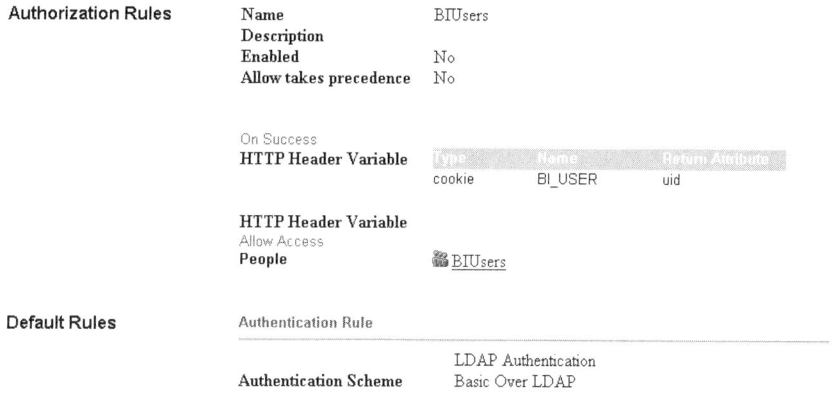

Authorization Rules	**Name**	BIUsers		
	Description			
	Enabled	No		
	Allow takes precedence	No		
	On Success			
	HTTP Header Variable	Type	Name	Return Attribute
		cookie	BI_USER	uid
	HTTP Header Variable			
	Allow Access			
	People	BIUsers		
Default Rules	Authentication Rule			
		LDAP Authentication		
	Authentication Scheme	Basic Over LDAP		

FIGURE 13-9 *OAM policy setup*

Configure the Impersonator User

Recall from earlier in this chapter that you must be logged into the Oracle BI server. When SSO is not configured, the Oracle BI presentation server will pass on the username and password that you provided to the BI server for authentication. When you enable SSO, the BI presentation server no longer knows the username and password of the end user. That information is captured and validated by the SSO server (OAM in our example). To overcome this situation, the presentation server will log into the BI server as a common user (called Impersonator) and will tell the BI server to run everything as the true end user.

First a user called Impersonator must be created in the RPD. This user should be placed in the Administrators group. This user is one of the few users that should be created in the RPD. At this point, you should have users called Administrator and Impersonator, and possibly some RPD developer accounts defined in your RPD. All other user accounts should be created and managed in the LDAP used by the SSO server.

For the presentation server to be able to log in as Impersonator, it must know Impersonator's password. This set of credentials is stored in a credential store (with the password encrypted). The credential store is used to store credentials for three users: the Impersonator user used here, the BI Publisher administrator, and the Oracle Delivers administrator. Use the cryptotools utility to put the Impersonator credentials into the credential store. Cryptotools is a command line utility that is used to generate encrypted credentials and store them in an XML-based credential store. You must also configure the presentation server to know where the credential store is located and how to open it (the encryption key). I recommend following steps in Chapter 8 of the deployment guide of the Oracle BI documentation library.

The following illustration shows the overall process of SSO integration with Oracle BI.

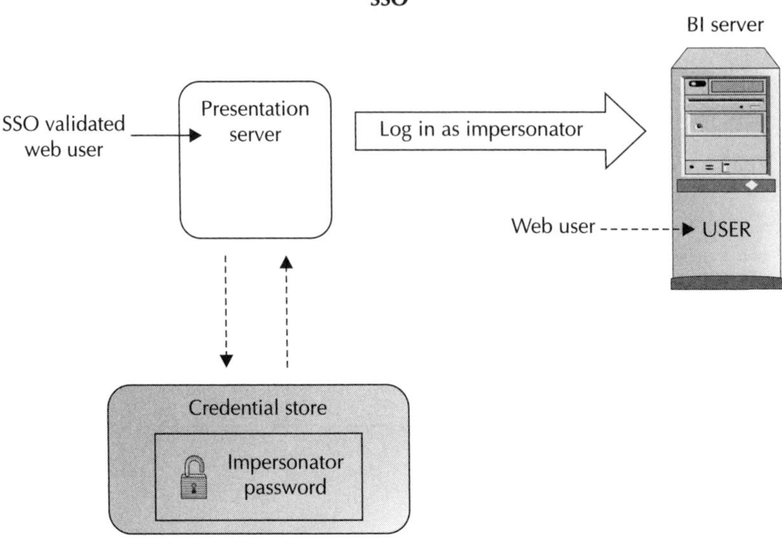

1. OAM sends the username of the authenticated user to the presentation server.
2. The presentation server looks up the credentials for the Impersonator user from the credential store.
3. The presentation server logs into the BI server as Impersonator and tells the BI server to execute all queries as the authenticated web user.

Configure the Presentation Server

As mentioned, the presentation server must be configured to use the credential store. Additional configuration steps are needed to complete the setup of SSO. Both of these changes are made by editing the instanceconfig.xml file. Recall that OAM is providing the end user's UID via a cookie variable called **BI_USER**. The presentation server needs to know where to get the end user's identity so that it can be passed on to the BI server together with Impersonator's credentials. (These steps are also documented in the deployment guide.) When you're finished making changes to the instanceconfig.xml file, it should include these sections:

```
<CredentialStore>
        <CredentialStorage type="file" path="/home/oracle/product/10.1.3/biee/OracleBIData/web/
config/credentialstore.xml" passphrase="secret"/>
</CredentialStore>
<Auth>
  <SSO enabled="true">
    <ParamList>
      <Param name="IMPERSONATE"
             source="cookie"
             nameInSource="BI_USER"/>
    </ParamList>
    <LogoffUrl>http://aosdb.us.oracle.com:7778/access/oblix/lang/en-us/logout.html</LogoffUrl>
    <LogonUrl>http://aosdb.us.oracle.com:7777/analytics</LogonUrl>
  </SSO>
</Auth>
<Listener>
```

```
  <Firewall>
    <Allow address="127.0.0.1"/>
    <Allow address="10.146.83.50"/>
  </Firewall>
</Listener>
```

Notice the **paramlist** in the **Auth** element. This tells Oracle BI to get the name of the user to be impersonated (the end user) from a cookie in the variable called **BI_USER**. The presentation server now has all the information it needs to log into the BI server as the user called impersonator and run everything as the end user.

Now we have set up our SSO server, OAM, to protect Oracle BI. We have also configured Oracle BI to log in automatically after OAM has authenticated the end user. To accomplish the Auto Login, the presentation server logged into Oracle BI as Impersonator and told the BI server to run everything as if the web user has actually logged into Oracle BI. The BI server will now perform the necessary initialization blocks to complete the setup of the end user's session. In particular, it will run the initialization blocks to set up group membership properly. All these initialization blocks are run as the real end user (not the Impersonator user). In fact, everything done by the BI server is run using the permissions of the real end user.

AnalyticsSOAP

After the configuration for SSO is finished, the presentation server now expects every user to access Oracle BI via the web and to have been authenticated via the SSO server. This may not always the case, however. For example, as discussed in the "SSO Setup Cautions" section, you might want to use the Oracle BI plug-in for Microsoft Office. When using this tool, you cannot authenticate via the SSO server. (Actually, this is possible in one situation: If you are using Microsoft NTLM as your SSO server, you can use your Windows desktop credentials to log in automatically to the Oracle BI Office plug-in.)

The following components of Oracle BI require special consideration to continue working in an SSO environment:

- Oracle BI plug-in for Microsoft Office
- Oracle BI Publisher
- The Oracle BI web services
- Oracle BI catalog manager in online mode

As you may recall from the brief architecture review at the beginning of this chapter, a component of Oracle BI called the presentation server plug-in is deployed to your application server. The plug-in is deployed to the URL /analytics. To keep all these components working in an SSO environment, you must deploy a second copy of this presentation server plug-in to your application server. Associate this second plug-in with the URL /analyticsSOAP.

Next, you want to make sure that the /analyticsSOAP URL is not protected by your SSO server. Each of the components should then be configured to communicate with Oracle BI using this new URL. Any component using this new URL will use the normal authentication mechanisms of Oracle BI. Because this new URL is not protected by your SSO server, you may want to consider imposing other restrictions on the use of the URL. For example, all requests from the Office Plug-in and BI Publisher will come from a known server: the BI Office server or the BI Publisher server. In that case, it would be easy to put an IP address restriction on the use of the /analyticsSOAP URL.

Deploying in a Secure Environment

Up to this point, we've discussed how to secure access to Oracle BI. It is also quite important that you secure the environment in which Oracle BI is running. This includes securing communication between the end user and Oracle BI, securing communication between various Oracle BI components, and securing communication between Oracle BI and authentication stores and backend databases.

SSL Everywhere

The Oracle BI feature SSL Everywhere is designed to provide secure communication between all Oracle BI components. This feature requires you to generate certificate requests, obtain certificates, configure certificate stores, and configure Oracle BI components to know how to locate and open certificate stores. These steps are detailed well in Chapter 6 of the deployment guide. Note that the SSL Everywhere feature covers communication only between Oracle BI components. It does not cover enabling HTTPS access to Oracle BI and encrypted communication between Oracle BI and external services: identity stores, e-mail servers, and databases. This coverage can be divided into three categories:

- **Client to Oracle BI communication** For example, the a web browser connecting to Oracle BI
- **Interprocess communication between the Oracle BI components** For example, the presentation server connecting to the scheduler service to submit a scheduled job
- **Oracle BI communication with external processes** For example, the BI server connecting to a database to retrieve data or to an LDAP server to authenticate a user

Actually, all three of these securing communication processes are independent of each other. This means that you may set up HTTPS access to Oracle BI and set up SSL communication to your LDAP server. This would enable encrypted communication for the first and third points, but not the second. If you decided it is important to provide encryption between the Oracle BI components—the second point—the SSL Everywhere feature documents how to set up that configuration.

Encrypted Outward Connections

Several components of the BI environment live outside the realm of Oracle BI. Secure communication with these components requires separate configuration. Three external components that come quickly to mind are LDAP, e-mail, and databases.

As you know, passwords are passed to the LDAP server in plaintext. The only way to protect the password as it is sent from the Oracle BI server and the LDAP server is to use SSL communication between them. This is configured in the Administrator tool while setting up the LDAP server.

E-mail is a common delivery mechanism for presenting content and alerts. When using Oracle Delivers, the scheduling and alerting component of Oracle BI, to run scheduled jobs and deliver reports via e-mail, you may consider encrypting the communication between Oracle BI and the e-mail server. SSL communication with the e-mail server is set up as part of the normal scheduler service configuration. Specifically, you specify SSL certificates on the Advanced tab of the Mail configuration section in Job Manager, as shown in Figure 13-10.

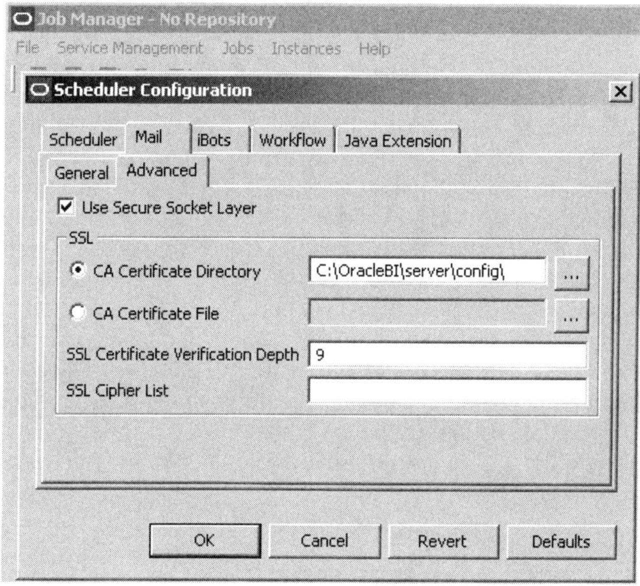

FIGURE 13-10 *Scheduler configuration*

Finally, the last chain of communication that you should consider securing is between the BI server and any database being queried. The process for doing this will be different for each database and depends on the method of communication used with the database. For example, with an Oracle database, Oracle BI uses the standard Oracle client. To secure communication between Oracle BI and an Oracle Database, you would use the Advanced Security option of the database. The Advanced Security option allows you to configure Public Key Infrastructure (PKI) or SSL communication between the Oracle client and database. This configuration occurs as part of the Oracle database client configuration.

Securing the BI Cache

One of Oracle BI's most unique features is the way that it handles the cache. Not only is it possible to perform derivations on the cache and use subsets of the cache, but the cache is also secure and sharable. The idea is that anyone who has access to the data will be able to use cache entries generated by other users. For example, if user A runs a report and user B has access to the same data as user A, then user B will be able to use user A's cache entries. However, if user B has different security permissions, he or she will not be allowed to use user A's cache.

What is truly amazing about this is that the BI server can even be made aware of database-level security policies and can make sure they are applied to the cache. This allows the cache to respect security policies that are set up external to the Oracle BI. We cover this in detail in Chapter 14.

While this section is not intended to be all about cache management, it is important that we mention a couple of features regarding cache management. The Oracle BI administrator must consider what gets cached and how long that cache is maintained. Data caching occurs at the table layer. This means that the Oracle BI administrator can set cache policies for each database table surfaced through Oracle BI. The administrator can also set time limits on how long cache entries can exist for a given table. Cache entries might be removed based on age limits, cache size limits, or the number of cached items, or they might be removed manually.

Cache management is normally a tuning exercise. However, this impacts security in one place. With each initialization block, you have the option of caching the results of the initialization block. Recall that initialization blocks are used to determine group membership. Also, as you will see in the next chapter, results of initialization blocks are also used when applying row-level security. While caching initialization blocks would speed up the session creation process, it may also introduce a security risk. For example, removing a user from a group in the external identity store would not immediately remove the user from the group in Oracle BI when caching the results of initialization blocks.

Another thing to consider when discussing Oracle BI cache is that these entries are written to the file system. While they are not easy to read, it is possible to glean some information from these files. For example, it is possible to see the query that generated the cache entry. It is also possible to see some data values just by looking at the cache files. It is recommended that access to the directories storing the cache entries be restricted. No one but the administrator should have file system access to the Oracle BI server.

Public-facing Applications

An emerging trend is to make BI systems available to the public. This is especially common among government agencies that have an official mandate to provide information to their constituents. For example, if you are moving into a new neighborhood, it is quite easy to get on the web and find information about crime and school performance in that neighborhood. Another great example of this is the reporting requirements that President Obama established for with the American Recovery and Reinvestment Act of 2009 (http://recovery.gov). New York City provides yet another example: Mayor Bloomberg, in an effort to increase the transparency of the city government, decided to make the city's Key Performance Indicators available to the public via a BI environment called Citywide Performance Reporting (www.nyc.gov/html/ops/cpr/html/home/home.shtml).

Firewalls and DMZs

When making data available via the Internet, our first and most obvious step is to decide exactly what information we want to make available to the public. (In the next chapter, we will focus on protecting the data in an Oracle BI system.) The next step is to minimize the public-facing components of the system itself.

In the beginning of this chapter, we gave a quick overview of the architecture of the Oracle BI system. In particular, we detailed three major server components of the Oracle BI architecture: the BI server, the presentation server, and the presentation server plug-in. We have talked quite a bit about the presentation server and the BI server; however, we have not mentioned much about the presentation server plug-in. The purpose of this plug-in is to provide a component of the Oracle BI that resides in a web tier and can be isolated in a DMZ. Most importantly, this allows the presentation server and BI server to be deployed completely behind the firewall.

Public User

With public-facing applications, it is often desirable to have certain components truly public—meaning no login is required. Oracle BI actually requires that every user log into the system. To work around this, it is recommend that you create a specific user for public access and create a way for this user to get automatically logged in. The best way to do this is to embed the BI content into another system such as a portal or web page. To accomplish this, you can use the URL API or the web services API. In each case, it is possible to log on the user automatically. These interfaces to Oracle BI also support normal authentication methods.

For example, with the URL API, the username and password can be embedded in the URL. In this case, the URL takes the form http://server/analyitcs/saw.dll?Dashboards&NQUser=PUBLIC_USER&NQPassword=LOCKED_DOWN_USER. I realize you might be hesitant to put a password in the URL, but it's not as bad as it sounds. Remember that you are trying to create a completely public set of BI content. It really doesn't matter if that user's password is known, because the information this user has access to was designed to be publicly available.

In the next chapter, you'll learn the specifics of how to lock down both content and permissions of this user. With the web services API, you can specify the username and password as part of the web service logic. In particular, the SAWSessionService is used to set up a session properly when using the web services API. This web service provides logon, logoff, and impersonate methods.

Summary

Designing security requirements for a BI system requires special considerations, and the requirements are different from those of a transactional system. The beginning of this chapter discussed these differences, including differences in user populations, differences in how the data is used, and differences caused by combining data from multiple transactional systems.

The rest of the chapter focused on securing access to Oracle BI. Before getting into the specifics, a brief architectural overview of Oracle BI was provided. Additionally, variables and initialization blocks were covered in depth, which provided the foundation for what was covered in the sections on authentication and authorization.

Next, several methods of authentication and authorization were discussed. Reasons for avoiding the built-in authentication in a production system were provided as well as detailed steps in setting up various external authentication schemes. Before detailing authorization steps, the two types of groups in Oracle BI were discussed: BI server groups and web catalog groups.

After detailing the setup of external authentication and authorization, integration with SSO servers was discussed. Generic SSO integration was discussed as well as specific steps on integration with OAM. Finally, details about deploying Oracle BI in various security configurations were discussed including SSL configuration and deploying Oracle BI across firewalls.

The primary focus of this chapter was on securing access to Oracle BI. In the next chapter, we will assume that the user has accessed Oracle BI in a secure way and focus on securing the data being presented to the user. This will include security mechanisms internal to Oracle BI as well as how to leverage security already set up within the database.

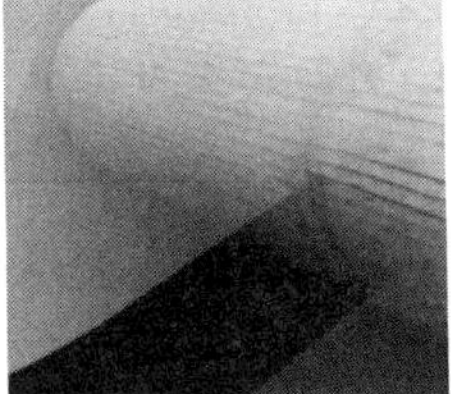

CHAPTER 14

Securing Oracle BI Content and Data

In Chapter 13, we talked about securing access to the Oracle Business Intelligence (BI) server itself. Much of the discussion focused on authentication and authorization, as these two topics represent the critical and important first steps of the security lifecycle. Now let's move into the realm of securing the actual data and content served up by Oracle BI.

At this point, Oracle BI knows who the end user is and knows the groups in which the user belongs. It will use this information to make sure that the end user sees only the content and data he or she is supposed to see. To run a report or dashboard successfully, the user must have access both to the web content (the dashboard or report definition) and the data being served up by that report.

The web catalog contains the definition of all of the dashboards and reports in the system. It does not contain any actual data. Securing web catalog content involves defining who can view or edit dashboard or report definitions, and this is covered in the first part of this chapter. Next, it focuses on securing the data presented through the web catalog content. Security must be applied to the data that is surfaced in the reports and dashboards defined in the web catalog. Fine-grained security for the data focuses on the security features that Oracle BI can add to the data and the features Oracle BI can leverage from the Oracle database. You'll learn about setting up Oracle BI to leverage Virtual Private Database (VPD) and fine-grained auditing (FGA).

Lastly, a number of necessary and often desirable Oracle BI features give users additional privileges required for performing specific tasks. These features have obvious security implications, and the chapter concludes by examining these features and identifying areas you may need to explore.

Securing Web Catalog Content

To run a report, you need permission to access both the report definition, or web catalog content, and the data that will be presented in the report. When we refer to the web catalog *content*, we are specifically referring to the definitions of the objects. So having read access to web catalog content means that you have read access to the report definition.

NOTE
BI Publisher content is secured in a way that's slightly different from all other types of content, because BI Publisher exists as both a stand-alone product and as an integrated component of Oracle BI. BI Publisher will be discussed last in the chapter. Until then, you can assume that unless BI Publisher is specifically mentioned, we are referring to securing non–BI Publisher content.

Content security policies can be applied to users or groups. It's best to start by securing content at the group level for two reasons: First, this is much easier to manage, because you are working with a much smaller set of policies. For example, an organization of thousands of users might have only 50 distinct groups of users, and 50 policies is much more manageable than thousands. Second, web catalog security policies cannot be applied to a user until the user has logged into Oracle BI for the first time. No matter what type of authentication you use (internal or external), the Oracle BI presentation server does not know about the user until the user logs in for the first time. Let's assume, for example, that we want all object-level permissions to be accomplished via direct grants to the user. Before the user logs in for the first time, the user does not exist in the web catalog, making it impossible to create the object-level grants in Oracle BI. The first time the user logs in, he would have access to publicly available objects only. After this first login, however, the administrator would be able to make the necessary object-level grants.

Web Catalog Groups

As mentioned, it is a best practice to apply security policies first at the group level—specifically for web catalog groups. In Chapter 13, you saw that groups are defined in the RPD and owned by the BI server. Web catalog groups are defined in the web catalog and owned by the presentation server. RPD group membership determines data-level security, because the BI server is responsible for retrieving and processing all data. Web catalog group membership determines web catalog content security because the presentation server is responsible for protecting all web catalog content.

Folder-based Security

Before we begin an in-depth discussion on securing web catalog content, let's review the web catalog itself. The web catalog consists of all the definitions of reports and dashboards in your Oracle BI system. You access the web catalog in two main ways: through the web interface and using the Catalog Manager client-server tool.

The web interface is useful for report developers to organize their content and perform basic administration, including security administration. Catalog Manager is useful for performing larger scale administration tasks. For example, you might use Catalog Manager to promote a new dashboard and all of its supporting content from the development server to the production server.

At the OS level, the web catalog is actually a directory full of XML files. Each report and dashboard gets its own XML file. The structure of the web catalog at the OS level exactly matches what you see in the web interface or in Catalog Manager.

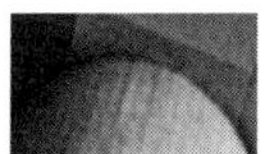

NOTE
Modifying the XML files that make up the web catalog is supported only via Catalog Manager—direct editing of the files using an XML editor or any other editor is not supported.

As mentioned, all content is stored in folders. Security can be applied at the individual object level or at the folder level. This is analogous to securing a file system—files and folders can have read or write permissions granted to specific users or groups. Oracle BI supports the following permissions:

- **Read** View an object.
- **Change/Delete** Modify or delete an object. Also, with Change/Delete permissions on a folder, you can create new objects in that folder.
- **Full Control** Read access, Change/Delete, and the ability to assign permissions.
- **No Access** No access to an object.
- **Traverse Folder** View objects at a lower level. For example, you might want to restrict access to /shared/SHReports but grant access to /shared/SHReports/public. In this case, you would need traverse folder permission on /shared/SHReports.

A detailed explanation of these permissions, complete with examples, is available in Chapter 8 of the Presentation Server Administration Guide (Oracle BI Documentation Library: www.oracle.com/technology/documentation/bi_ee.html). Here is one point worth citing from the documentation: "Explicitly denying access takes precedence over any other permissions or privileges." This is a very useful feature. If a group of users cannot be allowed to see certain web content, you can use No Access permission. This will always guarantee that these users will not be able to access to that content, no matter what permissions they might have inherited via group membership or parent folder permissions.

iBot Security

Simply put, an iBot is a job. It might be a simple scheduled job: Deliver report A to user B every Friday. It could also be a rather complex conditional job: If criteria A is met, deliver report B to the users defined by report C. Users create iBots via the web interface, and these are submitted to the scheduler service. The scheduler service will handle executing the scheduled job by submitting requests to the BI server on behalf of the user who created the iBot. When the job is complete, the scheduler service returns the results to the appropriate delivery profile. Let's run through a few of the specifics.

To create an iBot, you need access to the "Access to Delivers" system privilege. Being granted this permission allows you to access to the Oracle Delivers feature of Oracle BI—in other words, it lets you create iBots. When you attempt to open, edit, or save an iBot, the basic rules of web content security apply. In general, iBots are treated like any other object in the web catalog; however, you will notice two differences.

The first difference involves where iBots are stored in the web catalog. Normally, you can store an object in your personal folder or in a shared folder to which you have Change/Delete or Full Control permission. With iBots, your storage location is determined by whether you are making the iBot available for subscription. If you do not allow subscriptions, the iBot can be saved only in your personal folder. The iBot definition will be stored in a hidden subfolder, called _iBots, in your personal folder. You will be the only one who can edit the definition of this job, but you can still specify additional recipients. These recipients will get results, but they will not have access to the job definition. If you decide to publish the iBot for subscription, the job must be stored in the shared iBots folder. Additionally, if you allow a group or user to subscribe to a scheduled job, the user is automatically granted read access to the job definition.

The second major security consideration when working with iBots is the notion of data visibility. Data visibility is defined on the General tab on the Create iBot web interface, as shown in Figure 14-1. Three options can be set for data visibility, although only two choices will ever be presented at any one time.

iBot Data Visibility Options

The first option is to set the data visibility to Personalized. This is the default setting, and it creates the report using the permissions of the recipient. The recipient receives the data as if she had run the report herself. Assume, for example, that Beth creates an iBot and lists David as a recipient. When the data visibility is set to Personalized, the results that are generated and delivered to David using David's permissions.

The second option is to set the data visibility to Not Personalized (Use iBot Owner's Data Visibility). This runs the report with the permissions of the iBot owner and then delivers the result of the report to each recipient. Keep in mind that the recipient might be getting data that he might not normally be allowed to see. It is analogous to the iBot owner running a report, downloading a PDF copy of the results, and then e-mailing that PDF to each recipient. This option is available for

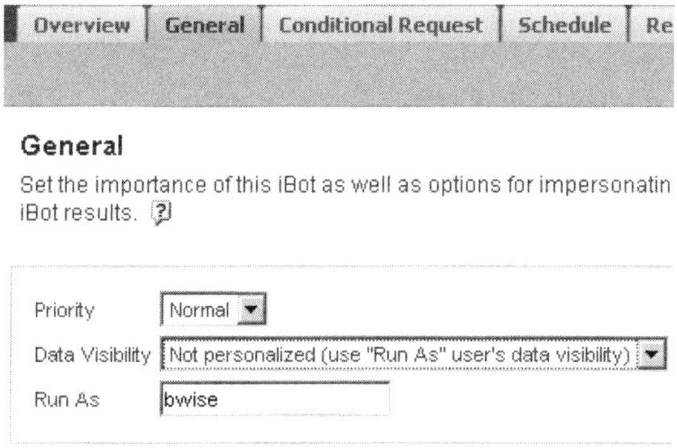

FIGURE 14-1 *The General tab in an iBot definition*

non-administrative users who have been granted the permission Publish iBots For Subscription or the permission Deliver iBots To Specific Or Dynamically Determined Users.

The third option is to set the data visibility to Not Personalized (Use The Run As User's Data Visibility). This is similar to the second option and requires the same permissions, but it also requires the user to be a Presentation Server Administrator. The difference here is that the iBot owner can run the report as any user, not just the iBot owner, and then deliver the results.

Securing BI Publisher Catalog Content

BI Publisher catalog content is different from the rest of Oracle BI content in several ways. These differences stem from the requirement that BI Publisher exist as both a stand-alone product and as a component of the Oracle BI Enterprise Edition suite. For example, when used as a standalone product, BI Publisher needs to have its own identity management infrastructure. When operating as part of the larger Oracle BI suite, it would be better to have an integrated security infrastructure. An awareness of these types of differences is extremely helpful as you plan your BI Publisher deployment.

BI Publisher supports a number of different security models, including BI server security, BI Publisher internal security, eBusiness Suite security, and Lightweight Directory Access Protocol (LDAP). For our discussion, we are using BI server security, as that is the recommended strategy when using BI Publisher and Oracle BI together. All groups in BI Publisher are actually BI server RPD groups. In fact, both BI Publisher catalog content security and data source security are controlled using RPD groups.

In addition, access to BI Publisher catalog content is always done at the group and folder level. This is different from access in Oracle BI, where security can be controlled at the group and folder level or at the user and object level. The final difference is that BI Publisher permissions are controlled completely by membership is special system groups. Membership in these system groups must be directly granted for the permission to be effective. The membership cannot be granted via membership in some other group. These groups are as follows:

- **XMLP_ADMIN** The administrator group
- **XMLP_DEVELOPER** Can create and edit reports
- **XMLP_SCHEDULER** Can schedule reports

- **XMLP_ANALYZER_EXCEL** Can use Excel Analyzer functionality
- **XMLP_ANALYZER_ONLINE** Can use the Online Analyzer
- **XMLP_TEMPLATE_DESIGNER** Reserved for a future feature

This section has presented only half of the security requirements: the web catalog content definition as well as the data presented through that content must be protected. The next section focuses completely on securing the data presented through Oracle BI.

Conveying Identity to the Database

As mentioned in Chapter 13, Oracle BI uses shared connection pools to communicate with the database. This is great for performance but requires a bit of extra setup work to ensure a secure and auditable environment. Steps should be taken to make sure that the underlying database knows who is actually querying the information so that proper database security can be applied. The easiest way to do this with an Oracle database is to set a client identifier. In this chapter, we will use client identifiers to make it possible to use Oracle's VPD functionality and Oracle Database Auditing with Oracle BI.

Setting Client Identifiers

When connecting to the database through a shared connection pool, it is quite common to use the client identifier as a way to capture the end user's true identity. The Oracle database provides a procedure to set the client identifier called **DBMS_SESSION.SET_IDENTIFIER**. Ideally, this would be called any time a user establishes or obtains a new connection to the database.

Oracle BI connection pools even offer the ability to call database functions at several different times: on connect, before query, after query, and on disconnect. One caveat, however, is that you cannot call Oracle procedures directly from these connection pool connection scripts. The connection pool scripts expect return values and therefore your procedures must be created or wrapped as PL/SQL functions.

It is a simple step to create a function to wrap **DBMS_SESSION.SET_IDENTIFIER**. In the sample RPDs provided on the Downloads page at www.OraclePressBooks.com, a database user called BI_SELECT does all data access (the data_access connection pool). This user has a function that takes in the BI end user's username and returns a string. It's not really important what the function returns, as we won't be using it for anything meaningful. For debugging and just as a general good practice, we'll set the return value to something that might one day be usable:

```
CREATE OR REPLACE
  FUNCTION bi_select.SET_IDENTIFIER
    (
      p_username_in IN VARCHAR2 )
    RETURN VARCHAR2
  AS
  BEGIN
    dbms_session.set_identifier(p_username_in);
    RETURN 'Function SET_IDENTIFIER Completed for ' || p_username_in;
  END;
/
```

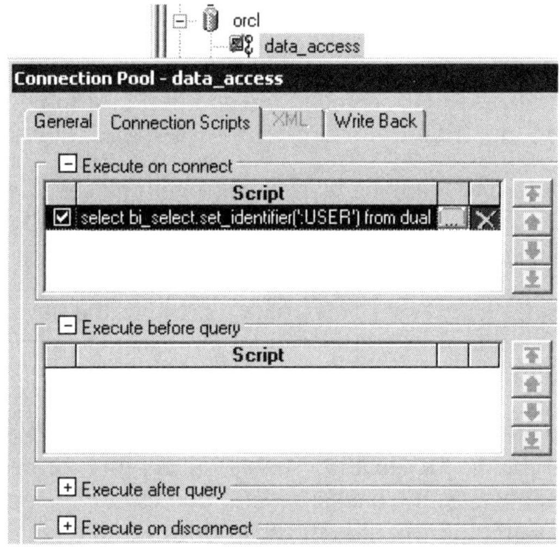

FIGURE 14-2 *Setting a client identifier by a connection script*

As shown in Figure 14-2, this function can then be called as part of the connection with a simple **SELECT bi_select.set_identifier(':USER') FROM dual**. As mentioned, this can be found in all of the sample RPDs provided at www.OraclePressBooks.com. Look at the Connection Scripts tab of the DATA_ACCESS connection pool for the ORCL database, shown in Figure 14-2.

You can test to see if this is working in a couple of ways. The easiest way is to log onto the database using SQL*Plus and query the v$session view. From the Oracle BI Administrator tool, right-click any table from the SH schema and choose View Data using the data_access connection pool. Then run the following query in the database in SQL*Plus:

```
SELECT username, client_identifier FROM v$session WHERE username = 'BI_SELECT'
```

You should see BI_SELECT as the username and Administrator (the user logged into the Administration tool) as the client identifier. You can also test this in the audit log. We'll look at this more closely in the section "Database Auditing."

Securing Data Presented by Oracle BI

The BI server handles all data retrieval. Data security policies can be enforced at the BI server level or at the database level. This section offers examples of both and concludes with a discussion on deciding where you can apply the security policy.

Chapter 13 reviewed the basics of query execution in Oracle BI, including the presentation server issuing a logical SQL statement and the BI server transforming that into one or more physical SQL statements that are issued to the database. Let's examine this in a bit more detail before getting into security policies.

When a user wants to create a new ad hoc data request, she must first choose a subject area. A subject area is a logical presentation of the data accessible via Oracle BI that the user accesses in the web interface. This subject area is the representation of a presentation catalog defined in the presentation layer of the BI server metadata. The BI server metadata consists of three layers:

- **Presentation layer** This layer consists of one or more presentation catalogs, collections of tables and columns presented to the end user as a subject area. The presentation server, or any ODBC or JDBC application, can issue logical SQL statements against these tables.
- **Business model and mapping layer** This intermediate layer sits between the presentation layer and the physical layer. Business rules, including drill paths, aggregation rules, and security policies, are applied at this layer.
- **Physical layer** This layer of metadata represents the physical tables against which the BI server will issue queries. This is normally created by importing metadata from the database's data dictionary.

The business model and mapping layer plays a critical part in determining how the logical SQL statement issued by the Presentation server will get transformed in a physical SQL statement issued by the BI server against the backend data sources.

It is also worth examining what the BI server does when it receives a logical SQL statement. In general, two things happen: a query plan is established and the possible use of the Oracle BI cache is evaluated. The BI server uses the metadata to determine how to satisfy the logical request, including any multi-pass SQL statements, fragmentation optimization (splitting the query across multiple systems), and aggregation navigation (rewriting queries against available aggregate data stores to improve performance). The BI server cache is extremely important in this section, because this cache is shared between users. We'll discuss how to ensure that the sharing of cache respects all security policies.

Security Policies Within the BI Server

Securing data is done at two levels in Oracle BI. The first level is a coarse level and involves giving people access to subject areas—similar to giving users access to a schema in a database. If a user has access to a subject area, he will be able to perform queries against that subject area. If a user does not have access to a subject area, he will not even see that the subject area exists. It will not be usable in any fashion in Oracle BI. The second level of data security occurs at a very fine level and is either row- or column-based security, and this is the primary focus of this chapter.

Subject Area Security

Setting up subject area security is quite simple. Technically, security is applied to the presentation catalog in the BI server metadata. As mentioned, a one-to-one correspondence exists between BI server metadata presentation catalogs and the subject areas that appear when using Oracle Answers. The terms "presentation catalogs" and "subject areas" are often used interchangeably, and they will both be used here as well. As shown in Figure 14-3, to set up subject area security, you modify the permissions in the Presentation Catalog properties dialog box in the Administration tool.

Read access to a subject area can be granted to a user or a group. Chapter 13 discussed the benefits of externalizing security. If you have externalized security, access to subject areas can be accomplished only at the group level, because users are not stored in the RPD. This same restriction does not apply in the same way to fine-grained security within the BI server, as you will see in the next section.

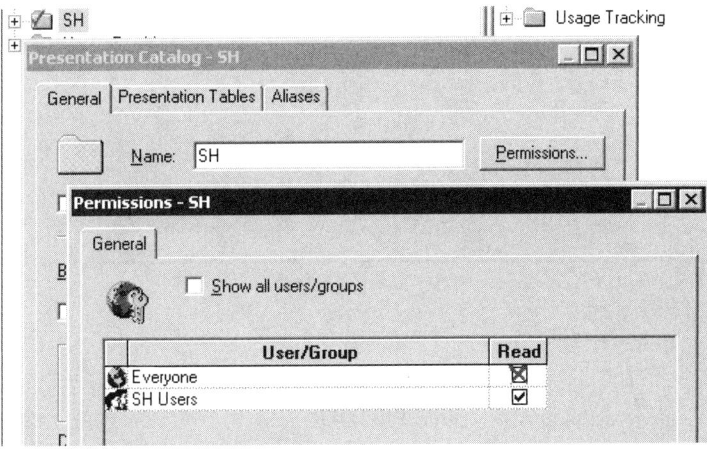

FIGURE 14-3 *Setting up subject area security in the Presentation Catalog dialog box*

Now let's move from the coarse-level security of securing access to subject areas to the fine-grained level of applying row- and column-level security. This approach follows the best practice of applying security at the most general level and then moving to the most specific level.

Oracle BI's Row-level Security

Adding row-level security using Oracle BI is accomplished by adding business model filters in the BI server metadata. These filters are defined at the group level. This does not mean that the filter is the same for everyone in the group—in fact, the opposite is almost always true: the filter being added is usually user-specific.

Let's look at an example. This example business model filter is found in each example RPD. The point of this simple example is to limit the data to which the product managers have access: product managers should be able to view sales data only for the products they manage. A database table called BI_TABLES.PRODUCT_MANAGERS will be used in conjunction with the SH sample schema. This table has a row for each product that each user is allowed to view. As you can see in Figure 14-4, the user biproduct1 manages Game Consoles and the user biproduct2 manages Portable PCs and Desktop PCs.

Now that the data is in place for this example, we can focus on the steps required to apply a business model filter. This will involve creating a session variable to hold information about which products a user manages and creating the business model filter that will be applied to the members of the Product Managers group.

Creating the GET_PRODUCT Session Variable Chapter 13 discussed how to set up session variables and offered several examples of using session variables. Specifically, they were used to assign group membership dynamically as the user logged into Oracle BI. In this example, we use a session variable to store information about which products a user manages. The sample RPDs provided at www.OraclePressBooks.com from the Downloads page include an initialization

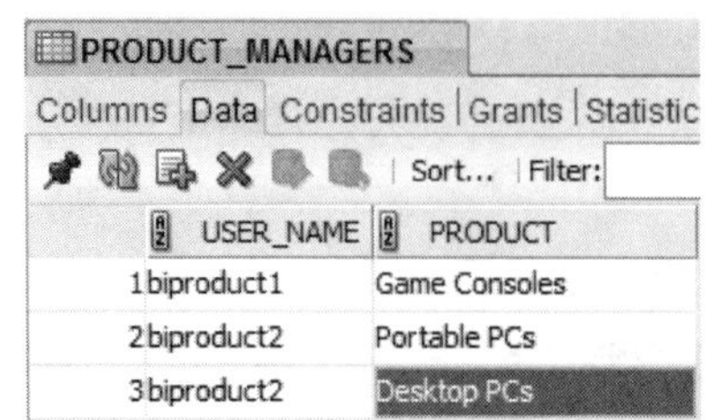

FIGURE 14-4 *The PRODUCT_MANAGERS table*

block titled GET_PRODUCTS. This initialization block uses row-wise initialization to create and populate a session variable called **PRODUCT**. Here is the query in that initialization block:

```
select 'PRODUCT' variable_name, product variable_value
from bi_tables.product_managers
where user_name = ':USER'
```

This query returns the appropriate products for each product manager. The predicate here, **user_name = ':USER'**, ensures that only the correct products are returned. Figures 14-5 and 14-6 show the Utilities dashboard included as part of this example. Figure 14-5 shows the variables when BIPRODUCT1 is logged into Oracle BI, and Figure 14-6 shows the variables when BIPRODUCT2 is logged into Oracle BI. Notice that BIPRODUCT1 has a session variable of **PRODUCT = Game Consoles** and BIPRODUCT2 has a session variable of **PRODUCT = Portable PCs;Desktop PCs**.

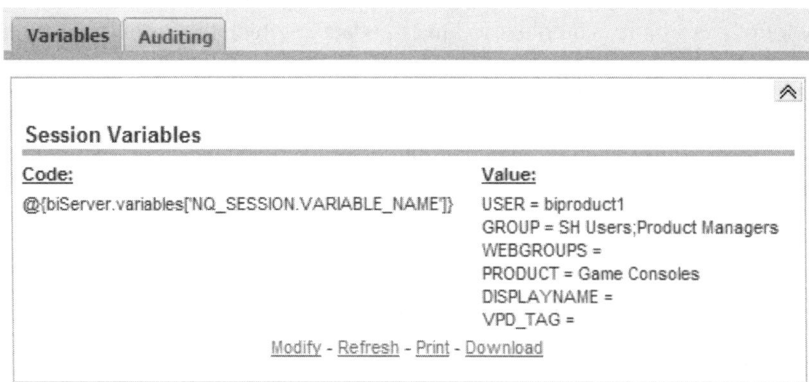

FIGURE 14-5 *The Utilities dashboard when BIPRODUCT1 is logged into Oracle BI*

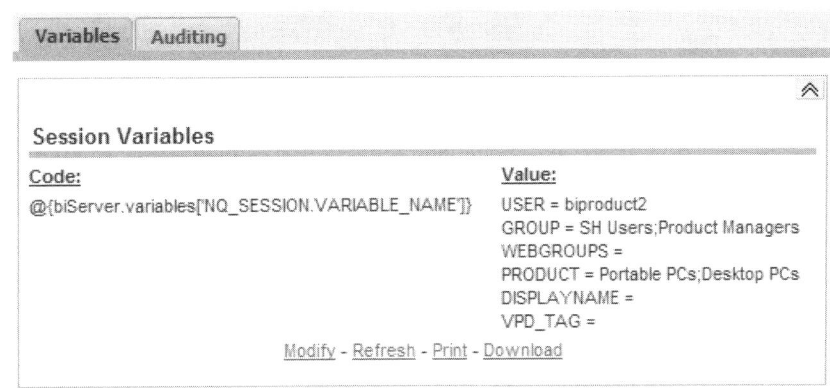

FIGURE 14-6 *The Utilities dashboard when BIPRODUCT2 is logged into Oracle BI*

Now that the session variable is set up and working, we can define the business model filter.

Applying the Business Model Filter Business model filters are set up in the Permissions dialog box for a given group. As you can see in Figures 14-7 and 14-8, several interesting security features are included in the Permissions dialog box. The General tab lists all subject area and column-level security restrictions (column-level security is discussed in the next section). Figure 14-7 shows the Query Limits tab, where you set limits on when databases can be queried, the maximum number of rows, and the maximum amount of time that can be spent on a query. The Populate Privilege refers to a feature used by the marketing feature of Oracle BI. The Execute Direct Database Requests privilege is discussed later in this chapter in the section "Direct Database Requests." In the Filters tab, shown in Figure 14-8, you can set up business model filters.

User/Group Permissions - Product Managers

General | Query Limits | Filters

Database	Restrict	Status Max Rows	Max Rows	Status Max Time	Max Time (Minutes)	Populate Privilege	Execute Direct Database Requests
A - Sample	...	Ignore	100000	Ignore	10	Ignore	Ignore
B - Sample Fc	...	Ignore	100000	Ignore	10	Ignore	Ignore
orcl	...	Ignore	100000	Ignore	10	Ignore	Ignore
Security Infor	...	Ignore	100000	Ignore	10	Ignore	Ignore

OK | Cancel | Help

FIGURE 14-7 *The Query Limits tab of the Product Managers group permissions dialog box*

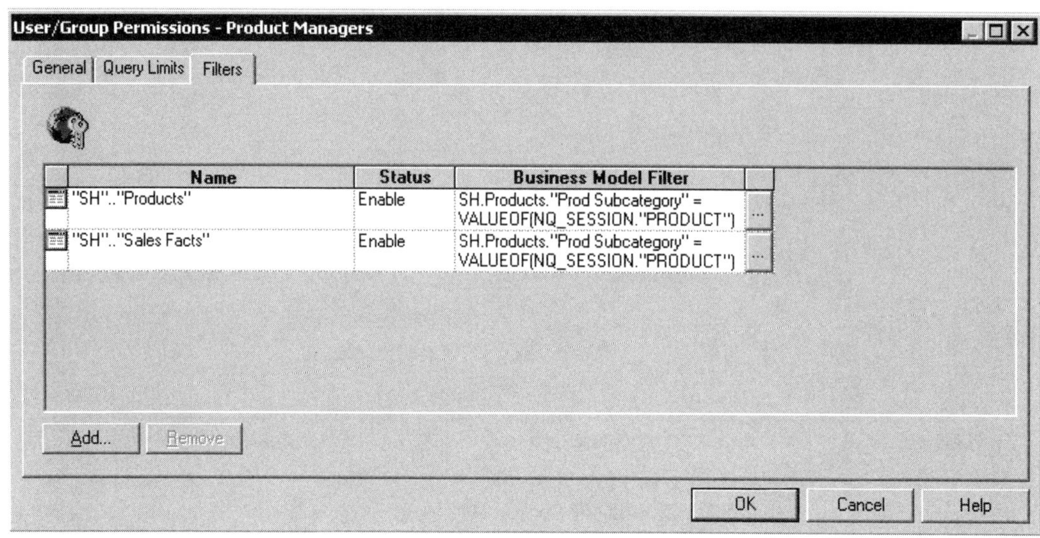

FIGURE 14-8 *Business model filters for the Product Managers group*

In this example, a business model filter is applied to the Products and Sales Facts table. Whenever a product manager includes a query against the Products or Sales Facts tables, the filter **SH.Products."Prod Subcategory" = VALUEOF(NQ_SESSION. "PRODUCT")** is added to the query. Notice a few interesting things. First, the filter is making use of the product session variable that we defined earlier. Second, the filter can use any column in the subject area even if the table containing that column is not included in the query. The BI server will automatically join in any necessary tables when it generates the physical query. In this example, the same filter, which uses a column in the Products table, is applied to both the Products and the Sales Facts tables. If the user queries only the Sales Facts table, the BI server will automatically join in the Products table so that the filter can be appropriately applied.

Finally, note that the equal sign works here even if the product session variable contains multiple values. The BI server is smart enough to know how to use row-wise initialized variables with equality checks.

In working through this example, you may have noticed that the syntax for accessing the session variable when using the web interface is different from the variable when using Administrator tool. To access a session variable while working in the web interface to Oracle BI, you use the syntax **@{biServer.variables['NQ_SESSION.PRODUCTS']}**. In the Administration tool, you use the syntax **VALUEOF(NQ_SESSION."PRODUCT")**.

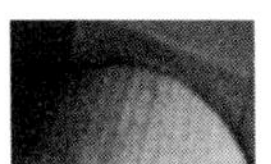

TIP

Be careful of the syntax when accessing session variables. The syntax in the web interface is different from the syntax used in the Administration tool.

Column-level Security

Oracle BI supports the ability to apply column-level security. The process of setting up column-level security is very similar to that of setting up subject area security. By default, if a user has access to a subject area, she would have access to all tables and columns in that subject area. If a column should not be seen by a user or group of users, Read access can be revoked. In the Administration tool, column-level security is defined in the Permissions dialog box of the column's properties.

The mechanics of securing access to a column is straightforward and requires nothing more than a few steps. After the column is secured, you'll need to take a few more steps to ensure a satisfying end user experience. Let's investigate two use cases to help you understand how this is done: an end user creating a new ad hoc request using a subject area containing secured columns, and an end user attempting to run a report or dashboard that uses a secured column.

The example RPD called AOS_INTERNAL_COLUMN_SEC.RPD, which is supplied at www.OraclePressBooks.com, has a secured column in the SH subject area. The "Sales Facts"."Amount Sold" column is not accessible to the users BICHANNEL1 and BICHANNEL2. If BICHANNEL1 tries to create a new ad hoc query using the SH subject area, this column will not appear in the list of available columns. This use case requires no additional work.

For the second use case, assume that an administrator creates a report that uses the column "Sales Facts"."Amount Sold". BICHANNEL1 is not allowed to use that column. Using the default setup of Oracle BI, if BICHANNEL tries to run this report, it will error out: "[nQSError: 27005] Unresolved column."

This result is not acceptable and better options are available. These options require some additional steps to set up, as outlined in the following.

First, turn on the BI Server parameter **PROJECT_INACCESSIBLE_COLUMN_AS_NULL**, found under the security section of the NQSConfig.ini file (located in the OraceBI_HOME/server/config directory). By default, this parameter is set to **NO**. Changing this to **YES** will stop the error from occurring. Instead, that column will be dropped from the report as if it were never included in the report at all. This is better than the preceding option, but it may still not be what you are looking for.

Let's consider an example report that has three columns: CUSTOMER_NAME, CUSTOMER_CREDIT_LIMIT, and TOTAL_ORDERED. If the secured column is CUSTOMER_CREDIT_LIMIT, the parameter setting solution might be acceptable. When BICHANNEL1 runs the report, this column will be missing, but CUSTOMER_NAME and TOTAL_ORDERED will still appear on the report and the report is useful. If the secured column was instead CUSTOMER_NAME or TOTAL_ORDERED, this would probably be a different story, because dropping CUSTOMER_NAME or TOTAL_ORDERED off the report would probably make the report unusable.

Oracle BI provides two functions to help deal with this column-level end-user experience problem: **choose** and **IndexCol**. With the following two examples, you should still make sure the parameter **PROJECT_INACCESSIBLE_COLUMN_AS_NULL** is set to YES.

The choose Function Oracle BI functions can be applied in two possible locations. A report developer can use a function while developing the report in the web interface, or a metadata developer can use a function in the business model layer of the BI server metadata. The **choose** function is usable by a report developer only in the web interface. It is not allowed as a business model function. The **choose** function takes a list of expressions as inputs and returns the first one in the list that the user actually has permission to see. In the example provided on the Web (AOS_INTERNAL_COLUMN_SEC.RPD) are three "Amount Sold" columns:

- **"Amount Sold"** Accessible to everyone except BICHANNEL1 and BICHANNEL2. This column includes all sales.

- **"Amount Sold TeleSales"** Accessible to everyone except BICHANNEL2. This column is based on a logical column that filters the sales only to sales from the TeleSales channel.
- **"Amount Sold Internet"** Accessible to everyone except BICHANNEL1. This column is based on a logical column that filters the sales only to sales from the Internet channel.

Let's assume that we want to create a report that shows the amount sold by product category. We also want this report to work for everyone, including the users BICHANNEL1 and BICHANNEL2. Using just the column "Amount Sold" will not work for BICHANNEL1 and BICHANNEL2, because they do not have access to this column. Instead, we should use the following function:

```
choose("Sales Facts"."Amount Sold","Sales Facts"."Amount Sold TeleSales",
"Sales Facts"."Amount Sold Internet")
```

When anyone other than BICHANNEL1 or BICHANNEL2 logs onto the system, they will see "Amount Sold." When BICHANNEL1 logs on and runs this report, "Amount Sold TeleSales" will be returned. When BICHANNEL2 logs on and runs this report, "Amount Sold Internet" will be returned. This technique handles the problem very nicely, but it requires that both the business model and the report be designed with column security in mind.

The IndexCol Function The last tool that Oracle BI provides to deal with this challenge is a function called **IndexCol**, which is designed to be used in the metadata at the business model layer. This function uses an external function to determine what column should be used. The syntax for the function is **IndexCol(*external function, column list*)**. The external function should return an integer that represents which column that should be used. A *0* means the first column will be used, a *1* means the second column will be used, and so on.

A common way to use this function is to use a session variable for the external function. In this case, an initialization block will run some type of query to determine which column should be used and populate the session variable with the appropriate integer.

You should note a couple of interesting things about this function. It is executed as part of the logical request generation, and this means that the logical SQL, including the query log and usage tracking, will contain the **IndexCol** function. However, cache hits will be determined after the **IndexCol** function is evaluated. In addition, the **IndexCol** function is designed to be used inside a hierarchy. Hierarchies are defined within the business model of the BI server metadata. They define the relationships between levels in a dimension. A hierarchy will manifest itself to the end user as a drill path. Because the **IndexCol** function can be used as part of a hierarchy, the evaluated expression will be drillable just as if the final resulting column were used directly in the report. This makes this type of column-level security very useful for hierarchy security.

Let's work through an example in which product managers should see the entire product hierarchy and all other users should see the product hierarchy only from the product subcategory level down. First, we'll create an initialization block that returns an integer and populates a session variable called **PRODUCT_LEVEL**. The following code sets the value to *0* for the users biproduct1 and biproduct2; otherwise it sets a default value of *1*:

```
SELECT DECODE(':USER','biproduct1',0,'biproduct2',0,1) FROM dual
```

Next, we create a new logical column that uses the **IndexCol** function and the **PRODUCT_LEVEL** session variable to return the appropriate function. Figure 14-9 shows how this is done.

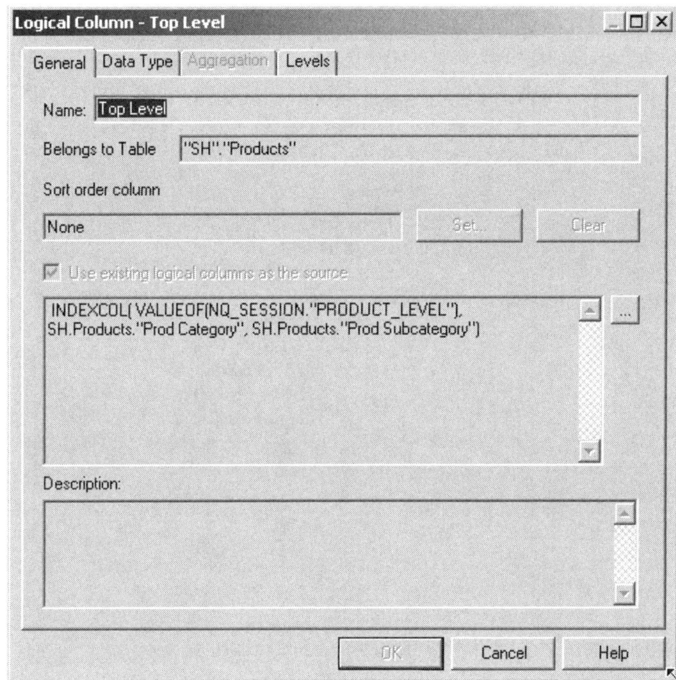

FIGURE 14-9 *The IndexCol function based on a session variable is an effective technique for implementing column-level security.*

With this function, we have created a new logical column called Top Level that can be used by the report developer.

To help you understand how this new logical column works, let's review the product hierarchy defined in the business model and shown in Figure 14-10. Before any column-level security is implemented, the hierarchy would represent the normal drill path available to end users. The Top Level column does not need to be placed in the hierarchy, but because it evaluates to columns that do live in the hierarchy, it will act like a member of the hierarchy.

If biproduct1 runs a report with Top Level in the report, Top Level will evaluate to Prod Category and biproduct1 will be able to drill down the product hierarchy from that point. Figure 14-11 shows a report after biproduct1 has drilled down twice from Top Level.

Now, if BIADMIN logs into Oracle BI and runs a report with the Top Level column in it, the results will be different. The Top Level column will evaluate to Prod Subcategory and BIADMIN will be able to drill down from there. Figure 14-12 shows this report for the user BIADMIN.

Column-level Security Summary Oracle BI supports column-level security. If you decide to set up column-level security in your metadata, you will need to decide how to handle users who do not have permission to view one or more columns in a report. You have three options: let Oracle BI remove the column from the report automatically, use the choose function in your report

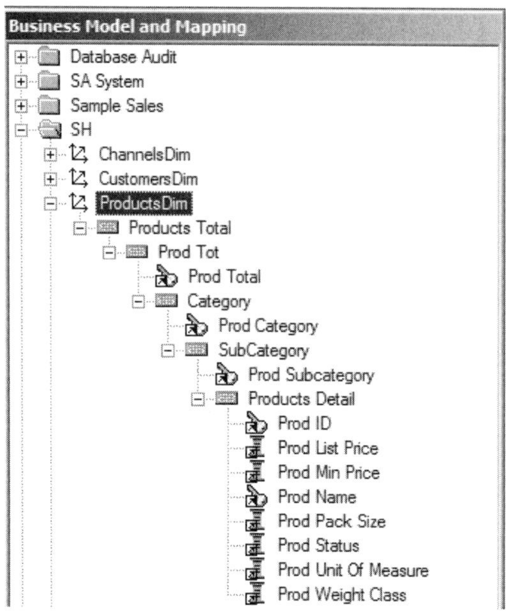

FIGURE 14-10 *The product hierarchy in the SH business model*

definition, or use the IndexCol function in your metadata. Automatically removing the column from the report may work for some column types, and an example was provided. The choose function works well with column-based security, but using it requires a lot of planning by both the RPD developer and the report developer. The IndexCol function is ideal in times when column-based security is needed for columns that are part of a hierarchy.

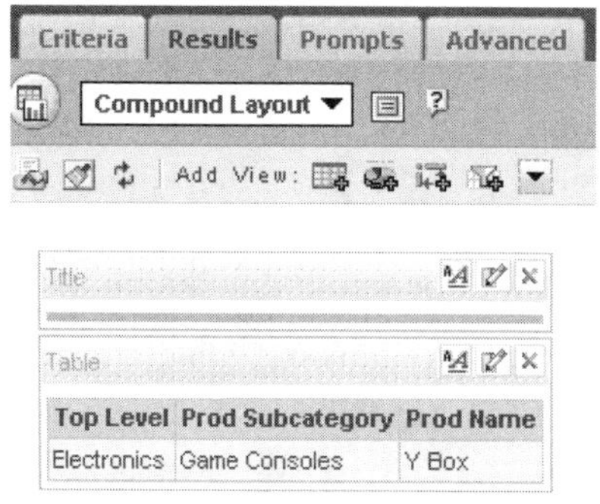

FIGURE 14-11 *The logical column Top Level evaluates to Prod Category for the user biproduct1.*

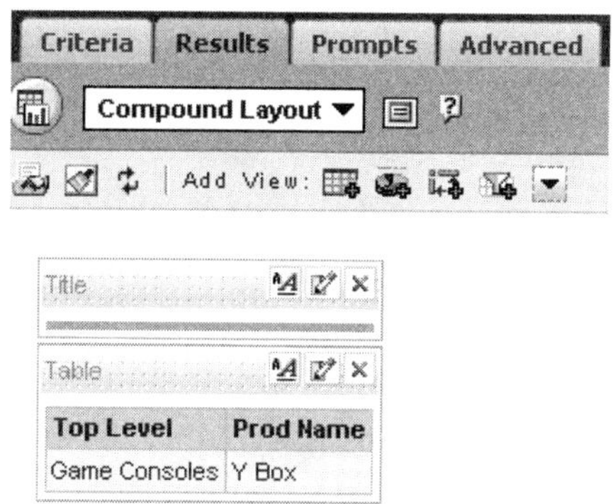

FIGURE 14-12 *The logical column Top Level evaluates to Prod Subcategory for the user BIADMIN.*

Integrating Oracle BI with Database Security Policies

So far, the focus has been on how to secure data presented through Oracle BI. We have explored security policies that were defined at the BI server level. Now we will examine the steps required integrate Oracle BI with database-level security policies. In particular, we will focus on how Oracle VPD can be used in conjunction with Oracle BI. This discussion of Oracle BI and data security concludes by comparing and contrasting Oracle BI's row-level security with Oracle Database row-level security.

Oracle BI and VPD

At a high level, the Oracle VPD feature is similar to business model filters. For example, VPD lets you apply row-level security—in other words, the exact same query will return different results for different users based on their permissions. The rules that define which users will see which rows are captured in a PL/SQL program called a *VPD policy* that is applied to database tables or views. VPD policies can affect all Data Manipulation Language (DML) statements, and not just queries; however, as this chapter is focused on securing the reporting environment, our discussion is limited to VPD policies applied to select statements.

Three steps are required to integrate Oracle BI with a VPD-enabled database:

1. Set up the database session properly.
2. Inform Oracle BI that it will be accessing a VPD-enabled database.
3. Make the BI server cache aware of the VPD policy.

Often, VPD policies make use of some attribute about the end user to determine the security enforced. For example, a VPD policy might make use of the end user's department to limit rows returned in a query. The RPD examples included with this book and found at www.OraclePressBooks.com from the Downloads page are all designed to work with a VPD policy that focuses on sales channels. This policy limits the sales data presented to the user based on the sales channels that the user manages. For this policy to be effective, the database must know who the end user is.

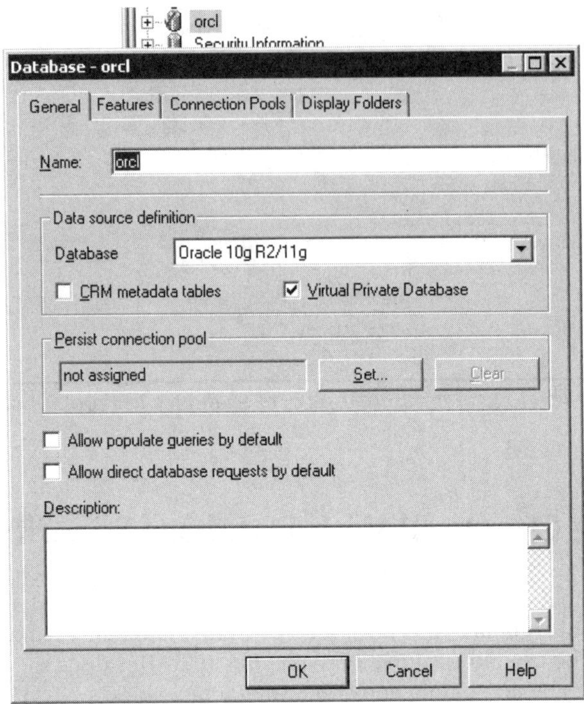

FIGURE 14-13 *Identifying a database as a VPD in the BI server metadata*

Recall that Oracle BI uses shared connection pools to connect to the database. So to make Oracle BI work with our example VPD policy, we need to convey the end user's identity to the database. (The mechanics of conveying this information to the database were covered earlier in the chapter.)

Next, we must inform the BI server that it is connecting to a VPD-enabled database in the database Properties dialog box in the Administrator tool. As shown in Figure 14-13, you need to mark the database as a Virtual Private Database. This informs the BI server that database security policies may affect the rows returned by a query. Knowing this, the BI server will take additional steps in deciding whether cache entries can be used to satisfy queries. The details of how the BI server cache works with VPD are covered next.

Oracle BI Cache and VPD

One very interesting feature of the BI server is its sharable cache feature, which allows cache entries to be shared by multiple BI users. This can drastically improve performance, even in high-user scenarios. This might leave you a bit concerned about security. Note that all BI Server security features work natively with the shared cache. In particular, business model filters work with the BI server cache, because business model filters are added to the query before checking to see whether the query can be satisfied by the cache.

The next big question that probably comes to mind is this: Does the BI cache work with database security features (such as Oracle VPD)? The answer is yes, which is quite amazing considering that the decision to use cache is made before any query is sent to the database where the VPD policy is applied.

The key to getting the BI server's sharable cache to work with Oracle VPD is to tag the cache entries. These tags are basically labels on the cache entries that let the BI server know who should be allowed to share the cache.

Let's look at another example provided on the Web. While examining the example, we will also run through a basic test to verify that the cache is working with the VPD policy. This example includes a simple VPD policy, and all of the example RPDs provided on the Web are designed to work with this VPD policy. We'll put a VPD policy in place that restricts the rows returned from the SH.SALES table. The rows returned will be restricted so that the end user can see the rows for only the channels that they manage. Figure 14-14 shows the CHANNEL_MANAGERS table that holds information necessary for the VPD policy.

Following the three steps listed earlier for integrating Oracle BI with a VPD-enabled database, let's first make sure that the database session is properly set up and that the user's identity is conveyed to the database. To do this, we execute the statement **select bi_select.set_identifier(': USER') from dual** in a connection script for the data access connection pool. The details of how to do this were covered in the section "Setting Client Identifiers."

Second, we mark the database as a VPD database in the BI server metadata. As shown in Figure 14-13, this is done on the Properties page for the ORCL database in the RPD. The Virtual Private Database checkbox must be selected when the underlying database uses VPD policies. This instructs the BI server to start tagging all BI server cache entries.

Third, we must make the BI server aware of the VPD policy and instruct the BI server on how exactly it will tag the cache entries. We do this by populating a security-sensitive session variable with information from the VPD policy. The code for the VPD policy used in the examples provided at www.OraclePressBooks.com is listed next. This is a simple policy and is not intended to represent any best practices with respect to VPD policy development. This policy simply applies a filter to the SH.SALES table so that only rows for the channels that the end user manages

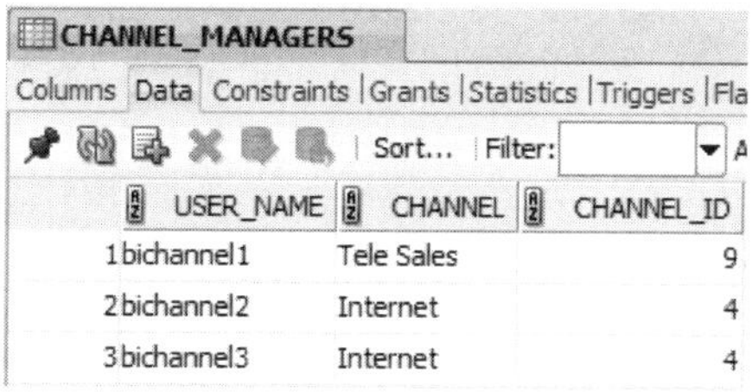

CHANNEL_MANAGERS

Columns | Data | Constraints | Grants | Statistics | Triggers | Fla

Sort... Filter:

	USER_NAME	CHANNEL	CHANNEL_ID
1	bichannel1	Tele Sales	9
2	bichannel2	Internet	4
3	bichannel3	Internet	4

FIGURE 14-14 *The CHANNEL_MANAGERS table used in the VPD policy*

are returned. The other important thing to notice in this package is the VPD tagging function called **VPD_TAG**:

```
CREATE OR REPLACE
PACKAGE bi_select.channel_policy
AS
FUNCTION vpd_whereclause
  (
    schema_name IN VARCHAR2,
    object_name IN VARCHAR2)
  RETURN VARCHAR2;
FUNCTION vpd_tag
  (
    v_channel_manager IN VARCHAR2)
  RETURN VARCHAR2;
END;
/

CREATE OR REPLACE
PACKAGE body bi_select.channel_policy
AS
FUNCTION vpd_whereclause
  (
    schema_name IN VARCHAR2,
    object_name IN VARCHAR2)
  RETURN VARCHAR2
AS
  v_whereclause VARCHAR2(2000):='';
  v_client_id   VARCHAR2(30)  :='';
BEGIN
  SELECT sys_context('USERENV','CLIENT_IDENTIFIER')
  INTO v_client_id
  FROM dual;
  IF v_client_id  IS NOT NULL THEN
    v_whereclause := 'channel_id in
                      (select channel_id from bi_tables.channel_managers
                       where upper(bi_tables.channel_managers.user_name)
                        = upper('''|| v_client_id||'''))';
  ELSE
    v_whereclause := '1=0';
  END IF;
  RETURN v_whereclause;
END;

FUNCTION vpd_tag
  (
    v_channel_manager IN VARCHAR2)
  RETURN VARCHAR2
AS
  v_return VARCHAR2(2000) := NULL;
```

```
BEGIN
  FOR r IN
  (SELECT TO_CHAR(channel_id) channel_id
  FROM bi_tables.channel_managers
  WHERE upper(user_name) = upper(v_channel_manager)
  ORDER BY 1
  )
  LOOP
    v_return := v_return || r.channel_id || ';';
  END LOOP;
  IF v_return IS NOT NULL THEN
    v_return  := SUBSTR(v_return,1,LENGTH(v_return)-1);
  END IF;
  RETURN v_return;
END;
END;
/
```

The tag on the Oracle BI cache entry will consist of the values of the security sensitive session variables for the user that issued the query. Figure 14-15 shows the definition of the session variable **VPD_TAG**—notice that Security Sensitive is selected. The code to populate this session variable, in the initialization block GET_VPD_TAG, makes use of the VPD tagging function:

```
select channel_policy.vpd_tag(':USER')
from dual
```

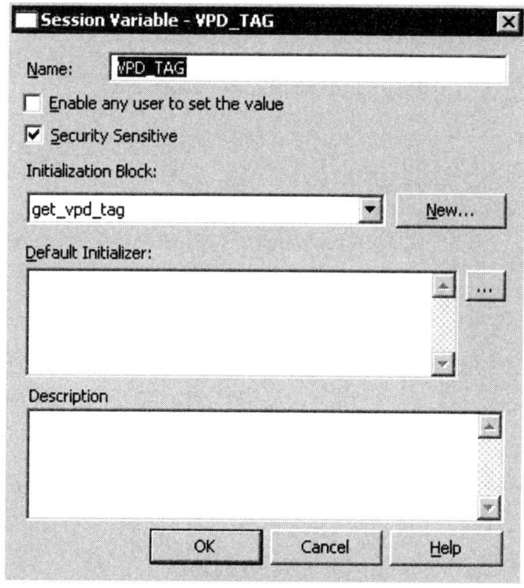

FIGURE 14-15 *The security session variable VPD_TAG that will be used to tag cache entries*

For the user BICHANNEL1, the **VPD_TAG** session variable is set to *9,* and for users BICHANNEL2 and BICHANNEL3, the value is set to *4.* When we test this, we should see that out of these three users, only BICHANNEL2 and BICHANNEL3 can share cache entries.

The mechanism for tagging the cache entries is the key to ensuring the Oracle BI cache does not violate VPD policies. If the effect of the VPD policy will yield different results for two different users, then the VPD tag should use different values for these two users. Because the logic that defines the VPD tag is tied so closely to the VPD policy itself, I decided to build this logic directly into my VPD policy PL/SQL package. The BI_SELECT.CHANNEL_POLICY PL/SQL package contains the logic to generate both the VPD predicate and the VPD tag. The function called **VPD_WHERECLAUSE** is used by the VPD policy to generate the predicate that will be appended to all queries against the SH.SALES_FACTS table. The function called **VPD_TAG** generates the value that should be used to tag cache entries.

Testing the VPD Example Testing this feature is worthwhile, because it helps you understand how it works. The goal of this test is to show that the BI server uses the cache only when it will not violate the VPD policy. This test requires three users: BICHANNEL1, BICHANNEL 2, and BICHANNEL 3 (see the appendix for more details on these users). If you take a quick look at the BI_SELECT.CHANNEL_MANAGERS table shown in Figure 14-14 and the SH.CHANNELS table, you will see that BICHANNEL1 manages the TeleSales channel, while BICHANNEL 2 and BICHANNEL 3 manage the Internet channel. We will run an Oracle BI Answers request for each user. This will be a very simple report that returns the sales for each channel. Figure 14-16 shows the definition of this report in Oracle Answers.

Figure 14-17 shows the results of this query when executed by BICHANNEL1.

Figure 14-18 shows the results of this query when executed by BICHANNEL2 or BICHANNEL3.

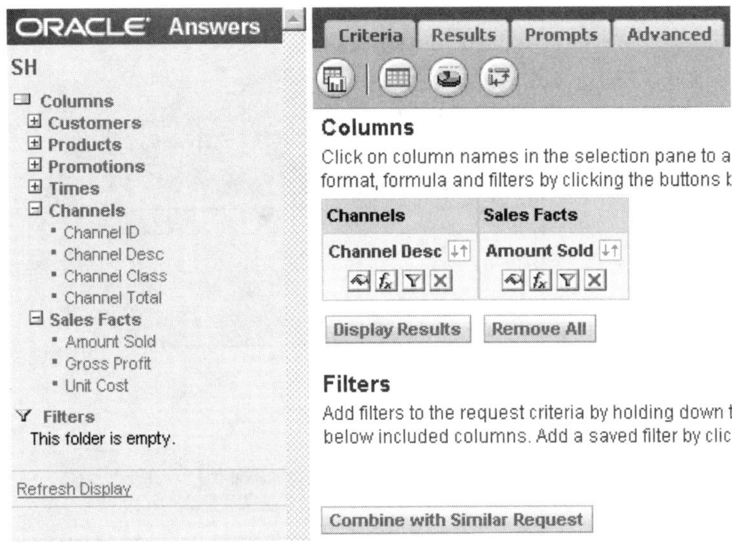

FIGURE 14-16 *The request that will be executed by all three users*

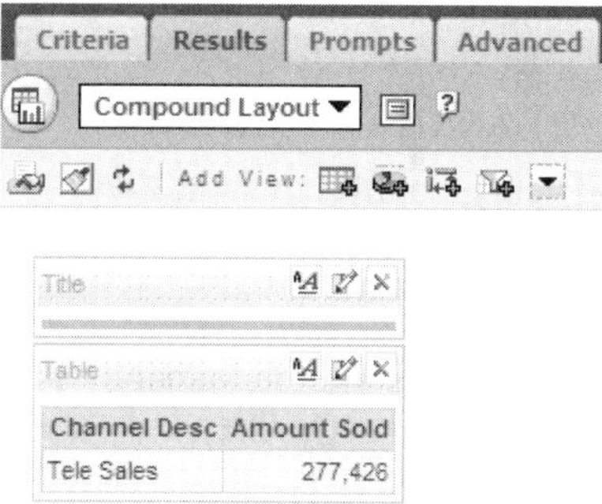

FIGURE 14-17 *The results when executed by BICHANNEL1*

These results are the exact results that we would expect to see with the VPD policy. The user BICHANNEL1 can see only the sales for the TeleSales division. The users BICHANNEL2 and BICHANNEL3 can see only one the sales for the Internet division. This tells us that the database is appropriately applying the VPD policy. It also tells us that BICHANNEL1 is not sharing a cache entry with BICHANNEL2 and BICHANNEL3. Had the BI server used the cache to satisfy the request, we would have seen the same results for all three users.

The last thing we need to check is that BICHANNEL2 and BICHANNEL3 are able to share cache entries, because the VPD policy limits both users to the same set of data. Here are the steps required to verify this:

1. Clear all cache entries.
2. Run the query as BICHANNEL1.
3. Check the logs and verify the BI server sends a query to the database (no cache entries are available).
4. Run the query as BICHANNEL2.

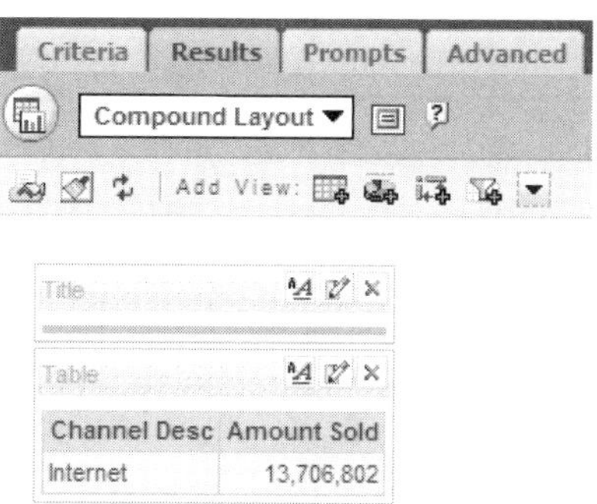

FIGURE 14-18 *The results when executed by BICHANNEL2 or BICHANNEL3*

5. Check the logs and verify the BI server sends a query to the database. BICHANNEL2's **VPD_TAG** session variable does not match the **VPD_TAG** attached to BICHANNEL1's cache entry.
6. Run the query as BICHANNEL3.
7. Check the logs and verify that BICHANNEL3 was able to use the cache entry generated by BICHANNEL2. BICHANNEL3's **VPD_TAG** session variable matches the **VPD_TAG** attached to BICHANNEL2's cache entry.

Now we'll clear all cache entries using the Manage Cache utility in the Administrator tool. Then, the log level needs to be raised for the three users we will use for our test: BICHANNEL1, BICHANNEL2, and BICHANNEL3. Log levels range from 0 to 7. Productions systems should run with a log level of 0 to avoid unnecessary overhead and should be raised for testing only for troubleshooting. The log level needs to be set to a value of at least 2 to see the physical queries that are issued to the database. If you are using the RPD with internal security, the log level for each user can be adjusted on the user property page in the RPD.

If we use any of the RPDs with externalized security, we need to set a session variable called **LOGLEVEL** equal to a value of 2 or higher for each user, to raise the log level for a user. We can temporarily turn on logging for a user easily by issuing the command **set variable LOGLEVEL=2;** in the Prefix box on the Advanced tab of an Answers request. You can see this in Figure 14-19.

To see the logs generated by each user, you will need to open a browser window and log in as an administrator (BIADMIN in the example RPDs). This allows you to get to the Manage Sessions screen from the Administration window. For each session, you can see the log files that are generated. Here is a snippet of the log file that BICHANNEL1 generated:

```
+++bichannel1:720000:720003:----2008/10/10 16:15:09
-------------------- Sending query to database named orcl (id: <<268155>>):
select T3192.CHANNEL_DESC as c1,
     sum(T3276.AMOUNT_SOLD) as c2,
     T3192.CHANNEL_ID as c3
from
     SH.CHANNELS T3192,
     SH.SALES T3276
where   ( T3192.CHANNEL_ID = T3276.CHANNEL_ID )
group by T3192.CHANNEL_DESC, T3192.CHANNEL_ID
order by c1
```

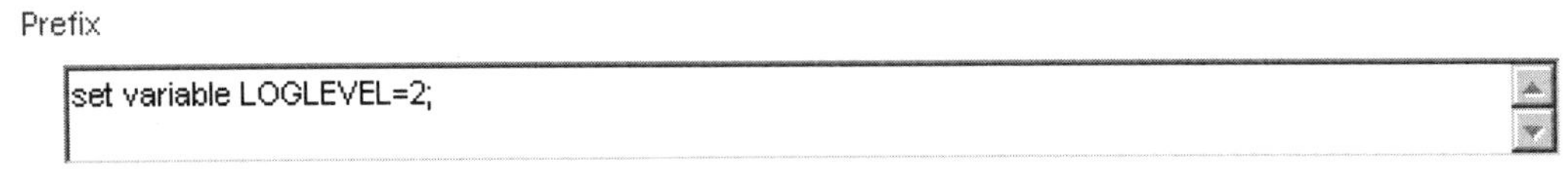

Prefix

set variable LOGLEVEL=2;

FIGURE 14-19 *Raise the user's log level by setting the LOGLEVEL variable on the Advanced tab in Answers.*

Next, here's BICHANNEL2's log file entry:

```
+++bichannel2:700000:700003:----2008/10/10 16:17:34
-------------------- Sending query to database named orcl (id: <<267859>>):
select T3192.CHANNEL_DESC as c1,
     sum(T3276.AMOUNT_SOLD) as c2,
     T3192.CHANNEL_ID as c3
from
     SH.CHANNELS T3192,
     SH.SALES T3276
where  ( T3192.CHANNEL_ID = T3276.CHANNEL_ID )
group by T3192.CHANNEL_DESC, T3192.CHANNEL_ID
order by c1
```

Finally, here's the log file for BICHANNEL3:

```
+++bichannel3:710000:710005:----2008/10/10 16:19:57
-------------------- Cache Hit on query:
Matching Query:  SET VARIABLE QUERY_SRC_CD='Report',LOGLEVEL=2; SELECT
Channels."Channel Desc" saw_0, "Sales Facts"."Amount Sold" saw_1 FROM SH ORDER
BY saw_0
Created by: bichannel2
```

To summarize, all three of these users ran the same report or logical query. User BICHANNEL2 was not able to use the BI server cache entry created by BICHANNEL1, because the two users' VPD tags do not match. However, user BICHANNEL3 is able to use the cache generated by BICHANNEL2 because they have the same VPD tags.

Deciding When to Use VPD or Oracle BI Row-level Security

At first glance, VPD and Oracle BI row-level security may seem a bit redundant. However, you might want to use both of these types of data security for several reasons. Following a basic good security practice, using both VPD and the BI filters, provides defense-in-depth for multiple layers of protection, as shown next:

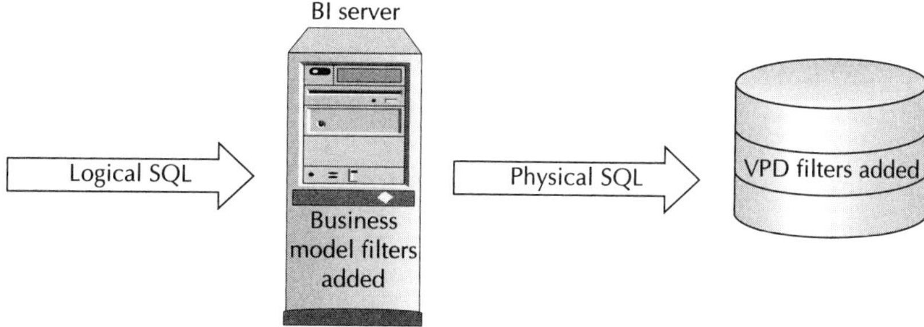

Applying security at the database (VPD) puts the security as close to the data as possible. This method's biggest advantage is that security is enforced no matter how the database is accessed: Oracle BI, SQL*Plus, a web application, or any other access method.

NOTE
VPD policies are applied to all applications that access the database. Oracle BI security filters are applied only to queries issued via Oracle BI.

Applying security at the BI layer provides its own benefits as well. For example, a business model filter might be applied to data that actually comes from multiple physical sources. In this case, the filters need to be defined only once: at the business model layer of the BI metadata. In addition, business model filters in Oracle BI allow VPD-like security to be added to any backend data source that Oracle BI supports (multidimensional data sources, relational database—both Oracle and non-Oracle, Access database, spreadsheets, and XML data files).

At this point, you may be wondering which of these two row-level security mechanisms you should implement. As we implied, they are not mutually exclusive. If, however, you find that one mechanism meets all your needs, it is unlikely that you would replicate the work in another layer.

So which should you implement? Here are a number of things you might consider:

- *Will the data be accessed by something other than the BI server applications?* It is absolutely critical that the data is secure at all times by all access mechanisms. Putting the security as close to the data as possible ensures that the security is not intentionally or inadvertently bypassed.
- *Will the backend database support row-level security?* Oracle BI allows for a number of backend databases. Using Oracle BI, you can apply row-level security no matter what the backend data source is (XML, Excel, Access, and so on).
- *How much work will be required to implement these features?* I've worked with some clients that already have the VPD policies in place and just needed to make sure that Oracle BI could respect those policies. Other clients are adding BI on top of existing systems where it would require a lot of work to add VPD. They tend to find Oracle BI business model filters easier to implement.
- *Who is responsible for the security?* If the DBA is responsible for the security, VPD would be the logical choice. If the BI application administrator is responsible for the database, it might be easier to implement security as part of the BI deployment.
- *What are the audit requirements?* Applying the security policy in the database using VPD allows all the security to be centralized. This not only makes it easier for auditors to inspect the security policies, but it also makes it easier to ensure that the policies are not bypassed or altered.
- *Does the data need to be protected from the administrators*? Oracle BI business model filters do not apply to administrators. If it is important to secure your data from administrators, database security options should be employed. In fact, this is the perfect situation for integrating Oracle BI with Database Vault.

In addition to these considerations is one more implementation consideration. Oracle BI business model filters and VPD polices are applied at different levels. VPD policies are applied at the object level. Every query issued by every user will be affected by the policy. If you want to exclude the policy from being applied to a user, that must be designed into the policy itself or you have to make use of the EXEMPT ACCESS POLICY privilege.

An Oracle BI business model filter is applied to an object at the group level. Business model filters will affect only members of the group where the filter is defined. Users that are not members of this group are completely unaffected by the business model filters attached to the group. You can, of course, make this group as large or as small as you want. You could design the group so that everyone is a member. In summary, VPD policies affect every user by default, whereas Oracle BI business model filters only affect the member of the group where the filter is defined.

In conclusion, Oracle VPD and Oracle BI business model filters are mechanisms used to enforce row-level security. Oracle BI is designed to work with VPD and even has a VPD-aware caching architecture. Oracle BI business model filters provide a quick and easy way to add row-level security to your BI environment, but the are applied only to data accessed through Oracle BI. In addition, they can be used with any supported Oracle BI data source. Oracle VPD has the distinct advantage of being closer to the data. VPD policies will be applied no matter how the data is being accessed.

NOTE
Oracle BI has been optimized to work with VPD.

Oracle BI and Database Vault

This section explains how the concepts introduced in Chapters 4 through 7 can be applied to the concepts discussed in this and the previous chapter. Chapter 6 focused on creating a security policy around a Sales Management application. This included transactional, batch, and reporting use cases. In this section, we focus primarily on the reporting use case, as Oracle BI is a reporting tool. However, as Oracle BI can be placed on top of transactional or warehouse data models, the other use cases in Chapter 6 can also be useful for someone attempting to integrate Oracle BI and Database Vault (DBV).

Factors and Oracle BI

Recall from Chapter 4 that factors are discrete security-related attributes that resolve to a specific value. In Oracle BI, factors can be used in number of ways. They might be used directly as part of the Oracle BI authentication and authorization process or to simplify the definition of Oracle BI session variables.

In Chapter 13, we used initialization blocks to authenticate and authorize users. Factor functions are ideal for initialization blocks. Using factor functions greatly simplifies the development of initialization blocks by allowing the Oracle BI administrator to reuse existing security code. This also allows you to put your security policies in a central place (the DBV), making it easier for auditors to verify compliance with security requirements. Finally, the definition of the factor function is protected by DBV. When the code used to retrieve security-related information is stored in an initialization block, any authorized BI server metadata developer can modify that code. Moving the code into a DBV-protected factor means that only authorized realm users will be able to modify the factor definition.

When using factors to establish Oracle BI session variables, remember that Oracle BI uses shared connection pools to retrieve database information. For example, if we wanted to use the factor User_Department_Name, as defined in Chapter 5, the initialization block query would simply be **select DVF.F$USER_DEPARTMENT_NAME FROM DUAL**. This factor function uses the database session to return the value of the factor. This will work only if we have properly conveyed the end user's identity to the database.

One way for Oracle BI to convey the end user's identity would be to use the technique discussed earlier in this chapter to set a client identifier. Another way to convey the end user's identity would be to use the technique discussed in Chapter 5 to set the CLIENT_IDENTIFIER factor. This technique discussed how to use the concepts of factor assignment and factor validation to set the client identifier in a more trusted manner. The example presented in Chapter 5 demonstrated how the factor could be assigned only from an application server that used a specific certificate as part of the database authentication process. In this case, the application server would be the BI server.

Before using the factor User_Department_Name with Oracle BI, we need to make one modification. The code that defined the factor called **hr.employee_utility.get_user_department_name** without any parameters. By default, this function uses **SYS_CONTEXT('USERENV', 'SESSION_USER')**) as input. But this will not work with the way Oracle BI uses connection pools, so the factor should call the **get_user_department_name** function passing the client identifier as input. In this case the factor definition would look like this:

```
dbms_macadm.create_factor(
factor_name => 'User_Department_Name' ,
factor_type_name => 'User',
description =>
'The name of the department the current user works in.',
rule_set_name => NULL ,
get_expr =>
'hr.employee_utility.get_user_department_name(
     sys_context(''USERENV'',''CLIENT_IDENTIFIER''))',
validate_expr => null,
identify_by => dbms_macutl.g_identify_by_method,
labeled_by => dbms_macutl.g_labeled_by_self,
eval_options => dbms_macutl.g_eval_on_access,
audit_options => dbms_macutl.g_audit_on_get_error,
fail_options => dbms_macutl.g_fail_with_message);
```

To set the **DEPARTMENT_NAME** session variable, we would use an initialization block to issue the query **select DVF.F$USER_DEPARTMENT_NAME FROM DUAL** via a connection pool. This connection pool would have a logon script that calls **dvsys.set_factor('Client_Identifier', ':USER')**. Actually, to use the procedure **dvsys.set_factor** as part of a logon script, it would need to be wrapped in a function just as we did with **dbms_session.set_identifier** earlier in the chapter. The logon script would ensure that the end user's identity is properly conveyed to the database before attempting to retrieve the department name factor. Once the Oracle BI session variable **DEPARTMENT_NAME** is set, it could be used as a part of a business model filter to appropriately limit the data the end user can see.

Realms and Oracle BI

In designing the examples included at www.OraclePressBooks.com, we took care to follow the principles discussed in Chapter 1. In particular, if you examine the setup scripts, you will find objects owner accounts and user access accounts.

Let's quickly review the database accounts used in the examples. For the application data, the object owner accounts used are SH and BI_TABLES, while the user access account is BI_SELECT. Earlier in the chapter we saw how every end user connected via a shared connection pool (BI_SELECT) to retrieve information from the database. We also examined how to convey the end user's identity to the database for the purposes of identification and auditing. A similar setup was used for the security-related information used in the examples. The object owner accounts are BI_SECURITY_TABLES and BI_USAGE_TRACKING and the user access account is BI_SECURITY_SELECT.

The next thing you will notice is that in just the first two setup scripts, it took 25 **grant** commands to set up the user access accounts properly, even for such a simple example. This is where the concept of DBV realms becomes very useful. In the security setup for these examples, we have effectively described two realms. All the application-related objects, all objects owned by SH and BI_TABLES, could be placed in one realm. All security-related objects, all objects owned by BI_SECURITY_TABLES and BI_USAGE_TRACKING, could be placed in another realm. The user access accounts would be added as realm participants. Chapter 5 gives examples of how to set up these realms and add objects and participants to the realm.

Without DBV protections, it is actually quite easy to circumvent our previous BI security setup. All it takes is a database user with the SELECT ANY privilege to bypass all the work we put into designing our architecture. Putting these objects in a realm fixes this problem by immediately controlling access via ANY privileges. In addition, the management of access to objects can be eased by granting the appropriate realm participant SELECT ANY TABLE without worrying about granting too many privileges to the participants. Once DBV is installed and configured, accounts with system ANY privileges can no longer access or manipulate objects protected by the realm.

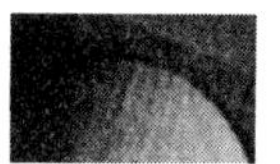

TIP

The benefit of placing the objects in realms is that it immediately and transparently protects all the BI data and security-related BI objects from other privileged database users.

Recall that more than just tables and views can be added to the realm. This is an important point. Another object to add to the realm would be the VPD policy; this ensures that the security policy protecting the data is also secured. The BI_ACCESS role used in the example could also be added to the realm; this would ensure that this role could be granted only by the accounts or roles authorized as owners of the realm.

Auditing

The caching capabilities of Oracle BI introduce some interesting security questions, and the same is true with auditing. It might seem like the hardest part of auditing when using Oracle BI would be capturing the end user's identity from within the database as the user has connected via a shared connection pool. Once the database knows who is running the query, it should be a simple matter of enabling database auditing.

As you know, caching exists to speed performance, and it does this by eliminating redundant work. In our examples, this means redundant queries. The consequence is that when the caching feature of Oracle BI is enabled, it is possible that queries will sometimes be satisfied without even accessing the database. In such cases, there is nothing to audit in the database, because the database has done no work. This leaves three options.

First, realize the limitation and understand that database auditing will work only when queries are actually sent to the database. This is not a bad option, however, an audit record of the first query (meaning the query that generated the cache entry) will exist, so it's not as if data can be viewed without your knowledge—you simply won't know everyone who looked at it.

Second, turn off caching and force all queries to the database. This will ensure auditing for all access by all users all the time but negates any performance enhancements to the application as well as the benefits of allowing the database to do other work instead of returning these (redundant) queries.

Third, combine the auditing that the BI server does with the auditing that the database does. This option, depicted in the following illustration, is discussed in the next two sections.

Auditing

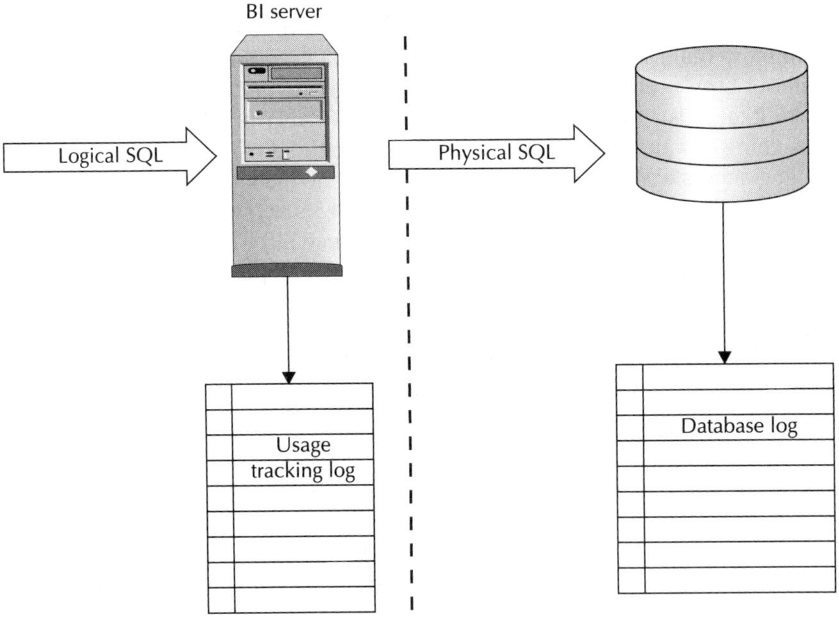

Usage Tracking

The usage tracking feature of the Oracle BI enables you to capture information about your environment that can be used for a variety of purposes:

- **Tracking actual performance data** Often performance data is conveyed through vague references to dashboards being slow. Usage tracking provides actual facts on how long queries take, where the time is being spent (database or BI server), and cache hit information. Not only can this provide useful performance information, but it can help you figure out what queries need to be tuned.

- **Tracking who is doing what from a security perspective** Usage tracking will record every logical SQL statement issued by a user. *This is the logical SQL issued against the BI server and not the physical SQL sent to the database.* The only place to find the physical SQL is in the BI server query logs or in the database audit logs.
- **Tracking who is doing what from a content perspective** Usage tracking records which subject areas and dashboard pages are being queried. You can see the most commonly used subject areas and dashboards. This can be useful in figuring out where development resources should be focused.

Usage tracking is documented in the Server Administration Guide of the Oracle BI Documentation Library (www.oracle.com/technology/documentation/bi_ee.html). The content captured in usage tracking is very well documented. The following steps represent a few additional notes on configuring usage tracking:

1. Create the usage tracking table. The SAACCT.*.sql script (use the one appropriate for your database) is located in the OracleBI_HOME/server/schema directory. This directory also contains scripts for setting up Oracle Delivers and Oracle BI Marketing.
2. Create a time dimension. The scripts for this are located in the OracleBI_HOME/server/Sample/usagetracking/SQL_Server_Time directory. Note that scripts are included for multiple databases in this directory and not just SQL Server. This will create and populate two tables: One table includes date information that extends from year down to the day. The other table is a dimension that includes all minutes in a 24-hour period.
3. Merge the usage tracking repository with your production repository. The usage tracking RPD can be found in the OracleBI_HOME/server/Sample/usagetracking directory.
4. Merge the usage tracking web catalog with your production web catalog. The usage tracking web catalog is found in the same location as the usage tracking RPD.
5. Configure the BI server to use usage tracking. This configuration change is done in the NQSConfig.ini file. An example of how to configure this is included in the comments of your default configuration file.

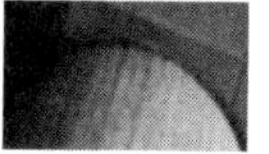

NOTE
Two important points about using usage tracking: First, this information is useful as a security tool. As such, read and write access to this information should be restricted to those with a need to know. Second, the usage tracking table will grow quite rapidly. You will need to monitor this and steps will need to be taken to manage the size of this table (such as partitions, archiving).

Database Auditing

The Oracle database has very robust auditing capabilities. When used properly, organizations have gleaned tremendous information about who is getting access to what, from where, when, and how. This section provides some basic insight into how Oracle database auditing can be used in conjunction with Oracle BI. Three basic steps are involved:

1. Verify that database auditing is enabled. Validating that the database is set up to audit is as simple as checking the value for the **AUDIT_TRAIL** parameter. The appendix of this book covers the details on how to check whether auditing is enabled and how to enable

it. The examples provided on the Web have the **AUDIT_TRAIL** set to **DB_EXTENDED** so that the physical SQL statements are captured.

2. Start auditing. Auditing can be done in various ways, and two possibilities work well for Oracle BI. You could audit all select statements on a specific table, or you could audit all queries issued by a specific user (the shared connection pool user in this case).
3. Convey the end user's identity to the database, as described earlier in this chapter.

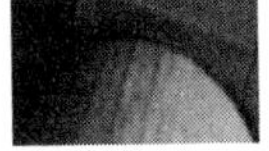

NOTE
Database auditing is transparent to Oracle BI as well as to any application. The database will audit any SQL statement that the BI server sends to the database that matches the audit criteria.

It's worth mentioning again that if the BI server is caching, not every user query will be sent to the database. If the BI server cache can satisfy the user query, it will do so without bothering the database. To get a complete picture of what the end user is accessing, you should enable both usage tracking and database auditing, as discussed next.

Combining Usage Tracking and Database Auditing

Usage tracking and database auditing are by default two completely independent features. You can enable one or both of them and they act independently of one another. However, as mentioned, to get a complete view of what a user is doing, you can use both features simultaneously and combine the output.

The easiest way to combine this data is to expose the database audit trail via Oracle BI. The database audit trail can be modeled in the BI server metadata just like any source. This can then be combined with the usage tracking metadata.

Combining data sources with Oracle BI can be done in a number of different ways. You could combine the two data sources in the business model layer of the BI server metadata. This would allow the BI server to present these two data sources as a single subject area. This technique requires a clear means of joining the data from the two different sources. Another way to combine multiple data sources is to merge the data at the answers request or dashboard level. Using this method, data from two or more sources could be displayed together on one dashboard page. Dashboard prompts can be used to link the information from the different sources.

In the examples provided on the Web, usage tracking and the database audit trail were modeled as two separate subject areas. The information was then merged on the dashboard by including reports from both subject areas, filtered by the same prompt. Figure 14-20 shows usage tracking and database audit information for user BIPRODUCT1.

Usage tracking and the database audit trail were modeled separately and combined at the dashboard layer for two reasons. First, this satisfies the requirement of being able to analyze both usage tracking and database audit information at the same time. To make this work, the column being filtered by the dashboard prompt must be named the same in each subject area. In this example, the dashboard prompt is filtering the column User Name. In the BI server metadata, the column User Name maps to the physical column LOGON in the usage tracking schema and CLIENT_ID in the database audit trail.

The second reason for modeling this as two subject areas is that modeling these two data sources as a single subject area could prove challenging for the following reasons:

- Not every logical SQL statement logged in usage tracking will generate a physical SQL statement captured in the database audit trail.

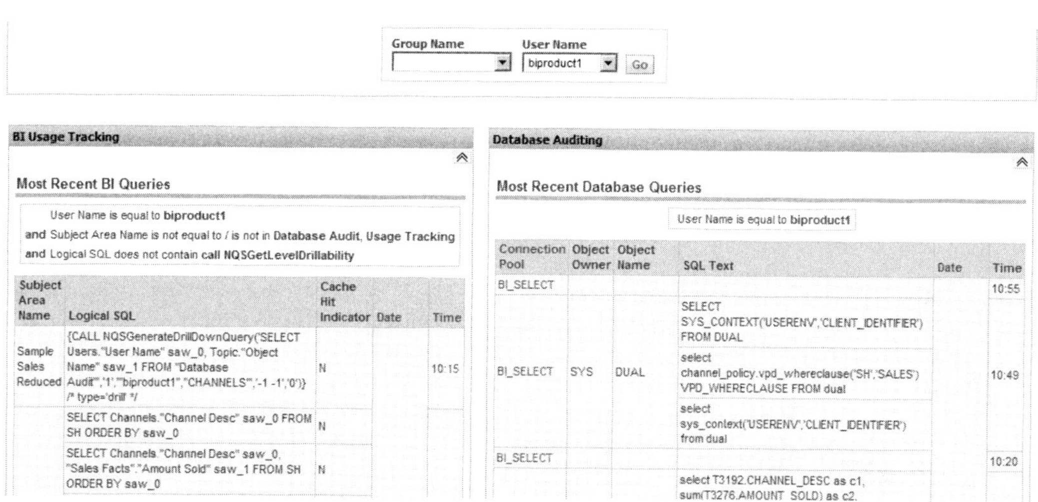

FIGURE 14-20 *Usage tracking and database audit information combined on a single dashboard*

- One logical SQL statement logged in usage tracking may generate multiple physical SQL statements in the database audit trail (multi-pass SQL, query fragmentation, or aggregate navigation).
- Usage tracking records access to the logical table accessed in the subject area and the database audit trail records access to physical tables in the database. To join these, it would be necessary to capture the relationship between logical tables in subject areas and physical tables in the database.

In conclusion, to get a complete audit record, you need to use a combination of Oracle BI Usage Tracking and the Oracle Database Auditing. Usage tracking records what is accessed at the logical level and database auditing captures what is accessed at the database level.

BI Features with Security Implications

A number of features of Oracle BI should be examined from a security perspective. Using these features does not imply a security risk. It is important that you understand exactly what each feature does and what it means from a security perspective.

Managing access to features is done via the web using the Manage Privileges screen on the Administration page. The first section of this screen allows you to control access to major applications within the suite. Just as you would with any other system, you turn off access to anything that is not explicitly required. Most features are fairly self-explanatory. Features requiring special attention are covered here.

Default Privileges

As is the case with any product, you should carefully examine the default security setup upon installation. In both the BI server and the presentation server, there are a number of things granted to Everyone. As mentioned, these permissions should be carefully analyzed to see if everyone really needs that functionality. As we go through the following sections, we will discuss many of these features in detail. Here are a few changes that you should consider making immediately:

- Revoke access to products from Everyone and grant access only when needed. By default, everyone has access to Oracle Answers, Oracle Delivers, Oracle BI Publisher, and Oracle Disconnected Analytics.
- Revoke access to the Advanced tab in Oracle Answers.
- Revoke the ability to issue direct database requests.

You can also make a configuration change at the BI server to help with appropriately setting default privileges. You can control the default privileges set on presentation catalogs in the RPD. This is done by setting the configuration option titled **DEFAULT_PRIVILEGES**. This parameter can be set to **NONE** or **READ**. By default, it is set to **READ**. When in this mode, each new presentation catalog is readable by everyone by default. To change this behavior, set the value to **NONE**.

Act as Proxy

Oracle BI can let users run a request on behalf of someone else. This feature is designed primary for two reasons. First, it allows and end user to delegate functionality to someone else. For example, a manager might be going on vacation and wants someone else to be able to run her reports while she is gone. The second possible use is for developer or administrators to test running reports using someone else's permissions.

To keep things clear in this section, we will refer to the user running reports for someone else as the "proxy user." We will refer to the impersonated user as the "target user" (this is the same notation used in the documentation). In this section, three topics are covered:

- The actual permissions that the proxy user gets when running reports for someone else
- The steps required to set up and maintain this feature
- The impact on usage tracking, database logs, and database security

A Proxy User's Permissions

When a proxy user requests that things are "run as" the target user, the proxy user gets one of two possible sets of privileges: full or restricted. This is called the proxy level. With restricted proxy level, the proxy user gets read access to everything the target user can see but does not get the privileges of the proxy user.

Let's assume that a manager has granted restricted proxy permissions to a subordinate. The employee can now see all the reports and data that the manager can see. However, the employee will still maintain his normal privileges. So if the manager had access to Oracle Dashboards and Oracle Delivers and the employee had access only to Oracle Dashboards, the employee will still be able to run only Oracle Dashboards.

On the other hand, if the manager had granted full proxy permissions, the employee would get all of the manager's permissions and privileges. If a proxy level is not specified, it is set to restricted by default.

Enabling Act as Proxy Functionality

Several steps are required to set up this functionality. First, you need to set up the database infrastructure to support it. Oracle BI does not contain the facilities for storing the allowed proxy users and the associated proxy levels. This must be stored and maintained in a database table external to Oracle BI. The table must contain three columns: PROXYID, TARGETID, and PROXYLEVEL. Note that since this table dictates the proxy arrangement—that is, which user can assume privileges of which other user—you need to ensure tight security controls on this table.

Next you need to modify the BI server. Two session variables must be set: **PROXY** and **PROXYLEVEL**. When you create these variables, you will get a notification that these variables have special purposes. This is exactly what they were designed for. Both of these variables are considered security-sensitive by default, meaning their values cannot be modified from the Web even if you forget to mark the Security Sensitive checkbox. Here is a sample initialization block for **PROXY**:

```
SELECT targetid
FROM bi_proxy.Proxies
WHERE 'VALUEOF(NQ_SESSION.RUNAS)'=targetid
  AND ':USER'=proxyId
```

Here is a sample initialization block for **PROXYLEVEL**:

```
SELECT proxylevel
FROM bi_proxy.Proxies
WHERE 'VALUEOF(NQ_SESSION.RUNAS)'=targetid
  AND ':USER'=proxyId
```

Notice the use of the session variable **RUNAS**. This will get defined and populated by the presentation server when the user initiates the Run As process from the settings menu on the Web.

Lastly, you need to modify the presentation server. To do this, you first create an XML file in the $OracleBI_HOME\web\msgdb\customMessages folder. You can call the file anything you want. This file defines what will show up in the Run As screen for the given user, and it needs to contain the following information:

```
<?xml version="1.0" encoding="utf-8" ?>
<WebMessageTables xmlns:sawm="com.siebel.analytics.web.messageSystem">
  <WebMessageTable system="SecurityTemplates" table="Messages">
       <WebMessage name="LogonParamSQLTemplate">
              <XML>
              <logonParam name="RUNAS">
                   <getValues>EXECUTE PHYSICAL CONNECTION POOL
                    "Security Information".bi_security_select
                    select targetid
                    from bi_proxy.proxies where proxyid='@{USERID}'
                  </getValues>
                   <verifyValue> EXECUTE PHYSICAL CONNECTION POOL
                     "Security Information".bi_security_select
                     select targetid
                     from bi_proxy.proxies where proxyid='@{USERID}'
                     and targetid='@{VALUE}'
                   </verifyValue>
                   <getDelegateUsers>EXECUTE PHYSICAL CONNECTION POOL
                    "Security Information".bi_security_select
                     select proxyid, PROXYLEVEL
                     from bi_proxy.proxies where targetid='@{USERID}'
                    </getDelegateUsers>
              </logonParam>
```

```
            </XML>
        </WebMessage>
        </WebMessageTable>
</WebMessageTables>
```

Notice a couple of interesting things in this file. First is the name of the web message: LogonParamSQLTemplate. This will be referenced in the instanceconfig.xml file shortly. Second, notice that the session variable title **RUNAS** is defined and will be populated with the **targetid** value that the user selects. Next, modify the instanceconfig.xml file so that this custom web message will be loaded. Add the following lines:

```
<LogonParam>
  <TemplateMessageName>LogonParamSQLTemplate</TemplateMessageName>
  <MaxValues>100</MaxValues>
</LogonParam>
```

MaxValues refers to the maximum number of users that will be shown in the drop-down list.

The final step is to make sure that you enable the Web privilege that allows a user or group of users to use the Act as Proxy functionality. By default, no one is allowed this privilege. As you can see from Figures 14-21 and 14-22, once the Web privilege is enabled, you will get a new option on the settings menu and a list of Act As users will be populated from the database table you created.

The examples shown in this section are included on the Downloads page at www.OraclePressBooks.com. See the section in the appendix titled "Internal Authentication with Act As Proxy Enabled" for information on using this example.

Act as Proxy Impact on Security

To help you understand the implications of using this feature, let's use some of the techniques developed in Chapter 13 to explore what happens when a user acts as another user.

First, you inspect the **USER** and **GROUP** session variables and notice that they actually change to the target user and the target user's groups. This is easily accomplished using the Utilities Dashboard in the examples included on the Web. This has a major impact on all things security related. In addition, all session variables are repopulated as though the target user had logged onto the system. This means all business model filters will now be applied as if the target user were actually logged onto the system.

Recall that we set the Client Identifier in the connection pool DB session to convey that the end user's identity to the database will send the target ID only to the database. The database will then apply VPD policies for the target ID, and all audit trails will reference only the target user. This is a good thing, because all security policies, both BI server–enforced and database-enforced, are being applied to the target user. It is worth noting that, from the database's perspective,

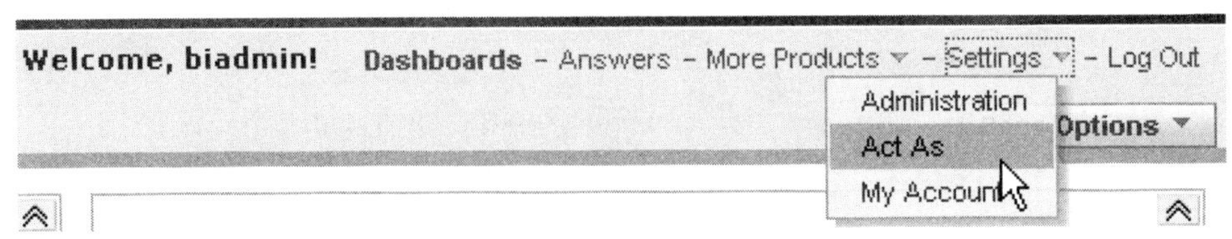

FIGURE 14-21 *Act As Proxy functionality enabled*

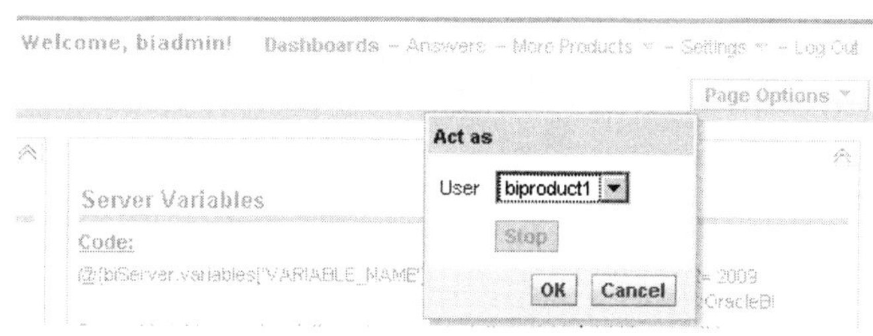

FIGURE 14-22 *The user biadmin running reports as the user biproduct1*

everything was done by the target user. It does not know that a proxy user is actually issuing queries on behalf of the target user.

In contrast, the BI server does record the fact that the Act As Proxy functionality is being used. If you take a look at the usage tracking, you will notice that the proxy user value is saved in the USER_NAME physical column and the target user value is saved in the RUNAS_USER_NAME physical column. This is very useful because it shows the true picture of what happened: the proxy user ran the query acting as the target user. Figure 14-23 shows both the proxy user and the target user recorded in the usage tracking logs after running the examples found at www.OraclePressBooks.com. The presentation layer column User Name corresponds to the physical column USER_NAME, and the presentation layer column Impersonated User corresponds to the physical column RUNAS_USER_NAME.

Direct Database Requests

The basic architecture of Oracle BI is designed to push all requests through the BI server and leverage the metadata defined there. However, it is possible to make direct database requests. This is a feature that is disabled by default and should be evaluated very carefully before being enabled. Direct database requests allow the user to enter a physical SQL statement via the Web. This statement is then sent directly to the database for execution.

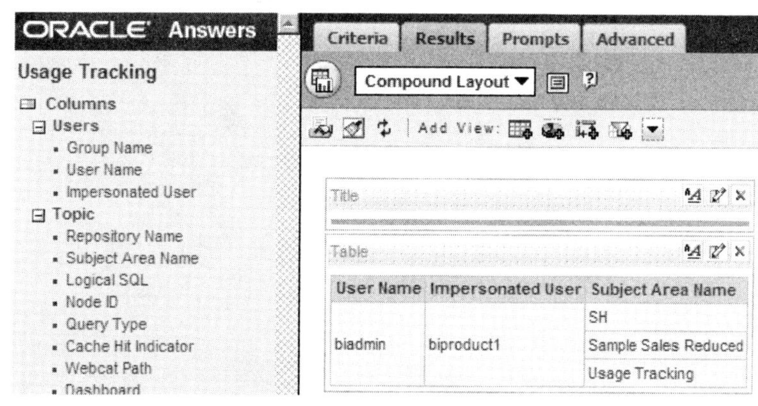

FIGURE 14-23 *Proxy and target user shown in usage tracking*

Before we discuss the steps required to enable or disable direct database requests, it is worth examining the impact of doing so. Forcing the query through the BI server does a number of things:

- Joins the tables as defined in the metadata
- Groups and aggregates the data as defined in the metadata
- Applies appropriate row- and column-level security as defined in the metadata

Allowing the user to issue direct database requests lets the user bypass all security and business rules that have been defined in the BI server metadata.

Three major components must be enabled before a direct database request can be issued:

- The database definition in the BI server metadata must allow direct database requests.
- The presentation server privilege Edit Direct Database Requests must be enabled.
- The presentation server privilege Execute Direct Database Requests must be enabled.

You can configure a database to allow direct database requests in the BI server metadata in two ways: You can check the Allow Direct Database Requests By Default checkbox, as shown in Figure 14-24, to enable direct database requests for all users against that database. Or you can enable direct database requests in the BI server metadata for a specific group. As shown in Figure 14-25, you do this in the Query Limits tab of the Group Permissions dialog box in the Administrator tool. For each group and database, you can specify whether direct database requests are ignored or allowed.

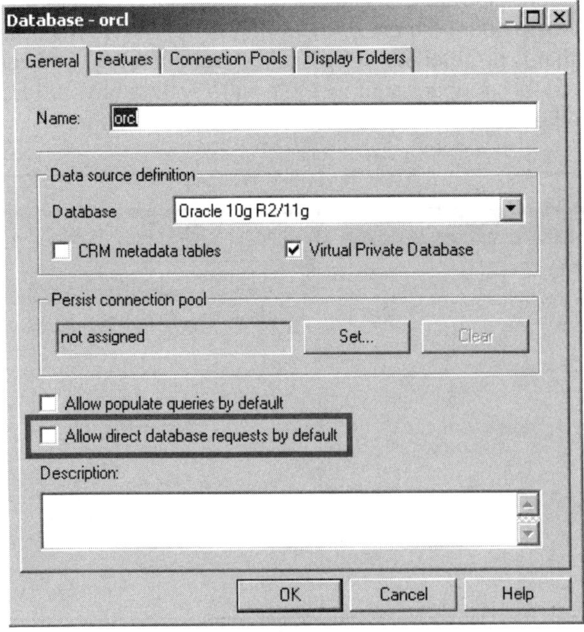

FIGURE 14-24 *Enabling direct database requests for all users*

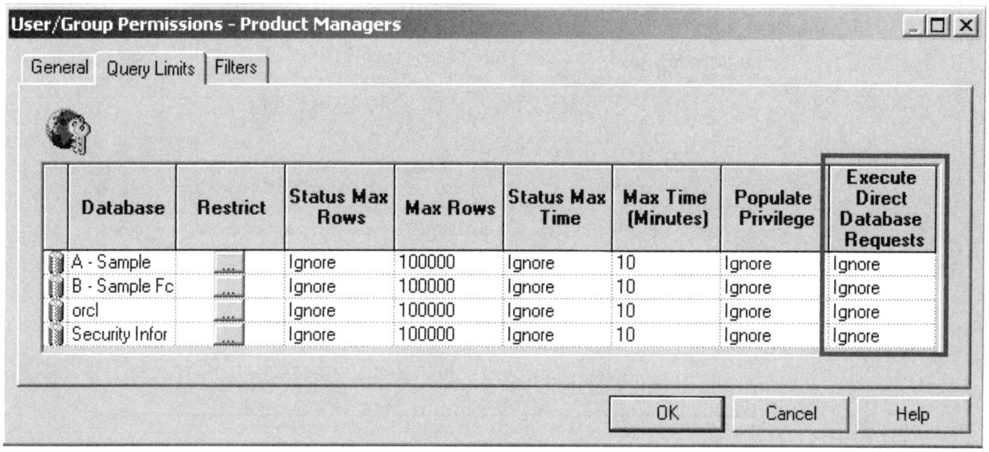

User/Group Permissions - Product Managers

General | Query Limits | Filters

Database	Restrict	Status Max Rows	Max Rows	Status Max Time	Max Time (Minutes)	Populate Privilege	Execute Direct Database Requests
A - Sample	...	Ignore	100000	Ignore	10	Ignore	Ignore
B - Sample Fc	...	Ignore	100000	Ignore	10	Ignore	Ignore
orcl	...	Ignore	100000	Ignore	10	Ignore	Ignore
Security Infor	...	Ignore	100000	Ignore	10	Ignore	Ignore

OK | Cancel | Help

FIGURE 14-25 *Enabling direct database requests by group*

After direct database requests are enabled in the RPD, two presentation server permissions must be enabled: a permission allowing users to edit or create direct database requests and a permission allowing users to execute answers requests based on direct database requests. These permissions are located under the Answers section on the Manage Privileges web page, as shown in Figure 14-26.

At the beginning of this section, the reasons for avoiding direct database requests were presented. At some time, you may need to use this feature, and the ability to separate the privileges associated with editing and executing direct database requests is very useful. As shown in Figure 14-26, Presentation Server Administrators are the only users allowed to create or edit a

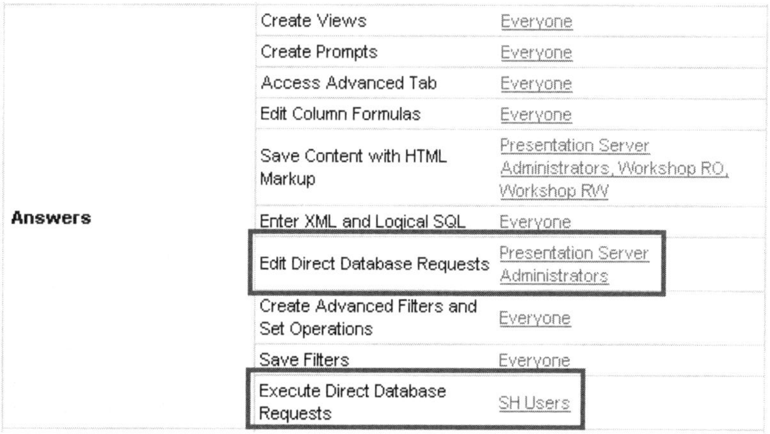

Answers	Create Views	Everyone
	Create Prompts	Everyone
	Access Advanced Tab	Everyone
	Edit Column Formulas	Everyone
	Save Content with HTML Markup	Presentation Server Administrators, Workshop RO, Workshop RW
	Enter XML and Logical SQL	Everyone
	Edit Direct Database Requests	Presentation Server Administrators
	Create Advanced Filters and Set Operations	Everyone
	Save Filters	Everyone
	Execute Direct Database Requests	SH Users

FIGURE 14-26 *Enabling direct database requests in the presentation server*

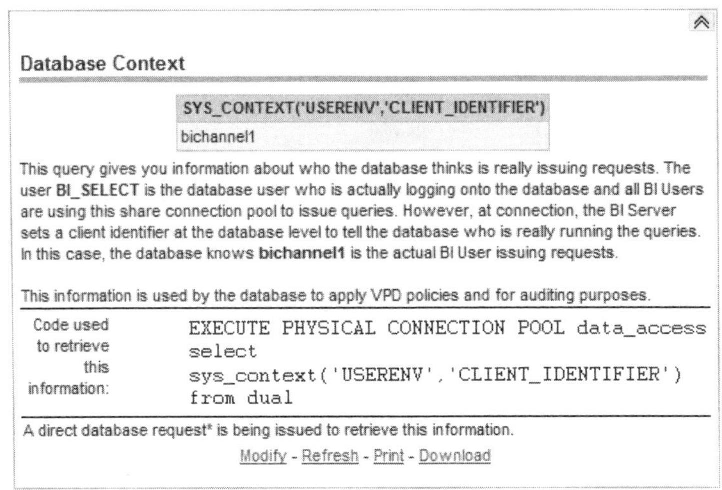

FIGURE 14-27 *An example of a direct database request*

direct database request, and member of the SH Users group are the only users allowed to execute the request. This allows the members of SH Users to run direct database requests without granting them permission to create these types of requests. This segregation of duties allows for a very controlled use of the privilege.

An example of a direct database request is included in the dashboards found on the Downloads page at www.OraclePressBooks.com. The Channel Managers tab of the SH dashboard has two requests that are based on direct database requests. Figure 14-27 shows one of these requests. This tab was designed to show data with VPD policies being enforced. As you saw earlier in the chapter, an important step is conveying the end user's identity to the database. In this example, to verify that the database was aware of the true end user, I wanted the BI Server to issue the query **select syscontext('USERENV','CLIENT_IDENTIFIER') from dual**.

In summary, the ability to execute a direct database request must first be enabled at the database level inside the RPD. Then, at the presentation server, users must be granted permission to edit or execute direct database requests. These permissions should be enabled with great care, because you are opening additional access to your backend data sources.

Advanced Tab

When you decide to give users access to Oracle Answers, you should evaluate several features within Answers, including the ability to set system-wide formats for columns. The general user should not have the ability to do this, because it would affect the look and feel of all reports. By default, only Presentation Server Administrators are granted this permission.

Another Answers feature that you should evaluate is ability to use the Advanced tab. By default, this tab is available to any user that has access to Answers. This should be changed. Only Presentation Server Administrators and advanced developers should have access to this tab. One reason for turning off access to the Advanced tab for general ad hoc query users is that they probably don't need it and it might confuse them. Another reason is because you can perform operations that the general user should not be allowed to do.

The Advanced tab contains the following capabilities:

- Directly edit the XML definition of a report.
- Directly edit the logical SQL of the report.
- Bypass the presentation server cache.
- Bypass the BI server cache. The BI server cache can be bypassed by including the statement **set variable DISABLE_CACHE_HIT=1;** in the Prefix box on the Advanced tab.
- Turn on logging. This is also very useful for developers and administrators and is discussed in the "Testing the VPD Example" section.
- Set session variables values.

Session variable values can be set using the **set variable** command in the Prefix box on the Advanced tab. Session variables are often used as security measures. We used them in this chapter to create business model filters and limit data returned to users. The ability to override the values of these session variables could possibly provide a means of overriding these security settings. To prevent the end user from changing the value of a session variable, it must be marked as security sensitive during the definition of the session variable.

Direct Access to the BI Server

The BI server presents itself as a database. It is not a database, however, because it does not actually store any data, and it is not possible to perform transactions against it. You can, however, query it like a database. JDBC and ODBC drivers are provided with Oracle BI and can be used to query the BI server directly.

Just as it is common to restrict direct access to your database and force general user interaction with the database through an application layer, you may consider restricting direct access to the BI server. You can restrict direct access to the BI server by restricting network access to the BI server listening port (default value of 9703) using standard firewall techniques. The components that require direct BI server access are the presentation server, the scheduler service, BI Publisher, and Hyperion Provider Services (if you want to use SmartView against the BI server).

To understand why you might want to limit direct access to the BI server, consider how a user might attempt to access the BI server directly. First, JDBC and ODBC drivers are shipped with the BI server, so any Java- and ODBC-based application such as Access or Excel could communicate with the BI server. In addition, the BI Administration tool makes direct access to the BI server and can manipulate the metadata. It is not uncommon for organizations to lock down direct access to the BI server to prohibit access to the BI server via the Administration tool. This is actually more of a configuration management restriction to prevent developers from making non-tested metadata manipulations to production servers.

Lastly, a command-line interface to the BI Server, nqCmd.exe, can be thought of as SQL*Plus for the BI server. It is most commonly used for running scripts to manage BI server cache or for managing aggregates defined by the Aggregate Persistence Wizard. Just as you might limit who has access to SQL*Plus in your organization, you should consider limiting access to nqCmd.exe.

We have focused on restricting direct access to the BI server. Most users will communicate with the BI server via some type of application layer: the presentation server, BI Publisher, or some custom application. One important thing to remember is that even if people do gain direct access to the BI server, all security rules still apply and usage tracking will still be enforced. Strong authentication and authorization policies are going to be your best means of protecting access to data. Preventing direct access to the BI server just adds one more layer of defense against unauthorized data access.

Web Services Access

Oracle BI includes a complete set of Web Services that include the ability to create a session, query the catalog, check permissions, modify the catalog, run reports, and schedule iBots. The ability to use the Web Services is controlled with a privilege called SOAP.

The ability to make web services calls to Oracle BI is controlled with this privilege. If you are not planning on using Web Services, you might be tempted to turn this feature off. However, many other features also use these Web Services, including the BI Office plug-in, BI Publisher (when using Answers as a data source), and the Oracle Business Indicators iPhone application. Turning off the ability to use Web Services will prevent you from using these applications.

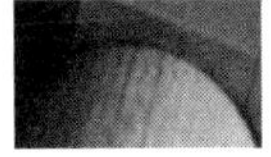

CAUTION
Turning off access to Oracle BI Web Services will impact other components of Oracle BI, including the Oracle BI Office plug-in, Oracle BI Publisher, and the Oracle Business Indicators iPhone application.

Summary

Let's summarize what you've learned so far with a scenario: Assume we are logging into Oracle BI. In Chapter 13, we covered all of the details of what happens during the login process. So now we have logged onto Oracle BI and are assigned to appropriate RPD groups and web catalog groups. Now we have access to a collection of dashboards, reports, iBots, and BI Publisher reports. All these components require the appropriate permissions for both the report definition and the data that will be presented through the report.

Our ability to access the report definition is determined by web catalog security. We may have been granted access to objects directly, or one of the groups of which we are a member might have been granted access to a folder of web catalog content. We may also have been granted any of the following permissions: Change/Delete, Full Control, No Access, or Read.

Assuming we have the appropriate access to the report definition, the next step is to ensure that we have access to the data that will be presented through the report. Security for the data can be applied at the BI server or at the database. At the BI server, coarse access to the data is controlled at the subject area level. Based on our RPD group membership, we will have read access to certain subject areas. At a more granular level, row- or column-level security may have been applied. The BI server implements row-level security via a feature called Business Model Filters. Column-level security is very easy to implement and several tools are provided to help make sure reports run correctly when column-level security is applied.

For security to be applied at the database level, the database must know who we are. For performance and ease of maintenance reasons, Oracle BI uses connection pools when connecting to the database. Connection scripts in the connection pool definition make it possible to convey the end user's identity to the database. For the Oracle database, the easiest way to do this is to set a client identifier in the connection script. For databases using Database Vault, factors should be set as part of this connection script. In either case, once the database knows our identity, database security and auditing can be leveraged.

This chapter covered a variety of Oracle BI features that require some considerations from a security perspective. One such feature is the sharable cache of Oracle BI. We explored the ability to make the cache aware of database security policies. We also recognized that if queries are being satisfied by cache, they will not get logged by database auditing procedures. Other topics included running reports as another user, executing direct database requests, and accessing web services in Oracle BI.

A successful implementation of Oracle BI should make it much easier for users to access data sources and, hopefully, increase the number and type of users with access to organizational information. The notion of providing enterprise-level, self-service BI can be your impetus to reevaluate existing security policies. The design and implementation stages of Oracle BI are the easiest times to implement new security policies. Chapters 13 and 14 identified several areas worthy of your attention and provided you with the necessary skills to put together an effective security plan for your Oracle BI implementation.

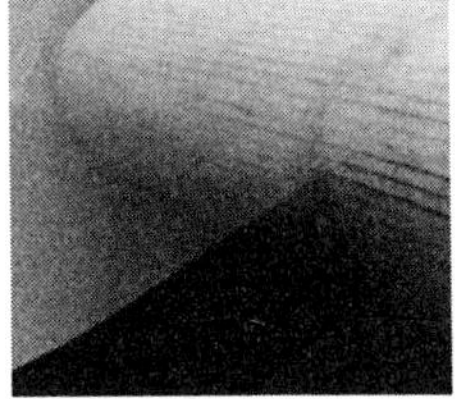

APPENDIX

Using the Oracle BI Examples

set of Oracle BI examples are provided with this book to help you set up various security configurations and to reinforce concepts discussed in Chapters 13 and 14. These examples are available on the Downloads page at www.OraclePressBooks .com. Specifically, these examples help with the concepts of variables, dynamic group membership, various authentication schemes, business model filters, Virtual Private Database (VPD) integration, and database auditing. They consist of a web catalog (with several dashboards and reports) and several RPDs. The web catalog works with each of the provided RPDs. Each RPD focuses on a different method of authentication or security feature. This appendix gives an overview of each example provided, notes on how to set up each example, and notes on interesting features that should be observed in each example.

In each example, I tried to minimize the amount of work necessary to maintain users and groups. User-group information is needed for authorization purposes, usage tracking, and SA System. The concept in every example is to have one place where you manage users and groups and then find a way that authorization, usage tracking, and SA System can all use that information. For example, when you're setting up database authentication, all users, groups, and user-to-group memberships are created in the database using database users and roles. Then, views based on the database dictionary are used for authorization, usage tracking, and SA System. This allows the information to be managed in one place and to be instantly available for use in several areas.

Users and Groups

Table A-1 lists the groups that are used in the examples. Depending on the RPD, these groups are implemented in different fashions (internal RPD groups, rows in a database tables, database groups, or LDAP groups).

Several more XMLP_* groups should also be used, in whichever authentication mode you choose. XMLP_ADMIN and XMLP_DEVELOPER were the only BI Publisher groups used in the examples. Refer to the BI Publisher documentation for a detailed list of the rest of the XMLP_* groups.

Table A-2 shows the users included in these examples. The password for each user is the same as the username. The Administrator account is the standard RPD Administrator account that

Group Name	Group Type	Description
Administrators	Group	BI Server Administrators
Presentation Server Administrators	Web group	Web Catalog Administrator
SH Users	Group and web group	Sales History BI User
Product Managers	Group	Sales History product managers; business model filters applied to members of this group
XMLP_ADMIN	Group	Required BI Publisher group
XMLP_DEVELOPER	Group	Required BI Publisher group

TABLE A-1 *The BI Groups Used in the Examples*

Username	Group Membership	Description
Administrator	Administrators, Presentation Server Administrators, XMLP_ADMIN	The internal Administrator account
biadmin	Administrators, Presentation Server Administrators, XMLP_ADMIN	The administrator for Oracle BI (BI Server, Presentation Server, BI Publisher, Delivers)
biwebadmin	Presentation Server Administrator	Full administrative privileges on the Presentation Server only
bishuser	SH Users, XMLP_DEVELOPER	Normal user allowed to use the SH subject area; user can also developer new reports in BI Publisher
biproduct1	SH Users, Product Managers	Business model filters limit user to game consoles; restrictions driven by rows in PRODUCT_MANAGERS table
biproduct2	SH Users, Product Managers	Business model filters limit user to portable and desktop PCs; restrictions driven by rows in PRODUCT_MANAGERS table
bichannel1	SH Users	VPD policies restrict user to Tele Sales channel; restrictions driven by rows in CHANNEL_MANAGERS table
bichannel2	SH Users	VPD policies restrict user to Internet channel; restrictions driven by rows in CHANNEL_MANAGERS table
bichannel3	SH Users	VPD policies restrict user to Internet channel; restrictions driven by rows in CHANNEL_MANAGERS table
binoshuser		User does not have access to the SH subject area

TABLE A-2 *Users and Their Roles in the Examples*

is created with any new repository. It is always defined internal to Oracle BI. All other users are defined in the place most appropriate for the authentication method that the RPD supports.

Database Preparations

These examples were tested on both Oracle 10*g* and Oracle 11*g* databases. To run the scripts in this example, you will need a database with the sample schemas installed. All the examples are built on the SH (sales history) schema. Several database scripts are provided to set up additional tables used in the examples.

Database Auditing

A dashboard in the examples focuses on BI usage tracking and database auditing. To use database auditing, you must ensure that this feature is enabled in the database. In particular, to see the SQL that is being executed, the database must be in extended auditing mode. You can check the status of your database by executing the following query:

```
SELECT name,value FROM v$parameter
WHERE name LIKE 'audit%'
```

If your database is not in extended auditing mode (DB_EXTENDED), issue this command:

```
alter system set audit_trail='DB_EXTENDED' scope=spfile;
```

You must restart the database for this to take effect. These commands to enable auditing were not included in the example install scripts because they require a database restart. Finally, you must specify exactly what is going to be audited. See the section "Useful Scripts" later in this appendix to see how to do this.

Database Scripts

Four setup scripts should be run for any example you want to use. For specific RPDs, you may need to run additional scripts. These are explained in the section "RPD-Specific Scripts." Finally, some scripts are provided to help test and enable various features.

Setup Scripts

Run the following scripts in this order:

- **1_install_script.sql** This script must be run as sys or another user that has permission to grant privileges on dbms_crypto. The users that Oracle BI will use to connect to the Oracle database are set up here. Tables that express user-to-group assignments for usage tracking and SA System are also set up here. When using internal authentication, user-to-group assignments must be maintained in two places: the RPD (for authentication and authorization) and a set of tables (for usage tracking and SA System). These tables are also used for table-based authentication.
- **2_usage_tracking_sa_system.sql** This script sets up the required infrastructure for usage tracking and the SA System subject area.
- **3_load_date.sql** This loads the date table used by usage tracking. If you have a date dimension in your data warehouse, you could use it instead.
- **4_load_time.sql** This loads the time table used by usage tracking, which includes a row for every minute in a day.

RPD-Specific Scripts

Following are the RPD-specific scripts:

- **database_account_roles.sql** This should be run before using aos_database.rpd. It creates database users and roles that will be used for Oracle BI authentication and authorization purposes. It also creates the necessary views so that usage tracking and SA System can pull user-to-group assignment information from the database dictionary.

- **ldap_setup_oid.sql** This should be run before using aos_ldap.rpd. Several things must also happen before attempting to use this script. First, you should populate your LDAP with the users and groups described in Table A-2. You should create one extra group in your LDAP called BIUsers and put all the Oracle BI end users in this group. Finally, you must modify this script so that it has the correct LDAP connection information and base DN information. If you are using Oracle Internet Directory as your LDAP, this script should be close to what you need.
- **ldap_setup_ad.sql** This is the same as the ldap_setup_oid.sql script, but it includes minor changes for Active Directory. You will need to make the same changes here as listed for the OID script.
- **act_as_proxy.sql** This should be run before using aos_internal_proxy.rpd. This creates the table that holds the proxy permissions necessary for this example.

Useful Scripts

Following are some other useful scripts:

- **vpd_setup.sql** This creates a VPD policy on SH.SALES. You should be aware of a few things when enabling this policy. After it is enabled, the only users that will be allowed to query the SH.SALES table will be users listed in the BI_TABLES.CHANNEL_MANAGERS table. If any other user queries SH.SALES, no rows will be returned. As discussed in Chapter 14, a well-designed VPD policy should handle all types of users and should make sure they see the appropriate information. This policy is quite simple and was designed to illustrate the ability to use VPD with Oracle BI's caching infrastructure in a secure way. This script also contains the code necessary to disable and drop the policy
- **vpd_tester.sql** Some useful SQL statements to test that the VPD policy is set up correctly.
- **audit_tester.sql** Some useful SQL statements to test that auditing is working properly.

Oracle BI Setup

Before beginning the process of setting up any of the provided examples, you should perform the following steps. Of particular importance is the information in the section "BI Publisher Super User." Skipping this step makes it easy to lock yourself completely out of BI Publisher. Scheduler configuration could actually be done anytime during the process. However, whenever you set up an authentication scheme, I recommend that you test all components—it's just nice to have Delivers completely set up before beginning.

Credential Store

In Chapter 13, you read how the presentation server uses a credential store to store encrypted passwords. Three sets of credentials need to go into this credential store. Each set is identified by an alias:

- **admin** The credentials for the Scheduler service

- **bipublisheradmin** The credentials for BI Publisher
- **impersonation** The credentials for the impersonator user used in single sign-on (SSO) configurations

You should run cryptotools three times to set up each of these three credentials. Also, the passphrase used to encrypt the password should be the same for each set of credentials—failure to do this actually results in a presentation server that will not start.

BI Publisher Superuser

Before making any changes to BI security settings, I highly recommend that you set up a BI Publisher superuser. As mentioned, if you do not do this, it will be easy to lock yourself out of BI Publisher completely. I also recommend using a username that is unique to BI Publisher (that is, a username that does not exist in your Oracle BI identity store). After setting up a superuser and password, you need to restart BI Publisher. Test this new user and make sure you can login as that user. The superuser is a back door into BI Publisher that will work no matter what security scheme BI Publisher is configured to use.

Other BI Publisher Configuration Steps

You should also make a few more changes to BI Publisher, after Oracle BI authentication is set up and working.

First, edit the BI EE JDBC data source to use the internal administrator account: Administrator. Make sure that you leave the Use Proxy Authentication option checked, as shown in Figure A-1. This should always be used for BI server data sources. When this is checked, queries against the BI server will use a shared connection pool but will execute under the permissions of the actual user logged into BI Publisher. This Proxy Authentication feature is also used when executing BI Publisher reports in a VPD-enabled Oracle Database. I like setting up the JDBC connection first, because I can test the connection there.

Next, you should perform the security configuration. Specify that you will use the BI server for your BI Publisher security model. BI Publisher supports a number of different security models.

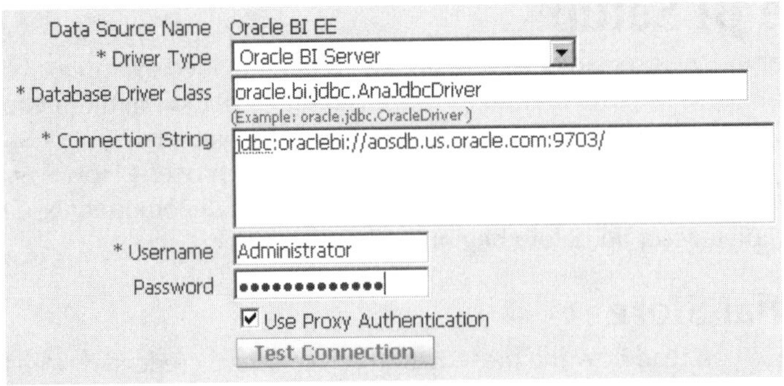

FIGURE A-1 *Setting up a JDBC connection to the BI server in BI Publisher*

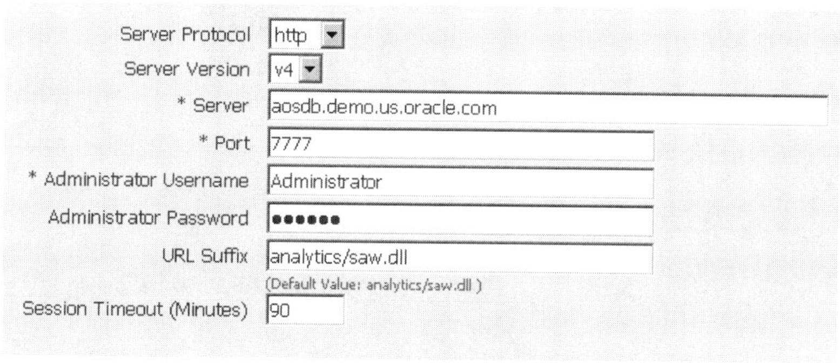

Server Protocol http
Server Version v4
* Server aosdb.demo.us.oracle.com
* Port 7777
* Administrator Username Administrator
Administrator Password ●●●●●●
URL Suffix analytics/saw.dll
(Default Value: analytics/saw.dll)
Session Timeout (Minutes) 90

FIGURE A-2 *Setting up integration with the presentation server*

However, if you are using BI Publisher in an integrated Oracle BI environment, it is recommended that you use the BI server for BI Publisher security. This allows BI Publisher to leverage the security you have set up for the BI server. The details you specify here are identical to those you used to set up your BI EE JDBC data source.

After BI Publisher is set up to use BI server security, you need to change one thing on your BI EE JDBC data source: Authorize the group SH Users to use this data source. Notice that BI Publisher is getting this list of groups from the BI server. If you tried to do this step prior to BI server security being set up, you would not have seen the proper list of groups.

Finally, you should set up integration with BI Presentation Services. This is required to be able to use Answers requests as a data source. As shown in Figure A-2, you should use the Administrator username and password again. Remember that if you are using SSO, this should actually point to the URL suffix that is not SSO protected, as discussed in Chapter 13.

Sample BI Publisher Report

After you have set up one of the RPDs and the web catalog, you need to load one BI Publisher report into the repository. To load this report, log into BI Publisher as BISHUSER and navigate to that user's My Folder. As shown in Figure A-3, click Upload A Report and upload the BIP test report.zip file provided with this text. This report is used on BISHUSERS's My Dashboard.

Scheduler Configuration

To set up the scheduler service, just use the standard setup instructions and scripts provided with Oracle BI.

Usage Tracking

The normal steps required to set up usage tracking are detailed in Chapter 14. These involve creating the usage tracking table and a time dimension, modifying the configuration of the BI server, integrating the usage tracking RPD with your production RPD, and integrating the usage tracking web catalog with your production web catalog. Most of this is already done in these examples. The setup scripts for the database will create the necessary database tables for usage tracking. All the RPDs and the web catalog provided with this book already have the usage tracking RPD and web catalog integrated into them. The only thing you will need to do is modify

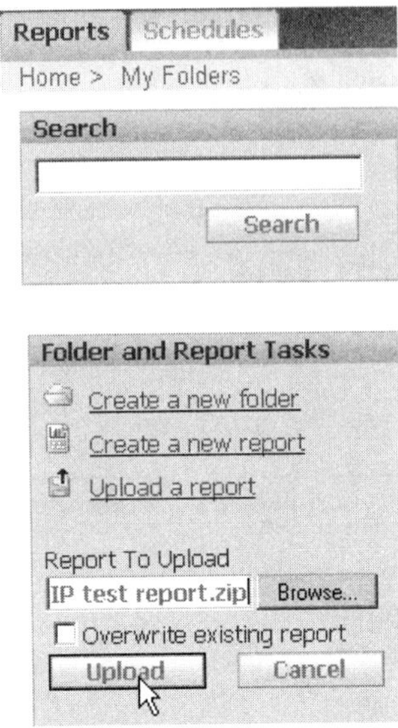

FIGURE A-3 *Uploading the sample BI Publisher report to your instance of BI Publisher*

the NQSConfig.INI settings for your BI server. You should modify the usage tracking section of this configuration file to read as follows:

```
[ USAGE_TRACKING ]
ENABLE = YES;
DIRECT_INSERT = YES;
PHYSICAL_TABLE_NAME = "Security Information"."BI_USAGE_TRACKING"."S_NQ_ACCT" ;
CONNECTION_POOL = "Security Information"."Usage Tracking Writer Connection Pool" ;
BUFFER_SIZE = 10 MB ;
BUFFER_TIME_LIMIT_SECONDS = 5 ;
NUM_INSERT_THREADS = 5 ;
MAX_INSERTS_PER_TRANSACTION = 1 ;
```

Recommend Testing

After trying these examples, I recommend running through a series of tests to make sure everything is working properly. I've seen quite a few people set up an authentication scheme and test only basic login functionality or test only features with an administrative account. Invariably, a minor configuration issue shows up when actual end users start using all the different parts of the system.

Oracle BI Tests

When testing Oracle BI, the most important thing you can do is to log in as every possible class of user. In these examples, that means logging in as an administrator, a product manager (to test business model filters), a channel manager (to test the VPD policy), and a normal SH User. After logging on as each user, you should check a few things:

1. Does the user have access to the appropriate system features? For example, logging on as an administrator, you should see the Setting – Administration utility. Non-administrative users should not have access to this.
2. Check the Settings – My Account page to see if web catalog group membership is set up properly. Keep in mind that membership in a web catalog group that is inherited from an RPD group will not show up here.
3. Check that session variables are getting set properly. I developed the Utilities dashboard included in the sample web catalog for exactly this purpose.
4. Finally, check data-level security by examining the Subject Areas available and testing any business model filters (product managers in our case) and VPD policies (channel managers).

BI Publisher Tests

When testing BI Publisher integration, you should test a few items for both administrative and non-administrative accounts:

1. Can you log into BI Publisher using Oracle BI credentials? This tests the security model setup.
2. Check that when you navigate from Oracle BI to BI Publisher using the More Products – BI Publisher link that you are automatically logged into BI Publisher. This will tell you that the credential store is configured properly for BI Publisher. Another way to test this is to embed a BI Publisher report onto a dashboard.
3. Finally, you should test the ability to create a report based on an Answers request. This will test BI Publisher integration with Presentation Services. If you log in as BISHUSER, you'll see a BI Publisher report on that user's My Dashboard page that checks all of these things.

Oracle Delivers Tests

To test Oracle Delivers, you need to test its ability to schedule a report. This actually tests a few things. Your ability to save an iBot tells you that the Presentation Service can communicate with the scheduler service (using the credential store). The job executing tells you that the scheduler is properly able to log onto the Oracle BI Server and successfully execute the job. Receiving the results or the alert tells you that Scheduler service was able to notify the presentation server that the job was finished. Again, make sure you test this for both administrative and non-administrative accounts.

Sample Web Catalog Description

The web catalog provided with this book is designed to be used with any of the provided RPDs. The SH dashboard is designed to showcase business model filters and VPD working with Oracle BI. The Utilities dashboard has some tools to help you test and see auditing in action. Keep in mind that these dashboards were designed to showcase specific BI security functionality and not elaborate dashboard techniques.

SH Dashboard

The Product Managers tab on the SH dashboard is designed to showcase business model filters. To see this work, you should log in as one of the product managers: BIPRODUCT1 or BIPRODUCT2. When you do, you will see the BI server automatically adding filters to existing reports based on the business model filters designed in the repository.

The Channel Managers tab showcases VPD functionality. To see this in action, you will need to enable the VPD policy (vpd_setup.sql). You will also need to log in as a channel manager (BICHANNEL1, BICHANNEL2, or BICHANNEL3). Two reports on this page use direct database requests that can be edited only by a Presentation Server Administrator and can be executed only by SH Users. This means that BIADMIN cannot run these reports. See Chapter 14 for a discussion on why the privileges were set up this way.

Utilities Dashboard

The Utilities dashboard consists of two tabs: Variables and Auditing. The Variables tab is extremely useful in checking your external authorization setup. The key to externalizing authorization is to set session variables properly. This screen will let you know if they are being set properly. The Auditing tab contains reports from both usage tracking and database auditing.

Other Dashboards

A couple of other dashboards are provided in the sample web catalog, including four dashboards that actually come with the product as part of the sample sales demo. The sample web catalog and RPDs were built on top of this sample sales RPD and web catalog. The Usage Tracking dashboard included with the product has also been integrated into the web catalog that comes with this book. Finally, BISHUSER's My Dashboard has a BI Publisher report on it to enable quick testing of BI Publisher integration. Before you log on as BISHUSER, make sure you upload the BI Publisher report as described in the section "Sample BI Publisher Report" earlier in this appendix.

Sample RPD Descriptions

Several RPDs are also included with this book. Each is designed for a specific authentication style or security feature. If you want to use any of these RPDs, you will need to make some modifications so that they will run on your system. Some of these changes are the same in each RPD and are listed in the section "Common to All RPDs." Other changes are specific to that RPD and can be found in their respective section. In each section, I list the changes that should be made and point out some features of which you should be aware.

Common to All RPDs

Make the following changes to each provided RPD that you want to use:

1. Change the default initializer of the **BI_EE_HOME** server variable. The sample sales databases use this variable to determine the location of the XML data sources. This should be set to the location of the OracleBI directory in your installation.
2. Change the data source name in each Oracle connection pool. The orcl and Security Information databases are the two Oracle databases. Each connection pool in these databases needs to be updated with information specific to your system.

While changing the data access connection pool of the orcl database, take a quick look at the Connections Scripts tab. You'll notice that I'm using the identity persistence method discussed in Chapter 14 (**select bi_select.set_identifier(':USER') from dual**). This is required for both VPD and database auditing. Both of these topics can be explored using any of the provided RPDs. If you look at the General tab of the properties for the orcl database, you will notice that it is identified as a Virtual Private Database. This will allow for the cache entry tagging discussed in Chapter 14.

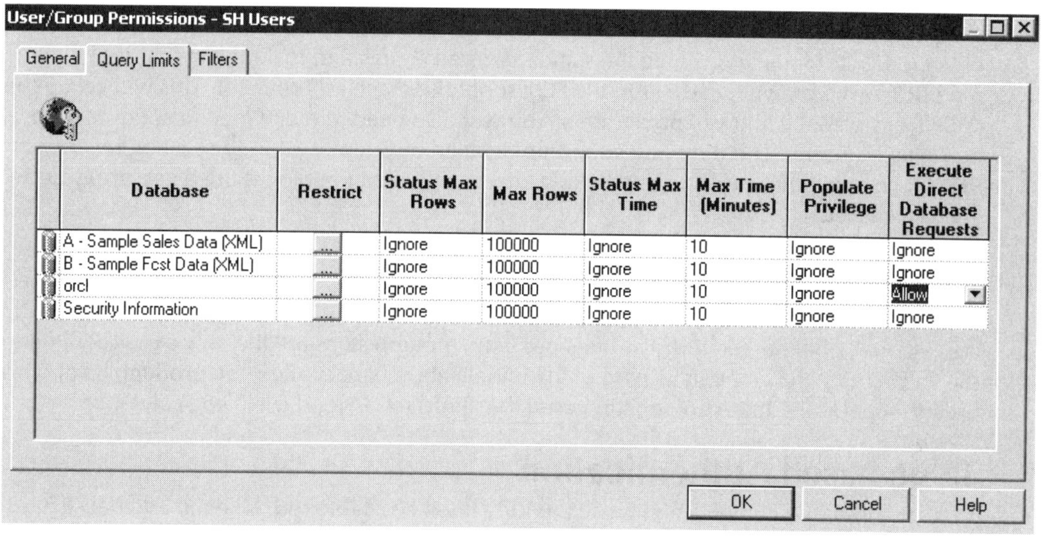

User/Group Permissions - SH Users

General | Query Limits | Filters

Database	Restrict	Status Max Rows	Max Rows	Status Max Time	Max Time (Minutes)	Populate Privilege	Execute Direct Database Requests
A - Sample Sales Data (XML)	...	Ignore	100000	Ignore	10	Ignore	Ignore
B - Sample Fcst Data (XML)	...	Ignore	100000	Ignore	10	Ignore	Ignore
orcl	...	Ignore	100000	Ignore	10	Ignore	Allow
Security Information	...	Ignore	100000	Ignore	10	Ignore	Ignore

OK | Cancel | Help

FIGURE A-4 *Direct Database Requests are enabled for the SH Users group*

Another thing to notice in all of the RPDs are the Groups. As mentioned in Chapter 13, groups must be defined in the RPD, and web catalog groups must be defined in the web catalog. Membership in these groups may be handled in different ways (depending on the authorization method), but they have to exist in the RPD and Web catalog. Notice the business model filter applied to the Product Managers group. Notice also that the SH Subject Area is available only to SH Users.

Finally, notice that Direct Database Requests have to be enabled in both the web catalog and the RPD. In the RPD, this is turned on by group. Examine the SH Users groups and look at the Query Limits tab of the Permissions dialog box. This is illustrated in Figure A-4. In the presentation server, permissions were granted to the SH Users web catalog group to allow members to execute Direct Database Requests.

Internal Authentication

To test internal authentication, use the RPD titled aos_internal.rpd. No additional modifications are required for this RPD. You should check that the web groups are properly set up for the administrative users. In all the other authentication methods, the web catalog group will be populated dynamically. However, with internal authentication, the web catalog group must be maintained manually. Log in as Administrator and put BIADMIN and BIWEBADMIN in the Presentation Server Administrators web catalog group. Note that users will show up in the web catalog only after they have logged in once. I have already logged in as each user, so you will not run into that issue with this web catalog. However, if you use internal security and want to use web catalog groups, you will need to log in as the user before you can assign that user to any web catalog groups. (This is one of the reasons listed in Chapter 13 for not using internal authentication in production environments.)

Internal Authentication with Act as Proxy Enabled

To use the Act as Proxy feature with these examples, you should use the RPD titled aos_internal_proxy.rpd. In addition to running the standard install scripts and making the standard RPD modifications, you will need to run the SQL script titled act_as_proxy.sql. This will set up the table that stores the allowed proxy users. You will also need to make modifications to your presentation server. These modifications are detailed in Chapter 14 in the section on "Act as Proxy." The two things to note in this RPD are the initialization blocks titled **get_proxy** and **get_proxylevel**.

Column-based Security

To test the column-based security discussed in Chapter 14, you will want to use the RPD titled aos_internal_column_sec.rpd. The standard configuration steps are the only steps required to use this RPD. You will want to take note of the initialization block called **get_product_level**. This is used to support the **IndexCol** function used the "Products"."Top Level" Logical column.

Table-based Authentication

To test table-based authentication, use the RPD titled aos_table.rpd. Like the internal security RPD, the only modifications you need to make to get this to work in your environment are the modifications listed in the section "Common to All RPDs." In the internal authentication RPD, it was suggested that you make sure users were in the proper web catalog group. This is not the case with this RPD. Users will be dynamically assigned to RPD groups and web catalog groups. This assignment is done based on the values in the BI_SECURITY_TABLES.BI_USER_GROUPS table. In fact, it is worth making sure users do not belong to any web catalog groups before beginning. Then you can be sure to see the dynamic group membership in action.

You should notice a few things in this RPD:

- An "authorization pool" connection pool is used by two initialization blocks: **check_user** and **get_groups**. This connection pool uses the database user BI_SECURITY_SELECT to log onto the database and query the tables in the BI_SECURITY_TABLES schema.
- The **check_use**r initialization block is worth examining. It uses the **NQS_PASSWORD_CLAUSE** and the **hash_password** function discussed in Chapter 13.
- The **get_groups** initialization block uses row-wise initialization to define and populate the **GROUP** and **WEBGROUPS** session variables. This dynamically assigns users to the proper RPD groups and web catalog groups.
- Groups are defined in the RPD and the web catalog groups are defined in the web catalog, but the users exist only in a database table. Also, group membership is managed in a database table.

Database Authentication

Before using the aos_database.rpd to test database authentication, you should run the script database_accounts_roles.sql as sys. This will set up database accounts and roles to match the users that we have been using for the examples. It also sets up some views on top of the data dictionary views so that the usage tracking and SA System tables do not have to be maintained. As mentioned in Chapter 13, database authentication requires that you externalize group membership in a table. We created views based on the data dictionary to accomplish this.

Here are some things you should notice in the RPD:

- The **check_user** initialization block uses the authentication connection pool to verify that the provided credentials are valid database credentials. This connection pool uses the provided credentials to log into the database and execute a simple query to populate the **USER** session variable.
- The **get_groups** initialization block uses the authorization connection pool to query group information. This connection pool connects as BI_SECURITY_SELECT and uses the views built on the database dictionary to get group information.
- The SA System subject area is now querying the database dictionary. In a production environment, you would need to combine the data dictionary information with extra information (such as e-mail address, cell phone number, and so on).

LDAP Authentication

You need to do several things before attempting to use aos_ldap.rpd. As mentioned in the "RPD-Specific Scripts" section earlier, you must first load users and groups into your Lightweight Directory Access Protocol (LDAP) server. Then you must create an LDAP group called BIUsers and put all you BI users into that group. You will also need to modify the provided LDAP setup script so that it will work with your LDAP and then run the script. Finally, you will need to modify the LDAP server setup in the RPD, as shown in Figure A-5, by modifying the LDAP server in the Administration tool's Security Manager. You will need to modify your hostname, Base DN, and Bind DN. In addition, on the Advanced tab, you can check ADSI if you are using Active Directory and set up SSL if required.

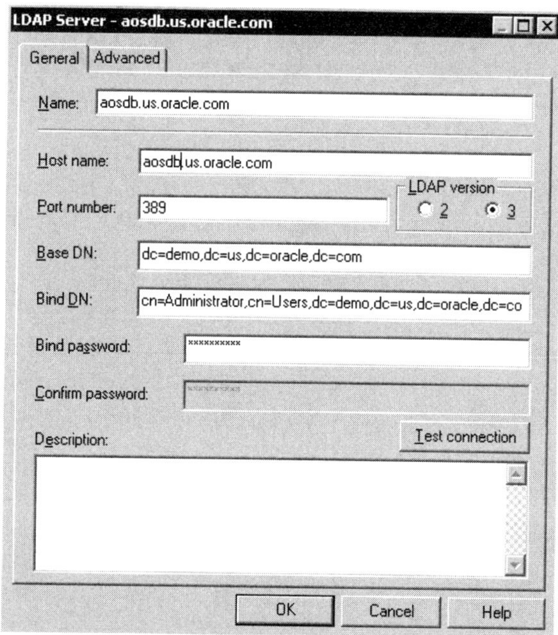

FIGURE A-5 *Modify the LDAP connection information to match your LDAP*

Once you have everything working, you should examine the following points in the aos_ldap rpd:

- The **check_user** initialization block is using the LDAP server that you set up.
- The **get_groups** initialization block is using the v_bi_groups_ldap and v_bi_user_groups_ldap views that sit directly on top of your LDAP server.
- Usage tracking and SA System are also using views built on top of your LDAP server.
- An RPD user called Impersonator was added to the RPD and placed in the Administrators group. This user is not required for LDAP but is required for SSO integration.

SSO Integration

Before you attempt SSO integration, make sure that LDAP integration is working completely, including dynamic group membership. If you got the aos_ldap.rpd working, everything is ready to begin SSO integration.

Use the following steps to set up SSO integration:

1. SSO protect the /analytics web resource. (Chapter 13 discusses how to do this for Oracle Access Manager, and the documentation discusses how to do this for Oracle Single Sign-On.)
2. Deploy the analytics.ear file as /analyticsSOAP. The /analytics URL will still be used for accessing Oracle BI via the Web. The new /analyticsSOAP URL will be used for BI Publisher, Catalog Manager, BI Office Server, and any web service–based application that integrates with your BI system. If you try to use /analytics with any of these applications, you will get an authorization error from the SSO server. This is because these applications do not know how to access the browser-based security token that the SSO server will set. The /analyticsSOAP URL should not be SSO protected.
3. Modify the instanceconfig.xml file according to the documentation. These changes tell Oracle BI that it will choose a security token from the SSO server rather than presenting the normal login page.

Summary

The examples provided with this book are intended to supplement the information presented in Chapters 13 and 14. This appendix details the steps you need to use for each of these examples. It also highlights the key parts of the code you should examine to get the most out of the examples. Hopefully, these examples will help you better understand the material presented in this book and will help you in deploying a secure Oracle Business Intelligence system.

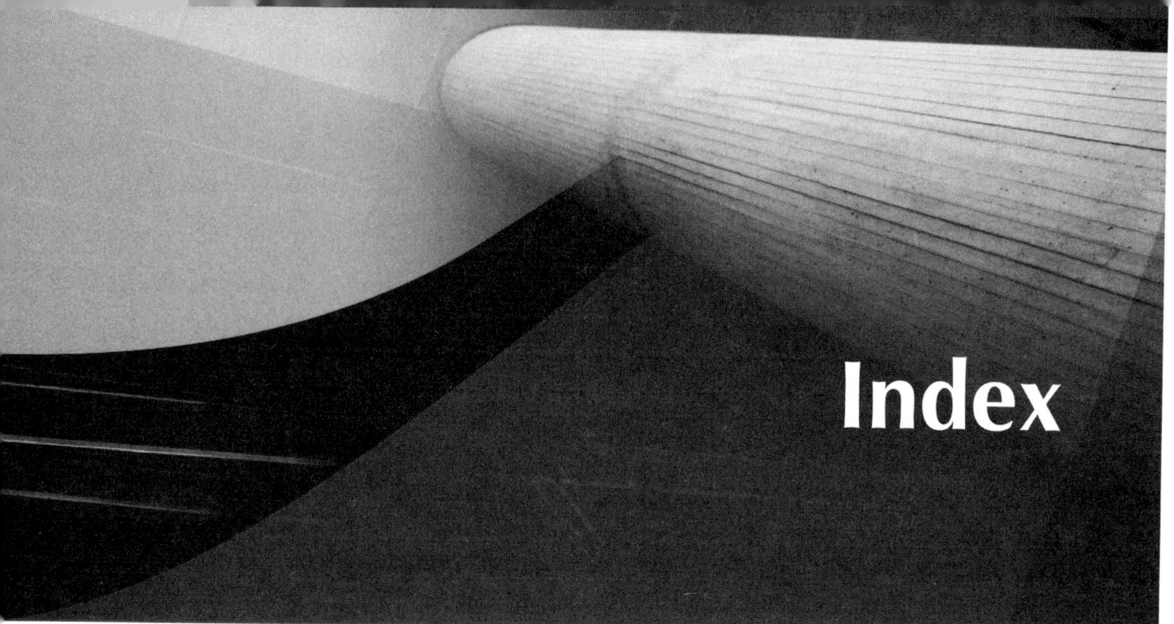

Index

A

B

C

D

E

F

G

O

S

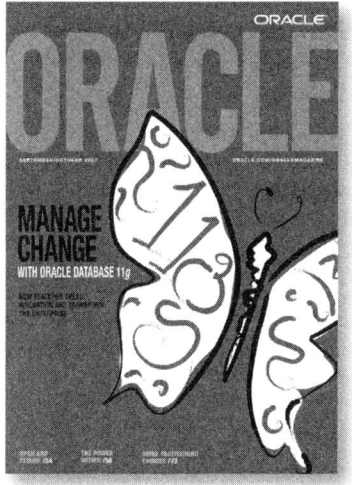

Want your own FREE subscription?

To receive a free subscription to *Oracle Magazine*, you must fill out the entire card, sign it, and date it (incomplete cards cannot be processed or acknowledged). You can also fax your application to +1.847.763.9638. **Or subscribe at our Web site at oracle.com/oraclemagazine**

○ **Yes, please send me a FREE subscription *Oracle Magazine*.** ○ No.

○ From time to time, Oracle Publishing allows our partners exclusive access to our e-mail addresses for special promotions and announcements. To be included in this program, please check this circle. If you do not wish to be included, you will only receive notices about your subscription via e-mail.

○ Oracle Publishing allows sharing of our postal mailing list with selected third parties. If you prefer your mailing address not to be included in this program, please check this circle.

If at any time you would like to be removed from either mailing list, please contact Customer Service at +1.847.763.9635 or send an e-mail to oracle@halldata.com. If you opt in to the sharing of information, Oracle may also provide you with e-mail related to Oracle products, services, and events. If you want to completely unsubscribe from any e-mail communication from Oracle, please send an e-mail to: unsubscribe@oracle-mail.com with the following in the subject line: REMOVE [your e-mail address]. For complete information on Oracle Publishing's privacy practices, please visit oracle.com/html/privacy/html

X

signature (required) date

name title

company e-mail address

street/p.o. box

city/state/zip or postal code telephone

country fax

Would you like to receive your free subscription in digital format instead of print if it becomes available? ○ Yes ○ No

YOU MUST ANSWER ALL 10 QUESTIONS BELOW.

① WHAT IS THE PRIMARY BUSINESS ACTIVITY OF YOUR FIRM AT THIS LOCATION? (check one only)

- □ 01 Aerospace and Defense Manufacturing
- □ 02 Application Service Provider
- □ 03 Automotive Manufacturing
- □ 04 Chemicals
- □ 05 Media and Entertainment
- □ 06 Construction/Engineering
- □ 07 Consumer Sector/Consumer Packaged Goods
- □ 08 Education
- □ 09 Financial Services/Insurance
- □ 10 Health Care
- □ 11 High Technology Manufacturing, OEM
- □ 12 Industrial Manufacturing
- □ 13 Independent Software Vendor
- □ 14 Life Sciences (biotech, pharmaceuticals)
- □ 15 Natural Resources
- □ 16 Oil and Gas
- □ 17 Professional Services
- □ 18 Public Sector (government)
- □ 19 Research
- □ 20 Retail/Wholesale/Distribution
- □ 21 Systems Integrator, VAR/VAD
- □ 22 Telecommunications
- □ 23 Travel and Transportation
- □ 24 Utilities (electric, gas, sanitation, water)
- □ 98 Other Business and Services ________

② WHICH OF THE FOLLOWING BEST DESCRIBES YOUR PRIMARY JOB FUNCTION? (check one only)

CORPORATE MANAGEMENT/STAFF

- □ 01 Executive Management (President, Chair, CEO, CFO, Owner, Partner, Principal)
- □ 02 Finance/Administrative Management (VP/Director/ Manager/Controller, Purchasing, Administration)
- □ 03 Sales/Marketing Management (VP/Director/Manager)
- □ 04 Computer Systems/Operations Management (CIO/VP/Director/Manager MIS/IS/IT, Ops)

IS/IT STAFF

- □ 05 Application Development/Programming Management
- □ 06 Application Development/Programming Staff
- □ 07 Consulting
- □ 08 DBA/Systems Administrator
- □ 09 Education/Training
- □ 10 Technical Support Director/Manager
- □ 11 Other Technical Management/Staff
- □ 98 Other

③ WHAT IS YOUR CURRENT PRIMARY OPERATING PLATFORM (check all that apply)

- □ 01 Digital Equipment Corp UNIX/VAX/VMS
- □ 02 HP UNIX
- □ 03 IBM AIX
- □ 04 IBM UNIX
- □ 05 Linux (Red Hat)
- □ 06 Linux (SUSE)
- □ 07 Linux (Oracle Enterprise)
- □ 08 Linux (other)
- □ 09 Macintosh
- □ 10 MVS
- □ 11 Netware
- □ 12 Network Computing
- □ 13 SCO UNIX
- □ 14 Sun Solaris/SunOS
- □ 15 Windows
- □ 16 Other UNIX
- □ 98 Other
- 99 □ None of the Above

④ DO YOU EVALUATE, SPECIFY, RECOMMEND, OR AUTHORIZE THE PURCHASE OF ANY OF THE FOLLOWING? (check all that apply)

- □ 01 Hardware
- □ 02 Business Applications (ERP, CRM, etc.)
- □ 03 Application Development Tools
- □ 04 Database Products
- □ 05 Internet or Intranet Products
- □ 06 Other Software
- □ 07 Middleware Products
- 99 □ None of the Above

⑤ IN YOUR JOB, DO YOU USE OR PLAN TO PURCHASE ANY OF THE FOLLOWING PRODUCTS? (check all that apply)

SOFTWARE

- □ 01 CAD/CAE/CAM
- □ 02 Collaboration Software
- □ 03 Communications
- □ 04 Database Management
- □ 05 File Management
- □ 06 Finance
- □ 07 Java
- □ 08 Multimedia Authoring
- □ 09 Networking
- □ 10 Programming
- □ 11 Project Management
- □ 12 Scientific and Engineering
- □ 13 Systems Management
- □ 14 Workflow

HARDWARE

- □ 15 Macintosh
- □ 16 Mainframe
- □ 17 Massively Parallel Processing
- □ 18 Minicomputer
- □ 19 Intel x86(32)
- □ 20 Intel x86(64)
- □ 21 Network Computer
- □ 22 Symmetric Multiprocessing
- □ 23 Workstation Services

SERVICES

- □ 24 Consulting
- □ 25 Education/Training
- □ 26 Maintenance
- □ 27 Online Database
- □ 28 Support
- □ 29 Technology-Based Training
- □ 30 Other
- 99 □ None of the Above

⑥ WHAT IS YOUR COMPANY'S SIZE? (check one only)

- □ 01 More than 25,000 Employees
- □ 02 10,001 to 25,000 Employees
- □ 03 5,001 to 10,000 Employees
- □ 04 1,001 to 5,000 Employees
- □ 05 101 to 1,000 Employees
- □ 06 Fewer than 100 Employees

⑦ DURING THE NEXT 12 MONTHS, HOW MUCH DO YOU ANTICIPATE YOUR ORGANIZATION WILL SPEND ON COMPUTER HARDWARE, SOFTWARE, PERIPHERALS, AND SERVICES FOR YOUR LOCATION? (check one only)

- □ 01 Less than $10,000
- □ 02 $10,000 to $49,999
- □ 03 $50,000 to $99,999
- □ 04 $100,000 to $499,999
- □ 05 $500,000 to $999,999
- □ 06 $1,000,000 and Over

⑧ WHAT IS YOUR COMPANY'S YEARLY SALES REVENUE? (check one only)

- □ 01 $500, 000, 000 and above
- □ 02 $100, 000, 000 to $500, 000, 000
- □ 03 $50, 000, 000 to $100, 000, 000
- □ 04 $5, 000, 000 to $50, 000, 000
- □ 05 $1, 000, 000 to $5, 000, 000

⑨ WHAT LANGUAGES AND FRAMEWORKS DO YOU USE? (check all that apply)

- □ 01 Ajax
- □ 02 C
- □ 03 C++
- □ 04 C#
- □ 05 Hibernate
- □ 06 J++/J#
- □ 07 Java
- □ 08 JSP
- □ 09 .NET
- □ 10 Perl
- □ 11 PHP
- □ 12 PL/SQL
- □ 13 Python
- □ 14 Ruby/Rails
- □ 15 Spring
- □ 16 Struts
- □ 17 SQL
- □ 18 Visual Basic
- □ 98 Other

⑩ WHAT ORACLE PRODUCTS ARE IN USE AT YOUR SITE? (check all that apply)

ORACLE DATABASE

- □ 01 Oracle Database 11*g*
- □ 02 Oracle Database 10*g*
- □ 03 Oracle9*i* Database
- □ 04 Oracle Embedded Database (Oracle Lite, Times Ten, Berkeley DB)
- □ 05 Other Oracle Database Release

ORACLE FUSION MIDDLEWARE

- □ 06 Oracle Application Server
- □ 07 Oracle Portal
- □ 08 Oracle Enterprise Manager
- □ 09 Oracle BPEL Process Manager
- □ 10 Oracle Identity Management
- □ 11 Oracle SOA Suite
- □ 12 Oracle Data Hubs

ORACLE DEVELOPMENT TOOLS

- □ 13 Oracle JDeveloper
- □ 14 Oracle Forms
- □ 15 Oracle Reports
- □ 16 Oracle Designer
- □ 17 Oracle Discoverer
- □ 18 Oracle BI Beans
- □ 19 Oracle Warehouse Builder
- □ 20 Oracle WebCenter
- □ 21 Oracle Application Express

ORACLE APPLICATIONS

- □ 22 Oracle E-Business Suite
- □ 23 PeopleSoft Enterprise
- □ 24 JD Edwards EnterpriseOne
- □ 25 JD Edwards World
- □ 26 Oracle Fusion
- □ 27 Hyperion
- □ 28 Siebel CRM

ORACLE SERVICES

- □ 28 Oracle E-Business Suite On Demand
- □ 29 Oracle Technology On Demand
- □ 30 Siebel CRM On Demand
- □ 31 Oracle Consulting
- □ 32 Oracle Education
- □ 33 Oracle Support
- □ 98 Other
- 99 □ None of the Above

08014004

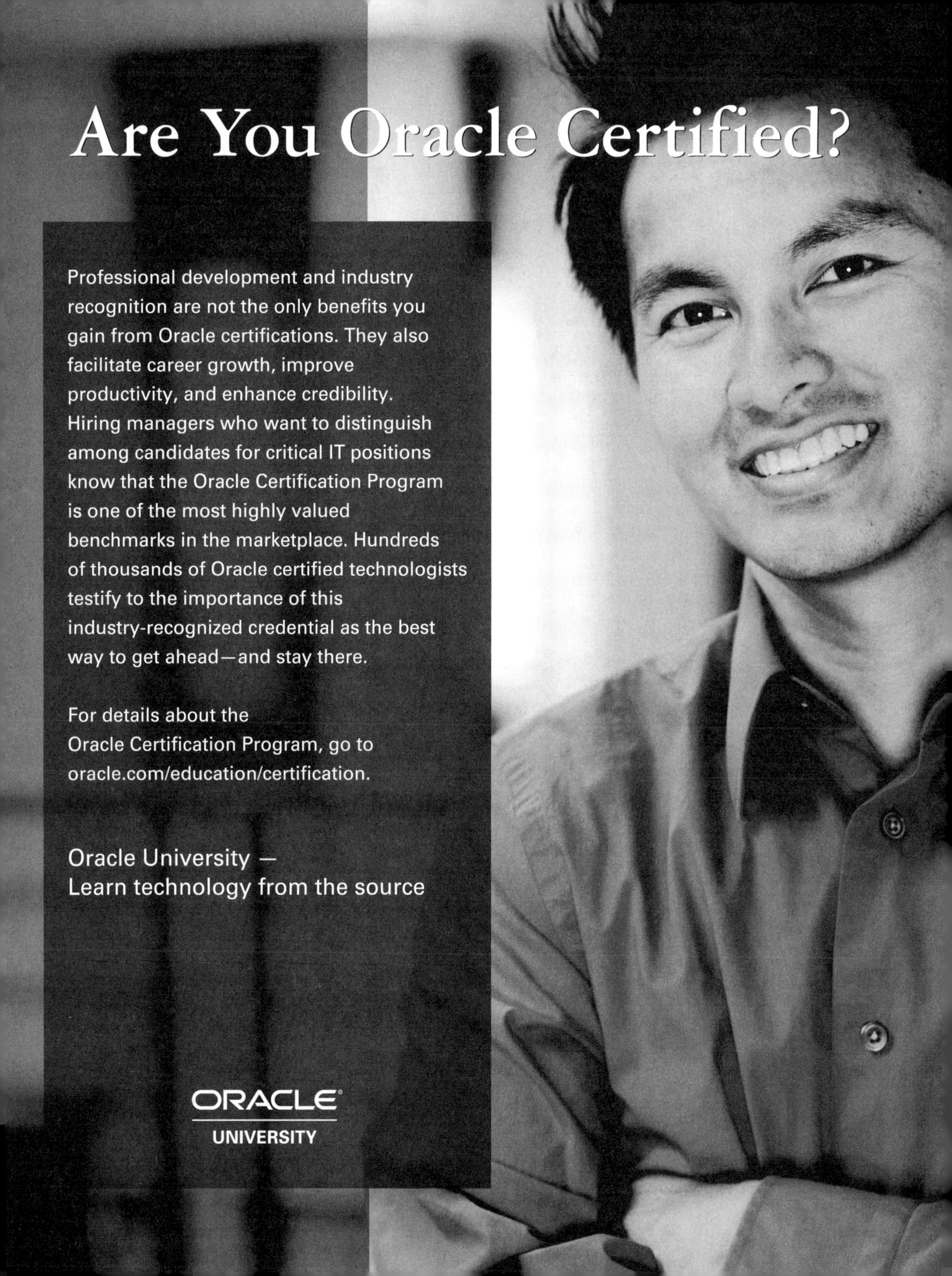
Are You Oracle Certified?
Professional development and industry recognition are not the only benefits you gain from Oracle certifications. They also facilitate career growth, improve productivity, and enhance credibility. Hiring managers who want to distinguish among candidates for critical IT positions know that the Oracle Certification Program is one of the most highly valued benchmarks in the marketplace. Hundreds of thousands of Oracle certified technologists testify to the importance of this industry-recognized credential as the best way to get ahead—and stay there.
For details about the Oracle Certification Program, go to oracle.com/education/certification.
Oracle University — Learn technology from the source
ORACLE
UNIVERSITY